Psychology Applied to Work

SEVENTH EDITION

Related Titles of Interest

- *Clear Thinking with Psychology: Separating Sense from Nonsense* by John Ruscio
- *Conducting Research in Psychology: Measuring the Weight of Smoke,* 2nd edition, by Brett W. Pelham and Hart Blanton
- *Culture and Psychology: People Around the World,* 2nd edition, by David Matsumoto
- *Experimental Design,* 3rd edition, by Roger Kirk
- *Forensic Psychology* by Larry Wrightsman
- *Group Dynamics,* 3rd edition, by Donelson Forsyth
- *Health Psychology,* 4th edition, by Linda Brannon and Jess Feist
- *Health Psychology* by Phillip Rice
- *A Lifetime of Relationships* by Nelly Vanzetti and Steve Duck
- *Psychological Testing: Principles, Applications, and Issues,* 5th edition, by Robert Kaplan and Dennis Saccuzzo
- *Psychology and the Legal System,* 5th edition, by Larry Wrightsman, Edie Greene, Michael Nietzel, and William Fortune
- *Research Methods in Social Psychology,* 7th edition, by Rick H. Hoyle, Monica J. Harris, and Charles M. Judd
- *Research Methods Laboratory Manual for Psychology and Software* by William Langston
- *Social Psychology* by Stephen Worchel, Joel Cooper, Al Goethals, and James Olson
- *A Simple Guide to SPSS for Windows 8.0, 9.0 & 10.0* by Lee A. Kirkpatrick and Brooke C. Feeney
- *Stress and Health,* 3rd edition, by Phillip Rice
- *Training in Organizations,* 4th edition, by Irwin L. Goldstein and Kevin Ford

Forthcoming Titles

- *Social Cognition* by Brett W. Pelham and David Bonninger

Psychology Applied to Work

AN INTRODUCTION TO INDUSTRIAL AND ORGANIZATIONAL PSYCHOLOGY

SEVENTH EDITION

Paul M. Muchinsky

University of North Carolina at Greensboro

THOMSON
™
WADSWORTH

Australia • Canada • Mexico • Singapore • Spain
United Kingdom • United States

THOMSON

WADSWORTH

Psychology Editor: *Marianne Taflinger*
Development Editor: *Jim Strandberg*
Technology Project Manager: *Darin Durstein*
Assistant Editor: *Dan Moneypenny*
Editorial Assistant: *Stacy Green*
Marketing Manager: *Kathleen Morgan*
Marketing Assistant: *Laurel Anderson*
Production Editor: *Kirk Bomont*
Production Service: *New Leaf Publishing Services, Nancy Shammas*

Manuscript Editor: *Carol Reitz*
Permissions Editor: *Sue Ewing*
Interior Design: *E. Kelly Shoemaker*
Cover Design: *Rokusek Design*
Cover Photo: *Roy Ooms/Masterfile*
Indexer: *Do Mi Stauber*
Print Buyer: *Kristine Waller*
Typesetting: *Lachina Publishing Services*
Printing and Binding: *Phoenix*

For more information about our products, contact us at:
Thomson Learning Academic Resource Center
1-800-423-0563
For permission to use material from this text,
contact us by: Phone: 1-800-730-2214
Fax: 1-800-730-2215
Web: http://www.thomsonrights.com

Library of Congress Control Number: 2002106176

ISBN 0-534-59625-8

Wadsworth/Thomson Learning
10 Davis Drive
Belmont, CA 94002-3098
USA

Asia
Thomson Learning
5 Shenton Way #01-01
UIC Building
Singapore 068808

Australia
Nelson Thomson Learning
102 Dodds Street
South Melbourne, Victoria 3205
Australia

Canada
Nelson Thomson Learning
1120 Birchmount Road
Toronto, Canada M1K 5G4
Canada

Europe/Middle East/Africa
Thomson Learning
High Holborn House
50/51 Bedford Row
London WC1R 4LR
United Kingdom

Latin America
Thomson Learning
Seneca, 53
Colonia Polanco
11560 Mexico D.F.
Mexico

To the victims and their families

of the terrorist attack on the United States

September 11, 2001

Paul M. Muchinsky was born and raised in Connecticut. He received his B.A. degree in psychology from Gettysburg College, his M.S. degree in industrial/organizational psychology from Kansas State University, and his Ph.D. from Purdue University. He was a faculty member of Iowa State University for twenty years. In 1993 he was appointed the Joseph M. Bryan Distinguished Professor of Business at the University of North Carolina at Greensboro. Throughout his career, Dr. Muchinsky has been very active in a wide range of professional activities within the field of industrial/organizational psychology. Many of the cases and examples of concepts presented in this book come directly from his professional experiences. When not engaged as an I/O psychologist, Dr. Muchinsky fantasizes about playing baseball for the New York Yankees.

BRIEF CONTENTS

C ONTENTS

C H A P T E R   5   **Personnel Decisions**   **136**

CHAPTER   6   **Training and Development**   **176**

P REFACE

An author always feels a great sense of excitement and gratification when a new edition is published. I am delighted to have written the 7th edition of *Psychology Applied to Work: An Introduction to Industrial and Organizational Psychology*. This edition retains many of the qualities that have been manifested in previous editions of the book over the past 20 years. It is the single most comprehensive portrayal of industrial/organizational (I/O) psychology in the field. The book is written from a research-based, scientific perspective with abundant applications to the world of work.

The revisions for this edition include the following:

■ **Chapter 1:** The Historical Background of I/O Psychology

New material on the history of I/O psychology and cross-cultural issues in our field; updates on the demographics of our membership and salaries paid.

■ **Chapter 2:** Research Methods in I/O Psychology

New material on the role of theory in I/O psychology, research in industry, survey research, qualitative research, and ethics in research.

■ **Chapter 3:** Criteria: Standards for Decision Making

New material on job analysis, the O*NET, dynamic performance criteria, and competency modeling; new field note and new case study.

■ **Chapter 4:** Predictors: Psychological Assessments

New material on a unified theory of validity, predictor constructs, Big 5 personality factors, faking on tests, integrity tests, Computerized Adaptive Testing, situational judgment tests, interviews, assessment centers, and work experience as a predictor of job performance.

■ **Chapter 5:** Personnel Decisions

New material on the social context of personnel decisions, how the changing nature of work is affecting personnel selection decisions, legal context of personnel decisions, ADA, affirmative action, and validity generalization.

■ **Chapter 6:** Training and Development

New material on self-efficacy in learning, Secretary's Commission on Achieving Necessary Skills (SCANS), training needs assessment, web-based training, and cultural diversity training.

■ **Chapter 7:** Performance Appraisal

New material on the theory of person perception as it relates to appraising job performance, 360-degree assessment, contextual performance, self-assessments, and appraisal "politics."

■ **Chapter 8:** Organizations and Organizational Change

New chapter: three theories of organizations, reorganizing and downsizing, components of social systems, organizational change, organizational resistance to change, organizational change interventions; new case study.

■ **Chapter 9:** Teams and Teamwork

New chapter: origins of work teams, level of analysis, types of teams, principles of teamwork, team structure, team processes, shared mental models, decision making in teams, virtual teams, social loafing, personnel selection for teams, training in teams, performance appraisal in teams; new case study and three new field notes.

■ **Chapter 10:** Organizational Attitudes and Behavior

New material on job satisfaction, emotions in the workplace, organizational commitment, organizational justice, organizational citizenship behavior, psychological contract, and antisocial behavior in the workplace.

■ **Chapter 11:** Occupational Health

New chapter: the concept of occupational health, positive psychology, work stress, work/family conflict, dual-career families, work schedules, alcoholism and drug abuse in the workplace, psychological effects of unemployment, child labor and exploitation; new field note.

■ **Chapter 12:** Work Motivation

New material on conceptual basis of work motivation, goal setting, self-regulation theory, job enrichment, synthesis and integration of motivational theories; new field note.

■ **Chapter 13:** Leadership

New material on leadership vs. management, charismatic leadership, leader–member exchange theory, transformational leadership, diversity in leadership issues, and integrating motivation and leadership.

- **Chapter 14:** The Changing Nature of Work

   New material on emotions in the workplace, rise of a temporary workforce, and the role time plays in our lives.

- **Appendix:** Union/Management Relations

   A new feature designed to be of optional use. Formerly a regular chapter in previous editions, this 7th edition appendix presents new material on I/O psychology used to assist "union-busting," the growing use of arbitration as a means of dispute settlement, and trying to implement organizational change in a unionized company.

InfoTrac College Edition

InfoTrac College Edition is available (free of charge) to students who purchase this book. InfoTrac is a fully searchable online university library that contains complete articles and images from more than 700 scholarly and popular publications. Such access can help students with independent study on topics relevant to I/O psychology. Journals of interest include *Science, Across the Board, Discover, Executive Female, Success, Working Woman, Training & Development, Commentary, Online, Policy Review, Social Justice, Human Relations, Social Policy, The Futurist, New Statesman, Washington Monthly, The Humanist, Dollars and Sense,* and *Reason.*

Learning Aids

I have provided several learning aids to help students understand the text material. New to this edition is a glossary that defines more than 250 terms used in the book. Consistent with previous editions, three field notes are presented per chapter that personalize the material for students and show practical illustrations of the conceptual material.

   A case study is presented at the end of each chapter. The case studies present real dilemmas that involve making tough but necessary decisions, such as the theft of company property and changing an organization. These cases are designed to involve the students in the practice side of I/O psychology, which draws upon the knowledge learned from the research side. One-third of the case studies are new to this edition. Over the years I've heard from students and teachers alike that the cartoons shed light on the more technical aspects of I/O psychology with some humor. Three new cartoons are added to this edition.

Ancillaries for Students and Teachers

As with the previous edition, a *Study Guide and Exercise Workbook* and an *Instructor's Manual/Test Bank* are both available. The *Study Guide and Exercise Workbook* consists of more examples and practical applications that reveal the potency of I/O psychological concepts in the contemporary work world. The *Instructor's Manual/ Test Bank* presents multiple-choice, true-false, fill-in, short-answer, and essay questions as well as transparency masters for the teachers. Topics are also presented for class discussion as well as instructor tips on how to make the best use of the exercises in the *Study Guide and Exercise Workbook*.

Three new ancillaries have been added to this edition:

1. Included free with every copy of the book, **Concept Charts for Study and Review** offers a two-page chart for each chapter that highlights the major concepts and visually reinforces the chapter content by showing how ideas and concepts are related.
2. **Lecture Outlines** in Microsoft® Powerpoint® can be downloaded from the text's Web site.
3. A new release in the **CNN® Today Industrial/Organizational Psychology video series,** Volume 4 offers approximately 45 minutes of news clips originally broadcast on CNN.

ACKNOWLEDGEMENTS

The revisions for this edition were guided by some extraordinarily thoughtful and detailed suggestions by reviewers. Colleagues who invest the time and energy needed to provide high-quality reviews are greatly appreciated. They were:

Meredith Auerbach, University of New Haven
John Binning, Illinois State University
Karen Holcombe Ehrhart, University of Maryland–College Park
Mike Horvath, Clemson University
Fred Oswald, Michigan State University
Karen Williams, Illinois State University

I would like to express my love and gratitude to my wife Noël for her unrelenting support and encouragement in writing this book. In many ways this is "our" book. Finally, I hope one day they create a "Secretaries Hall of Fame." My secretary, Lynn Southard, would be a first-round, unanimous-vote, charter member. I couldn't have written this book without her extraordinary skills.

Paul M. Muchinsky

The Historical Background of I/O Psychology

CHAPTER OUTLINE

LEARNING OBJECTIVES

- Explain how I/O psychology relates to the profession of psychology as a whole.
- Be able to identify the major fields of I/O psychology.
- Understand how and why psychologists are licensed and certified.
- Learn the history of I/O psychology, including the major people, events, and eras.
- Give the reasons for cross-cultural interest in I/O psychology.

Psychology is defined as the scientific study of thinking and behavior. It is a science because psychologists use the same rigorous methods of research found in other areas of scientific investigation. Some of their research is more biological in nature (such as the effects of brain lesions on a rat's food consumption); other research is more social in nature (such as identifying the factors that lead to bystander apathy). Because psychology covers such a broad spectrum of content areas, it is difficult to have a clear and accurate image of what a psychologist does. Many people think that every psychologist "is a shrink," "has a black couch," "likes to discover what makes people tick," and so on. In fact, these descriptions usually refer to the specialty of clinical psychology—the diagnosis and treatment of mental illness or abnormal behavior. Most psychologists do not treat mental disorders, nor do they practice psychotherapy. In reality, psychologists are a very diversified lot with many specialized interests.

Many psychologists are united professionally through membership in the American Psychological Association (APA), founded in 1892. As of 2001 the APA had more than 85,000 members, 53% men and 47% women. The broad diversity of interests among psychologists is reflected by the fact that the APA has 53 divisions representing special-interest subgroups. Matarazzo (1987) noted there are not really so many different specialty areas of psychology, just many fields in which the same basic psychological principles are applied. Though some APA members have no divisional affiliation, others belong to more than one. The APA publishes several journals—vehicles through which psychologists can communicate their research findings to other scholars. The APA also holds regional and national conventions, sets standards for graduate training in certain areas of psychology (that is, clinical, counseling, and school), develops and enforces a code of professional ethics, and helps psychologists find employment. In 1988 the American Psychological Society (APS) was founded, in part because the membership and emphasis of the APA had shifted significantly toward the health care practice areas of psychology. The purpose of the APS is to advance the discipline of psychology primarily from a scientific perspective. Most of its members are academic psychologists.

INDUSTRIAL/ORGANIZATIONAL PSYCHOLOGY

Society for Industrial and Organizational Psychology (SIOP) the professional organization that represents I/O psychologists in the United States

One of the specialty areas of psychology is industrial/organizational (I/O) psychology (represented by Division 14 of the APA, the **Society for Industrial and Organizational Psychology**, or **SIOP**). In 2001 SIOP had about 3,400 professional members and approximately 1,900 student members. The percentage of women entering the field has greatly accelerated in recent years. For example, in 2001 over half of those who received doctorates in I/O psychology were women. SIOP is the primary professional organization for I/O psychologists in this nation. SIOP has developed a website on the Internet, *www.siop.org*, which provides information about careers in I/O psychology. In other countries what we call *I/O psychology* is referenced by other names. In the United Kingdom it is called *occupational psychology*, in many European countries *work and organizational psychology*, and in

South Africa *industrial psychology*. While the terminology may vary around the world, the members of our profession share common interests.

Approximately 4% of all psychologists are in the I/O area. Our relatively small representation in the total population of psychologists probably helps to explain why some people are unaware of the I/O area. About half of all psychologists work in the specialty areas of clinical and counseling psychology, which probably contributes to the stereotype of psychologists in general.

I/O psychology
an area of scientific study and professional practice that addresses psychological concepts and principles in the work world

As a specialty area, **I/O psychology** has a more restricted definition than psychology as a whole. Many years ago Blum and Naylor (1968) defined it as "simply the application or extension of psychological facts and principles to the problems concerning human beings operating within the context of business and industry" (p. 4). In broad terms, the I/O psychologist is concerned with behavior in work situations. There are two sides of I/O psychology: science and practice. I/O psychology is a legitimate field of scientific inquiry, concerned with advancing knowledge about people at work. As in any area of science, questions are posed by I/O psychologists to guide their investigation, and scientific methods are used to obtain answers. Psychologists try to form the results of studies into meaningful patterns that will be useful in explaining behavior and to replicate findings to make generalizations about behavior. In this respect, I/O psychology is an academic discipline.

The other side of I/O psychology—the professional side—is concerned with the application of knowledge to solve real problems in the world of work. I/O psychological research findings can be used to hire better employees, reduce absenteeism, improve communication, increase job satisfaction, and solve countless other problems. Most I/O psychologists feel a sense of kinship with both sides: science and practice. Accordingly, the education of I/O psychologists is founded on the **scientist–practitioner model**, which trains them in both scientific inquiry and practical application.

scientist–practitioner model
a framework for education in an academic discipline based on understanding the scientific principles and findings evidenced in the discipline and how they provide the basis for the professional practice

As an I/O psychologist, I am pleased that the results of my research can be put to some practical use. But by the same token, I am more than a technician—someone who goes through the motions of finding solutions to problems without knowing why they "work" and what their consequences will be. I/O psychology is more than just a tool for business leaders to use to make their companies more efficient. So the I/O psychologist has a dual existence. Well-trained I/O psychologists realize that an effective application of knowledge can come only from sound knowledge, and they can therefore both contribute to knowledge and apply it. Dunnette (1998) believes that an emerging trend in I/O psychology is greater fusion of the science and practice aspects of our profession than we have witnessed in the past.

Figure 1–1 shows the main work settings of I/O psychologists. They fall into four main areas, with universities and consulting firms being the primary employers. Across these four areas, I/O psychologists are unevenly split in their scientist–practitioner orientation. Universities employ more scientists; consulting firms employ more practitioners; business and government have a good mix of both. As of 2001 the average annual income for M.S. graduates in I/O psychology was approximately $68,000, whereas Ph.D. graduates earned approximately $90,000.

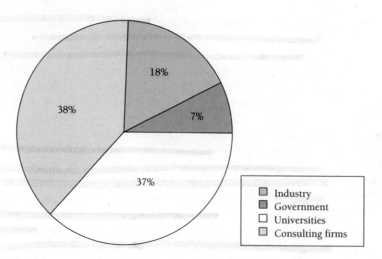

FIGURE 1–1 ■ Principal work settings of I/O psychologists
SOURCE: Society for Industrial and Organizational Psychology, member database, 2001

Some members of our profession who work in consulting firms earn more than $1 million annually.

Fields of I/O Psychology

Like psychology in general, I/O psychology is a diversified science containing several subspecialties. The professional activities of I/O psychologists can be grouped into six general fields.

Selection and Placement. I/O psychologists who work in this field are concerned with developing assessment methods for the selection, placement, and promotion of employees. They are involved in studying jobs and determining to what degree tests can predict performance in those jobs. They are also concerned with the placement of employees, which is directed toward identifying those jobs that are most compatible with the individual's skills and interests.

Training and Development. This field is concerned with the identification of employee skills that need to be enhanced to improve job performance. The areas of training include technical skills enhancement (e.g., computer operations), managerial development programs, and training of all employees to work together effectively. I/O psychologists who work in this field must design ways to determine whether training and development programs have been successful.

Performance Appraisal. Performance appraisal is the process of identifying criteria or standards for determining how well employees are performing their jobs. I/O psychologists who work in this field are also concerned with determining the utility or value of job performance to the organization. They may be involved with measuring the performance of work teams, units within the organization, or the organization itself.

DILBERT by Scott Adams

SOURCE: Dilbert® reprinted by permission of United Feature Syndicate, Inc.

Organization Development. Organization development is the process of analyzing the structure of an organization to maximize the satisfaction and effectiveness of individuals, work groups, and customers. Organizations grow and mature just as people do; thus, the field of organization development is directed toward facilitating the organizational growth process. I/O psychologists who work in this field are sensitized to the wide array of factors that influence behavior in organizations.

Quality of Worklife. I/O psychologists who work in this field are concerned with factors that contribute to a healthy and productive workforce. They may be involved in redesigning jobs to make them more meaningful and satisfying to the people who perform them. A high-quality worklife contributes to greater productivity of the organization and to the emotional health of the individual.

Ergonomics. Ergonomics is a multidisciplinary field that includes I/O psychologists. It is concerned with designing tools, equipment, and machines that are compatible with human skills. I/O psychologists who work in this field draw upon knowledge derived from physiology, industrial medicine, and perception to design work systems that humans can effectively operate.

   In summary, psychology as a discipline is composed of many specialty areas, one of which is I/O psychology. And I/O psychology consists of several subspecialties. Although some of these subspecialties overlap, many are distinct from one another. Thus, I/O psychology is not really a single discipline; it is a mix of subspecialties bonded together by a concern for people at work. Each of the subspecialties of I/O psychology will be explored to various degrees in this book.

LICENSING AND CERTIFICATION OF PSYCHOLOGISTS

What makes a psychologist a psychologist? What prevents people with no psychological training from passing themselves off as psychologists? One way professions offer high-quality service to the public is by regulating their own membership. Selective admission into the profession helps protect the public against quacks and charlatans who risk doing great damage not only to their clients but also to the profession they allegedly represent.

The practice of professional psychology is regulated by law in every state. When both the title and practice of psychology are regulated, the law is called a *licensing law.* When only the title of psychologist is regulated, the law is called a *certification law.* Laws limit licensure to those qualified to practice psychology as defined by state law. Each state has its own standards for licensure, and these are governed by regulatory boards. The major functions of any professional board are to determine the standards for admission into the profession and to conduct disciplinary actions when professional standards are violated.

licensure

the process by which a professional practice is regulated by law to ensure quality standards are met to protect the public

Typically, **licensure** involves education, experience, examination, and administrative requirements. A doctoral degree in psychology from an approved program is usually required, as well as one or two years of supervised experience. Applicants must also pass an objective, written examination covering many areas of psychology, although the majority of questions pertain to the health care (i.e., clinical and counseling) areas of psychology. Specialty examinations (for example, in I/O psychology) usually are not given. Currently, psychologists must pass a uniform national examination to obtain a license (Hoffman, 1980). Finally, the applicant must meet citizenship and residency requirements and be of good moral character.

Licensing and certification are intended to ensure that clients receive services from qualified practitioners. However, scrupulous I/O psychologists can never guarantee results, and they should never try. Companies have been duped by consulting firms and individuals into believing a wide range of claims that simply cannot be substantiated. The problems that the I/O psychologist faces are too complex for guarantees. Reasonable expectations on the part of both the I/O psychologist and the company are the best way to avoid such difficulties.

There is a controversy regarding the licensure of I/O psychologists. The original purpose of licensure in psychology was to protect the public in the health care areas of psychology. Because I/O psychologists are not health care providers, there is not a pressing need for licensure to protect the public (Howard & Lowman, 1985). Also, some I/O psychologists object to the heavy emphasis placed on clinical and counseling psychology in the licensure process. Most states regard I/O psychologists as they do other types of applied psychologists who offer services to the public, however, and thus require them to be licensed. A few states regard I/O psychologists as having a sufficiently different mandate to exempt them from licensure.

THE HISTORY OF I/O PSYCHOLOGY

It is always difficult to write *the* history of anything; there are different perspectives with different emphases. It is also a challenge to divide the historical evolution of a discipline into units of time. In some cases, time itself is a convenient watershed (decades or centuries); in others, major events serve as landmarks. In the case of I/O psychology, the two world wars were major catalysts for changing the discipline. This historical overview will show how the field of I/O psychology came to be what it is and how some key individuals and events helped shape it.[1]

---

[1] A more detailed treatment of the history of I/O psychology can be found in the excellent books by Ferguson (1962) and Napoli (1981) and in the article by Katzell and Austin (1992).

The Early Years (1900–1916)

In its beginnings, what we know today as I/O psychology didn't even have a name; it was a merging of two forces that gathered momentum before 1900. One force was the pragmatic nature of some basic psychological research. Most psychologists at this time were strictly scientific and deliberately avoided studying problems that strayed outside the boundaries of pure research. However, a psychologist named W. L. Bryan published a paper (Bryan & Harter, 1897) about how professional telegraphers develop skill in sending and receiving Morse code. A few years later in 1903, Bryan's presidential address to the American Psychological Association (Bryan, 1904) touched on having psychologists study "concrete activities and functions as they appear in everyday life" (p. 80). Bryan did not advocate studying problems found in industry per se, but he stressed examining real skills as a base upon which to develop scientific psychology. Bryan is not considered the father of I/O psychology but rather a precursor.[2]

The second major force in the evolution of the discipline came from the desire of industrial engineers to improve efficiency. They were concerned mainly with the economics of manufacturing and thus the productivity of industrial employees. A husband and wife team, Frank and Lillian Gilbreth, contributed pioneering knowledge about time and motion in industrial production. They are perhaps best known for their research on the elements of human motion, which they called "therbligs" (*Gilbreth* spelled backward, almost). Koppes (1997) reported that Lillian Gilbreth was one of several female psychologists who made substantial contributions in the early era of I/O psychology. Koppes noted that Gilbreth made a historic speech at a meeting of industrial engineers in 1908. She was asked for her opinion because she was the only woman attending the meeting. According to Yost (1943), Lillian Gilbreth "rose to her feet and remarked that the human being, of course, was the most important element in industry, and that it seemed to her this element had not been receiving the attention it warranted. The engineer's scientific training, she said, was all for the handling of inanimate objects. She called attention to the fact that psychology was fast becoming a science and that it had much to offer that was being ignored by management engineers. The plea in her impromptu remarks was for the new profession of scientific management to open its eyes to the necessary place psychology had in any program industrial engineers worked out" (Koppes, 1997, p. 511).

Thus, the merging of psychology with applied interests and concern for increasing industrial efficiency was the impetus for the emergence of I/O psychology. Koppes (2002) observed that in the late 19th century, America's society experienced rapid changes and developments because of industrialization, immigration, a high birthrate, education, and urban growth. A drive for social reform prevailed, and Americans looked toward science for practical solutions. These societal demands forced psychologists to popularize their science and demonstrate the value of psychology in solving problems and helping society. By 1910 "industrial

---

[2] The term *industrial psychology* was apparently used for the first time in Bryan's 1904 article. Ironically, it appeared in print only as a typographical error. Bryan was quoting a sentence he had written five years earlier (Bryan & Harter, 1899), in which he spoke of the need for more research in individual psychology. Instead, Bryan wrote "industrial psychology" and did not catch his mistake.

■ **Walter Dill Scott**

SOURCE: Archives of the History of American Psychology

psychology" (the "organizational" appendage did not become official until 1970) was a legitimate specialty area of psychology.

Three individuals stand out as the founding fathers of I/O psychology. They worked independently; in fact, their work barely overlapped. The major contributions of these individuals deserve a brief review.

Walter Dill Scott. Scott, a psychologist, was persuaded to give a talk to some Chicago business leaders on the need for applying psychology to advertising. His talk was well received and led to the publication of two books: *The Theory of Advertising* (1903) and *The Psychology of Advertising* (1908). The first book dealt with suggestion and argument as means of influencing people. The second book was aimed at improving human efficiency with such tactics as imitation, competition, loyalty, and concentration. By 1911 Scott had expanded his areas of interest and published two more books: *Influencing Men in Business* and *Increasing Human Efficiency in Business*. During World War I, Scott was instrumental in the application of personnel procedures in the army. Landy (1997) described Scott as the consummate scientist–practitioner who was highly respected in both spheres of professional activity. Scott had a substantial influence on increasing public awareness and the credibility of industrial psychology.

Frederick W. Taylor. Taylor was an engineer by profession. His formal schooling was limited, but through experience and self-training in engineering he went

■ **Frederick W. Taylor**

SOURCE: Stevens Institute of Technology

on to obtain many patents. As he worked himself up through one company as a worker, supervisor, and finally plant manager, Taylor realized the value of redesigning the work situation to achieve both higher output for the company and a higher wage for the worker. His best-known work is his book *The Principles of Scientific Management* (1911). Van De Water (1997) reported these principles as: (1) science over rule of thumb, (2) scientific selection and training, (3) cooperation over individualism, and (4) equal division of work best suited to management and employees. In perhaps the most famous example of his methods, Taylor showed that workers who handled heavy iron ingots (pig iron) could be more productive if they had work rests. Training employees about when to work and when to rest increased average worker productivity from 12.5 to 47.0 tons moved per day (with less reported fatigue), which resulted in increased wages for them. The company also drastically increased efficiency by reducing costs from 9.2 cents per ton to 3.9 cents per ton.

As a consequence of this method, it was charged that Taylor inhumanely exploited workers for a higher wage and that great numbers of workers would be unemployed because fewer were needed. Because there was rampant unemployment at this time, the attacks on Taylor were virulent. His methods were eventually investigated by the Interstate Commerce Commission (ICC) and the U.S. House of Representatives. Taylor replied that increased efficiency led to greater, not less, prosperity and that workers not hired for one job would be placed in another that would better use their potential. The arguments were never really resolved—World War I broke out and the controversy faded.

Hugo Münsterberg. Münsterberg was a German psychologist with traditional academic training. The noted American psychologist William James invited Münsterberg to Harvard University, where he applied his experimental methods to a variety of problems, including perception and attention. He was a popular figure in American education, a gifted public speaker, and a personal friend of President Theodore Roosevelt. Münsterberg was interested in applying traditional psychological methods to practical industrial problems. His book *Psychology and Industrial Efficiency* (1913) was divided into three parts: selecting workers, designing work situations, and using psychology in sales. One of Münsterberg's most renowned studies involved determining what makes a safe trolley car operator. He systematically studied all aspects of the job, developed an ingenious laboratory simulation of a trolley car, and concluded that a good operator could comprehend simultaneously all of the influences that bear on the car's progress. Some writers consider Münsterberg the father of industrial psychology.

Landy (1992) reported that many prominent I/O psychologists throughout the 20th century can trace their professional roots back to Münsterberg. Münsterberg's influence in the history of the field is well evidenced by the coterie of I/O psychologists who were guided by his teachings.

When World War I broke out in Europe, Münsterberg supported the German cause. He was ostracized for his allegiance, and the emotional strain probably contributed to his death in 1916. Only the U.S. involvement in the war gave some unity to the profession. The primary emphasis of the early work in I/O psychology was on the economic gains that could be accrued by applying the ideas and methods of psychology to problems in business and industry. Business leaders began to employ psychologists, and some psychologists entered applied research.

■ **Hugo Münsterberg**

SOURCE: Archives of the History of American Psychology

However, World War I caused a shift in the direction of industrial psychological research.

World War I (1917–1918)

World War I was a potent impetus to psychology's rise to respectability. Psychologists believed they could provide a valuable service to the nation, and some saw the war as a means of accelerating the profession's progress. Robert Yerkes was the psychologist most instrumental in involving psychology in the war. As president of the APA, he maneuvered the profession into assignments in the war effort. The APA made many proposals, including ways of screening recruits for mental deficiency and of assigning selected recruits to jobs in the army. Committees of psychologists investigated soldier motivation, morale, psychological problems of physical incapacity, and discipline. Yerkes continued to press his point that psychology could be of great help to our nation in wartime.

The army, in turn, was somewhat skeptical of the psychologists' claims. It eventually approved only a modest number of proposals, mostly those involving the assessment of recruits. Yerkes and other psychologists reviewed a series of general intelligence tests and eventually developed one that they called the **Army Alpha.** When they discovered that 30% of the recruits were illiterate, they developed the **Army Beta,** a special test for those who couldn't read English. Meanwhile, Walter Dill Scott was doing research on the best placement of soldiers in the army. He classified and placed enlisted soldiers, conducted performance ratings of officers, and developed and prepared job duties and qualifications for over 500 jobs.

Plans for testing recruits proceeded at a slow pace. The army built special testing sites at its camps and ordered all existing officers, officer candidates, and newly drafted recruits to be tested. Both the Army Alpha and Army Beta group intelligence tests were used, as were a few individual tests. The final order authorizing the testing program came from the adjutant general's office in August 1918. However, the Armistice was signed only three months later, and World War I was over. Testing was terminated just as it was finally organized and authorized. As a result, the intelligence testing program didn't contribute as much to the war as Yerkes would have liked. Even though 1,726,000 individuals were ultimately tested in the program, actual use of the results was minimal.

Although psychology's impact on the war effort was not substantial, the very process of giving psychologists so much recognition and authority was a great impetus to the profession. Psychologists were regarded as capable of making valuable contributions to society and of adding to a company's (and in war, a nation's) prosperity. Also in 1917 the oldest and most representative journal in the field of I/O psychology—the *Journal of Applied Psychology*—began publication. Some of the articles in the first volume were "Practical Relations Between Psychology and the War" by Hall, "Mentality Testing of College Students" by Bingham, and "The Moron As a War Problem" by Mateer. The first article published in the *Journal of Applied Psychology* not only summarized the prevailing state of industrial psychology at the time but also addressed the science-versus-practice issue that still faces I/O psychologists today.

Army Alpha
an intelligence test developed during World War I by I/O psychologists for the selection and placement of military personnel

Army Beta
a nonverbal intelligence test developed during World War I by I/O psychologists to assess illiterate recruits

The past few years have witnessed an unprecedented interest in the extension of the application of psychology to various fields of human activity. . . . But perhaps the most strikingly original endeavor to utilize the methods and the results of psychological investigation has been in the realm of business. This movement began with the psychology of advertising. . . . Thence the attention of the applied psychologist turned to the more comprehensive and fundamental problem of vocational selection—the question, namely, of making a detailed inventory of the equipment of mental qualities possessed by a given individual, of discovering what qualities are essential to successful achievement in a given vocation, and thus of directing the individual to the vocational niche which he is best fitted to fill. . . . Every psychologist who besides being a "pure scientist" also cherishes the hope that in addition to throwing light upon the problems of his science, his findings may also contribute their quota to the sum-total of human happiness; and it must appeal to every human being who is interested in increasing human efficiency and human happiness by the more direct method of decreasing the number of cases where a square peg is condemned to a life of fruitless endeavor to fit itself comfortably into a round hole. (Hall, Baird, & Geissler, 1917, pp. 5–6)

After the war, there was a boom in the number of psychological consulting firms and research bureaus. The birth of these agencies ushered in the next era in I/O psychology.

Between the Wars (1919–1940)

Applied psychology emerged from World War I as a recognized discipline. Society was beginning to realize that industrial psychology could solve practical problems. Following the war, several psychological research bureaus came into full bloom. The Bureau of Salesmanship Research was developed by Walter Bingham at the Carnegie Institute of Technology. There was little precedent for this kind of cooperation between college and industry. The bureau intended to solve problems with psychological research techniques, problems that had never been examined scientifically. Twenty-seven companies cooperated with Bingham, each contributing $500 annually to finance applied psychological research. One of the early products of the bureau was the book *Aids in Selecting Salesmen*. For several years the bureau concentrated on the selection, classification, and development of clerical and executive personnel as well as salespeople. When the Carnegie Institute stopped offering graduate work in psychology, the bureau was disbanded.

Another influential company during the period was the Psychological Corporation, founded by James Cattell in 1921. Cattell formed it as a business corporation and asked psychologists to buy stock in it. The purpose of the Psychological Corporation was to advance psychology and promote its usefulness to industry. The corporation also served as a clearinghouse for information. As protection against quacks and charlatans, who were becoming increasingly prevalent, it provided companies with reference checks on prospective psychologists. Unlike many agencies that began at the time, the Psychological Corporation has remained in business. Over the years it has changed its early mission, and today it is one of the country's largest publishers of psychological tests.

In 1924 a series of experiments began at the Hawthorne Works of the Western Electric Company. Although initially they seemed to be of minor scientific

Hawthorne studies
a series of research studies that refocused the interests of I/O psychologists to how work behavior manifests itself in an organizational context

significance, they became classics in industrial psychology. In the opinion of many writers, the **Hawthorne studies** "represent the most significant research program undertaken to show the enormous complexity of the problem of production in relation to efficiency" (Blum & Naylor, 1968, p. 306).

The Hawthorne studies were a joint venture between Western Electric and several researchers from Harvard University (none of whom were industrial psychologists by training). The original study attempted to find the relationship between lighting and efficiency. The researchers installed various sets of lights in workrooms where electrical equipment was being produced. In some cases, the light was intense; in other cases, it was reduced to the equivalent of moonlight. Much to the researchers' surprise, productivity seemed to have no relationship to the level of illumination. The workers' productivity increased whether the illumination was decreased, increased, or held constant. The results of the study were so bizarre that the researchers hypothesized some other factors as being responsible for productivity.

The results of the first study initiated four other major studies that were conducted over a 12-year period: (1) relay assembly test room, (2) mass interviewing program, (3) bank wiring observation room, and (4) personnel counseling. (For more information on these studies, see the original text by Roethlisberger and Dickson, 1939.) In essence, the Hawthorne studies revealed many previously unrecognized aspects of human behavior in a workplace. Researchers hypothesized that the study's results were caused by the employees' desire to please them. Flattered at having distinguished investigators from Harvard University take the time to study them, the workers had gone out of their way to do what they thought would impress them—namely, to be highly productive. They therefore had produced at a high level whether the room was too light or too dark. The researchers learned that factors other than purely technical ones (for example, illumination) influence productivity.

One of the major findings from the studies was a phenomenon labeled the **Hawthorne effect.** The workers' job performance began to improve following the start of the researchers' intervention and continued to improve in part because of the novelty of the situation; that is, the employees responded positively to the novel treatment they were getting from the researchers. Eventually, however, the novelty began to wear off, and productivity returned to its earlier level. This phenomenon of a change in behavior following the onset of novel treatment, with a gradual return to the previous level of behavior as the effect of the novelty wears off, is the Hawthorne effect.

Hawthorne effect
a positive change in behavior that occurs at the onset of an intervention followed by a gradual decline, often to the original level of the behavior prior to the intervention

As Adair (1984) observed, however, the precise reason for the change in behavior (for example, the novelty of the situation, special attention, or prestige from being selected for study) is not always clear. Sometimes behavior change is due just to a change in the environment (for example, the presence of the researchers) and not to the effect of some experimentally manipulated variable (for example, the amount of illumination). The psychological literature indicates that Hawthorne effects may last anywhere from a few days to two years, depending on the situation. Throughout this book, research findings that appear attributable to Hawthorne effects will be cited.

The Hawthorne studies also revealed the existence of informal employee work groups and their controls on production, as well as the importance of employee attitudes, the value of having a sympathetic and understanding supervisor, and the need to treat workers as people instead of merely as human capital. Their revelation of the complexity of human behavior opened up new vistas for industrial psychology, which for nearly 40 years had been dominated by the desire to improve company efficiency. Today the Hawthorne studies, while regarded by some contemporary psychologists as having been based on flawed research methods (e.g., Bramel & Friend, 1981), are considered to be the greatest single episode in the formation of industrial psychology. They also showed that researchers sometimes obtain totally unexpected results. Because the investigators were not tied to any one explanation, their studies took them into areas never before studied by industrial psychology and raised questions that otherwise might never have been asked. Industrial psychology was never the same again.

This era in industrial psychology ended with the coincidental conclusion of the Hawthorne studies and the outbreak of World War II. Industrial psychologists were now faced with an immense task: helping to mobilize a nation for a two-continent war.

World War II (1941–1945)

When the United States entered World War II, industrial psychologists were more prepared for their role in the war effort than they had been in 1917. By this time, psychologists had studied the problems of employee selection and placement and had refined their techniques considerably.

Walter Bingham chaired the advisory committee on classification of military personnel that had been formed in response to the army's need for classification and training. Unlike in World War I, this time the army approached the psychologists first. One of the committee's earliest assignments was to develop a test that could sort new recruits into five categories based on their ability to learn the duties and responsibilities of a soldier. The test that was finally developed was the **Army General Classification Test (AGCT)**, a benchmark in the history of group testing. Harrell (1992), in reflecting on his own involvement in developing the AGCT 50 years earlier, reported that 12 million soldiers were classified into military jobs on the basis of the test. The committee also worked on other projects, such as methods of selecting people for officer training, trade proficiency tests, and supplemental aptitude tests.

Psychologists also worked on the development and use of situational stress tests, a project undertaken by the U.S. Office of Strategic Services (OSS) (Murray & MacKinnon, 1946). The purpose of this testing program was to assess candidates for assignment to military intelligence units. During a three-day session of extremely intensive testing and observation, the candidates lived together in small groups under almost continuous observation by the assessment staff. Specially constructed situational tests, many modeled after techniques developed in the German and British armies, were used to assess candidates in nontraditional ways. One test, for example, involved constructing a 5-foot cube from a collection of

Army General Classification Test (AGCT)
a test developed during World War II by I/O psychologists for the selection and placement of military personnel

wooden poles, pegs, and blocks. It was impossible for one person to assemble the cube in the allotted time, so two "helpers" were provided. These were actually psychologists who played prearranged roles. One helper acted very passive and contributed little; the other obstructed work by making impractical suggestions and ridiculing and criticizing the candidate. Of course, no candidate could complete the project with this kind of "help." The real purpose of the test was not to see whether the candidates could construct the cube but to assess their emotional and interpersonal reactions to stress and frustration. In general, the OSS assessment program was judged to be quite successful.

Another area of work was the selection and training of pilots to fly warplanes. The committee formed for this purpose consisted of psychologists, military personnel, and civilian pilots. The committee's policy was to move the traditional experimental test setting from the laboratory to the cockpit. Airplanes were outfitted with recording and monitoring devices to assess the problems and reactions of student pilots. This research resulted in two products. First, good candidates were selected and trained as pilots (the traditional domain of personnel psychology). Second, equipment was designed to make the pilot's job easier and safer (a contribution of the new field of engineering psychology).

Throughout the war, industrial psychology was also being used in civilian life. The use of employment tests in industry increased greatly. Because the nation needed a productive workforce, psychologists were called on to help reduce employee absenteeism. Industry discovered that many of the techniques of industrial psychologists were useful, especially in the areas of selection, training, and machine design, and industrial leaders were particularly interested in the applications of social psychology. New methods of measuring soldier attitude and morale could also be used in industry. In short, the techniques developed during the war could be applied to business and industry in peacetime. World War II was a springboard for refining industrial psychological techniques and honing the skills of applied psychologists.

Each of the two world wars had a major effect on industrial psychology but in a somewhat different way. World War I helped form the profession and give it social acceptance. World War II helped develop and refine it. The next era in the history of I/O psychology saw the discipline evolve into subspecialties and attain higher levels of academic and scientific rigor.

Toward Specialization (1946–1963)

In this era, industrial psychology evolved into a legitimate field of scientific inquiry, having already established itself as an accepted professional practice. More colleges and universities began to offer courses in "industrial psychology," and graduate degrees (both M.S. and Ph.D.) were soon given. The Division of Industrial Psychology of the American Psychological Association was created in 1946. Benjamin (1997) reported that earlier I/O psychologists had less professional identity, being represented in the family of "applied psychologists."

As with any evolving discipline, subspecialties of interest began to crystallize, and industrial psychology became splintered. New journals emerged along with new professional associations. Engineering psychology (or ergonomics), born during World War II, was recognized as a separate area, in part due to such seminal books as *Applied Experimental Psychology* (Chapanis, Garner, & Morgan, 1949) and the *Handbook of Human Engineering Data* (1949). Engineering psychology went through an explosive period of growth from 1950 to 1960. This was due mainly to research done in affiliation with the defense industries. Engineering psychology's heritage was a mixture of both experimental and industrial psychology, as seen in its early label, "applied experimental psychology." That part of industrial psychology specializing in personnel selection, classification, and training also got its own identity, "personnel psychology." Sometime in the 1950s, interest grew in the study of organizations. Long the province of sociologists, this area caught the interest of psychologists. Elton Mayo was a founder of what became known as the human relations movement. Drawing upon the findings from the Hawthorne studies, it emphasized individual needs, informal groups, and social relationships as the primary basis for behavior within organizations. In the 1960s, industrial psychology research took on a stronger organizational flavor. Investigators gave more attention to social influences that impinge on behavior in organizations. Terms such as *organizational change* and *organization development* appeared in the literature regularly. Industrial psychology addressed a broader range of topics. Classic textbooks of the 1950s, such as *Personnel and Industrial Psychology* by Ghiselli and Brown (1955), gave way in title (as well as in substance) to books with more of an organizational thrust. Traditional academic boundaries between disciplines began to blur in this postwar period. Engineering psychology was a fusion of experimental and industrial psychology; organizational behavior was a mix of industrial psychology, social psychology, and sociology. This melding of disciplines was healthy because it decreased the use of narrow, parochial attempts to address complex areas of research.

The Modern Era (1964–Present)

In the late 1950s and early 1960s, the nation was swept up in what became known as the "civil rights movement." As a nation we became more sensitized to the plight of minorities who had systematically been denied equal opportunities to various sectors of life, including housing, education, and employment. In 1964 Congress passed the Civil Rights Act, a far-reaching piece of legislation designed to reduce unfair discrimination against minorities. One component of the Civil Rights Act, Title VII, addressed the issue of discrimination in employment. The significance of the law to I/O psychologists is explained as follows: For years I/O psychologists were given a relatively free rein to use a wide variety of psychological assessment devices (that is, tests, interviews, and so on) to make employment decisions. The result of these employment decisions was the disproportionately small representation of minorities (most notably Blacks and women) in the workplace, particularly in positions above lower-level jobs. Since historically these decisions seemed to result in discrimination against minorities, the government entered the picture to monitor (and, if necessary, remedy) employers' personnel practices.

By 1978 the government had drafted a uniform set of employment guidelines to which employers were bound. Companies were legally mandated to demonstrate that their employment tests did not uniformly discriminate against any minority group. In addition, the new government standards were not limited to just paper-and-pencil tests or the personnel function of selection; they addressed all devices (interviews, tests, applications) used to make all types of personnel decisions (selection, placement, promotion, discharge, and so on).

The discipline of I/O psychology now had to serve two ultimate authorities. The first authority is what all disciplines must serve—namely, to perform high-quality work, be it conducting scientific research or providing services to clients. The second authority added was government scrutiny and evaluation. I/O psychologists now had to accept the consequences of being legally accountable for their actions. As a profession, we would continue to evaluate ourselves, but government policies and agencies would also judge our actions. In 1990 President George H. Bush signed into law the Americans with Disabilities Act and in 1991 an updated version of the Civil Rights Act. Both acts were designed to remedy further inequities in the workplace.

Much has been discussed about the overall effect of government intervention on the profession of I/O psychology. Some people believe it has been an impetus to the profession, compelling us to address issues and develop solutions that we might otherwise have ignored. Others believe that the profession has been compromised by the intrusion of political and legal influences that serve to deflect activities into areas beyond our traditional domain. Some of the greatest advances in I/O psychology have been made in the past 20 years, and I attribute these advances, in part, to our being accountable to forces beyond our own profession. Legal oversight has, in my opinion, prompted I/O psychologists to broaden their horizons in terms of the problems they address and the solutions they propose. In any case, the reality of being an I/O psychologist in the 21st century involves attentiveness to legal standards, parameters that our professional predecessors never had to deal with.

I/O psychology made a major contribution to the military during this era of our history. Campbell (1990a) described the efforts of I/O psychologists to develop a test for the selection and classification of military personnel. This project involved many psychologists and took almost ten years to complete. Called "Project A," it involved developing the **Armed Services Vocational Aptitude Battery (ASVAB).** Every year the ASVAB is administered to 300,000–400,000 people; of that number, 120,000–140,000 individuals are selected.

It must also be recognized that computer technology has had a profound impact on the conduct of work. Craiger (1997) reported that from the 1950s to 1980s computers used for military purposes were converted for business purposes. Initially, only the most technically skilled individuals could use this complex technology. In 1981 the first stand-alone desktop personal computer was introduced, however, which allowed all employees to work directly with the new technology. Later in that decade client-server networks were introduced, permitting workers to share information. Work units became transformed from individuals to teams that functioned as integrated components of the larger organization. The arrival of the "information age" produced an emphasis on the generation, sharing, and management of information as a vital dimension of work. Jobs were created, some in very high levels of the organization, that had not even existed a generation earlier. Thus, the traditional chief executive officer (CEO) and chief

Armed Services Vocational Aptitude Battery (ASVAB)
a test developed in the 1980s by I/O psychologists for the selection and placement of military personnel

operating officer (COO) jobs were joined by the job of chief information officer (CIO).

There has been a major shift in the primary theoretical basis of I/O psychology in the past 20 years. For many years psychology had been dominated by behaviorism, where psychologists were concerned with the social and environmental factors that shape behavior. In the 1980s psychologists, including I/O psychologists, shifted their focus to the cognitive factors that cause behavior. Such a theoretical orientation spurs interest in how individuals receive information from their environment, how they process that information, and in turn how they manifest behavior. Some scholars have referred to the shift from a behavioral orientation to a cognitive orientation as the "cognitive revolution" in psychology.

Overview

The history of I/O psychology is rich and diverse. The field was born at the confluence of several forces, developed and grew through global conflict, and was woven into the societal fabric of which it is a part. Our history is relatively brief and our members are not great in number, but I believe I/O psychologists have contributed greatly to both economic and personal welfare. The year 1992 marked the 100th anniversary of the American Psychological Association. In celebration of our centennial, Katzell and Austin (1992) wrote a major review of the history of I/O psychology. They noted that our history is marked by a continuous interweaving of scientific and professional contributions. At certain points in our history the practice of I/O psychology has been at the vanguard of our professional efforts (particularly during wars). At other times, our scientific advances have been more noteworthy. However, as stated previously in this chapter, the science and practice of I/O psychology can never be too far apart from each other. Katzell and Austin (1992) quoted a memorable statement by Morris Viteles, one of the early pioneers of our field, who aptly summarized the two domains of I/O psychology: "If it isn't scientific, it's not good practice, and if it isn't practical, it's not good science" (p. 826). Likewise, Farr and Tesluk (1997) cited the comment by the first president of Division 14, Bruce Moore, on the duality of the science and practice of I/O psychology: "The extreme applied practitioner is in danger of narrow, myopic thinking, but the extreme pure scientist is in danger of being isolated from facts" (p. 484).

Our profession, like many others, is also subject to cycles of interest and activity. For example, Highhouse (1999) reported that the Great Depression in the 1930s led to the development of personnel counseling within organizations for helping employees solve personal problems. Questionable managerial support for such activity eventually led to its disappearance within the field of I/O psychology by the 1960s. However, the past decade our profession has seen a renewed interest in work/family conflict and the mental health of employees. In 1990 the *Handbook of Industrial and Organizational Psychology* was published (Dunnette & Hough), the first of a four-volume set that documents some of our profession's finest scientific achievements. Today I/O psychology is multidisciplinary in both its content and its methods of inquiry. On reflection, it was the same at the turn of the century—a confluence of interest in advertising research, industrial efficiency, and mental testing. In a sense, the evolution of I/O psychology is the chronicle of mushrooming interests along certain common dimensions as molded by a few seismic events. As we enter what some call the "global era" of civilization, where national and cultural boundaries are less confining, I/O psychology has also expanded its domains of interest and involvement. Entrance into the "global era" has compelled I/O psychologists to become more knowledgeable of cultures other than those typified by Western civilization. We have learned that there are broad cultural differences in the importance people place on work in life.

CROSS-CULTURAL I/O PSYCHOLOGY

cross-cultural psychology
an area of research that examines the degree to which psychological concepts and findings generalize to people in other cultures and societies

Cross-cultural psychology studies "similarities and differences in individual psychological and social functioning in various cultures and ethnic groups" (Kagitcibasi & Berry, 1989, p. 494). Given the central role that work plays in our lives, it is not surprising that I/O psychologists are being compelled to examine cross-cultural factors in work behavior. Erez (1994) described the following significant changes in world conditions that affect our worklives.

Cultural Diversity of the Labor Force. Demographic data in the United States revealed that by the year 2000 about one-third of the labor force was Black and Hispanic. The unification of Europe and the political changes in the former Soviet republics have resulted in waves of immigrants across cultural boundaries.

Scope of the Work Environment. More than 100,000 U.S. companies do business overseas. It is estimated that one-third of the profit of U.S. companies is derived from international business, along with one-sixth of the nation's jobs. The competitive global market requires greater knowledge of cultures, values, and business practices other than our own.

Mergers, Acquisitions, and Joint Ventures. In recent years a substantial number of companies have gone through the processes of mergers, acquisitions, and downsizing. More U.S. companies were acquired by foreign businesses than vice versa. Mergers and acquisitions have resulted in organizational downsizing and massive layoffs; millions of workers have been affected. Joint ventures are planned business activities between two or more organizations, often involving different cultures. They work together as partners on a specific project; for example, a Swiss organization provides the financial support for a U.S. electronics company to develop a telecommunications system for a manufacturing organization in China. Very often a confrontation between organizational cultures results when two or more companies are merged or work together.

Emergence of High Technology and Telecommunication Systems. The revolution in telecommunication systems has introduced electronic mail, fax machines, cellular phones, and teleconferences. New technology has facilitated global communication and reduced the time needed for communication. Such changes have accelerated cross-cultural communication and exposure to different values, norms, and behaviors.

Erez (1994) sounded a warning note about why I/O psychologists must be aware of cultural differences as they propose solutions to problems of work behavior. "The successful implementation of managerial techniques depends on their congruence with cultural values. Cultural values serve as criteria for evaluating the contributions of various managerial practices to employee well-being" (p. 601). Triandis (1994) described several practical examples of work-related problems that arise from insensitivity to cultural differences. For example, 25%–40% of U.S. managers selected for overseas assignments have failed because of "culture shock" associated with their new assignment. Values and customs prevalent in our society do not necessarily generalize to other cultures. Additionally, what constitutes satisfying work differs across cultures. Jobs that provide a sense of challenge are more appealing in Western cultures, whereas jobs that provide opportunities for affiliation are more appealing in other cultures. There is also evidence that cultural differences are not limited by geographic boundaries. Ronen (1997) observed that culture does not differ by country, per se, because subcultures within nations are often influenced by level of industrialization, religious affiliation, and economic wealth. Furthermore, Earley and Randel (1997) noted that there can be both intracultural and intercultural variation in topics of interest to I/O psychologists, and that culture is loosely and incompletely shared among individuals. As the growing globalization of society continues, psychologists are beginning to question some long-held beliefs about cross-cultural issues, such as whether cultures are necessarily geographically based (Hermans & Kempen, 1998) and the generalizability of Western theories to non-Euroamerican societies (Poortinga, 1999).

It is abundantly clear that the very meaning and nature of work are not universal. I/O psychologists are called upon to assist in the process of developing work procedures that span diverse cultural groups to produce a uniformly desired outcome—our economic and personal well-being.

THE MANDATE OF I/O PSYCHOLOGY

I/O psychology is confronted with a daunting task—to increase the fit between the workforce and the workplace at a time when the composition of both is rapidly changing. Today's workforce is unlike any other in our history. More people are seeking employment than ever before, and they have higher levels of education. There are more women entering the workforce seeking full-time careers, more dual-income couples, and more individuals whose native language is not English. Likewise, the nature of work is changing. There are an increasing number of jobs in service industries, jobs that require computer literacy, and part-time jobs. Rapid economic changes are forcing large-scale layoffs, often requiring individuals to learn new job skills at midlife. Societal changes also influence employment, as evidenced by the growing problem of drug use in the workplace.

Another feature of the employment picture is the rate or speed of change. Although work has always had a sense of urgency, time pressures are seemingly becoming more acute. Rapid large-scale changes in automation and computerization are changing the skill levels needed by employees. Life expectancy is increasing, and many once-retired people are returning to the workforce. Medical costs are escalating at an alarming rate, and employers feel compelled to find ways to limit their liability for employee health-related expenses. Business mergers and acquisitions are at an all-time high, and the affected employees must find ways to address the trauma of job loss, transfers, and reassignments. Factors and conditions such as these add to the pressures of designing work that is both economically efficient and personally satisfying. The year 2000 was once held out as a futuristic date and symbolized an era when life would be very different. Whether I/O psychology is ready for it or not, the new millennium has arrived.

I/O psychologists have a growing realization that our worklives are intimately tied to our personal lives. It is just not realistic to try to segment our work and personal lives. We take our work problems home with us, and our personal problems can and sometimes do affect our worklives. We are now witnessing more of an integrated, holistic approach to the psychology of work and its impact on our total well-being. I/O psychologists are currently studying such topics as leisure, emotional support provided by family members, and how job stress is dealt with at home. We have learned that our scope of concern as I/O psychologists extends beyond the traditional 8:00 a.m. to 5:00 p.m. hours of employment.

I/O psychology is concerned with the worklives of people, and because those worklives are changing, so too is I/O psychology. As a profession, we find ourselves on the threshold of some areas where we have little prior experience. We would be remiss if we did not venture into these new territories, for they are legitimate and important concerns within the world of work. Furthermore, all of our work must be conducted according to our professional code of ethics (American Psychological Association, 1992). I find the mandate of I/O psychology to be very challenging, with the unending variety of issues we address being a great source of stimulation. While some disciplines rarely change their content, I/O psychology most certainly is not the "same old stuff."

I can think of few other fields of work that are as critical to human welfare as I/O psychology. We spend more of our lifetimes engaged in working than in any other activity. Thus, I/O psychology is devoted to understanding our major mission in life. As our nation faces increasing problems of economic productivity, the field of I/O psychology continues to contribute to making our world a better place in which to live. Indeed, Katzell and Guzzo (1983) reported that 87% of the psychological approaches to improving employee productivity have been successful. Furthermore, Colarelli (1998) asserted that across the full spectrum of work organizations in society, psychological interventions designed to solve social and organizational problems are underutilized. Additionally, the scientific contributions that I/O psychologists have made are regarded as sufficiently noteworthy to occasion the revision of federal laws governing fair employment practices.

In general, we as professionals are striving to gain a complete understanding of the problems and issues associated with the world of work, embracing both its quantitative and humanistic dimensions. When you have finished reading this book, you should have a much better understanding of human behavior in the workplace. Perhaps some of you will be stimulated enough to continue your work in I/O psychology. It is a most challenging, rewarding, and useful profession.

Research Methods in I/O Psychology

LEARNING OBJECTIVES

- ■ Understand the empirical research cycle.
- ■ Know the relative advantages and disadvantages of the laboratory experiment, quasi-experiment, questionnaire, and observation research methods.
- ■ Understand meta-analysis and qualitative research methods.
- ■ Explain the statistical concepts of central tendency and variability.
- ■ Understand the concept of correlation and its interpretation.
- ■ Have an awareness and appreciation of the ethical issues associated with research.

research
a formal process by
which knowledge is
produced and
understood

We all have hunches or beliefs about the nature of human behavior. Some of us believe that red-haired people are temperamental, dynamic leaders are big and tall, blue-collar workers prefer beer to wine, the only reason people work is to make money, and the like. The list is endless. Which of these beliefs are true? The only way to find out is to conduct **research,** or the systematic study of phenomena according to scientific principles. Much of this chapter is devoted to a discussion of research methods used in I/O psychology. Understanding the research process helps people solve practical problems, apply the results of studies reported by others, and assess the accuracy of claims made about new practices, equipment, and so on.

I/O psychologists are continually faced with a host of practical problems. Knowledge of research methods makes us better able to find useful solutions to problems rather than merely stumbling across them by chance. An understanding of research methods also helps us apply the results of studies reported by others. Some factors promote the generalizability of research findings; others retard it. **Generalizability** is defined as the degree to which the conclusions based on one research sample are applicable or generalizable to another, often larger, population. People often assert the superiority of some new technique or method; a knowledge of research methods helps us determine which ones are truly valuable. It has been suggested that science has three goals: description, prediction, and explanation. The descriptive function is like taking a photograph—a picture of a state of events. Researchers may describe levels of productivity, numbers of employees who quit during the year, average levels of job satisfaction, and so on. The second function is prediction. Researchers try to predict which employees will be productive, which ones are likely to quit, and which ones will be dissatisfied. This information is then used to select applicants who will be better employees. The explanatory function is perhaps the most difficult to unravel; it is a statement of why events occur as they do. It tries to find causes: why production is at a certain level, why employees quit, why they are dissatisfied, and so forth.

This chapter will give you some insight into the research process in I/O psychology. The process begins with a statement of the problem and ends with the conclusions drawn from the research. This chapter should help you become a knowledgeable consumer of I/O psychological research.

generalizability
the extent to which
conclusions drawn
from one research
study spread or apply
to a larger population

THE EMPIRICAL RESEARCH PROCESS

Figure 2–1 shows the steps that scientists take in conducting empirical research. The research process is basically a five-step procedure with an important feedback loop; that is, the results of the fifth step influence the first step in future research studies. First, the research process begins with a statement of the problem: What question or problem needs to be studied? Second, how do you design a study to answer the question? Third, how do you measure the variables and collect the necessary data? Fourth, how do you apply statistical procedures to analyze the data? (In other words, how do you make some sense out of all the information collected?) Finally, how do you draw conclusions from analyzing the data? Let's look at each of these steps in more detail.

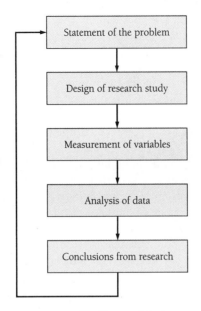

FIGURE 2–1 ■ **The empirical research cycle**

theory
a statement that proposes to explain relationships among phenomena of interest

inductive method
a research process in which conclusions are drawn about a general class of objects or people based on knowledge of a specific member of the class under investigation

deductive method
a research process in which conclusions are drawn about a specific member of a class of objects or people based on knowledge of the general class under investigation

Statement of the Problem

Questions that initiate research don't arise out of thin air. They are based on existing knowledge—your own and others' experiences with the problem, personal intuition or insight, or a theory. A **theory** is a statement that proposes to explain relationships among phenomena—for example, a theory of why individuals are attracted to each other. As researchers conduct their studies, they become more familiar with the problem and may expand the scope of their questions. One person's research may stimulate similar research by someone else; thus, researchers often benefit from their colleagues' studies. After conducting much research on a topic, researchers may propose a theory about why the behavior occurs. The sequence that starts with data and culminates in theory is the **inductive method** of science. The opposite sequence is the **deductive method.** In the deductive method, a researcher first forms a theory (perhaps by intuition or by studying previous research) and then tests the theory by collecting data. If the theory is accurate, the data will support it; if it is inaccurate, they will not.

The value of theory in science is that it integrates and summarizes large amounts of information and provides a framework for the research. Campbell (1990b) noted, however, that as a scientific discipline, psychology is much more difficult to investigate than physics or chemistry. People are far too variable, both across individuals and from day to day within one person, to be defined by a single formula or equation. The situation is not the same in physics or chemistry. A molecule of water has the same formula no matter where in the world it might be. Psychology has no equivalent of universal natural laws, such as Newton's three laws of motion. The following quotations illustrate three different yet valid views on theory:

- "There is nothing quite so practical as a good theory."—Kurt Lewin, noted social psychologist
- "Research designed with respect to theory is likely to be wasteful."—B. F. Skinner, noted experimental psychologist
- "Theory, like mist on eyeglasses, obscures facts."—Charlie Chan, noted fictional detective

Lewin's statement is often cited in psychology. Its essence is that a theory is useful for guiding research. A theory synthesizes information, organizes it into logical components, and directs the researcher's efforts in future studies. But Skinner believes that too much effort is spent on "proving" theories; that is, the theory is master of the research. Skinner feels that most theories eventually fall out of favor and that productive research does not require a theory. His position is an extreme case of empiricism. Charlie Chan thinks that researchers become too committed to proving their theories and become blinded to information that doesn't conform to what they want to believe. A good researcher doesn't let the theory obscure the facts. Rather than thinking of theories as "right" or "wrong," we try to think of them in terms of their usefulness. A useful theory helps give meaning to the problem; it helps the subject matter make more sense.

Campbell (1990b) believes that theories are only a means to an end and thus have no inherent value. He stated that theories should "help us develop better research questions, provide more useful interpretation of data, or guide the future investment of research resources" (pp. 66–67). A theory is an important tool in specifying research questions; nevertheless, a theory is only one way to formulate a research problem. Other methods can also result in high-quality research. This is especially true in a pragmatic area like I/O psychology, where some research problems come from everyday experiences in industry. If 50% of a company's workforce quit every year, one doesn't need a theory to realize that this is a serious problem. However, a theory of turnover can help explain why the turnover is occurring. I believe the value of theory in I/O psychology is to provide a useful explanation for work-related behaviors as opposed to being the sole source of a research idea.

Design of the Research Study

research design
a plan for conducting scientific research for the purpose of learning about a phenomenon of interest

A **research design** is a plan for conducting a study. A researcher can use many strategies; the choice of method depends on the nature of the problem being studied as well as cost and feasibility. Research strategies may be compared along several dimensions, but two are most important: (1) the naturalness of the research setting and (2) the investigator's degree of control over the study. No one strategy is the best under all conditions; there are always tradeoffs. These two dimensions affect both the internal and external validity of the research. **Internal validity** refers to the extent to which the results of the research can be attributed to the variables investigated rather than to other possible explanations for the results. **External validity** refers to the extent to which the findings from a research study are relevant to individuals and settings beyond those specifically examined in the study. External validity is synonymous with generalizability. If a study lacks internal validity, it can have no external validity.

internal validity
the degree to which the relationships evidenced among variables in a particular research study are accurate or true

external validity
the degree to which the relationships evidenced among variables in a particular research study are generalizable or accurate in other contexts

Naturalness of the Research Setting. In some research strategies, the problem can be studied in the environment in which it naturally occurs. This is desirable because we don't want the research strategy to destroy or distort the phenomenon under study. Some research strategies appear phony because the problem is studied in unnatural ways. In contrast, for example, the Hawthorne studies were conducted right in the plant with actual employees performing their normal jobs. Some studies do not need to be conducted in a natural environment, however, because the behavior under investigation is assumed to be independent of the setting. For example, an engineering psychology study to test whether people react faster to red or green lights could be conducted as appropriately in a laboratory as in a natural field setting.

Degree of Control. In some research strategies, the researcher has a high degree of control over the conduct of the study. In others, very little control is possible. In the Hawthorne studies, the researchers could control the exact amount of lighting in the work area by installing (or removing) lights, although it turned out that factors other than lighting affected the workers' performance. But suppose you want to study the relationship between people's ages and their attitudes toward I/O psychology. You are particularly interested in comparing the attitudes of people over age 40 with those under 40. You develop a questionnaire that asks their opinions about I/O psychology (is it interesting, difficult to understand, and so on) and distribute it to your classmates. It turns out that every person in the class is under 40. Now you have no information on the over-40 group, so you can't answer your research question. This is an example of a low degree of control (you cannot control the age of the people in the study). Low control is particularly endemic to the questionnaire research method.

Primary Research Methods

primary research method
a class of research methods that generates new information on a particular research question

This section is a discussion of four primary research methods used in I/O psychology. A **primary research method** is one that provides an original or principal source of data bearing on a particular research question. No one method is perfect; that is, none offers a high degree of both naturalism and control. Each method will be described and illustrated with an example.

laboratory experiment
a type of research method in which the investigator manipulates independent variables and assigns subjects to experimental and control conditions

Laboratory Experiment. **Laboratory experiments** are conducted in contrived settings as opposed to naturally occurring organizational settings. In a laboratory, the researcher has a high degree of control over the conduct of the study, especially over those conditions associated with the observations of behavior. The experimenter designs the study to test how certain aspects of an actual environment affect behavior. The laboratory setting must mirror certain dimensions of the natural environment where the behavior normally occurs. A well-designed laboratory experiment will have some of the conditions found in the natural environment but will omit those that would never be present. Furthermore, in a laboratory experiment, the researcher randomly assigns the study participants to the various treatment conditions, which enhances control and facilitates drawing causal inferences.

Streufert et al. (1992) conducted a laboratory experiment on the effects of alcohol intoxication on visual-motor performance. A sample of adult men participated for two days; one day they consumed alcohol and the other day they consumed mineral water (disguised with a mild ethanol spray to provide the odor of alcohol). The mineral water served as a control condition against which to compare alcohol intoxication. The alcohol dosage was designed to produce breath alcohol levels of either .05 or .10 (the conventional legal standard for alcohol intoxication). Visual-motor performance was measured on a task similar to the Pac-Man video game. The researchers studied several aspects of performance, including risk taking and errors. They compared performance under alcohol intoxication with performance under the control condition for each person. The results showed that error rates were dramatically higher under conditions of alcohol consumption. Serious performance deterioration was found to occur even at the lower (.05) intoxication level. Under the influence of alcohol, some individuals exhibited greater cautiousness (i.e., slower reaction time) to the visual-motor task, trading off speed of response for fewer errors. The researchers regarded errors in the task to be equivalent to an air traffic controller's failure to ward off aircraft that have come too close to each other. Additionally, although reduced speed of response may decrease errors, it also may prevent engaging in needed defense maneuvers.

This study illustrates the defining characteristics of a laboratory experiment. By controlling for other factors, the researchers were able to determine the causal link between alcohol consumption and performance on a visual-motor task. They could also control the dosage of alcohol to produce precise breath alcohol levels of .05 or .10, typical levels of intoxication associated with drinking alcohol in naturalistic settings. Nevertheless, one can question the generalizability of the skills needed to perform the selected visual-motor task to real jobs. Some jobs, such as a surgeon, require even greater concentration and coordination. In such a case, the magnitude of the "errors" caused by alcohol intoxication would be greater. Other jobs, such as a manual laborer, have fewer visual-motor skill requirements, in which case the errors would be less. In short, the findings from the study pertain to the effects of alcohol on visual-motor performance, not the total spectrum of skills needed for performance across many jobs. Nevertheless, the laboratory experiment is a classic research method for addressing highly specific research questions, and the results from such experiments can often be interpreted with a high degree of clarity.

Quasi-Experiment. *Quasi* is defined as "seemingly but not actually"; therefore, a **quasi-experiment** resembles an experiment but actually offers less control over the variables under investigation. A quasi-experiment is a research strategy in which some variables are manipulated in a natural setting (that is, the people in the study do not perceive the setting as having been created to conduct the research). As in a laboratory experiment, the researcher tests the effects of a few variables on the subjects' behavior. But there is also less control. In a laboratory experiment, all the variables are manipulated at the researcher's discretion and can be included or excluded according to the design of the study. However, in a quasi-experiment, variables that occur in the natural setting are also part of the investigation. Though they add to the richness and realism of the study, they also lessen the researcher's control. Furthermore, random assignment of study participants is often not possible in a field setting, which leads to less generalizable conclusions by the researcher.

Latham and Kinne (1974) reported a study that clearly demonstrates the quasi-experiment as a research method. It examined how a one-day training program on goal setting affected the job performance of pulpwood workers. The subjects in the study were 20 pulpwood logging crews. Their behavior was observed as they performed their normal job duties harvesting lumber in a forest. The experimenters split the subjects into two groups of ten crews each. They matched the two groups on a number of factors so that they would be equal in terms of

quasi-experiment
a type of research method for conducting studies in field situations where the researcher may be able to manipulate some independent variables

ability and experience. One group was given a one-day course on how to set production goals—that is, how many cords of wood to harvest per hour. The other group was not given any special instructions and worked in the usual way. The experimenters then monitored the job performances of the wood crews over the next three months. Results showed that the crews who were trained to set production goals for themselves harvested significantly more wood than the other crews. The study supported the use of goal setting in an industrial context.

The major strength of this study in terms of demonstrating the quasi-experiment method is that the context was very real. Actual workers were used in the context of their everyday jobs. The setting was a forest, not a laboratory where the crews would have been pretending. Although the study's design was not complex enough to rule out competing explanations for the observed behavior, it did allow the researchers to conclude that the goal-setting technique probably caused the increase in job performance. This study also illustrates some weaknesses of the quasi-experiment method. Some workers who were supposed to participate in the goal-setting group decided not to. This forced the researchers to redesign part of the study. Also, few I/O psychologists are able to influence a company to change its work operations for research purposes. (In fact, one of the authors of this study was employed by the lumber company, which undoubtedly had some effect on the company's willingness to participate.)

questionnaire
a type of research method in which subjects respond to written questions posed by the investigator

Questionnaire. **Questionnaires** rely on individuals' self-reports as the basis for obtaining information. They can be constructed to match the reading ability level of the individuals being surveyed. Questionnaires represent a means of maintaining the anonymity of respondents if the subject matter being covered is sensitive. Furthermore, they are a highly effective means of data collection.

Murphy, Thornton, and Prue (1991) used the questionnaire method to ascertain the acceptability of employee drug testing. The authors asked two samples of individuals (college-aged students and older, nontraditional students) to indicate the degree to which they view testing for illicit drug use as justified in each of 35 jobs (such as salesperson, surgeon, mechanic, and airline pilot). The students rated each job on a 7-point scale from low to high acceptance of drug testing. The jobs were carefully selected to represent different types of skills and temperaments needed for their successful conduct, as well as physical conditions under which the jobs are performed. The results indicated that the degree to which different jobs involved danger to the worker, coworkers, or the public was most strongly related to the acceptability of employee drug testing. The authors concluded that it would be relatively easy to justify drug testing for some jobs, whereas substantial efforts may be necessary to overcome resistance to drug testing for other jobs. Furthermore, the responses by both sets of students were virtually the same; that is, the attitudes of college-aged students were the same as those of older individuals (average age of 35). However, the results also revealed a high degree of variability in attitudes toward drug testing among members of both groups. Some individuals were in favor of drug testing across all jobs, whereas other individuals were opposed to drug testing for any job.

Questionnaires are a very popular method of research in I/O psychology; however, they do suffer from several practical limitations. Some people are not willing to complete a questionnaire and return it to the researcher. Roth and BeVier (1998) reported that a 50% return rate is considered adequate in survey research, yet the return rate of mailed questionnaires is often less than 50%. For example, in the Murphy et al. (1991) study, the return rate of questionnaires mailed to the homes of the nontraditional students was 31%. Such a low response rate raises the question of how representative or unbiased the responses are for the group as a whole. Indeed, Rogelberg, Luong, Sederburg, and Cristol (2000) found that nonrespondents to an organizational survey exhibited more negative attitudes about various aspects of their work than did respondents to the survey. The researchers were able to ascertain the attitudes of both groups by means of inter-views. Their findings cast doubt on the generalizability of the answers from respondents of some surveys to the larger population in question. More positively, Stanton (1998) found that responses to a survey using the Internet contained fewer incomplete or missing answers than responses to the same survey adminis-tered via the mail. The author supported using the Internet as an efficient means of collecting survey data. Rising postal rates are also a concern for mail surveys. Researchers usually pay the postage both ways. Despite their limitations, ques-tionnaires are used extensively in I/O psychology to address a broad range of research questions.

observation
a type of research method in which the investigator observes subjects for the purpose of under-standing their behavior and culture

Observation. **Observation** is a method that can be used when the research is examining overt behaviors. In natural field settings, behavior may be observed over extended periods of time and then recorded and categorized. As a research method, observation is not used very frequently in I/O psychology, primarily because it requires substantial amounts of time and energy.

Komaki (1986) sought to identify the behaviors that differentiate effective and ineffective work supervisors. She had observers record the behaviors of 24 man-agers: 12 previously had been judged as effective in motivating others and 12 judged as relatively ineffective. Approximately twenty 30-minute observations were made of each manager's behavior over a seven-month period (232 hours of obser-vation in total). The managers were observed as they conducted their normal day-to-day job duties. The observer stood out of sight but within hearing distance of the manager and used a specially designed form for recording and coding the observations. Komaki found the primary behavior that differentiated the effective and ineffective managers was the frequency with which they monitored their employees' performance. Compared with ineffective managers, effective managers spent more time sampling their employees' work. The findings were interpreted as underscoring the importance of monitoring critical behaviors in producing effec-tive supervisors. However, this conclusion requires corroborating empirical evi-dence because the two groups of managers were merely observed with no attempt to control for other variables that might account for the results.

Observation is often a fruitful method for generating ideas that can be further tested with other research methods. The observation method is rich in providing data from environments where the behavior in question occurs. But how success-ful can observers be in acting like "flies on the wall," observing behavior but not influencing it? In the Komaki study, the managers were highly aware that they were being observed. Given this, to what degree did the managers modify their

TABLE 2–1 ■ Comparison of primary research strategies

	Laboratory Experiment	Quasi-Experiment	Questionnaire	Observation
Control (potential for testing causal relationships)	High	Moderate	Low	Low
Realism (naturalness of setting)	Low	High	Moderate	High

conduct to project socially desirable behaviors (e.g., monitoring of their subordinates)? Perhaps effective managers are more sensitive to social cues than ineffective managers and thus are better able to be perceived in a positive fashion. Note that we are dealing with interpretations of the behavior (the "why"), not merely the behavior itself (the "what"). It has been suggested that acceptance and trust of the observers by the study participants are critical to the success of this research method.

Table 2–1 compares the four primary research methods on two major dimensions: researcher control and realism. No method is high on both factors. There is always a tradeoff; a researcher may sacrifice realism for control or vice versa, depending on the study's objectives. The choice of a strategy should be guided by the purpose of the research and the resources available. A well-trained I/O psychologist knows the advantages and disadvantages of each method.

Secondary Research Methods

secondary research method
a class of research methods that examines existing information from research studies that used primary methods

meta-analysis
a quantitative secondary research method for summarizing and integrating the findings from original empirical research studies

While a primary research method is one that gathers or generates new information on a particular research question, a **secondary research method** looks at existing information from studies that used primary methods. One particular secondary research method, meta-analysis (Hunter & Schmidt, 1990; Rosenthal, 1991), is being used with increasing frequency in I/O psychology. **Meta-analysis** is a statistical procedure designed to combine the results of many individual, independently conducted empirical studies into a single result or outcome. The logic behind meta-analysis is that we can arrive at a more accurate conclusion regarding a particular research topic if we combine or aggregate the results of many studies that address the topic, instead of relying on the findings of a single study. The result of a meta-analysis study is often referred to as an "estimate of the true relationship" among the variables examined because we believe such a result is a better approximation of the "truth" than would be found in any one study. A typical meta-analysis study might combine the results from 25 or more individual empirical studies. As such, a meta-analysis investigation is sometimes referred to as "a study of studies." Although the nature of the statistical equations performed in meta-analysis is beyond the scope of this book, they often entail adjusting for characteristics of a research study (for example, the quality of the measurements used in the study and the sample size) that are known to influence the study's results.

Despite the apparent objectivity of this method, the researcher must make a number of subjective decisions in conducting a meta-analysis. For example, one decision involves determining which empirical studies to include. Every known study ever conducted on the topic could be included or only those studies that meet some criteria of empirical quality or rigor. The latter approach can be justified on the grounds that the results of a meta-analysis are only as good as the quality of the original studies used. The indiscriminate inclusion of low-quality empirical studies lowers the quality of the conclusion reached. Another issue is referred to as the "file drawer effect." Research studies that yield negative or nonsupportive results are not published (and thus not made widely available to other researchers) as often as studies that have supportive findings. The nonpublished studies are "filed away" by researchers, resulting in published studies being biased in the direction of positive outcomes. Thus, a meta-analysis of published studies could lead to a conclusion distorted because of the relative absence of (unpublished) studies reporting negative results. Additionally, Ostroff and Harrison (1999) noted that original research studies on a similar topic sometimes differ in the **level of analysis** used by the researchers. For example, one original study may have examined the individual attitudes of employees in a work team, while another original study may have examined the attitudes of different teams working with each other. It would not be appropriate to meta-analyze the findings from these two studies because the level (or object) of analysis in the first study was the individual, but in the second study it was the work team. Ostroff and Harrison argued that researchers must be careful meta-analyzing findings from original studies that addressed different topics. These are examples of the issues that must be addressed in conducting a meta-analysis (Wanous, Sullivan, & Malinak, 1989).

level of analysis
the unit that is the object of the researchers' interest and about which conclusions are drawn from the research

Despite the difficulty in making some of these decisions, meta-analysis is a popular research procedure in I/O psychology. Refinements and theoretical extensions in meta-analytic techniques (Raju, Burke, Normand, & Langlois, 1991) attest to the sustained interest in this method across the areas of psychology. For example, many companies have sponsored smoking cessation programs for their employees to promote health and reduce medical costs. Viswesvaran and Schmidt (1992) meta-analyzed the results from 633 studies of smoking cessation involving more than 70,000 individual smokers. They found that 18.6% of smokers quit after participation in a cessation program, but the results differed by type of program. Instructional programs were found to be twice as effective as drug-based programs. The results of this meta-analysis can be of considerable practical value in assisting organizations to develop effective smoking cessation programs for their employees.

Hunter and Schmidt (1996) are very optimistic about the scientific value of meta-analysis. They believe it has the power to change how we conduct our research and to provide guidance on major social policy issues. Shadish (1996) contended that meta-analysis can also be used to infer causality through selected statistical and research design procedures. It is clear that meta-analysis has become a prominent data-analytic method for researchers and will undoubtedly continue to be so in the future.

Qualitative Research

qualitative research
a class of research methods in which the investigator takes an active role in interacting with the subjects he or she wishes to study

In recent years there has been an increase in interest among some disciplines in what is called **qualitative research.** The name is somewhat of a misnomer because it implies the absence of any quantitative procedures (i.e., statistical analyses), which is not true. Qualitative research involves new ways of understanding research questions and how these ways influence the conclusions we reach about the topic under investigation. Qualitative research (compared with traditional research methods) requires the investigator to become more personally immersed in the entire research process, as opposed to being just a detached, objective investigator.

Maxwell (1998) stated that qualitative research often begins with an examination of why the investigator is interested in conducting the research in the first place. He proposed three kinds of purposes for conducting a scientific study: personal, practical, and research. Personal purposes are those that motivate *you* to conduct a study; they can include a desire to change some existing situation or simply to advance your career as a researcher. Such personal purposes often overlap with the practical and research purposes. It is critical that you be aware of your personal purposes and how they may shape your research. To the extent that data analysis procedures are based on personal desires and you have not made a careful assessment of their implications for your methods and results, you are in danger of arriving at invalid conclusions. Practical purposes focus on accomplishing something—meeting some need, changing some situation, or achieving some goal. Research purposes, on the other hand, focus on understanding something—gaining some insight into what is going on and why it is happening. Maxwell advised researchers to be fully cognizant of the multiple purposes for doing a study, and of how these purposes can interact to influence the conclusions we reach in our research.

ethnography
a research method that utilizes field observation to study a society's culture

emic
an approach to researching phenomena that emphasizes knowledge derived from the participants' understanding of their own culture

etic
an approach to researching phenomena that emphasizes knowledge derived from the perspective of an objective investigator in understanding a culture

The essence of qualitative research is to recognize the number of different ways we can attain an understanding of a phenomenon. We can learn through watching, listening, and in some cases participating in the phenomenon we seek to understand. One qualitative research approach is ethnography. Fetterman (1998) described **ethnography** as the art and science of describing a group or culture. The description may be of any group, such as a work group or an organization. An ethnographer details the routine daily lives of people in the group, focusing on the more predictable patterns of behavior. Ethnographers try to keep an open mind about the group they are studying. Preconceived notions about how members of the group behave and what they think can severely bias the research findings. It is difficult, if not impossible, however, for a researcher to enter into a line of inquiry without having some existing problem or theory in mind. Ethnographers believe that both the group member's perspective and the external researcher's perspective of what is happening can be melded to yield an insightful portrayal of the group. The insider's view is called the **emic** perspective, whereas the external view is the **etic** perspective. Since a group has multiple members, there are multiple emic views of how group insiders think and behave in the different ways they do. Differing perceptions of what is going on in the group can help a researcher understand maladaptive behavior patterns. Most ethnographers begin their research process from the emic perspective, and then try to understand their data from the scientific or etic perspective. High-quality ethnographic research requires both perspectives: an insightful and sensitive interpretation of group processes combined with data collection techniques.

The field of I/O psychology has been relatively slow to adopt qualitative research methods. Historically our discipline has taken a quantitative approach to understanding phenomenon; meta-analysis is an example. However, I/O psychology is relying increasingly on more qualitative methods to facilitate our understanding of organizational issues. One example is researchers attempting to understand the processes of recruitment and selection from the perspective of the job applicant, not just the organization. With the growing use of work teams in organizations, ethnographic research methods may well aid us in understanding the complex interactions within a group (Brett, Tinsley, Janssens, Barsness, & Lytle, 1997). In the final analysis, there is no need to choose between qualitative and traditional research methods. We need to realize that both approaches can help us understand topics of interest to us. Lee, Mitchell, and Sablynski (1999) suggest that the use of qualitative methods may be growing in I/O psychology because researchers want additional methods to better understand the topics of interest to them. In this book, case studies and field notes are used along with empirical research findings to facilitate an understanding of issues in I/O psychology.

Measurement of Variables

variable
an object of study whose measurement can take on two or more values

After developing a study design, the researcher must carry it out and measure the variables of interest. A **variable** is represented by a symbol that can assume a range of numerical values. **Quantitative variables** (age, time) are those that are inherently numerical (21 years or 16 minutes). **Qualitative variables** (gender, race) are not inherently numerical, but they can be "coded" to have numerical meaning: female = 0, male = 1; or White = 0, Black = 1, Hispanic = 2, Asian = 3; and so forth. For research purposes, it doesn't matter what numerical values are given to the qualitative variables because they merely identify these variables for measurement purposes.

quantitative variable
an object of study that inherently has numerical values associated with it

qualitative variable
an object of study that does not inherently have numerical values associated with it

Variables Used in I/O Psychological Research. The term *variable* is often used in conjunction with other terms in I/O psychological research. Four such terms that will be used throughout this book are *independent, dependent, predictor,* and *criterion.* Independent and dependent variables are associated in particular with experimental research strategies. **Independent variables** are those that are manipulated or controlled by the researcher. They are chosen by the experimenter, set or manipulated to occur at a certain level, and then examined to assess their effect on some other variable. In the laboratory experiment by Streufert et al. (1992), the independent variable was the level of alcohol intoxication. In the quasi-experiment by Latham and Kinne (1974), the independent variable was the one-day training program on goal setting.

independent variable
a variable that can be manipulated to predict the values of the dependent variable

dependent variable
a variable whose values are predicted by the independent variable

Experiments assess the effects of independent variables on the dependent variable. The **dependent variable** is most often the object of the researcher's interest. It is usually some aspect of behavior (or, in some cases, attitudes). In the Streufert et al. study, the dependent variable was the subjects' performance on a visual-motor task. In the Latham and Kinne study, the dependent variable was the number of cords of wood harvested by the lumber crews.

The same variable can be selected as the dependent or the independent variable depending on the goals of the study. Figure 2–2 shows how a variable (employee performance) can be either dependent or independent. In the former case, the researcher wants to study the effect of various leadership styles (independent variable) on employee performance (dependent variable). The researcher might select two leadership styles (a stern taskmaster approach versus a relaxed, easygoing one) and then assess their effects on job performance. In the latter case, the researcher wants to know what effect employee performance (independent variable) has on the ability to be trained (dependent variable). The employees are divided into "high-performer" and "low-performer" groups. Both groups then attend a training program to assess whether the high performers learn faster than the low performers. Note that variables are never inherently independent or dependent. Whether they are one or the other is up to the researcher's discretion.

Predictor and criterion variables are often used in I/O psychology. When scores on one variable are used to predict scores on a second, the variables are called **predictor** and **criterion** variables, respectively. For example, a student's high school grade point average might be used to predict his or her college grade point average. Then high school grades are the predictor variable; college grades are the criterion variable. As a rule, criterion variables are the focal point of our study. Predictor variables may or may not be successful in predicting what we want to know (the criterion). Predictor variables are similar to independent variables; criterion variables are similar to dependent variables. The distinction between the two is a function of the research strategy. Independent and dependent variables are used in the context of experimentation. Predictor and criterion variables are used in any research strategy where the goal is to determine the status of subjects on one variable (the criterion) as a function of their status on another variable (the predictor).

predictor variable
a variable used to predict a criterion variable

criterion variable
a variable that is a primary object of a research study

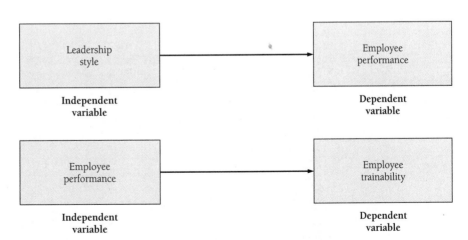

FIGURE 2–2 ■ **Employee performance used as either a dependent or an independent variable**

Independent variables are associated with making causal inferences; predictor variables may not be.

Analysis of Data

After the data have been collected, the researcher has to make some sense out of them. This is where statistics come in. Many students get anxious over the topic of statistics. Although some statistical analytic methods are quite complex, most are reasonably straightforward. I like to think of statistical methods as golf clubs—tools for helping do a job better. Just as some golf shots call for different clubs, different research problems require different statistical analyses. Knowing a full range of statistical methods will help you better understand the research problem. It is impossible to understand the research process without some knowledge of statistics. A brief exposure to statistics follows.

descriptive statistics
a class of statistical analyses that serves to describe the variables under investigation

Descriptive statistics simply describe data. They are the starting point in the data analysis process; they give the researcher a general idea of what the data are like. Descriptive statistics can show the shape of a distribution of numbers, measure the central tendency of the distribution, and measure the spread or variability in the numbers.

Distributions and Their Shape. Suppose a researcher measures the intelligence of 100 people with a traditional intelligence test. Table 2–2 is a list of those 100 scores. To make some sense out of all these numbers, the researcher arranges the numbers according to size and then plots them in a scatter diagram. Figure 2–3

TABLE 2–2 ■ One hundred intelligence test scores

133	141	108	124	117
110	92	88	110	79
143	101	120	104	94
117	128	102	126	84
105	143	114	70	103
151	114	87	134	81
87	120	145	98	95
97	157	99	79	107
108	107	147	156	144
118	127	96	138	102
141	113	112	94	114
133	122	89	128	112
119	99	110	118	142
123	67	120	89	118
90	114	121	146	94
128	125	114	91	124
121	125	83	99	76
120	102	129	108	98
110	144	89	122	119
117	127	134	127	112

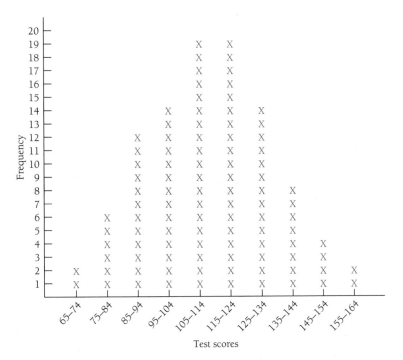

FIGURE 2–3 ■ **Frequency distribution of 100 test scores (grouped data)**

shows what those 100 test scores look like in a frequency distribution. Because so many scores are involved, they are grouped into categories of equal size, with each interval containing ten possible scores.

The figure tells us something about the intelligence test scores. We can see that the most frequently occurring scores are in the middle of the distribution; extreme scores (both high and low) taper off as we move away from the center. The general shape of the distribution in Figure 2–3 is called *normal* or *bell shaped*. Many variables in psychological research are distributed normally—that is, with the most frequently occurring scores in the middle of the distribution and progressively fewer scores at the extreme ends. Figure 2–4a shows a classic normal distribution. The curve in Figure 2–4a is smooth compared with the distribution in Figure 2–3 because the inclusion of many test scores takes the "kinks" out of the distribution.

Not all distributions of scores are normal in shape; some are lopsided or pointed. If a professor gives an easy test, a larger proportion of high scores results in a pointed or *skewed* distribution. Figure 2–4b shows a negatively skewed distribution (the tail of the distribution is in the negative direction). The opposite occurs if the professor gives a difficult test; the result is a positively skewed distribution (the tail points in the positive direction), as in Figure 2–4c. Thus, plotting the distribution of data is one way to understand them. We can make inferences based on the shape of the distribution. (In the case of the negatively skewed distribution of test scores, we infer that the test was easy.)

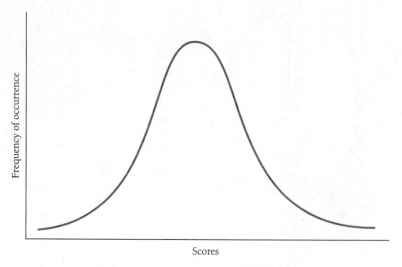

FIGURE 2–4a ■ **A normal or bell-shaped distribution of scores**

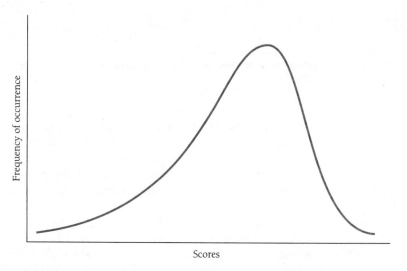

FIGURE 2–4b ■ **A negatively skewed distribution of scores**

Measures of Central Tendency. After we learn the shape of the distribution, the next step is to find the typical score. One of three measures of central tendency is usually used for this, depending on the shape of the distribution.

The **mean** is the most common measure of central tendency. The mean is the arithmetic average score in the distribution. It is computed by adding all of the individual scores and then dividing the sum by the total number of scores in the distribution. The formula for computing the mean is

mean
the arithmetic average of a distribution of numbers

$$\bar{X} = \frac{\Sigma X}{N}$$

[Formula 2–1]

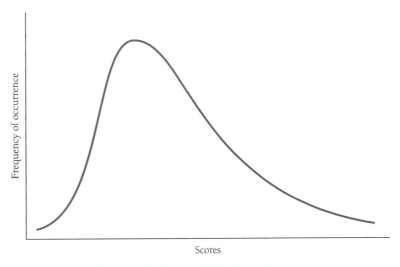

FIGURE 2–4c ■ A positively skewed distribution of scores

where $\overline{X}$ is the symbol for the mean, Σ is the symbol for summation, X is the symbol for each individual score, and N is the total number of scores in the distribution. The mean for the data in Table 2–2 is found as follows:

$$\overline{X} = \frac{11{,}322}{100} = 113.22 \qquad\qquad \text{[Formula 2–2]}$$

The average intelligence test score in the sample of people tested is 113.22 (or 113 rounded off). The entire distribution of 100 scores can be described by one number: the mean. The mean is a useful measure of central tendency and is most appropriately used with normally distributed variables.

median
the midpoint of all
the numbers in a
distribution

     The **median** is the midpoint of all the scores in the distribution, so 50% of all scores are above the median and 50% are below. If we have a distribution of four scores, 1, 2, 3, and 4, the median is 2.5; that is, half the scores (3 and 4) are above this point and half (1 and 2) are below it. (The statistical procedure used to compute the median for graphed data is quite lengthy and will not be presented

FRANK AND ERNEST   by Bob Thaves

SOURCE: Reprinted by permission of Newspaper Enterprise Association, Inc.

here. For your information, the median of the data presented in Table 2–2 is 112.9.) The median is the best measure of central tendency for skewed distributions that contain some extreme scores. The median is relatively insensitive to extreme scores, whereas the mean is affected by them. For example, if we have a distribution of three scores, 1, 2, and 3, the mean is 2. Alternatively, if the distribution of three scores were 1, 2, and 30, the mean would be 11.

The **mode** is the least used measure of central tendency. The mode is defined as the most frequently occurring score in a distribution. The mode is not used for many statistical analyses, but it may have a practical purpose. Some concepts are best understood in whole numbers (that is, integers), not in fractions or decimals. For example, it makes more sense to say "The modal number of children in a family is 3" rather than "The mean number of children in a family is 2.75." It is difficult to imagine three-fourths of a child. In cases such as this, the mode is the preferred measure of central tendency. Although the mean is more appropriate than the mode for describing the data in Table 2–2, the mode is 114.

In the normal distribution, the mean ($\overline{X}$), median (*Md*), and mode (*Mo*) are equal, as shown in Figure 2–5a. In a skewed distribution, the mean and median are pulled toward the tail of the distribution, as shown in Figure 2–5b.

One of the three measures of central tendency can be used to describe a typical score in a distribution.

Measures of Variability.   In addition to describing a set of scores by the shape of their distribution and their central tendency, we can talk about the spread of the scores or their variability. The scores' **variability** is an indication of how representative the mean is as a measure of central tendency. There are several numerical indices to describe variability in scores. The simplest index, the **range**, is obtained

mode
the most frequently occurring number in a distribution

variability
the dispersion of numerical values evidenced in the measurement of an object or concept

range
a descriptive statistical index that reflects the dispersion in a set of scores; arithmetically, the difference between the highest score and the lowest score

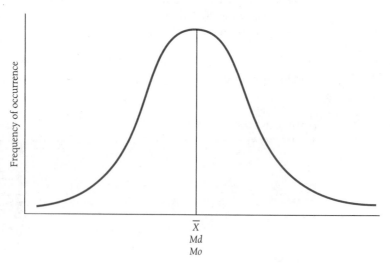

FIGURE 2–5a ■ Position of the mean, median, and mode in a normal distribution

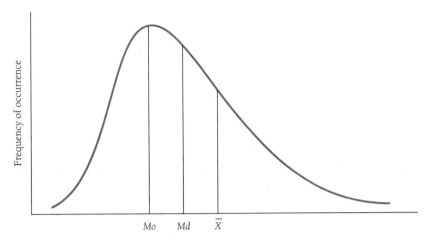

FIGURE 2–5b ■ Positions of the mean, median, and mode in a skewed distribution

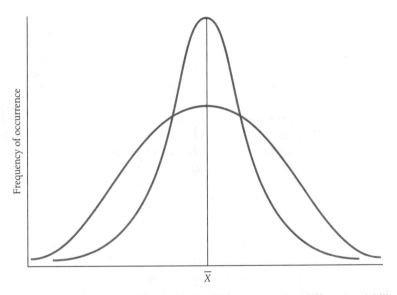

FIGURE 2–6 ■ Two distributions with the same mean but different variability

by subtracting the lowest score from the highest. The range of the data in Table 2–2 is $157 - 67 = 90$.

Consider Figure 2–6. The two normal distributions have equal means but unequal variability. One distribution is very peaked with a smaller range; the other is quite flat with a larger range. In addition to having different ranges, these distributions differ with regard to another measure of variability, the standard deviation.

standard deviation
a statistic that shows the dispersion of scores around the mean in a distribution of scores

The **standard deviation** is a measure of the spread of scores around the mean. The formula for the standard deviation is

$$s = \sqrt{\frac{\Sigma(X - \overline{X})^2}{N}}$$

[Formula 2–3]

where s is the standard deviation, X is each individual score, Σ is the symbol for summation, $\overline{X}$ is the mean of the distribution, and N is the total number of scores in the distribution. To compute the standard deviation, we subtract the mean ($\overline{X}$) from each individual score (X) in the distribution, square that number, add up all the numbers, divide that total by the number of scores in the distribution, and then take the square root of the figure. By applying this formula to the data in Table 2–2, we find the standard deviation for that distribution is 19.96 (or 20 rounded off).

The standard deviation is particularly important when used with the normal distribution. Given the mathematical properties of the normal curve, we know that theoretically 68% of all the scores should fall within ±1 standard deviation of the mean. So from the data in Table 2–2 (which has a mean of 113 and a standard deviation of 20), we know that theoretically 68% of all the scores should fall between 93 (113 − 20) and 133 (113 + 20). Furthermore, the mathematical derivation of the normal curve indicates that theoretically 95% of all the scores should fall within ±2 standard deviations from the mean—that is, between 73 (113 − 40) and 153 (113 + 40). Finally, theoretically 99% of all the scores should fall within ±3 standard deviations from the mean, between 53 (113 − 60) and 173 (113 + 60). The actual percentages of scores from the data in Table 2–2 are very close to the theoretical values; 69% of the scores fall within 1 standard deviation, 96% fall within 2 standard deviations, and 100% fall within 3 standard deviations. Although other measures of variability besides the range and standard deviation are also used, these two measures will suffice for the purposes of this book. Variability is important because it tells about the spread of scores in a distribution. And this can be just as important as knowing the most typical score in a distribution.

Correlation. So far we have been concerned with the statistical analysis of only one variable: its shape, typical score, and dispersion. But most I/O psychological research deals with the relationship between two (or more) variables. In particular, we are usually interested in the extent that we can understand one variable (the criterion or dependent variable) on the basis of our knowledge about another (the predictor or independent variable). A statistical procedure useful in determining this relationship is called the correlation coefficient. A **correlation coefficient** is a measure of the degree of linear relationship between two variables, which we shall refer to as X and Y. The symbol for a correlation coefficient is r, and its range is from −1.00 to +1.00. A correlation coefficient tells two things about the relationship between two variables: the direction of the relationship and its magnitude.

correlation coefficient
a statistical index that reflects the degree of relationship between two variables

The direction of a relationship is either positive or negative. A positive relationship means that as one variable increases in magnitude, so does the other. An example of a positive correlation is between height and weight. As a rule, the taller a person is, the more he or she weighs; increasing height is associated with increasing weight. A negative relationship means that as one variable increases in magnitude, the other gets smaller. An example of a negative correlation is between production workers' efficiency and scrap rate. The more efficient workers are, the less scrap is left. The less efficient they are, the more scrap is left.

The magnitude of the correlation is an index of the strength of the relationship. Large correlations indicate greater strength than small correlations. A correlation of .80 indicates a very strong relationship between the variables, whereas a correlation of .10 indicates a very weak relationship. Magnitude and direction are independent; a correlation of −.80 is just as strong as one of +.80.

The four parts of Figure 2–7 are graphic portrayals of correlation coefficients. The first step in illustrating a correlation is to plot all pairs of variables in the study. For a sample of 100 people, record the height and weight of each person. Then plot the pair of data points (height and weight) for each person. The stronger the relationship between the two variables, the tighter is the spread of data points around the line of best fit that runs through the scatterplot.

Figure 2–7a shows a scatterplot for two variables that have a high positive correlation. Notice that the line through the data points slants in the positive

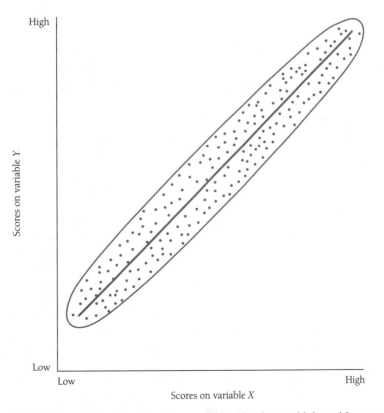

FIGURE 2–7a ■ **Scatterplot of two variables that have a high positive correlation**

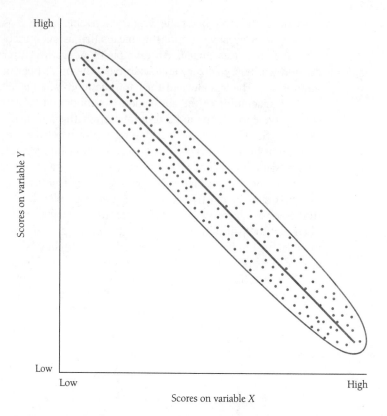

High

Low

Scores on variable Y

Low   High

Scores on variable *X*

FIGURE 2–7b ■ **Scatterplot of two variables that have a high negative correlation**

direction, and most of the data points are packed tightly around the line. Figure 2–7b shows a scatterplot for two variables that have a high negative correlation. Again, notice that the data points are packed tightly around the line, but in this case, the line slants in the negative direction. Figure 2–7c shows a scatterplot for two variables that have a low positive correlation. Although the line slants in the positive direction, the data points in the scatterplot are spread out quite widely around the line of best fit. Finally, Figure 2–7d shows a scatterplot for two variables that have a low negative correlation. The line of best fit slants in the negative direction, and the data points are not packed tightly around the line.

The stronger the correlation between two variables (either positive or negative), the more accurately we can predict one variable from the other. The statistical formula used to compute the correlation coefficient will not be presented in this book because it is available in statistics books and it will not be necessary for you, as you read this book, to compute any correlations. However, it is important that you know what a correlation is and how to interpret one. The only way to derive the exact numerical value of a correlation coefficient is to apply the statistical formula. Although the eyeball-inspection method of looking at a scatterplot gives some idea of what the correlation is, research has shown that people are generally not very good at inferring the magnitude of correlations by using this method.

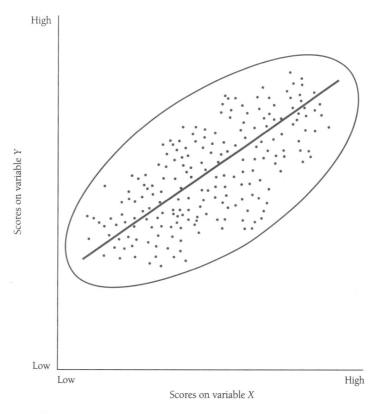

High

Low

Low High

Scores on variable X

Scores on variable Y

FIGURE 2–7c ■ **Scatterplot of two variables that have a low positive correlation**

The correlation coefficient does not permit any inferences to be made about *causality*—that is, whether one variable caused the other to occur. Even though a causal relationship may exist between two variables, just computing a correlation will not reveal this fact.

Suppose you wish to compute the correlation between the amount of alcohol consumed in a town and the number of people who attend church there. You collect data on each of these variables in many towns in your area. The correlation coefficient turns out to be .85. On the basis of this high correlation, you conclude that because people drink all week, they go to church to repent (alcohol consumption causes church attendance). Your friends take the opposite point of view. They say that because people have to sit cramped together on hard wooden pews, after church they "unwind" by drinking (church attendance causes alcohol consumption). Who is correct? On the basis of the existing data, no one is correct because causality cannot be inferred from a single correlation coefficient. Proof of causality must await experimental research. In point of fact, the causal basis of this correlation is undoubtedly neither of the opinions offered. It is due to the fact that the various towns in the study have different populations, which produces a systematic relationship between these two variables along with many others, such as the number of people who eat out in restaurants or attend movies. Just the

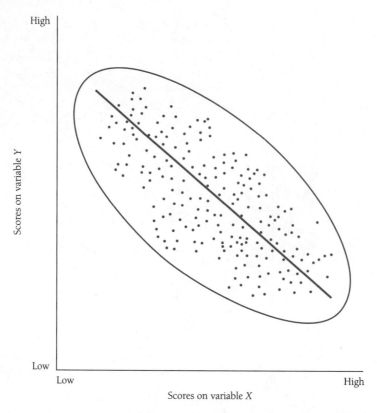

FIGURE 2–7d ■ **Scatterplot of two variables that have a low negative correlation**

computation of a correlation in this example does not even determine whether the churchgoers are the drinkers. The effect of a third variable on the two variables being correlated can cloud our ability to understand the relationship between the variables in purely correlational research.

To what degree can we determine causality in I/O psychological research? Making a clear determination of causality in research is never easy, but two basic approaches have been developed. Both involve the critical factor of control—to control for other explanations for the obtained results. The classic approach is the laboratory experiment. In this case, a small number of factors are selected for study, the experiment is carefully designed to control other variables, and the causal-based conclusions are limited to only the variables examined in the study. The Streufert et al. (1992) study on the effects of alcohol intoxication on visual-motor performance is one example. The second approach to assessing causality is more recent. It is based on advances in mathematical techniques for abstracting causal information from nonexperimental data. These mathematical approaches require restrictive assumptions, such as the availability of well-developed theoretical formulations, the measurement of all critical variables, and high precision of measurement. Under these conditions, assessments of causality are permissible.

Answering the question "why" is not only the ultimate objective of scientific research but also the means by which we make sense out of the events in our environment (Silvester & Chapman, 1997).

Because correlation is a common analytical technique in I/O psychological research, many of the empirical findings in this book will be expressed in those terms. However, the concept of correlation will not magically yield accurate inferences in I/O psychological research. As Mitchell (1985) noted, a poorly designed research study cannot be "saved" by the use of correlation to draw valid conclusions. Researchers must plan studies carefully, use sound methodological procedures, and use appropriate statistical analyses to arrive at meaningful conclusions. Over the past few decades our profession has made major advances in the sophistication and precision of our statistical methods. This increased precision can lead to increased understanding of the phenomena we seek to understand. Murphy and DeShon (2000) argue that such advances are of sufficient magnitude to cause us to question some long-held assumptions about major topics of interest to us. Kirk (1996) added that statistical results must also be judged in terms of their practical significance—that is, whether the result is useful in the real world. Practical significance is a most reasonable standard to use to judge research findings in I/O psychology.

Conclusions from Research

After analyzing the data, the researcher draws conclusions. A conclusion may be that alcohol intoxication impairs certain skills more than others, or jobs that require skills more adversely impaired by alcohol consumption warrant more restrictive standards than other jobs. Latham and Kinne's study (1974) concluded that goal setting increased the rate of wood harvesting. So a company might decide to implement the goal-setting procedure throughout the firm. Generally, it is unwise to implement any major changes based on the results of only one study. As a rule, we prefer to know the results from several studies. We want to be as certain as possible that any organizational changes are grounded in repeatable, generalizable results.

Sometimes the conclusions drawn from a study modify beliefs about a problem. Note in Figure 2–1 that a feedback loop extends from "Conclusions from research" to "Statement of the problem." The findings from one study influence the research problems in future studies. Theories may be altered if empirical research fails to confirm some of the hypotheses put forth. One of the most critical issues in conducting research is the quality of the generalizations that can be drawn from the conclusions. A number of factors determine the boundary conditions for generalizing the conclusions from a research study to a broader population or setting. One factor is the representativeness of individuals who serve as the research subjects. The generalizability of conclusions drawn from research on college students has been questioned on the grounds that college-aged students are not representative of the population. This is why it is advisable to explicitly assess the generalizability of findings across groups, as was done in the Murphy et al. (1991) study on attitudes toward drug testing. A second factor is the degree of fit between the subjects and the research task. Studying what college students believe is important in finding a job is a reasonable fit between subjects and the task. Studying what leisure activities college students will engage in after they retire from the workforce is not. A third factor that determines the generalizability of conclusions is the research method. Dipboye (1990) argued that research topics get studied in either laboratory *or* field (i.e., naturally occurring) settings. He suggested that laboratory *and* field research strategies should be used in coordination with each other rather than in competition. Dipboye believes that each basic strategy has something to offer and that researchers can gain understanding by studying a problem with both methods. Laboratory research has traditionally been regarded as more scientifically rigorous, whereas field research is seen as more representative of real-world conditions. Locke (1985) reached the conclusion that most findings from laboratory experiments can be generalized beyond the lab, but other individuals (for example, Mook, 1983) are more skeptical.

A related issue is the generalizability of research conclusions based on college students (typically 18–22 years old) and nonstudent participants. Much research is conducted in university settings, and university students often serve as subjects in research studies because they are an available sample. It has been a matter of great debate within the entire field of psychology whether the conclusions reached based on studying 18–22-year-olds can be generalized to a larger and more diverse population. There is no simple answer to this question; it depends greatly on the research topic under consideration. Asking typical college students to describe their vocational aspirations is highly appropriate. Asking typical college students to describe how they will spend their retirement, 50 years from now, would have limited scientific value. Because I/O psychology is concerned with the world of work, and thus the population of concern to us is the adult working population, we are generally cautious in attempting to generalize findings based on studies of college students.

Research is a cumulative process. Researchers build on one another's work in formulating new research questions. They communicate their results by publishing articles in journals. A competent researcher must keep up to date in his or her area of expertise to avoid repeating someone else's study. The conclusions drawn from research can affect many aspects of our lives. Research is a vital part of industry; it is the basis for changes in products and services. Research can be a truly exciting activity, although it is seemingly tedious if you approach it only from the perspective of testing stuffy theories, using sterile statistics, and inevitably reaching dry conclusions. Daft (1983) suggested that research is a craft, and a researcher, like an artist or craftsperson, has to pull together a wide variety of human experiences to produce a superior product. Being a researcher is more like unraveling a mystery than following a cookbook (see Field Note 1). However, research is not flash-in-the-pan thrill seeking; it involves perseverance, mental discipline, and patience. There is also no substitute for hard work. I can recall many times when I anxiously anticipated seeing computer analyses that would foretell the results of a lengthy research study. This sense of anticipation is the fun of doing research—and research, in the spirit of Daft's view of researchers being craftspersons, is a craft I try to pass on to my students. Klahr and Simon (1999) believe

eing a good researcher is a lot like being a good detective. You have to use all of your senses to buttress information collected by traditional research methods. I often administer and interpret attitude surveys for my industrial clients. The results of these surveys reveal a wealth of information about the companies. However, if it is judged only in statistical terms, this information often seems somewhat dry and bland. Therefore, I decided to experience the organizations in person to better understand and appreciate the statistical results. I have smelled acid fumes in a metal fabricating company that burned my nose and eyes after only a few minutes of exposure. I have tasted a rancid bologna sandwich from a vending machine situated by a big window in the company cafeteria (the sun shining through the window heated the machine and spoiled the food). I have walked (and slipped) across a company parking lot that was a solid 2- to 3-inch sheet of ice during the months of January and February. I have been in a "sound-sensitive" room that was so quiet I could hear my heartbeat. And in the president's office of one status-conscious organization, I have seen a white llama-wool carpet thick enough to swallow most of your shoes as you walked across it. In and of themselves, these events have little meaning, but when considered as part of the total organizational fabric, they provide a rich texture to I/O psychological research findings.

researchers from all scientific disciplines, while differing in the methods used in their respective disciplines, are all basically problem solvers. Research methods are invoked to solve problems and answer questions of interest to the researcher. As such we are driven by a sense of curiosity, like that of a child. Klahr and Simon add: "Perhaps this is why childlike characteristics, such as the propensity to wonder, are so often attributed to creative scientists and artists" (p. 540).

McCall and Bobko (1990) also noted the importance of serendipity in scientific research. *Serendipity* refers to a chance occurrence or happening that influences the research process. The history of science is filled with chance discoveries. For example, a contaminated culture eventually led Alexander Fleming to learn about and recognize the properties of penicillin. Rather than discarding the culture because it was contaminated, Fleming sought to understand how it had become so. The lesson is that we should allow room for lucky accidents and unexpected observations to occur and be prepared to pursue them when they do.

ETHICAL PROBLEMS IN RESEARCH

Research participants have certain legal rights pertaining to their physical treatment during a study, confidentiality of information, privacy, and voluntary consent (no one can be forced to take part in a study). Researchers who violate these rights, particularly in studies that involve physical or psychological risk, can be subject to professional censure and possible litigation. It is not at all unusual for psychologists to face ethical conflicts in the conduct of their work, including in research (Bersoff, 1999). The American Psychological Association (1992) has a code of ethics that must be honored by all APA members who conduct research. Among the researcher responsibilities covered by the code of ethics are the accurate advertising of psychological services, the confidentiality of information collected during the research, and the rights of human participants. The code of ethics was created to protect the rights of subjects and to avoid the possibility of having research conducted by unqualified people. It is the responsibility of the researcher to balance ethical accountability and the technical demands of scientific research practices (Rosnow, 1997). Wright and Wright (1999) argue that organizational researchers should be concerned with the welfare of research participants not only *during* the research but also *after* it. They assert the participants should benefit from the research as well as the researchers.

The researcher is faced with additional problems with employees of companies. Even when managers authorize research, it can cause problems in an organizational context. Employees who are naive about the purpose of research are often suspicious when asked to participate. They wonder how they were "picked" for inclusion in the study and whether they will be asked difficult questions. Some people even think a psychologist can read their minds and thus discover all sorts of private thoughts. Research projects that arouse emotional responses may place managers in an uncomfortable interpersonal situation.

Mirvis and Seashore (1979) described some of the problems facing those who conduct research with employees. Most problems involve role conflict, the dilemma of being trained to be a good researcher yet having to comply with both company and professional standards (London & Bray, 1980). For example, consider a role-conflict problem I faced in doing research with industrial employees. I used a questionnaire to assess the employees' opinions and morale. Management had commissioned the study. As part of the research design, all employees were told that their responses would be confidential. One survey response revealed the existence of employee theft. Although I did not know the identity of the employee, with the information given and a little help from management, that person could have been identified. Was I to violate my promise and turn over the information to management? Should I tell management that some theft had occurred but I had no way to find out who had done it (which would not have been true)? Or was I to ignore what I knew and fail to tell management about a serious problem in the company? In this case, I informed the company of the theft, but I refused to supply any information about the personal identity of the thief. This was an uneasy compromise between serving the needs of my client and maintaining the confidentiality of the information source.

Lowman (1999) presented a series of cases on ethical problems for I/O psychologists. Taken from real-life experiences, the multitude of ethical dilemmas cover such issues as conflict of interest, plagiarizing, and "overselling" research results. The pressures to conduct high-quality research, the need to be ethical, and the reality of organizational life sometimes place the researcher in a difficult situation (see Field Note 2). These demands place constraints on the I/O psychologist that researchers in other areas do not always face. Freeman (1990) noted a trend of increasing concern for ethics in all facets of I/O psychological research, including drug testing and the moral rights of employees.

FIELD NOTE 2   **An Ethical Dilemma**

ost ethical problems do not have clear-cut solutions. Here is one I ran into. I was trying to identify some psychological tests that would be useful in selecting future salespeople for a company. As part of my research, I administered the tests in question to all the employees in the sales department. With the company's consent, I assured the employees that the test results would be confidential. I explained that my purpose in giving the tests was to test the tests—that is, to assess the value of the tests—and that no one in the company would ever use the test results to evaluate the employees. In fact, no one in the company would even know the test scores. The results of my research were highly successful. I was able to identify which tests were useful in selecting potentially successful salespeople.

A few weeks later the same company's management approached me and said they now wanted to look into the value of using psychological tests to promote salespeople to the next higher job in the department, sales manager. In fact, they were so impressed with the test results for selecting new salespeople that they wanted to assess the value of these very same tests for identifying good sales managers. And since I had already given the tests to their salespeople and had the scores, all I would have to do is turn over the scores to the company, and they would determine whether there was any relationship between the scores and promotability to sales manager. I said I couldn't turn over the test results because that would violate my statement that the results were confidential and that no one in the company would ever know how well the employees did on the tests. I offered two alter-

natives. One was to readminister the same tests to the employees under a different set of test conditions— namely, that the company would see the test results, and in fact the results could be used to make promotion decisions. The second alternative was for me (not the company) to determine the value of these tests to make promotion decisions. In that way I would maintain the confidentiality of the test scores.

Management totally rejected the first alternative, saying it made no sense to readminister the same tests to the same people. I already had the test results, so why go back and get them a second time? The second alternative was also not approved. They said I was deliberately creating a need for the company to pay me for a second consulting project when they were perfectly capable of doing the work, with no outside help and at no extra cost. They said, in effect, I was holding the test results "hostage" when I would not release them. In my opinion, the company's management was asking me to compromise my professional integrity by using the test results in a way that violated the agreement under which the tests were originally administered.

The issue was never really resolved. The company soon faced some major sales problems caused by competitors and lost interest in the idea of using psychological tests for identifying sales managers. The management is still angered by my decision, asserting that I am assuming ownership of "their" test results. I have not been asked to do any more consulting work for them, but it is also quite possible that they would no longer have needed my services even if I had turned the test results over.

RESEARCH IN INDUSTRY

Although the empirical research steps in Figure 2–1 are followed in most I/O psychological research, research conducted in industry (as opposed to universities or research centers) often has some additional distinguishing features. First, Boehm (1980) observed that research questions in industry inevitably arise from organizational problems. For example, problems of excessive employee absenteeism, turnover, job dissatisfaction, and so on may prompt a research study designed to reduce their severity. Rarely are research questions posed just to "test a theory." In fact, a study by Flanagan and Dipboye (1981) revealed that psychologists who view organizations simply as laboratories to test theories are not looked on favorably. Hulin (2001) claims the goals of science and the goals of practice are different. Specifically, the goal of research is to contribute to knowledge, not simply to find solutions for practice. Rynes, McNatt, and Bretz (1999) investigated the process of academic research conducted within work organizations. They found that such collaborative research serves to narrow the gap between the science and practice of I/O psychology, in part by increasing the likelihood of implementation of the research findings by the organizations. Latham (2001) asserted that the goals of the science and practice of I/O psychology are overlapping, and research benefits both sides of the profession.

A second distinguishing feature of research in industry is how the results will be used. In industry, if the results of the study turn out to be positive and useful, the research unit of the organization will then try to "sell" (that is, gain acceptance of) the findings throughout the organization. For example, if providing job applicants with a very candid and realistic preview of the organization reduces turnover, then the researchers will try to persuade the rest of the organization to use such procedures in recruiting new employees. If the results of a study turn out negative, then the organization will look for side products or secondary ideas that will be of value. In research outside industry, less attention is given to implementing the findings and convincing other people of their utility.

Third, industry has practical motives for conducting research. Industrial research is conducted to enhance the organization's efficiency. Among private-sector employers, this usually translates into greater profitability. For example, research can be of vital importance in finding out consumer responses to new products and services, identifying ways to reduce waste, and making better use of employees. In university settings, research may not have such an instrumental purpose. The research questions have relevance to industry, but the link between the findings and their implementation may not be as direct (see Field Note 3).

I am reminded of a student who approached an organization with a research idea. The student needed a sample of managers to test a particular hypothesis. After patiently listening to the student's request, the organization's representative asked, "Why should we participate in this study? How can this study help us?" Industries that sponsor and participate in research do so for a reason: to enhance their welfare. Universities also conduct research for a reason, but it may be nothing more than intellectual curiosity. Some studies have examined the extent to which research influences policy makers—that is, how much the results of research studies influence important decisions. Hogan and Sinclair (1996) reported that organizations are generally reluctant to alter their practices based on the results of empirical research. Argyris (1996) noted that we need to acquire more **actionable knowledge**—knowledge that helps implement relevant research findings in organizations. Ruback and Innes (1988) concluded that to have the greatest impact, we need to study dependent variables that are important to decision makers, such as human lives and dollars saved. They also believe we should focus our attention on independent variables that policy makers have the power to change.

actionable knowledge
knowledge produced from research that helps formulate policies or action to address a particular issue

,Although academic and industrial research may be guided by somewhat different factors, both have contributed heavily to the I/O psychological literature. The infusion of research from both sectors has in fact been very healthy and stimulating for the profession. Jahoda (1981) commented that more psychological research needs to be done in anticipation of future work problems rather than as a reaction to current problems. Industrial researchers seem to be in the best position to forecast future organizational concerns. Thus, they may be able to find answers to problems before they become crises.

What should I/O psychologists study? Strasser and Bateman (1984) surveyed both managers and nonmanagers as to what they would like to see researched. The predominant answer from both groups related to how people can learn to get along with one another in a work context. As one respondent in their survey said, "People all have different personalities and some people we just can't get along with. How can we avoid personality conflicts and still have a good working relationship?" (p. 87). The second most pressing research need was communication among people.

Thomas and Tymon (1982) believe there is an unhealthy split between academicians who research topics (the "knowledge producers") and practitioners who want to implement research findings (the "knowledge users"). Those authors feel that individuals tend to fall into one of the camps, and we need a closer interplay between producing knowledge and using it. Other researchers have echoed these

---

FIELD NOTE 3   **Win the Battle but Lose the War**

ndustry-based research is always embedded in a larger context; that is, it is conducted for a specific reason. Sometimes the research is successful, sometimes it isn't, and sometimes you can win the battle but lose the war. A client of mine gave promotional tests—tests that current employees take to be advanced to higher positions in the company at higher rates of pay. These tests were important to the employees because only through the tests could they be promoted. The company gave an attitude survey and discovered that many employees did not like the tests. They said many test questions were outdated, there were no correct answers to some questions, and most questions were poorly worded. As a result of all these "bad" questions, employees were failing the tests and not getting promoted. I was hired to update and improve the promotional tests (there were 75 of them). Using the full complement of psychological research procedures, I analyzed every question on every test, eliminated the poor questions, had new questions

developed, and in general "cleaned up" each of the tests. By every known standard the tests were now of very high quality. Both the company's management and I felt confident the employees would be delighted with these revised tests. We were wrong. In the next attitude survey given by the company, the employees still thought poorly of the (new) tests, but their reasons were different than before. Now they complained that the tests were too hard and too technical and required too much expertise to pass. The employees failed the new tests with the same frequency as they had failed the old tests and were just as unhappy. In fact, they may have been even more unhappy; their expectations about the tests had been elevated because the company had hired me to revise them. I felt I had done as good a job in revising the tests as I possibly could have, but in the final analysis I didn't really solve the company's problem. I was hired to revise the tests, but what the management really wanted was to have the employees be satisfied with the tests, which didn't occur.

same thoughts (e.g., Harmon, 1991). While it may be tempting to say that researchers should tackle big, socially important problems, such problems are usually very complex and difficult to research. However, the contributions that I/O psychologists have made to such areas are among our profession's proudest achievements. I/O psychological research has been instrumental in enhancing our nation's productivity (Guzzo, Jette, & Katzell, 1985) and the quality of our worklife (Lawler, 1982). An understanding of research methods is vital for psychologists to resolve problems that confront humankind in an increasingly complex world.

CASE STUDY   ■ **How Should I Study This?**

Robin Mosier had just returned from her psychology class and was eager to tell her roommate about an idea she had. Julie Hansen had taken the same class the previous semester, so Robin was hopeful that Julie could help her out. The psychology professor gave the class an assignment to come up with a research design to test some hypothesis. Robin's idea stemmed from the job she had held the past summer.

Robin began to describe her idea. "Last summer I worked as a clerk in the bookkeeping department of a bank. Sometimes it wasn't always clear how we should fill out certain reports and forms. I was always pretty reluctant to go to my supervisor, Mr. Kast, and ask for help. So were the other female workers. But I noticed the guys didn't seem to be reluctant at all to ask him for help. So I got this idea; see, I think women are more reluctant than men to ask a male superior for help."

"Okay," replied Julie. "So now you have to come up with a way to test that idea?"

"Right," said Robin. "I was thinking maybe I could make up a questionnaire and ask students in my class about it. I think people would know if they felt that way or not."

"Maybe so," Julie said, "but maybe they wouldn't want to admit it. You know, it could be one of those things that either you don't realize about yourself or, if you do, you just don't want to say so."

"Well, if I can't just ask people about it, maybe I could do some sort of experiment," Robin commented. "What if I gave students some tasks to do, but the instructions weren't too clear? If I'm right, more men than women will ask a male experimenter for help."

"Do you think you'd get the opposite effect with a female experimenter?" asked Julie.

"You mean, would more women than men ask a female experimenter for help? I don't know. Maybe," answered Robin.

"If that's the case," said Julie, "you might want to test both male and female experimenters with both male and female subjects."

Robin scratched some notes on a pad. Then she said, "Do you think an experimenter in a study is the same thing as a boss on a job? You see your boss every day, but you may only be in an experiment for about an hour. Maybe that would make a difference in whether you sought help."

"I'm sure it could," replied Julie. "I know I would act differently toward someone I might not see again than toward someone I'd have to work with a long time."

"I know what I'll do," Robin responded. "I won't do the experiment in a lab setting, but I'll go back to the company where I worked last summer. I'll ask the male and female office workers how they feel about asking Mr. Kast for help. I saw the way they acted last summer, and I'd bet they tell me the truth."

"Wait a minute," cautioned Julie. "Just because some women may be intimidated by Mr. Kast doesn't mean that effect holds for all male supervisors. Mr. Kast is just one man. How do you know it holds for all men? That's what you want to test, right?"

Robin looked disconsolate. "There's got to be a good way to test this, although I guess it's more complicated than I thought."

Study Questions

1. What research method should Robin use to test her idea? How would you design the study?
2. What other variables might explain the employees' attitude toward Mr. Kast?
3. If this idea were tested using a laboratory or quasi-experiment method, what variables should be eliminated or controlled in the research design?
4. If this idea were tested with a questionnaire, what questions should be asked?
5. If this idea were tested with the observation method, what behaviors would you look for?

SUGGESTED INFOTRAC TOPICS

psychological research
behavioral research
research design
causality
questionnaire

observation
meta-analysis
qualitative research
correlation
research ethics

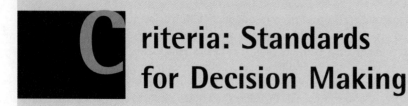

C H A P T E R 3

Criteria: Standards for Decision Making

LEARNING OBJECTIVES

- ■ Understand the distinction between conceptual and actual criteria.
- ■ Understand the meaning of criterion deficiency, relevance, and contamination.
- ■ Explain the purpose of a job analysis and the various methods of conducting one.
- ■ Explain the purpose of a job evaluation and the issues associated with determining the worth of a job.
- ■ Identify the major types of criteria examined by I/O psychologists.

54

criteria
standards used to help make evaluative judgments about objects, people, or events

Each time you evaluate someone or something, you use criteria. **Criteria** (the plural of *criterion*) are best defined as evaluative standards; they are used as reference points in making judgments. We may not be consciously aware of the criteria that affect our judgments, but they do exist. We use different criteria to evaluate different kinds of objects or people; that is, we use different standards to determine what makes a good (or bad) movie, dinner, ball game, friend, spouse, or teacher. In the context of I/O psychology, criteria are most important for defining the "goodness" of employees, programs, and units in the organization as well as the organization itself.

When you and some of your associates disagree in your evaluations of something, what is the cause? Chances are good the disagreement is caused by one of two types of criterion-related problems. For example, take the case of rating Professor Jones as a teacher. One student thinks he is a good teacher; another disagrees. The first student defines "goodness in teaching" as (1) preparedness, (2) course relevance, and (3) clarity of instruction. In the eyes of the first student, Jones scores very high on these criteria and receives a positive evaluation. The second student defines "goodness" as (1) enthusiasm, (2) capacity to inspire students, and (3) ability to relate to students on a personal basis. This student scores Jones low on these criteria and thus gives him a negative evaluation. Why the disagreement? Because the two students have different criteria for defining goodness in teaching.

Disagreements over the proper criteria to use in decision making are common. Values and tastes also dictate people's choice of criteria. For someone with limited funds, a good car may be one that gets high gas mileage. But for a wealthy person, the main criterion may be physical comfort. Not all disagreements are caused by using different criteria, however. Suppose that both students in our teaching example define goodness in teaching as preparedness, course relevance, and clarity of instruction. The first student thinks Professor Jones is ill-prepared, teaches an irrelevant course, and gives unclear instruction. But the second student thinks he is well-prepared, teaches a relevant course, and gives clear instruction. Both students are using the same evaluative standards, but they do not reach the same judgment. The difference of opinion in this case is due to the discrepancies in the meanings attached to Professor Jones's behavior. These discrepancies may be due to perceptual biases, differential expectations, or operational definitions associated with the criteria that cause them. Thus, even people who use the same standards in making judgments do not always reach the same conclusion.

The profession of I/O psychology does not have a monopoly on criterion-related issues and problems. They occur in all walks of life, ranging from the criteria used to judge interpersonal relationships (for example, communication, trust, respect) to the welfare of nations (for example, literacy rates, per capita income, infant mortality rates). Since many important decisions are made on the basis of criteria, it is difficult to overstate their significance in the decision-making process. Because criteria are used to render a wide range of judgments, I define them as the evaluative standards by which objects, individuals, procedures, or collectivities are assessed for the purpose of ascertaining their quality. Criterion issues have major significance in the field of I/O psychology.

CONCEPTUAL VERSUS ACTUAL CRITERIA

Psychologists have not always thought that criteria are of prime importance. Before World War II, they were inclined to believe that "criteria were either given of God or just to be found lying about" (Jenkins, 1946, p. 93). Unfortunately, this is not so. We must carefully consider what is meant by a "successful" worker, student, parent, and so forth. We cannot plunge headlong into measuring success, goodness, or quality until we have a fairly good idea of what (in theory, at least) we are looking for.

conceptual criterion
the theoretical standard that researchers seek to understand through their research

A good beginning point is the notion of a conceptual criterion. The **conceptual criterion** is a theoretical construct, an abstract idea that can never actually be measured. It is an ideal set of factors that constitute a successful person (or object or collectivity) as conceived in the psychologist's mind. Let's say we want to define a successful college student. We might start off with intellectual growth; that is, capable students should experience more intellectual growth than less capable students. Another dimension might be emotional growth. A college education should help students clarify their own values and beliefs, and this should aid in emotional development and stability. Finally, we might say that a good college student should want to have some voice in civic activities, be a "good citizen," and contribute to the well-being of his or her community. As an educated person, the good college student will assume an active role in helping to make society a better place in which to live. We might call this dimension a citizenship factor.

Thus, these three factors become the conceptual criteria for defining a "good college student." We could apply this same process to defining a "good worker," "good parent," or "good organization." However, because conceptual criteria are theoretical abstractions, we have to find some way to turn them into measurable, real factors. That is, we have to obtain **actual criteria** to serve as measures of the conceptual criteria that we would prefer to (but cannot) assess. The decision is then which variables to select as the actual criteria.

actual criteria
the operational or actual standard that researchers measure or assess

A psychologist might choose grade point average as a measure of intellectual growth. Of course, a high grade point average is not equivalent to intellectual growth, but it probably reflects some degree of growth. To measure emotional growth, a psychologist might ask a student's adviser to judge how much the student has matured over his or her college career. Again, maturation is not exactly the same as emotional growth, but it is probably an easier concept to grasp and evaluate than the more abstract notion of emotional growth. Finally, as a measure of citizenship, a psychologist might count the number of volunteer organizations (student government, charitable clubs, and so on) the student has joined over his or her college career. It could again be argued that the sheer number (quantity) of joined organizations is not equivalent to the quality of participation in these activities, and that "good citizenship" is more appropriately defined by quality rather than quantity of participation. Nevertheless, because of the difficulties inherent in measuring quality of participation, plus the fact that one cannot speak of quality unless there is some quantity, the psychologist decides to use this measure. Table 3–1 shows the conceptual criteria and the actual criteria of success for a college student.

TABLE 3–1 ■ Conceptual and actual criteria for a successful college student

Conceptual Criteria	Actual Criteria
Intellectual growth	Grade point average
Emotional growth	Adviser rating of emotional maturity
Citizenship	Number of volunteer organizations joined in college

How do we define a "good" college student in theory? With the conceptual criteria as the evaluative standard, a good college student should display a high degree of intellectual and emotional growth and should be a responsible citizen in the community. How do we operationalize a good college student in practice? Using the actual criteria as the evaluative standard, we say a good college student has earned high grades, is judged by an academic adviser to be emotionally mature, and has joined many volunteer organizations throughout his or her college career. In a review of the relationship between the two sets of criteria (conceptual and actual), remember that the goal is to obtain an approximate estimate of the conceptual criterion by selecting one or more actual criteria that we think are appropriate.

CRITERION DEFICIENCY, RELEVANCE, AND CONTAMINATION

We can express the relationship between conceptual and actual criteria in terms of three concepts: deficiency, relevance, and contamination. Figure 3–1 shows the overlap between conceptual and actual criteria. The circles represent the contents of each type of criterion. Because the conceptual criterion is a theoretical abstraction, we can never know exactly how much overlap occurs. The actual criteria selected are never totally equivalent to the conceptual criteria we have in mind, so there is always a certain amount (though unspecified) of deficiency, relevance, and contamination.

criterion deficiency
the part of the conceptual criterion that is not measured by the actual criterion

Criterion Deficiency. **Criterion deficiency** is the degree to which the actual criteria fail to overlap the conceptual criteria—that is, how deficient the actual criteria are in representing the conceptual ones. There is always some degree of deficiency in the actual criteria. By careful selection of the actual criteria, we can reduce (but never eliminate) criterion deficiency. Conversely, criteria that are selected because they are simply expedient, without much thought given to their match to conceptual criteria, will be grossly deficient.

criterion relevance
the degree of overlap or similarity between the actual criterion and the conceptual criterion

Criterion Relevance. **Criterion relevance** is the degree to which the actual criteria and the conceptual criteria coincide. The greater the match between the conceptual and the actual criteria, the greater is the criterion relevance. Again, because the conceptual criteria are theoretical abstractions, we cannot know the exact amount of relevance.

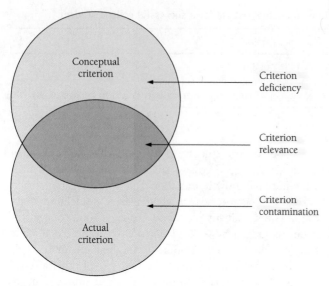

Criterion Contamination. **Criterion contamination** is that part of the actual criteria that is unrelated to the conceptual criteria. It is the extent to which the actual criteria measure something other than the conceptual criteria. Contamination consists of two parts. One part, called *bias,* is the extent to which the actual criteria systematically or consistently measure something other than the conceptual criteria. The second part, called *error,* is the extent to which the actual criteria are not related to anything at all.

FIGURE 3–1 ■ **Criterion deficiency, relevance, and contamination**

Both contamination and deficiency are undesirable in the actual criterion, and together they distort the conceptual criterion. Criterion contamination distorts the actual criterion because certain factors are included that don't belong (that is, they are not present in the conceptual criterion). Criterion deficiency distorts the actual criterion because certain important dimensions of the conceptual criterion are not included in the actual criterion.

criterion contamination
the part of the actual criterion that is unrelated to the conceptual criterion

Let us consider criterion deficiency and contamination in the example of setting criteria for a good college student. How might the actual criteria we chose be deficient in representing the conceptual criteria? Students typically begin a class with differing amounts of prior knowledge of the subject matter. One student may know nothing of the material, while another student may be very familiar with it. At the end of the term, the former student might have grown more intellectually than the latter student, but the latter student might get a higher grade in the course. By using the grade point average as our criterion, we would (falsely) conclude that the latter student grew more intellectually. So the relationship between grades and intellectual growth is not perfect (that is, it is deficient). A rating of emotional maturity by an academic adviser might be deficient because the adviser is not an ideal judge. He or she might have only a limited perspective of the student. Finally, it is not enough to just count how many volunteer groups a student belongs to. Quality of participation is as important as (if not more important than) quantity.

How might these actual criteria be contaminated? If some academic majors are more difficult than others, then grades are a contaminated measure of intellectual growth; students in "easy" majors will be judged to have experienced more intellectual growth than students in difficult majors. This is a bias between earned grade point averages and the difficulty of the student's academic major. The source of the bias affects the actual criterion (grades) but not the conceptual criterion (intellectual growth). A rating of emotional maturity by the student's adviser could be contaminated by the student's grades. The adviser might believe that students with high grades have greater emotional maturity than students with low grades. Thus, the grade point average might bias an adviser's rating even though it probably has no relationship to the conceptual criterion of emotional growth. Finally, counting the number of organizations a student joins might be contaminated by the student's popularity. Students who join many organizations may simply be more popular rather than better citizens (which is what we want to measure).

If we know that these criterion measures are contaminated, why would we use them? In fact, when a researcher knows that a certain form of contamination is present, its influence can be controlled through experimental or statistical procedures. The real problem lies in anticipating the occurrence of contaminating factors. Komaki (1998) noted that a problem with some criteria is that they are not under the direct control of the person being evaluated. For example, two salespeople may differ in the amount of their overall sales volume because they have different-sized sales territories, not because one is a better salesperson than the other.

As Wallace (1965) observed, psychologists have spent a great deal of time trying to discover new and better ways to measure actual criteria. They have used various analytical and computational procedures to get more precise assessments. Wallace recommended that rather than dwelling on finding new ways to measure actual criteria, psychologists should spend more time choosing actual criteria that will be adequate measures of the conceptual criteria that they really seek to understand. The adequacy of the actual criterion as a measure of the conceptual criterion is always a matter of professional judgment—no equation or formula will determine it. As Wherry (1957) said in a classic statement, "If we are measuring the wrong thing, it will not help us to measure it better" (p. 5).

JOB ANALYSIS

job analysis
a formal procedure by which the content of a job is defined in terms of tasks performed and human qualifications needed to perform the job

I/O psychologists must often identify the criteria of effective job performance. These criteria then become the basis for hiring people (choosing them according to their ability to meet the criteria of job performance), training them (to perform those aspects of the job that are important), paying them (high levels of performance warrant higher pay), and classifying jobs (jobs with similar performance criteria are grouped together). A procedure useful in identifying the criteria or performance dimensions of a job is called job analysis; it is conducted by a job analyst. Harvey (1991) defined **job analysis** as "the collection of data describing (a) observable (or otherwise verifiable) job behaviors performed by workers, including both *what is accomplished* as well as *what technologies are employed* to accomplish the end results, and (b) verifiable characteristics of the job environment with which workers interact, including physical, mechanical, social, and informational elements" (p. 71). A thorough job analysis documents the tasks that are performed on the job, the situation in which the work is performed (for example, tools and equipment present, working conditions), and the human attributes needed to perform the work. These data are the basic information needed to make many personnel decisions. Their use is mandated by legal requirements, and estimated annual costs for job analyses have ranged from $150,000 to $4,000,000 in a large organization (Levine, Sistrunk, McNutt, & Gael, 1988).

Sources of Job Information

subject matter expert (SME)
a person knowledge-able about a topic who can serve as a qualified information source

The most critical issue in job analysis is the accuracy and completeness of the information about the job. There are three major sources of job information, and each source is a **subject matter expert (SME).** The qualifications for being termed an SME are not precise, but a minimum condition is that the person has direct, up-to-date experience with the job for a long enough time to be familiar with all of its tasks (Thompson & Thompson, 1982).

The most common source of information is the *job incumbent*—that is, the holder of the job. The use of job incumbents as SMEs is predicated upon their implicit understanding of their own jobs. Landy and Vasey (1991) believe that the sampling method used to select SMEs is very important. They found that experienced job incumbents provide the most valuable job information. Given the rapid changes in work caused by changing technology, however, Sanchez (2000) questioned whether job incumbents are necessarily qualified in some cases to serve as SMEs. New jobs, jobs that don't currently exist in an organization and for which there are no incumbents, also have to be analyzed. Sanchez proposed the use of statistical methods to forecast future needed employee characteristics as technology shifts the way work is conducted. A second source of information is the *supervisor* of the job incumbent. Supervisors play a major role in determining what job incumbents do on their jobs, and thus they are a credible source of information. While supervisors may describe jobs somewhat more objectively than incumbents, there can be legitimate differences of opinion between incumbents and supervisors. It has been my experience that most differences occur not in what is accomplished in a job, but in the critical abilities actually needed to perform the job. The third source of job information is a trained *job analyst*. Job analysts are used as SMEs when comparisons are needed across many jobs. Because of their familiarity with job analysis methods, analysts often provide the most consistent across-job ratings. Job analyst expertise lies not in the subject matter of various jobs per se, but in their ability to understand similarities and differences across jobs in terms of the tasks performed and abilities needed.

In general, incumbents and supervisors are the best sources of descriptive job information, whereas job analysts are best qualified to comprehend the relationships among a set of jobs. The most desirable strategy in understanding a job is to collect information from as many qualified sources as possible, as opposed to relying exclusively on just one source.

task
the lowest level of analysis in the study of work; a basic component of work

position
a set of tasks performed by a single employee

Job Analysis Procedures

The purpose of job analysis is to explain the tasks that are performed on the job and the human attributes needed to perform the job. A clear understanding of job analysis requires knowledge of four job-related concepts, as shown in Figure 3–2. At the lowest level of aggregation we have tasks. **Tasks** are the basic units of work that are directed toward specific job objectives. A **position** is defined as a set

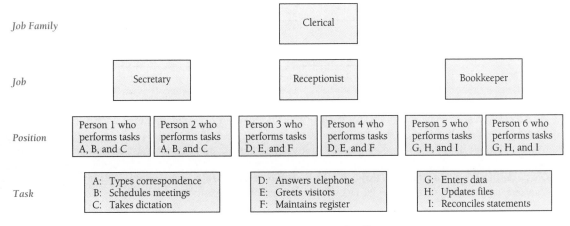

FIGURE 3–2 ■ **Relationships among tasks, positions, jobs, and job families**

job
a set of similar positions in an organization

of tasks performed by a single employee. There are usually as many positions in an organization as there are employees. However, many positions may be similar to one another. In such a case, similar positions are grouped or aggregated to form a **job**. An example is the job of secretary; another job is that of bookkeeper. Similar jobs may be further aggregated based on general similarity of content to form a **job family**—in this case, the clerical job family.

It is possible to understand jobs from either a task-oriented or a worker-oriented perspective. Both procedures are used in conducting job analyses.

job family
a grouping of similar jobs in an organization

Task-Oriented Procedures. A **task-oriented procedure** seeks to understand a job by examining the tasks performed, usually in terms of *what* is accomplished. The procedure begins with a consideration of job duties, responsibilities, or function. Williams and Crafts (1997) defined a job duty as "a major part of the work that an incumbent performs, comprised of a series of tasks, which together accomplish a job objective" (p. 57). Tasks thus become the basic unit of analysis for understanding a job using task-oriented procedures. The job analyst develops a series of *task statements,* which are concise expressions of tasks performed. Examples include "splice high-voltage cables," "order materials and supplies," and "grade tests." Task statements should not be written in too general terminology, nor should they be written in a very fine level of detail. They should reflect a discrete unit of work with appropriate specificity. Clifford (1994) estimated that the number of tasks required to describe most jobs typically is between 300 and 500.

task-oriented procedure
a procedure or set of operations in job analysis designed to identify important or frequently performed tasks as a means of understanding the work performed

Following the development of task statements, SMEs (most often incumbents) are asked to rate the task statements on a series of scales or dimensions. The scales reflect important dimensions that facilitate understanding the job. Among the common scales used to rate task statements are frequency, importance, difficulty, and consequences of error. An example of the frequency scale is shown in Table 3–2. Based on an analysis of the ratings (especially with regard to the mean and standard deviation), we acquire an understanding of a job in terms of the rated frequency, importance, difficulty, and other dimensions of the tasks that make up the job.

TABLE 3–2 ■ Frequency scale for rating tasks

Frequency—How often do you perform this task?

Rate the task from 0 to 5 using the following scale:

0—*Never perform.* Use this rating for tasks you do not perform.

1—*A few times per year or less.* Use this rating for tasks that are performed less frequently than any other tasks. You may perform these tasks a few times per year (up to six), or even less.

2—*Once a month.* Use this rating for tasks that you usually perform about once a month, or at least every other month, but not every week.

3—*Once a week.* Use this rating for tasks that you perform several times a month, usually every week, but not every day.

4—*Once a day.* Use this rating for tasks that you usually perform every day.

5—*More than once a day.* Use this rating for tasks you perform most frequently. On most days, you perform these tasks more than once.

SOURCE: From "Inductive Job Analysis" by K. M. Williams and J. L. Crafts, 1997, in *Applied Measurement Methods in Industrial Psychology* (pp. 51–88), edited by D. L. Whetzel and G. R. Wheaton, Palo Alto, CA: Consulting Psychologists Press.

functional job analysis (FJA)
a method of job analysis that describes the content of jobs in terms of People, Data, and Things

A classic example of a task-oriented method of job analysis is **functional job analysis (FJA)**, developed by Fine and his associates (1989). Two types of task information are obtained from FJA: (1) *what a worker does*—the procedures and processes engaged in by a worker as a task is performed, and (2) *how a task is performed*—the physical, mental, and interpersonal involvement of the worker with the task. These types of information are used to identify what a worker does and the results of those job behaviors. The critical component in analyzing a job is the proper development of task statements. These task statements are then rated by SMEs using specific rating scales. The ratings serve as a basis for inferring worker specifications needed to perform the tasks.

Perhaps the most notable characteristic of FJA is that tasks are rated along three dimensions: People, Data, and Things. When a task requires involvement with People, the worker needs interpersonal resources (sensitivity, compassion, etc.). When a task requires involvement with Data, the worker needs mental resources (knowledge, reasoning, etc.). When a task is defined primarily in relation to Things, the worker needs physical resources (strength, coordination, etc.). Each of these three dimensions (People, Data, Things) is presented in a hierarchy ranging from high to low. Thus, a given job may be defined as requiring a medium level of People, a high level of Data, and a low level of Things, for example. Figure 3–3 portrays the three dimensions and their associated levels. FJA has been used to analyze jobs in many sectors of society, but most frequently in the federal government. The method is regarded as one of the major systematic approaches to the study of jobs.

worker-oriented procedure
a procedure or set of operations in job analysis designed to identify important or frequently utilized human attributes as a means of understanding the work performed

Worker-Oriented Procedures. A **worker-oriented procedure** seeks to understand a job by examining the human attributes needed to perform it successfully. The human attributes are classified into four categories: knowledge (K), skills (S), abilities (A), and other (O) characteristics. *Knowledge* is specific types of informa-

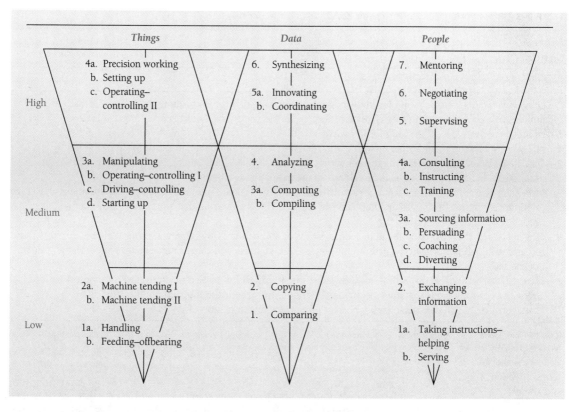

FIGURE 3–3 ■ **Hierarchy of Things, Data, and People dimensions of work**

SOURCE: From *Functional Job Analysis Scales: A Desk Aid* (rev. ed.) by S. Fine, 1989, Orlando, FL: Dryden.

KSAOs

an abbreviation for "knowledge, skills, abilities, and other" characteristics

tion people need in order to perform a job. Some knowledge is required of workers before they can be hired to perform a job, while other knowledge may be acquired on the job. *Skills* are defined as the proficiencies needed to perform a task. Skills are usually enhanced through practice—for example, skill at typing and skill at driving an automobile. *Abilities* are defined as relatively enduring attributes that generally are stable over time. Examples are cognitive ability, physical ability, and spatial ability. Skills and abilities are confused often and easily, and the distinction is not always clear. It is useful to think of skills as cultivations of innate abilities. Generally speaking, high levels of (innate) ability can be cultivated into high skill levels. For example, a person with high musical ability could become highly proficient in playing a musical instrument. However, low levels of (innate) ability preclude the development of high skill levels. *Other* characteristics are all other personal attributes, most often personality factors (e.g., remaining calm in emergency situations) or capacities (e.g., withstanding extreme temperature conditions). Collectively these four types of attributes, referred to as **KSAOs**, reflect an approach to understanding jobs by analyzing the human attributes needed to perform them.

TABLE 3–3 ■ Importance scale for rating KSAOs for electrician tasks

Importance—How important is this knowledge, skill, ability, or other characteristic for performing the job tasks of an electrician?

Rate the KSAOs from 0 to 5 using the following scale:

0—*Of no importance.* Use this rating for knowledge that is unnecessary for performing the job, skills that are unnecessary, or abilities and other characteristics that an electrician does not need.

1—*Of little importance.* Use this rating for knowledge that is nice to have but not really necessary, skills that are rarely used, or abilities and other characteristics that are of little importance in relationship to the job.

2—*Of some importance.* Use this rating for knowledge, skills, or abilities and other characteristics that have some importance, but still would be ranked below average in relation to others.

3—*Moderately important.* Use this rating for knowledge, skills, or abilities and other characteristics that are of average importance in terms of successful completion of the job. These KSAOs are not the most critical, but still are needed to be successful on the job.

4—*Very important.* Use this rating for knowledges, skills, or abilities and other characteristics that are very important for successful job performance. These knowledges, skills, abilities, and other characteristics are essential, but are not the most critical.

5—*Extremely important.* Use this rating for knowledge that is critical for an electrician to have in order to perform safely and correctly, skills that are essential and are used throughout the job, and abilities and other characteristics that all electricians must possess for successful completion of job tasks.

SOURCE: From "Inductive Job Analysis" by K. M. Williams and J. L. Crafts, 1997, in *Applied Measurement Methods in Industrial Psychology* (pp. 51–88), edited by D. L. Whetzel and G. R. Wheaton, Palo Alto, CA: Consulting Psychologists Press.

Similar to task statements, KSAO statements are written to serve as a means of understanding the human attributes needed to perform a job. They are written in standard format, using the wording "Knowledge of," "Skill in," or "Ability to." Examples include "Knowledge of city building codes," "Skill in operating a pneumatic drill," and "Ability to lift a 50-pound object over your head." The KSAO statements are also rated by SMEs. An example of an importance scale for rating KSAOs for the job of electrician is shown in Table 3–3. Similar to analyzing the ratings of task statements, the ratings of KSAO statements are analyzed (i.e., mean and standard deviation) to provide an understanding of a job based on the human attributes needed to successfully perform the job.

Other analytic procedures can be followed to gain further understanding of a job. A **linkage analysis** unites the two basic types of job analysis information: task-oriented and worker-oriented. A linkage analysis examines the relationship between KSAOs and tasks performed. The results of this analysis reveal which particular KSAOs are linked to the performance of many important and frequently performed tasks. For example, a knowledge that is linked to many important and frequently performed tasks should be included in an employee selection test, while knowledges of lesser importance may not be included.

linkage analysis
a technique in job analysis that establishes the connection between the tasks performed and the human attributes needed to perform them

How to Collect Job Analysis Information

The first step in conducting job analyses is to review written materials that contain information about the job. Such materials may include position descriptions, training manuals, and other information provided by the organization. After reading these materials, the job analyst is prepared to collect more extensive information about the job to be analyzed. Three procedures are typically followed: the interview, direct observation, and a questionnaire.

Procedures for Collecting Information. In the first procedure, the interview, SMEs are asked questions by the job analyst about the nature of their work. They may be interviewed individually, in small groups, or through a series of panel discussions. The job analyst questions the SMEs to get an understanding of the tasks performed on the job and the KSAOs needed to perform them. The individuals selected to be interviewed are regarded as SMEs, people qualified to render informed judgments about their work. Desirable characteristics in SMEs include verbal ability, a good memory, and cooperativeness. Also, if SMEs are suspicious of the motives behind a job analysis, they are inclined to magnify the importance or difficulty of their abilities as a self-protective tactic (see Field Note 1).

The second method is direct observation: Employees are observed as they perform their jobs. Observers try to be unobtrusive, observing the jobs but not getting in the workers' way (see Field Note 2). Observers generally do not talk to the employees because it interferes with the conduct of work. They sometimes use cameras or videotape equipment to facilitate the observation. Direct observation is

---

FIELD NOTE 1   **A Memorable Lesson**

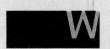

When interviewing employees about their jobs, job analysts should explain what they are doing (and why they are doing it). If they do not fully explain their role, employees may feel threatened, fearing the analysts may somehow jeopardize their position by giving a negative evaluation of their performance, lowering their wages, firing them, and so on. Although job analysts do not have the power to do these things, some employees assume the worst. When employees feel threatened, they usually magnify the importance or difficulty of their contributions to the organization in an attempt to protect themselves. Therefore, to ensure accurate and honest responses, all job analysts should go out of their way to disarm any possible suspicions or fears.

I learned the importance of this point early in my career. One of my first job analyses focused on the job of a sewer cleaner. I had arranged to interview three sewer cleaners about their work. However, I had neglected to provide much advance notice about myself, why I would be talking to them, or what I was trying

to do. I simply arrived at the work site, introduced myself, and told the sewer cleaners that I wanted to talk to them about their jobs. Smelling trouble, the sewer cleaners proceeded to give me a memorable lesson on the importance of first establishing a nonthreatening atmosphere. One sewer cleaner turned to me and said: "Let me tell you what happens if we don't do our job. If we don't clean out the sewers of stuff like tree limbs, rusted hubcaps, and old tires, the sewers get clogged up. If they get clogged up, the sewage won't flow. If the sewage won't flow, it backs up. People will have sewage backed up into the basements of their homes. Manhole covers will pop open, flooding the streets with sewage. Sewage will eventually cover the highways, airport runways, and train tracks. People will be trapped in their homes surrounded by sewage. The entire city will be covered with sewage, with nobody being able to get in or out of the city. And that's what happens if we don't do our job of cleaning the sewers." Sadder but wiser, I learned the importance of not giving employees any reason to overstate their case.

an excellent method for appreciating and understanding the adverse conditions (such as noise or heat) under which some jobs are performed; however, it is a poor method for understanding *why* certain behaviors occur on the job.

The third procedure for collecting job information is a structured questionnaire or inventory. The analyst uses already existing knowledge or taxonomies of job information to analyze a job. A **taxonomy** is a classification scheme useful in organizing information—in this case, information about jobs. The information collected about the job is automatically organized within the already existing system of measurement and can be integrated into a database of scores describing other jobs previously analyzed. Peterson and Jeanneret (1997) referred to this procedure as being *deductive* in nature because the job analyst can deduce an understanding of a job from a preexisting framework for analyzing jobs. Alternatively, the interview and direct observation procedures are *inductive* in nature because the job analyst has to rely on newly created information about the job being analyzed. Because job analysts are often interested in understanding more than one job, the structured inventory is a very useful way to examine the relationships among a set of jobs. Most of the recent professional advances in job analysis within the field of I/O psychology have occurred with deductive procedures.

taxonomy
a classification of objects designed to enhance understanding of the objects being classified

Taxonomic Information. There are several examples of taxonomic information for job analysis. The first is the **Position Analysis Questionnaire (PAQ)** (McCormick & Jeanneret, 1988), which consists of 195 statements used to describe the human attributes needed to perform a job. The statements are organized into six major categories: information input, mental processes, work output, relationships with other persons, job context, and other requirements. Some sample statements from the Relationships with Other Persons category are shown in Figure 3–4. Based on a database of thousands of similar jobs that have been previously analyzed with the PAQ, the job analyst can come to understand the focal job.

Position Analysis Questionnaire (PAQ)
a method of job analysis that assesses the content of jobs on the basis of approximately 200 items in the questionnaire

---

FIELD NOTE 2 **Unintentional Obstruction of Work**

 lthough logically it may not seem so, it takes talent to watch people at work. Observation is one of the methods job analysts use to study jobs. The object is to unobtrusively observe the employee at work. The analyst doesn't need to hide; he or she simply needs to blend in. In attempts to avoid interfering with employees, I have inadvertently positioned myself too far away to see what was really happening. I have also learned to bring earplugs and goggles to work sites because, when watching people at work, the observer is exposed to the same environmental conditions they are. Although you can be "too far" from a worker to make accurate observations, you can also get "too close." Cascio (1982) described this true story:

While riding along in a police patrol car as part of a job analysis of police officers, an analyst and an officer were chatting away when a call came over the radio regarding a robbery in progress. Upon arriving at the scene the analyst and the officer both jumped out of the patrol car, but in the process the overzealous analyst managed to position himself between the robbers and the police. Although the robbers were later apprehended, they used the analyst as a decoy to make their getaway from the scene of the crime (p. 56).

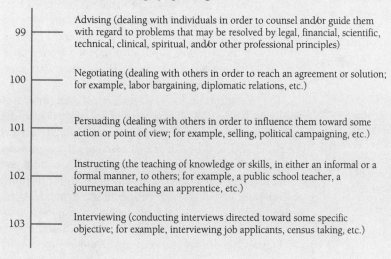

Relationships with Other Persons

This section deals with different aspects of interaction between people involved in various kinds of work.

Code	Importance to this job
DNA	Does not apply
1	Very minor
2	Low
3	Average
4	High
5	Extreme

4.1 Communications

Rate the following in terms of how important the activity is to the completion of the job. Some jobs may involve several or all of the items in this section.

4.1.1 Oral (communicating by speaking)

99 — Advising (dealing with individuals in order to counsel and/or guide them with regard to problems that may be resolved by legal, financial, scientific, technical, clinical, spiritual, and/or other professional principles)

100 — Negotiating (dealing with others in order to reach an agreement or solution; for example, labor bargaining, diplomatic relations, etc.)

101 — Persuading (dealing with others in order to influence them toward some action or point of view; for example, selling, political campaigning, etc.)

102 — Instructing (the teaching of knowledge or skills, in either an informal or a formal manner, to others; for example, a public school teacher, a journeyman teaching an apprentice, etc.)

103 — Interviewing (conducting interviews directed toward some specific objective; for example, interviewing job applicants, census taking, etc.)

FIGURE 3-4 ■ Sample items from the PAQ

SOURCE: From Position Analysis Questionnaire. Copyright 1969 by Purdue Research Foundation. All rights reserved. Reprinted by permission.

A second example of taxonomic information is the research of Fleishman and his associates in developing a taxonomy of human abilities needed to perform tasks (Fleishman & Quaintance, 1984). Fleishman identified 52 abilities required in the conduct of a broad spectrum of tasks. Examples of these abilities are oral expression, arm–hand steadiness, multilimb coordination, reaction time, selective attention, and night vision. Fleishman calibrated the amount of each ability needed to perform tasks. For example, with a scale of 1 (low) to 7 (high), the following amounts of *arm–hand steadiness* are needed to perform these tasks:

Cut facets in diamonds 6.32
Thread a needle 4.14
Light a cigarette 1.71

Fleishman's method permits jobs to be described in terms of the tasks performed and the corresponding abilities and levels of those abilities needed to perform them. Such a taxonomic approach classifies jobs on the basis of requisite human abilities.

The third example of taxonomic information available for job analyses is provided by the U.S. Department of Labor. Based on job analyses of millions of incumbents, these massive compilations of information provide users with broad job and occupational assessments. Two such resources are available. The first is the **Dictionary of Occupational Titles (DOT)** (U.S. Department of Labor, 1991). The DOT describes thousands of jobs in terms of the worker traits needed to perform each job. The DOT is based, in part, on the framework of functional job analysis with regard to the People, Data, and Things dimensions of work. Eleven worker traits are given, including intelligence, verbal ability, numerical ability, finger dexterity, and motor coordination. Job analysts compiled the trait requirement ratings by estimating how much of each of the 11 traits were needed for each job. Made on a 5-point scale, the ratings show the amount of each trait possessed by various segments of the working population, ranging from 1 (the top 10% of the population) to 5 (the lowest 10%). The DOT also describes jobs in terms of occupational groups, based on similarity of job content.

The second resource is the Occupational Information Network **(O*NET)**, developed by the U.S. Department of Labor. It is intended to be a comprehensive national database of worker attributes and job characteristics. It is designed to replace the DOT and be the primary source of occupational information. The initial version of O*NET has been developed, with a more complete database updated on an ongoing basis. The database contains information about KSAOs, interests, general work activities, and work context. It provides the essential foundation for facilitating career counseling, education, employment, and training activities. Additional information about the O*NET can be found at *www.onetcenter.org.*

Figure 3–5 shows the conceptual model upon which the O*NET is based. There are six domains of descriptions (e.g., worker requirements) containing more refined information within each domain (e.g., basic skills within worker requirements). The worker requirements and worker characteristics of the O*NET contain the kind of descriptions called "worker-oriented," while the occupational requirements, occupational-specific requirements, and organizational characteristics contain the kind of descriptions called "task-oriented." The experience requirements domain presents descriptions that are positioned between the worker- and task-oriented domains.

The O*NET offers a series of assessment instruments designed to assist individuals in exploring careers and making career decisions. The instruments are designed to help individuals assess their skills and interests and to help them identify occupations that match their profiles. Information is also available on the O*NET pertaining to characteristics of an organization that affect all jobs within the organization (Peterson et al., 2001). The DOT includes very little information about the overall organizational context in which jobs are embedded. An individual's performance within a job and satisfaction with it have been found to be related to organizational-level variables. Additionally, the O*NET presents economic information on labor markets, levels of compensation, and an occupational

Dictionary of Occupational Titles (DOT)
a classic reference book in I/O psychology that presents information on the content and characteristics of thousands of jobs

O*NET
abbreviation for the Occupational Information Network, an on-line computer-based source of information about jobs

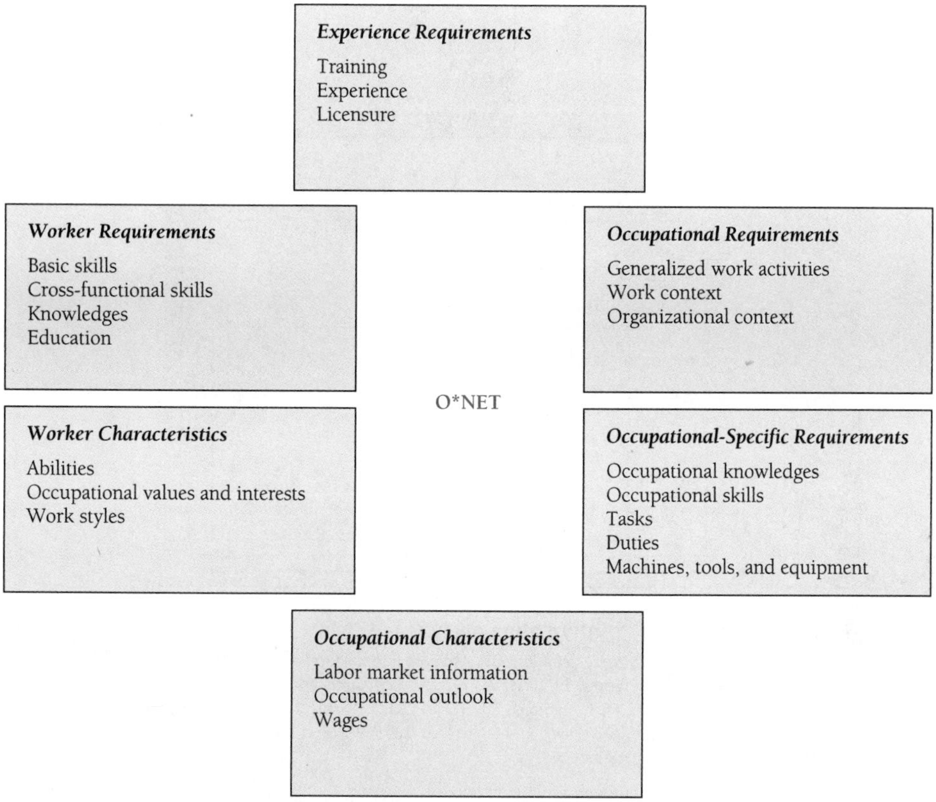

FIGURE 3–5 ■ **Content model of the O*NET**

SOURCE: From "The O*NET Content Model: Structural Considerations in Describing Jobs" by M. D. Mumford and N. G. Peterson, 1999, in *An Occupational Information System for the 21st Century: The Development of O*NET,* edited by N. G. Peterson, M. D. Mumford, W. C. Borman, P. R. Jeanneret, and E. A. Fleishman, Washington, DC: American Psychological Association. © 1999. Reprinted by permission.

outlook for the future. Figure 3–6 shows the multiple levels of analysis of job information presented in the O*NET. As such, the O*NET provides a highly integrated approach to the world of work, greatly expanding upon previous taxonomic approaches to presenting job information. Furthermore, the O*NET is much more invitational and user-friendly in its design (compared with the DOT), which should greatly enhance its practical value.

It is intended that a large number of applications will be developed that utilize the O*NET data, including job descriptions, job classification schemes, selection, training, and vocational counseling. The O*NET is anticipated to be a major contribution of I/O psychology to enhancing our knowledge and use of job-related information (Peterson, Mumford, Borman, Jeanneret, & Fleishman, 1999).

Managerial Job Analysis

With an emphasis on work activities that are performed on the job, traditional job analysis methods are typically well suited to traditional blue-collar and clerical

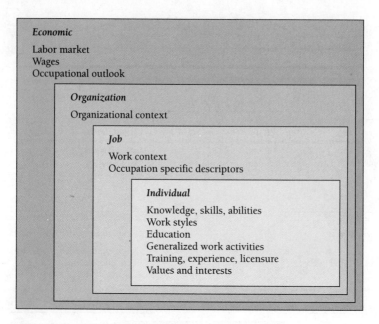

FIGURE 3–6 ■ Levels of information analysis in O*NET

SOURCE: From "Understanding Work Using the Occupational Information Network (O*NET) Implications for Research and Practice" by N. G. Peterson, M. D. Mumford, W. C. Borman, P. R. Jeanneret, E. A. Fleishman, M. A. Campion, M. S. Mayfield, F. P. Morgeson, K. Pearlman, M. K. Gowing, A. R. Lancaster, M. B. Silver, and D. M. Dye, 2001, *Personnel Psychology, 54,* pp. 451–492. Reprinted with permission.

jobs. In such jobs the work performed is evidenced by overt behaviors, such as hammering, welding, splicing wires, typing, and filing. These behaviors are highly observable, and the product of the work (e.g., a typed letter) flows directly from the skill (e.g., typing). In managerial-level jobs, the link between the KSAOs and the work output is not nearly so direct. Managerial work involves such factors as planning, decision making, forecasting, and maintaining harmonious interpersonal relations. Managerial work heavily involves cognitive and social skills, which are not so readily observable or identifiable. As such, it is often more difficult to conduct an accurate job analysis for managerial-level jobs because of the greater inferential leap between the work performed and the KSAOs.

Several job analysis methods have been developed to assist in understanding managerial jobs. Mitchell and McCormick (1990) developed the *Professional and Managerial Position Questionnaire,* which examines work along the dimensions of complexity, organizational impact, and level of responsibility. Raymark, Schmit, and Guion (1997) developed the *Personality-Related Position Requirements Form,* which analyzes jobs on the basis of the personality factors needed to perform them. Some of the personality dimensions measured are general leadership, interest in negotiation, sensitivity to interest of others, thoroughness and attention to details, and desire to generate ideas. These personality dimensions are based upon previous research that links them to managerial-level job activities. As a rule, however, the precision and accuracy of managerial job analyses are not as high as for clerical jobs because of the abstractness of the variables measured.

Uses of Job Analysis Information

Job analysis information produces the criteria needed for a wide range of applications in I/O psychology, as the ensuing chapters will show. A brief introduction to its uses is instructive.

First, an analysis of KSAOs reveals those attributes that are needed for successful job performance, including those needed upon entry into the job. The identification of these attributes provides an empirical basis to determine what personnel selection tests should assess. Thus, rather than selection tests being based on hunches or assumptions, job analytic information offers a rational approach to test selection. This topic will be described in Chapter 4. Second, job analytic information provides a basis for organizing different positions into a job, and different jobs into a job family. Such groupings provide a basis for determining levels of compensation because one factor in compensation is the attributes needed to perform the work. This topic will be discussed in the next section on job evaluation. Third, job analytic information helps determine the content of training needed to perform the job. The tasks identified as most frequently performed or most important become the primary content of training. This topic will be discussed in Chapter 6. Finally, job analytic information provides one basis to determine the content of performance evaluation or appraisal. A job analysis reveals the tasks most critical to job success, so the performance appraisal is directed at assessing how well the employee performs those tasks. This topic will be discussed in Chapter 7. In addition to these uses of job analytic information, the information can be used in vocational counseling, offering insight into the KSAOs needed to perform successfully in various occupations. Although not discussed in this book, the application of job analytic information in vocational counseling provides guidance in career selection. It is anticipated that one of the major uses of O*NET will be for vocational counseling.

Evaluating Job Analysis Methods

It should be evident that there are multiple ways of analyzing jobs. Are some methods better than others? Most of what we know about the relative merits of job analysis methods comes from questionnaires. For example, Arvey, Passino, and Lounsbury (1977) showed that the PAQ gave job analysis information that was not strongly biased by the gender of either the employee or the analyst. Conley and Sackett (1987) demonstrated that high-performing and low-performing job incumbents gave equivalent descriptions of their job; that is, job analytic information was not biased by the performance level of the incumbent. Cornelius, DeNisi, and Blencoe (1984) reported differences in the PAQ conclusions reached by expert job analysts and college students. As with most sophisticated measuring instruments, PAQ conclusions are influenced by the qualifications of the user.

The results of a study by Levine, Ash, Hall, and Sistrunk (1983), comparing seven major questionnaire methods of job analysis, reflect what the I/O profession as a whole has come to understand about job analysis methods. The authors found that different methods are regarded as differentially effective and practical depending on the purposes for which they may be used. No one method consistently surfaces as the best across the board. I believe that a well-trained job analyst could draw accurate inferences and conclusions using any one of several questionnaire methods. The converse is also true. No method can ensure accurate results when used by someone who is inexperienced with job analysis. A related opinion was reached by Harvey and Lozada-Larsen (1988), who concluded that the most accurate job analysis ratings are provided by raters who are highly knowledgeable about the job. Spector, Brannick, and Coovert (1989) described using computers to develop an artificial intelligence system to perform a job analysis. If successful, the computer would model the human judgment process in assembling information about jobs, and thereby remove the human job analyst from the process of analyzing jobs. Morgeson and Campion (1997) outlined a series of potential inaccuracies in job analytic information caused by such factors as biases in how job analysts process information about the jobs they are analyzing, and loss of motivation among SMEs who are less than enthusiastic about participating in job analyses. Morgeson and Campion believe the chances for inaccuracies are considerably less in task-oriented job analysis than in worker-oriented job analysis. That is, the ratings of observable and discrete tasks are less subject to error than the ratings of some abstract KSAOs.

Sanchez and Levine (2000) believe that our profession is greatly concerned with the standards for correctness or accuracy of job analysis data. However, we seem less concerned with establishing standards or rules by which we can use the data to set relevant personnel procedures. They argue that we should devote as much attention to examining how job analysis data are used in selection and training programs as in the accuracy of the information collected. Finally, Morgeson and Campion (2000) state that we have a better understanding of *what* work gets performed on a job than of *how* selected KSAOs operate to effectively perform tasks. They believe we need to have a clearer understanding of how KSAOs specifically enable us to perform tasks.

Competency Modeling

competency modeling
a process for determining the human characteristics needed to successfully perform a job

A recent trend in identifying the desired attributes of employees is called **competency modeling.** A *competency* is considered to be a characteristic or quality of people that a company wants its employees to manifest. As such, in traditional job analytic terms, a competency is a critical KSAO. Modeling refers to identifying the array or profile of competencies that an organization desires in its employees. Experts (e.g., Schippmann, 1999; Schippmann et al., 2000) agree that job analysis and competency modeling share some similarities in their approaches. Job analysis examines both the work that gets performed and the human attributes needed to perform the work, however, while competency modeling does not consider the work performed. The two approaches differ in three main areas: the generalizability of the information across jobs within an organization, the method by which the attributes are derived, and the degree of acceptance within the organization for the identified attributes.

First, job analysis tends to identify specific and different KSAOs that distinguish jobs within an organization. For example, one set of KSAOs would be identified for a secretary, while another set of KSAOs would be identified for a manager. In contrast, competencies are generally identified to apply to employees in all jobs within an organization or perhaps a few special differentiations among groups of jobs, as for senior executives. These competencies tend to be far more universal and abstract than KSAOs, and as such are often referenced as the "core competencies" of an organization. Here are some examples of competencies for employees:

- Exhibiting the highest level of professional integrity at all times
- Being sensitive and respectful of the dignity of all employees
- Staying current with the latest technological advances within your area
- Placing the success of the organization above your personal individual success

As can be inferred from this profile or "model," such competencies are applicable to a broad range of jobs and are specifically designed to be as inclusive as possible. KSAOs are designed more to be exclusive, differentiating one job from another. As Schippmann et al. (2000) stated, "Although job analysis can at times take a broad focus (e.g., when conducting job family research), the descriptor items serving as a basis for the grouping typically represent a level of granularity that is far more detailed than is achieved by most competency modeling efforts" (p. 727).

Second, KSAOs are identified by job analysts using technical methods designed to elicit specific job information. As such, the entire job analysis project is often perceived to be arcane by employees. In contrast, competency modeling is likely to include review sessions and group meetings of many employees to ensure that the competencies capture the language and spirit that are important to the organization. As a result, employees readily identify with and relate to the resulting competencies, an outcome rarely achieved in job analysis.

Third, competency modeling tries to link personal qualities of employees to the larger overall mission of the organization. The goal is to identify those characteristics that tap into an employee's willingness to perform certain activities or to "fit in" with the work culture of the organization (Schippmann et al., 2000). We will discuss the important topic of an organization's culture in Chapter 8. Job analysis, on the other hand, does not try to capture or include organizational level issues of vision and values in its conduct. Traditional job analysis does not have the "populist appeal" of competency modeling by members of the organization.

Schippmann et al. (2000) pose the question as to whether competency modeling is just a trend or fad among organizations. Competency modeling does not have the same rigor or precision found in job analysis. However, competency modeling does enjoy approval and adoption by many organizations. These authors note somewhat ironically that "the field of I/O psychology has not led the competency modeling movement, despite the fact that defining the key attributes needed for organizational success is a 'core competency' of I/O psychology" (p. 731). They believe the future might see a blurring of borders as the competency modeling and job analysis approaches evolve over time.

JOB EVALUATION

Different jobs have different degrees of importance or value to organizations. Some jobs are critically important, such as company president, and command the highest salary in the organization. Other jobs are less important to the organization's

job evaluation
a procedure for assessing the relative value of jobs in an organization for the purpose of establishing levels of compensation

external equity
a theoretical concept that is the basis for using wage and salary surveys in establishing compensation rates for jobs

internal equity
a theoretical concept that is the basis for using job evaluation in establishing compensation rates for jobs

compensable factors
dimensions of work used to assess the relative value of a job for determining compensation rates

success and thus pay lower salaries. **Job evaluation** is a procedure that is useful for determining the relative value of jobs in the organization, which in turn helps determine the level of compensation. It is beyond the scope of this book to present a complete discourse on compensation. An excellent analysis of compensation from an I/O psychology perspective has been written by Gerhart and Milkovich (1992). This section will simply review one component of the compensation process: job evaluation.

Organizations that wish to attract and retain competent employees have to pay competitive wages. If wages are set too low, competent people will obtain better-paying jobs elsewhere. Similarly, if wages are set too high, the organization will pay more than is necessary to staff itself. How, then, does an organization determine what is a fair and appropriate wage? Basically, two different operations are required. One is to determine external equity. Equity means fairness, so **external equity** is a fair wage in comparison to what other employers are paying. A wage survey (that is, a survey that reveals what other companies pay employees for performing their jobs) is used to determine the "going rate" for jobs in the business community. The second operation is to determine **internal equity,** or the fairness of compensation levels within the organization. Job evaluation is used to determine the relative positions (from highest paid to lowest paid) of the jobs in the organization; thus, it is used to assess internal equity.

Methods of Job Evaluation

The several methods of job evaluation all rely heavily, either implicitly or explicitly, on using criteria to assess the relative worth of jobs. Their differences rest primarily on the degree of specificity involved in the comparison process; that is, jobs may be compared either in some global fashion (as in their overall value to the company's success) or along certain specific dimensions (as in how much effort they require and the working conditions under which they are performed).

In practice, most organizations use job evaluation methods that examine several dimensions or factors of work. These dimensions are called **compensable factors,** or those factors for which employers pay compensation; that is, various levels of compensation are paid for jobs depending on "how much" of these compensable factors are present in each. Please note a fine distinction here that people often confuse. With a few notable exceptions, organizations do not pay individuals; organizations pay jobs, which individuals fill. The jobs determine the level of compensation, not the people in them.

There is no one fixed set of compensable factors. In theory, organizations can pay jobs for whatever reasons they want. In practice, however, *effort, skill, responsibility,* and *working conditions* are typical compensable factors.

Another related set of four compensable factors, often used in the compensation of managers and executives, is the Hay Plan (named after the Hay Group consulting firm). The first, *know-how,* is the total of all skills and knowledge required to do the job. The second factor, *problem solving,* is the amount of original thinking required to arrive at decisions in the job. The third factor, *accountability,* is being answerable for actions taken on the job. The fourth factor, *additional compensable elements,* addresses exceptional contexts in which the jobs are performed.

Here is one way in which job evaluation works. Let us say the organization has selected four compensable factors: skill, effort, responsibility, and working conditions. Although most or all of the jobs in the organization would be evaluated, our discussion is limited to two jobs: office secretary and security officer. The results of a job analysis might reveal that the major criteria for a secretary's performance are typing, filing, and supervising a clerk. For the security officer, the criteria of job performance might be physically patrolling the office building, remaining vigilant, and maintaining security records. The criteria for both jobs would be evaluated or scored in terms of the degree to which the compensable factors are present. For example, the secretary's job might be evaluated as requiring considerable skill, little effort, modest responsibility, and performance under temperate working conditions. The security officer's job might be evaluated as requiring little skill, modest effort, considerable responsibility, and performance under potentially hazardous working conditions.

Thus, the level of compensation paid for jobs is a function of their status on the compensable factors. Jobs that have high levels of the compensable factors (for example, high effort, great skill) receive higher rates of pay than jobs that have low levels of these factors. All the jobs in the company would be evaluated in this fashion and then arranged in a hierarchy from high to low. A job evaluation method called the Factor Evaluation System (FES) developed by the U.S. Civil Service Commission (1977) is used to evaluate jobs in the federal government. The method is based on assessing nine factors (or criteria). Each factor is broken down into levels (low, medium, and high), with a corresponding point value for each level. Every job is evaluated using this method, with the result that every job is assigned a point total based on the scores from the nine factors. The point total is then used to set the salary paid to the job. Table 3–4 shows the nine factors and their corresponding points.

TABLE 3–4 ■ Factor description table for factor evaluation system

Factor	Possible Points for Factor	Value of Factor as Percentage of Total (Weight of Factor)	Number of Levels	Points for Each Level
Knowledge required by the position	1,850	41.3%	9	50, 200, 350, 550, 750, 950, 1250 1550, 1850
Supervisory control	650	14.5%	5	25, 125, 275, 450, 650
Guidelines	650	14.5%	5	25, 125, 275, 450, 650
Complexity	450	10.0%	6	25, 75, 150, 225, 325, 450
Scope and effect	450	10.0%	6	25, 75, 150, 225, 325, 450
Personal contact	110	2.5%	4	10, 25, 60, 110
Purpose of contact	220	4.9%	4	20, 50, 120, 220
Physical demand	50	1.1%	3	5, 20, 50
Work environment	50	1.1%	3	5, 20, 50
Total	4,480	99.9%		

SOURCE: From U.S. Civil Service Commission, *Instructions for the Factor Evaluation System,* May 1977, Washington, DC: U.S. Government Printing Office.

Other methods of job evaluation do not require the use of compensable factors, but all methods require that jobs be evaluated on one or more criteria. A (dollar) value is then ultimately attached to the relative position of every job in the hierarchy. Job evaluation attempts to ensure some correspondence between the compensation paid for the job and the value of the job to the organization.

Obviously a key to any job evaluation system is whether the "right factors" are being considered. The evaluations should be made on the basis of factors that truly reflect the jobs' worth, importance, or value. Also, unlike job analysis, which is basically a value-free operation (that is, an analysis), job evaluation is heavily loaded with values (that is, an evaluation). Values are evidenced in the selection of job factors to be evaluated and whether certain factors are considered more important than others. Therefore, job evaluation is an extension of job analysis applied to determining the relative worth of jobs in an organization for the purpose of providing equitable pay.

Research on Job Evaluation

I/O psychological research on job evaluation is not as extensive as the research on job analysis. However, we will describe a few studies. Gomez-Mejia, Page, and Tornow (1982) compared the relative accuracy and practical utility of seven different job evaluation approaches. Their results indicated that although several methods provided useful information, a critical factor was the job analysis data on which the job evaluation system was based. If the job analysis data are of poor quality, their use in job evaluation makes that process suffer. Hahn and Dipboye (1988) reported that the most accurate and reliable job evaluation ratings were provided by people who received training in how to evaluate as well as extensive information about the jobs to be evaluated. Collins and Muchinsky (1993) reported that job evaluation ratings provided consistent assessments of job worth *within* a job family (e.g., secretary vs. clerk) but produced considerable disagreement about job worth *across* job families (e.g., secretary vs. electrician). Since large companies often organize their jobs into multiple job families, the finding suggests that it will be unlikely to find a single job evaluation instrument to provide consistent and accurate assessments of worth across all jobs in a company.

I/O psychologists typically regard agreement among people in describing work-related issues as evidence of the "correctness" of their opinions. However, research on job evaluation reveals the potential fallibility of this perspective. Schwab and Wichern (1983) suggested that systematic bias may be operating in the determination of compensation. For example, let us assume that most secretaries are women and that society as a whole does not highly value the work that women typically perform. Therefore, the wages paid to female secretaries are lower than they "should" be. Additionally, this same bias operates to uniformly suppress the judged value of a secretarial job vis-à-vis the compensable factors; that is, secretarial jobs are judged to be relatively low in required effort, skill, and responsibility. Therefore, what looks like a "fair" relationship between the value of the job and the wages paid for it is actually the product of linking biased job evaluation results with biased wages. In other words, as Schwab and Wichern indicated, agreement may masquerade as truth or fairness when it is actually indicating systematic bias. Rynes and Milkovich (1986) concluded that market wages, which often serve as criteria in job evaluation, can be biased by many factors. For example, geographical differences and company pay practices influence market wages, as do the supply and demand of labor, thus dispelling the myth that market wages reflect the true worth of a job.

Comparable Worth. The issue of systematic bias in job evaluation also relates to the doctrine of comparable worth, called a "doctrine" because it represents a philosophy of how jobs should be paid. **Comparable worth** means giving people equal pay for performing comparable work (Mahoney, 1983). This is in contrast to giving equal pay for equal work, which is the doctrine underlying the Equal Pay Act, a federal law regarding compensation. The Equal Pay Act states that men and women who perform equal work are to receive equal pay. Proponents of comparable worth believe that two jobs are rarely ever truly equal. They believe it is more reasonable to speak of jobs as having comparable or equivalent worth. Jobs that are of comparable worth should be paid the same.

To determine the worth of all jobs would require a common measuring device, such as job evaluation. However, comparable worth proponents believe that many current job evaluation methods are inherently biased against the work typically performed by women. These people point to labor statistics indicating that women on the average earn about 75 cents for every $1 earned by men (Martocchio, 2001). This, they assert, is de facto evidence that women are the victims of discrimination caused by job evaluation methods that unfairly undervalue the work they perform. Indeed, Arvey (1986) suggested that the factors selected for consideration in job evaluation may be biased against women. For example, the physical strength exerted in a job is often used as one factor in job evaluation. Since most men are physically stronger than most women, the rated value of female-dominated jobs may suffer on this factor. Alternatively, many women work in jobs in which eyestrain is a problem, yet amount of eyestrain is typically not a factor included in job evaluation (see Field Note 3). Proponents of comparable worth propose the need for a bias-free system to evaluate jobs that would reduce the male/female pay differential by increasing the wages paid to women.

Opponents of the doctrine of comparable worth believe no systematic bias is operating against "female" jobs. They believe that women are as free to choose whatever jobs they want as men are; they simply settle for lower-paying jobs that allow them more latitude for other obligations, such as family duties. Economic forces are always operating in a free society. Companies that implement a comparable worth policy would be at a disadvantage for hiring some types of employees. In short, the opponents believe the job evaluation system is not at fault; rather, society has socialized men and women to pursue different types of jobs. They further believe there is no way to ever measure jobs in a way that is totally free of any values—that is, to have a totally bias-free assessment.

Most discussions of comparable worth are presented by people who feel strongly about the topic, one way or the other (England, 1992). There are currently no correct answers to this heated debate. At its core is the issue of values applied to job evaluation.

comparable worth
a belief that jobs of comparable value to the organization should be compensated equally

FIELD NOTE 3   **What to Compensate?**

At the core of the debate on comparable worth is the question of how the worth of a job is determined. A traditional way of determining job worth is through job evaluation. It is common to rate jobs on certain factors (such as effort and working conditions), with each rating being worth a certain number of points. The points are then summed, and the total point value of the job becomes the measure of its relative worth. Comparable worth advocates believe that the very factors on which jobs are evaluated often slant the final results in favor of jobs traditionally held by men.

For example, on the effort factor, jobs that involve heavy lifting are worth more than jobs that involve light lifting. On the working conditions factor, jobs that are performed under adverse physical conditions (such as outdoor work) are worth more than jobs performed under temperate conditions (such as an air-conditioned or heated office). Who is more likely to fill a job requiring heavy lifting—men or women? Typically men. Who is more likely to work outdoors? Typi-

cally men. Therefore, men's jobs are more likely to be worth more points, and thus receive higher wages, than jobs traditionally filled by women.

But what if we changed the very factors on which jobs are rated? Two possible factors are mental stress and the handling of sensitive/confidential information. Jobs that subject workers to high mental stress and the handling of confidential information would be worth more than jobs that don't. Secretaries often work under stressful conditions (that is, a hectic work pace and continual deadlines) and deal with confidential information. Most secretarial jobs are held by women. Therefore, depending on the job factors you wish to consider (effort and working conditions versus mental stress and confidential information), you could arrive at two quite different conclusions regarding the worth of a secretary's job. Job factors are nothing more than criteria, the criteria by which the worth of a job is determined. As stated earlier in this chapter, differences of opinion about criteria are at the heart of many disputes. Such is certainly the case with comparable worth.

JOB PERFORMANCE CRITERIA

Desirable job performance criteria can be defined by three general characteristics; the criteria must be appropriate, stable, and practical. The criteria should be relevant and representative of the job. They must endure over time or across situations. Finally, they should not be too expensive or hard to measure. Other authors think that different issues are important—for example, the time at which criterion measures are taken (after one month on the job, six months, and so on), the type of criterion measure taken (performance, errors, accidents), and the level of performance chosen to represent success or failure on the job (college students must perform at a C level in order to graduate). Criteria are often chosen by either history or precedent; unfortunately, sometimes criteria are chosen because they are merely expedient or available.

objective performance criteria
a set of factors used to assess job performance that are (relatively) objective or factual in character

subjective performance criteria
a set of factors used to assess job performance that are the product of someone's (e.g., supervisor, peer) subjective rating of these factors

Job performance criteria may be objective or subjective. **Objective performance criteria** are taken from organizational records (payroll or personnel) and supposedly do not involve any subjective evaluation. **Subjective performance criteria** are judgmental evaluations of a person's performance (such as a supervisor might render). Although objective criteria may involve no subjective judgment, some degree of assessment must be applied to give them meaning. Just knowing that an employee produced 18 units a day is not informative; this output must be compared with what other workers produce. If the average is 10 units a day, 18 units clearly represents "good" performance. If the average is 25 units a day, 18 units is not good.

Objective Criteria

Production. Using units of production as a criterion is most common in manufacturing jobs. If an organization has only one type of job, then setting production criteria is easy. But most companies have many types of production jobs, so productivity must be compared fairly. That is, if average productivity in one job is 6 units a day and in another job it is 300 units a day, then productivities must be equated to adjust for these differences. Statistical procedures are usually used for this. Other factors can diminish the value of production as a criterion of performance. In an assembly-line job, the speed of the line determines how many units are produced per day. Increasing the speed of the line increases production. Furthermore, everyone who works on the line has the same level of production. In a case like this, units of production are determined by factors outside of the individual worker. So errors that are under the worker's control may be the criterion of job performance. However, this is no cure-all for the criterion problem either. Errors are not fair criteria if they are more likely in some jobs than others. Due to automation and work simplification, some jobs are almost "goof-proof." In such jobs error-free work has nothing to do with the human factor.

Sales. Sales are a commonly used performance criterion for wholesale and retail sales work, but variations must be considered. Using the sheer number of sales as a criterion is appropriate only if everyone is selling the same product(s) in comparable territories. A person who sells toothbrushes should sell more units than a person who sells houses. Also, someone selling tractors in Iowa should sell more than a person whose sales territory is Rhode Island. Not only is Iowa bigger than Rhode Island but also more farming is done proportionately in Iowa than in Rhode Island. Total sales volume is equally fallible as a criterion. A real estate salesperson can sell a $100,000 house in one afternoon, but how long would it take to sell $100,000 worth of toothbrushes?

The solution to these types of problems is to use norm groups for judging success. A real estate salesperson should be compared to other real estate salespeople in the same sales territory. The same holds for other sales work. If comparisons have to be drawn across sales territories or across product lines, then statistical adjustments are needed. Ideally, any differences in sales performance are then due to the ability of the salesperson, which is the basis for using sales as a criterion of job performance.

Tenure or Turnover. Length of service is a very popular criterion in I/O psychological research. Turnover not only has a theoretical appeal (for example, Hom & Griffeth, 1995) but also is a practical concern. Employers want to hire people who will stay with the company. For obvious practical reasons, employers don't want to hire chronic job-hoppers. The costs of recruiting, selecting, and training new hires can be extremely high. Turnover is perhaps the most frequently used

CNN video

A production worker making parts for a Harley-Davidson motorcycle.
SOURCE: CNN

nonperformance criterion in the psychological literature. It is a valuable and useful criterion because it measures employment stability.

Campion (1991) suggested that many factors should be considered in the measurement of turnover. One is *voluntariness* (whether the employee was fired, quit to take another job with better promotional opportunities, or quit because of dissatisfaction with a supervisor). Another factor is *functionality* (whether the employee was performing the job effectively or ineffectively). Williams and Livingstone (1994) meta-analyzed studies that examined the relationship between turnover and performance, and concluded that poor performers were more likely to voluntarily quit their jobs than good performers.

Absenteeism. Absence from work, like turnover, is an index of employee stability. Although some degree of employee turnover is good for organizations, unexcused employee absenteeism invariably has bad consequences for the organization. Excused absenteeism (e.g., personal vacation time) is generally not a problem, as it is sanctioned and must be approved by the organization. Rhodes and Steers (1990) and Martocchio and Harrison (1993) reviewed many studies on why people are absent from work. Absence appears to be the product of many factors, including family conflicts, job dissatisfaction, alcohol and drug abuse, and personality. However, as Johns (1994) noted, employees are likely to give self-serving justifications for their absence. For example, being absent from work to care for a sick child is more socially acceptable than acknowledging deviant behavior such as drug use. Accordingly, self-reports of why employees are absent can be highly inaccurate.

Absenteeism is a pervasive problem in industry; it costs employers billions of dollars a year in decreased efficiency and increased benefit payments (for example, sick leave) and payroll costs. Absenteeism has social, individual, and organizational causes, and it affects individuals, companies, and even entire industrial societies.

Accidents. Accidents are sometimes used as a criterion of job performance, although they have a number of limitations. First, accidents are used as a measure mainly for blue-collar jobs. (While white-collar workers can be injured at work, the frequency of such accidents is small.) Thus, accidents are a measure of job performance for only a limited sample of employees. Second, accidents are difficult to predict, and there is little stability or consistency across individuals in their occurrence (Senders & Moray, 1991). Third, accidents can be measured in many ways: number of accidents per hours worked, miles driven, trips taken, and so on. Different conclusions can be drawn depending on how accident statistics are calculated. Employers do not want to hire people who, for whatever reason, will incur job-related accidents. But in the total picture of job performance, accidents are not used as a criterion as often as is production, turnover, or absence.

Theft. Employee theft is a major problem facing organizations, with annual losses estimated to be $200 billion annually (Greenberg & Scott, 1996). Hollinger and

Clark (1983) administered an anonymous questionnaire about theft to employees at three types of organizations. The percentages of employees who admitted to stealing from their employer were 42% in retail stores, 32% in hospitals, and 26% in manufacturing firms. Thus, employee theft is a pervasive and serious problem. From an I/O psychologist's perspective, the goal is to hire people who are unlikely to steal from the company, just as it is desirable to hire people who have a low probability of having accidents. The problem with using theft as a criterion is that we know very little about the individual identity of employees who do steal. Hollinger and Clark based their survey results on anonymous responses. Furthermore, those responses came from people who were willing to admit they stole from the company. Those employees who were stealing but chose not to respond to the survey or who did not admit they stole were not included in the theft results. Greenberg and Scott (1996) asserted that some employees resort to theft as a means of offsetting perceived unfairness in how their employer treats them.

A drawback in using theft as a job performance criterion is that only a small percentage of employees are ever caught stealing. The occurrence of theft often has to be deduced on the basis of calculated shortages from company inventories of supplies and products. In addition, many companies will not divulge any information about theft to outside individuals. Although companies often share information on such criteria as absenteeism and turnover, theft records are too sensitive to reveal. Despite these limitations, I/O psychologists regard theft as an index of employment suitability, and we will probably witness much more research on theft in the years ahead (see Field Note 4).

In conclusion, the objective criteria reviewed can indeed be relevant measures of job performance. In fact, the single most important criterion of job performance

---

FIELD NOTE 4 Theft of Waste

any organizations experience problems of theft by employees. Thefts include office supplies used in work, such as staplers and tape dispensers, as well as items that are intended for sale to customers. Sometimes cash is stolen. What all these items have in common is that they are assets or resources of the company.

I once had an experience with a company where the biggest concern was not the theft of resources, but the theft of waste! A company printed U.S. postage stamps. The worth of each stamp is the value printed on the stamp—usually the cost of 1 ounce of first-class postage, currently 34¢. While there was some concern that employees would steal the postage stamps for their personal use, the bigger concern was the theft of misprints or errors. Printing errors occur when a stamp is printed off-center or, in extreme cases, when the printing on the stamp is correct but the image is inverted, or upside-down. One 34¢ stamp printed with an inverted image may be worth thousands of dollars to philatelists, or stamp collectors. In the printing of postage stamps, errors occur as they do in all other types of printing. In this case, however, the errors have very high market value. To reduce the possibility of theft of misprints that were scheduled to be destroyed, the company had three elaborate and extensive sets of search and security procedures for anyone *leaving* the company. Somewhat paradoxically, there was no security for people entering the building. All the security procedures involved people leaving the building, as they were searched for the theft of highly valuable waste or scrap.

"We've done a computer simulation of your projected performance in five years. You're fired."

for a sales job is often total sales volume. However, many jobs don't involve making sales, producing objects, stealing property, or incurring accidents. Thus, objective job performance criteria can be misleading measures of how well people perform their jobs. Subjective job performance criteria are often used because of their wide applicability.

Subjective Criteria

Subjective criteria are judgments made of an employee's performance. The judgment is usually a rating or ranking. For example, a supervisor might rate the employees in a department on the basis of overall effectiveness. This rating would then be the standard of job performance. Supervisor ratings are by far the most frequently used judgmental criteria; however, ratings may also be supplied by peers, subordinates, and workers themselves. The ratings may be on a general factor, such as overall effectiveness, or on specific factors, such as quantity of work, quality of work, creativity, practical judgment, and so forth. Some studies have even compared judgments made by two or more sets of raters (for example, supervisors and peers) who evaluate several dimensions of behavior. Such studies normally show that certain raters are more consistent in rating certain aspects of job performance. Supervisors may agree in rating the quality of work; peers agree in rating interpersonal relations. Chapter 7 will discuss this issue in greater detail.

Because judgmental criteria are used so often, a great deal of attention has been given to improving the quality of these judgments. If the people doing the judging don't know how to make such evaluations, the quality of their decisions will be very poor. Spool (1978) reviewed the research on training people to make more accurate judgments of behavior. He found that people can indeed learn to be accurate evaluators. People who are more involved and interested in evaluating behavior make more careful and accurate judgments. Research (for example, Pursell, Dossett, & Latham, 1980) revealed that a one-day training program can greatly enhance people's skills in observing and interpreting behavior.

From this discussion, it is clear that no single measure of job performance is totally adequate. While each criterion may have merit, each can also suffer from weakness along other dimensions. For instance, few people would say that an employee's absence has no bearing on overall job performance, but no one would say that absence is a complete measure of job performance. Absence, like production or job level, is but one piece of the broader picture. Don't be discouraged that no one criterion meets all our standards. It is precisely because job performance is multidimensional (and each single dimension is a fallible index of overall performance) that we are compelled to include many relevant aspects of work in establishing criteria.

Relationships Among Job Performance Criteria

Several job performance criteria can be identified for many jobs, and each criterion frequently assesses a different aspect of performance. These criteria are usually independent of one another. If they were all highly positively correlated—say, $r = .80$ or $r = .90$—there would be no point in measuring them all. Knowing an employee's status on one criterion would give his or her status on the others. Several studies have tried to identify interrelationships among criteria.

A classic study by Seashore, Indik, and Georgopoulos (1960) revealed multiple job performance criteria and also showed that the criteria were relatively independent of one another. For example, Seashore and associates studied delivery men for whom five job performance criteria were available: productivity (objectively measured by time standards), effectiveness (subjectively rated based on quality of performance), accidents, unexcused absences, and errors (based on the number of packages not delivered). The correlations among these five criteria appear in Table 3–5. The data show that the five criteria were relatively independent of one another. The highest correlation coefficients were found among the variables of productivity, effectiveness, and errors ($.28$, $-.26$, and $-.32$). These results demonstrate that there really is no single measure of overall performance on the job; each criterion measures a different facet.

Bommer, Johnson, Rich, Podsakoff, and MacKenzie (1995) conducted a meta-analytic study examining the relationship between subjective ratings of job performance and objective measures of job performance. They reported an average correlation coefficient of $.39$ between these two types of assessment. Quite clearly, you can arrive at different conclusions about a person's job performance depending on how you choose to assess it.

There is also a relationship between job level and the number of criteria needed to define job performance. Lower-level, relatively simple jobs do not have many dimensions of performance; more complex jobs have many. In fact, the number of job performance criteria can separate simple jobs from complex ones. Manual laborers who unload trucks might be measured by only three criteria: attendance (they have to show up for work), errors (they have to know how to stack the material), and speed. More complex jobs, as in the medical field, might be defined by as many as 15 independent criteria. The more complex the job, the more criteria are needed to define it and the more skill or talent a person has to have to be successful.

Dynamic Performance Criteria

dynamic performance criteria aspects of job performance that change over time for individuals, as does their predictability

The concept of **dynamic performance criteria** applies to job performance criteria that change over time. It is significant because job performance is not stable or consistent over time, and this dynamic quality of criteria adds to the complexity of making personnel decisions. Steele-Johnson, Osburn, and Pieper (2000) identified three potential reasons for systematic changes in job performance over time. First, employees might change the way they perform tasks as a result of repeatedly conducting them. Second, the knowledge and ability requirements needed to perform the task might change due to changing work technologies. Third, the knowledge and abilities of the employees might change as a result of additional training.

TABLE 3–5 ■ Correlations among five criterion variables

	Productivity	Accidents	Absences	Errors
Effectiveness	.28	−.02	−.08	−.32
Productivity		.12	−.01	−.26
Accidents			.03	−.18
Absences				.15

SOURCE: Adapted from "Relationship Among Criteria of Job Performance" by S. E. Seashore, B. P. Indik, and B. S. Georgopoulos, 1960, *Journal of Applied Psychology, 44,* pp. 195–202.

Consider Figure 3–7, which shows the levels of three job performance criteria—productivity, absence, and accidents—over an eight-year period. The time period represents a person's eight-year performance record on a job. You will notice that the patterns of behavior for the three criteria differ over time. The individual's level of accidents is stable over time. In this case, accidents is not a dynamic performance criterion because of its stability over time. However, a very different pattern emerges for the other two criteria. The individual's level of productivity increases over the years, more gradually in the early years and then more rapidly in the later years. Absence, on the other hand, follows the opposite pattern. The employee's absence was greatest in the first year of employment and progressively declined over time. Absence and productivity are dynamic performance criteria, while accidents is a static criterion.

When a job applicant is considered for employment, the organization attempts to predict how well that person will perform on the job. A hire/no hire decision is then made on the basis of this prediction. If job performance criteria are static (like accidents in Figure 3–7), the accuracy of the prediction is aided by the stability of the behavior. However, if job performance criteria are dynamic, a critical new element is added to the decision, *time.* It may be that initially productivity would not be very impressive, but over time the employee's performance would rise to and then surpass a satisfactory level. Dynamic performance criteria are equivalent to "hitting a moving target," as the level of the behavior being predicted is continuously changing. Furthermore, the pattern of change may be different *across* individuals. That is, for some people productivity may start off low and then get progressively higher, while for others the pattern may be the opposite.

To what degree are dynamic performance criteria an issue in I/O psychology? The profession is divided. Some researchers (e.g., Barrett, Alexander, & Doverspike, 1992; Barrett, Caldwell, & Alexander, 1985) contend that job performance criteria aren't very dynamic at all, and the problem is not severe. Others (Deadrick & Madigan, 1990; Hofmann, Jacobs, & Baratta, 1993) provide research findings indicating that various criteria of job performance do change over time, as does their predictability. Hulin, Henry, and Noon (1990) believe that time is an underresearched topic in understanding the relationship between concepts. They assert that over time some criteria become more predictable while others decline in predictability. The investigation into dynamic criteria requires examining complex

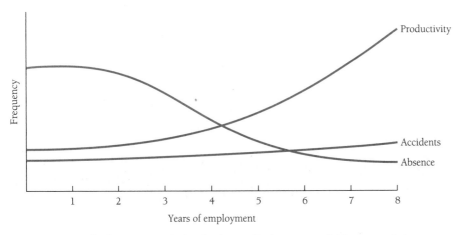

FIGURE 3–7 ■ **Performance variation in three criteria over an eight-year period**

research questions that do not lend themselves to simple answers. In general, if criteria operate in a dynamic fashion over time, this underscores our need to be sensitive to the difference in the prediction of behavior in the short term versus the long term.

EXPANDING OUR VIEW OF CRITERIA

Throughout the history of I/O psychology, our concept of criteria has been primarily *job-related*. That is, we have defined the successful employee primarily in terms of how well he or she meets the criteria for performance on the job. However, as Borman (1991) noted, it is possible to consider ways employees contribute to the success of the work group or organization that are not tied directly to *job* performance criteria. One example is being a "good soldier"—demonstrating conscientious behaviors that show concern for doing things properly for the good of the organization. Another example is prosocial behavior—doing little things that help other people perform their jobs more effectively.

Brief and Motowidlo (1986) found that in some organizations it is explicitly stated that part of an employee's own job performance is to support and provide guidance to other individuals. A military combat unit is one such example. However, in many other organizations, going beyond the call of duty to help out a fellow employee or the organization is outside the formally *required* job responsibilities. The proclivity of some individuals in a group to help out others can at times be detrimental to the organization, as when a group member helps a coworker with a problem and in the process fails to complete an important job-related task. Nevertheless, Borman (1991) concluded, in most cases the welfare of the organization is enhanced by prosocial behavior. The topic of prosocial behavior will be discussed in more detail in Chapter 10.

Research on prosocial behavior shows that the criteria for a successful employee may transcend performance on job tasks. It is thus conceivable that some employees may be regarded as valuable members of the organization because they are quick to assist others and be "good soldiers"—not because they perform their own job tasks very well. The concept of a "job" has historically been a useful framework for understanding one's duties and responsibilities, and accordingly for employees to be held accountable for meeting job performance criteria. However, there are circumstances and conditions (such as demonstrating prosocial behavior) that lead I/O psychologists to question the value of criteria strictly from a job perspective. Some researchers believe it is more beneficial to think of employees as performing a series of roles for the organization, as opposed to one job. The relationship between roles and jobs will be discussed in Chapter 8.

CONCLUDING COMMENTS

Austin and Villanova (1992) traced the history of criterion measurement in I/O psychology over the past 75 years. The conceptual problems associated with accurate criterion representation and measurement of today are not all that different from those faced at the time of the birth of I/O psychology. However, I believe I/O psychology may be at the dawn of a new criterion for determining the successful employee. Actually, it is not a *new* criterion so much as a reemphasis and generalization of a criterion that has always been with us. The growing importance of this criterion results from the changing conditions of contemporary work, the subject of Chapter 14. The criterion has two components: the ability to learn and grow, and the willingness to do so. The world of work as we know it is constantly changing, and the rate of change is accelerating. Few things are as they used to be. Technological advances in communication and production have revolutionized the way we work. The means by which organizations utilize their employees have changed likewise. No longer are we in static, stable environments. New employees are required to be able to learn quickly on the job. Older employees are expected (and in some cases required) to learn new systems and ways of conducting business. We have entered an era of required growth and learning. The successful employee must have not only the capacity to learn and grow, but also the desire and willingness to do so. As our work environment continues to change, so too must employees change with them. Offices and factories are becoming learning sites, and employees must engage in "learning a living." Ways of measuring both the capacity to learn and the willingness to learn will be discussed in the next chapter.

CASE STUDY   ■   **Theft of Company Property**

Wilton Petroleum Company was a wholesale distributor of a major brand of gasoline. Gasoline was shipped via barges from the refinery to the company. The company then delivered the gasoline to retail gas stations for sale to motorists. The gasoline tanker trucks were huge, 18-wheel vehicles that held 9,000 gallons of gasoline. The gasoline that was pumped out of the truck into underground holding tanks at the gas stations was monitored very precisely. The company knew exactly how many gallons of gasoline were pumped into the holding tanks at each gas station, and it knew exactly how many gallons were pumped out of the tanker trucks. A meter on the tanker truck recorded the amount of gasoline leaving the tanker. A 20-foot hose extending from the truck permitted the driver to fill the tanks at each gas station. Every day each driver recorded the total volume of gasoline delivered. The total volume pumped out of the truck had to equal the total volume of gasoline deposited into the holding tanks. Any discrepancy would be regarded as evidence of theft of the gasoline by the drivers.

Based on years of experience the company knew there was a slight flaw in the system used to monitor the flow of gasoline out of the tanker. The meter recorded the flow of gasoline out of the tanker; however, there were always about 3 gallons of gasoline in the 20-foot hose that went unrecorded. That was the gasoline that had flowed out of the truck but did not enter the holding tanks.

One truck driver, Lew Taylor, believed he knew a way to "beat the system" and steal gasoline for his personal use. After making all his scheduled deliveries for the day, he would extend the full length of the hose on the ground and let gravity drain out the 3 gallons of gasoline in the hose. The pump and the meter were never turned on, so there was no record of any gasoline leaving the tank. Company officials knew that Taylor was siphoning the gasoline based on the very small but repeated shortage in Taylor's records compared with other drivers. The value of the stolen gasoline each day was only about $5, but the cumulative value of the losses was considerable.

Michael Morris, operations manager of the company, knew Taylor was stealing the gasoline but couldn't prove it. Taylor had found a loophole in the monitoring system and had a way to steal gasoline. Morris decided to lay a trap for Taylor. Morris "planted" a company hand tool (a hammer) on a chair at the entrance to the room where the drivers changed their clothes after work. Morris had a small hole drilled in the wall to observe the chair. He thought that if Taylor stole the gasoline, he might be tempted to steal the hammer. The trap worked. Taylor was spied placing the company tool under his jacket as he walked out the door. On a signal from Morris, security officers approached Taylor and asked about the hammer. Taylor produced the hammer, was led by the security officers to Morris's office, and was immediately fired from his job. Although Taylor had stolen hundreds of dollars worth of gasoline from his employer, he was terminated for the theft of a hand tool worth about $10.

Study Questions

1. If Taylor had a perfect attendance record, made all his deliveries on time, had effective interpersonal skills, and in all other ways was a conscientious employee, would you still have fired Taylor for committing theft if you had been Morris? Why or why not?

2. Do you think Taylor "got what was coming to him" in this case, or was he "set up" by Morris and thus a victim of entrapment?

3. What do you think of the ethics of companies spying on their employees with peepholes and cameras to detect the occurrence of theft by employees? Why do you feel as you do?
4. What effect might Taylor's dismissal by Wilton Petroleum have on other employees of the company?
5. Have you ever "taken" a paper clip, pencil, or sheet of paper home with you from your place of work? If so, do you consider it to be a case of theft on your part? Why or why not, and what's the difference between the "theft" of a paper clip versus a hammer?

SUGGESTED INFOTRAC TOPICS

criteria

job analysis

Occupational Information Network

competency modeling

job evaluation

comparable worth

employee turnover

employee absenteeism

employee accidents

employee theft

Predictors: Psychological Assessments

LEARNING OBJECTIVES

- ■ Identify the major types of reliability and what they measure.
- ■ Understand the major manifestations of validity and what they measure.
- ■ Know the major types of psychological tests categorized by administration and content.

■ Explain the role of psychological testing in making assessments of people, including ethical issues and predictive accuracy.

■ Explain nontest predictors such as interviews, assessment centers, work samples, biographical information, and letters of recommendation.

■ Understand the new or controversial methods of assessment.

A *predictor* is any variable used to forecast a criterion. In weather prediction, barometric pressure can be used to forecast rainfall. In medical prediction, body temperature can be used to predict (or diagnose) illness. In I/O psychology, we seek predictors of job performance criteria as indexed by productivity, absenteeism, turnover, and so forth. There is no limit to the variables we can use for this purpose. Although we do not use tea leaves and astrological signs as fortune-tellers do, we have explored a multitude of devices to use as potential predictors of job performance criteria. This chapter will review the variables traditionally used, examine their success, and discuss some professional problems inherent in their application.

ASSESSING THE QUALITY OF PREDICTORS

All predictor variables, like other measuring devices, can be assessed in terms of their quality or goodness. We can think of several features of a good measuring device. We would like it to be consistent and accurate; that is, it should repeatedly yield precise measurements. In psychology we judge the goodness of our measuring devices by two psychometric criteria: reliability and validity. If a predictor is not both reliable and valid, it is useless.

Reliability

reliability
a standard for evaluating tests that refers to the consistency, stability, or equivalence of test scores

Reliability is the consistency or stability of a measure. A measure should yield the same estimate on repeated use when the measured trait has not changed. Even though that estimate may be inaccurate, a reliable measure will always be consistent. Three major types of reliability are used in psychology to assess the consistency or stability of the measuring device, and a fourth assessment of reliability is often used in I/O psychology.

test-retest reliability
a type of reliability that reveals the stability of test scores upon repeated applications of the test

Test-Retest Reliability. **Test-retest reliability** is perhaps the simplest assessment of a measuring device's reliability. We measure something at two times and compare the scores. We can give an intelligence test to the same group of people at two different times and then correlate the two sets of scores. This correlation is called a *coefficient of stability* because it reflects the stability of the test over time. If the test is reliable, those who scored high the first time will also score high the second time, and vice versa. If the test is unreliable, the scores will "bounce around" in such a way that there is no similarity in individuals' scores between the two trials.

When we say a test (or any measure) is *reliable,* how high should the coefficient of stability be? The answer is the higher the better. A test cannot be too reliable. As a rule, reliability coefficients around .70 are professionally acceptable, though some frequently used tests have test-retest reliabilities of only around .50. Furthermore, the length of time between administrations of the test must be considered in the interpretation of a test's test-retest reliability. Generally the shorter the time interval between administrations (e.g., one week vs. six months), the higher will be the test-retest reliability.

equivalent–form reliability
a type of reliability that reveals the equivalence of test scores between two versions of the test

Equivalent–Form Reliability. A second type of reliability is parallel or **equivalent-form reliability**. Here a psychologist develops two forms of a test to measure the same attribute and gives both forms to a group of people. The psychologist then correlates the two scores for each person. The resulting correlation, called a *coefficient of equivalence,* reflects the extent to which the two forms are equivalent measures of the same concept. Of the three major types of reliability, this type is the least popular because it is usually challenging to come up with one good test, let alone two. Many tests do not have a "parallel form." Furthermore, research (e.g., Clause, et al., 1998) reveals it is by no means easy to construct two tests whose scores have similar meanings and statistical properties such that they are truly parallel or equivalent measures. However, in intelligence and achievement testing (to be discussed shortly), equivalent forms of the same test are sometimes available. If the resulting coefficient of equivalence is high, the tests are equivalent and reliable measures of the same concept. If it is low, they are not.

internal–consistency reliability
a type of reliability that reveals the homogeneity of the items in a test

Internal–Consistency Reliability. The third major assessment is the **internal-consistency reliability** of the test—the extent to which it has homogeneous content. Two types of internal-consistency reliability are typically computed. One is called split-half reliability. Here a test is given to a group of people, but in scoring the test (though not administering it), the researcher divides the items in half, into odd- and even-numbered items. Each person thus gets two sets of scores (one for each half), which are correlated. If the test is internally consistent, there should be a high degree of similarity in the responses (that is, right or wrong) to the odd- and even-numbered items. All other things being equal, the longer a test is, the greater is its reliability.

A second technique for assessing internal-consistency reliability is to compute one of two coefficients: Cronbach's alpha or Kuder-Richardson 20 (KR20). Both procedures are similar, though not statistically identical. Conceptually, each test item is treated as a minitest. Thus, a 100-item test consists of 100 minitests. The response to each item is correlated with the response to every other item. A matrix of interitem correlations is formed whose average is related to the homogeneity of the test. If the test is homogeneous (the item content is similar), it will have a high internal-consistency reliability. If the test is heterogeneous (the items cover a wide variety of concepts), it is not internally consistent and the resulting coefficient will be low. Internal-consistency reliability is frequently used to assess a test's homogeneity of content in I/O psychology.

Inter-Rater Reliability. When assessments are made on the basis of raters' judgments, it is possible for the raters to disagree in their evaluations. Two different raters may observe the same behavior yet evaluate it differently. The degree of correspondence between judgments or scores assigned by different raters is most commonly referred to as **inter-rater reliability**, although it has also been called *conspect reliability*. There are some situations in which raters must exercise judgment in arriving at a score. Two examples are multiple raters analyzing a job and multiple interviewers evaluating job candidates. The score or rating depends not only on the job or candidate but also on the persons doing the rating. The raters' characteristics may produce distortions or errors in their judgments. Estimation of inter-rater reliability is usually expressed as a correlation and reflects the degree of agreement among the ratings. Evidence of high inter-rater reliability establishes a basis to conclude that the behavior was reliably observed, and in turn we conclude that such observations are accurate. It is a frequently assessed type of reliability in I/O psychology.

inter-rater reliability
a type of reliability that reveals the degree of agreement among the assessments of two or more raters

Validity

Reliability refers to consistency and stability of measurement; validity refers to accuracy. A valid measure is one that yields "correct" estimates of what is being assessed. However, another factor distinguishes validity from reliability. Reliability is inherent in a measuring device, but validity depends on the use of a test. **Validity** refers to the test's appropriateness for predicting or drawing inferences about criteria. A given test may be highly valid for predicting employee productivity but totally invalid for predicting employee absenteeism. In other words, it would be appropriate to draw inferences about employee productivity from the test but inappropriate to draw inferences about absenteeism. There are several different ways of assessing validity, and they all involve determining the appropriateness of a measure (test) for drawing inferences.

validity
a standard for evaluating tests that refers to the accuracy or appropriateness of drawing inferences from test scores

Validity has been a controversial topic within the field of psychology. For many years psychologists believed there were "types" of validity, just as there are types of reliability (test-retest, internal consistency, etc.). However, psychologists have come to believe there is but a single or unitary conception of validity. Psychologists are involved in the formulation, measurement, and interpretation of constructs. A *construct* is a theoretical concept we propose to explain aspects of behavior. Examples of constructs in I/O psychology are intelligence, motivation, mechanical comprehension, and leadership. Because constructs are abstractions (ideas), we must have some real, tangible ways to assess them; that is, we need an actual measure of the proposed construct. Thus, a paper-and-pencil test of intelligence is one way to measure the psychological construct of intelligence. The overarching explanation of the degree to which an actual measure (i.e., a test of intelligence) is an accurate and faithful representation of its underlying construct (i.e., the construct of intelligence) is **construct validity**.

construct validity
the degree to which a test is an accurate and faithful measure of the construct it purports to measure

Construct Validity. The construct validity process is the quest to ascertain the linkage between what is measured by the test and the theoretical construct. Let us assume we wish to understand the construct of intelligence, and to do so we develop a paper-and-pencil test that we believe assesses that construct. To establish the construct validity of our test, we want to compare scores on our test with known measures of intelligence, such as verbal, numerical, and problem-solving ability. If our test is a faithful assessment of intelligence, then the scores on our test should converge with these other known measures of intelligence. More technically, there should be a high correlation between the scores from our new test of intelligence and the existing measures of intelligence. These correlation coefficients are referred to as *convergent validity coefficients* because they reflect the degree to which these scores converge (or come together) in assessing a common concept, intelligence.

Likewise, scores on our test should not be related to concepts that we know are not related to intelligence, such as physical strength, eye color, and gender. That is, scores on our test should diverge (or be separate) from these concepts that are unrelated to intelligence. More technically, there should be very low correlations between the scores from our new test of intelligence and these concepts. These correlation coefficients are referred to as *divergent validity coefficients* because they reflect the degree to which these scores diverge from each other in assessing unrelated concepts. Other statistical procedures may also be used to establish the construct validity of a test.

After collecting and evaluating much information about the test, we accumulate a body of evidence supporting the notion that the test measures a psychological construct. In turn, we say the test manifests a high degree of construct validity. Tests that manifest a high degree of construct validity are among the most widely respected and frequently used assessment instruments in I/O psychology.

Binning and Barrett (1989) described construct validation as the process of demonstrating evidence for five linkages or inferences, as illustrated in Figure 4–1. Figure 4–1 shows two empirical measures and two constructs. *X* is a measure of construct 1, as a test of intelligence purports to measure the psychological construct of intelligence. *Y* is a measure of construct 2, as a supervisor's assessment of an employee's performance purports to measure the construct of job performance. Linkage 1 is the only one that can be tested directly because it is the only inference involving two variables that are directly measured (*X* and *Y*). In assessing the construct validity of *X* and *Y*, one would be most interested in assessing linkages 2 and 4, respectively. That is, we would want to know that the empirical measures of *X* and *Y* are faithful and accurate assessments of the constructs (1 and 2) they purport to measure. Because our empirical measures are never perfect indicators of the constructs we seek to understand, Edwards and Bagozzi (2000) believe researchers should devote more attention to assessing linkages 2 and 4. For the purpose of constructing theories of job performance, one would be interested in linkage 3, the relationship between the two constructs. Finally, Binning and Barrett noted that in personnel selection, we are interested in linkage 5—that is, the inference between an employment test score and the domain of performance on the job. Thus, the process of construct validation involves examining the linkages among multiple concepts of interest to us. We always operate at the empirical level (*X* and *Y*), yet we wish to draw inferences at the conceptual level (constructs 1 and 2). Construct validation is the continuous process of verifying the accuracy of an inference among concepts for the purpose of furthering our ability to understand

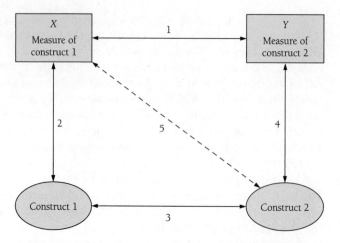

FIGURE 4–1 ■ Inferential linkages in construct validation

SOURCE: From "Validity of Personnel Decisions: A Conceptual Analysis of the Inferential and Evidential Bases" by J. F. Binning and G. V. Barrett, 1989, *Journal of Applied Psychology, 74,* p. 480. Copyright © 1989 American Psychological Association. Reprinted by permission.

those concepts (Pulakos, Borman, & Hough, 1988). Messick (1995) furthermore believes that issues of construct validation extend to how test scores are interpreted and the consequences of test use.

Criterion–Related Validity. One manifestation of construct validity is the **criterion-related validity** of a test. As its name suggests, criterion-related validity refers to how much a predictor relates to a criterion. It is a frequently used and important manifestation of validity in I/O psychology. The two major kinds of criterion-related validity are concurrent and predictive. Concurrent validity is used to diagnose the existing status on some criterion, whereas predictive validity is used to forecast future status. The primary distinction is the time interval between collecting the predictor and criterion data.

In measuring *concurrent* criterion-related validity, we are concerned with how well a predictor can predict a criterion at the same time, or concurrently. Examples abound. We may wish to predict a student's grade point average on the basis of a test score. So we collect data on the grade point averages of many students, and then we give them a predictor test. If the predictor test is a valid measure of grades, there will be a high correlation between test scores and school grades. We can use the same method in an industrial setting. We can predict a worker's level of productivity (the criterion) on the basis of a test (the predictor). We collect productivity data on a current group of workers, give them a test, and then correlate their scores with their productivity records. If the test is of value, we can draw an inference about a worker's productivity on the basis of the test score. In measurements of concurrent validity, there is no time interval between collecting the predictor and criterion data. The two variables are assessed concurrently, which is how the method gets it name. Thus, the purpose of assessing concurrent criterion-

criterion-related validity
the degree to which a test forecasts or is statistically related to a criterion

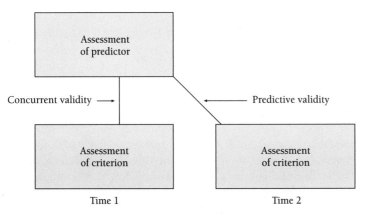

FIGURE 4–2 ■ **Portrayal of concurrent and predictive criterion-related validity**

related validity is so the test can be used at a later time with the knowledge that it is predictive of the criterion.

In measuring *predictive* criterion-related validity, we collect predictor information and use it to forecast future criterion performance. A college might use a student's high school class rank to predict the criterion of overall college grade point average four years later. A company could use a test to predict whether job applicants will complete a six-month training program. Figure 4–2 graphically illustrates concurrent and predictive criterion-related validity.

The conceptual significance of predictive and concurrent validity in the context of personnel selection will be discussed in the next chapter. The logic of criterion-related validity is straightforward. We determine whether there is a relationship between predictor scores and criterion scores based on a sample of employees for whom we have both sets of scores. If there is a relationship, we use scores on those predictor variables to select applicants on whom there are no criterion scores. Therefore, we can predict the applicants' future (and thus unknown) criterion performance from their known test scores based on the relationship established through criterion-related validity.

validity coefficient
a statistical index that reveals the degree of association between two variables

When predictor scores are correlated with criterion data, the resulting correlation is called a **validity coefficient.** Although an acceptable reliability coefficient is in the .70–.80 range, a desirable validity coefficient is in the .30–.40 range. Validity coefficients less than .30 are not uncommon, but those over .50 are rare. Just as a predictor cannot be too reliable, it also cannot be too valid. The greater the correlation between the predictor and the criterion, the more we know about the criterion on the basis of the predictor. By squaring the correlation coefficient (r), we can calculate how much variance in the criterion we can account for by using the predictor. For example, if a predictor correlates .40 with a criterion, we can explain 16% (r^2) of the variance in the criterion by knowing the predictor. This particular level of predictability (16%) would be considered satisfactory by most psychologists, given all the possible causes of performance variation. A correlation of 1.0 indicates perfect prediction (and complete knowledge). However, as Lubinski and Dawis (1992) noted, tests with moderate validity coefficients are not necessarily flawed or inadequate. The results attest to the complexity of human behavior. Our behavior is influenced by factors not measured by tests, such as motivation and luck. We should thus have realistic expectations regarding the validity of our tests.

Some criteria are difficult to predict no matter what predictors are used; other criteria are fairly predictable. Similarly, some predictors are consistently valid and are thus used quite often. Other predictors do not seem to be of much predictive value no matter what the criteria are, and thus they fall out of use. Usually, however, certain predictors are valid for predicting only certain criteria. Later in this chapter we will review the predictors typically used in I/O psychology and examine how valid they are for predicting criteria.

Content Validity.   Another manifestation of construct validity is **content validity.** Content validity involves the degree to which a predictor covers a representative sample of the behavior being assessed. It is limited mainly to psychological tests, but it can also be extended to interviews or other predictors. Historically, content validity was most relevant in achievement testing. Achievement tests are designed to indicate how well a person has mastered a specific skill or area of content. In order to be "content valid," an achievement test on Civil War history, for example, must contain a representative sample or mix of test items covering the domain of Civil War history, such as battles, military and political figures, and so on. If all of the questions were about the dates of famous battles, the test would not be a balanced representation of the content of Civil War history. If a person scores high on a content-valid test of Civil War history, we can infer that he or she is very knowledgeable about the Civil War.

How do we assess content validity? Unlike criterion-related validity, we do not compute a correlation coefficient. Content validity is assessed by subject matter experts in the field the test covers. Civil War historians would first define the domain of the Civil War and then write test questions covering it. These experts would then decide how content valid the test is. Their judgments could range from "not at all" to "highly valid." Presumably, the test would be revised until it showed a high degree of content validity.

A similar type of validity based on people's judgments is called **face validity.** This is concerned with the appearance of the test items: Do they look appropriate for such a test? Estimates of content validity are made by test developers; estimates of face validity are made by test takers. It is possible for a test item to be content valid but not face valid, and vice versa. In such a case, the test developers and test takers would disagree over the relevance or appropriateness of the item for the domain being assessed. Within the field of psychology content validity is generally thought to be of greater significance or importance than face validity. However, the face validity of a test can greatly affect whether individuals perceive the test to be an appropriate, legitimate means of assessing them for some important decision (as a job offer). Individuals are more likely to bring legal challenges against companies for using tests that are not face valid. Thus, issues of content validity are generally more relevant for the science of I/O psychology, while issues of face validity are generally more relevant for the practice of I/O psychology.

Content validity has importance for I/O psychology. Once used mainly for academic achievement testing, it is also relevant for employment testing. There is a strong and obvious link between the process of job analysis (discussed in Chapter 3) and the concept of content validity. Employers develop tests that assess the knowledge, skills, and abilities needed to perform a job. How much the content of these tests is related to the actual job is assessed by content-validation procedures. First,

content validity
the degree to which subject matter experts agree that the items in a test are a representative sample of the domain of knowledge the test purports to measure

face validity
the appearance that items in a test are appropriate for the intended use of the test by the individuals who take the test

the domain of job behavior is specified by employees and supervisors. Then test items are developed to assess the factors needed for success on the job. The content validity of employment tests is thus a function of the extent to which the content of the job is reflected in the content of the test. Goldstein, Zedeck, and Schneider (1993) asserted that content validity is established by the careful linkage between the information derived from job analysis and its associated use in test construction. Content validity purports to reveal that the knowledge and skills required to perform well on the job and on the employment test are interchangeable.

There is the tendency to think of test validity as being equivalent to an on/off light switch—either a test is valid or it isn't. The temptation to do so is probably based on other uses of the word *valid* in our language, such as whether or not a person has a valid driver's license. However, this either/or type of thinking about test validity is not correct. It is more accurate to think of test validity as a dimmer light switch. Tests manifest various degrees of validity, ranging from none at all to a great deal. At some point along the continuum of validity, practical decisions have to be made about whether a test manifests "enough" validity to warrant its use. To carry the light switch analogy further, a highly valid test sheds light on the object (construct) we seek to understand. Thus, the test validation process is the ongoing act of determining the amount of "illumination" the test projects on the construct. Another analogy is to think of validity as the overall weight of evidence that is brought before a jury in a legal trial. Different types of evidence may be presented to a jury, such as eyewitness reports, fingerprint analysis, and testimony. No one piece of evidence may be compelling to the jury; however, the weight of all the evidence, taken in its totality, leads the jury to reach a decision. In this case we can think of the validity of a test as the overall weight of the evidence showing that it measures the construct it purports to measure. The very meaning of the term *validity* in psychology is continually evolving and being refined (Jonson & Plake, 1998) due to the inherent complexity of the concept.

PREDICTOR CONSTRUCTS

The goal of psychological assessment is to know something about the individual being assessed for the purpose of making an inference about that person. In I/O psychology the inference to be made often pertains to whether the individual is likely to perform well in a job. What the "something" is that we seek to know is a construct we believe is important to success on the job. That "something" could be the individual's intelligence, ambition, interpersonal skills, ability to cope with frustration, willingness to learn new concepts or procedures, and so on. How do we assess these characteristics of individuals? I/O psychologists have developed a broad array of predictor measures designed to help us make decisions (i.e., hire or not hire) about individuals. A discussion of these predictor measures is presented in the rest of this chapter. For the most part, these predictor measures can be classified along two dimensions.

The first dimension is whether the predictor seeks to measure directly the underlying psychological construct in question (e.g., mechanical comprehension), or whether it seeks to measure a sample of the same behavior to be exhibited on the job. For example, let us assume we want to assess individuals to determine if they are suitable for the job of a mechanic. On the basis of a job analysis we know the job of mechanic requires the individual to be proficient with tools and equipment, and to have proficiency in diagnosing mechanical problems. We could elect to assess mechanical ability with a paper-and-pencil test of mechanical comprehension. Such a test would reveal to what degree the individual possesses mechanical knowledge, but it would not assess proficiency in the use of tools (i.e., because it is a paper-and-pencil test). Alternatively, we could present the individual with a mechanical object in a state of disrepair and say, "This appears to be broken. Figure out what is wrong with it and then fix it." The individual's behavior in diagnosing and repairing the object would be observed and rated by knowledgeable individuals (i.e., subject matter experts). This latter type of assessment is called "behavioral sampling" because it samples the types of behavior exhibited on the job (in this case, diagnosing and repairing mechanical objects). This particular assessment would measure the individual's proficiency with tools used in diagnosis and repair. However, it is limited to only one particular malfunctioning mechanical object. The assessment lacks the breadth of coverage of a paper-and-pencil test. Furthermore, the behavior sampling method of assessment measures whether the individual can perform the diagnosis and repair at this time, not whether he or she could learn to do so with proper training. These types of issues and others will be presented in the discussion of predictor methods.

A second distinction among predictors is whether they seek to measure something about the individual currently, or whether they assess something about the individual in the past. A job interview is a current measure of a person's characteristics, as the interviewer assesses voice quality, interpersonal demeanor, and poise. An assessment of these factors would be used to predict whether the individual would succeed in a job. Alternatively, a predictor measure could assess if the individual exhibited these behaviors in the past, not concurrently. An example would be a letter of recommendation solicited from a former employer who supervised the individual in a previous job. Here the intent is to make a prediction about future behavior (in the new job) on the basis of past behavior (in the old job). Thus, predictor measures are used to make inferences about future behavior on the basis of current or past behavior. Some predictor measures can be developed that measure both past and current behaviors. The job interview is one such example. The interviewer can assess the individual's behavior in the interview as it is happening, and can also ask questions regarding the individual's previous work history.

All predictor measures do not fall neatly into either the construct/behavioral sampling categories or the assessment of past/present characteristics of individuals. However, this classification approach is a reasonable way to understand the varieties of predictor measures and their respective intents. In all cases predictor measures are designed to forecast future behavior. They differ in the approaches taken in making these predictions. The degree to which these approaches differ in reliability, validity, fairness, social acceptability, legal defensibility, time, and cost has been the subject of extensive research in I/O psychology.

PSYCHOLOGICAL TESTS AND INVENTORIES

paper-and-pencil test
a method of assessment in which the responses to questions are evaluated in terms of their correctness

inventory
a method of assessment in which the responses to questions are recorded and interpreted but are not evaluated in terms of their correctness

Psychological tests and inventories have been the most frequently used predictors in I/O psychology. The difference between the two is that in a **paper-and-pencil test** the answers are either right or wrong; in an **inventory** there are no right or wrong answers. Usually, though, the terms *tests* and *psychological testing* refer to the family of both tests and inventories.

History of Psychological Testing

Testing has a long multinational history in the field of psychology. Sir Francis Galton, an English biologist, was interested in human heredity. During the course of his research, he realized the need for measuring the characteristics of biologically related and unrelated persons. He began to keep records of people on such factors as keenness of vision and hearing, muscular strength, and reaction time. By 1880 he had accumulated the first large-scale body of information on individual differences. He was probably the first scientist to devise systematic ways of measuring people. In 1890 the American psychologist James Cattell introduced the term *mental test*. He devised an early test of intelligence based on sensory discrimination and reaction time. Hermann Ebbinghaus, a German psychologist, developed math and sentence-completion tests and gave them to schoolchildren. In 1897 he reported that the sentence-completion test was related to the children's scholastic achievement.

The biggest advances in the early years of testing were made by the French psychologist Alfred Binet. In 1904 the French government appointed Binet to study procedures for the education of retarded children. To assess mental retardation, Binet (in collaboration with Theodore Simon) developed a test of intelligence. It consisted of 30 problems covering such areas as judgment, comprehension, and reasoning, which Binet regarded as essential components of intelligence. Later revisions of this test had a larger sampling of items from different areas. Binet's research on intelligence testing was continued by the American psychologist Lewis Terman, who in 1916 developed the concept of IQ (intelligence quotient). These early pioneers paved the way for a wide variety of tests that would be developed in the years to come, many of which were used by industrial psychologists to predict job performance. Although most of the early work in testing was directed at assessing intellect, testing horizons expanded to include aptitude, ability, interest, and personality.

speed test
a type of test that has a precise time limit; a person's score on the test is the number of items attempted in the time period

Types of Tests

Tests can be classified either by their administration or by their content. Both methods will be used here.

Speed Versus Power Tests. **Speed tests** have a large number of easy questions; the questions are so easy that the test taker will always get them right. The test is timed (for example, 5-minute limit) and has more items than can possibly be answered in the allotted time period. The total score on such a test is the number of items answered and reflects the test taker's speed of work.

power test
a type of test that usually does not have a precise time limit; a person's score on the test is the number of items answered correctly

Power tests have questions that are fairly difficult; that is, the test taker usually cannot get them all right. Usually there is no time limit. The total score on such a test is the number of items answered correctly. Most tests given in college are power tests. If time limits are imposed, they are mostly for the convenience of the test administrator.

Individual Versus Group Tests. **Individual tests** are given to only one person at a time. Such tests are not common because of the amount of time needed to administer them to all applicants. For example, if a test takes one hour and ten people are to take it, ten hours of administration time will be required. The benefits of giving such a test must be balanced against the costs. Certain types of intelligence tests are individually administered, as are certain tests for evaluating high-level executives. In these tests the administrator has to play an active part (for example, asking questions, demonstrating an object) as opposed to just monitoring them.

individual test
a type of test that is administered to one individual test taker at a time

group test
a type of test that is administered to more than one test taker at a time

Group tests are administered to several people simultaneously and are the most common type of test. They do not involve the active participation of an administrator. The Army Alpha and Army Beta tests were early group intelligence tests used in World War I. Most tests used in educational and industrial organizations are group tests because they are efficient in terms of time and cost.

Paper-and-Pencil Versus Performance Tests. *Paper-and-pencil tests* are the most common type of test used in industrial and educational organizations. They do not involve the physical manipulation of objects or pieces of equipment. The questions asked may require answers in either multiple-choice or essay form. The individual's physical ability to handle a pencil should not influence his or her score on the test. The pencil is just the means by which the response is recorded on a sheet of paper.

performance test
a type of test that requires the test taker to exhibit physical skill in the manipulation of objects

In a **performance test** the individual has to manipulate an object or a piece of equipment. The score is a measure of the person's ability to perform the manipulation. A typing test and a test of finger dexterity are examples of performance tests. Sometimes paper-and-pencil and performance tests are used jointly. To get a driver's license, for example, most people have to pass both a written and a behind-the-wheel performance test.

ETHICAL STANDARDS IN TESTING

To prevent the misuse of psychological tests, the American Psychological Association has developed standards (AERA, APA, NCME, 1999). The ethics of psychological testing are a major responsibility of psychologists, as seen in the APA code of professional ethics (*Standards for Educational and Psychological Testing*, 1985). Maintaining ethical standards in testing is one of the more important issues confronting the entire profession of psychology (American Psychological Association, 1992).

Depending on the purpose of the testing, test users must have certain qualifications. Sometimes the user must be a licensed professional psychologist, particularly in clinical psychology. However, in industry fewer qualifications are required to administer employment tests. To prevent their misuse and to maintain test security, restrictions are also placed on who has access to tests (Author, 1999). However, Moreland et al. (1995) concluded that educational efforts will ultimately be more effective in promoting good testing practices than efforts to limit the use of tests. Test publishers are discouraged from giving away free samples or printing detailed examples of test questions as sales promotions, which could invalidate future test results.

invasion of privacy
a condition associated with testing pertaining to the asking of questions on a test that are unrelated to the test's intent or are inherently intrusive to the test taker

Other ethical issues are the invasion of privacy and confidentiality. **Invasion of privacy** occurs when a psychological test reveals more information about a person than is needed to make an informed decision. Tests should be used for precise purposes; they should not be used to learn information irrelevant to performing the job. For example, if a mechanical comprehension test is used to hire mechanics, the company should not also give an interest inventory just to learn about potential employees' hobbies and recreational activities. Using an interest inventory that has no relationship to job performance could be an invasion of the applicant's privacy. Furthermore, some types of questions are inherently invasive (for example, about one's religious beliefs), regardless of the merit or intent of the questions.

confidentiality
a condition associated with testing pertaining to which parties have access to test results

Confidentiality refers to who should have access to test results. When a person takes an employment test, he or she should be told the purpose of the test, how the results will be used, and which people in the company will see the results. Problems arise if a third party (another prospective employer, for example) wants to know the test results. The scores should be confidential, unless the test taker gives a written release.

Another ethical problem in this area is the retention of records. Advances in computer technology have made it possible to store large quantities of information about people. Who should have access to this information, and what guarantees are there that it will not be misused? The results of an intelligence test taken in sixth grade may become part of a student's permanent academic record. Should a potential employer get the results of this elementary school test? Furthermore, the test probably couldn't predict job performance, so why would anyone want the results? Indeed, recent research (e.g., Chan, Drasgow, & Sawin, 1999; Farrell & McDaniel, 2001) revealed that time diminishes the predictive accuracy of cognitive ability measures over time. These types of questions are central to problems of confidentiality.

SOURCES OF INFORMATION ABOUT TESTING

Mental Measurements Yearbooks (MMY)
a classic set of reference books in psychology that provide reviews and critiques of published tests

Because testing is a rapidly changing area, it is important to keep up with current developments in the field. Old tests are revised, new tests are introduced, and some tests are discontinued. Fortunately, several key references are available. Perhaps the most important source of information is the series of **Mental Measurements Yearbooks (MMY).** The MMY was first published in 1938, and it has been revised in roughly a five-year cycle. Each yearbook includes tests published during a specified period, thus supplementing the tests reported in previous yearbooks. The *Fourteenth Mental Measurements Yearbook* (Plake & Impara, 2001), for example, deals mainly with tests that appeared between 1996 and 1999. Each test is critically reviewed by an expert in the field and documented with a complete list of references. Information about price, publisher, and versions of the test is also given. The MMY series is the most comprehensive review of psychological tests available in the field.

Less-detailed books, such as *Tests in Print V* (Murphy, Impara, & Plake, 1999), resemble bibliographies and help locate tests in the MMY. Other resource books review tests relevant for more restricted applications, as in business and industry (Hogan & Hogan, 1990; Sweetland & Keyser, 1991). Some psychological journals review specific tests, and various professional test developers publish test manuals. The test manual should give the information needed to administer, score, and evaluate a particular test, as well as data on the test's reliability and validity. Although these manuals are useful, they are usually not as complete and critical as reviews in the MMY.

The test user has an obligation to use the test in a professional and competent manner. Tests should be chosen with extreme care and concern for the consequences of their use. Important decisions are based on test scores, and the choice of test is important. A test should be thoroughly analyzed before it is considered for use. Whittington (1998) reported that test developers and test reviewers should be more thorough in providing information to help potential users make more informed decisions about test usage. Figure 4–3 illustrates the range of pro-

FIGURE 4–3 ■ **Code of professional responsibilities in psychological assessment**

SOURCE: Adapted from NCME Ad Hoc Committee on the Development of a Code of Ethics, 1995, National Council on Measurement in Education.

fessional responsibilities in psychological assessment, including test development, marketing and selling the tests, scoring, interpretation and use, and educating others about psychological assessment.

TEST CONTENT

Tests can be classified according to their content. The next sections will discuss the major types of constructs assessed by tests used in industry. Also presented will be information on how valid the various types of tests have been in personnel selection as documented from their use in the psychological literature.

Intelligence Tests

Intelligence or cognitive ability is perhaps the most heavily researched construct in all of psychology. Interest in the assessment of intelligence began more than 100 years ago. Despite the length of time the construct of intelligence has been assessed, however, there remains no singular or standard means to assess it. Furthermore, recent research suggests intelligence is even more complex than we have believed.

What is generally agreed upon regarding intelligence? Intelligence traditionally has been conceptualized as having a singular, primary basis. This concept is known as *general mental ability* and is symbolized by **g**. By assessing *g*, we gain an understanding of a person's general level of intellectual capability. Tests that measure *g* have been found to be predictive of performance across a wide range of occupations (e.g., Ree, Earles, & Teachout, 1994). The criterion-related validity of *g* is impressive, oftentimes in the range of .40–.60. Many researchers believe it is the single most diagnostic predictor of future job performance. Simply put, if we could know only one attribute of a job candidate upon which to make a prediction, we would want an assessment of intelligence. General intelligence is regarded to be a ubiquitous predictor of a wide variety of performance criteria, prompting Brand (1987) to observe: "*g* is to psychology what carbon is to chemistry" (p. 257). Furthermore, Hunter (1986) showed that the predictive power of intelligence *increases* with higher degrees of job complexity.

However, while research clearly supports the validity of general intelligence as a predictor, some researchers believe that conceptualizing intelligence merely as *g* encourages oversimplification of the inherent complexity of intelligence. Murphy (1996) asserted that intelligence is not a unitary phenomenon, and other dimensions of intelligence are also worthy of our consideration. Ackerman (1992), for example, reported the superior predictive power of multiple abilities over general intelligence in complex information-processing tasks, as in the job of air traffic controller. Ackerman and Kanfer (1993) developed a useful selection test for air traffic controllers based in large part on the assessment of spatial ability. From an I/O psychology perspective, therefore, the controversy regarding the assessment of intelligence rests primarily on the adequacy of measuring (just) general intelligence (*g*) or assessing multiple cognitive abilities in forecasting job behavior. The current

g
the symbol for "general mental ability," which has been found to be predictive of success in most jobs

TABLE 4–1 ■ Sample test questions for a typical intelligence test

1. What number is missing in this series?
   3–8–14–21–29–(?)

2. SHOVEL is to DITCHDIGGER as SCALPEL is to:
   (a) knife (b) sharp (c) butcher (d) surgeon (e) cut

body of research seems to indicate that in most cases measuring the g factor of intelligence offers superior predictive accuracy in forecasting success in training and job performance over the measurement of specific (math, spatial, and verbal) cognitive abilities (Carretta & Ree, 2000; Roznowski et al., 2000).

In a recent development, Sternberg (1997) proposes a triarchic (or three-part) theory of intelligence. Sternberg contends that there are multiple kinds of intelligence. He posits academic intelligence as representing what intelligence tests typically measure, such as fluency with words and numbers. Table 4–1 shows two sample test questions from a typical intelligence test. However, Sternberg proposes two other important kinds of intelligence that conventional intelligence tests don't measure. One is *practical intelligence,* which he states is the intelligence needed to be competent in the everyday world and is not highly related to academic intelligence. The second (nontraditional) kind of intelligence Sternberg calls *creative intelligence,* which pertains to the ability to produce work that is both novel (i.e., original or unexpected) and appropriate (i.e., useful). Manifestations of this kind of intelligence are critical in writing, art, and advertising. Sternberg believes that all three kinds of intelligence may be necessary for lifelong learning and success, depending upon the nature of our vocation. As Daniel (1997) stated, our means of assessing intelligence (i.e., a test) are heavily guided by how we view what we are trying to assess (see Field Note 1). A view of intelligence dominated by academic intelligence will lead us to assess that particular kind to the relative exclusion of practical and creative intelligence. Wagner (1997) asserted we need to expand our criteria to show the various manifestations of intelligence, such as over time and over different aspects of job performance (e.g., task proficiency versus successfully interacting with other people). Hedlund and Sternberg (2000) assert that the contemporary world of business seeks employees who can adapt to highly changing conditions. Real-life problems tend to be ill-defined, ambiguous, and dynamic, and such problems do not match the types of problems on which intelligence traditionally has been assessed. Hedlund and Sternberg believe the concept of practical intelligence is intended to complement, rather than to contradict, the narrower views of g-based theories of intelligence.

As can be inferred from the foregoing discussion, the construct of intelligence is highly complex. From an I/O psychology perspective, we are concerned with the degree to which cognitive ability forecasts job performance. Murphy (1996) summarized the prevailing conclusion: "Research on the validity of measures of cognitive ability as predictors of job performance represents one of the 'success stories' in I/O psychology" (p. 6).

Mechanical Aptitude Tests

Mechanical aptitude tests require a person to recognize which mechanical principle is suggested by a test item. One of the more popular tests of mechanical reasoning is the Bennett Test of Mechanical Comprehension (Bennett, 1980). The test is a series of pictures reflecting various mechanical facts and principles. Sample questions from the Bennett Test are shown in Figure 4–4. Other tests of mechanical comprehension have also been developed.

Muchinsky (1993) reported that the Bennett Test was most effective in predicting the job performance of manufacturing employees who produce electromechanical components. A concurrent criterion-related validity coefficient of .38 was reported in the study. Schmitt, Gooding, Noe, and Kirsch (1984) reported an average validity coefficient of .27 for mechanical aptitude tests across many studies. The highest validity coefficients are typically found for vehicle operators as well as trade and craft employees.

Sensory/Motor Ability Tests

Sensory ability tests assess visual acuity, color vision, and hearing sensitivity. These abilities are related to success in certain types of jobs. Perhaps the best-known test of visual acuity is the Snellen Eye Chart, a display with rows of letters that get

---

FIELD NOTE 1   What Is Intelligence?

The construct of intelligence is highly complex, perhaps more complex than researchers have previously realized. Theorists have long debated whether intelligence is a unitary concept or whether there are various forms of intelligence, such as verbal and quantitative. Tests of intelligence are designed and interpreted based on these theoretical formulations. The questions on traditional tests of intelligence have a correct answer and only one correct answer. Examples include the answers to questions about mathematics and vocabulary. However, recent research by Sternberg suggests that there are other manifestations of intelligence. Many problems in life do not have a single correct answer; other problems may have more than one correct answer. Furthermore, in real life, solutions to problems are not so much "correct" or "incorrect" as they are "feasible" and "acceptable." Examples include dealing with interpersonal problems at the individual level and with global problems at the national level. It takes intelligence to solve such problems, but these types of questions do not appear on typical tests of intelligence. There is an adage that "young people are smart and old people are wise." Perhaps wisdom is a form of intelligence that is derived through many years of successfully dealing with problems that lack single correct solutions. Psychologists refer to knowledge that helps solve practical problems as procedural knowledge or tacit knowledge. Indeed, Sternberg and Horvath (1999) have described how tacit knowledge contributes to success in a broad array of occupations, such as law, medicine, military command, and teaching. As Marchant and Robinson (1999) state on the subject of legal expertise, all lawyers are knowledgeable of law. That is what they are taught in law school. But the truly successful lawyers understand how to interpret the law and the dynamics of the entire legal system. The capacity to derive feasible and acceptable solutions to complex problems that have no single correct answers is, as current research supports, a legitimate form of intelligence.

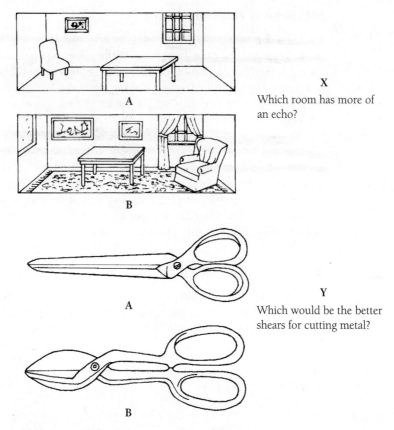

X

Which room has more of an echo?

Y

Which would be the better shears for cutting metal?

FIGURE 4–4 ■ **Sample test questions from the Bennett Test of Mechanical Comprehension**

SOURCE: From *Bennett Mechanical Comprehension Test.* Copyright 1942, 1967–1970, 1980 by the Psychological Corporation. Reproduced by permission. All rights reserved.

increasingly smaller. The test taker stands 20 feet away from the chart and reads each row until the letters are indistinguishable. A ratio is then computed to express acuity:

$$\text{Acuity} = \frac{\text{Distance at which a person can read a certain line of print (usually 20 feet)}}{\text{Distance at which the average person can read the same line of print}}$$

For example, if the smallest line of print a person can read from 20 feet is the line most people can read from 40 feet, then the person's score is 20/40. Each eye is tested separately, and normal vision is 20/20. Buffardi, Fleishman, Morath, and McCarthy (2000) reported that differences in vision were associated with the occurrence of human errors in jobs in the Air Force.

The most common way to measure hearing sensitivity is with an instrument called an *audiometer.* An audiometer produces tones of different frequencies and

"Let's put it this way—if you can find a village without an idiot, you've got yourself a job."

SOURCE: Reprinted from *The Industrial-Organizational Psychologist.*

loudness. The tone is gradually raised in intensity. When the test taker signals that the note has been heard, the examiner records the level of intensity on an audiogram, which shows the intensity of sound needed to hear tones of different frequency. An audiogram is prepared for each ear. Hearing loss is detected by comparing one person's audiogram with the results from a tested population.

Researchers have also devised paper-and-pencil tests of perceptual accuracy. In these tests two stimuli are presented, and the test taker must judge whether they are the same or different. The stimuli may be numbers or names. Table 4–2 shows one type of item in a perceptual accuracy test.

Tests of motor ability assess fine or gross motor coordination. Two frequently used motor ability tests are the Purdue Pegboard and the Crawford Small Parts Dexterity Test. In the first part of the Purdue Pegboard, the test taker places pins into small holes in a pegboard using first the right hand, then the left hand, and then both hands together. In the second part, the pins are again placed in the holes but with the addition of collars and washers. The first part of the test measures manual dexterity; the second part measures finger dexterity. In the Crawford Small Parts Dexterity Test, the test taker first places pins in holes in the board and then places metal collars over the pins. In the second part of the test, a screwdriver is used to insert small screws after they have been placed by hand into threaded holes.

Sensory/motor ability tests manifest a typical validity coefficient between .20 and .25. They are most predictive of job success in clerical occupations.

TABLE 4–2 ■ Sample test question from a typical perceptual accuracy test

Which pairs of items are identical?

> 17345290—17342590
> 2033220638—2033220638
> WPBRAEGGER—WPBREAGGER
> CLAFDAPKA26—CLAPDAFKA26

Personality Inventories

Unlike the previously cited tests, which have objective answers, personality inventories do not have right or wrong answers. Test takers answer how much they agree with certain statements (e.g.,"People who work hard get ahead"). In personality inventories similar types of questions normally make up a scale, which reflects a person's introversion, dominance, confidence, and other traits. Items are scored according to a predetermined key such that responding one way or another to an item results in a higher or lower score on a respective scale. These scale scores are then used to predict job success. The basic rationale is that successful employees possess a particular personality structure, and scales reflective of that structure become the basis for selecting new employees.

Today personality assessment is one of the fastest-growing areas in personnel selection. A comprehensive five-factor model of personality structure has been proposed as being useful for predicting job performance. It is often referred to as the **"Big 5" theory of personality**. These are the five personality factors:

"Big 5" theory of personality
a theory that defines personality in terms of five major factors: neuroticism, extraversion, openness to experience, agreeableness, and conscientiousness

> *Neuroticism*—the person's characteristic level of stability versus instability
> *Extraversion*—the tendency to be sociable, assertive, active, talkative, energetic, and outgoing
> *Openness to experience*—the disposition to be curious, imaginative, and unconventional
> *Agreeableness*—the disposition to be cooperative, helpful, and easy to get along with
> *Conscientiousness*—the disposition to be purposeful, determined, organized, and controlled

Extensive empirical support for its validity was provided by McCrae and Costa (1987) and R. T. Hogan (1991). Personality inventories have also been developed based upon this model—for example, the NEO-PI (P. T. Costa, 1996) and the Hogan Personality Inventory (Hogan & Hogan, 1992). Barrick and Mount (1991) concluded from a meta-analysis that extraversion is a valid predictor of performance in occupations that involve social interactions, such as managers and salespeople. Tokar, Fisher, and Subich (1998) revealed that personality is linked to many aspects of work behavior, including job performance, career progression, and vocational interests. Conscientiousness shows consistent correlation with job performance criteria for all occupations and across different cultures (Salgado, 1997). In a major meta-analytic review of the five-factor model, Hurtz and Donovan (2000) cautioned that the magnitude of the validity coefficients for predicting job performance criteria were only modest, about .20. Collins and Gleaves (1998) reported the five personality factors were equally applicable for evaluating black and white job applicants. These five factors are a durable framework for considering personality structure among people of many nations, and they have prompted McCrae and Costa (1997) to refer to their pattern of interrelationships as a "human universal." Furthermore, such personality measures provide *incremental* predictive validity beyond measures of intelligence (Judge, Higgins, Thoresen, & Barrick, 1999).

A long-standing concern with using personality tests for personnel selection is that job applicants might not give truthful responses. Rather, applicants may fake their responses to give what they believe are socially desirable answers. Ones, Viswesvaran, and Reiss (1996) examined this issue through a meta-analysis of research studies and concluded that social desirability does not have a significant influence on the validity of personality tests for personnel selection. They believe a person who would attempt to "fake" a personality selection test would also be inclined to "fake" job performance. However, Rosse, Stecher, Miller, and Levin (1998) reached a somewhat different conclusion. The authors found that response distortion or faking was more prevalent among job applicants than job incumbents, as job applicants seek to create a favorable impression in the assessment. Rosse et al. believe that faking by job applicants on personality inventories is a matter that warrants continued professional attention.

Hogan, Hogan, and Roberts (1996) concluded that personality tests should be used in conjunction with other information, particularly the applicant's technical skills, job experience, and ability to learn. More specifically, Ackerman and Heggestad (1997) believe "abilities, interests, and personality develop in tandem, such that ability level and personality dispositions determine the probability of success in a particular task domain, and interests determine the motivation to attempt the task" (p. 239). Simply put, the influence of personality in job performance should not be overestimated, but it should also not be underestimated.

On a conceptual level intelligence and personality have typically been viewed as separate constructs. Intelligence traditionally has reflected the "can do" dimension of an individual; namely, the person "can do" the work because he or she is judged to possess an adequate level of intelligence. Personality traditionally has reflected the "will do" dimension of an individual; namely, the person "will do" the work because he or she is judged to possess the demeanor to do so. Until very recently researchers have not considered to what degree intelligence and personality might be related. As Hofstee (2001) stated, "Intelligence and personality suffer from the salad-dressing syndrome. Certain dressings based on oil and vinegar form an unstable emulsion; they have to be shaken forcefully prior to usage, and even so, they separate within seconds. Similarly, there seems to be little attraction between personality and intelligence" (p. 43). However, researchers (Collis & Messick, 2001) are now examining the theory and measurement of both intelligence and personality to determine if there are patterns of association between them. Hofstee has proposed the existence of a "*p* factor" (a general personality factor reflecting the ability to cope), which is parallel to the *g* factor in intelligence. Further research may lead to a melding of these two constructs, which have typically been viewed as distinct.

Integrity Tests

The reemergence of using personality assessment for personnel selection is also demonstrated in the recent development and growing use of honesty or integrity tests. **Integrity tests** are designed to identify job applicants who will not steal from their employer or otherwise engage in counterproductive behavior on the job. These tests are paper-and-pencil tests and generally fall into one of two types (Sackett & Wanek, 1996). In the first type, an *overt integrity test,* the job applicant clearly understands that the intent of the test is to assess integrity. The test typically has two sections: One deals with attitudes toward theft and other forms of dishonesty (namely, beliefs about the frequency and extent of employee theft, punitiveness toward theft, perceived ease of theft, and endorsement of common rationalizations about theft), and a second section deals with admissions of theft and other illegal activities (such as dollar amounts stolen in the past year, drug use, and gambling). There is some evidence (Cunningham, Wong, & Barbee, 1994) that the responses to such tests are distorted by the applicants' desire to create a favorable impression. Alliger, Lilienfeld, and Mitchell (1995) found that the questions in integrity tests are value laden and transparent (e.g., "Are you a productive person?"), which makes it easy for applicants to distort their responses to affect the desired result. The second type of test, called a *personality-based measure,* makes no reference to theft. These tests contain conventional personality assessment items that have been found to be predictive of theft. Because this type of test does not contain obvious references to theft, it is less likely to offend job applicants. These tests are primarily assessments of conscientiousness and emotional stability personality factors (Hogan & Brinkmeyer, 1997).

Research findings have shown that integrity tests are valid. Bernardin and Cooke (1993) found that scores on an honesty test successfully predicted theft among convenience store employees. Collins and Schmitt (1993) conducted a study of incarcerated offenders convicted of white-collar crimes, such as embezzlement and fraud. Compared with a control sample of employees in upper-level positions of authority, offenders had greater tendencies toward irresponsibility, lack of dependability, and disregard of rules and social norms. In a meta-analytic review, Ones, Viswesvaran, and Schmidt (1993) concluded that integrity tests effectively predict the broad criterion of organizationally disruptive behaviors like theft, disciplinary problems, and absenteeism. Self-reported measures of counterproductive behavior were found to be more predictable than objective measures (such as detected workplace theft). However, Ones and Viswesvaran (1998) found gender differences in integrity tests, with women scoring higher than men. Differences in honesty scores by race and age were negligible.

Problems are inherent in validating tests designed to predict employee theft. First, the issue is very sensitive, and many organizations don't care to make information public. Organizations may readily exchange information on employee absenteeism, but employee theft statistics are often confidential. Second, the criterion isn't really theft so much as being caught stealing, because many thefts go undetected. Third, the percentage of employees caught stealing in an organization is usually very small—2% to 3% is the norm. Consequently, there are statistical difficulties in trying to predict what is essentially a rare event. Furthermore,

integrity test
a type of paper-and-pencil test that purports to assess a test taker's honesty, character, or integrity

Camara and Schneider (1994) noted that test publishers classify integrity tests as proprietary, meaning that access to these tests is not provided to researchers interested in assessing their validity. Some people argue that the value of integrity tests for personnel selection is greater than the typical validity coefficient suggests. They argue that applicants who pass an integrity test are sensitized to the organization's concern for honesty and that other theft-reducing measures (such as internal surveillance systems) may well be used to monitor employees. Such procedures reduce the occurrence of employee theft but are not evidenced in the predictive accuracy of the honesty test.

Wanek (1999) offered the following summation on the use of integrity tests for personnel selection: "Between otherwise equal final candidates, choosing the candidate with the highest integrity test score will lead, over the long run, to a work force comprised of employees who are less likely to engage in counterproductive activities at work, and more likely to engage in productive work behaviors" (p. 193).

Physical Abilities Testing

Psychological assessment has long been directed toward cognitive abilities and personality characteristics. However, research (e.g., Fleishman & Quaintance, 1984) has also examined the assessment of physical abilities, and in particular how these physical abilities relate to performance in some jobs. J. Hogan (1991a) presented the set of physical abilities relevant to work performance:

- *Static strength*—the ability to use muscle force to lift, push, pull, or carry objects
- *Explosive strength*—the ability to use short bursts of muscle force to propel oneself or an object
- *Gross body coordination*—the ability to coordinate the movement of the arms, legs, and torso in activities where the whole body is in motion
- *Stamina*—the ability of the lungs and circulatory (blood) systems of the body to perform efficiently over time

An analysis (J. Hogan, 1991b) revealed that the total set of physical abilities could be reduced to three major constructs: strength, endurance, and movement quality. These three constructs account for most of the variation in individual capacity to perform strenuous activities. Arvey, Landon, Nutting, and Maxwell (1992) established the construct validity of a set of physical ability tests for use in the selection of entry-level police officers. The findings suggested that two factors—strength and endurance—underlie performance on the physical ability tests and performance on the job of police officers. The results further showed that women scored considerably lower than men on the physical ability tests. However, the findings did not suggest how much importance physical abilities compared with cognitive abilities should be accorded in the selection decision. In general the research on physical abilities reveals that they are related to successful job performance in physically demanding jobs, such as firefighters, police officers, and factory workers. Indeed, Hoffman (1999) successfully validated a series of physical ability tests for selecting employees for construction and mechanical jobs. Future research needs to consider the effects of aging on the decline of physical abilities and the legal implications of differences in physical abilities across groups.

Multiple–Aptitude Test Batteries

Tests may also be categorized on the basis of their structural composition rather than their item content. Test "batteries" consist of many of the types of tests already discussed: intelligence, mechanical aptitude, personality, and so on. These tests are usually quite long, often taking several hours to complete. Each part of the test measures such factors as intellectual ability and mechanical reasoning. The tests are useful because they yield a great deal of information that can be used later for hiring, placement, training, and so forth. The major disadvantages of the tests are the cost and time involved. The two most widely known multiple-aptitude batteries are the Armed Services Vocational Aptitude Battery (ASVAB) and the Differential Aptitude Test (DAT).

Computerized Adaptive Testing

computerized adaptive testing (CAT)
a form of assessment using a computer in which the questions have been precalibrated in terms of difficulty, and the examinee's response to one question determines the selection of the next question

One of the major advances in psychological testing is called **computerized adaptive testing (CAT)**, or "tailored testing" (Wainer, 2000). Here is how it works: CAT is an automated test administration system that uses a computer. The test items appear on the video display screen, and the examinee answers using the keyboard. Each test question presented is prompted by the response to the previous question. The first question given to the examinee is of medium difficulty. If the answer given is correct, the next question selected from the item bank of questions has been precalibrated to be slightly more difficult. If the answer given to that question is wrong, the next question selected by the computer is somewhat easier. And so on.

The purpose of the CAT system is to get as close a match as possible between the question-difficulty level and the examinee's demonstrated ability level. In fact, by the careful calibration of question difficulty, one can infer ability level from the difficulty level of the questions answered correctly. CAT systems are based on complex mathematical models. Proponents believe that tests can be shorter (because of higher precision of measurement) and less expensive and have greater security than traditional paper-and-pencil tests. The military is the largest user of CAT systems, testing thousands of examinees monthly. In an example of CAT being used in the private sector, Overton, Harms, Taylor, and Zickar (1997) found their CAT system did achieve greater test security than traditional paper-and-pencil tests. Additionally, traditional academic tests like the Graduate Record Exam (GRE) are now available for applicants using an on-line CAT system. An added benefit is that the results of the test are available to the applicant in a much shorter time than with the paper-and-pencil administration.

CAT systems will never completely replace traditional testing, but they do represent the cutting edge of psychological assessment (Meijer & Nering, 1999). Computers have made possible great advances in science, as evidenced in I/O psychology by this major breakthrough in testing. Furthermore, with the creation of national information networks, the traditional practice of using psychological tests late in the selection process may change as it becomes possible to have access to test results at the time a job application is made. There have also been recent technical advances in the use of pen-based notebook computer testing (Overton, Taylor, Zickar, & Harms, 1996).

THE VALUE OF TESTING

As Haney (1981) observed, society has tended to imbue psychological tests with some arcane mystical powers, which, as the evidence reviewed in this chapter indicates, is totally unwarranted. There is nothing mysterious about psychological tests; they are merely tools to help us make better decisions than we could make without them. The psychological testing profession has a large number of critics. Criticism relates more to the inappropriate use of good tests than to poor quality. For example, since tests of vocational interest were never originally intended to predict managerial success, we really shouldn't be too surprised or unhappy when we find they do not. Testing has been oversold as a solution to problems. Many people have decried the "tyranny of testing"—the fact that critical decisions (say, entrance into a college or professional school) that affect an entire lifetime are based on a single test. Testing has its place in our repertoire of diagnostic instruments; tests should help us meet our needs and not be the master of our decisions. This is sound advice that psychologists have long advocated. However, it is advice that both the developers and users of psychological tests have occasionally ignored or forgotten. It is also the case that many people don't like to be tested, find the process intimidating or anxiety-producing, and are highly concerned about what use will be made of their test results. Tenopyr (1998) described organized efforts by some groups of people opposed to testing to get laws passed pertaining to the legal rights of test takers, bearing such titles as "The Test Takers' Bill of Rights." We cannot seriously hope to abolish testing in society because the alternative to testing is not testing at all. What we can strive to accomplish is to make testing highly accurate and fair to all parties concerned.

Advances are also being made in the format of test questions. Traditionally multiple-choice test questions have one correct answer. Given this characteristic, test questions have to be written such that there is indeed a correct answer to the question, and only one correct answer (Haladyna, 1999). However, in real life many problems and questions don't have a single correct answer. Rather, an array of answers is possible, some more plausible or appropriate than others. There is a growing interest in designing tests that require the test taker to rate a series of answers (all correct to some degree) in terms of their overall suitability for resolving a problem. One name given to this type of assessment is **situational judgment test** (McDaniel et al., 2001). Research on this type of test reveals that it measures a construct similar to intelligence, but not the same as our traditional conception of *g*. Situational judgment tests reflect the theoretical rationale of practical intelligence discussed earlier in the chapter.

situational judgment test a type of test that describes a problem situation to the test taker and requires the test taker to rate various possible solutions in terms of their feasibility or applicability

In a major review of psychological testing, Meyer et al. (2001) concluded that psychological test validity is compelling and comparable to medical test validity. In practice we often get validity coefficients in the .10–.40 range. If we compare these correlations with the perfect upper limit of 1.00, we may feel disappointed with our results. Meyer et al. stated, "However, perfect associations are never encountered in applied psychological research, making this benchmark unrealistic. Second, it is easy to implicitly compare validity correlations with reliability coefficients, because the latter are frequently reported in the literature. However, reliability coefficients (which are often in the range of $r = .70$ or higher) evaluate only the correspondence between a variable and itself. As a result, they cannot provide a reasonable standard for evaluating the association between two distinct real-world variables" (pp. 132–133).

What we have learned about psychological tests from an I/O psychological perspective is that some tests are useful in forecasting job success and others are not. As an entire class of predictors, psychological tests have been moderately predictive of job performance. Yet some authors (for example, Hunter & Hunter, 1984) believe that, all things considered, psychological tests have outperformed all other types of predictors across the full spectrum of jobs. Single-validity coefficients in excess of .50 are as unusual today as they were in the early years of testing. While test validity coefficients are not as high as we would like, it is unfair to condemn tests as useless. Also, keep in mind that validity coefficients are a function of both the predictor and the criterion. A poorly defined and constructed criterion will produce low validity coefficients no matter what the predictor is like. Because of the limited predictive power of tests, psychologists have had to look elsewhere for forecasters of job performance. The balance of this chapter will examine other predictors that psychologists have investigated.

INTERVIEWS

In terms of sheer frequency, interviews are the most popular method of selecting employees. The popularity of the employment interview may be enhanced by legal problems with paper-and-pencil tests. Although most court cases regarding discrimination have involved paper-and-pencil tests, interviews along with other predictors are still regarded as tests by the government and, as such, are subject to the same judicial review. Interviews are more subjective than tests, so chances for unfair discrimination seem to be greater, particularly among untrained interviewers (Huffcutt & Woehr, 1999). As such, it is advisable to have information derived from a job analysis be a primary basis for the questions posed in an interview. Because interviews are used so often in employment decisions, many research studies on them have been conducted. Some of the major issues related to the employment interview will be discussed next.

Degree of Structure

Interviews can be classified along a continuum of structure, where *structure* is defined as the amount of procedural variability across job applicants. In a highly

unstructured interview

a format for the job interview in which the questions are different across all candidates

structured interview

a format for the job interview in which the questions are consistent across all candidates

unstructured interview, the interviewer typically asks the applicant to "tell me about yourself" and the applicant can provide responses ranging from hobbies and goals to previous work experience. The interviewer may or may not ask follow-up questions and has a great deal of discretion in what questions are asked (Whetzel & McDaniel, 1997). Highly **structured interviews** have predetermined procedures for eliciting, observing, and evaluating responses. The questions to be asked have been determined in advance, and all applicants are asked the same questions. It is not unusual for the interviewer to use a standardized rating scale to assess the answers given by each candidate. In reality, most employment interviews fall somewhere along the continuum between the "highly unstructured" and the "highly structured" interview. However, research results indicate the higher validity of the structured interview over the unstructured type. Huffcutt et al. (2001) determined that the predictor constructs most often assessed by interviewers of candidates were personality traits (conscientiousness, agreeableness, etc.) and applied social skills (interpersonal relations, team focus, etc.). However, highly unstructured and highly structured interviews do not tend to measure the same constructs. In particular, highly unstructured interviews often focus more on constructs such as general intelligence, education, work experience, and interests, whereas highly structured interviews often focus more on constructs such as job knowledge, interpersonal and social skills, and problem solving.

Campion, Palmer, and Campion (1997) examined procedures to increase the degree of structure in the interview. Among the suggestions are to base the questions on an analysis of the job, to limit prompting by the interviewer, to rate the answers given to each question asked, and to use multiple interviewers per candidate. Campion et al. reported that while some techniques increase structure, such as limiting prompting and not accepting any questions from the applicant, neither the interviewer nor the applicant likes being so constrained. Thus, while these procedures reduce the likelihood that different applicants are treated unequally in the interview, they also produce negative reactions among the participants. The preference for more unstructured interviews by participants was confirmed by Kohn and Dipboye (1998). In a study that examined interview structure and litigation outcomes, Williamson et al. (1997) reported that organizations were more likely to win when their interviews were job related (e.g., the interviewer was familiar with the job requirements) and based on standardized administration (e.g., minimal interviewer discretion) and also the interviewer's decision was reviewed by a superior. Furthermore, research on the validity of structured interviews (e.g., Cortina, Goldstein, Payne, Davison, & Gilliland, 2000) indicates that they predict job performance as well as mental ability does. Increasing the degree of structure in the interview is also associated with greater fairness among minority group members (Huffcutt & Roth, 1998; Moscoso, 2000).

Despite these reasons for supporting the use of the structured interview, Dipboye (1997) reported there are also reasons that unstructured interviews have value to the organization. A primary reason is that interviews can serve purposes besides assessing the candidate's suitability for a job. They also provide an opportunity for the interviewer to convey information about the organization, its values, and its culture. The unstructured interview can be akin to a ritual conveying to others the important attributes of the organization and sending the message that great care is being taken to select a qualified applicant. Dipboye concluded that perhaps a semistructured interview procedure may be the best compromise for meeting the multiple purposes of the employment interviews.

Situational Interviews

situational interviews
a type of job
interview in which
candidates are
presented with a
problem situation
and asked how they
would respond to it

Situational interviews present the applicant with a situation and ask for a description of the actions he or she would take in that situation. Some situational interviews focus on hypothetical, future-oriented contexts in which the applicants are asked how they would respond if they were confronted with these problems. Other situational interviews focus on how the applicants have handled situations in the past that required the skills and abilities necessary for effective performance on the job. Pulakos and Schmitt (1995) referred to the latter type of interviews as "experienced-based," and they offered the following examples to illustrate the difference in focus (p. 292):

- *Experience-based question:* Think about a time when you had to motivate an employee to perform a job task that he or she disliked but that you needed the individual to do. How did you handle that situation?
- *Situational question:* Suppose you were working with an employee who you knew greatly disliked performing a particular job task. You were in a situation where you needed this task completed, and this employee was the only one available to assist you. What would you do to motivate the employee to perform the task?

The candidate's responses to such questions are typically scored on the type of scale shown in Figure 4–5. The interviewer has to use his or her best judgment to evaluate the candidate's response because there is clearly no one correct answer to the question. Thus, the situational judgment interview is the oral counterpart of the written situational judgment test. Each candidate responds to several such situational questions, and the answers to each question might be evaluated on different dimensions, such as "Taking Initiative" and "Problem Diagnosis."

The situational interview grows in frequency of use and has been found particularly helpful in evaluating candidates for supervisory jobs. Latham and Finnegan (1993) reported that the use of the situational interview as a selection method was a source of pride among those who passed and were hired. The current employees who had gone through it themselves believed the people being hired were well qualified for the job. There is also recent evidence (Weekley & Jones, 1997) that situational judgments can be assessed through video-based tests. Thus, the use of situational contexts, which was originally developed through the interview format, is now being expanded with different technologies. While visual and vocal cues in an interview have been found predictive of job success (DeGroot & Motowidlo, 1999), research shows that interviews have validity even when the interviewer and candidate don't meet face to face. Schmidt and Rader (1999) reported in a meta-analysis a validity coefficient of .40 for tape-recorded interviews that are scored based on a transcript of a telephone interview.

Low	*Medium*	*High*
Responses showed limited awareness of possible problem issues likely to be confronted. Responses were relatively simplistic, without much apparent thought given to the situation.	Responses suggested considerable awareness of possible issues likely to be confronted. Responses were based on a reasonable consideration of the issues present in the situation.	Responses indicated a high level of awareness of possible issues likely to be confronted. Responses were based on extensive and thoughtful consideration of the issues present in the situation.
1	2 3 4	5

FIGURE 4–5 ■ **Example of rating scale for scoring a situational interview**

The interview remains one of the most (if not the most) commonly used personnel selection methods. Arvey and Campion (1982) postulated three reasons for its persistent use. First, the interview really is more valid than our research studies indicate. However, due to methodological problems and limitations in our research, we can't demonstrate how valid it actually is (Dreher, Ash, & Hancock, 1988). Second, people generally are likely to place confidence in highly fallible interview judgments; that is, we are not good judges of people, but we think we are—a phenomenon called the *illusion of validity*. Finally, the interview serves other personnel functions unrelated to employee selection, such as selling candidates on the value of the job and of the organization as an attractive employer. Judge, Higgins, and Cable (2000) proposed that the interview is perceived to be an effective means for both the candidate and the organization to gauge the degree of fit or congruence between them, which in large part accounts for the popularity of the method. Whatever the reasons for the interview's popularity, few companies are willing to do something as important as extending a job offer without first seeing a person "in the flesh."

ASSESSMENT CENTERS

Assessment centers involve evaluating job candidates, most typically for managerial-level jobs, using several methods and raters. They were originally developed by researchers at AT&T who were interested in studying the lives of managers over the full duration of their careers. **Assessment centers** are a group-oriented, standardized series of activities that provide a basis for judgments or predictions of human behaviors believed or known to be relevant to work performed in an organizational setting. They may be a physical part of some organizations, such as special rooms designed for the purpose. They may also be located in a conference center away from the normal workplace. Because these centers are expensive, they have been used mainly by large organizations; however, private organizations now conduct assessment center appraisals for smaller companies.

Here are four characteristics of the assessment center approach:

1. Those individuals selected to attend the center (the assessees) are usually management-level personnel the company wants to evaluate for possible

assessment center
a method of assessing job candidates via a series of structured, group-oriented exercises that are evaluated by raters

selection, promotion, or training. Thus, assessment centers can be used to assess job applicants for hire or current employees for possible advancement.

2. Assessees are evaluated in groups of 10 to 20. They may be divided into smaller groups for various exercises, but the basic strategy is to appraise individuals against the performance of others in the group.

3. Several raters (the assessors) do the evaluation. They work in teams and collectively or individually recommend personnel action (for example, selection, promotion). Assessors may be psychologists, but usually they are company employees unfamiliar with the assessees. They are often trained in how to appraise performance. The training may last from several hours to a few days.

4. A wide variety of performance appraisal methods are used. Many involve group exercises—for example, leaderless group discussions in which leaders "emerge" through their degree of participation in the exercise. Other methods include in-basket tests, projective personality inventories, personal history information forms, and interviews. The program typically takes from one to several days.

Given the variety of tests, the assessee provides substantial information about his or her performance. Raters evaluate the assessees on performance dimensions judged relevant for the job in question. These dimensions involve leadership, decision making, practical judgment, and interpersonal relations skills—the typical performance dimensions for managerial jobs. Based on these evaluations, the assessors prepare a summary report for each assessee and then feed back portions of the report to the assessee. Raters forward their recommendations for personnel action to the organization for review and consideration.

In theory, an assessee's evaluation on a particular dimension (e.g., leadership) will be consistent across the different exercises in which the dimension is observed and rated by the assessor. Thus, if an assessee is judged to have high leadership ability, this high level of leadership ability will manifest across different assessment exercises. In the same way, if an assessee is judged to have low interpersonal skills, this low level of interpersonal skills will also manifest across different assessment exercises. However, in practice research shows that assessors tend to give more uniform evaluations of dimensions within a single exercise, and different evaluations of the same dimensions across exercises. Sackett and Tuzinski (2001) stated, "The persistence of exercise factors despite interventions as . . . assessor training and reductions in the number of dimensions to be rated in an exercise suggests that assessors do not make finely differentiated dimensional judgments" (p. 126). It is thus concluded that assessors tend to evaluate assessees in terms of their overall effectiveness, despite the intent of the assessment center method to make fine-grained evaluations of different skills and abilities. Despite their limitations, assessment centers offer promise for identifying persons with potential for success in management. Assessment centers seem to be successful in their major goal of selecting talented people. Assessment ratings predict advancement more strongly than performance. For example, Jansen and Stoop (2001) found that assessment center ratings correlated .39 with career advancement over a seven-year period. The validity of assessment center ratings to predict job performance is less positive.

Assessment center evaluations are particularly susceptible to criterion contamination. One source of contamination is basing overall judgments of performance on many evaluation methods (tests, interviews, and so on). The validity of the evaluations may stem from the validity of these separate appraisal methods; that is, a valid interview or test might be just as capable of forecasting later job success as the resulting evaluation. But because the incremental value of these methods is "buried" in the overall assessor judgments, it is debatable how much assessors' ratings contribute to predicting future performance beyond these separate methods. There is also evidence (Kleinmann, 1993) that assessees can fashion their behavior to impress assessors when the assessees know what dimensions of their performance are being evaluated.

Klimoski and Strickland (1977) proposed a second source of contamination that is far more subtle. They contended that assessment center evaluations are predictive because both assessors and company supervisors hold common stereotypes of the effective employee. Assessors give higher evaluations to those who "look" like good management talent, and supervisors give higher evaluations to those who "look" like good "company" people. If the two sets of stereotypes are held in common, then (biased) assessment center evaluations correlate with (biased) job performance evaluations. The danger is that organizations may hire and promote those who fit the image of the successful employee. The long-term effect is an organization staffed with people who are mirror images of one another. Opportunity is greatly limited for creative people who "don't fit the mold" but who might be effective if given the chance.

After reviewing the literature on assessment centers, Klimoski and Brickner (1987) concluded that assessment evaluations are indeed valid but I/O psychologists still do not really know why. The authors proposed five possible explanations.

1. *Actual criterion contamination.* Companies use assessment evaluations to make decisions regarding promotions, pay raises, and rated job performance, so it is hardly surprising that assessment evaluations would predict such criteria.

2. *Subtle criterion contamination.* As explained by Klimoski and Strickland (1977), both assessors and company supervisors hold common stereotypes of the successful employee, so biased assessment evaluations are related to biased performance evaluations.

3. *Self-fulfilling prophecy.* Companies designate their "up-and-coming" employees to attend assessment centers, and after assessment these same people are indeed the ones who get ahead in the company.

4. *Performance consistency.* People who succeed in work-related activities do so in many arenas—in assessment centers, in training, on the job, and so on. They are consistently good performers, so success in assessment relates to success on the job.

5. *Managerial intelligence.* The skills and abilities needed to be successful in assessment centers and on the job have much in common. Such talents as verbal skills, analytic reasoning, and well-developed plans of action are acquired and cultivated by more intellectually capable people. The authors refer to this construct as "managerial intelligence."

Research on assessment centers has been evolving. Early research addressed whether assessment evaluations were predictive of job success and found they were. More recent research addresses the limitations of this method of assessment and the reasons that assessment evaluations are predictive. As our knowledge about assessment centers continues to grow, we are beginning to address some complex and intriguing questions of both theoretical and practical significance.

WORK SAMPLES AND SITUATIONAL EXERCISES

Work Samples

work samples
a type of personnel selection test in which the candidate demonstrates proficiency with a task representative of the work performed in the job

Motowidlo, Hanson, and Crafts (1997) classified **work samples** as "high-fidelity simulations," where *fidelity* refers to the level of realism in the assessment. Work samples present applicants with carefully developed examples of work-related problems and require the applicant to solve the problems as if they were on the job, but without actually putting them on the job.

An excellent example of a work sample was reported by Campion (1972), who wanted to develop a predictor of job success for mechanics. Using job analysis techniques, he learned that the mechanic's job was defined by success in the use of tools, accuracy of work, and overall mechanical ability. He then designed tasks that would show an applicant's performance in these three areas. Through the cooperation of job incumbents, he designed a work sample that involved such typical tasks as installing pulleys and belts and taking apart and repairing a gearbox. The proper steps necessary to perform these tasks were identified and given numerical values according to their appropriateness (for example, 10 points for aligning a motor with a dial indicator, 1 point for aligning it by feeling the motor, 0 points for just looking at the motor). Campion used a concurrent criterion-related validity design, and each mechanic in the shop took the work sample. Their scores were correlated with the criterion of supervisor ratings of their job performance. The validity of the work sample was excellent: It had a coefficient of .66 with use of tools, .42 with accuracy of work, and .46 with overall mechanical ability. Campion showed that there was a strong relationship between how well mechanics did on the work sample and how well they did on the job. In general, work samples are among the most valid means of personnel selection.

But work samples do have limitations (Callinan & Robertson, 2000). First, they are effective primarily for blue-collar jobs that involve either the mechanical trades (for example, mechanics, carpenters, electricians) or the manipulation of objects. They are not very effective when the job involves working with people rather than things. Second, work samples assess what a person can do; they don't assess potential. They seem best suited to evaluating experienced workers rather than trainees. Finally, work samples are time-consuming and costly to administer. Because they are individual tests, they require a lot of supervision and monitoring. Few work samples are designed to be completed in less than one hour. If there are 100 applicants to fill five jobs, it may not be worthwhile to give a work sample to all applicants. Perhaps the applicant pool can be reduced with some other selection instrument (for example, a review of previous work history). Yet, despite their limitations, work samples are useful in personnel selection.

Robertson and Kandola (1982) reported another advantage of work samples: Applicants respond to them very favorably. Work samples engender a positive reaction from applicants because of their high face validity. Applicants perceive a direct linkage between how well they perform on a work sample and how well they would perform on the job (that is, the concept of criterion-related validity). Indeed, Cascio and Phillips (1979) reported that one major U.S. city has instituted work-sample selection tests for many city jobs, in part because of the appeal of the method to applicants.

Situational Exercises

situational exercise a method of assessment in which examinees are presented with a problem situation and asked how they would respond to it

Situational exercises are roughly the white-collar counterpart of work samples; that is, they are used mainly to select people for managerial and professional jobs. Unlike work samples, which are designed to be replicas of the job, situational exercises mirror only part of the job. Accordingly, Motowidlo et al. (1997) referred to them as "low-fidelity simulations" because they present applicants with only a description of the work problem and require them to describe how they would deal with it.

Situational exercises involve a family of tests that assess problem-solving ability. Two examples are the In-Basket Test and the Leaderless Group Discussion. The In-Basket Test involves having applicants sort through an in-basket of things to do. The contents are carefully designed letters, memos, brief reports, and the like that require the applicant's immediate attention and response. The applicant goes through the contents of the basket and takes the appropriate action to solve the problems presented, such as making a phone call, writing a letter, or calling a meeting. Observers score the applicant on such factors as productivity (how much work got done) and problem-solving effectiveness (versatility in resolving problems). The In-Basket Test is predictive of the job performance of managers and executives, a traditionally difficult group of employees to select. But a major problem with the test is that it takes up to three hours and, like a work sample, is an individual test. If there are many applicants, too much time is needed to administer the test. Schippman, Prien, and Katz (1990) reported that the typical validity coefficient for the In-Basket Test is approximately .25.

In a Leaderless Group Discussion (LGD), a group of applicants (normally two to eight) engage in a job-related discussion in which no spokesperson or group leader has been named. Raters observe and assess each applicant on such factors as individual prominence, group goal facilitation, and sociability. Scores on these factors are then used as the basis for hiring. The reliability of the LGD increases with the number of people in the group. The typical validity coefficient is in the .15–.35 range.

Although neither the In-Basket Test nor the LGD has the validity of a typical work sample, remember that the criterion of success for a manager is usually more difficult to define. The lower validities usually found in the selection of managerial personnel are as attributable to problems with the criterion and its proper articulation as anything else. However, as Motowidlo et al. noted, high-fidelity simulations (like work samples) are often very expensive to develop and use.

Thus, the gains in validity that come from their use might not offset their cost. Accordingly, the authors believe that low-fidelity simulations can be adapted to a wide variety of jobs and, because of their lower cost, may be a promising alternative to the high-fidelity simulations.

BIOGRAPHICAL INFORMATION

biographical information
a method of assessing individuals in which information pertaining to past activities, interests, and behaviors in their lives is recorded

The theory of using biographical information as a method of personnel selection is based upon our development as individuals. Our lives represent a series of experiences, events, and choices that define our development. Past and current events shape our behavior patterns, attitudes, and values. Because there is consistency in our behaviors, attitudes, and values, an assessment of these factors from our past experiences should be predictive of such experiences in the future. **Biographical information** assesses constructs that shape our behavior, such as sociability and ambition. To the extent these constructs are predictive of future job performance, through biographical information we assess previous life experiences that were manifestations of these constructs.

Biographical information is frequently recorded on an application blank. The application blank, in turn, can be used as a selection device on the basis of the information presented. The questions asked on the application blank are predictive of job performance criteria. Mael (1991) recommended that all biographical questions pertain to historical events in the person's life, as opposed to questions about behavioral intentions or presumed behavior in a hypothetical situation. Table 4–3 lists 16 dimensions of biographical information and an example item for each dimension, as reported by Schoenfeldt (1999).

There are many examples of useful applications of biographical information. Cascio (1976) reported validity coefficients of .77 and .79 for predicting the turnover of white and black workers, respectively. While the magnitude of these validity coefficients is extremely impressive, what is also desirable is that the biographical questionnaire method was fair to members of both racial groups. Childs and Klimoski (1986) demonstrated that selected early life experiences predicted not only later success in a job but also feelings of personal and career accomplishments throughout a lifetime. Sarchione, Cuttler, Muchinsky, and Nelson-Gray (1998) reported that specific biographical information scales measuring drug use history and criminal history were predictive of subsequent dysfunctional behavior among law enforcement officials (e.g., excessive use of force, theft of agency property). Other researchers (e.g., Carlson et al., 1999; Brown & Campion, 1994) have reported the success of biographical questionnaires in predicting promotion, salary, absenteeism, and productivity. Furthermore, research has shown that the criterion variance predicted by biographical information is not redundant with the criterion variance predicted by other types of selection methods, such as personality (McManus & Kelly, 1999) and general mental ability (Mount, Witt, & Barrick, 2000).

While using biograghical information for personnel selection has generated considerable interest on the part of researchers (e.g., Gunter, Furnham, & Drakely, 1993; Stokes, Mumford, & Owens, 1994), there are concerns about fairness, legal issues, and honesty of responses. One aspect of the fairness problem concerns equal accessibility of the behavior or experience being questioned by all respondents.

TABLE 4–3 ■ **16 Biographical information dimensions**

Dimension	Example Item
Dealing with people	
1. Sociability	Volunteer with service groups
2. Agreeableness/cooperation	Argue a lot compared with others
3. Tolerant	Response to people breaking rules
4. Good impression	What a person wears is important
Outlook	
5. Calmness	Often in a hurry
6. Resistance to stress	Time to recover from disappointments
7. Optimism	Think there is some good in everyone
Responsibility/dependability	
8. Responsibility	Supervision in previous jobs
9. Concentration	Importance of quiet surroundings at work
10. Work ethic	Percent of spending money earned in high school
Other	
11. Satisfaction with life	How happy in general
12. Need for achievement	Ranking in previous job
13. Parental influence	Mother worked outside home when young
14. Educational history	Grades in math
15. Job history	Likes/dislikes in previous job
16. Demographic	Number in family

SOURCE: Adapted from "From Dustbowl Empiricism to Rational Constructs in Biographical Data" by L. F. Schoenfeldt, 1999, *Human Resource Management Review, 9,* pp. 147–167.

For example, assume the response to a question about participation in high school football is found to be predictive of subsequent performance on a job. The strategy would then be to include this question on an application blank to evaluate job candidates. The problem is that only males are allowed to play high school football, thereby prohibiting females from having potential access to this type of experience. Female job applicants would be disadvantaged in being evaluated by this question. The problem is not that females *didn't have* this experience but that they *couldn't have* it (i.e., females didn't have equal access). The "solution" to this problem is not to ask different questions of male and female applicants because laws governing fair employment practice emphasize consistency of treatment to all job applicants.

Another concern is that the questions should not be invasive. Invasiveness addresses whether the respondent will consider the item content to be an invasion of his or her privacy. As Nickels (1994) noted, items inquiring about religious affiliations, marital status, or dating habits are potentially invasive. Mael, Connerley, and Morath (1996) reported two types of biodata questions that are regarded as intrusive: a question that refers to an event that could have been explained away if the applicant had the chance to do so, and a question with a response that is not reflective of the type of person the respondent has since become. Questions that are perceived to invade privacy invite litigation against the hiring organization by job applicants (see Field Note 2).

FIELD NOTE 2   **Inappropriate Question?**

iographical items sometimes lack content validity and face validity for the job in question even though they manifest empirical criterion-related validity. The potential irrelevance of biographical questions is always a concern in personnel selection. Here is a case in point.

A city had developed a biographical inventory that was to be used along with some psychological tests to evaluate police officers for promotion to police detectives. All the questions in the biographical inventory were predictive of job performance as a detective, as determined by a criterion-related validity study. One of the questions on the inventory was: "Did you have sexual intercourse for the first time before the age of 16?" Some police officers who took this promotional exam and failed it sued the city for asking such a question in an employment test, a question so obviously lacking in face validity. The officers said the question had absolutely no relevance to the conduct of a detective's job, and furthermore it was an inva-

sion of their privacy. They had been denied a detective's job because of a totally inappropriate question, and therefore they wanted the entire test results thrown out.

The case was heard at the district court. The judge ruled in favor of the officers, saying that the question was totally lacking in content validity and was an invasion of their privacy. Therefore, the officers should be reconsidered for promotion to detective. The city appealed the verdict to the state supreme court. The judge there reversed the lower court ruling and allowed the test results to stand, meaning the officers would not get promoted. The state supreme court judge based his decision on the grounds that the answer to that question did correlate with job performance as a detective. From a practical and legal standpoint, it is advisable to avoid asking such invasive questions in the first place, even though in this case a lengthy legal battle ultimately resulted in a decision favorable to the city.

A final issue is the question of fakability. To what extent do individuals distort their responses to create a more socially desirable impression? Research (Kluger, Reilly, & Russell, 1991; Becker & Colquitt, 1992) reveals that faking does occur in responses to certain types of questions. The questions most likely to be faked in a socially desirable direction are those that are difficult to verify for accuracy and have the appearance of being highly relevant to the job.

Despite these limitations, using biographical information is a logically defensible strategy in personnel selection. Mumford and Stokes (1992) portrayed biographical information as revealing consistent patterns of behavior that are interwoven throughout our lives. By assessing what applicants have done, we can gain great insight into what they will do.

LETTERS OF RECOMMENDATION

One of the most commonly used and least valid of all predictors is the letter of recommendation. Letters of recommendation and reference checks are as widespread in personnel selection as the interview and the application blank. Unfortunately, they usually lack comparable validity. Letters of recommendation are written on behalf of an applicant by a current employer, professional associate, or personal friend. The respondent rates the applicant on such dimensions as leadership ability and written and oral communication skills. The responses are then used as a basis for hiring.

One review of letters of recommendation (Muchinsky, 1979) reported an average validity coefficient of .13. Some people even make recommendations that have an inverse relationship with the criterion; that is, if the applicant is recommended for hire, the company would do best to reject him or her! One of the biggest problems with letters of recommendation is their restricted range. As you might expect, almost all letters of recommendation are positive. Most often, the applicants themselves choose who will write the letters, so it isn't surprising that they pick people who will make them look good. Because of this restriction (that is, almost all applicants are described positively), the lack of predictive ability of the letter of recommendation is not unexpected.

While a few studies using specially constructed evaluation forms have reported moderate validity coefficients, the typical validity coefficient is very low. Because of their limited validity, letters of recommendation should not be taken too seriously in making personnel selection decisions. The only major exception to this statement is the following condition: When applicants are described in positive terms, you will not know whether they will be successful on the job. However, on those rare occasions when the applicant is described in negative terms (even if only mildly), such an assessment is usually indicative of future problems on the job. Those types of letters should be taken seriously. On average, though, very few letters of recommendation contain nonsupportive information about an applicant (see Field Note 3).

FIELD NOTE 3 **Intentional Deception in Letters of Recommendation**

 was the director of a graduate program to which about 100 students seek admission annually. One of the requirements for admission is a letter of recommendation. Over the years I received several memorable letters of recommendation, but on one occasion I received a letter (actually two) that clearly illustrates why such letters have little predictive value. This letter came from the president of a foreign university where the student was enrolled. It made the student sound incredibly strong academically: the class valedictorian, the only recipient of the native king's fellowship program, the only student who received a special citation from the university, and so forth. Needless to say, I was most impressed by this letter.

About two weeks later I got another application for admission from a second student from that same university. Accompanying this application was another letter supposedly written by the university president. This letter was identical to the first. The only difference was the name of the student typed at the top of the letter. Thus, both students had been the class valedictorian, both were the only recipient of the fellowship, and so on.

I then called a different academic department and discovered that it had received the identical letter on yet a third student from that university who was applying for graduate work in that department. What we had was literally a form letter in which every student in the university was described, word for word, as the best. The university apparently provided this "service" to its students seeking admission to graduate schools in the United States. Such attempts at deception do nothing to portray fairly a candidate's strengths and weaknesses—and most certainly do not enhance the validity of the letter of recommendation as a personnel selection method.

DRUG TESTING

drug testing
a method of assessment typically based on an analysis of urine that is used to detect illicit drug use by the examinee

Drug testing is the popular term for efforts to detect *substance abuse,* the use of illegal drugs and the improper and illegal use of prescription and over-the-counter medications, alcohol, and other chemical compounds. Substance abuse is a major global problem with far-reaching societal, moral, and economic consequences. The role that I/O psychology plays in this vast and complex picture is to detect substance abuse in the workplace. Employees who engage in substance abuse jeopardize not only their own welfare but also potentially the welfare of fellow employees and other individuals. I/O psychologists are involved in screening out substance abusers among both job applicants and current employees.

Unlike other forms of assessment used by I/O psychologists that involve estimates of cognitive or motor abilities, drug testing embraces chemical assessments. The method of assessment is typically based on a urine sample (hair samples can also be used). The rationale is that the presence of drugs will be revealed in a person's urine. Therefore, a sample of urine is treated with chemicals that will reveal the presence of drugs if they have been ingested by the person. There are two basic types of assessments. A *screening test* assures the potential presence of a wide variety of chemicals. A *confirmation test* on the same sample identifies the presence of chemicals suggested by the initial screening test. I/O psychologists are not directly involved with these tests because they are performed in chemical laboratories by individuals with special technical training. The profession of I/O psychology does become involved in drug testing because it assesses suitability for employment, with concomitant concern about the reliability, validity, legality, and cost of these tests.

Drug abuse issues are very complex, and there are some real concerns. The reliability of the chemical tests is much higher than the reliability of traditional paper-and-pencil psychological assessments. However, the reliability is not perfect, which means that different conclusions can be drawn about substance abuse depending on the laboratory that conducts the testing. Questions of validity are much more problematic. The accurate detection of drug use varies as a function of the type of drug involved, because some drugs remain in our systems for days and others remain for weeks. Thus, the timing of taking the urine sample is critical. It is also possible that diet can falsely influence the results of a drug test. For example, eating poppy-seed cake may trigger a confirmatory response to heroin tests because heroin is derived from poppy seeds. The legality of drug testing is also highly controversial. Critics of drug testing contend it violates the U.S. Constitution with regard to unreasonable search and seizure, self-incrimination, and the right to privacy. It is also a matter of debate which jobs should be subject to drug testing. Some people argue for routine drug testing; others say drug testing should be limited to jobs that potentially affect the lives of others (for example, transportation workers). Yet another issue is the criteria for intoxication and performance impairment. What dosage of a drug constitutes a level that would impair job performance? Thus, the validity of drug tests for predicting job performance may well vary by the type of job and the criteria of job performance. Drug usage may be a valid predictor of accidents among truck drivers or construction workers, but not predict gradations of successful job performance among secretaries. Finally, there is the matter of cost. Screening tests cost about $10 per specimen, but confirmatory tests can cost up to $100 per specimen. These costs will eventually have to be passed on to consumers as part of the price they pay for having their goods and services rendered by a drug-free workforce. A major investigation by the National Research Council (Normand, Lempert, & O'Brien, 1994) on drug testing underscored the particular danger of unfairness to job applicants who are falsely classified as drug users. Drug testing thus must balance the economic goals of workforce productivity with individual rights to fair treatment in the workplace.

Some recent research on drug testing has revealed applicant reactions to such testing and its effectiveness. Murphy, Thornton, and Prue (1991) found that drug testing was judged most acceptable for jobs in which there was the potential for danger to others. Uniform drug testing for all jobs was not viewed favorably. Stone and Kotch (1989) reported that the negative reaction to drug testing by companies can be reduced by giving employees advance notice of scheduled drug tests and responding to detected drug use with treatment programs rather than the discharge of employees. Normand, Salyards, and Mahoney (1990) conducted a study on the effects of drug testing and reported sobering results. A total of 5,465 job applicants were tested for the use of illicit drugs. After 1.3 years of employment, employees who tested positive for illicit drugs had an absenteeism rate 59.3% higher than employees who tested negative. The involuntary turnover rate (namely, employees who were fired) was 47% higher among drug users than nonusers. The estimated cost savings of screening out drug users in reducing absenteeism and turnover costs for one cohort of new employees was $52,750,000. This figure does not reflect the compounded savings derived by cohorts of new employees added each year the drug-testing program is in existence.

As can be seen, drug testing is an exceedingly complex and controversial issue. While the analysis of urine is beyond the purview of I/O psychology, making decisions about an applicant's suitability for employment is not. I/O psychology is being drawn into a complicated web of issues that affects all of society. Our profession may be asked to provide solutions to problems we couldn't even have imagined 20 years ago.

NEW OR CONTROVERSIAL METHODS OF ASSESSMENT

This final section is reserved for three new or controversial methods of assessing job applicants.

polygraph
an instrument that assesses characteristics of an individual's central nervous system that are supposedly indicative of giving false responses to questions

Polygraph or Lie Detection

A **polygraph** is an instrument that measures aspects of the autonomic nervous system—physiological reactions of the body such as heart rate and perspiration. In theory these autonomic responses will "give you away" when you are telling a lie. The polygraph is attached to the body with electronic sensors for detecting the physiological reactions. Polygraphs are used more to evaluate people charged with criminal activity in a post hoc fashion (for example, after a robbery within a company has occurred) than to select people for a job, although it is used in the latter capacity as well.

Is a polygraph foolproof? No. People can appear to be innocent of any wrongdoing according to the polygraph but in fact be guilty of misconduct. Research conducted by the Federal Bureau of Investigation (Podlesny & Truslow, 1993) based on a crime simulation reported that the polygraph correctly identified 84.7% of the guilty group and 94.7% of the innocent group. Bashore and Rapp (1993) suggested that alternative methods that measure brain electrical activity can be used to complement the polygraph and would be particularly effective in revealing the possession of information in persons attempting to conceal it (i.e., the guilty group). Many psychologists are skeptical of the scientific value of the polygraph, believing people can readily learn countermeasures to invalidate the results (Iacono & Lykken, 1997). In 1988 President Reagan signed into law a bill banning the widespread use of polygraphs for preemployment screening among private-sector employers. However, as Honts (1991) reported, polygraph use by the federal government continues to grow. It is used extensively in the hiring process of government agencies involved in national security, as well as in the area of law enforcement.

Graphology

graphology
a method of assessment in which characteristics of a person's handwriting are evaluated and interpreted

Graphology or handwriting analysis is very popular in Europe as a selection method. Here is how it works: A person trained in handwriting analysis (called a *graphologist*) examines a sample of a candidate's handwriting. Based on such factors as the specific formation of letters, the slant and size of the writing, and how hard the person presses the pen or pencil on the paper, the graphologist makes an assessment of the candidate's personality. This personality assessment is then correlated with criteria of job success.

Rafaeli and Klimoski (1983) had 20 graphologists analyze handwriting and then correlated their assessments with three types of criteria: supervisory ratings, self-ratings, and sales production. Although the authors found some evidence of inter-rater agreement (meaning the graphologists tended to base their assessments on the same facets of handwriting), the handwriting assessments did not correlate with any criteria. Ben-Shakhar et al. (1986) reported that graphologists did not perform significantly better than chance in predicting the job performance of bank employees. Graphology has been found to be predictive of affective states such as stress (Keinan & Eilat-Greenberg, 1993), but its ability to predict job performance has not been empirically established.

Tests of Emotional Intelligence

Recently I/O psychology has begun to address what has historically been regarded as the "soft" side of individual differences, including moods, feelings, and emotions. For many years the relevance of these constructs to the world of work was denied. They were regarded as transient disturbances to the linkages between abilities (e.g., intelligence) and performance. However, we are beginning to realize that moods, feelings, and emotions play a significant role in the workplace, just as

emotional intelligence
a construct that reflects a person's capacity to manage emotional responses in social situations

they do in life in general. The concept of **emotional intelligence** was initially proposed by Salovey and Mayer (1990).

It is proposed that individuals differ in how they deal with their emotions, and those who effectively manage their emotions are said to be "emotionally intelligent." Some theorists believe that emotions are within the domain of intelligence, rather than viewing "emotion" and "intelligence" as independent or contradictory. Goleman (1995) proposed five dimensions to the construct of emotional intelligence. The first three are classified as intrapersonal, and the last two are interpersonal.

1. *Knowing one's emotions.* Self-awareness, recognizing a feeling as it happens, is the cornerstone of emotional intelligence. The ability to monitor feelings from moment to moment is hypothesized to be crucial to psychological insight and self-understanding.
2. *Managing one's emotions.* Handling feelings so they are appropriate is an ability that builds on self-awareness. People who are low in this ability are prone to feelings of distress, whereas those who are high are more resilient to life's setbacks and upsets.
3. *Motivating oneself.* Marshaling emotions in pursuit of a goal is essential for paying attention, for self-motivation, and for creativity. People who have this ability tend to be more productive and effective in whatever they undertake. More will be said about this topic in Chapter 12 on work motivation.
4. *Recognizing emotions in others.* Empathy is the fundamental "people skill." People who are empathetic are more attuned to the subtle social signals that indicate what others need or want. This skill makes them well suited for the caring professions such as nurses and social workers.
5. *Handling relationships.* Proficiency in social relationships is, in large part, the ability to manage emotions in others. People who excel in this ability do well in tasks that rely on interacting smoothly with others.

Goleman differentiated people who are high in traditional intelligence (i.e., cognitive ability) from those high in emotional intelligence as follows: People with high cognitive ability (alone) are ambitious and productive, unexpressive, detached, and emotionally bland and cold. In contrast, people who are high in emotional intelligence are socially poised, outgoing, and cheerful. They are sympathetic and caring in their relationships. They are comfortable with themselves, others, and the social environment they live in. These portraits are of extreme types, when in reality most of us are a mix of traditional and emotional intelligence. However, each construct adds separately to a person's attributes. Goleman (1995) believes "of the two, emotional intelligence adds far more of the qualities that make us more fully human" (p. 45).

Because the concept of emotional intelligence is very new, we don't know a great deal about it. Currently there are no well-established tests or inventories to measure it, although some initial attempts have been made (i.e., Goleman, 1998; Weisinger, 1998). Furthermore, it is a matter of professional debate whether emotional intelligence is a distinct construct (Barrett, 2001), or whether it is already understood under the rubric of personality theory. There is conceptual overlap between personality and emotions, but they are not identical. While psychology has not yet reached a verdict on the scientific status of emotional intelligence, what it addresses is certainly not well understood within the field of I/O psychology. In a rare empirical study on emotional intelligence, Fox and Spector (2000) reported that emotional intelligence was positively related to performance in an employment interview. I anticipate that the relationship between emotional intelligence and job performance will be more fully explored in the near future.

OVERVIEW AND EVALUATION OF PREDICTORS

Personnel selection methods can be evaluated by many standards. I have identified four major standards that I think are useful in organizing all the information we have gathered about predictors.

1. *Validity,* as defined in this book, refers to the ability of the predictor to forecast criterion performance accurately. Many authorities argue that validity is the predominant evaluative standard in judging selection methods; however, the relevance of the other three standards is also substantial.

2. *Fairness* refers to the ability of the predictor to render unbiased predictions of job success across applicants in various subgroups of gender, race, age, and so on. The issue of fairness will be discussed in greater detail in Chapter 5.

3. *Applicability* refers to whether the selection method can be applied across the full range of jobs. Some predictors have wide applicability in that they appear well suited for a diverse range of jobs; other methods have particular limitations that affect their applicability.

4. The final standard is the *cost* of implementing the method. The various personnel selection methods differ markedly in their cost, which has a direct bearing on their overall value.

Table 4–4 presents the 12 personnel selection methods appraised on each of the four evaluative standards. Each standard is partitioned into three levels: low, moderate, and high. This classification scheme is admittedly oversimplified, and in some cases the evaluation of a selection method did not readily lend itself to a uniform rating. Nevertheless, this method is useful in providing a broad-brush view of all the personnel selection methods.

Average validities in the .00–.20, .21–.40, and over .40 ranges were labeled low, moderate, and high, respectively. Selection methods that have many, some, and few problems of fairness were labeled low, moderate, and high, respectively. The applicability standard, the most difficult one to appraise on a single dimension, was classified according to the ease of using the method in terms of feasibility and generalizability across jobs. Finally, direct cost estimates were made for each selection method. Methods estimated as costing less than $20 per applicant were labeled low; $20 to $50, moderate; and over $50, high. The ideal personnel selection method would be high in validity, fairness, and applicability and low in cost. Inspection of Table 4–4 reveals that no method has an ideal profile. The 12 methods produce a series of tradeoffs among validity, fairness, applicability, and cost. This shouldn't be surprising; if there were one uniformly ideal personnel selection method, there probably would be little need to consider 11 others.

TABLE 4–4 ■ **Assessment of 12 personnel selection methods along four evaluative standards**

Selection Method	Evaluative Standards			
	Validity	*Fairness*	*Applicability*	*Cost*
Intelligence tests	High	Moderate	High	Low
Mechanical aptitude tests	Moderate	High	Low	Low
Sensory/motor ability tests	Moderate	High	Low	Low
Personality inventories	Moderate	High	Moderate	Moderate
Physical abilities tests	High	Moderate	Low	Low
Interviews	Moderate	Moderate	High	Moderate
Assessment centers	High	High	Moderate	High
Work samples	High	High	Low	High
Situational exercises	Moderate	(Unknown)	Low	Moderate
Biographical information	High	Moderate	High	Low
Letters of recommendation	Low	(Unknown)	High	Low
Drug tests	Moderate	High	Moderate	Moderate

In terms of validity, the best methods are intelligence tests, work samples, biographical information, assessment centers, and physical abilities tests. However, each of these methods is limited by problems with fairness, applicability, or cost. Ironically, the worst selection method in terms of validity, letters of recommendation, is one of the most frequently used. This method is characterized by high applicability and low cost, which no doubt accounts for its popularity.

Fairness refers to the likelihood that the method will have differential predictive accuracy according to membership in any group, such as gender or race. While the issue of fairness has generated a great deal of controversy, no method is classified in Table 4–4 as having low fairness. Insufficient information is available on two of the methods (situational exercises and letters of recommendation) to render an evaluation of their fairness, but it seems unlikely they would be judged as grossly unfair. Although several methods have exhibited some fairness problems (thus warranting caution in their use), the problems are not so severe as to reject any method as a means of selecting personnel.

The applicability dimension was the most difficult to assess, and evaluation of this dimension is most subject to qualification. For example, work samples are characterized by low applicability because they are highly limited to certain types of jobs (that is, jobs involving the mechanical manipulation of objects). However, this limitation appears to be more than offset by the method's high validity and fairness. Simply put, the problem with this method is its feasibility for only a selected range of jobs. In contrast, other methods have high applicability (such as the interview) and qualify as almost universal means of selection.

The cost dimension is perhaps the most arbitrary. Indirect or hidden costs may be associated with selection methods—costs that were not included in their evaluation but perhaps could have been. The break points in the classification scheme are also subjective. For example, I considered a $40-per-applicant cost to be moderate; others might say it is low or high. These issues notwithstanding, one can see a full range of cost estimates in Table 4–4. Some methods do not cost much (for example, letters of recommendation), but they do not appear to be worth much either.

This chapter has examined several major types of predictors used in personnel selection. These predictors have been validated against a number of different criteria for a variety of occupational groups. Some predictors have been used more extensively than others. Furthermore, certain predictors have historically shown more validity than others. The ideal predictor would be an accurate forecaster of the criterion, equally applicable across different groups of people, and not too lengthy or costly to administer. But predictors rarely meet all these standards in practice.

This chapter has described the diversity of methods that organizations use to predict whether an individual will succeed on the job. All of the methods involve candidates being administered assessments (e.g., test, interview, work sample, etc.), and receiving scores on those assessments, and then examiners deciding whether a candidate's score profile meets the organization's standards for selection. However, there is another way that suitability for employment can be judged—an examination of work experience (Quinones, Ford, & Teachout, 1995). The logic of this selection method is captured by a quotation from the philosopher Orison Swett Marden:

> Every experience in life, everything with which we have come in contact in life, is a chisel which has been cutting away at our life statue, molding, modifying, shaping it. We are part of all we have met. Everything we have seen, heard, felt, or thought has had its hand in molding us, shaping us.

There are many varieties and degrees of work experience, however. Tesluk and Jacobs (1998) have proposed a three-component framework for conceptualizing work experience. The first component is *quantitative,* and it reflects primarily the length of time a person has spent working on a task or in a job. The *qualitative* component reflects the variety and breadth of tasks and responsibilities performed in a job. The third component is the *interaction* between the quantitative and qualitative, and might best be explained by an example. Assume a person has worked in the same job for five years. The content of the job is very static and can be learned in one year. Such a person has not had "five years of work experience" as much as "one year of work experience five times." Assume a second person has also worked in a job for five years, but the challenges and responsibilities of the job evolved over the five-year period. This second person has more accurately had "five years of job experience." The component that differentiates the two cases is the qualitative component.

As Tesluk and Jacobs stated, I/O psychology is just beginning to understand the linkage between work experience and future job behavior. Our discipline has much to learn about candidates who, for example, have rich and lengthy work experience, yet score poorly on some form of psychological assessment. Currently we have no professionally established and accepted system for equating or even comparing assessment results with work experience.

As noted in Chapter 1, I/O psychology has entered the global era. As such we have become aware of business customs and practices that are considerably different from those practiced in Western cultures. These include the methods by which employees are selected and promoted. Currently in Japan personnel decisions are made, in part, on the basis of blood type. There are four types of blood: O, A, B, and AB. D'Adamo (1996) offers the following explanation: "Termed *ketsu-eki-gata*, Japanese blood type analysis is serious business. Corporate managers use it to hire workers, market researchers use it to predict buying habits, and most people use it to choose friends, romantic partners, and lifetime mates. Vending machines that offer on-the-spot blood type analysis are widespread in train stations, department stores, restaurants, and other public places. There is even a highly respected organization, the ABO Society, dedicated to helping individuals and organizations make the right decisions, consistent with blood type. . . . This happens every day in Japan—for example, when a company advertises that it is looking for Type Bs to fill middle management positions" (pp. 46–47). While the methods used to select employees may vary across cultures, what is constant is the need for all organizations to make good personnel decisions. This process is the subject of the next chapter.

CASE STUDY ■ **How Do We Hire Police Officers?**

Bay Ridge, a city with a population of about 125,000, experienced remarkable growth over a short time for two major reasons. First, several large industries had been attracted to the area; with more jobs, there were more people. Second, due to a rezoning plan, several small townships were incorporated into Bay Ridge, which caused a sudden burgeoning in the city's official population. As a consequence of this growth, the city needed to expand its police force. For many years, Bay Ridge had only a relatively small force and used only a brief interview to select the officers. Recently, however, there had been several complaints about the city's selection interview. Due to the complaints and the need to hire many more officers, the city council decided to abandon the old method of hiring. The city commissioned a job analysis for police officers and determined that three major factors contributed to success on the job. The next step was to develop selection measures to assess each of the three factors. The city council called a meeting with the city personnel director to get a progress report on the selection measures being proposed. Four city council members and Ron Davenport, the city personnel director, attended.

> *Davenport:* I'm pleased to report to you that we have made substantial progress in our study. The job analysis revealed that the following factors determine success on the police force: physical agility, sensitivity to community relations, and practical judgment. We are fairly pleased with the tests developed to assess two of the factors, although one of them is causing us some problems.
>
> *Councilmember DeRosa:* Would you kindly elaborate on what these factors mean?

Davenport: Certainly. Physical agility is important in being able to apprehend and possibly disarm a suspect. It is also important in being able to carry a wounded officer out of the line of hostile fire. Sensitivity to community relations involves knowledge of racial and ethnic problems in the city, plus an ability to work with the community in preventing crime. Practical judgment reflects knowing when it is advisable to pursue a criminal suspect and what methods of action to use in uncertain situations.

Councilmember Flory: How do you propose to measure physical agility?

Davenport: It looks as if we'll go with some physical standard—being able to carry a 150-pound dummy 25 yards, or something similar. We might also use some height and weight requirements. We could have some problems with gender differences in that women are not as strong as men, but I think we can work it out.

Councilmember Reddinger: Are all of these tests going to be performance tests?

Davenport: No, that's the only one so far. For the community relations factor, we're going to use a situational interview. We'll ask the candidates how they would go about dealing with some hypothetical but realistic problem, such as handling a domestic argument. The interviewers will grade their answers and give them a total score.

Councilmember Hamilton: What will be a passing score in this interview?

Davenport: We haven't determined that yet. We're still trying to determine if this is the best way to measure the factor.

Councilmember Flory: How do you plan to measure practical judgment?

Davenport: That's the problem case. We really haven't figured out a good test of that yet.

Councilmember DeRosa: How about a test of general intelligence?

Davenport: It appears that practical judgment is related to intelligence, but it's not the same thing. A person can be very intelligent in terms of verbal and numerical ability but not possess a great deal of practical judgment.

Councilmember Reddinger: Hasn't some psychologist developed a test of practical judgment?

Davenport: Not that we know of. You also have to remember that the type of judgment a police officer has to demonstrate is not the same thing as the type of judgment, say, a banker has to show. I guess I'm saying there appear to be different kinds of practical judgment.

Councilmember Hamilton: Could you use some personality inventory to measure it?

Davenport: I don't think so. I doubt that practical judgment is a personality trait. At least I'm not aware of any direct measures of it.

Councilmember Flory: How about using the interview again? A police officer has to demonstrate practical judgment in handling community relations. Can't you just expand the interview a bit?

Davenport: That's a possibility we're considering. Another possibility is to put candidates in a test situation where they have to demonstrate their practical judgment. It could be a pretty expensive method, all things considered, but it may be the best way to go.

Councilmember DeRosa: I have a feeling, Mr. Davenport, that your success in measuring practical judgment will determine just how many good officers we get on the force.

Study Questions

1. The city will have to validate whatever predictors it develops to select police officers. What method or methods of validation do you think it should use?
2. Do you think that biographical information might be useful in predicting one's success as a police officer? If so, what types of items might be useful?
3. Describe a work sample or situational exercise that might measure practical judgment.
4. What might be a problem in using a physical ability test to select police officers?
5. The personnel department has asked you to assist in developing or selecting predictors of police officer performance. What advice would you give?

SUGGESTED INFOTRAC TOPICS

psychological testing
intelligence tests
personality tests
integrity tests
job interview

assessment centers
letters of recommendation
drug testing
graphology
polygraph

Personnel Decisions

CHAPTER OUTLINE

LEARNING OBJECTIVES

■ Explain the social and legal contexts for personnel decisions.

■ Describe the processes of personnel recruitment and affirmative action.

■ Understand the statistical concepts of regression analysis and multiple regression analysis.

■ Explain the concept and significance of validity generalization.

■ Describe the selection of employees and the process of assessing job applicants.

■ Identify issues pertaining to the determination of the passing score.

■ Explain the concept and significance of test utility related to organizational efficiency.

■ Describe the personnel functions of placement and classification.

THE SOCIAL CONTEXT FOR PERSONNEL DECISIONS

I/O psychologists have historically contributed to the process of making personnel decisions by developing assessment instruments, conducting validational research on the boundaries of an instrument's usability, and explaining the consequences of how the instrument is used (e.g., the implications of determining the passing score). Other organizational members are also involved in making personnel decisions, including professionals in human resources, managers of the prospective employees, and in some cases coworkers of the prospective employees. Furthermore, personnel decisions are influenced by organizational values, such as the organization's preference for hiring only applicants who possess very high credentials. Organizations operate within the social or cultural context in which they are embedded. These larger-scale forces have a direct bearing on who gets hired and who doesn't. For example, hiring only the best applicants will invariably create a chronically unemployed segment of society. Every applicant can't be the "best," yet all people benefit from employment. Unemployment results in a host of serious ills for individuals and society as a whole, a topic we will discuss in a later chapter. There are also cultural differences in what makes for a desirable employee. Many Western cultures question the value of hiring the family members of employees. The term *nepotism* refers to showing favoritism in the hiring of family members. In the United States nepotism is usually viewed negatively because it results in unequal opportunity among job applicants, which is anathema to our cultural values. In some non-Western cultures, however, nepotism in hiring is viewed positively. The logic is that a family member is a known commodity who can be trusted to be committed, not an anonymous applicant. Why *not* give preferential treatment to applicants who are associated by birth or marriage with members of the hiring organization? Personnel decisions are always embedded in a larger organizational and social context. They do not "stand apart" in a vacuum unrelated to the larger social system.

Guion (1998a) has developed a schematic representation of the forces that act on personnel decisions, as shown in Figure 5–1. At the top of the diagram is the organization, which reflects that all personnel decisions are designed to serve the needs of the organization. I/O psychology draws heavily upon scientific theory (e.g., the concept of validity) to conduct research and develop assessment instruments. The instruments are used to assess candidates and help reach a decision about those candidates, which results in the outcome that some people get offered employment and others do not. The shaded boxes in Figure 5–1 represent the traditional areas of activity among I/O psychologists in making personnel decisions. However, there is another important concept shown in the diagram that typically does not draw as much attention among I/O psychologists. It is the social and cultural context in which the total organization exists. The end product of the personnel selection process is to offer employment to some candidates and deny it to others. Some issues that affect this outcome transcend the scientific and technical. The science of personnel selection is sometimes dismissed because it does not reflect the way hiring occurs "in the real world." There is truth to the assertion that some organizations make hiring decisions without regard to the forces presented in Figure 5–1. Guion (1998b) has noted that the way some organizations

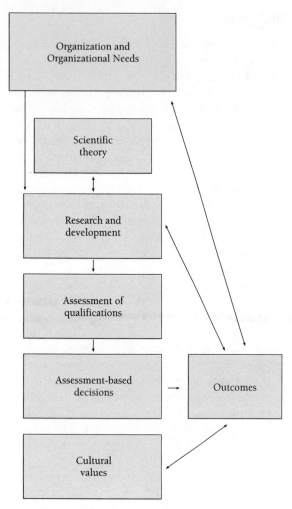

FIGURE 5–1 ■ **Schematic representation of the forces in personnel decisions and outcomes**

SOURCE: Adapted from *Assessment, Measurement, and Prediction for Personnel Decisions* by R. M. Guion, 1998, Lawrence Erlbaum and Associates.

hire people in real life tends to be more intuitive, nonquantitative, and often not based on validated, empirically derived factors. This chapter will examine the science and practice of making personnel decisions with the full realization that some organizations' practices are only loosely linked to science.

PERSONNEL DECISIONS IN THE NEW MILLENNIUM

As we discussed in Chapter 1, life in the 21st century is very different than it was even one generation ago. Schmitt and Chan (1998) identified five major changes in society that will affect the ways personnel decisions are made in many organizations. The first is the *speed of technological change.* With computer-based technology work is conducted today in ways that we didn't even imagine 25 years ago. The emphasis on the rapid rate of change compels us to hire workers who can adapt to ever-evolving work conditions. Emphasis is thus placed on a person's willingness and capacity to learn new job skills on a continual basis. Second is the growing reliance on the *use of teams to accomplish work.* Coordinated and integrated teams responsible for accomplishing work tasks are replacing individual workers and their supervisors. Teams and teamwork are the subject of Chapter 9. The cultural values of the United States have traditionally rewarded individual achievement, and our personnel selection methods have been geared toward that objective. Now we must select individuals who will fit well into the team concept. The third factor is *changes in communication technology.* Faxes, e-mail, and handheld electronic devices permit us to communicate with people instantaneously around the world. It is no longer necessary to meet face to face or even communicate by telephone. What is the result of this new impersonal communication on such classic issues as the bond between coworkers, morale, and organizational commitment? The fourth change is that *most large corporations are now global in nature.* Over half of Ford Motor Company's employees work outside of the United States. The products of many organizations are sold and serviced throughout the world. We need to hire employees who are adaptable and open to cultures other than their own. As previously described, we also need to be sensitive to differing cultural values and their effect on individuals and organizations.

Finally, the U.S. economy is making the transition from primarily a manufacturing orientation to a *service orientation.* Organizations that provide services must hire employees who have a customer orientation; that is, they are sensitive to the customers' needs and adept at satisfying them. Emphasis is now more heavily placed on interpersonal (i.e., personality) skills. As Schmitt and Chan described, these changes in the 21st century lead us, on average, to select employees with different KSAOs than we sought in the past.

These new societal trends affect our choice of desirable candidates in personnel selection. If jobs are ever-changing, the emphasis will be on hiring people with high intelligence (or *g*). Teaching them the specific knowledge or skill required on the job will be left to post-hiring training. If jobs are increasingly service oriented, the emphasis will be on hiring people who are conscientious and interpersonally flexible as measured by personality inventories. However, as Behling (1998) described, these skills are most appropriate when new employees will have to do a lot of problem solving, will have a lot of autonomy, will learn skills and knowledge on the job that are more important than those brought to the job, and will need to learn and adapt rapidly. As Guion (1998b) said, currently not all jobs in society are so characterized. In some jobs it is still critical for job success to get a match between the specific qualifications of the person and the specific job requirements. Thus, in rapidly changing work the desired match is more between the person and the organization, whereas in less rapidly changing work the desired match is more between the person and the job. As Campbell, Hanson, and Oppler (2001) stated, most models or conceptions of effective job performance ultimately boil down to whether an applicant possesses the "can do" (e.g., technical ability, intelligence) and "will do" (e.g., ambition, willingness to learn) factors.

The quest to find a good match between the qualifications of people and the demands of work are seemingly more daunting today than ever before. However, in truth the process of trying to figure out the best way to select people for organizations is ancient. The means of matching people and work are the subject of cultural lore since antiquity. Salgado (2000) recounts the following tale from long ago:

> A farmer did not know what profession he should choose for his son. One day, in order to orient himself, he gave a Bible, an apple and a coin to the boy. The farmer thought: If the boy eats the apple, he will be a gardener; if he reads the Bible, he will serve to be ecclesiastic; and if he puts the money in his pocket, he will be a merchant. Some time later, the farmer found the boy seated on the Bible, with the money in his pocket, and eating the apple. "Aha—said the farmer—a clever boy. He has the makings of a politician." (p. 191)

As described in Chapter 4, our predictors have evolved from apples, coins, and bibles to tests of mental ability, tests of personality, and interviews. However, the fundamental issue has remained unchanged throughout history—finding the best match between the qualifications of people and the demands of work. Personnel decisions affect people's worklives. Becker and Gerhart (1996) asserted that if personnel decisions influence organizational performance, they must either improve efficiency or contribute to profitability. The amount of money organizations pay to their employees is the single largest operating cost in many organizations.

Therefore, it is to the advantage of both the individual and the organization that personnel decisions be made wisely. For individual employees, it is best that they be selected for jobs that utilize their abilities. For organizations, it is best that they hire qualified individuals who will contribute to the success of the organization. Furthermore, there are international and cultural differences in how organizations make personnel decisions. Ryan, McFarland, Baron, and Page (1999) reported cultural differences in the acceptance of traditional personnel selection methods (e.g., evaluation of the candidate's work history, the interview) versus less popular methods (e.g., biodata). The authors recommend greater awareness of differing international practices regarding personnel selection as business is increasingly conducted on a global basis. This chapter will examine the process of making personnel decisions and the factors associated with determining their quality.

THE LEGAL CONTEXT FOR PERSONNEL DECISIONS

Civil Rights Act of 1964

For the first 60 years or so of I/O psychology, there was virtually no connection between psychologists and the legal community. Psychological tests were developed, administered, and interpreted by psychologists, and as a profession psychologists governed themselves. However, during the late 1950s and early 1960s, the nation was swept up in the civil rights movement. At that time civil rights concerned primarily the conditions under which Blacks lived and worked in this country. Blacks were denied access to colleges, restaurants, and jobs—in short, their civil rights were denied. Presidents Kennedy and Johnson were interested in changing this aspect of American society. In 1964 the Civil Rights Act, a major piece of federal legislation aimed at reducing discrimination in all walks of life, was passed. The section of the law pertaining to discrimination in employment is Title VII, and it is the section most relevant to I/O psychology. In essence, this was the message: Blacks were grossly underemployed throughout the country in both private- and public-sector jobs, particularly in jobs above the lower levels of organizations. To reduce discrimination in employment (one of the mandates of the Civil Rights Act), the federal government began to intervene in employment hiring; in essence, it would monitor the entire procedure to ensure fairness in selection. Thus, personnel decisions became deeply embedded within a legal context in the 1960s. As Guion (1998a) asserted, previously the federal government had regulated things (e.g., food and drugs), but with this act it regulated behavior. The Civil Rights Act was expanded to cover other people as well. In fact, five charateristics were used to identify groups: race, gender, religion, color, and national origin. Those designated for legal recognition were referred to as **protected groups.** The Civil Rights Act included all personnel functions—training, promotion, retention, and performance appraisal—in addition to selection. Furthermore, any methods used for making personnel decisions (tests, interviews, assessment centers, etc.) were subject to the same legal standards.

protected groups
a designation for the members of society who are granted legal recognition by virtue of a demographic characteristic, such as race, gender, national origin, color, religion, age, and disability

FRANK AND ERNEST   by Bob Thaves

SOURCE: Reprinted by permission of Newspaper Enterprise Association, Inc.

Title VII specifies several unlawful employment practices, including the following:

- Employers may not fail or refuse to hire, or discharge, anyone on the basis of the five protected groups.
- Employers may not separate or classify employees or applicants so as to deprive anyone of employment opportunities on the basis of any of the five protected groups.
- Advertising employment or training opportunities may not indicate preferences for any group, as witnessed, for example, in separate classified advertisements for "Help Wanted—Men" and "Help Wanted—Women."

Adverse Impact

adverse impact
a type of unfair discrimination in which the result of using a particular personnel selection method has an adverse effect on protected group members compared with majority group members

disparate treatment
a type of unfair discrimination in which protected group members are afforded differential procedures in consideration for employment compared with majority group members

Under the Civil Rights Act discrimination may be charged under two legal theories. One is **adverse impact** (also called *disparate impact*), in which discrimination affects different groups (vis-à-vis the five protected groups) differently. Evidence that one group (e.g., women) as a whole is less likely to be hired is evidence of discrimination against those group members. The second theory is **disparate treatment**, which refers to evidence that a member of a protected group is treated differently from other job applicants in the employment process. All job applicants should receive the same treatment with regard to selection methods and hiring standards. Singling out some applicants for different employment procedures is evidence of disparate treatment.

Of the two legal bases of discrimination, adverse impact has garnered the greater attention among I/O psychologists. Adverse impact exists when employment procedures result in a differential effect between protected and majority group members. A simple rule of thumb was created to operationalize the concept of adverse impact: the "80%" (or "4/5ths") rule. The rule states that adverse impact occurs if the selection ratio (that is, the number of people hired divided by the number of people who apply) for any group of applicants (such as Blacks) is less than 80% of the selection ratio for another group. Suppose 100 Whites apply for a job and 20 are selected. The selection ratio is thus 20/100, or .20. By multiplying

.20 by 80%, we get .16. This means that if fewer than 16% of the Black applicants are hired, the selection test produces adverse impact. So if 50 Blacks apply for the job and if at least 8 (50 × .16) Blacks are not selected, then the test produces adverse impact.

If adverse impact is found to exist, the organization faces two alternatives. One is to demonstrate that the test is a valid predictor of job performance. The second alternative is to use a different test that has no adverse impact (but may also be less valid than a test that does manifest adverse impact). If adverse impact does not result from the selection method, the organization is not required to validate it. Obviously, however, it is a sound business decision to validate any selection method at any time. A company would always want to know whether its method is identifying the best candidates for hire. As our understanding of the concept of validity has evolved over the years, psychologists have advocated the use of other manifestations of validity. One of these is the concept of validity generalization, which will be discussed shortly.

As part of the Civil Rights Act, the Equal Employment Opportunity Commission (EEOC) was established to investigate charges of prohibited employment practices and to use conciliation and persuasion to eliminate prohibited practices. The EEOC subsequently produced the *Uniform Guidelines on Employee Selection Procedures* for organizations to follow in making employment decisions. When there is a conclusion of "just cause" to believe charges of employment discrimination are true, the EEOC can file suit in court. If the organization cannot be persuaded to change its employment practices, then the issue is brought before the court for adjudication. Organizations that lose such cases are obligated to pay financial damages to the victims of their employment practices. The financial awards in these cases can be class-action settlements (the individual who is suing represents a class of similar people) or back-pay settlements (the organization has to pay a portion of what victims would have earned had they been hired), or both. The courts have granted multi-million-dollar awards in single cases. However, not everyone who fails an employment test automatically gets his or her day in court. A lawsuit must be predicated on just cause, and sometimes the two parties may reach an agreement without resorting to litigation.

Major Court Cases

If a case proceeds to trial, the body of facts presented and how the court ultimately evaluates those facts become the judicial interpretation of the law. The decisions rendered by the courts become part of what is called *case law*. Several landmark decisions rendered by the U.S. Supreme Court have shaped the interpretation of the Civil Rights Act. In *Griggs v. Duke Power Company*, the Court ruled in 1971 that individuals who bring suit against a company do not have to prove that the company's employment test is unfair; rather, the company has to prove that its test is fair. Thus, the burden of proving the fairness of the test rests with the employer. This finding was referred to as "Griggs' Burden." In *Albemarle v. Moody*, the Court ruled on just how much judicial power the employment guidelines really have. Although they were called guidelines, the Court ruled that they be granted the "deference of law," meaning they were in effect the law on employment testing. In *Bakke v. University of California,* the Court ruled that Whites can be the victims of discrimination as well as Blacks. Bakke (a white man) sued the University of California on the grounds that his race had been a factor in his being denied admission to their medical school. The Court ruled in Bakke's favor and required the University of California to admit Bakke to the medical college. This case was heralded as a classic case of "reverse discrimination," which technically is incorrect. First, the name connotes that only Blacks can be discriminated against, which obviously is not true. Second, reversal of the process of discrimination results in nondiscrimination. In *Watson v. Fort Worth Bank & Trust,* the Court ruled that the *cost* of alternative selection procedures must be considered in making decisions about selection methods. Previously, matters of cost had not been a concern of the courts or the EEOC. Furthermore, the Court modified its stance regarding burden of proof. Literally thousands of cases have been adjudicated in the district, appellate, state supreme courts, and U.S. Supreme Court based on litigation spawned by employment law. These four cases (all from the U.S. Supreme Court) represent a very small sampling.

Other employment laws followed the passage of the Civil Rights Act, but none had the same far-reaching impact on employment practices. In 1967 the Age Discrimination in Employment Act (ADEA) was passed, which extends to people aged 40 and over the same legal protection granted to the five protected groups under the Civil Rights Act. The body of employment law cases grows annually, some cases are appealed to a higher court, and some lower court rulings are reversed upon appeal. It is a major challenge for professionals involved with the legal system to keep current with the ever-expanding body of employment law (Author, 2000).

Americans with Disabilities Act

In 1990 the Americans with Disabilities Act (ADA) was signed into law by President George H. Bush. The ADA is the most important piece of legislation ever enacted for persons with disabilities (O'Keeffe, 1994). A *disability* is defined by ADA as "a physical or mental impairment that substantially limits one or more (of the) major life activities; a record of such impairment; or being regarded as having such an impairment." A major life activity is seeing, hearing, walking, learning, breathing, and working. An employment test that screens out an individual with a disability must be job-related and consistent with business necessity. The law states that employers must provide disabled persons *reasonable accommodation* in being evaluated for employment and in the conduct of their jobs. Employers are required to modify or accommodate their business practices in a reasonable fashion to meet the needs of disabled persons. This can include providing elevators or ramps for access to buildings for those who cannot walk, and also providing readers for those with dyslexia or who are blind. The ADA extends protection to individuals who are alcoholics and former illegal drug users (Jones, 1994) as well as to individuals with psychiatric disabilities (Carling, 1994). The fundamental premise of the law is that disabled individuals can effectively contribute to the workforce, and they cannot be discriminated against in employment decisions because of their disabilities. If a reasonable accommodation on the employer's part is needed to meld these individuals into the workforce, it is so prescribed by the ADA law. As Klimoski and Palmer (1994) noted, organizations are expected to act with goodwill in responding to the ADA and be committed to make it work effectively. At this time there appear to be legitimate differences of opinion regarding the legal interpretation of the law. These interpretations will become clearer as the courts address cases brought before them regarding the employment rights of disabled persons. As with all employment laws, the ultimate goal of the ADA is to produce a more just and productive society.

In 2001 the U.S. Supreme Court ruled on the case of *Martin v. PGA Tour*. Martin is a professional golfer who suffers from a physical disability in his right leg that restricts his ability to walk a golf course. He asked The PGA of America for permission to ride a golf cart during tour competition. The PGA refused on the grounds that riding in a cart would give Martin an unfair advantage over other golfers who are compelled by PGA rules to walk the course. Martin sued the PGA for the right to use a golf cart under ADA, claiming that his riding in a cart was a reasonable accommodation the PGA could make in his pursuit of earning a living as a golfer. Furthermore, Martin contended it would not be an "undue burden" (or hardship) on the PGA to allow Martin to ride. The U.S. Supreme Court ruled in favor of Martin, saying that making shots was an essential job function but walking between shots was not.

Societal Values and Employment Law

Employment laws reflect our society's values about what we regard as "fairness" in the work world. As our conceptions of fairness have changed over time, so have employment laws. Guion (1998a) stated, "Changes follow or accompany (or are accompanied by) changes in the ideas and attitudes of society in general, whether emerging spontaneously or in response to leadership. Even imperfect law is an expression of, and an understanding of, social policy" (p. 205). Tenopyr (1996) asserted that there is a strong linkage between measurement issues in psychology (e.g., validity) and social policy pertaining to employment. Tenopyr argued that psychologists should have addressed many of the issues long before national policy debates practically mandated the research. She believes psychologists "should undertake an organized effort to anticipate social issues of the future and to begin the research necessary to address them" (p. 360).

The Civil Rights Act of 1964 provides for equal access to employment by all protected groups. Access to employment is often gained by passing tests used to make employment decisions. Psychological research has revealed that different groups of people do not score equally on all standard employment tests. An example is a test of physical fitness for the job of firefighter. Because men have, on average, greater upper body strength than women, more men than women pass a test requiring the lifting of a heavy object. This difference between genders in upper body strength increases the likelihood that both men and women are not hired in equivalent proportions, thereby increasing the likelihood of adverse impact against women. Psychologists are thus sometimes compelled to consider two undesirable options: Either use tests that have validity but produce adverse impact, or use tests that do not produce adverse impact but are less valid. Selection methods that uniformly have high validity and no adverse impact are elusive, although various strategies have been proposed (e.g., Hattrup, Rock, & Scalia, 1997; Hoffman & Thornton, 1997). One strategy is to set different passing scores for various groups to avoid adverse impact. However, in 1991 President George H. Bush signed into law an amendment to the Civil Rights Act that prohibited test score adjustments as a means of attaining employment fairness. Specifically, the amended Civil Rights Act stated it shall be an unlawful practice for an employer "in connection with the selection or referral of applicants or candidates for employment or promotion to adjust the scores of, use different cutoffs for, or otherwise alter the results of employment related tests on the basis of race, color, religion, sex, or national origin."

Varca and Pattison (1993) presented a cogent discussion of how the amended Civil Rights Act and more recent court cases, such as *Wards Cove Packing Company v. Antonio,* have modified both the applicant's and employer's responsibilities in employment discrimination litigation, pertaining to such issues as burden of proof. Wigdor and Sackett (1993) described the development of employment laws as reflecting attempts to reach ultimate societal goals of workforce productivity and provide opportunities for all social groups to achieve their employment potential. Some authors are of the opinion there is no likely way to resolve the conflict between these goals in a fashion that is mutually satisfying to both sides. Our society is divided on the relative importance that should be attached to attaining these two goals (e.g., Gottfredson, 1994; Sackett & Wilk, 1994). The ensuing years will witness how the courts adjudicate the complicated interplay among the societal goals that surround employment testing. The profusion of laws and court cases testifies to the continuing debate within our country over issues of *social justice* in employment. The matter of social justice in employment will be discussed in several contexts throughout this book.

Affirmative Action

affirmative action a social policy that advocates members of protected groups will be actively recruited and considered for selection in employment

Affirmative action is a social policy aimed at reducing the effects of prior discrimination. It is not a requirement under the Civil Rights Act, although it is included in the EEOC guidelines. The original intent of affirmative action was aimed primarily at the recruitment of new employees—namely, that organizations should take positive (or affirmative) action to bring members of minority groups into the workforce that had previously been excluded.

Campbell (1996) described four goals of affirmative action:

1. *Correct present inequities.* If one group has "more than its fair share" of jobs or educational opportunities because of current discriminatory practices, then the goal is to remedy the inequity and eliminate the discriminating practices.
2. *Compensate past inequities.* Even if current practices are not discriminatory, a long history of past discrimination may serve to put members of a minority group at a disadvantage.
3. *Provide role models.* Increasing the frequency of minority group members acting as role models could potentially change the career expectations,

educational planning, and job-seeking behavior of younger minority group members.

4. *Promote diversity.* Increasing the minority representation in a student body or workforce may act to increase the range of ideas, skills, or values that can be brought to bear on organizational problems and goals.

As straightforward as these goals may appear, there is great variability in the operational procedures used to pursue the goals. The most passive interpretation is to follow procedures that pertain strictly to recruitment, such as extensive advertising in sources most likely to reach minority group members. A stronger interpretation of the goals is *preferential selection:* Organizations will select minority group members from the applicant pool if they are judged to have substantially equal qualifications with nonminority applicants. The most extreme interpretation is to set aside a specific number of job openings or promotions for members of specific protected groups. This is referred to as the *quota interpretation* of affirmative action: Organizations will staff themselves with explicit percentages of employees representing the various protected groups, based on local or national norms, within a specific time frame. Quotas are legally imposed on organizations as a severe corrective measure for prolonged inequities in the composition of the workforce. Quotas are not the typical interpretation of affirmative action.

Affirmative action has been hotly debated by proponents and critics. In particular, over the past ten years the subject of affirmative action has been a major political issue (Crosby & VanDeVeer, 2000). Criticism of the quota interpretation in particular has been strident, claiming the strategy ignores merit or ability. Under a quota strategy it is alleged that the goal is merely "to get the numbers right." Proponents of affirmative action believe steps are needed to offset the effects of many years of past discrimination against specific protected groups. The State of California recently reversed its commitment to affirmative action in the admission of students into its universities. Preliminary evidence indicates the new admission policy has resulted in less representation of some minority groups in the student population.

Has affirmative action been effective in meeting national goals of prosperity in employment for all people? Some experts (e.g., Guion, 1998a; Heilman, 1996) question its overall effectiveness, asserting that unemployment rates are much higher and average incomes much lower now for some groups (particularly Blacks) than they were at the inception of affirmative action over 30 years ago. Furthermore, the perceived beneficiaries of affirmative action are often stigmatized as being incompetent, as nonbeneficiaries attribute minority employment in large part to group membership (Heilman, McCullough, & Gilbert, 1996; Heilman & Alcott, 2001). While there appears to be consensus that affirmative action has not produced its intended goals (Murrell & Jones, 1996), there is considerable reluctance to discard it altogether. President Clinton stated the nation should "amend it, not end it." It is feared that its absence may produce outcomes more socially undesirable than have occurred with its presence, however flawed it might be. Dovidio and Gaertner (1996) asserted that affirmative action policies are beneficial in that they emphasize outcomes rather than intentions and they establish monitoring systems that ensure accountability.

Kravitz et al. (1997) documented a large quantity of psychological and behavioral research conducted on affirmative action. Among the issues studied are reactions to individuals and by individuals hired because of affirmative action policies. Heilman and Herlihy (1984) investigated the reactions of individuals to women who got their jobs on the basis of merit or because of preferential treatment based on gender. Neither men nor women were attracted to jobs when it was believed that women in those jobs had been hired because of their gender. Heilman, Simon, and Repper (1987) examined the effects of gender-based selection. In a laboratory study they led women to believe they were selected for a group leader position because of either their gender or their ability. When selected on the basis of gender, women devalued their leadership performance, took less credit for successful outcomes, and reported less interest in persisting as leaders. The findings suggest that when individuals have doubts about their competence to perform a job effectively, gender-based preferential selection is likely to have adverse consequences on how they view themselves and their performance. Heilman, Block, and Lucas (1992) reported that individuals viewed as having been hired because of affirmative action were not believed to have had their qualifications given much weight in the hiring process. The stigma of incompetence was found to be fairly robust, and the authors questioned whether the stigma would dissipate in the face of disconfirming information about the individuals' presumed incompetence. Highhouse et al. (1999) found that subtle differences in the way jobs were advertised reflecting the company's commitment to affirmative action influenced the attitudes of black engineers to pursue employment with the company. The authors concluded that minority applicants are sensitive to the manner in which a company projects its stance on minority recruitment and selection. Kravitz and Klineberg (2000) identified differences within minority group populations with regard to their support for affirmative action. Blacks were found to be more strongly supportive of affirmative action than Hispanics. In summary, currently our society has made the subject of affirmative action a volatile issue in a national debate. Many of the conflicting issues will undoubtedly be addressed by the U.S. Supreme Court.

RECRUITMENT

recruitment
the process by which individuals are solicited to apply for jobs

The personnel function of **recruitment** is the process of attracting people to apply for a job. Organizations can select only from those candidates who apply. With the growing ease of use and social acceptability of conducting business via the Internet, organizations are now developing features of websites to attract job applicants. Graham (2000) reports that on-line recruiting is the fastest growing medium for recruiting and is particularly popular among candidates in their 20s and 30s. If few people apply for a job, the odds of finding a strong candidate are lower than if many candidates apply. Organizations often have preferences for recruiting recent college graduates versus individuals with work experience. Rynes, Orlitzky, and Bretz (1997) reported that experienced hires were regarded by staffing specialists as having a stronger work ethic and more realistic expectations than recent

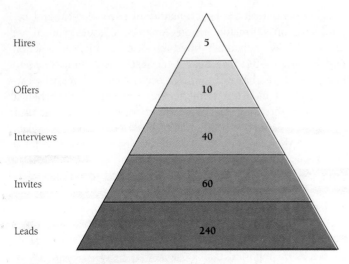

Hires — 5

Offers — 10

Interviews — 40

Invites — 60

Leads — 240

FIGURE 5–2 ■ Recruiting yield pyramid

SOURCE: From *The Recruitment Function* by R. H. Hawk, 1967, New York: AMACOM, a division of American Management Association. All rights reserved. Reprinted by permission.

recruiting yield pyramid
a conceptualization of the recruiting process that reveals the ratio of initial contacts to individuals hired

college graduates. However, new graduates were regarded more highly than experienced hires on their willingness and ability to learn new things.

There is more to recruiting than you might think. The **recruiting yield pyramid,** shown in Figure 5–2, is useful in hiring candidates. Let us say that the goal is to hire 5 managers. The company has learned from past experience that for every 2 managers who are offered jobs, only 1 will accept. Therefore, the company will need to make 10 offers. Furthermore, the company has learned that to find 10 managers who are good enough to receive an offer, 40 candidates must be interviewed; that is, only 1 manager out of 4 is usually judged acceptable. However, to get 40 managers to travel to the company for an interview, the company has to invite 60 people; that is, typically only 2 out of 3 candidates are interested enough in the job to agree to be interviewed. Finally, to find 60 potentially interested managers, the company needs to get four times as many contacts or leads. Some people will not want to change jobs, others will not want to move, and still others will simply be unsuitable for further consideration. Therefore, the company has to make initial contacts with about 240 managerial candidates. Note the mushrooming effect in recruiting applicants. Stated in reverse order, 240 people are contacted to find 60 who are interested, to find 40 who agree to be interviewed, to find 10 who are acceptable, to get the 5 people who will accept the offer.

Obviously the yield ratios (in this case, 240:5) differ depending on the organization and the job in question. Highly attractive employers have fewer people decline their offers, and less demanding jobs are filled with less selectivity. Also, economic conditions play a big role in whether the company must pursue the applicant, or vice versa. Nevertheless, a poor job of recruiting greatly limits the caliber of people available for hire. Also, the time from when a company realizes it needs new employees until the employees show up for work is typically measured in weeks or months rather than days.

Rynes (1993) noted that most of the emphasis on personnel decisions from an I/O psychology perspective centers on how employers can make better decisions in assessing applicants. However, as Rynes observed, the process can be viewed from the opposite perspective—that is, the extent to which applicants consider the company to be a desirable employer. Specifically, what impressions of the company are generated by the company's recruitment and assessment practices?

Schuler (1993) referred to the quality of a selection process that makes it acceptable to job applicants as "social validity," an extension of face validity discussed in Chapter 4. Steiner and Gilliland (1996), for example, reported that the social validity of selection procedures was the strongest correlate of applicants' favorable reactions to the organization. Furthermore, there were cultural differences in the social validity of various selection procedures. French college students were more favorably disposed to graphology as a selection method, whereas U.S. college students were more accepting of biographical information. Ployhart and Ryan (1998) found that job applicants held negative views of an organization for using what they considered unfair selection procedures, even when the applicants were hired. Klein and Weaver (2000) demonstrated that new employees who attended a volunteer organizational-level orientation program became more quickly socialized and exhibited greater commitment to the organization than nonattendees. Applicant reactions to assessment procedures are often vividly personal and highly emotional. Harris (2000) observed that it might be a wiser investment for organizations to explain to rejected candidates why they were denied employment in a way that reduces negative feelings and damage to self esteem than to gird for potential litigation. Rynes (1993) offered the following examples of applicant reactions to the recruiting and assessment tactics of companies:

- A married graduate student with a 3.9 grade point average reported that the first three questions in a company's psychological assessment procedure involved inquiries about her personal relationship with her husband and children. Although the company asked her what she thought of the procedure before she left, she lied because she was afraid that telling the truth would eliminate her from future consideration. Because of dual-career constraints, she continued to pursue an offer, but noted that if she got one, her first on-the-job priority would be to try to get the assessor fired.
- A student told how he had originally planned to refuse to submit to psychological testing, but was persuaded by his girlfriend that it would be a more effective form of protest to pursue the offer and then pointedly turn it down.
- The first interview question asked of a female student was, "We're a pretty macho organization. . . . Does that bother you?" Unfortunately it did, and she simply wrote the company out of her future interviewing plans. (p. 242)

These examples illustrate that job applicants are not merely passive "receptors" of selection procedures. Rather, applicants react to what they are asked to do or say to get a job. Sometimes a negative experience causes them to withdraw from the application process. Smither et al. (1993) found that applicant reactions to selection methods were positively related to their willingness to recommend the employer to others. Companies and applicants should realize that the recruitment and selection process is *mutual*—both parties are engaged in assessing the degree of fit with each other (see Field Note 1).

FIELD NOTE 1 **The Left-Handed Dentist**

One of the more unusual personnel selection consulting projects I've worked on involved hiring a dentist. A dentist in my town had just experienced an unpleasant breakup with his partner. They disagreed on many major issues surrounding dentistry, including the relative importance of preventive dental maintenance versus treatment, pain management for patients, and so on. Their parting was not amicable. The dentist who remained solicited my help in getting a new partner. He described at great length the characteristics he was looking for in a new partner. Some related to certain dentistry skills, while others dealt with attitudinal or philosophical orientations toward dentistry.

I didn't envision any major problems in picking a new partner because the desired characteristics seemed reasonable, and I knew dental schools turned out many graduates each year (thus, I would have a large applicant pool). Then came a curve ball I neither anticipated nor understood initially. The dentist said to me, "And, of course, my new partner must be left-handed." The dumb look on my face must have told the dentist I didn't quite catch the significance of left-handedness. The dentist then explained to me something I had never realized despite all the years I have gone to dentists. Dental partners often share instruments in their practice, and there are both left-handed and right-handed dental instruments. The dentist was left-handed himself, so therefore his new partner would also have to be left-handed. I then asked the dentist what proportion of dentists were left-handed. He said he didn't know for sure, but knew it was a small percentage. Suddenly, my task had become much more difficult.

It was one thing to find a new dentist who met the specifications for the job and who would like to set up a practice in a small Iowa town. It was another thing to have the size of the potential applicant pool greatly reduced by such a limiting factor as left-handedness. There is a technical term for a trait such as left-handedness in this case: "bona fide occupational qualification" (BFOQ). For a qualification to be a BFOQ, it must be "reasonably necessary to the operation of that particular business or enterprise." Thus, an employer could use left-handedness as a BFOQ in dentistry, but left-handedness would not be a BFOQ in accounting, for example. I am happy to tell you I found a dentist who met all the qualifications. The two dentists have been partners for over 20 years now.

A MODEL OF PERSONNEL DECISIONS

Figure 5–3 is a model that shows the sequence of factors associated with making personnel decisions. Several of these factors have been discussed in earlier chapters. The process of job and organizational analysis initiates the sequence and was described in Chapter 3. An analysis of the job and organization establishes the context in which the personnel decisions will be made. The results of these analyses provide information useful in determining the criteria of job performance (also discussed in Chapter 3), as well as provide insights into those predictor constructs useful in forecasting job performance (as discussed in Chapter 4). The linkage between the predictors and criteria is the essence of validity—the determination of how well our predictors forecast job performance (as also discussed in Chapter 4). We are now in a position to continue the sequence used by I/O psychologists: examining issues pertaining to recruiting, designing selection systems, and assessing the utility of those systems. However, before a discussion of these issues, the next topic is a method of statistical analysis often used by I/O psychologists in assessing the linkage between predictors and criteria. It is called regression analysis.

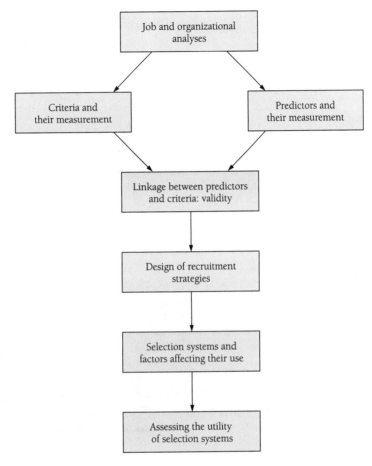

FIGURE 5–3 ■ **Model of personnel decisions in organizations**

REGRESSION ANALYSIS

regression analysis
a statistical procedure
used to predict one
variable on the basis
of another variable

The statistical technique used to predict criterion performance on the basis of a predictor score is called **regression analysis**. Although a correlation coefficient is useful for showing the degree of relationship between two variables, it is not useful for predicting one variable from the other. Regression analysis, however, does permit us to predict a person's status on one variable (the criterion) based on his or her status on another variable (the predictor). If we assume that the relationship between the two variables is linear (as it usually is), it can be described mathematically with a regression equation:

$$\hat{Y} = a + bX$$ [Formula 5–1]

where

$\hat{Y}$ = the predicted criterion score

a = a mathematical constant reflecting where the regression line intercepts the ordinate (or Y axis)

b = a mathematical constant reflecting the slope of the regression line
X = the predictor score for a given individual

The values of a and b are derived through mathematical procedures that minimize the distance between the regression line (that is, a line useful for making predictions) and the pairs of predictor–criterion data points.

To develop a regression equation, we need predictor and criterion data on a sample of people. Let us say we have a sample of 100 employees. Supervisor ratings of job performance are the criterion, and the predictor test we wish to investigate is an intelligence test. We administer the intelligence test to the workers, collect the criterion data, and then see if we can predict the criterion scores on the basis of the intelligence test scores. From the predictor–criterion data, we derive the following regression equation:

$$\hat{Y} = 1 + .5X \qquad\qquad \text{[Formula 5–2]}$$

The relationship between the two variables is shown in Figure 5–4. Note that the regression line crosses the Y axis at a value of 1 (that is, a = 1). Also, for every 2-unit increase in X, there is a corresponding 1-unit increase in Y. Thus, the slope of the regression line, defined as the change in Y divided by the change in X, equals $\frac{1}{2}$ or .5 (that is, b = .5).

For any value of X, we can now predict a corresponding Y score. For example, if someone scores 12 on the intelligence test, the predicted criterion rating is

$$\hat{Y} = 1 + .5(12) = 7 \qquad\qquad \text{[Formula 5–3]}$$

If a supervisor rating of 5 represents adequate job performance (and we do not want anyone with a lower rating), the regression equation can be worked backward to get the minimum passing score:

$$5 = 1 + .5X$$
$$X = 8$$

So, if we use the intelligence test to hire, we will not accept any applicant who scores less than 8 because lower scores would result in a predicted level of job performance lower than we want. There is also another way to find the passing score. In Figure 5–4, locate the value of 5 on the Y axis (the criterion). Move horizontally to the regression line, and then drop down to the corresponding point on the X axis (the predictor). The score is 8.

Multiple Predictors

Better personnel decisions are made on the basis of more than one piece of information. How well two or more predictors combined improve the predictability of the criterion depends on their indi-

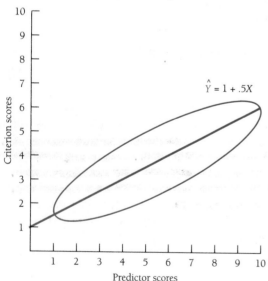

FIGURE 5–4 ■ **Predictor–criterion scatterplot and regression line of best fit**

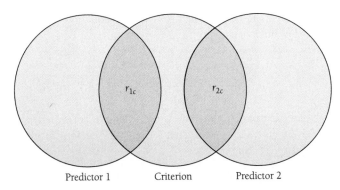

Predictor 1   Criterion   Predictor 2

FIGURE 5–5 ■ **Venn diagram of two uncorrelated predictors**

multiple correlation
the degree of predict-
ability (ranging from
0 to 1.0) in forecast-
ing one variable on
the basis of two or
more other variables

vidual relationships to the criterion and their relationship to each other. Suppose two predictors both correlate with the criterion but do not correlate with each other. This relationship is illustrated by the Venn diagram in Figure 5–5. The shaded area on the left shows how much the first predictor overlaps the criterion. The overlap area is the validity of the first predictor, symbolized by the notation r_{1c}, where the subscript 1 stands for the first predictor and the subscript c stands for the criterion. The shaded area on the right shows the extent to which the second predictor overlaps the criterion; its validity is expressed as r_{2c}. As can be seen, more of the criterion can be explained by using two predictors. Also note that the two predictors are unrelated to each other, meaning that they predict different aspects of the criterion. The combined relationship between two or more predictors and the criterion is referred to as a **multiple correlation** (R). The only conceptual difference between r and R is that the range of R is from 0 to 1.0, while r ranges from -1.0 to 1.0. When R is squared, the resulting R^2 value represents the total amount of variance in the criterion that can be explained by two or more predictors. When predictors 1 and 2 are not correlated with each other, the squared multiple correlation (R^2) is equal to the sum of the squared individual validity coefficients, or

$$R^2_{c.12} = r^2_{1c} + r^2_{2c}$$ [Formula 5–4]

For example, if r_{1c} = .60 and r_{2c} = .50, then

$$\begin{aligned} R^2_{c.12} &= (.60)^2 + (.50)^2 \\ &= .36 + .25 \\ &= .61 \end{aligned}$$ [Formula 5-5]

The notation $R^2_{c.12}$ is read "the squared multiple correlation between the criterion and two predictors." In this condition (when the two predictors are unrelated to each other), 61% of the variance in the criterion can be explained by two predictors.

In most cases, however, it is rare that two predictors related to the same criterion are unrelated to each other. Usually all three variables share some variance with one another; that is, the intercorrelation between the two predictors (r_{12}) is not zero. Such a relationship is presented graphically in Figure 5–6. In the figure each predictor correlates substantially with the criterion (r_{1c} and r_{2c}), and the two predictors also overlap each other (r_{12}). The addition of the second predictor adds more criterion variance than can be accounted for by one predictor alone. Yet all of the criterion variance accounted for by the second predictor is not new variance; part of it was explained by the first predictor. When there is a correlation

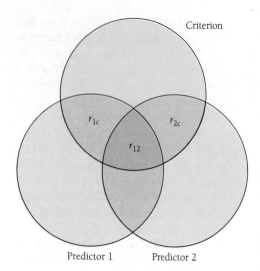

Criterion

r_{1c} r_{2c}

r_{12}

Predictor 1   Predictor 2

FIGURE 5–6 ■ **Venn diagram of two correlated predictors**

between the two predictors (r_{12}), the equation for calculating the squared multiple correlation must be expanded to

$$R^2_{c.12} = \frac{r^2_{1c} + r^2_{2c} - 2r_{12}r_{1c}r_{2c}}{1 - r^2_{12}} \qquad \text{[Formula 5–6]}$$

For example, if the two predictors intercorrelated .30, given the validity coefficients from the previous example and $r_{12} = .30$, we have

$$R^2_{c.12} = \frac{(.60)^2 + (.50)^2 - 2(.30)(.60)(.50)}{1 - (.30)^2}$$

$$= .47 \qquad \text{[Formula 5–7]}$$

As can be seen, the explanatory power of two intercorrelated predictor variables is diminished compared with the explanatory power when they are uncorrelated (.47 versus .61). This example provides a rule about multiple predictors: It is generally advisable to seek predictors that are related to the criterion but are uncorrelated with each other. However, in practice, it is very difficult to find multiple variables that are statistically related to another variable (the criterion) but at the same time statistically unrelated to each other. Usually variables that are both predictive of a criterion are also predictive of each other. Also note that the abbreviated version of the equation used to compute the squared multiple correlation with independent predictors is just a special case of the expanded equation when r_{12} is equal to zero.

Multiple Regression Analysis

multiple regression analysis
a statistical procedure used to predict one variable on the basis of two or more other variables

The relationship between correlation and regression is the foundation for the relationship between multiple correlation and multiple regression. Just as regression analysis permits prediction on the basis of one predictor, **multiple regression analysis** permits prediction on the basis of multiple predictors. The logic for using multiple regression is the same as the logic for using multiple correlation: It usually enhances prediction of the criterion.

As we noted before, the formula for a regression equation with one predictor is

$$\hat{Y} = a + bX \qquad \text{[Formula 5–8]}$$

When we expand this to the case of two predictors, we have

$$\hat{Y} = a + b_1X_1 + b_2X_2 \qquad \text{[Formula 5–9]}$$

where X_1 and X_2 are the two predictors and b_1 and b_2 are the regression weights associated with the two predictors. As before, the b values are based in part on the correlation between the predictors and the criterion. In multiple regression the b values are also influenced by the correlation among the predictors. However, the procedure for making predictions in multiple regression is similar to that used in one-predictor (or simple) regression.

Suppose we have criterion data on a sample of industrial workers who take two tests we think may be useful for hiring future workers. We analyze the data to derive the values of a, b_1, and b_2 and arrive at this regression equation:

$$\hat{Y} = 2 + .4X_1 + .7X_2 \qquad \text{[Formula 5–10]}$$

If a person scores 30 on test 1 and 40 on test 2, his or her predicted criterion performance is

$$\hat{Y} = 2 + .4(30) + .7(40) = 42$$

The degree of predictability afforded by the two predictors is measured by the multiple correlation between the predictors and the criterion. If the multiple correlation is large enough to be of some value for prediction purposes, we might use the two tests to hire future workers. The company would undoubtedly set a minimum predicted criterion score at a certain value—say, 40. In this example, the person's predicted job performance score (42) was higher than the minimum score set by the company (40), so the person would be hired.

Multiple regression is not limited to just two predictors; predictors can be added to the regression equation until they no longer enhance prediction of the criterion. The k-predictor regression equation is simply an extension of the two-predictor regression equation, and all terms are interpreted as before. The equation looks like this:

$$\hat{Y} = a + b_1X_1 + b_2X_2 + b_3X_3 + \cdots + b_kX_k \qquad \text{[Formula 5–11]}$$

Usually, there comes a point at which adding more predictors will not enhance the prediction of the criterion. Regression equations with four or five predictors usually do as good a job as those with more. The reason is that the shared variance among the predictors becomes very large after four to five predictors, so adding more does not add unique variance in the criterion. If we could find another predictor that was (1) uncorrelated with the other predictors and (2) correlated with the criterion, it would be a useful addition to the equation. Multiple regression is a very popular prediction strategy in I/O psychology and is used extensively.

VALIDITY GENERALIZATION

validity generalization
a concept that reflects the degree to which a predictive relationship empirically established in one context spreads to other populations or contexts

The concept of **validity generalization** refers to a predictor's validity spreading or generalizing to other jobs or contexts beyond the one in which it was validated. For example, let us say that a test is found valid in hiring secretaries in a company. If that same test is found useful for hiring secretaries in another company, we say its validity has generalized. That same test could also be useful in selecting people for a different job, such as clerks. This is another case of the test's validity generalizing. Schmitt and Landy (1993) graphically depicted the domains across which validity can generalize, as shown in Figure 5–7. Validity generalization has long been a goal of I/O psychologists because its implication would certainly make our jobs easier. However, the problem is that when we examined whether a test's validity would generalize across either companies or jobs, we often found that it

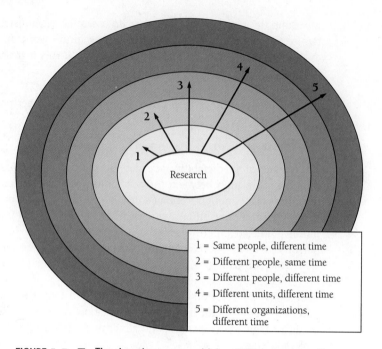

FIGURE 5–7   ■   The domains across which validity can generalize

SOURCE: From *Personnel Selection in Organizations* by N. Schmitt and F. J. Landy.
Copyright © 1993, John Wiley & Sons, Inc. This material is used by permission of
John Wiley & Sons, Inc.

did not; that is, the test's validity was specific to the situation in which it was originally validated. The implication, of course, was that we had to validate every test in every situation in which it was used. We could not assume that its validity would generalize.

Schmidt and Hunter (1978, 1980) support validity generalization as a means of selecting personnel. They argue that the problem of situational specificity of test validity is based on psychologists' erroneous belief in the "law of small numbers," which is the belief that whatever results hold for large samples will also hold for small samples. They think this belief is incorrect—that small-sample results are highly unstable and give highly variable test validities. Schmidt and Hunter believe that in most cases psychologists use small samples (40 to 50) to validate tests. Indeed, Salgado (1998) reported the average sample size in typical criterion-related validity studies is too small to produce stable, generalizable conclusions, resulting in the (erroneous) conclusion that test validity is situation specific. Schmidt and Hunter argue that if tests were validated in large samples, the results would generalize (not be situation specific).

Validity generalization means that there is a single "true" relationship between a test and job performance, as for a secretary. Let us say that relationship has a correlation of .40 based on validity studies involving thousands of subjects each. In theory, we could generalize the validity of these findings from huge sample sizes to more typical employment situations with small samples. Organizations with immense sample sizes (such as the military or federal government) would validate certain tests; the rest of the business world would simply "borrow" these validities as a basis for using the tests for hiring. Alternatively, appropriately large samples can be found by pooling results from many smaller studies through meta-analysis.

In support of their position, Schmidt and Hunter (1978) presented data based on a sample of more than 10,000 individuals. The sample was drawn from the army. Data were reported on ten predictors that were used to forecast success in 35 jobs. The results indicated highly similar validity coefficients across different jobs, meaning that differences among jobs did not moderate predictor–criterion relationships. The researchers concluded that the effects of situational moderators disappear with appropriately large sample sizes. One psychological construct that is supposedly common for success in all jobs (and that accounts for validity generalizing or spreading) is intelligence and, in particular, the dimension of intelligence relating to information processing.

Meta-analyses of the relationship between tests of cognitive ability and job performance have consistently yielded evidence that the validity of intelligence does indeed generalize across a wide variety of occupations. Schmidt and Hunter (1981) stated, "Professionally developed cognitive ability tests are valid predictors of performance on the job and in training for all jobs" (p. 1128). This conclusion increases our reliance on measures of g to forecast job performance. However, as Guion (1998a) observed, the validity generalization conclusion about cognitive ability does not indicate that all cognitive tests are *equally* valid predictors across all jobs, all criteria, or all circumstances. Thus, while cognitive ability does predict job performance across many occupations, it is not comparably predictive in all cases. Even in lower-level jobs, however, cognitive ability still exhibits respectable levels of predictive validity.

Murphy (1997) concluded that the most important message of validity generalization research is that "validation studies based on small samples and unreliable measures are simply a bad idea" (p. 337). Such studies are more likely to mislead us into believing validity varies greatly across situations. The impact of validity generalization research has been to improve the way researchers design validation studies. When research is designed improperly, the conclusions will most likely be erroneous. Guion (1998a) believes that validity generalization is one of the major methodological advances in personnel selection research in the past 20 years. It has allowed personnel selection specialists to infer criterion-related evidence and therefore use cognitive ability tests in situations where a local validity study would have been infeasible and might therefore preclude the use of cognitive ability testing. Murphy (2000) stated:

> The greatest single contribution of validity generalization analyses to personnel selection is the demonstration that the results of empirical research can indeed be applied, with considerable success, to help solve important and practical problems. . . . One implication is that hiring organizations do not have to "reinvent the wheel" every time a new selection system is developed. Rather, they can often use the accumulated literature on the validity of selection tests to make reasonably accurate forecasts of how well particular tests or methods of assessment will work for them. (p. 204)

PERSONNEL SELECTION

personnel selection
the process of
determining those
applicants who are
selected for hire
versus those who are
rejected

Personnel selection is the process of identifying from the pool of recruited applicants those to whom a job will be offered. As long as there are fewer job openings than applicants, some applicants will be hired and some won't. Selection is the process of separating the selected from the rejected applicants. Ideally, the selected employees will be successful on the job and contribute to the welfare of the organization. Two major factors determine the quality of the newly selected employees and the degree to which they can affect the organization: the validity of the predictor and the selection ratio.

Predictor Validity. Figure 5–8 shows a predictor–criterion correlation of .80, which is reflected in the oval shape of the scatterplot of the predictor and criterion scores. Along the predictor axis is a vertical line—the **predictor cutoff**—that separates passing from failing applicants. People above the cutoff are accepted for hire; those below it are rejected. Also, observe the three horizontal lines. The solid line, representing the criterion performance of the entire group, cuts the entire distribution of scores in half. The dotted line, representing the criterion performance of the rejected group, is below the performance of the total group. Finally,

predictor cutoff
a score on a test that
differentiates those
who passed the test
from those who failed

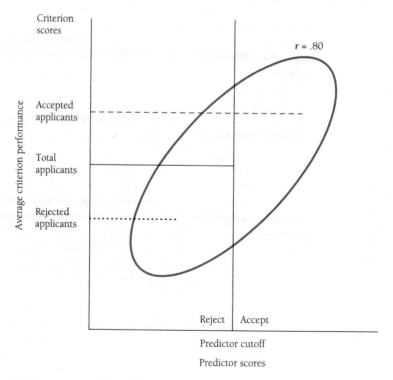

FIGURE 5–8 ■ Effect of a predictor with a high validity (*r* = .80) on test utility

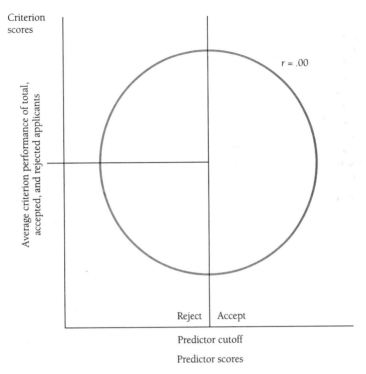

Criterion
scores

Average criterion performance of total,
accepted, and rejected applicants

r = .00

Reject | Accept

Predictor cutoff

Predictor scores

FIGURE 5–9 ■ **Effect of a predictor with no validity (*r* = .00) on test utility**

the dashed line, which is the average criterion performance of the accepted group, is above the performance of the total group. The people who would be expected to perform the best on the job fall above the predictor cutoff. In a simple and straightforward sense, that is what a valid predictor does in personnel selection: It identifies the more capable people from the total pool.

A different picture emerges for a predictor that has no correlation with the criterion, as shown in Figure 5–9. Again, the predictor cutoff separates those accepted from those rejected. This time, however, the three horizontal lines are all superimposed; that is, the criterion performance of the accepted group is no better than that of the rejected group, and both are the same as the performance of the total group. The value of the predictor is measured by the difference between the average performance of the accepted group and the average performance of the total group. As can be seen, these two values are the same, so their difference equals zero. In other words, predictors that have no validity also have no value.

On the basis of this example, we see a direct relationship between a predictor's value and its validity: The greater the validity of the predictor, the greater its value as measured by the increase in average criterion performance for the accepted group over that for the total group.

Selection Ratio.

Selection Ratio. A second factor that determines the value of a predictor is the selection ratio (SR). The **selection ratio** is defined as the number of job openings (*n*) divided by the number of job applicants (*N*):

$$SR = \frac{n}{N}$$ [Formula 5–12]

When the SR is equal to 1 (there are as many openings as there are applicants) or greater (there are more openings than applicants), the use of any selection device has little meaning. The company can use any applicant who walks through the door. But most often, there are more applicants than openings (the SR is somewhere between 0 and 1), and the SR is meaningful for personnel selection.

The effect of the SR on a predictor's value can be seen in Figures 5–10 and 5–11. Let us assume we have a validity coefficient of .80 and the selection ratio is .75, meaning we will hire three out of every four applicants. Figure 5–10 shows the predictor–criterion relationship, the predictor cutoff that results in accepting the top 75% of all applicants, and the respective average criterion performances of the total group and the accepted group. If a company hires the top 75%, the average criterion performance of that group is greater than that of the total group (which is weighted down by the bottom 25% of the applicants). Again, value is measured by this difference between average criterion scores. Furthermore, when the bottom

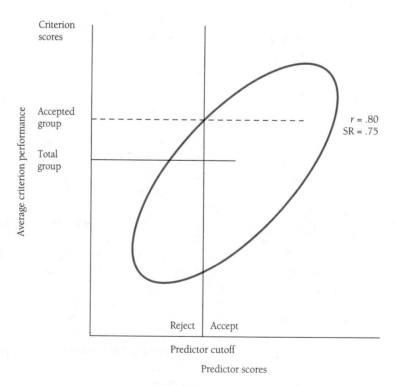

FIGURE 5–10 ■ Effect of a large selection ratio (SR = .75) on test utility

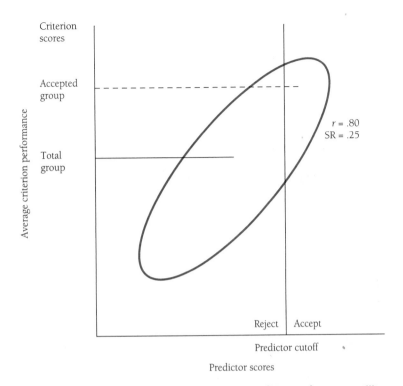

Criterion
scores

Accepted
group

Total
group

r = .80
SR = .25

Average criterion performance

Reject | Accept

Predictor cutoff

Predictor scores

FIGURE 5–11 ■ **Effect of a small selection ratio (SR = .25) on test utility**

25% is lopped off (the one applicant out of four who is not hired), the average criterion performance of the accepted group is greater than that of the total group.

In Figure 5–11 we have the same validity coefficient (*r* = .80), but this time the SR is .25; that is, out of every four applicants, we will hire only one. The figure shows the location of the predictor cutoff that results in hiring only the top 25% of all applicants and the average criterion performances of the total and accepted groups. The average criterion performance of the accepted group is not only above that of the total group as before, but the difference is also much greater. In other words, when only the top 25% are hired, their average criterion performance is greater than the performance of the top 75% of the applicants, and both of these values are greater than the average performance of the total group.

The relationship between the SR and the predictor's value should be clear: The smaller the SR, the greater the predictor's value. This should also make sense intuitively. The fussier we are in admitting people (that is, the smaller the selection ratio), the more likely it is that the people admitted (or hired) will be of the quality we desire. A third factor (albeit of lesser significance) also affects the value of a predictor in improving the quality of the workforce. It is called the **base rate**, defined as the percentage of current employees who are performing their jobs successfully. If a company has a base rate of 99% (that is, 99 out of every 100 employees perform their jobs successfully), it is unlikely that any new selection method can improve

base rate
the percentage of current employees in a job who are judged to be performing their jobs satisfactorily

upon this already near-ideal condition. If a company has a base rate of 100%, obviously no new selection system can improve upon a totally satisfactory work-force. The only "improvement" that might be attained with a new test is one that takes less time to administer or one that costs less (but still achieves the same degree of predictive accuracy).

Selection Decisions

As long as the predictor used for selection has less than perfect validity ($r = 1.00$), we will always make some errors in personnel selection. The goal is, of course, to make as few mistakes as possible. With the aid of the scatterplot, we can examine where the mistakes occur in making selection decisions.

Part (a) of Figure 5–12 shows a predictor–criterion relationship of about .80 where the criterion scores have been separated by a criterion cutoff. The criterion

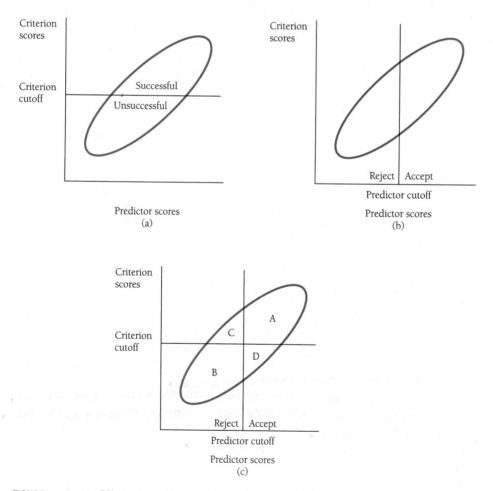

FIGURE 5–12 ■ Effect of establishing (a) criterion cutoff, (b) predictor cutoff, and (c) both cutoffs on a predictor–criterion scatterplot

cutoff is the point that separates successful (above) from unsuccessful (below) employees. Again, management decides what constitutes successful and unsuccessful performance (see Field Note 2). Part (b) shows the same predictor–criterion relationship, except this time the predictor scores have been separated by a predictor cutoff. The predictor cutoff is the point that separates accepted (right) from rejected (left) applicants. The score that constitutes passing the predictor test is determined by the selection ratio, cost factors, or occasionally law.[1] Part (c) shows the predictor–criterion relationship intersected by both cutoffs. Each of the resulting four sections of the scatterplot is identified by a letter representing a different group of people:

> *Section A:* Applicants who are above the predictor cutoff and above the criterion cutoff are called **true positives**. These are the people who we think will succeed on the job because they passed the predictor test, and who in fact turn out to be successful employees. This group represents a correct decision: We correctly decided to hire them.
>
> *Section B:* The people in this group are those who we thought would not succeed on the job because they failed the predictor test and who, if hired anyway, would have performed unsatisfactorily. This group represents a correct decision: We correctly predicted they would not succeed on the job. These people are **true negatives**.

true positives
a term to describe individuals who were correctly selected for hire because they became successful employees

true negatives
a term to describe individuals who were correctly rejected for employment because they would have been unsuccessful employees

---

[1]In some public-sector organizations (for example, state governments), the passing score for a test is determined by law. Usually a passing score is set at 70% correct.

FIELD NOTE 2   Raising the Bar

popular expression heard in organizations is the desire to "raise the bar"—meaning to elevate the organization's standards above current levels. If the organization believes it is necessary to have higher standards associated with its operations, then it will "raise the bar" regarding what it considers to be acceptable or satisfactory. A good way to visualize this metaphor (both literally and figuratively) is with regard to personnel selection. Assume an organization uses a test that manifests criterion-related validity to select employees for its sales jobs. Let us further assume that the standard of satisfactory performance (or the criterion cutoff) is selling $1,000,000 in products per year. Assume the minimum score that corresponds to that sales figure is 87 on the test. However, the company decides that $1,000,000 per year no longer represents acceptable job performance; it now

decides to elevate the sales standard to $1,250,000 per year. Think of the horizontal line reflecting the criterion cutoff in Figure 5–12(a) as the "bar." By "raising the bar," or elevating the minimum standard from $1,000,000 to $1,250,000, the organization seeks a higher level of job performance. To select employees who can attain this new higher level of job performance also entails raising the passing score on the test, for example, from 87 to 92. Because the test manifests criterion-related validity, the better people perform on the test, the better they perform on the job. To perform on the job at a level of $1,250,000 in sales per year now requires scoring 92 on the test. The expression "raising the bar" in this case refers to elevating the standard, first the criterion and then the concomitant effect of that decision on raising the standard passing score on the test.

false negatives
a term to describe
individuals who were
incorrectly rejected
for employment
because they would
have been successful
employees

false positives
a term to describe
individuals who were
incorrectly accepted
for employment
because they were
unsuccessful
employees

Section C: People who failed the predictor test (and are thus predicted not to succeed on the job) but who would have succeeded had they been given the chance are called **false negatives**. We have made a mistake in our decision-making process with these people. They would really turn out to be good employees, but we mistakenly decided they would not succeed. These are "the good ones we let get away."

Section D: The people who passed the predictor test (and are thus predicted to succeed on the job) but perform unsatisfactorily after being hired are called **false positives**. We have also erred with these people. They are really ineffective employees who should not have been hired, but we mistakenly thought they would succeed. They are "the bad ones we let in."

Positive/negative refers to the result of passing/failing the predictor test; *true/false* refers to the quality (good/bad) of our decision to hire the person. In personnel selection we want to minimize the number of false positives and false negatives.

If there is no difference between making false positive and false negative decisions (that is, letting a bad worker in is no worse than letting a good one get away), it does no good to "juggle" the predictor cutoff scores. By lowering the predictor cutoff in part (c) of Figure 5–12 (moving the line to the left), we *decrease* the size of section C, the false negatives. But by reducing the number of false negatives, we *increase* the space in section D, the false positives. The converse holds for raising the predictor cutoff (moving the line to the right). Furthermore, classification errors (false positives and false negatives) are also influenced by extreme base rates. For example, when the behavior being predicted occurs very rarely (as employees who will commit violent acts in the workplace), the differential likelihood of one type of error over the other is great (Martin & Terris, 1991). However, cutoff scores cannot be established solely for the purpose of minimizing false positives or false negatives. Cascio, Alexander, and Barrett (1988) indicated that there must be some rational relationship between the cutoff score and the purpose of the test. Issues pertaining to the cutoff score will be discussed in the next section.

For many years, employers were not indifferent between making false positive and false negative mistakes. Most employers preferred to let a good employee get away (in the belief that someone else who is good could be hired) rather than hire a bad worker. The cost of training, reduced efficiency, turnover, and so on made the false positive highly undesirable. Although most employers still want to avoid false positives, false negatives are also important. The applicant who fails the predictor test and sues the employer on the grounds of using unfair tests can be very expensive. If people do fail an employment test, employers want to be as sure as possible that they were not rejected due to unfair and discriminatory practices. Denying employment to a qualified applicant is tragic; denying employment to a qualified minority applicant can be both tragic and expensive. Both types of selection errors can be reduced by increasing the validity of the predictor test. The greater the validity of the predictor, the smaller the chance that people will be mistakenly classified.

Determination of the Cutoff Score

Have you ever wondered how certain cutoff or passing scores came to be? Why is 70% correct associated with passing a test (such as a driving test)? In educational institutions, why are the cutoffs of 90%, 80%, and 70% usually associated with the grades of A, B, and C, respectively? It has been reported that several thousand years ago a Chinese emperor decreed that 70% correct was needed to successfully pass a test. That 70% correct figure, or relatively close approximations, has been used throughout history in a wide range of assessment contexts as representing a standard to guide pass/fail decisions. While I/O psychologists are primarily limited to assessment decisions in employment contexts, we too have had to wrestle with issues pertaining to the determination of where to set the cutoff score, and how to interpret differences in test scores (e.g., Stricker, 2000).

Cascio, Alexander, and Barrett (1988) addressed the legal, psychometric, and professional issues associated with setting cutoff scores. As they reported, there is a wide variation regarding the appropriate standards to use in evaluating the suitability of established cutoff scores. In general, a cutoff score should normally be set to be reasonable and consistent with the expectations of acceptable job proficiency in the workplace. Also, the cutoff should be set at a point that selects employees who are capable of learning a job and performing it in a safe and efficient manner. Thus, undesirable selection consequences are associated with setting the cutoff score "too low" (an increase in false positive selection decisions) or "too high" (an increase in false negative selection decisions).

When there is criterion-related evidence of a test's validity, it is possible to demonstrate a direct correspondence between performance on the test and performance on the criterion, which aids in selecting a reasonable cutoff score. Take, for example, the case of predicting academic success in college. The criterion of academic success is college grade point average, and the criterion cutoff is a C average, or 2.0 on a 4.0 scale. That is, students who attain a grade point average of 2.0 or higher graduate, whereas those with a grade point average of less than 2.0 do not graduate from college. Furthermore, assume the selection (admission) test for entrance into the college is a 100-point test of cognitive ability. With a criterion-related validation paradigm, it is established that there is an empirical linkage between scores on the test and college grade point average. The statistical analysis of the scores reveals the relationship shown in Figure 5–13. Because a minimum grade point average of 2.0 is needed to graduate and there is a relationship between test scores and college grade point average, we can determine (through regression analysis) the exact test score associated with a predicted grade point average of 2.0. In this example, a test score of 50 is predictive of a grade point average of 2.0. Therefore, a score of 50 becomes the cutoff score on the cognitive ability test.

The task of determining a cutoff score is much more difficult when only content-related evidence of the validity of a given test is available. In such cases it is important to consider the level of ability associated with a certain test score that is judged suitable or relevant to job performance. However, obvious subjectivity is associated with such decisions. In general, there is no such thing as a single,

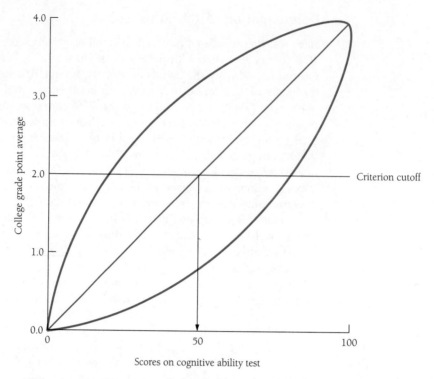

College grade point average (y-axis: 0.0, 1.0, 2.0, 3.0, 4.0)

Criterion cutoff

Scores on cognitive ability test (x-axis: 0, 50, 100)

FIGURE 5–13 ■ **Determining the cutoff score through a test's criterion-related validity**

uniform, correct cutoff score. Nor is there a single best method of setting cutoff scores for all situations. Cascio et al. (1988) made several suggestions regarding the setting of cutoff scores. Here are three:

- The process of setting a cutoff score should begin with a job analysis that identifies relative levels of proficiency on critical knowledge, skills, and abilities (KSAs).
- When possible, data on the actual relationship of test scores to criterion measures of job performance should be considered carefully.
- Cutoff scores should be set high enough to ensure that minimum standards of job performance are met.

In summarizing the process of determining a passing score, Ebel (1972) noted: "Anyone who expects to discover the 'real' passing score . . . is doomed to disappointment, for a 'real' passing score does not exist to be discovered. All any examining authority . . . can hope for, and all any of their examinees can ask, is that the basis for defining the passing score be defined clearly, and that the definition be as rational as possible" (p. 496).

In addition to measurement issues associated with determining a cutoff score, there are legal issues to consider. Many of these legal issues pertain to adverse impact. It will be recalled that adverse impact is determined by the "80% rule";

that is, adverse impact is said to exist if the selection ratio associated with a particular passing score on a test for one subgroup of job applicants is less than four-fifths (or 80%) of the selection ratio for the largest subgroup of job applicants. Suppose, for example, the passing score on a selection test results in a selection ratio of 70% for male applicants but only 40% for female applicants. Because 40% is less than four-fifths of 70% ($4/5 \times 70\% = 56\%$), that particular passing score has an adverse impact against female applicants. Some organizations mistakenly believed that they could avoid the issue of adverse impact by setting a cutoff score so low that virtually all of the applicants pass the test (i.e., the selection ratio is extremely high). The courts have recognized this procedure to be futile, for if an organization is unable to weed out those individuals who are minimally qualified, there is no justification for using the test in the first place. Setting a very low cutoff score tends, in the opinion of the courts, to destroy the credibility of the entire testing process.

banding
a method of interpreting test scores such that scores of different magnitude in a numeric range or band are regarded as being equivalent

An alternative to setting low cutoff scores is a procedure called **banding** (Murphy, Osten, & Myors, 1995). The traditional approach to personnel selection is to rank applicants on the basis of their test scores and select the applicants with the highest scores. An alternative approach involves test score banding, in which some differences in test scores are ignored, and individuals whose scores fall within the same band are selected on some basis other than the test score (such as gender or race), thereby eliminating or greatly reducing adverse impact. The width of the band is a function of the reliability of the test. Highly reliable tests produce relatively narrow bands, while less reliable tests produce wider test score bands. Thus, a one-point difference in test scores (e.g., a score of 90 versus 89) is not judged to be of sufficient magnitude to reflect a meaningful difference in the applicants' respective abilities. One then extends this logic to a two-point difference in test scores, a three-point difference, and so on. Eventually, a certain magnitude of differences in test scores *is* determined to reflect a meaningful difference in ability. It is at this point where this band ends, and other bands may be formed from the distribution of test scores.

Banding is a controversial interpretation of test scores. The fundamental purpose of banding is to meet the dual objectives of hiring qualified workers and promoting diversity within the workforce (Campion et al., 2001). Proponents of the method (e.g., Siskin, 1995; Zedeck, Outtz, Cascio, & Goldstein, 1995) argue that banding achieves the objectives of hiring able candidates while avoiding adverse impact. Critics of the method (e.g., Schmidt, 1991; Schmidt & Hunter, 1995) contend that banding leads to the conclusion that random selection (i.e., ignoring test scores altogether) is logically defensible, which is anathema to the classic principles of measurement. There is also concern (Gottfredson, 1994; Sackett & Wilk, 1994) that banding may lead to an overemphasis on certain types of selection errors relative to others. The ultimate resolution of the question on whether banding is advisable is likely to depend on the organization's values regarding social and economic issues. The controversy also underscores the point raised by Ebel (1972) that there is no one professionally agreed-upon method to determine passing scores on tests. Furthermore, sometimes selection decisions are made for reasons having little to do with passing scores (see Field Note 3).

FIELD NOTE 3 **Dirty Politics**

his chapter is devoted to explaining how personnel decisions are made. Many factors have been identified and explained, but one has been left out. I've rarely seen it discussed in any book or article on personnel selection, but (unfortunately) it is sometimes a critical, if not deciding, factor. It is called politics. Consider this experience I had.

I was hired for a very important consulting project: to pick the chief of police for a large city. The job has tremendous visibility, high influence, and great responsibility. I didn't want to "blow it" as the consultant. The city recruited applicants for the opening, and a total of 50 applicants met the minimum qualifications for consideration set by the city. I was handed the 50 applications and told to identify the best candidates in the applicant pool.

My first step was to evaluate each candidate in terms of education and experience using a weighted application-blank procedure. That got the applicant pool down to 25. These 25 quarter-finalists then had to submit written answers to three essay test questions about how they would handle some difficult police problems. These answers were evaluated, and the 15 best applicants proceeded to the semifinalist stage. Here the candidates took a series of personality inventories and intelligence tests. Based on those results, 10 finalists were selected and in turn were subjected to a lengthy oral interview. From all the assessment results, I rank ordered the 10 finalists and submitted the list to the city council, which had the judicial authority to approve the new chief of police. The candidate ranked first was from a different state; the candidate ranked second was the current assistant chief of police, the second in command. The candidate ranked first was clearly the best person for the job, far and away better than anyone else. I thought the city council (composed of seven people) had an easy job: to approve the top candidate as the new chief of police. It is here that politics came in, and it got rather dirty.

The assistant chief of police was a close friend of three city council members. They played cards together, as did their wives. From the very beginning, the three city council members had known the assistant chief of police would rank high in the selection process. In fact, nearly everyone had thought he would be the next chief of police. When I presented the city council with my list of the 10 candidates, things got very awkward: "Their man" was not first on

the list. The press followed the selection process carefully because it was a hot news item. The media announced the rank order of the 10 finalists. The public's general reaction was to have the city council approve the candidate who had been ranked first. But the head of the city council was not about to sell out his old friend.

The head of the city council (one of the three friends) then made this startling announcement. Because every rookie cop on the force dreams about one day rising to be the chief, to award the chief's job to an "outsider" (that is, a candidate not native to the city) would destroy the morale of the police force and take away every rookie's dream forever. Therefore, he was going to advise the city council to select as the next chief of police not the person ranked first (the outsider) but the person ranked second (the assistant chief, and his friend). This was the first time anyone had made any reference at all to the insider/outsider distinction. It was a new hurdle imposed at the eleventh hour as a means of bumping the top-ranked candidate from the list. Some members of the community howled in protest at this announcement, as did the media, declaring it was a "fix" to install the council's personal choice. All the three city council members had to do was convince a fourth member to vote for the second-ranked person and he would be in. In a highly electrified meeting of the city council in a council chamber jam-packed with reporters and camera crews, the city council members publicly cast their votes. By a 4–3 vote, the number-one-ranked candidate (the outsider) was approved and became the new chief of police.

I would like to believe the four "yes" votes came from people who recognized the quality of the top candidate, but I know better. Politics being what it is, strange things can happen. They voted the way they did not simply because they supported the stronger candidate but because they wanted to even a score with the three council members against whom they had held a grudge from a previous political episode. In short, the right decision was made, but for the wrong reason.

I wish to emphasize that there was absolutely nothing in my graduate training to prepare me for this experience. Similarly, there is no section of this book titled "How to Cope with Political Intrigue." But politics is a driving force in all organizations at all levels. Given this fact, sometimes I wonder how I/O psychologists accomplish as much as they do.

OVERVIEW OF PERSONNEL SELECTION

The foregoing discussion of personnel selection addressed several interrelated issues. These issues will be briefly reviewed and summarized to capture the empirical, social, and legal context in which personnel selection decisions are made.

The two goals of any personnel selection system are to hire qualified applicants and to fairly assess the ability of all applicants. The issue of "hiring qualified applicants" is subsumed under validity and reflects that there is a correspondence between how well people perform on a test and how well they perform on the job. The issue of "fairly assessing the ability of all applicants" is subsumed under test fairness and reflects that tests are not biased against selected groups of people in our society. Furthermore, these two goals are embedded not only in a social context, but also in a legal one. Laws have been passed to help achieve social goals, and personnel selection decisions are held to these legal standards.

What we have learned about the value of our tests is that they are very good. Schmidt and Hunter (1998) reviewed 85 years of research on many personnel selection methods. Their findings led them to conclude that general mental ability (g) was the single most valid predictor ($r = .51$) of job performance. When g was combined with a second predictor, the three best combinations in terms of maximizing validity (expressed as a multiple correlation) were g plus an integrity test (.65), g plus a structured interview (.63), and g plus a work sample test (.63). The vast majority of other predictor variables also increased the overall predictive accuracy of a selection system beyond g. Personnel selection tests are as accurate as diagnostic tests in medicine, but they are far from perfect. Accordingly, selection errors (i.e., false negatives and false positives) always occur. Do these errors occur evenly across all group of applicants, or do they fall disproportionately more on some groups than others? This is the subject of the fairness of our tests. The population of the United States is a melting pot or amalgam of a broad range of racial, ethnic, and religious groups. As a nation we want that diversity reflected in our workforce. The constant tension in our society regarding personnel selection revolves around meeting these two goals—selecting qualified applicants and achieving diversification in the workforce.

There is often a direct relationship between people's preference for one of these two goals and their stance on affirmative action. Over the past 40 years (since passage of the Civil Rights Act of 1964) the pendulum of the relative social preference for these two goals has swung back and forth. Sackett, Schmitt, Ellingson, and Kabin (2001) described what they call "high stakes testing," which reflects that important decisions in life (e.g., admission into a school or job) often depend upon the results of a test. Caught in the bind of using valid tests to make hiring decisions that produce adverse impact, some institutions have sought to use less valid tests that produce less adverse impact. However, doing so weakens the institution's commitment to selecting the most qualified applicant. Some universities have abandoned the use of tests (e.g., the SAT) in making admissions decisions to increase their chances of having diversified student populations. Sackett et al. believe the massive amount of research findings on psychological assessment reveals that it is not possible to simultaneously maximize the twin goals of having a highly diversified workforce (or student population) and selecting the most qualified applicants. Nevertheless, attempts continue to find ways to both maximize the quality of the selected workforce and reduce the level of adverse impact (e.g., Ryan, Ployart, & Friedel, 1998; De Corte, 1999).

The conflict between the pursuit of these two goals is addressed within the legal system. Ultimately the courts decide what is judged to be the fairest resolution of the conflict. In an employment context, the *Uniform Selection Guidelines* define the standards for validating tests. In reality, it is often very difficult for employers to validate tests because of the large sample sizes needed to do so accurately. Simply put, most organizations don't employ enough people in specific jobs to satisfy the conditions needed to conduct empirical validation research. The problem of insufficient sample sizes in validation has been a subject of great concern among employers (i.e., Hoffman, Holden, & Gale, 2000; Peterson, Wise, Arabian, & Hoffman, 2001). Psychologists have proposed the concept of validity generalization as a means of demonstrating the validity of tests, and the concept enjoys support among I/O psychologists. However, court cases are judged by legal standards, not psychological concepts, and it is a matter of debate whether the courts would fully accept validity generalization as a means of demonstrating the appropriateness of a personnel selection method. As Hoffman and McPhail (1998) stated, "Depending on the stringency with which the job analysis and investigation of fairness [of the *Guidelines*] are enforced, the use of validity generalization arguments in support of test use in a particular setting may or may not be acceptable. . . . (S)ole reliance on validity generalization to support test use is probably premature" (p. 990).

In conclusion, personnel selection is predicated upon a complex mix of technical and social factors embedded in a legal framework. I/O psychologists are called upon to render our best professional judgments to facilitate the flow of people into the workforce. Doing so involves being highly aware of the dual goals of any selection system, with the full realization that simultaneously achieving both goals is often very difficult. While our profession can contribute knowledge regarding the scientific and technical aspects of personnel selection, social preferences for what constitutes justice or fairness are at the core of the issues to be addressed.

TEST UTILITY AND ORGANIZATIONAL EFFICIENCY

It is important to remember that a human resources office is only one part of an organization. Each part must contribute to the organization's overall success. If the company is a profit-making firm (as many are) or just wants to improve its operating efficiency (as all organizations should), a basic question is how much improved personnel-selection techniques contribute to its overall profitability or efficiency. If more productive workers are hired as a result of a new selection technique, how much utility will they add to the company? The **utility** of a test literally refers to its value—where "value" is measured in monetary or economic terms. Several studies have shown just how much utility a valid testing program can provide.

Schmidt, Hunter, McKenzie, and Muldrow (1979) estimated the dollar value to the company of using a valid employee-selection program. They analyzed the job of a computer programmer. They asked supervisors to estimate the "worth" (in

utility
a concept reflecting the economic value of making personnel decisions

dollars) of good, average, and poor computer programmers. Supervisors considered such factors as work speed, number of errors, and so on. The authors used the responses along with the following information they had collected: (1) a certain test useful in hiring computer programmers had a validity of .76; (2) it cost $10 to administer the test to each applicant; (3) over 4,000 computer programmers were employed by the company (which was, in this case, the federal government); (4) over 600 new programmers were hired each year; and (5) once on the job, the average programmer stayed about ten years.

Using all this information, the authors compared the expected utility of the test with other tests that had been used in the past and had validities ranging from .00 to .50. They also examined the effect of various selection ratios ranging from .05 to .80. The dollar value to the government of using the more valid test was astonishing. When the previously used test was assumed to have a validity of .50 and the selection ratio was .80, the incremental gain in efficiency (that is, the result of hiring better-quality people) was $5.6 million in one year. This was the smallest dollar gain because the previous testing conditions were quite favorable ($r = .50$). Given the poorest testing condition (a previous test with no validity) and a selection ratio of .05, the dollar gain was $97.2 million in one year.

Keep in mind that these dollar values pertain to using just one test to hire people in one job in one organization for one year. If you extend these principles to testing in general across many jobs and many companies (and also across time), the dollar value extends into the billions. Other studies have shown that the utility of valid tests enhances efficiency by reducing turnover, training time, and accidents. The key element in improved utility is test validity. The impact of test validity on subsequent job performance is dramatic; there is no substitute for using "good" selection techniques.

The concept of assessing the dollar value of using valid selection tests has also prompted some admonitions. Cascio (1993) challenged the assumption that all applicants who are offered jobs accept and are hired. In practice, lower-scoring applicants must be accepted in place of higher-scoring applicants who decline offers of employment. When unemployment is low, companies may be forced to lower their minimum hiring requirements in order to fill vacancies. Lower hiring requirements mean higher selection ratios. Smith, Farr, and Schuler (1993) discussed the difference between considering utility for a particular organization versus for society as a whole. In a single organization, the worst candidates can be selected out. In the economy as a whole, this is only marginally possible. Even in times of high unemployment (10%), 90% of the economically active population are at work. Selection merely shifts the static pool of talent toward organizations that have high selection standards, without any net gain to the economy as a whole. The underlying significance of all these findings is that while utility is a valuable concept for guiding personnel decisions, a number of factors make utility estimates inexact, or at the least contingent upon complicating issues.

Hazer and Highhouse (1997) concluded that the complexity of utility analysis makes potential users of the method skeptical, and they recommended using the simplest approaches to the method. Although Carson, Becker, and Henderson (1998) were able to make some progress in getting managers to understand utility analysis, they concluded that the acceptability of the procedure to managers was "disappointingly low." Whyte and Latham (1997) referred to the reluctance of managers to understand and accept the rational, statistically based conclusions of the procedure as the "futility of utility analysis." Cronshaw (1997) suggested that the best feature of utility analysis might be its informational value provided by psychologists to assist managers in making personnel decisions. This use is in contrast to presenting utility analysis as a sales and marketing technique to persuade managers to adopt a particular selection method.

PLACEMENT AND CLASSIFICATION

The vast majority of research in personnel psychology is on selection, the process by which applicants are hired. Another personnel function (albeit less common) involves deciding which jobs people should be assigned to after they have been hired. This personnel function is called either *placement* or *classification,* depending on the basis for the assignment. In many cases selection and placement are not separate procedures. Usually people apply for certain fixed jobs. If they are hired, they fill the jobs they were applying for. However, in some organizations (and at certain times in our nation's history), decisions about selection and placement have to be made separately.

Placement and classification decisions are usually limited to large organizations that have two or more jobs an applicant could fill. It must be decided which job best matches the person's talents and abilities. A classic example is the military. Thousands of applicants used to be selected each year, either voluntarily or through the draft. The next question was where to assign them. Placement and classification procedures are designed to get the best match between people and jobs.

placement
the process of assigning individuals to jobs based on one test score

Placement differs from classification on the basis of the number of predictors used to make the job assignment. **Placement** involves allocating people to two or more groups (or jobs) on the basis of a single predictor score. Many junior high school students are placed into math classes on the basis of a math aptitude test.

classification
the process of assigning individuals to jobs based on two or more test scores

Classification involves allocating people to jobs on the basis of two or more valid predictor factors. For this reason, classification is more complex; however, it results in a better assignment of people to jobs than placement does. Classification uses smaller selection ratios than placement, which accounts for its greater utility. The reason classification is not always used instead of placement is that it is often difficult to find more than one valid predictor to use in assigning people to jobs. The military has been the object of most classification research. Military recruits take a battery of different tests covering such areas as intelligence, ability, and aptitude. On the basis of these scores, recruits are assigned to jobs in the infantry, medical corps, military intelligence, and so on. Other organizations that have to assign large numbers of people to large numbers of jobs also use this procedure. Given this constraint, relatively few companies need to use classification procedures.

Two issues are particularly important in placement and classification. The first issue is the nature of the jobs that need to be filled. Placement and classification decisions are easier when the jobs are very different. It is easier to decide whether a person should be assigned as a manager or a clerk than to decide between a secretary and a clerk. The manager and clerk jobs require different types of skills, whereas the secretary and clerk jobs have similar job requirements. These decisions become more complex when the jobs require successive operations (such as on an assembly line) or coordination among work units. In these cases, we are also concerned about how well all of the people in the work unit fit together to form a cohesive team.

The second issue is values. What is best in terms of satisfaction and productivity for the individual may not be best for the company, and vice versa. There can be conflicts between individuals and organizations about which values underlie manpower allocation decisions. Basically three strategies are possible; each reflects different values.

The *vocational guidance strategy* aims to maximize the values of the individual in terms of his or her wants or preferences. College students select their own majors based on the careers they wish to pursue. In other words, no college ever states that a student "must" major in a certain area; the decision is strictly an individual one.

The *pure selection strategy* maximizes organizational values. In this case only the best-qualified people are placed in a job. Although the placed people are indeed very good, the method is somewhat impractical. Large numbers of people might not be placed into any job because they are not the "best" of the applicants. The method is inherently wasteful because many applicants remain unemployed. Both the vocational guidance and pure selection strategies have weaknesses. While the vocational guidance method may work well in educational institutions, it does not work well in industry. If all the applicants wanted to be the company president, large numbers of jobs would go unfilled.

The *successive selection strategy* is a compromise between the two extremes. In this method all jobs are filled by at least minimally qualified people, and, given the available jobs, people are placed into those that will make the best use of their talents. Successive selection is a good compromise because the jobs get filled (the organization's needs are met) and the individuals get assigned to jobs for which they are suited (the individual's needs are met).

At one time, placement and classification were as important as (if not more so than) selection. During World War II, industry needed large numbers of people to produce war materiel. The question was not whether people would get a job but what kind of job they would fill. A similar situation occurred in the military as thousands of recruits were being inducted every month. It was of paramount importance to get the right people into the right jobs. Today the greatest amount of interest in classification continues to be in the military (Campbell, Harris, & Knapp, 2001). The problems and issues faced in the classification of military personnel are traditional, trying to balance the needs of the military with the abilities of the individual (Rosse, Campbell, & Peterson, 2001). Attending to the preferences and aspirations of individuals who enter the military is not a trivial matter, however. As Walker and Rumsey (2001) noted, military recruiters and guidance counselors must fill openings with candidates from an all-volunteer applicant pool. This contrasts with time in U.S. history when military service was compulsory.

Researchers interested in classification have addressed many of the same issues that are confronted in selection. For example, Bobko (1994) reported that the most vexing issues facing classification decisions revolve around values, such as attaining ethnic and gender balance versus maximizing performance. The relative importance of general mental ability (g) versus consideration of other factors as well is also a matter of debate in making classification decisions. Zeidner and Johnson (1994) believe other factors besides g must be considered in efficiently assigning individuals to jobs. In addition to cognitive ability, Alley (1994) recommended the assessment of personality, interests, and knowledge. The rationale behind placement and classification remains the same: Certain people will perform better in certain jobs than others. To this end, placement and classification are aimed at assigning people to jobs in which their predicted job performance will be the best.

CASE STUDY   ■   ## Just Give Me a Chance

Hugh Casey slumped at his desk, totally dejected. He just read the letter from Fulbright University informing him that his application for admission into the school of medicine had been rejected. It had been his dream since high school to become a doctor, and in particular to be a heart surgeon. Hugh had been an excellent student in high school and was admitted to the highly selective Seymour College despite achieving only a modest score on the college admission test. His interest in medicine was sparked when his father had triple-bypass heart surgery. The surgeon who performed the operation, Dr. Charles Dressen, was a friend of the family. Dr. Dressen had graduated from Fulbright University's medical school, which was nationally renowned for its high standards. Fulbright was the premier medical school in the region. Hugh wanted to emulate Dr. Dressen, to become a heart surgeon who saved lives, just as Dr. Dressen had saved his father's life. Fulbright was not only his first choice for medical school, it was his only choice. Hugh felt it almost was his destiny to graduate with a medical degree from Fulbright and follow in Dr. Dressen's footsteps.

At Seymour College, Hugh made the dean's list the previous four semesters. His overall grade point average was 3.60. After a rough freshman year, which many first-year students experience, he settled down and performed very well in the pre-med curriculum. At the start of his senior year he took the medical college admission test and did not score extremely well. It was the same story with the admissions test used by Seymour. He just didn't test well in standardized three-hour examinations. However, Hugh felt he had more than proved himself by his performance at Seymour. He believed that doing well over a four-year period should count more in his application to medical school than his performance in a three-hour test.

Furthermore, three professors at Seymour wrote what they said were very positive letters of recommendation on his behalf. Additionally, even Dr. Dressen, a graduate of Fulbright's medical school, wrote a letter to his alma mater in support of Hugh. Finally, Hugh traveled to Fulbright for an interview with the medical school's admissions committee. While he was admittedly nervous, Hugh felt the interview had gone very well. He was particularly delighted to tell the committee about his coming to know Dr. Dressen, and how Dr. Dressen had become his inspirational role model. Hugh got goose bumps when he walked through the halls of the medical school during his visit to Fulbright. He just knew Fulbright was the place for him.

Hugh stared at the rejection letter feeling devastated and angry. How could Fulbright do this to him? How did the admissions committee reach its decision? Hugh had earned excellent grades in high school and undergraduate school, and he just knew he would be equally good in medical school. Hugh reasoned their rejection implied they thought he wouldn't make it through medical school. What would he have to do to prove himself, to prove to the admissions committee he would be a successful medical school student and then a successful heart surgeon? Hugh decided he would ask Fulbright to admit him on a conditional basis, not even knowing whether the medical school had such a policy. He would agree to be evaluated after one year in medical school. If he were performing poorly, he would leave Fulbright and accept that the admissions committee's initial decision on his application was correct. But if he performed well in that year, then he would want to be fully admitted to the medical school and no longer be under their scrutiny. Hugh wanted to prove to himself, to Fulbright, and to the world that he would become as great a heart surgeon as Dr. Dressen. All he wanted was a chance.

Study Questions

1. Which type of selection mistake (false positive or false negative) do you think Fulbright wants to avoid? Why does Fulbright feel this way?
2. Do you believe Fulbright thinks Hugh won't be successful in medical school, and that is why they rejected his application? Or do you believe Fulbright probably concluded Hugh would be successful in medical school, but there were simply other candidates who had better credentials?
3. If organizations are faced with evaluating many qualified applicants and they have more qualified applicants than there are openings, should a personal experience of the type Hugh had with Dr. Dressen be a factor in determining admission? Why or why not?
4. If you were on the admissions committee at Fulbright, how would you make decisions about applicants in a way that is fair and reasonable to both the medical school and the applicants?
5. What do you think about Hugh's plea to be given a chance to prove himself? Is he unreasonable? Given the imperfect validity of selection methods, should organizations give applicants a chance to prove themselves in a trial period on the job (or in school)? Why or why not?

SUGGESTED INFOTRAC TOPICS

affirmative action

Civil Rights Act

recruitment

adverse impact

Americans with Disabilities Act

passing score

employment discrimination

preferential treatment

personnel selection

personnel classification

C H A P T E R 6

Training and Development

LEARNING OBJECTIVES

- ■ Explain the relationship between learning and task performance.
- ■ Understand the strategic value of training and development to organizations.
- ■ Describe the assessment of training needs through organizational, task, and person analysis.
- ■ Know the major methods of training and their associated strengths and weaknesses.
- ■ Describe the importance of cultural diversity training, sexual harassment training, and mentoring in management development.
- ■ Explain the evaluation of training and development programs.

Organizations select employees on the basis of their predicted likelihood of succeeding on the job. Although some employees are expected to perform their jobs well immediately upon hire, the vast majority of employees are granted time to grow into their new jobs. This growth process is expedited by formal organizational training processes designed for that purpose. Goldstein and Ford (2002) define **training** as "the systematic acquisition of skills, rules, concepts, or attitudes that result in improved performance in another environment" (p. 1).

training
the process through which the knowledge, skills, and abilities of employees are enhanced

Entry-level employees are hired on the basis of their ability to be successfully trained. The key qualification is their predicted capability to learn how to perform the job. At other job levels, the knowledge and skill demands of work are continually escalating. Martocchio and Baldwin (1997) expressed this perspective clearly: "In an age of technological innovation in which robots, telecommunications, artificial intelligence, software, and lasers perform routine tasks, worker skills soon become obsolete. Put bluntly, today's jobs require new and different skills at all levels of an organization" (p. 6). Accordingly, employees in these jobs must enhance their capabilities to perform their jobs satisfactorily. Training provides opportunities for people to enter the job market with needed talents and to perform in new functions.

I share the opinion of others that the relative importance of training to enhance job performance is increasing. A major reason for this emphasis is the growing reliance on computers in the conduct of work and its associated repercussions on the human requirements of work. Computer-assisted manufacturing and computer-assisted design are two major technological innovations in production. Manufacturing employees are now often expected to have some fluency in computer-based operations. Such talents can be acquired only through additional preparation for work.

The government has sponsored activities for providing better vocational training to high school students. The Secretary's Commission on Achieving Necessary Skills (SCANS) is a national project started in 1990 by the U.S. Department of Labor. The SCANS Commission contends that more than half of the people leaving high school do not have the knowledge or foundation required to find or hold a good job. SCANS identified a set of competencies common across a broad range of occupations. SCANS (1991) concluded that high school students need to learn not only basic academic skills but also workplace know-how skills. Its report defined workplace competencies (resources, interpersonal skills, information, systems, technology) and foundation skills (basic reading and writing skills, thinking skills, and personal qualities such as responsibility, self-esteem, sociability, self-management, and integrity) necessary for worker success. There are growing pressures in all areas of work to operate more efficiently (i.e., work procedures must require less time or produce less waste) and to enhance the overall quality of our goods and services. Such changes require enhanced organizational performance in increasingly competitive markets. Training, therefore, is a process to improve the fit between job demands and human attributes.

The title of this chapter is "Training and Development." Training and development are both processes for enhancing employee skills, but historically they have a somewhat different focus. The term *development* was generally reserved for skill-enhancing processes for managerial-level personnel, whereas *training* was generally applied to skill-enhancement processes in jobs lower in the organizational hierarchy. That is, managers (and above) are "developed"; nonmanagers are "trained." Today this distinction is not as meaningful as it once was. The need is acute for skill enhancement for employees at *all* organizational levels, and all employees should be engaged in the process of expanding their capabilities. Universities and colleges are no longer regarded as exclusive centers of "learning." Learning needs to occur in all organizations on a continuous basis. It might be advisable to think of your college years as "learning through education" and of your working years as "learning through training and development." Because some of the classic distinctions between training and development are still relevant, both processes will be described. Recognizing the need for skill enhancement and having the processes to do so are more important than the labels affixed to them.

LEARNING AND TASK PERFORMANCE

learning
the process by which change in knowledge or skills is acquired through education or experience

Learning can be defined as the process of encoding, retaining, and using information. This perspective of learning prompted Howell and Cooke (1989) to refer to individuals as "human information processors." The specific procedures by which we process information for both short-term and long-term use has been the subject of extensive research in cognitive psychology (Weiss, 1990). This section will examine some useful findings from this body of research that facilitate our understanding of how learning affects the training and development process.

Anderson (1985) suggested that skill acquisition be segmented into three phases: declarative knowledge, knowledge compilation, and procedural knowledge. **Declarative knowledge** is defined as knowledge about facts and things. The declarative knowledge of skill acquisition involves memorizing and reasoning processes that allow the individual to attain a basic understanding of a task. During this phase the individual may observe demonstrations of the task and learn task-sequencing rules. Individuals must devote nearly all of their attention to understanding and performing the task. Performance in the declarative knowledge stage is slow and error prone. Only after the person has acquired an adequate understanding of the task can he or she proceed to the second phase, the **knowledge compilation** phase.

declarative knowledge
a body of knowledge about facts and things

knowledge compilation
the body of knowledge acquired as a result of learning

During this second stage of skill acquisition, individuals integrate the sequences of cognitive and motor processes required to perform the task. Various methods for simplifying or streamlining the task are tried and evaluated. Performance then becomes faster and more accurate than in the declarative knowledge phase. The attentional demands on the individual are reduced as the task objectives and procedures are moved from short-term to long-term memory.

procedural knowledge
a body of knowledge about how to use information to address issues and solve problems.

Procedural knowledge is knowledge about how to perform various cognitive activities. This final phase of skill acquisition is reached when the individual has essentially automatized the skill and can perform the task efficiently with little attention (Kanfer & Ackerman, 1989). After considerable practice, the person can do the task with minimal impairment while devoting attention to other tasks.

Furthermore, Ackerman (1987) proposed that three major classes of abilities are critically important for performance in the three phases of skill acquisition. *General intellectual ability* is posited to be the most important factor in acquiring declarative knowledge. When the individual first confronts a novel task, the attentional demands are high. As he or she begins to understand the demands of the task and develops a performance strategy, the attentional demands decrease and the importance of intellectual ability for task performance is lessened.

As the individual moves along the skill acquisition curve from declarative to procedural phases, *perceptual speed abilities* become important. The individual develops a basic understanding of how to perform the task but seeks a more efficient method for accomplishing the task with minimal attentional effort. Perceptual speed abilities seem most critical for processing information faster or more efficiently at this phase.

Finally, as individuals move to the final phase of skill acquisition, their performance is limited by their level of *psychomotor ability.* "Thus individual differences in final, skilled performance are not necessarily determined by the same abilities that affect the initial level of task performance or the speed of skill acquisition" (Kanfer & Ackerman, 1989, p. 664). Psychomotor abilities (such as coordination) determine the final level of task performance in the procedural knowledge phase.

It should be evident based upon these research findings from cognitive psychology that there are complex relationships between individual abilities and phases of task performance. These findings offer an explanation of why some individuals may be quick to acquire minimal competency in a task, but do not subsequently develop a high degree of task proficiency. Alternatively, other individuals may initially learn a task slowly, but gradually develop a high level of task proficiency. Research by Morrison and Brantner (1992) revealed that learning the requirements of jobs in the military occurred in stages, with plateaus in learning followed by subsequent periods of growth. It appears that the relationship between learning and task performance is more complex than many researchers have believed. These findings bear not only on why certain individuals learn at different rates of speed but also on how training and development processes have to be targeted to enhance selected individual abilities. This conclusion was also supported by the research of Kluger and DeNisi (1996). Their meta-analysis of the effects of feedback on performance revealed that learning to perform tasks depends on a complex set of factors that affect gains in performance as well as the duration of the performance. The process of how we learn to perform tasks appears more complex than we have long believed.

Recently several major studies have been conducted that reveal the process by which learning occurs and transfers to the job. Ford and Kraiger (1995) identified three distinguishing characteristics between people who are regarded as experts on a topic and novices. The first is proceduralization and automaticity. Proceduralization refers to a set of conditional action rules—if Condition A exists, then Action B is needed. Automaticity refers to a state of rapid performance that requires little cognitive effort. Automaticity enables a person to accomplish a task without conscious monitoring and thus allows concurrent performance on additional tasks. Experts not only "know" things, but also know when that knowledge is applicable and when it should not be used. Novices may be equally competent at recalling specific information, but experts are much better at relating that information in cause-and-effect sequences. The second characteristic is mental models, which is the way knowledge is organized. The mental models of experts are qualitatively better because they contain more diagnostic cues for detecting meaningful patterns in learning. Experts have more complex knowledge structures, resulting in faster solution times. The third characteristic is meta-cognition. Meta-cognition is an individual's knowledge of and control over his or her cognitions. Experts have a greater understanding of the demands of a task and their own capabilities. Experts are more likely to discontinue a problem-solving strategy that would ultimately prove to be unsuccessful.

Ford et al. (1998) and Chen, Gully, Whiteman, and Kilcullen (2000) both described the importance of a task-specific individual attribute for learning. Chen et al. distinguish "trait-like" and "state-like" individual differences. Trait-like attributes include cognitive ability and personality, which are not specific to a certain task or situation and are stable over time. State-like attributes are task-specific. The most critical state-like attribute for learning is self-efficacy. **Self-efficacy** is the belief in one's capabilities to mobilize the motivation, cognitive resources, and courses of action needed to meet given situational demands. A sense of self-efficacy, tied to a specific task, is reflected in the belief that "I can do this" and a feeling of getting "up" for a task. Alternatively, low self-efficacy is reflected in the belief that there are some types of tasks (e.g., math problems) you are not good at. Ford et al. asserted it is important to develop a sense of self-efficacy in trainees—namely, that they feel confident and positive about being able to learn the material. The authors advise trainers to teach not only knowledge and skills but also other learning traits that facilitate the development of self-efficacy. Trainees should be given explicit instruction on meta-cognitive activities that increase self-efficacy, confidence, and the likelihood that newly learned skills will generalize beyond training.

> **self-efficacy**
> a sense of personal control and being able to master one's environment

In support of this position, Colquitt, LePine, and Noe (2000) conducted a meta-analysis of 20 years of research on training motivation. They empirically confirmed the importance of motivation to learn in successful training. General cognitive ability (g) correlated .76 with learning declarative knowledge, while the motivation to learn (as measured in part by self-efficacy) correlated .39 with declarative knowledge. When the two factors (g, the "can do" factor, and motivation to learn, the "will do" factor) were combined in a multiple regression analysis, they explained 63% (i.e., $R^2 = .63$) of the variance in learning declarative knowledge.

THE STRATEGIC VALUE OF TRAINING AND DEVELOPMENT

Organizations do not train and develop their employees for the sheer sake of doing so. Rather, it is because employees represent a competitive advantage that enhances organizational performance when managed wisely. The competitive strategy an organization uses is the means by which it competes for business in the marketplace. There is a linkage between the type of competitive strategy an organization uses and its training and development practices (Jackson & Schuler, 1990).

A **speed strategy** is designed to offer the customer a competitive value in terms of reduced time for products or services. A training practice that serves this strategic function emphasizes teamwork among employees and methods of stream-lined production, designed to reduce the time it takes to meet a customer's needs. An **innovation strategy** is used to develop products or services that differ from the competition. Its primary business objective is to offer something new and different. The focus of training in this context is on developing new products, services, or technologies. A **quality-enhancement strategy** is designed to provide value by offering a product or service of higher quality than that offered by competitors. To reach that objective, employees are trained to provide a consistently high level of service quality with no defects. Finally, the objective of a **cost-reduction strategy** is to gain a competitive advantage by being a low-cost provider of services. Under this business strategy, relatively little emphasis is placed on enhancing employee skills through training. Employees with higher skill levels warrant higher levels of compensation, which serves to increase costs. Since this is the opposite of the desired outcome, organizations that pursue cost-reduction strategies tend to invest few resources in enhancing the skills of their employees.

In reality most organizations adopt a mix of competitive business strategies. Accordingly, training and development activities are directed to meeting multiple objectives. The fast-food industry is a good example. However, you should note there is an overarching pattern between what organizations are trying to accomplish (i.e., their strategy for competing) and their philosophy toward training and development. Certain business strategies (innovation) are far more dependent on the quality of their employees than others (cost reduction). Therefore, the greatest advances and emphases in training technologies occur in those organizations that most highly value their human resources to sustain a competitive advantage.

speed strategy
a business strategy directed at providing customers with rapid delivery of products or services

innovation strategy
a business strategy directed at providing customers with innovative or novel products or services

quality-enhancement strategy
a business strategy directed at providing customers with high-quality products or services

cost-reduction strategy
a business strategy directed at providing customers with low-cost products or services

THE PRETRAINING ENVIRONMENT

Tannenbaum and Yukl (1992) reviewed evidence suggesting that events that take place prior to training (i.e., the pretraining environment) can influence the effectiveness of training. Management actions and decisions provide cues that signal employee motivation for training. Employees start to learn about the way training is viewed in the organization early in the socialization process and continue to gather information with each training activity they attend. Some actions signal to trainees whether training is important (e.g., supervisory and peer support). Other actions reveal to employees the amount of control, participation, or input they have in the training process (e.g., participation in needs assessment).

Cohen (1990) found that trainees with more supportive supervisors entered training with stronger beliefs that training would be useful. Supportive supervisors would discuss an upcoming training course with the employees, establish training goals, provide them release time to prepare, and generally encourage the employees. Baldwin and Magjuka (1991) found that trainees who entered training expecting some form of follow-up activity or assessment afterward reported stronger intentions to transfer what they learned back on the job. The fact that their supervisor would require them to prepare a posttraining report meant they were held accountable for their own learning and apparently conveyed the message that the training was important. The converse is also true. Mathieu, Tannenbaum, and Salas (1990) found that trainees who reported many limitations in their job (e.g., lack of time, equipment, and resources) entered training with lower motivation to learn. These trainees had little incentive to learn new skills in an environment where the skills could not be applied.

Another factor that defines the pretraining environment is trainee input and choice in training. Baldwin, Magjuka, and Loher (1991) found that allowing trainees to specify what training they wanted increased their motivation to learn, provided they were given the training of their choice. However, trainees who were allowed to choose a course but were then assigned to a different course were less motivated and learned less than the trainees who did not participate at all in the choice of training. Similarly, Quinones (1995) concluded that one way employee motivation in training can be enhanced is by giving individuals the chance to choose their own training programs and ensuring that these preferences are honored. Although giving employees a choice of training does enhance motivation, it doesn't guarantee that employees receive the most appropriate training, since they may not choose a training program that deals with their perceived weaknesses.

As Tannenbaum and Yukl (1992) articulated, several factors representative of the organizational environment in which training occurs bear directly on its effectiveness. Training does not occur in a vacuum; it is but a means to an end. Factors that strengthen the linkage between training and relevant outcomes can be as critical as the training itself.

ASSESSING TRAINING NEEDS

The entire personnel training process has a rational design (see Figure 6–1) as proposed by Goldstein and Ford (2002). The design of personnel training begins with an analysis of training needs and culminates in the assessment of training results. Important steps in between involve developing objectives, choosing methods, and designing an evaluation. Training directors must keep up with the current literature on training methods because previous successes or failures can help shape the selection or design of a training program. It is equally important to determine a means of evaluating the program before it is implemented; that is, evaluative criteria must be selected to serve as the program's scorecard. The bulk of this chapter will discuss the major steps in the design of personnel training.

The assessment of training needs is a classic three-step process: organizational analysis, task analysis, and person analysis.

Organizational Analysis

In the evolution of thinking on training and development, the early focus of organizational analysis was on factors that provided information about where and

Needs Assessment

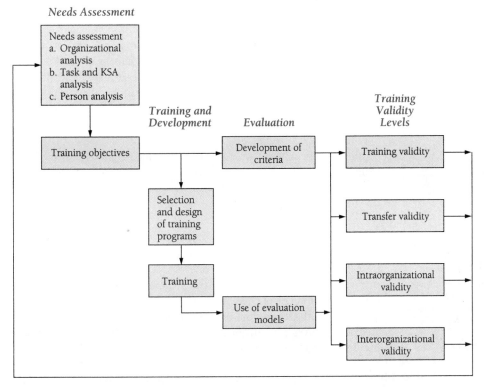

FIGURE 6–1 ■ **The classic training system**

SOURCE: Adapted from *Training in Organizations,* 4th ed., by I. L. Goldstein and J. K. Ford, p. 24. Copyright © 2002. Adapted with permission of Wadsworth, an imprint of the Wadsworth Group, a division of Thomson Learning.

organizational analysis
a phase of training needs analysis directed at determining whether training is a viable solution to organizational problems, and if so, where in the organization training should be directed

when training could be used in the organization. More contemporary thinking has transformed **organizational analysis** into an examination of systemwide components that determine whether the training program can produce behavior that will transfer to the organization. Organizational analysis should provide information on whether training is even necessary, whether training is the right approach, whether resources are available to develop and conduct training, and whether management and employees will support its implementation. Goldstein (1991) observed that persons who participate in training are faced with a problem: They are required to learn something in one environment—the training situation—and to use it in another—on the job. This problem requires an examination of the systemwide components of the organization that affect a trainee who arrives with newly learned skills. Training programs can fail because of organizational constraints that they were not intended to address. For example, trainees may learn a set of behaviors that are inconsistent with the way a manager prefers to have the job performed. The topic of transfer of training will be discussed in more detail later in the chapter.

Michalak (1981) believes trainers overemphasize the portion of training that deals with acquisition of skill and place too little emphasis on what happens afterward. Rouillier and Goldstein (1990) proposed the concept of an organizational

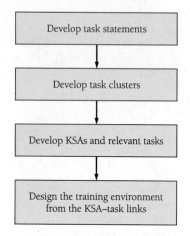

task analysis
a phase of training needs analysis directed at identifying which tasks in a job should be targeted for improved performance

transfer climate to explain why training can differ in its effectiveness. They determined that trainees demonstrated more transfer of skills from training to the job in organizational units where they were encouraged to use what they had learned and were rewarded for doing so. It was concluded that the transfer climate was a potentially powerful tool that organizations should consider to facilitate training transfer.

In summary, organizational analysis examines systemwide factors that facilitate or retard the transfer of skills from training to the job. Whatever factors facilitate the development of new skills in training should also be present on the job to facilitate maintenance of those skills.

Task Analysis

A **task analysis** is used to determine the training objectives that are related to the performance of particular activities or job operations. Information relevant to a task analysis could conceivably be taken from a job analysis, as discussed in Chapter 3. The task analysis results in a statement of the activities or work operations performed on the job and the conditions under which the job is performed. Task analysis involves four major steps as input for the design of training programs, as shown in Figure 6–2.

Development of Task Statements. The first step in task analysis is to completely specify the tasks performed on the job. Chapter 3 discussed task analysis. The goal is to write a sentence that conveys *what* the worker does, *how* the worker does it, to *whom* or *what,* and *why* the worker does it. The following two examples of task statements were provided by Goldstein (1991, p. 529):

> From the job of a secretary: "Sorts correspondence, forms, and reports to facilitate filing them alphabetically."

> From the job of a supervisor: "Inform next shift supervisor of departmental status through written reports so that the number of employees needed at each workstation can be determined."

It would not be unusual to have as many as 100 task statements written to describe the tasks performed in a job. The more varied the job, the greater the number of task statements.

Development of Task Clusters. In this step task statements are grouped into homogeneous clusters to make them more usable and manageable. Subject matter experts (SMEs) are responsible for sorting the task statements into meaningful categories that reflect important dimensions of work. For example, for the job of a secretary one cluster might pertain to tasks involving maintenance of records.

Knowledge, Skill, and Ability Analysis. A useful way for specifying the human capabilities needed to perform tasks is through knowledge, skills, and abilities (KSAs). *Knowledge* (K) refers to a body of information that, if applied, makes adequate job performance possible. *Skill* (S) refers to the capability to perform job operations with ease and precision and typically refers to psychomotor abilities. *Ability* (A) refers to cognitive and physical capabilities necessary to perform a job function. Most often, abilities require the application of knowledge. The purpose of this analysis is to establish the KSAs needed to perform particular tasks. Most often, persons who directly supervise the job being analyzed serve as SMEs to provide this information because they often think about what a job incumbent needs to know or what skills and abilities the incumbent needs in order to perform the tasks. Among the questions asked of SMEs to elicit KSA information are these:

- What are the characteristics of good and poor employees on [tasks in cluster]?
- Think of someone you know who is better than anyone else at [tasks in cluster]. What is the reason he or she does it so well?
- What does a person need to know in order to [tasks in cluster]?

The researcher then develops a linkage between the tasks performed on a job and the knowledge, skills, and abilities needed to perform them.

Development of Training Programs from the KSA–Task Links. The linkage between the KSAs and tasks provides the basis for directing training to enhance those KSAs that are critical to job performance. The relevance of the training for KSA enhancement is established through the linkage. Mager (1984) has recommended that after the tasks have been specified and the KSAs have been identified, effective behaviors should be established that indicate the task has been performed correctly. It can also be helpful to identify what ineffective behaviors are being exhibited when a task is performed incorrectly. It is to the advantage of both the trainer and trainee that there be agreement and understanding of those specific behaviors that must be acquired and the standards to which the trainee will be held. A task-based system of training needs cannot usually provide the entire foundation for a training system. If training were provided on the exact tasks that exist on the job, the training system would have very high **physical fidelity**. However, most training systems cannot achieve perfect physical fidelity. Therefore, training usually consists of some variation in the tasks or conditions found on the job. The goal is to design training in such a way that permits the calling forth of the skills and abilities that need to be learned. An effective training environment has high **psychological fidelity** in that it sets the stage for the trainee to learn the KSAs that will be applied on the job. Goldstein and Ford (2002) graphically depicted the linkages among KSAs, tasks, and training, as shown in Figure 6–3.

Person Analysis

Person analysis seeks to answer two questions: Who within the organization needs training, and what kind of training do they need? Most of the assessment questions for person analysis are based on the use of performance appraisal systems because it is necessary to appraise employees to determine their training needs. Performance appraisal is the subject of Chapter 7, and the issues inherent

---

physical fidelity
a concept from training pertaining to the degree of similarity between the physical characteristics of the training environment and the work environment

psychological fidelity
a concept from training pertaining to the degree of similarity between the knowledge, skills, and abilities (KSAs) learned in training and the KSAs needed to perform the job

person analysis
a phase of training needs analysis directed at identifying which individuals within an organization should receive training

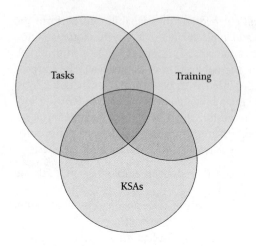

FIGURE 6–3 ■ **Psychological fidelity of training programs**

SOURCE: *Training in Organizations,* 4th ed., by I. L. Goldstein and J. K. Ford, p. 65. Adapted with permission of Wadsworth.

in its use will be discussed soon. For the moment, however, realize that performance appraisal is typically conducted for two reasons. One is to diagnose the employees' strengths and weaknesses as an aid in their development. The other reason is to evaluate the employees for the purpose of making administrative decisions, such as pay raises and promotions. Person analysis is predicated upon the diagnostic purpose of performance appraisal—to provide learning experiences helpful to the employee. To the extent that person analysis is directed solely to developmental issues and not administrative ones, there is usually little employee resistance to it. There is also some evidence that self-evaluations of ability (Mabe & West, 1982) may be of value in identifying individual training needs. Finally, it is possible to direct a person analysis of training needs not only to the present but also to the future in terms of what KSAs need to be learned to reach the next level of the organization. In this case, SMEs, usually upper-level managers, articulate the KSAs needed to perform future job requirements. An example (Frisch, 1998) of the results of a person analysis that shows the developmental needs of the employees is shown in Figure 6–4.

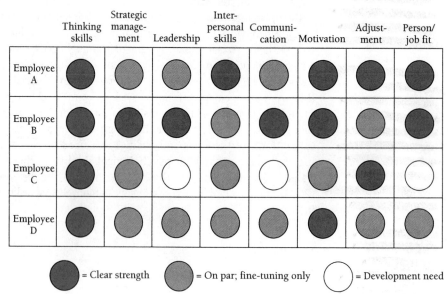

FIGURE 6–4 ■ **Results of person analysis**

SOURCE: Adapted from "Designing the Individual Assessment Process," by M. H. Frisch, 1999, in *Individual Psychological Assessment,* edited by R. Jeanneret and R. Silzer, San Francisco: Jossey-Bass.

In summary, Ostroff and Ford (1989) concluded that the classic tripartite approach of needs analysis (organization, task, and person) is entrenched in the literature as the basis upon which all subsequent training issues are based. While we still regard these three perspectives as a useful framework for determining training needs, the specific content of each continues to evolve over time. The most recent advances in training have demonstrated the critical importance of cues and consequences that promote the transfer of skills from training to the job. We are now more aware of the need to examine factors that enable training to be successfully applied to the job. These factors are just as critical as (if not more so than) the specific nature of the training.

METHODS AND TECHNIQUES OF TRAINING

After an organization determines its training needs and translates them into objectives, the next step is to design a training program to meet these objectives. This isn't an easy task because each training method has its own strengths, weaknesses, and costs. Ideally, we seek the "best" method—the one that meets our objectives in a cost-efficient manner. Many training methods are available. They can be classified in a number of ways, though probably the best way is according to where the training takes place.

On-Site Training Methods

on-site training methods
a set of training methods associated with individuals learning how to perform a job at the work site

As the name suggests, **on-site training methods** are conducted on the job site. On-site methods usually involve training in the total job, whereas off-site instruction often involves only part of the job.

On-the-Job Training. **On-the-job training** is perhaps the oldest and most common form of instruction. Usually no special equipment or space is needed because new employees are trained at the actual job location. The instructors are usually more established workers, and the employees learn by imitation. They watch an experienced worker perform a task and try to imitate the behavior. This method ensures one classic principle of training—transfer of training. Since the training content and location are the same as the job content, there are usually few problems with transfer.

on-the-job training
a method of learning a job by performing it at the work site

But on-the-job training has several limitations. It is often brief and poorly structured, often little more than "Watch me, and I'll show you how to do it." Also, many established workers find teaching a new recruit to be a nuisance, and the new employee may be pressured to master the task too quickly. On-the-job training is popular partly because it is so easy to administer. But since many new recruits make mistakes during training, the consequences of error must be evaluated.

job rotation
a method of learning two or more jobs by performing them in sequence

Job Rotation. **Job rotation** is a method of training in which workers rotate through a variety of jobs. They may be in the same job anywhere from a week to a year before they rotate. Job rotation is used with both blue-collar production

FRANK AND ERNEST by Bob Thaves

SOURCE: Reprinted by permission of Newspaper Enterprise Association, Inc.

workers and white-collar managers, and it has several organizational benefits. It acquaints workers with many jobs in a company and gives them the opportunity to learn by doing. Job rotation creates flexibility; during worker shortages, workers have the skills to step in and fill open slots. The method also provides new and different work on a systematic basis, giving employees a variety of experiences and challenges. Employees increase their flexibility and marketability because they can perform a wide array of tasks. Campion, Cheraskin, and Stevens (1994) found that job rotation was more common for employees early in their career rather than later. One explanation for this may be that younger employees are more interested in rotation because they see it as having greater value to their careers than do older employees. Another explanation is that senior management may view job rotation as a better investment when used with early-career employees (i.e., there is a bigger organizational payoff due to a longer payback period).

Like any training method, job rotation also has its limitations. If workers are paid on a piece-rate or commission basis, they can earn more money on some jobs and less on others; that is, due to individual differences, people are not equally suited for all jobs. Workers are then reluctant to rotate out of their "best" job. Job rotation also challenges one of the basic principles of personnel placement: Assign workers to jobs that best match their talents and interests. Some employees are wary of a training system that puts them in jobs they are not good at or do not like. Workers' willingness to learn new jobs is a key factor in the success of a job-rotation system.

apprentice system
a method of training in which the trainee (or apprentice) learns to perform a job by serving under the supervision of an experienced worker who provides guidance, direction, and support

Apprentice Training. The **apprentice system** is one of the oldest types of training programs. It is particularly common in the skilled trades. A new worker is "tutored" by an established worker for a long period (sometimes up to five years). The apprentice serves as an assistant and learns the craft by working with a fully skilled member of the trade called a *journeyman*. Apprenticeship programs are often used in the plumbing, carpentry, and electrical trades. At the end of the apprenticeship program, the person is "promoted" to journeyman. Training is intense, lengthy, and usually on a one-to-one basis. Generally one apprentice is assigned to one journeyman.

One weakness of the method is that the amount of time an apprenticeship lasts is predetermined by the members of the trade. Individual differences in learning time are generally not allowed for, so all apprentices have to work for a fixed time before they are upgraded. It has been argued that the apprentice program should be modified to allow more rapid rates of progress for faster learners.

Off–Site Training Methods

off-site training methods
a set of training methods associated with individuals learning how to perform a job at a place removed from the work site

There is more diversity in **off-site training methods,** and they differ markedly in their content and approach to learning. We will present two examples.

Lectures. As all students know, the lecture method is a popular form of instruction in educational institutions. It is also used in industry. With this method, large numbers of people can be taught at the same time; in that sense, it is quite cost efficient. However, the more diversified the audience, the more general the content usually becomes. Hence, its utility for imparting specialized knowledge is limited. A frequent reaction to a lecture on improving sales techniques is, "That idea sounds okay in principle, but how do I put it into operation in my company?" With a more homogeneous audience, a trainer (or teacher) can direct the lecture to specific topics and techniques, which is often more beneficial than using broad-based material. Thus, lectures are an effective way to train large numbers of people at once, particularly if they have a specific training need.

On the negative side, lectures are usually one-way communication. There is little chance for dialogue, questions, or discussions of individual problems and special interests. Trainees themselves have to understand and personalize the content of the lecture. Although popular, lecturing is not the best method to use for skill acquisition.

Audiovisual Material. Audiovisual material covers an array of training techniques, such as films, slides, and videotapes. It allows participants to see as well as hear, and it is usually good at capturing their interest. This underscores the importance of motivation and interest as necessary conditions for learning. After the initial expense of creating such a program, the cost of repeated use is usually minimal. Audiovisual material is particularly useful for training people in a work process or sequence. People can more readily trace the pattern of work flow when it is laid out graphically.

On the negative side, it is difficult to modify audiovisual material. If the training content changes, a whole new film has to be made. Slide presentations are more modifiable because the outdated slides can be replaced with more current ones. Also, the production cost of training films can be substantial. A half-hour color film with a soundtrack can cost $100,000 to produce. However, if the task or job is very important to the company, then the film is cost effective. With the aid of close-up images, stop action, slow motion, and instant replay, delicate and complex tasks can be broken down into discrete and understandable units.

computer-based training (CBT)
a method of training that utilizes computer technology to enhance the acquisition of knowledge and skills

Computer–Based Training

Computer-based training (CBT) is the most recently developed training method. CBT has exploded in its frequency of use with the advent of microcomputers and

CD-ROM technology. CBT has been used to teach a wide variety of skills, ranging from how to speak a foreign language to how to fly a helicopter. One CBT program begins by flashing the words "Good Morning." If the trainee fails to press a key that says "Good Morning" in five seconds, the computer flashes a second message: "What's the matter—kind of grumpy today?" All this has been programmed to make the trainee feel that the computer is not totally impersonal. This, in turn, is designed to enhance motivation.

The advantages of CBT include individualized instruction, reduced training time, and elimination of travel for training. Some advantages to the trainee are being able to work at his or her own pace, to begin and end a lesson when convenient, and to enter a program at his or her current level of achievement. Indeed, Dossett and Hulvershorn (1983) reported the average training time with CBT was less than with the lecture method for training military recruits in electronics. However, training program development lags far behind computer development, and programming for training purposes is still in its early stages. Goldstein (1991) also cautioned that successful learning in training systems is not guaranteed by the advent of a new, revolutionary technique alone. It requires careful needs assessment, careful design of training based on those needs, and evaluation efforts to fine-tune the program. Although much more work needs to be directed toward meeting the potential promise of this method, CBT appears to be a very viable technique for enhancing complex skills.

web-based training (WBT)
a method of training that utilizes the World Wide Web as the medium through which individuals acquire knowledge and skills

A derivative of CBT is **web-based training (WBT).** WBT is an innovative approach to distance learning (see Field Note 1) in which CBT is transformed by the technologies and methodologies of the World Wide Web. WBT presents live content in a structure that allows self-directed, self-paced instruction on any topic. WBT is designed for delivering training to individuals anywhere in the world at any time. Advances in computer network technology provide such features as 3-D

FIELD NOTE 1   Distance Learning

Computers are having a profound impact in the field of education at all levels. Children in the early grades of elementary school are learning how to operate a computer. High school graduates of today have a level of computer literacy that greatly exceeds that of college graduates less than a generation ago. Computer-aided instruction is changing the very nature of the educational process at the college level. An increasingly large number of students want a college education, yet they work during the day and may not have a university nearby that offers evening instruction. A solution to this problem is called *distance learning,* meaning that students can enroll in college courses yet not be physically present at the college. Course lectures offered at the college are videotaped and made available for viewing by students on their personal computers, at whatever time the students have available. Thus, a course can be offered without regard to time or space because computer technology delivers the course to the student. Some universities are now offering entire degree programs to students through this technology. A student can earn a degree from a university without ever having physically attended the university. Such degree programs are in their infancy, and they do require the technical support needed to make such an offering possible. However, their very existence attests to the power of the computer in being the dominant technological innovation in the past 50 years.

virtual reality, animation, interactions, chat and conferencing, and real-time audio and video. At the present time instructional designers and trainers are primarily in the developmental stages of learning how to write and produce WBT. WBT is expected to be the fastest growing arena for training over the next decade. The advantages of WBT include ease of delivery of training, rapid updating of content, less technical support compared with CBT, and flexibility of instructional mode. For example, people who prefer to learn visually can receive graphic illustrations to understand concepts and relationships. People who prefer to learn verbally can receive text and narration to enhance understanding.

The disadvantages of the WBT include its obvious reliance on computer technology such as icons, buttons, and navigational aids. People who are not comfortable with computer technology can be dissuaded from trying to use the method (i.e., they lack self-efficacy with regard to computers). WBT is still in its infancy as a training method, and we have no rigorous research to assess its value. However, as society becomes increasingly accustomed to using computers as part of daily living, WBT will play a greater role as an established training method.

Simulation

simulation
a training method whereby selected aspects of the work environment are replicated or modeled in a training environment

A **simulation** is designed to replicate the essential characteristics of the real world necessary to produce learning and transfer. The purpose of the simulation is to produce psychological fidelity—that is, to reproduce in the training tasks those KSAs necessary to perform the job. As Goldstein (1991) noted, one important aspect of simulators is that they permit the environment to be reproduced under the control of the trainer. Environments are created by careful design and planning to provide variation in the essential characteristics of the real situation. Simulation also permits the trainer to expand, compress, or repeat time, depending on the needs of the trainees. Nevertheless, simulations can still be effective with low physical fidelity (as a "mockup" or replica of the actual environment) if psychological fidelity is high.

The final job behavior to be learned is often too complex to be handled safely by a trainee in a real-life situation. Simulations permit the trainee to be introduced slowly to the essential task characteristics without danger to the trainee, coworkers, or expensive equipment. Simulations also permit the trainee to practice emergency procedures before being exposed to hazardous situations in real life. Flight simulations, for example, manifest a high degree of physical fidelity—the accurate representation of the real world of operational equipment. Flight simulations are so complex that nearly all aspects of flight training can be practiced on them. Goldberg, Mastaglio, and Johnson (1995) described the development of the Distributed Interactive Simulation (DIS) used by the military to train armored and mechanized infantry units in weapons systems. The DIS combines aviation, combat engineering, air defense, and field artillery simulators to represent the combined arms battlefield. DIS allows trainees in different geographical locations to interact in real time such that their actions are displayed to other trainees.

Many simulations use games. Business games train employees in certain skills. Within the rules of the game, participants try to meet the exercise's stated objectives. Business games can be used to train individuals or groups. Games have been developed to simulate interpersonal relations problems, financial and budgeting issues, and resource allocation decisions. Participants are told the objective (for example, to reach a certain profit level or to maximize financial return with a fixed budget), and then they are evaluated on whether they achieve it. Business games are popular for training managers and executives, particularly in financial matters.

A problem with simulations that have a game component is that the participants know it is only a game. Failing at a game is not the same as failing on the job. Participants sometimes behave differently than they would in real life. For example, in a marketing course a business game was created to simulate marketing a product. The class was divided into work teams. The team that achieved the greatest profit at the end of the semester received an award. Within the rules of the game (advertising the product, spending on research to improve the product, and so on), the "sales volume" of each work team was posted weekly. As the weeks went by, some work teams gradually fell behind in profit. So members of the losing teams began to take unnatural risks with their companies, risks they probably would not take on a real job. They did not care if their actions failed (the company went bankrupt) because it was only a game. And if their wild risks came through, they would receive the award. In this case, the game did not include some key elements of the job. Unlike a semester, the life span of a real company does not end on a predetermined date. The consequences of losing one's job (as well as destroying a company) are not the same as simply failing to win a class award. The best simulations are "best" because they provide for a high degree of transfer of training to the actual job. Needless to say, some simulations are easier than others to construct to maximize this transfer.

Role Playing. **Role playing** is a training method often aimed at enhancing either human relations skills or sales techniques. As opposed to programmed instruction, which is deliberately aimed at the individual, role playing involves many people. Role playing originally evolved out of clinical psychology, in which problems involving human interaction, real or imaginary, are presented and then spontaneously acted out. The enactment is normally followed by a discussion to determine what happened and why. Participants suggest how the problem could be handled more effectively in the future.

role playing
a training method directed primarily at enhancing interpersonal skills whereby training participants adopt various roles in a group exercise

Role playing is less tightly structured than acting, where performers have to say set lines on cue. Participants are assigned roles in the scenario to be enacted. For example, the scenario may be a department store. One person takes the role of an irate customer who is dissatisfied with a recently purchased product. A second person is assigned the role of the clerk who has to attend to the customer's complaint. Aside from observing some general guidelines about the product, the participants are free to act out their roles however they wish. Their performance is judged by people who do not have an active part in the role playing. In an educational setting the observers may be other students in the class; in a business setting they might be supervisors.

Many variations of role playing are possible. In some exercises participants repeat the enactment several times but switch roles. In other cases participants reverse the role they play in real life; for example, the supervisor plays a union representative. The role forces the participant to adopt the other side's position and then defend it.

Goldstein (1980) described advances with a technique called *behavioral role modeling,* which uses role playing as one of its parts. In behavioral role modeling, some points or principles to be stressed in training are identified. The participants watch a model use the principles (often on film) and then rehearse the principles by role playing. The trainer and other group members provide social reinforcement. Latham and Saari (1979) reported on a study of behavioral role modeling that was designed to increase interpersonal skills in dealing with employees. Forty first-line supervisors were assigned to either the modeling group or a control group, which received another form of training to meet the same objectives. Results showed that the supervisors trained with behavioral role modeling were more impressed with the training, scored higher on a learning test six months after training, and were judged to be performing better on the job a year later.

One advantage of role playing is that participants are highly active. By "putting their feet in the other person's shoes," participants gain some understanding of what it is like to experience interpersonal conflict in someone else's position. Interpersonal relations skills are among the more difficult ones to enhance with any training method. Despite legitimate criticism that some people put more emphasis on acting than problem solving, the method has been useful.

MANAGEMENT DEVELOPMENT ISSUES

management development
the process by which individuals serving in management or leadership positions are trained to better perform the job

Management development is the process by which individuals learn to perform effectively in managerial roles. Organizations are interested in management development in large part because they recognize its value as a strategy to improve organizational performance. Kotter (1988) argued the one factor that seems to distinguish excellent companies from others is the amount of time and energy spent in the planning, design, and execution of developmental activities. Baldwin and Padgett (1993) estimated that over 90% of organizations worldwide engage in some form of development activities for managers. Tharenou (1997) reported that many managers seek advancement continually, not just until they reach a particular level in the organization. For them, successful development activities are particularly critical because they contribute greatly to what Tharenou called "career velocity." The literature on management development tends to focus on major issues or processes managers address as part of their professional maturation. In contrast, the literature on personnel training often tends to be more concerned with specific methods or techniques of training. However, the larger systems issues of needs assessment, skill enhancement, and transfer are equally applicable to both training and development.

Whetten and Cameron (1991) identified critical management skills and linked them to successful performance on the job. Three *personal skills* were noted: developing self-awareness, managing stress, and solving problems creatively. Four *interpersonal skills* were also identified: communicating supportively, gaining power and influence, motivating others, and managing conflict. The authors pointed out that these skills overlap and managers must draw upon all of them to perform effectively in a managerial role. Yukl, Wall, and Lepsinger (1990) developed a survey that assesses managerial practices based upon these skills. Subordinates and peers describe how much a manager uses these practices and make recommendations on whether the manager's behavioral style should be modified. Managers compare this feedback with their own self-assessment of behavior. Ratings of the importance of these behaviors for the manager's job provide additional information for identifying relevant developmental activities. Lombardo and McCauley (1988) proposed that underutilization of selected managerial skills and practices contributes to *derailment*. Derailment occurs when a manager who has been judged to have the ability to go higher fails to live up to his or her full potential and is fired, demoted, or plateaued below the expected level of achievement.

There is also considerable interest in gender differences in management development (Ragins & Sundstrom, 1989). Many organizations have created a male managerial hierarchy—one composed predominantly of men—which is thought to be a critical structural feature influencing the processes that affect men's and women's managerial advancement. There is evidence that a "glass ceiling" exists for women in their professional advancement through an organization. This transparent barrier is fostered by organizations that regulate access to developmental experiences as part of a pattern that grooms men for powerful positions. Lyness and Thompson (1997) found that even women who "broke through" the glass ceiling into the highest-level executive jobs reported having less authority, fewer stock options, and less international mobility than men. Tharenou, Latimer, and Conroy (1994) reported that developmental activities had a more positive influence on the managerial advancement of men than of women. Men were more likely than women to attend company-sponsored training courses, especially between the ages of 35 and 54. Development may lead to more advancement for men than for women because men are thought to gain more skills and knowledge from professional development than women do. In turn, men gain skill and knowledge that are more relevant to managerial work, thus becoming better prepared for advancement than women. The authors believe organizations need to ensure that women's contributions of education, work experience, and development are perceived as similarly conducive to productivity as men's, and thus are rewarded with similar advancement.

Three issues of contemporary relevance to the management development process are deserving of discussion: cultural diversity, sexual harassment, and mentoring.

Cultural Diversity Training

Triandis, Kurowski, and Gelfand (1994) offered an insightful analysis of the consequences of our nation's increasing cultural heterogeneity or diversity. However, dealing with diversity is not a novel issue in this country; cultural diversity has characterized this nation since its founding. What is novel about modern diversity is that managers are encountering it more frequently both within their organization (their employees) and among their customers. Changes in the composition of the workforce are driven by labor and market trends, legislation, and demographics. For example, Brief and Barsky (2000) reported that 45% of all net additions to the labor force in the 1990s were non-White and almost two-thirds were women. Multinational companies increasingly have multinational management, with some top managers who come from the companies' homelands and some from other countries. The composition of the workforce is also changing in the United States at the entry level. White men, who traditionally have constituted the majority of new entrants into the labor force, are projected to be a minority among the new entrants in the 21st century (Goldstein & Gilliam, 1990). Likewise, the Americans with Disabilities Act may lead to an increase in the percentages of disabled workers. However, Baldridge and Veiga (2001) found that people with disabilities have been reluctant to make requests for assistance because of their belief that organizations will be slow to accommodate them. The authors believe organizations must create a supportive environment for people with disabilities, rather than just engage in legal compliance to avoid monetary penalties. Colella (2001) reported that some coworkers react negatively to requests by disabled people for accommodations, which may further decrease the likelihood of a request. Indeed, the professional golfer Casey Martin reported being rebuked by his fellow golfers for requesting to use a golf cart to accommodate the disability in his legs.

Historically, there have been two ways to approach cultural differences. One is the color-blind perspective (Ferdman, 1992), which advocates ignoring cultural differences. Its basic rationale is thus "Do not pay attention to differences." The second approach accepts the presence of cultural differences and proposes to improve relationships by teaching people from each culture to appreciate the perspectives of people from other cultures. Triandis (1995) classified these two approaches as the **melting pot conception,** where cultural differences are homogenized, versus the **multicultural conception,** which assumes each cultural group should maintain as much of its original culture as possible while contributing to the smooth functioning of society. Research indicates that both perspectives have merit, and an optimal approach may emphasize both what people universally have in common and what makes them different. Triandis et al. (1994) suggested that approximately half of all psychological theories are universally relevant and the other half are the products of Western cultures. The task of cross-cultural psychology is to sort out the two halves.

Triandis (1975) suggested that the ideal problem-solving group is diverse, with members who have been trained to understand the others' points of view. However, diversity has a price: Communication becomes more difficult and interpersonal attraction is likely to be lower. To increase interpersonal attraction, Triandis recommended individuals be trained to view the behavior of members of other cultures as functional and reasonable within a particular environment. That is, to be able to say, "If I faced that set of circumstances, I would also behave that way." Such a process produces a sense of *similarity* across culturally diverse people, where the psychological processes of adoption are similar but the situations are different. When similarities are emphasized, attraction can be created in two ways: by showing that there are universals and by indicating that the existing cultural differences "make sense." Despite sincere attempts to understand the underlying causes of why people react negatively to cultural differences, Brief and Hayes

melting pot conception
a concept behind facilitating relationships among people of different cultures based on them relinquishing their individual cultural identities to form a new, unified culture as a means of coexisting

multicultural conception
a concept behind facilitating relationships among people of different cultures based on them retaining their individual cultural identities as a means of coexisting

(1997) regard racial discrimination as an enduring employment problem in the United States. They believe manifestations of racism have evolved over the past 50 years from the blatant to the subtle, but racism continues to exist.

Schneider, Hitlan, and Radhakrishnan (2000) developed a survey to measure racial and ethnic harassment. The survey includes questions pertaining to whether a person has encountered the following types of experiences:

- Someone at work makes derogatory comments, jokes, or slurs about your ethnicity.
- Someone at work excludes you from social interactions during or after work because of your ethnicity.
- Someone at work fails to give you information you need to do your job because of your ethnicity.
- Someone at work makes you feel as if you have to give up your ethnic identity to get along at work.

The goal of diversity training programs is to reduce barriers, such as values, stereotypes, and managerial practices, that constrain employee contributions to organizational goals and personal development (Noe & Ford, 1992). Diversity training programs differ on whether attitude or behavior change is emphasized to achieve these goals.

Attitude change programs focus on an awareness of diversity and the personal factors that most strongly influence our behavior toward others. Many programs involve self-assessment of perceived similarities and differences between different groups of employees, and attributions for success and failure of minority employees. These programs may use videotapes and experiential exercises to increase employees' awareness of the negative effects of stereotypes on minority group members. It is assumed that this heightened awareness will result eventually in behavior change.

The *behavior change* approach emphasizes changing organizational policies and individual behaviors that limit employee productivity. Programs with the behavioral emphasis identify incidents that discourage employees from working to their potential. Perceptions regarding the degree to which the work environment and management practices are congruent with a philosophy of valuing differences among employees are often collected. Specific training programs are then directed at developing employee skills that are needed to create a workplace that supports diversity.

Rynes and Rosen (1995) conducted a major survey of human resource professionals about diversity issues in their organizations. Organizations that had successfully adopted diversity programs had strong support from top management and placed a high priority on diversity relative to other competing organizational objectives. Diversity training success was also associated with mandatory attendance for all managers, long-term evaluation of training results, managerial rewards for increasing diversity, and a broad inclusionary definition of what is meant by "diversity" in the organization. However, some critics believe that diversity training has been largely unsuccessful. Hemphill and Haines (1997) cited that Texaco paid a record settlement of $176 million in a racial discrimination suit, and the U.S. Army has been confronted with potential sexual harassment claims from over

5,000 women. Both of these organizations had previously implemented diversity training. The authors believe organizations can do little to force changes in how people feel about each other, but organizations should adopt a zero-tolerance policy for discrimination and harassment practices.

Ronen (1989) discussed a more specialized area of cultural diversity training—the individual assigned to an international position. The need for such training has grown for two reasons. The first is the increase in the number of individuals so assigned, and the second is the relatively high failure rate of managers in such assignments. Spreitzer, McCall, and Mahoney (1997) developed an assessment for the early identification of international executive potential. It is based on rating aspiring international executives on selected competencies and the ability to learn from experience. Dotlich (1982) reported the findings from a survey of U.S. managers who lived or traveled abroad on the reasons for difficulties in overseas assignments. The following two quotations were representative of the findings:

> Time as a cultural value is something which we don't understand until we are in another culture. It took me six months to accept the fact that my staff meeting wouldn't begin on time and more often would start 30 minutes late and nobody would be bothered but me.

> Communication can be a problem. I had to learn to speak at half the speed I normally talk. (p. 28)

Another problem area is family members adjusting to a different physical or cultural environment. Arthur and Bennett (1995) determined from a study of internationally assigned managers from many countries that family support is the most critical factor in accounting for successful international assignments. The results suggest the advisability of including one's spouse and other family members in cross-cultural training and, if feasible, sending them overseas to preview their new environment. Shaffer and Harrison (2001) studied the spouses (typically women) who accompany their partners in international assignments. The authors concluded that for the most part international organizations do relatively little to help the spouses understand the needs of their expatriot spouses and to help the spouses adjust to new cultures. The following discussion by an expatriot spouse depicts the spouse as an organizational asset and highlights the costs associated with being an expatriot spouse:

> The very worst aspect of being an expat spouse is that one is completely disenfranchised. You become a nonperson. For 30 years, I have moved my kids, my pets, my household, trailing after my husband to places where there are few other expats, no work permit for me, therefore, no job opportunities. I could not get money (he gets it from the company), am at the beck and call as a "corporate wife" (unpaid!), could not leave a country without permits or air tickets. I've moved to lands where no one spoke English (where we were living), many foods were unavailable, *very* poor health facilities, electricity and water would go off for hours or days. The few friends one might make leave for long vacations and leave permanently. One spends one's time volunteering, fund raising for the destitute, etc., and filled with guilt! After all, you *do* have water which occasionally comes out of a tap—you didn't have to walk one mile each way for it—you are not watching your child die of starvation or for lack of a measles shot. So you spend your time slogging away to help a few when thousands need it. The plusses?

Drop me down in any culture, any language, unknown script—I am not afraid and neither are my now adult kids. I've learned to live without a support system of people who care about me. I've also learned that the world is peopled with lovely people. Sound bitter? You bet! I'm 52 soon—still have no college degree, no equity, no profession, no home (not even a house of my own). The people I care about are thousands of miles away. I once told a banker at one of the hundreds of corporate functions I attend and organize when asked what I do: "Oh, I move!" That's my job—unpaid. It's a shame my husband's company doesn't pay wives for all the "corporate" work we do—I'd be worth a fortune paid by the hour! (Shaffer & Harrison, p. 252)

Ronen identified four abilities considered critical for successful overseas assignments: tolerance for ambiguity, behavioral flexibility, nonjudgmentalism, and cultural empathy. The selection decision for overseas assignments is usually predicated upon the candidate's technical skills in applied functional areas (such as engineering or finance), but usually the reasons for a failed assignment have little to do with deficient technical skills. Major areas recommended for enhancement through training include information about the host country's geography, political system, history, religion, and generalized customs and habits. It is also recommended that managers learn to understand their own listening ability, reaction to feedback, and predisposition toward judgmental attitudes. Black and Mendenhall (1990) suggested that cultural novelty, expected degree of interpersonal interaction in the foreign assignment, and the novelty of new jobs and tasks are situational factors that likely influence the appropriateness and effectiveness of cross-cultural training.

Hesketh and Bochner (1994) proposed that the process of cultural adjustment be viewed as a special case of being socially skilled, reflecting the more basic principle that when individuals interact, they are engaged in a mutually organized, skilled performance. Social competence is the ability to produce the desired effects on others in social situations. Thus, individuals who are socially inadequate have not mastered the conventions of their society, either because they are unaware of the prevailing rules of social behavior or because they are unwilling to abide by them. Therefore, success in international assignments is posited to be a function of one's capacity and willingness to learn new social skills. Many specific work-related social skills and attitudes are highly culture-based. For example, Adler, Doktor, and Redding (1986) reported the Japanese prefer to go from the general to the specific, whereas Westerners like to get the details out of the way before tackling the larger issues. Other cultural differences exist with regard to strategies of conflict resolution, bargaining style, and cognitive information processing. Thus, training in social skills can be developed to teach specific culturally relevant behaviors designed to enhance the person's repertoire.

The current emphasis on cultural diversity training seems attributable in part to two general factors. The first is the increasing awareness of our "differentness" as people, and the second is the reality that we all have to get along with one another to have an amicable and productive society. In a sense it is somewhat of a paradox—seeking ways to find similarities among differences. I believe the importance of addressing this paradox will intensify in the years to come, a conclusion supported by Bhawuk and Brislin (2000).

Sexual Harassment Training

sexual harassment
unwelcome sexual
advances, requests for
sexual favors, and
other verbal or
physical conduct of a
sexual nature when
such conduct creates
a hostile or offensive
work environment

**quid pro quo
harassment**
a legal classification
of harassment in
which specified orga-
nizational rewards are
offered in exchange
for sexual favors

**hostile environment
harassment**
a legal classification
of sexual harassment
in which individuals
regard conditions in
the workplace as
offensive

The Equal Employment Opportunity Commission (EEOC) (1980) defined **sexual harassment** as

> unwelcome sexual advances, requests for sexual favors, and other verbal or phys-
> ical conduct of a sexual nature when submission to or rejection of this conduct
> explicitly or implicitly affects an individual's employment, unreasonably interferes
> with an individual's work performance, or creates an intimidating, hostile, or
> offensive work environment.

In this definition are the two kinds of sexual harassment actionable under federal law: *quid pro quo* sexual harassment and hostile environment harassment. **Quid pro quo harassment** occurs when sexual compliance is made mandatory for promotion, favors, or job retention. **Hostile environment harassment** is less blatant than *quid pro quo* and refers to conditions in the workplace that are regarded as offensive, such as unwanted touching and off-color jokes. In the vast majority of cases on this issue, women rather than men have suffered from sexual abuse at work. Such abuse may constitute illegal sex discrimination in the form of unequal treatment on the job. More than 18,000 complaints were filed with the EEOC in 2000, and the cost of investigating and resolving claims of sexual harassment is in the millions of dollars annually. Sexual harassment is not so much about sex as about power and the power differential between managers and employees (Cleveland & Kerst, 1993). Organizations are devoting considerable training resources to deter the likelihood of sexual harassment in the workplace.

Much of the research on sexual harassment has focused on how men and women define it and whether men's definitions differ markedly from women's. Gutek (1985) reported that women consistently were more likely than men to label a behavior as sexual harassment. Men and women tend to disagree on whether uninvited sexual teasing, jokes, remarks, or questions represent sexual harassment. Generally, as an act becomes more overt and coercive, women and men are more likely to agree that it is sexual harassment (Wiener & Hurt, 2000). Nevertheless, Schneider, Swan, and Fitzgerald (1997) found that low-level but frequent types of sexual harassment can have significant negative consequences for working women. Wasti et al. (2000) found that the detrimental outcomes of sexual harassment experienced by U.S. women generalized to a sample of women in Turkey.

Tangri, Burt, and Johnson (1982) described three models used to explain sexual harassment. The *natural/biological model* asserts that sexual harassment is simply natural sexual attraction between two people. The *organizational model* argues that sexual harassment is the result of certain opportunities created by the organizational climate, hierarchy, and specific authority relationships. The *sociocultural model* states that sexual harassment reflects the larger society's differential distribution of power and status between the genders. A test of these models revealed that all three approaches have some empirical support, which leads the authors to conclude there is no single explanation for sexual harassment. Fitzgerald, Drasgow, Hulin, Gelfand, and Magley (1997) found that sexual harassment was associated with female perceptions of the risk of reporting harassing events, the likelihood of being taken seriously, and the probability of sanctions against the alleged harasser. They also demonstrated that gender composition (ratio of men to women in a work group) is associated with sexual harassment.

Physical attractiveness has also been examined as a factor influencing third-party judgments of sexual harassment. Quinn and Lees (1984) asserted that personnel departments are less likely to take seriously sexual harassment complaints from unattractive female employees than from attractive women. Castellow, Wuensch, and Moore (1990) found that female sexual harassment victims are more likely to win lawsuits against their harassers when the victims are attractive and the harassers are unattractive.

Training in the area of sexual harassment frequently consists of teaching sensitivity to other people's values and preferences. It should not be assumed, for example, that people prefer to be touched (as on the hand or arm) when engaged in conversation. There are also broad cultural differences in the degree to which physical contact between people is regarded as acceptable. People differ in the degree to which verbal statements, including profanity, are considered offensive or inappropriate. One organizational response to fear of allegations of sexual harassment is to engage in highly defensive behavior, including having a third party present when one talks with a member of the opposite sex and interacting with people only in an open, highly visible work area. Other examples are prohibiting any comments regarding physical appearance (e.g., "Those are attractive shoes you are wearing") and the reciprocal exchange of gifts among employees on special occasions (e.g., flowers or cards on birthdays). Some defensive behaviors are more personalized, such as a male manager refusing to mentor any female protégé. Lobel (1993) questioned the long-term benefit of these types of prohibitions on male/female relationships in the workplace. In an attempt to limit opportunities for potentially sexual harassing behaviors to occur, we may also be precluding opportunities for beneficial across-gender relationships to develop. Furthermore, the workplace can be a setting where people meet and mutually enter into a romantic relationship. Pierce, Byrne, and Aguinis (1996) proposed an explanation of workplace romance. They asserted that while a successful relationship can be beneficial to both parties, the breakup of a relationship can lead to charges of sexual harassment. Thus, allegations of sexual harassment can be spawned by what were once mutually positive experiences.

mentor
typically an older and more experienced person who helps to professionally develop and train a less experienced person

protégé
typically a younger and less experienced person who is helped and developed in job training by a more experienced person

Mentoring

A method growing in use for facilitating management development is mentoring. **Mentors** are older, more experienced individuals who advise and shepherd new people (**protégés**) in the formative years of their careers. Mentors are professionally paternalistic and serve in a "godparent" role. Hunt and Michael (1983) identified four states of the mentor relationship. The first is the *initiation phase,* when the more powerful and professionally recognized mentor recognizes the apprentice as a protégé. The second is the *protégé phase,* when the apprentice's work is recognized not for its own merit but as the by-product of the mentor's instruction, support, and advice. The third is the *breakup stage,* when the protégé goes off on his or her own. If the mentor–protégé relationship has not been successful, this is the final stage. If it has been successful, however, both parties continue on to the *lasting-friendship stage.* Here the mentor and the protégé have more of a peer relationship. The protégé may become a mentor but does not sever ties with the former mentor.

Noe (1988) determined two major dimensions to the mentoring relationship. One is psychosocial, where the mentor serves as a role model who provides counseling, acceptance, and coaching. The other dimension is job related, where the mentor provides exposure and visibility, sponsorship, and challenging assignments to augment the protégé's career. Most studies report positive results from mentoring. Fagenson (1989) found that mentored individuals had more satisfaction, career mobility and opportunity, recognition, and a higher promotion rate than nonmentored individuals. Similarly, Dreher and Ash (1990) found that individuals with extensive mentoring relationships had higher incomes and were more satisfied with their pay and benefits than individuals who had less extensive mentoring relationships. Chao, Walz, and Gardner (1992) demonstrated that informal mentoring programs (e.g., a senior-level and a junior-level manager share similar goals and values) produced more career-related support for the protégé than formal mentoring programs (e.g., a pool of potential protégés submit résumés for review by a "matchmaker committee"). Further support for the value of informal mentors was reported by Ragins and Cotton (1999). It appears that problems such as personality conflicts and lack of mentor commitment are more likely to occur with assigned mentors than with informal mentors unless the assigned mentors are carefully selected and trained. Eby (1997) reported that mentors can be at either the same organizational level or at a higher organizational level than the protégé. Also, the mentor can give the protégé guidance on the development of job skills or career skills. Eby found that mentoring was particularly helpful in getting individuals to adapt to rapidly changing organizational conditions.

Research has also been directed to across-race and across-gender mentoring issues. Thomas (1990) reported that White protégés had almost no developmental relationships with persons of another race. Blacks were more likely than Whites to form relationships outside the formal lines of authority and their own departments. Same-race relationships were found to provide significantly more psychosocial support than across-race relationships did. Feldman, Folks, and Turnley (1999) found substantial nationality and gender effects between mentors and protégés on international internships. Interns who differed in nationality and gender from their mentors were much less likely to receive task, social, and career support from them. This deficit in mentoring was associated with poorer socialization to internship assignments, less learning about international business, and less likelihood of receiving and accepting job offers from internship employers.

Thomas (1993) concluded that the two parties' preferred strategy for dealing with racial difference (either denying and suppressing it or discussing it openly) and whether both parties preferred the same strategy influenced the kind of relationship that developed. In some relationships, the senior person becomes merely a sponsor for the protégé, providing career support through advocacy for promotions, feedback, and coaching. In others, the senior person becomes a mentor, offering psychosocial support and friendship along with instrumental career support. Ragins and McFarlin (1990) found that across-gender protégés were less likely than same-gender protégés to report engaging in after-work social activities with their mentors. Compared with other gender combinations, female protégés with female mentors were more likely to agree with the idea that their mentors served a role-model function. Ragins and Cotton (1991) reported that women were more likely than men to report restricted access to mentors, in part because initiating a relationship with a mentor might be misinterpreted as a sexual advance.

Given the sensitivity of gender issues and the power differential between senior and junior managers, women may be more likely than men to pursue peer relationships to facilitate their career development. Kram and Isabella (1985) described how peer relationships are important. They found three types of peers. One is the *information peer,* a person with whom you can exchange information about work in the organization. You share a low level of disclosure and trust, and there is little mutual emotional support. The second type is the *collegial peer,* with whom you have a moderate level of trust and engage in some self-disclosure. Collegial peers provide increased emotional support and feedback and engage in more intimate discussions. The third type is the *special peer,* with whom there are no pretenses and formal roles. You reveal ambivalence and personal dilemmas as you would to few other people in your life. You need not limit peer relationships to members of the same gender, but special peers are most likely of your gender. The value of peer relationships to career development is not limited to women. However, because of the constraints women have in mentoring relationships, the importance of the peer relationship in career development is accentuated for women.

THE POSTTRAINING ENVIRONMENT

Tannenbaum and Yukl (1992) noted that the effectiveness of a training program can be influenced by events that occur after a trainee returns to the job. Some employees leave training with new skills and with strong intentions to apply those skills to their job, but limitations in the posttraining environment interfere with the actual transfer of training (see Field Note 2).

transfer of training
the degree of generalizability of the behaviors learned in training to those behaviors evidenced on the job that enhance performance

Transfer of training is defined as the extent to which trainees effectively apply the knowledge, skills, and attitudes gained in a training context back to the job. Baldwin and Ford (1988) noted the distinction between *generalization,* the extent to which trained skills and behaviors are exhibited in the transfer setting, and *maintenance,* the length of time that trained skills and behaviors continue to be used on the job. They believe that supervisory support is a major environmental factor that can affect the transfer process. In the posttraining environment, supervisor support includes reinforcement, modeling of trained behaviors, and goal-setting activities. Another factor that can influence transfer is the extent to which the posttraining environment provides opportunities for trainees to apply what they have learned. Ford et al. (1991) studied technical trainees after they completed training and found significant differences in opportunities to apply the training and wide variations in the lengths of time before trainees first performed the tasks for which they had been trained. Tracey, Tannenbaum, and Kavanagh (1995) concluded that posttraining knowledge and behavior are more likely to

FIELD NOTE 2   **The Willingness to Be Trained**

hen I was in graduate school, I helped a professor with a study of the coal mining industry. Many on-the-job accidents occurred in coal mines, and our assignment was to develop a safety training program to reduce them. My personal assignment was to observe and interview the coal miners about their work. While down in the mines, I noticed that the miners engaged in dangerous behaviors, such as not wearing their hard hats, leaving off their masks (which filtered out coal dust), and smoking in the mine (where an open flame could trigger an explosion). In addition to being unsafe, some of these behaviors were blatant violations of safety rules.

After the miners finished their work shifts, I interviewed them about their jobs. I was particularly interested in why they did such seemingly hazardous things. Since our goal was to develop a training program to reduce accidents, I felt that eliminating these unsafe behaviors was an obvious place to start. So I asked them why they didn't wear safety equipment at times. I did not expect their answer. They said they believed there was no relationship between what they did in the mine and what happened to them. They felt their lives were in the hands of luck, fate, or God, and it did not really matter how they conducted themselves. They all seemed to have personal anecdotes about other miners who were extremely safety conscious (that is, always wore all the safety equipment and were exceedingly cautious people in general) yet suffered serious injuries or death in accidents through no fault of their own, such as a cave-in. In short, the miners were highly fatalistic. They believed that if "your number was up," you would get hurt or killed, and there was nothing you could do about it. While a hard hat was a fine thing to wear, it would not do much good if five tons of rock fell on you. Therefore, they were not interested in engaging in safe behavior because their behavior did not matter one way or another.

This experience taught me many lessons about training. The major one is that if people are not motivated to be trained, to learn some new behaviors, it is pointless to try. As every teacher can tell you, if students do not want to learn or just do not care, there is nothing you can do to force them to learn. The coal miners simply did not want to learn new behaviors because in their minds their lives and welfare were determined by factors beyond their control. Trainers are like chefs: They can prepare the finest meals, but they cannot make you eat if you are not hungry.

perseverate in organizations that have strong social support systems. Specifically, transfer of training is enhanced in organizations that regard themselves as having a culture that recognizes the importance of continuous learning.

Some studies have examined whether transfer is facilitated by relapse-prevention training, an approach derived from research on physical addictions (Marx, 1982). Relapse-prevention training is designed to prepare trainees for the posttraining environment and to anticipate and cope with "high-risk" situations. Marx and Karren (1988) found that trainees who received relapse-prevention training after a regular training seminar demonstrated more of the trained behaviors than trainees with no relapse-prevention training.

It appears that limitations in the posttraining environment may inhibit the application of skills acquired during training. Furthermore, supervisory actions taken after one training course may become pretraining cues for subsequent training courses. Tannenbaum and Yukl (1992) recommended that the transfer environment be examined carefully to identify situational facilitators and inhibitors, and they proposed means either to prepare trainees to deal with the inhibitors or to modify the posttraining environment to encourage transfer.

EVALUATION CRITERIA OF TRAINING PROGRAMS

As is the case with any assessment or evaluation, some measure of performance must be obtained. Measures of performance refer to criteria, and the criteria used to evaluate training are just as important as those used in personnel selection. Relevance, reliability, and freedom from bias are all important considerations. One distinction between criteria used in personnel selection and criteria used to evaluate training is that training criteria are more varied and are used to evaluate multiple aspects of a training program.

Alliger et al. (1997) developed a taxonomy of training criteria based on the original research of Kirkpatrick (1976). Four types of training criteria are represented in the taxonomy. **Reaction criteria** refer primarily to the participants' reaction to the training program. These criteria measure impressions and feelings about the training; for example, did participants believe it was useful or added to their knowledge? Reaction criteria are treated as a measure of the face validity of the training program. Most trainers believe that initial receptivity provides a good atmosphere for learning in the instructional program, but as Goldstein (1991) cautioned, it does not necessarily cause high levels of learning. An evaluation form used to assess participants' reactions is shown in Figure 6–5.

Learning criteria refer to what has been learned as a result of training. Three measures can be taken. The first is immediate knowledge learned, which is often assessed at the conclusion of the training. The second is knowledge retention, where evaluators assess what has been learned at a later time. The third measure, as proposed by Alliger et al., is a behavioral/skill demonstration. This measure would be more than a score on a knowledge test, perhaps a demonstration in a role-playing exercise or a simulation that is a behavioral manifestation of the knowledge learned in training. Collectively, reaction and learning criteria are called *internal criteria*; that is, they refer to assessments internal to the training program itself.

Behavioral criteria refer to actual changes in performance once the employee is back on the job. These criteria are most clearly reflected in the concept of transfer of training. These criteria address such questions as to what extent the desired changes in the job behaviors of the trainee are realized by the training program. If the goal of the training program is to increase production, the behavioral criterion assesses output before and after training. Other types of behavioral criteria are absenteeism, scrap rate, accidents, and grievances. All of these are objective criteria. They can be measured easily and have relatively clear meaning, as discussed in Chapter 3. But if the goal of the training program is to increase managers' sensitivity toward people with handicaps, "increased sensitivity" has to be translated into some objective behavioral criteria. Note that scores on learning criteria and on behavioral criteria do not always correspond to a high degree. Some people who perform well in training do not transfer their new knowledge or skills back to the job. This is particularly true with training programs aimed at changing attitudes or feelings.

Results criteria relate to the economic value of the training program to the company. Cascio (1989) developed a procedure to apply utility analysis to the assessment of training outcomes. One premise is if the training program has any

reaction criteria
a standard for judging the effectiveness of training that refers to the reactions or feelings of individuals about the training they received

learning criteria
a standard for judging the effectiveness of training that refers to the amount of new knowledge, skills, and abilities acquired through training

behavioral criteria
a standard for judging the effectiveness of training that refers to the new behaviors that are exhibited on the job as a result of training

results criteria
a standard for judging the effectiveness of training that refers to the economic value that accrues to the organization as a result of the new behaviors exhibited on the job

The following evaluation form was established for use by the Training Department. Your cooperation will be appreciated and will help us to improve existing training courses.

At the end of each statement below, please fill in the blank with the number (according to the scale) that most accurately describes your reactions

Strongly Agree	Agree	Slightly Agree	Neutral	Slightly Disagree	Disagree	Strongly Disagree
7	6	5	4	3	2	1

Response

Course, Purpose, Objectives, and Structure

1. The purpose of the session was stated.   _____
2. The session's objectives were stated.   _____
3. An outline was provided to participants.   _____

Course Content

4. The material covered was important.   _____
5. The material covered was adequate to meet my job needs.   _____
6. The session was valuable for the information it contained.   _____
7. The material should be covered in the future, with others bearing my job title. _____

Course Delivery

8. The training leader(s) knew the subject well.   _____
9. Training methods helped meet course objectives.   _____
10. Presentations were effectively delivered.   _____
11. The course helped me understand important ideas.   _____
12. Instructional aids (e.g., overhead projector, slides, videotapes) were used effectively to emphasize key ideas. _____
13. The training leader(s) maintained a positive attitude toward participants. _____
14. Participants felt free to talk among themselves.   _____
15. I was free to discuss areas I had difficulty understanding before the course. _____
16. The training leader(s) showed sensitivity to participant feedback.   _____
17. The presentation methods helped to hold my interest.   _____

Use of Time

18. Time was effectively used.   _____

Overall Course Evaluation

19. The session's objectives were accomplished.   _____
20. I recommend this training program to others.   _____

FIGURE 6–5 ■ Participant evaluation form

SOURCE: From *Professional Training Roles and Competencies,* Vol. II, by H. J. Sredl and W. J. Rothwell, 1987, Amherst, MA: HRD Press.

effect, then the average job performance of the trained group should exceed that of the untrained group. Cascio proposed the use of a break-even analysis to determine that the economic value of the training program to the organization is greater than zero. Utility analyses are based upon a careful assessment of the costs associated with developing training, training materials, training time, and production losses. While such analyses are often difficult to perform, the failure to analyze training programs in dollars makes it more likely that training will be viewed as a cost rather than a benefit to the organization.

Collectively, behavioral and results criteria are called *external criteria*; they are evaluations external to the training program itself. Consideration of these four criteria sometimes produces different conclusions about the effectiveness of training than a judgment reached by just one or two criteria. For example, Campion and Campion (1987) compared two methods for improving a person's interview skills. An experimental group received instruction from multiple techniques on improving their interview skills, while a control group engaged in a self-study of relevant material. The results revealed that the experimental group performed better on reaction and learning criteria, but the two groups were equivalent with regard to behavioral and results criteria. Alliger and Janak (1989) concluded that there is not a causal flow among the four types of criteria, but that each serves as a standard by which training can be evaluated. Warr, Allan, and Birdi (1999) found that reaction criteria were more strongly related to learning criteria than subsequent job behavior criteria.

Saari, Johnson, McLaughlin, and Zimmerle (1988) examined the management training practices of 1,000 U.S. companies. Less than one-third conducted a needs assessment to determine the training needs of their managers. Relatively few companies attempted to evaluate training programs, and among those that did, most evaluations assessed only the participants' reactions to training. Goldstein (1978) illustrated the importance of assessing training effectiveness from multiple perspectives. He created some hypothetical complaints to show the many viewpoints by which the success of any training program can be judged:

> From a trainee: "There is a conspiracy. I just finished my training program. I even completed a pretest and a posttest. My posttest score was significantly better than the scores of my friends in the on-the-job control group. However, I lost my job because I could not perform the work."

> From a trainer: "There is a conspiracy. Everyone praised our training program. They said it was the best training program they ever attended. The trainees even had a chance to laugh a little. Now the trainees tell me that management will not let them perform their job the way we trained them."

> From an administrative officer in the company: "There is a conspiracy. My competition used the training program, and it worked for them. They saved a million. I took it straight from their manuals, and my employees still cannot do the job."

Each of these people asserted that the program did not have the intended effect. Goldstein (1991) says that the validity of any training program can be assessed along four dimensions:

1. *Training validity.* Did the trainees match the criteria established for them in the training program? This dimension is concerned with internal criteria and addresses the extent to which the trainees mastered the training.
2. *Transfer validity.* Did the trainees match the criteria for success when they were back on the job? This dimension involves external criteria and addresses the extent to which employee performance on the job was enhanced by training.
3. *Intraorganizational validity.* Is the training program equally effective with different groups of trainees within the same organization? This dimension is concerned with the internal generalizability of the training, such as the effectiveness of sensitivity training for sales versus production workers in the same organization.
4. *Interorganizational validity.* Is the training program equally effective with different trainees in companies other than the one that developed the training program? This dimension involves the external generalizability of the training, such as the degree to which a training program that is successful for a manufacturing company would also be successful for a financial organization.

In a review of studies that examined the effectiveness of managerial training programs, Burke and Day (1986) concluded that managerial training is moderately effective in improving learning and job performance but found relatively little knowledge about the intra- and interorganizational validity of such programs. The question of training program success is not simple. One study that did address intraorganizational validity was reported by Morrow, Jarrett, and Rupinski (1997). They concluded after a four-year study that managerial training had less effect and utility than sales/technical training. However, the results may be partly attributable to the greater difficulty of measuring the criteria of managerial job performance.

In the final analysis, the success of any training and development system is intimately tied to the culture of the organization. The organization sets the tone for the relative importance and need placed on enhancing the skills of its employees. Training and development activities are but a mirror of the organization's deeper values. Smith, Ford, and Kozlowski (1997) spoke to the need for *alignment* between the organization's culture and training initiatives. For example, a traditional authoritarian organization may not be supportive of individuals who attempt to take risks and try out new strategies. Mistakes and errors may be viewed as actions to be avoided rather than as opportunities from which to learn and develop. Also, given what we have discovered recently about the complexities of how and what we learn, our systems for evaluating learning should not be simplistic. Kraiger and Jung (1997) described the importance of linking training objectives to training evaluation criteria. Given the subtleties of how we learn, what we learn, and the duration of our learning, methods of assessing learning must be appropriately refined. Learning is the foundation of training and development. The recent advances we have made in understanding learning have their commensurate influences in our understanding of training and development.

C A S E   S T U D Y   ■   **Train or Select?**

The senior management staff at Barstow Industries faced an ongoing problem within the company. The company was large, employing approximately 11,000 people nationwide. Barstow hired a large number of people into the professional and scientific classification of employees: salespeople, engineers, accountants, and chemists. The management staff differed on the type of person to hire. About half the staff favored hiring people directly out of college and having the company train them in their jobs. The emphasis would be on training. The basic requirement was that the people had to be bright—bright enough to learn the job quickly. The other half of the staff favored hiring people with extensive job experience. There would be little need for training because the new employees had already demonstrated their ability to perform the job.

Both sides had good arguments. Those who favored the training approach argued that the company could save money on payroll costs because new, unproven employees could be hired at lower salaries than their experienced counterparts. Furthermore, by making the training company-specific, there was less chance the employees would be hired away by a competitor. It was also argued that the company had good training facilities, including trainers, which were resources the company should not underutilize.

Those who favored the selection of experienced employees proposed powerful counterarguments. They cited statistics showing that a sizable proportion of new college graduates don't last long with their first employer. They didn't want the company to act as a proving ground by weeding out the unsuccessful employees. Whatever increased salary costs were associated with hiring proven, experienced employees would be offset by their increased job performance. It was argued that their competitors could identify the "keepers," and Barstow would raid those companies' talent by offering a higher salary.

It was difficult to argue against the lower payroll costs the company would incur by hiring new, unproven people. But it was also difficult to argue with the better job performance and lower turnover obtained by hiring experienced employees. Every time it came to filling an open position the same arguments were presented by both sides. Individual managers in charge of filling positions within their departments had their own views on the issue, but it seemed there was always a person in authority above them who supported the other approach. Everyone seemed to believe there should be a uniform company position on the matter, but there certainly was no consensus on what the company should do. The only group that held a single view was the Human Resources Department, which was highly understandable because one of its major functions was to provide training. Everyone hoped the senior management staff would reach a decision shortly, but everyone also knew that many people would be unhappy with whatever decision was made.

Study Questions

1. What are some additional benefits and liabilities of hiring young employees and training them to fit a company's needs?

2. What are some additional benefits and liabilities of hiring experienced employees who have received most of their professional training elsewhere?
3. What are the benefits and liabilities of Barstow Industries staffing the organization using both approaches?
4. Do you think certain types of jobs (for example, sales) more readily lend themselves to one approach over the other? Why?
5. Give some examples of company-specific training and consider to what degree the training could be generalized to another company.

SUGGESTED INFOTRAC TOPICS

personnel training

management development

training needs

computer-based training

distance learning

web-based training

simulation

cultural diversity training

sexual harassment training

mentoring

C H A P T E R 7

Performance Appraisal

LEARNING OBJECTIVES

- Understand the reasons organizations have performance appraisal systems.
- Know the sources of performance appraisal data and the limitations of each.
- Explain the purpose of rater training.
- Understand the bases of rater motivation.
- Understand self-appraisal, peer appraisal, and 360-degree feedback.
- Explain the use of performance appraisal interviews.

Employees continually have their job performance appraised, whether on a formal or an informal basis. Informal appraisals may be made from haphazard observation, memory, hearsay, or intuition. Alternatively, with a formal and rational system, appraisals are more accurate, fair, and useful to all concerned. This chapter deals with formal programs, methods, and techniques for appraising employee performance.

Before the discussion of performance appraisal, it should be noted that there is no uniform understanding of what constitutes "performance," let alone how to appraise it. Campbell, McCloy, Oppler, and Sager (1993) asserted that the concept of performance is poorly understood. They stated that performance is to be distinguished from effectiveness. *Performance* is synonymous with behavior; it is what people actually do, and it can be observed. Performance includes those actions that are relevant to the organization's goals and can be measured in terms of each individual's proficiency (that is, level of contribution). *Effectiveness,* on the other hand, refers to the evaluation of the results of performance, and it is beyond the influence or control of the individual. Measures of effectiveness, while of major importance to the organization, are contaminated by factors over which the employee has little influence. An example of effectiveness is how many promotions an employee has had over a certain period of time—say, three years. The number of promotions a person has is affected by the availability of job openings to which one can be promoted and the qualifications of other candidates. Furthermore, it is the organization and not the individual that makes promotion decisions. Rewarding or punishing individuals on the basis of their effectiveness may be unfair and counterproductive. While there is a relationship between performance and effectiveness, the two concepts should not be confounded. The significance of the distinction is that appraisals of employee performance should be directed at job-related behaviors that are under the control of the employee.

Murphy and Cleveland (1995) believe that performance appraisals can help organizations in several ways. These factors are the primary reasons most organizations have formal performance appraisal systems. First, they can enhance the quality of organizational decisions, ranging from pay raises to promotions to discharges. The purpose of the human resource function in an organization is to maximize the contributions of employees to the goals of the organization, and assessments of employee job performance can play a major role in accomplishing that function.

Second, performance appraisals can enhance the quality of individual decisions, ranging from career choices to the development of future strengths. Accurate performance feedback is an important component of success in training and provides critical input for forming realistic self-assessments in the workplace. Performance feedback is also a key to maintaining high levels of work motivation.

Third, performance appraisals can affect employees' views of and attachment to their organization. An organization's successful performance appraisal system may help to build employee commitment and satisfaction. Employees who believe that an organization's decisions are irrational or unfair are unlikely to develop a strong commitment to that organization.

Finally, formal performance appraisals provide a rational, legally defensible basis for personnel decisions. As discussed in Chapter 5, personnel decisions must

TABLE 7–1 ■ **Employer and employee reasons for conducting appraisals**

Employer Perspective

1. Despite imperfect measurement, individual differences in performance make a difference.
2. Documentation of performance appraisal and feedback may be needed for legal defense.
3. Appraisal provides a rational basis for constructing a bonus or merit system.
4. Appraisal dimensions and standards can operationalize strategic goals and clarify performance expectations.
5. Providing individual feedback is part of a performance management process.
6. Despite the traditional individual focus, appraisal criteria can include teamwork and teams can be the focus of appraisal.

Employee Perspective

1. Performance feedback is needed and desired.
2. Improvement in performance requires assessment.
3. Fairness requires that differences in performance levels across workers be measured and have an impact on outcomes.
4. Assessment and recognition of performance levels can motivate improved performance.

SOURCE: From "Performance Appraisal in a Quality Context: A New Look at an Old Problem" by R. L. Cardy, 1998, in *Performance Appraisal* (p.142), edited by J. W. Smither, San Francisco: Jossey-Bass. Reprinted with permission.

be based on reason, not capriciousness. There must be a defensible explanation for why some employees are promoted, discharged, or receive differential pay raises compared with others. As will be discussed shortly, personnel decisions based on performance appraisals are subject to the same legal standards as tests. Both tests and performance evaluations are used as techniques in the personnel function. While performance appraisals may trigger discordant reactions from some employees, the alternative of making personnel decisions with no rational basis is simply unacceptable. Cardy (1998) summarized employer and employee reasons for conducting appraisals, as shown in Table 7–1.

USING THE RESULTS OF PERFORMANCE APPRAISALS

The results of a performance appraisal program may be applied to many other management functions (see Figure 7–1). As discussed in Chapter 3, criteria are derived from job analysis procedures; the criteria, in turn, are the basis for appraisals. The major uses of performance appraisal information are described in the following paragraphs.

Personnel Training. Perhaps the main use of performance appraisal information is for employee feedback; this is the basis for the person analysis discussed in the preceding chapter. Feedback highlights employees' strengths and weaknesses. Of course, the appraisal should pertain to job-related characteristics only. Defi-

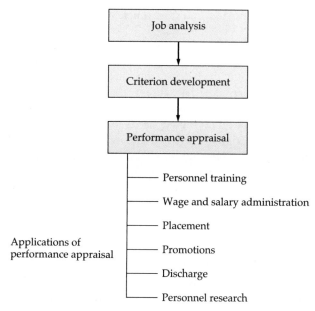

FIGURE 7–1 ■ Development of performance appraisal information and its applications

ciencies or weaknesses then become the targets for training. Training should involve only those areas where poor performance can be attributed to the individual and not to aspects of the work environment. The supervisor plays a key role in helping to develop the employee's skills. Although, by definition, performance appraisals are evaluative, in this context they serve more as diagnostic aids. Since some employees will not acknowledge their weaknesses, a supportive supervisor is more effective than one who is threatening or critical. More will be said about this later in the chapter.

Wage and Salary Administration. Perhaps the second most common use of performance appraisals is to determine raises. Pay increases are often made, in part, on the basis of job performance. Appraisal programs can be designed so that there is a direct relationship between the evaluation and the size of the raise. For example, an employee who is judged to be performing in the top 10% of the workforce might get a 12% raise. Conversely, an employee who performs in the bottom 10% might get only a 2% raise.

Unfortunately, the "personnel development" and "salary administration" aspects of appraisal are often uncomfortable partners. Many employees attach far more meaning to raises because they are more immediate and real than revelations about weaknesses on the job. If the two functions are combined in the same appraisal, employees can become defensive. When admitting weaknesses means getting a smaller raise, personnel development may take a backseat.

In a classic article, Meyer, Kay, and French (1965) talked about the need for "split roles" for supervisors in conducting appraisals. One role is a counselor or coach in discussing employee development or performance improvement. The other is a judge in making salary decisions. Evidence shows that most supervisors cannot play both roles simultaneously. The problem may be addressed by having two appraisals—for example, one in January for employee development and the other in June for salary. Or the supervisor may handle development while the personnel department handles salary. Although both functions are important, it is customary practice that they not be conducted at the same time by the same person.

Placement. Performance appraisal information is vital for placement decisions. New employees (such as management trainees) are often exposed to many tasks or jobs at first. Over a 12-month period, a trainee might have jobs in marketing, finance, and accounting. After being appraised in each, the trainee might be permanently assigned to that area where he or she performed best. By identifying the employee's strengths, performance appraisal indicates where the person's talents might best be used.

Promotions.   Promotions may be based on how well an employee performs on his or her current job. Appraisals identify the better-performing employees, and an employee who cannot perform well on his or her current job will not be considered for promotion. Succession planning is a concept in which fairly long-term projections (typically 3–5 years) about future staffing needs in an entire company are based upon the anticipated promotion of current employees. However, performance is not the sole determinant of promotion. Promotions are usually granted based on a combination of seniority and merit. If they are based strictly on seniority, there is nothing to ensure that competent people get promoted. Promotions based strictly on performance are more defensible, but most experts agree that experience in a job is also worth considering. Promotions have often served as the criterion in validating assessment center ratings.

Discharge.   Termination of employment must be predicated on just cause. A typical just cause is inadequate job performance, as determined through performance appraisal. It is also highly advisable for organizations to document that efforts were made to enhance the employee's performance and that the decision to terminate employment was the organization's last resort. Many lawsuits stemming from performance appraisals allege the fired employee was the victim of a "wrongful discharge." In such cases the organization must demonstrate the fairness, job-relatedness, and accuracy of the performance appraisal process that led to the termination decision.

Personnel Research.   In many criterion-related validity studies, assessments of the criterion are derived from performance appraisals. Recall that the criterion is a measure of job performance, and that is what performance appraisals are supposed to measure. When I/O psychologists want to validate a new predictor test, they correlate scores with criterion measures, which are often exhumed from a company's performance appraisal files. Any selection device is only as good as the criterion it tries to predict, so the appraisal must be a relevant measure of job success. Research (e.g., Harris, Smith, & Champagne, 1995) has found that for the purpose of personnel research, specially constructed performance appraisal instruments yielded more useful and less biased information than evaluations originally collected for administrative purposes (for example, salary administration). Harris et al. recommended that more attention be given to the purposes behind performance appraisal, and how these purposes influence the quality and usefulness of the evaluation.

PERFORMANCE APPRAISAL AND THE LAW

Federal law on fair employment practices also pertains to performance appraisal. Unfair discrimination can occur not only on the predictor (test) side of the equation but also in the job behavior the test is trying to predict.

Malos (1998) stated that the importance of legal issues in performance appraisal has "skyrocketed" in recent years. He reviewed many court cases involving alleged discrimination and found that charges of discrimination were frequently related to the assessment of the employee's job performance. Charges of discrimination may be brought under the laws discussed in Chapter 5, including Title VII of the Civil Rights Act of 1964, the Civil Rights Act of 1991, the Age Discrimination in Employment Act (ADEA), and the Americans with Disabilities Act (ADA). Litigation can also result from charges of employer *negligence* (breach of duty to conduct appraisals with due care), *defamation* (disclosure of untrue unfavorable performance information that damages the reputation of the employee), and *misrepresentation* (disclosure of untrue favorable performance information that presents a risk of harm to prospective employees or third parties).

Malos synthesized the findings from many court cases involving performance appraisal and arrived at recommendations for employers regarding both the content and the procedure of performance appraisals. The *content* of performance appraisal refers to the criteria of job performance that are evaluated. Malos made the recommendations for legally sound performance appraisals listed in Table 7–2. Conducting the appraisals on job-related factors, usually derived from a job analysis, is particularly important. Werner and Bolino (1997) likewise found that whether or not the company based its performance appraisals on criteria derived from job analyses was often a deciding factor in court rulings. Malos also made *procedural* recommendations for legally sound performance appraisals. These recommendations are presented in Table 7–3. Malos concluded by stating that as our economy continues to move toward a service and information emphasis, there will be the tendency to use subjective performance criteria, particularly at the professional and managerial levels. Also, more organizations are increasingly relying on multiple sources of evaluation (customers, subordinates, and peers). Using subjective criteria and untrained raters can lead to discrimination claims that are difficult to defend. It is recommended that when such criteria and raters are used, they should be used in conjunction with objective criteria and trained raters whose input is given greater weight.

TABLE 7–2 ■ **Content recommendations for legally sound performance appraisals**

Appraisal Criteria

- Should be objective rather than subjective
- Should be job-related or based on job analysis
- Should be based on behaviors rather than traits
- Should be within the control of the ratee
- Should relate to specific functions, not global assessments

SOURCE: From "Current Legal Issues in Performance Appraisal" by S. B. Malos, 1998, in *Performance Appraisal* (p. 80), edited by J. W. Smither, San Francisco: Jossey-Bass. Reprinted with permission.

TABLE 7–3 ■ **Procedural recommendations for legally sound performance appraisals**

Appraisal Procedures

- Should be standardized and uniform for all employees within a job group
- Should be formally communicated to employees
- Should provide notice of performance deficiencies and of opportunities to correct them
- Should provide access for employees to review appraisal results
- Should provide formal appeal mechanisms that allow for employee input
- Should use multiple, diverse, and unbiased raters
- Should provide written instructions for training raters
- Should require thorough and consistent documentation across raters that includes specific examples of performance based on personal knowledge
- Should establish a system to detect potentially discriminatory effect or abuses of the system overall

SOURCE: From "Current Legal Issues in Performance Appraisal" by S. B. Malos, 1998, in *Performance Appraisal* (p. 83), edited by J. W. Smither, San Francisco: Jossey-Bass. Reprinted with permission.

THEORY OF PERSON PERCEPTION

person perception
the processes by which individuals form impressions and make inferences about other people

At a fundamental level performance appraisal involves the perception of people. That is, how you appraise a person is related to how you perceive that person. Psychologists have developed a theory of **person perception** that is useful for providing a foundation for understanding performance appraisal. The theory is also called social cognition or attribution theory of person perception.

London (2001) outlines the theory as follows. We all have fairly fixed views of the way things should be when we enter into interpersonal interactions. These views act as filters to help us process large amounts of information about other people. We thereby tend to eliminate or ignore information that doesn't fit our initial views. We process information automatically whenever we can, avoid cognitive effort, and maintain consistency in our judgments. When something happens out of the ordinary, we may be compelled to think more carefully to interpret the unusual information and reformulate our opinions of a person or group. Automatic processing of information and the biases and distortions that result from it can be avoided with various interventions, such as training.

Klimoski and Donohue (2001) developed a framework to understand person perception. It is shown graphically in Figure 7–2. There are three parts to the framework: inputs, processes, and outputs. Inputs are characteristics of the perceiver, characteristics of the person being perceived (the target), and contextual factors.

Perceivers differ from each other with regard to their level of affect toward others, their level of motivation, and their cognitive abilities. Characteristics of the target include age, race, and gender, as well as nonverbal cues such as physical attractiveness, eye contact, body orientation, and interpersonal warmth. Context factors are represented by the presence of other group members, who influence

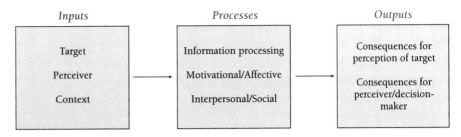

FIGURE 7–2 ■ **Input–processes–output framework of person perception**

SOURCE: Adapted from "Person Perception in Organizations: An Overview of the Field," by R. J. Klimoski and L. M. Donahue, 2001, in *How People Evaluate Others in Organizations* (p. 6), edited by M. London, Mahwah, NJ: Erlbaum.

the judgment of the target and provide the perceiver with information for making cognitive judgments. The second component of the framework, processes, includes a broad range of variables pertaining to the way the perceiver uses information to make a judgment. Perceivers use approaches to social cognition that are good enough to accomplish their goals for the setting, which for the most part involve trying to "make sense" out of another person so they can make better choices. For example, a perceiver would use a certain cognitive approach to assess the potential physical threat of a passerby on the sidewalk, a social exchange lasting only a few seconds. Alternatively, another cognitive approach would be used in a situation of greater length and purpose, such as a job interview in which the person wants to create a favorable impression. These cognitive structures are called **schemas**. Schemas are used to understand people in situations where the perceiver is confronted with incomplete or ambiguous information. They allow the perceiver to make rapid inferences about the characteristics and intentions of the target. Sometimes these inferences are correct and sometimes they are not. The third component of the person-perception framework is outputs, which are the consequences of the processing to the perceiver and the target. The consequences for the perceiver might include less monitoring of a target who is perceived to be highly trustworthy. The consequences for the target are performance ratings and written evaluations that formally document a worker's performance. Jelley and Goffin (2001) advised designing performance appraisal methods to more closely parallel the cognitive processes by which memory is stored and retrieved by raters in making evaluations.

Barnes-Farrell (2001) noted that changing demographics are creating a workforce in which supervisors and work-group members may have little common background to draw upon when making inferences, thus increasing the potential for using stereotypes to make appraisals. As will be discussed in Chapter 9, the emphasis on teamwork in organizations provides incentives for interpersonal functioning, and the appraisal of performance in a team, not an individual, context. The current overall importance of performance appraisal in the design of work contexts in which these judgments are made is changing. The input–process–output framework proposed by Klimoski and Donahue offers a basis to understand the

schema
a cognitive approach to processing information that results in making sense of events and actions that in turn influence how decisions are made on the basis of that information

underlying psychological mechanisms associated with how people form judgments of others.

SOURCES OF PERFORMANCE APPRAISAL INFORMATION

As stated in Chapter 3, job performance can be characterized by many criteria. Three different types of data are used: objective production data, personnel data, and judgmental data.

Objective Production Data

Objective production data used as an index of how well an employee is performing on the job is limited in its frequency and value. For a person in the job of a machine operator, job performance may be measured by counting the number of objects produced per day, per week, and so forth. Similarly, salespeople are appraised by assessing (counting) their sales volume over a given period. It is even possible to evaluate the performance of firefighters by counting the number of fires they extinguish.

Although each of these objective production measures has some intuitive appeal, none is usually a complete measure of job performance. Two problems in particular affect each of these measures. First, we would like to assume that differences in performance across people reflect true differences in how well these people perform their jobs. Unfortunately, variability in performance can be due to factors beyond the individual's control. One machine operator may produce more because he or she works with a better machine. A salesperson might have a larger sales volume because his or her territory is better. Firefighters who put out few fires might be responsible for an area with relatively few buildings. This problem of variation in performance stemming from external factors should sound familiar: It represents a form of criterion contamination (a topic discussed in Chapter 3).

The second problem with objective performance measures is that they rarely tell the whole story. A machine operator who produces more objects per day but who also produces more defective objects should not be described as the "best." Quality may be as important as quantity, but this cannot be recorded in a simple count of objects produced. A salesperson spends a lot of time recruiting new customers, an aspect that must be weighed against simply making calls on established customers. Creating new customers can be as important as maintaining business with old ones. The sales volume might be lower at first, but in the long run, the new customers will increase total sales volume. Extinguishing fires is but one aspect of a firefighter's job; preventing fires is another one. The "best" firefighters conceivably may not have put out many fires but might have contributed heavily toward preventing fires in the first place. There is growing use of electronic performance monitoring (EPM) to assess the performance of workers engaged in computer-based tasks. An EPM system records the objective aspects of performance on computer-based tasks, such as volume and speed of entries (Lund, 1992). Research (Westin, 1992) has revealed that such systems are regarded as unfair and inaccurate assessments of work performance because they ignore the discretionary or judgmental component of work, which is inherent to all jobs. In short, all of these actual criteria suffer from criterion deficiency. They are deficient measures of the conceptual criteria they seek to measure.

Relevance of Objective Production Data.   For the jobs mentioned, objective production data have some relevance. It would be absurd to say that sales volume has no relationship to a salesperson's performance. The salesperson's job is indeed to sell. The issue is the degree of relevance. It is a mistake to give too much importance to objective production data in performance appraisal (see Field Note 1). This is sometimes a great temptation because these data are usually very accessible, but the meaning of those clear-cut numbers is not always so evident. Finally, for many jobs, objective performance measures do not exist or, if they do, they have little relevance to actual performance. Criterion relevance is a question of judgment. For some jobs, objective performance data are partially relevant measures of success; in many others, such relevance is lacking.

Personnel Data

The second type of appraisal information is personnel data, the data retained by a company's personnel office. The two most common indices of performance are absenteeism and accidents. The critical issue with these variables is criterion relevance. To what extent do they reflect real differences in job performance?

Absenteeism is probably the most sensitive measure of performance. In almost all jobs, employees who have unexcused absence are judged as performing worse than others, all other factors being equal. Indeed, an employee can be fired for excessive absence. Most organizations have policies for dealing with absenteeism, which attests to its importance as a variable in judging overall performance. However, the measurement and interpretation of absenteeism are not clear-cut. Absences can be "excused" or "unexcused" depending on many factors pertaining to both

---

FIELD NOTE 1   What Is "High" Performance?

Usually we think of high performance as a positive score, a gain, or some improvement over the status quo. Conversely, when individuals perform "worse" than they did last year, it is tempting to conclude they didn't perform as well. However, such is not always the case. Performance must be judged in terms of what is under the control of the individuals being evaluated rather than those influences on performance that are beyond their control. There can be broad, pervasive factors, sometimes of an economic nature, that suppress the performance of everyone being judged. One example is in sales. If there is a general downturn in the economy and products or services are not being purchased with the same frequency as in the previous year, sales could be down, for example, by an average of 15%. This 15% (actually –15%) figure would then represent "average" performance. Perhaps the best salesperson in the year had only a 3% drop in sales over the previous year. Thus, "good" performance in this situation is a smaller loss compared with some average or norm group. This example illustrates that there is always some judgmental or contextual component to appraising performance and that sole reliance on objective numbers can be misleading.

the individual (for example, seniority) and the job (for example, job level). An employee who has ten days of excused absence may still be appraised as performing better than an employee with five days of unexcused absence. Whether the absence was allowed must be determined before performance judgments are made. Measuring absenteeism is a thorny problem, but it is seen as a highly relevant criterion variable in most organizations.

Accidents can be used as a measure of job performance but only for a limited number of jobs. Frequency and severity of accidents are both used as variables, as are accidents resulting in injury or property damage. Accidents are a more relevant criterion variable for blue-collar than for white-collar jobs. People who drive delivery trucks may be evaluated in part on the number of accidents they have. This variable can be contaminated by many sources, though. Road conditions, miles driven, time of day, and condition of the truck can all contribute to accidents. While relevance is limited to certain jobs, accidents can contribute greatly to appraisal. Companies often give substantial pay raises to drivers with no accidents and fire those with a large number.

Relevance of Personnel Data.   There is no doubt that factors such as absence and accidents are meaningful measures of job performance. Employees may be discharged for excessive absences or accidents. Employers expect employees to come to work and not incur accidents on the job. Therefore, these indicators are more likely to reflect levels of poor performance rather than good performance. However, as was the case with production data, personnel data rarely give a comprehensive picture of the employee's performance. Other highly relevant aspects of job performance often are not revealed by personnel data. It is for this reason that judgmental data are relied upon to offer a more complete assessment of job performance.

Rating Errors

The most common means of appraising performance are judgmental data and evaluations from raters. Because errors occur in making ratings, it is important to understand the major types of rating errors. In making appraisals with rating scales, the rater may unknowingly commit errors in judgment. These can be placed into three major categories: halo errors, leniency errors, and central-tendency errors. All three stem from rater bias and misperception.

halo error
a type of rating error in which the rater assesses the ratee as performing well on a variety of performance dimensions despite having credible knowledge of only a limited number of performance dimensions

Halo errors are evaluations based on the rater's general feelings about an employee. The rater may have a favorable attitude toward the employee that permeates all evaluations of this person. Typically, the rater has strong feelings about at least one important aspect of the employee's performance. The feelings are then generalized to other performance factors, and the employee is judged (across many factors) as uniformly good or bad. The rater who is impressed by an employee's idea might allow those feelings to carry over to the evaluation of leadership, cooperation, motivation, and so on. This occurs even though the "good idea" is not related to the other factors. The theory of person perception offers a conceptual basis to understand halo error. In the schemas we use to assess other people, it may make sense to us that they would be rated highly across many different dimensions of performance, even dimensions we have little or no opportunity to observe.

Raters who commit halo errors do not distinguish among the many dimensions of employee performance. A compounding problem is that there are two types of halo. One type is truly a rating error and involves the failure to differentiate an employee's performance across different dimensions. The second type is giving uniformly consistent ratings to an employee when these ratings are in fact justified; that is, the employee truly performs well across many dimensions. These effects are referred to as *invalid* and *valid* halo, respectively. Solomonson and Lance (1997) concluded that a valid halo (actual job dimensions that are positively interrelated) does not affect halo rater error (raters who allow general impressions to influence their ratings). In general, halo errors are considered to be the most serious and pervasive of all rating errors (Cooper, 1981). Recent research on halo error has revealed it as a more complex phenomenon than initially believed. Murphy and Anhalt (1992) concluded that halo error is not a stable characteristic of the rater or ratee, but rather is the result of an interaction of the rater, ratee, and evaluative situation. Balzer and Sulsky (1992) contended that halo error may not be a rating "error" so much as an indicator of how we cognitively process information in arriving at judgments of other people. That is, the presence of a halo does not necessarily indicate an inaccuracy in the ratings. In a related view, Lance, LaPointe, and Fisicaro (1994) noted there is disagreement as to whether halo error can be attributed to the rater or to the cognitive process of making judgments of similar objects.

leniency error
a type of rating error in which the rater assesses a disproportionately large number of ratees as performing well (positive leniency) or poorly (negative leniency) in contrast to their true level of performance

Leniency errors are the second category. Some teachers are "hard graders" and others "easy graders," so raters can be characterized by the leniency of their appraisals. Harsh raters give evaluations that are lower than the "true" level of ability (if it can be ascertained); this is called *severity* or *negative leniency*. The easy rater gives evaluations that are higher than the "true" level; this is called *positive leniency*. These errors usually occur because the rater applies personal standards derived from his or her own personality or previous experience. Kane, Bernardin, Villanova, and Peyrefitte (1995) found that the tendency to make leniency errors was stable with individuals; that is, people tend to be consistently lenient or harsh in their ratings. Bernardin, Cooke, and Villanova (2000) found that the most lenient raters were those who had the personality characteristics of being low in Conscientiousness and high in Agreeableness.

central-tendency error
a type of rating error in which the rater assesses a disproportionately large number of ratees as performing in the middle or central part of a distribution of rated performance in contrast to their true level of performance

Central-tendency error refers to the rater's unwillingness to assign extreme—high or low—ratings. Everyone is "average," and only the middle (central) part of the scale is used. This error may happen when raters are asked to evaluate unfamiliar aspects of performance. Rather than not respond, they play it safe and say the person is average in this "unknown" ability.

Even though we have long been aware of halo, leniency, and central-tendency errors, there is no clear consensus on how these errors are manifested in ratings. Saal, Downey, and Lahey (1980) observed that researchers define these errors in somewhat different ways. For example, leniency errors are sometimes equated with skew in the distribution of ratings; that is, positive skew is evidence of negative leniency and negative skew of positive leniency. Other researchers say that an average rating above the midpoint on a particular scale indicates positive leniency.

The exact meaning of central tendency is also unclear. Central-tendency errors occur if the average rating is around the midpoint of the scale but there is not much variance in the ratings. The amount of variance that separates central-tendency errors from "good" ratings has not been defined. Saal and associates think that more precise definitions of these errors must be developed before they can be overcome. Finally, the absence of these three types of rating errors does not necessarily indicate *accuracy* in the ratings. The presence of the rating errors leads to inaccurate ratings, but accuracy involves other issues besides the removal of these three error types. I/O psychologists are seeking to develop statistical indicators of rating accuracy, some based on classical issues in measurement (Cronbach et al., 1972).

Judgmental Data

Judgmental data are commonly used for performance appraisal because finding relevant objective measures is difficult. Subjective assessments can apply to almost all jobs. Those who do the assessments are usually supervisors, but some use has also been made of self-assessment and peer assessment. A wide variety of measures have been developed, all intended to provide accurate assessments of how people are performing (Pulakos, 1997). These are the major methods used in performance appraisal:

1. Graphic rating scales
2. Employee-comparison methods
   a. Rank order
   b. Paired comparison
   c. Forced distribution
3. Behavior checklists and scales
   a. Critical incidents
   b. Behaviorally anchored rating scale (BARS)
   c. Behavior-observation scale (BOS)

Graphic Rating Scales.   Graphic rating scales are the most commonly used tools in performance appraisal. Individuals are rated on a number of traits or factors. The rater judges "how much" of each factor the individual has. Usually performance is judged on a 5- or 7-point scale, and the number of factors ranges between 5 and 20. The more common dimensions rated are quantity of work, quality of work, practical judgment, job knowledge, cooperation, and motivation. Examples of typical graphic rating scales are shown in Figure 7–3.

Employee–Comparison Methods.   Rating scales provide for evaluating employees against some defined standard. With employee comparison methods, individuals are compared with one another; variance is thereby forced into the appraisals. Thus, the concentration of ratings at one part of the scale caused by rating error is avoided. The major advantage of employee-comparion methods is the elimination of central tendency and leniency errors because raters are compelled to differentiate among the people being rated. However, halo error is still

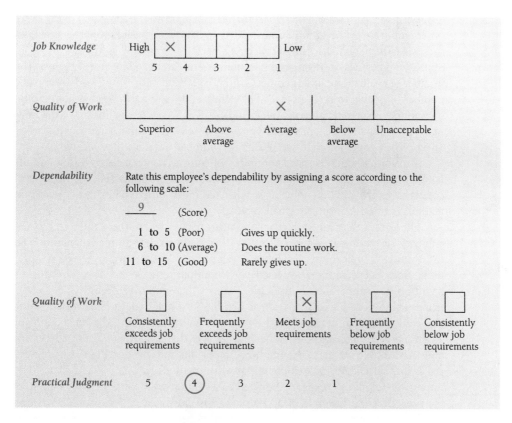

FIGURE 7–3 ■ **Examples of graphic rating scales for various performance dimensions**

possible because it manifests itself across multiple evaluations of the same person. However, all methods of employee comparison involve the question of whether variation represents true differences in performance or whether it creates a false impression of large differences when they are in fact small. There are three major employee-comparison methods: rank order, paired comparison, and forced distribution.

With the *rank-order method*, the rater ranks employees from high to low on a given performance dimension. The person ranked first is regarded as the "best" and the person ranked last as the "worst." However, we do not know how good the "best" is or how bad the "worst" is. We do not know the level of performance. For example, the Nobel Prize winners in a given year could be ranked in terms of their overall contributions to science. But we would be hard-pressed to conclude that the Nobel laureate ranked last made the worst contribution to science. Rank-order data are all relative to some standard—in this case, excellence in scientific research. Another problem is that it becomes tedious and perhaps even meaningless to rank order large numbers of people. What usually happens is that the rater can sort out the people at the top and bottom of the pile. However, for the rest with undifferentiated performance, the rankings may be somewhat arbitrary.

With the *paired-comparison method*, each employee is compared with every other employee in the group being evaluated. The rater's task is to select which of the two is better on the dimension being rated. The method is typically used to evaluate employees on a single dimension: overall ability to perform the job. The number of evaluation pairs is computed by the formula $n(n - 1)/2$, where n is the number of people to be evaluated. For example, if there are 10 people in a group, the number of paired comparisons is $10(9)/2 = 45$. At the conclusion of the evaluation, the number of times each person was selected as the better of the two is tallied. The people are then ranked by the number of tallies they receive.

A major limitation is that the number of comparisons mushrooms dramatically with large numbers of employees. If 50 people are to be appraised, the number of comparisons is 1,225; this obviously takes too much time. The paired-comparison method is best for relatively small samples.

The *forced-distribution method* is most useful when the other employee-comparison methods are most limited—that is, when the sample is large. Forced distribution is typically used when the rater must evaluate employees on a single dimension, but it can also be used with multiple dimensions. The procedure is based on the normal distribution and assumes that employee performance is normally distributed. The distribution is divided into five to seven categories. Using predetermined percentages (based on the normal distribution), the rater evaluates an employee by placing him or her into one of the categories. All employees are evaluated in this manner. The method "forces" the rater to distribute the employees across all categories (which is how the method gets its name). Thus, it is impossible for all employees to be rated excellent, average, or poor. An example of the procedure for a sample of 50 employees is illustrated in Figure 7–4.

Some raters react negatively to this method, saying that the procedure creates artificial distinctions among employees. This is partly because the raters feel that performance is not normally distributed but rather negatively skewed; that is, most of their employees are performing very well. The dissatisfaction can be partially allayed by noting that the lowest 10% are not necessarily performing poorly, just not as well as the others. The problem (as with all comparison methods) is that performance is not compared with a defined standard. The meaning of the differences among employees must be supplied from some other source.

Behavioral Checklists and Scales. Most recent advances in performance appraisal involve behavioral checklists and scales. The key term is *behavior*. Behaviors are less vague than other factors. The greater the agreement on the meaning of the performance appraised, the greater the chance that the appraisal will be accurate. All of the methods in this category have their origin directly or indirectly in the critical-incidents method.

Critical incidents are behaviors that result in good or poor job performance. Anderson and Wilson (1997) noted that the critical-incident technique is flexible and can be used for performance appraisal as well as job analysis. Supervisors record behaviors of employees that greatly influence their job performance. They either keep a running tally of these critical incidents as they occur on the job or recall them at a later time. Critical incidents are usually grouped by aspects of performance: job knowledge, decision-making ability, leadership, and so on. The end

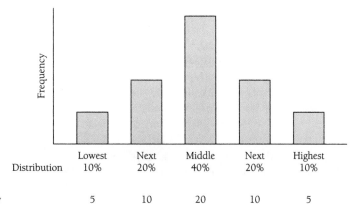

Distribution	Lowest 10%	Next 20%	Middle 40%	Next 20%	Highest 10%
Number of employees to be placed in each category based on 50 employees	5	10	20	10	5

FIGURE 7–4 ■ The forced-distribution method of performance appraisal

behaviorally anchored rating scales (BARS)

a type of performance appraisal rating scale in which the points or values are descriptions of behavior

product is a list of behaviors (good and bad) that constitute effective and ineffective job performance.

The original critical-incidents method did not lend itself to quantification (that is, a score reflecting performance). It was used to guide employees in the specifics of their job performance. Each employee's performance can be described in terms of the occurrence of these critical behaviors. The supervisor can then counsel the employee to avoid the bad and continue the good behaviors. For example, a negative critical incident for a machine operator might be "leaves machine running while unattended." A positive one might be "always wears safety goggles on the job." Discussing performance in such clear terms is more understandable than using such vague statements as "poor attitude" or "careless work habits."

Behaviorally anchored rating scales (BARS) are a combination of the critical-incident and rating-scale methods. Performance is rated on a scale, but the scale points are anchored with behavioral incidents. The development of BARS is time-consuming, but the benefits make it worthwhile. BARS are developed in a five-step process:

1. A list of critical incidents is generated in the manner discussed previously.

2. A group of people (usually supervisors—either the same people who generated the critical incidents initially or another group) clusters the incidents into a smaller set of performance dimensions (usually five to ten) that they typically represent. The result is a given number of performance dimensions, each containing several illustrative critical incidents.

3. Another group of knowledgeable people is instructed to perform the following task: The critical incidents are "scrambled" so that they are no longer listed under the dimensions described in step 2. The critical incidents might be written on separate note cards and presented to the people in random order. The raters' task is to reassign or retranslate all the critical incidents back to the original performance dimensions. The goal is to have critical incidents that clearly represent the performance dimensions under consideration. A critical incident generally is

said to be retranslated successfully if some percentage (usually 50% to 80%) of the raters reassign it back to the dimension from which it came. Incidents that are not retranslated successfully (that is, there is ample confusion as to which dimension they represent) are discarded.

4. The people who retranslated the items are asked to rate each "surviving" critical incident on a scale (typically seven or nine points) of just how effectively or ineffectively it represents performance on the appropriate dimension. The ratings given to each incident are then averaged, and the standard deviation for each item is computed. Low standard deviations indicate high rater agreement on the value of the incident. High standard deviations indicate low rater agreement. A standard deviation criterion is then set for deciding which incidents will be retained for inclusion in the final form of the BARS. Incidents that have a standard deviation in excess of 1.50 typically are discarded because the raters could not agree on their respective values.

5. The final form of the instrument consists of critical incidents that met both the retranslation and standard deviation criteria. The incidents serve as behavioral anchors for the performance dimension scales. The final BARS instrument is a series of scales listed vertically (one for each dimension) and anchored by the retained incidents. Each incident is located along the scale according to its established rating. An example of BARS for patrol officer performance is shown in Figure 7–5. As can be seen, behaviors are listed with respect to what the employee is expected to do at various performance levels. For this reason, BARS are sometimes referred to as "behavioral expectation scales."

One of the major advantages of BARS is unrelated to performance appraisal. It is the high degree of involvement of persons developing the scale. The participants must carefully examine specific behaviors that lead to effective performance. In so doing, they may reject false stereotypes about ineffective performances. The method has face validity for both the rater and ratee and also appears useful for training raters. However, one disadvantage is that BARS are job specific; that is, a different behaviorally anchored rating scale must be developed for every job. Furthermore, it is possible for employees to exhibit different behaviors (on a single performance dimension) depending upon situational factors (such as the degree of urgency), and as such there is no one single expectation for the employee on that dimension. For example, consider the dimension of interpersonal relations. When conditions at work are relatively free of tensions, a person may be expected to behave calmly. However, when operating under stress, a person may act irritably. Thus, the expectation of behavior depends on the circumstances in effect.

Another development in appraisal is the *behavioral-observation scale (BOS)*. Like BARS, it is based on critical incidents. With BOS the rater must rate the employee on the frequency of critical incidents. The rater observes the employee over a certain period, such as a month. Here is an example of a five-point critical-incident scale used in appraising salespeople, as provided by Latham and Wexley (1977):

Knows the price of competitive products

Never	Seldom	Sometimes	Generally	Always
1	2	3	4	5

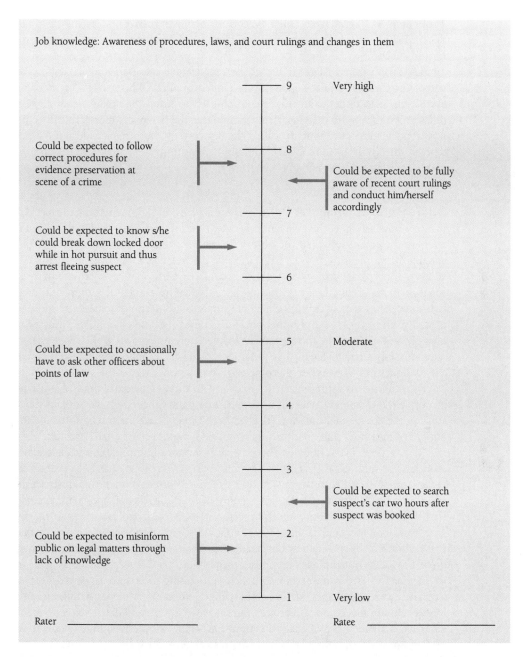

Job knowledge: Awareness of procedures, laws, and court rulings and changes in them

— 9   Very high

Could be expected to follow
correct procedures for
evidence preservation at
scene of a crime

— 8

Could be expected to be fully
aware of recent court rulings
and conduct him/herself
accordingly

— 7

Could be expected to know s/he
could break down locked door
while in hot pursuit and thus
arrest fleeing suspect

— 6

— 5   Moderate

Could be expected to occasionally
have to ask other officers about
points of law

— 4

— 3

Could be expected to search
suspect's car two hours after
suspect was booked

Could be expected to misinform
public on legal matters through
lack of knowledge

— 2

— 1   Very low

Rater _____   Ratee _____

FIGURE 7–5 ■ **Example of a behaviorally anchored rating scale for appraising patrol officers**

SOURCE: From *Psychology of Work Behavior,* rev. ed. (p. 128), by F. J. Landy and D. A. Trumbo, 1980, Pacific Grove, CA: Brooks/Cole.

Raters evaluate the employees on several such critical incidents, recording how often they observed the behavior. The total score is the sum of all the critical incidents. The final step is to correlate the response for each incident (a rating of 1, 2, 3, 4, or 5) with the total performance score. This is called *item analysis*. It is meant to detect the critical incidents that most influence overall performance.

Those incidents that have the highest correlations with the total score are the most discriminating factors in performance. They would be retained to develop criteria for job success.

Latham, Fay, and Saari (1979) suggested advantages to performance appraisals with BOS. First, like BARS, BOS are developed by those who use the method for evaluation, who understand they are committed to using the scales. Second, BOS information can be used to teach new employees the behaviors most critical to the job. Finally, BOS are content valid; the aspects of performance appraised are derived directly from the job. The authors believe this satisfies the EEOC requirement that appraisal methods be job relevant.

Relevance of Judgmental Data.

The relevance of judgmental data in performance appraisal, like the relevance of any type of performance appraisal data, refers to the extent to which the observed data are accurate measures of the "true" variable being measured. The "true" variable can refer to a global construct, such as overall job performance, or a dimension of job performance, such as interpersonal relations ability. One method of assessing the relevance of judgmental data is to correlate them with performance appraisals from another method, such as objective production or personnel data. In studies that have conducted this type of analysis, the resulting correlations have been only moderate. While these results may be interpreted to mean that judgmental data have only moderate relevance, the key question is whether the objective production data or the personnel data can be assumed to represent "true" ability. Those types of data might be just as incomplete or remotely relevant as judgmental data. Since we never obtain measures of the conceptual criterion (that is, "true" ability), we are forced to deal with imperfect measures that, not surprisingly, yield imperfect results. Research (e.g., Weekley & Gier, 1989) showed the existence of rater disagreement and halo error even among such expert raters as Olympic judges who were intensely trained to make accurate evaluations. DeNisi and Peters (1996) reported that instructing raters to keep a structured diary for continuous record keeping of performance (rather than using memory recall) produced more accurate assessments of the employees. Wagner and Goffin (1997) concluded that performance appraisal ratings produced by behavioral-observation methods are no more accurate than those produced by employee comparison methods.

Borman (1978) had another approach to assessing the relevance of judgmental data. He made videotapes of two employment situations: a manager talking with a problem employee and a recruiter interviewing a job candidate. Sixteen videotapes were made, eight of each situation. Each tape showed a different degree of performance—from a highly competent recruiter to a totally inept one. Similar degrees of performance were shown of the manager–subordinate meeting. Professional actors were used in the tapes. The same actor played the recruiter in all eight tapes, but a different actor played the new employee in each tape. Thus, the performance level (the "true" ability of the manager or recruiter) was "programmed" into the scripts.

"Barkley, I perceive my role in this institution not as a judge but merely as an observer and recorder. I have observed you to be a prize boob and have so recorded it."

Raters were asked to rate the performance of the manager and recruiter with a series of rating scales. The evaluations were correlated with the performance levels depicted. Correlations between ratings and levels of performance across several job dimensions (organizing the interview, establishing rapport, and so on) ranged from .42 to .97. The median was .69. Although this study used a simulation as opposed to actual job performance, it did show that various types of rating procedures are susceptible to differences in validity. The study also revealed that certain dimensions of performance are more accurately evaluated ("answering recruitee's questions," $r = .97$) than others ("reacting to stress," $r = .42$). Borman was led to conclude that raters are limited in their ability to appraise performance; they could not accurately evaluate the levels of "true" performance that were acted out in the scripts. He suggested a practical upper limit to validity that is less than the theoretical limit ($r = 1.0$) (see Field Note 2). After many years of research on various types of performance appraisal rating scales, I/O psychologists have concluded that the variance in rated performance due to the rating scale format is slight, typically less than 5%. Other sources of variance in rated performance are more substantial. These topics will be discussed next.

FIELD NOTE 2   Good Research Isn't Cheap

Many times unexpected costs are associated with performance appraisal. Here is the story of one of the more unusual expenses I have ever encountered in a research study.

One of the uses of performance appraisal information is as a criterion of job performance. In turn, criteria of job performance may be used to validate selection tests. I had a colleague who needed to collect both performance appraisal (criterion) data and test score (predictor) data to develop a selection test battery for a company. He traveled to the company and had all the supervisors convene in the company cafeteria. He explained the nature of the performance ratings he wanted them to make. Then he explained that all their subordinates would be taking a 30-minute test, and the scores would be correlated with the supervisors' performance appraisal ratings, as is done in a concurrent criterion-related validity study. My colleague then asked the supervisors whether they wanted to take the same test their subordinates would be taking just to get a feel for what it was like. They agreed. He

passed out the test and informed them they would have 30 minutes to complete it. He wanted the testing procedure to be very exact, giving everyone precisely 30 minutes. His watch did not have a second hand, so he was about to ask if he could borrow someone else's watch, when he spied the company's microwave oven on the wall in the cafeteria. He went over to the microwave, set the timer for 30 minutes, told the supervisors to begin the test, and started the microwave.

About 20 minutes into the test, a terrible odor began to fill the cafeteria. Somebody noticed it was coming from the microwave. My colleague had failed to place anything into the microwave when he started it, so for 20 minutes the microwave cooked itself, ultimately suffering terminal meltdown. The microwave cost $800 to replace and is one of the more unusual test-validation expense items I have ever heard of. Incidentally, the test turned out to be highly predictive of the performance appraisal ratings, so the exercise was not a complete waste.

RATER TRAINING

rater training
the process of training raters to make more accurate ratings of performance, typically achieved by reducing the frequency of halo, leniency, and central-tendency errors

Can you train raters to make better performance appraisals? The answer appears to be yes. **Rater training** is a formal process in which appraisers are taught to make fewer halo, leniency, and central-tendency errors. For example, Latham, Wexley, and Pursell (1975) randomly assigned 60 managers who appraised performance to one of these three groups:

- *Workshop group.* This group was shown videotapes on evaluating individuals. Members then discussed appraisal procedures and problems in making appraisals, with the intent of reducing rating errors.
- *Discussion group.* This group received training similar in content, but the main method was discussion.
- *Control group.* This group received no training.

Six months later, the three groups were "tested." They were shown videotapes of several hypothetical job candidates along with job requirements. The managers were asked to evaluate the candidates' suitability for the jobs in question. The groups showed major differences in the rating errors they made. The workshop group had no rating errors, and the control group performed the worst, making all three types of errors.

Zedeck and Cascio (1982) considered the purpose for which performance appraisal ratings are made—merit raise, retention, and development—and found that training works better for some purposes than others. Training typically enhances the accuracy of performance appraisals as well as their acceptability to those who are being appraised.

However, not all research on rater training is positive. Bernardin and Pence (1980) reported that raters who were trained to reduce halo errors actually made less accurate ratings after training. This seems due to the fact that, as Bartlett (1983) noted, there are two types of halo; reduction of invalid halo increases accuracy, but reduction of valid halo decreases it. Hedge and Kavanagh (1988) concluded that certain types of rater training reduce classical rating errors such as halo and leniency but do not increase rating accuracy. It is possible to reduce the occurrence of rating errors and also reduce accuracy because other factors besides the three classic types of rating errors affect accuracy. The relationship between rating errors and accuracy is uncertain because of our inability to know what "truth" is (Sulsky & Balzer, 1988).

One type of rater training appears particularly promising. Frame-of-reference training (Sulsky & Day, 1992) involves providing raters with common reference standards (i.e., frames) by which to evaluate performance. Raters are shown vignettes of good, poor, and average performances and are given feedback on the accuracy of their ratings of the vignettes. The intent of the training is to "calibrate" raters so that they agree on what constitutes varying levels of performance effectiveness for each performance dimension. Research by Woehr (1994) and Day and Sulsky (1995) supported the conclusion that frame-of-reference training increases the accuracy of individual raters on separate performance dimensions. In a meta-analytic review of rater training for performance appraisal, Woehr and Huffcutt (1994) examined the effectiveness of rater training methods on the major dependent variables of reduced halo error, reduced leniency error, and increased rating accuracy. The authors concluded that rater training has a positive effect on each dependent variable. However, the training strategies are differentially effective in addressing the aspect of performance ratings they are designed to meet. Because raters are influenced by numerous attribution errors or biases, Kraiger and Aguinis (2001) encourage evaluators to rely on multiple sources of information and question the veracity of judgments made by raters.

RATER MOTIVATION

It is not unusual for the majority of employees in a company to receive very high performance evaluations. These inflated ratings are often interpreted as evidence of massive rater errors (i.e., leniency or halo) or a breakdown in the performance appraisal system. The typical organizational response to rating inflation is to make some technical adjustment in the rating scale format or to institute a new training program for raters. However, there is another explanation for rating inflation that is unrelated to rater errors.

Murphy and Cleveland (1995) posited that the tendency to give uniformly high ratings is an instance of adaptive behavior that is, from the rater's point of

rater motivation
a concept that refers to organizationally induced pressures that compel raters to evaluate ratees positively

view, an eminently logical course of action. These deficiencies in ratings are more likely to be a result of the rater's *willingness* to provide accurate ratings than of the *capacity* to rate accurately. If the situation is examined from the rater's perspective, there are many sound reasons to provide inflated ratings. **Rater motivation** is often adjusted to achieve some particular result.

First, there are typically no rewards from the organization for accurate appraisals and few if any sanctions for inaccurate appraisals. Official company policies often emphasize the value of good performance appraisals, but organizations typically take no specific steps to reward this supposedly valued activity. Second, the most common reason cited for rating inflation is that high ratings are needed to guarantee promotions, salary increases, and other valued rewards. Low ratings, on the other hand, result in these rewards being withheld from subordinates. Raters are thus motivated to obtain valued rewards for their subordinates. Third, raters are motivated to give inflated ratings because the ratings received by subordinates are a reflection of the *rater's* job performance (Latham, 1986). One of the duties of managers is to develop their subordinates. If managers consistently rate their subordinates as less than good performers, it can appear that the managers are not doing their jobs. Thus, high ratings make the rater look good and low ratings make the rater look bad. Fourth, raters tend to inflate their ratings because they wish to avoid the negative reactions that accompany low ratings (Klimoski & Inks, 1990). Negative evaluations typically result in defensive reactions from subordinates, which can create a very stressful situation for the rater. The simplest way to avoid unpleasant or defensive reactions in appraisal interviews is to give uniformly positive feedback (i.e., inflated ratings).

Kozlowski, Chao, and Morrison (1998) describe the process of "appraisal politics" in organizations. If there is a sense that most other raters are inflating their ratings of their subordinates, a good rater has to play politics to protect and enhance the careers of his or her own subordinates. To the extent that a rating inflation strategy actually enhances the prospects of the better subordinates, it may be interpreted as being in the best interests of the organization to do so. Kozlowski et al. stated: "Indeed, if rating distortions are the norm, a failure to engage in appraisal politics may be maladaptive" (p. 176). Supporting this conclusion, Jawahar and Williams (1997) meta-analyzed performance appraisals given for administrative purposes (e.g., promotions) versus developmental or research purposes. Their results showed that performance appraisals conducted for administrative purposes were one-third of a standard deviation higher than those obtained for development or research purposes. As these authors stated, performance appraisals will be much more lenient when those appraisals are "for keeps" (see Field Note 3).

There is no simple way to counteract a rater's motivation to inflate ratings. The problem will not be solved by just increasing the capability of raters. In addition, the environment must be modified in such a way that raters are motivated to provide accurate ratings. Murphy and Cleveland (1995) believe accurate rating is most likely to occur in an environment where the following conditions exist:

- Good and poor performance are clearly defined.
- Distinguishing among workers in terms of their levels of performance is widely accepted.

FIELD NOTE 3   Are High Ratings a "Problem"?

esearch on performance appraisal ratings has typically regarded high ratings as reflecting some kind of error. This error then becomes the focus of corrective action, as methods (i.e., different rating techniques, rater training) are applied to produce lower evaluations. However, an examination of just the statistical properties of ratings, apart from the organizational context in which they are rendered, fails to capture *why* they occur. As recent research has revealed, managers who give high evaluations of their employees are behaving in an eminently reasonable fashion, not making errors per se. Managers (or other supervisors) have a vested interest in the job performance of their subordinates. The subordinates are socialized and coached to exhibit desired behaviors on the job. Those who don't exhibit these behaviors are often dismissed. Those who do are rewarded with social approval, if nothing more than being allowed to retain their jobs. The performance of subordinates is also regarded as a measure of the manager's own job performance. It is then logical for a manager to cultivate an efficient work group. Finally, managers often feel a sense of sponsorship for their employees. They want their employees to do well and have in fact often invested a sizable portion of their own time and energy to produce that outcome. Thus, when it comes time for a formal performance review of their subordinates, managers often respond by rating them highly. Rather than errors of judgment, the high evaluations could represent little more than the outcome of a successful socialization process designed to achieve that very outcome.

- There is a high degree of trust in the system.
- Low ratings do not automatically result in the loss of valued rewards.
- Valued rewards are clearly linked to accuracy in performance appraisal.

The authors know of organizations in which *none* of these conditions is met, but they don't know of any in which *all* of them are met. It is clear that we need more research on the organizational context in which performance appraisals are conducted. Mero and Motowidlo (1995) also reported findings that underscore the importance of the context in which ratings are made. They found that raters who are held accountable for their performance ratings make more accurate ratings than raters who are not held accountable. The problem of rating inflation will ultimately be solved by changing the context in which ratings are made, and not by changing the rater or the rating scale.

CONTEXTUAL PERFORMANCE

contextual performance behavior exhibited by an employee that contributes to the welfare of the organization but is not a formal component of an employee's job duties

Borman and Motowidlo (1993) contended that individuals contribute to organizational effectiveness in ways that go beyond the activities that make up their jobs. They can either help or hinder efforts to accomplish organizational goals by doing many things that are not directly related to their main functions. However, these contributions are important because they shape the organizational or psychological context that serves as a catalyst for work. The authors argued that these contributions are a valid component of overall job performance, yet they transcend the assessment of performance in specific tasks. This aspect of performance is referred to as **contextual performance**, organizational citizenship behavior, and extra-role performance. We will also discuss this topic in more detail in a later chapter.

These are some examples of contextual performance:

- Persisting with enthusiasm and extra effort as necessary to complete one's own task activities successfully
- Volunteering to carry out task activities that are not formally part of one's own job
- Helping and cooperating with others
- Endorsing, supporting, and defending organizational objectives

Borman and Motowidlo (1993) believe that an accurate assessment of job performance must include such contextual factors as well as task performance. Motowidlo and Van Scotter (1994) found that both task performance and contextual performance contributed independently to overall performance in a sample of U.S. Air Force mechanics. Experience was more highly related to task performance than to contextual performance, while personality variables were more highly related to contextual performance than to task performance. Borman, White, and Dorsey (1995) concluded that supervisors weight contextual performance approximately as highly as task performance when making overall performance ratings. Conway (1999) found that peers were particularly sensitive to the contextual job performance of managers. In general, it appears that knowledgeable raters are sensitized to the general contributions employees make in enhancing organizational welfare. Consideration of these contributions is as important in an overall evaluation as performance in the more narrow and specific behavior associated with task performance. However, to the extent that contextual performance is formally evaluated in making appraisals of job performance, it is no longer contextual. Rather, contextual performance becomes part of the formal job requirements, even though the behaviors are exhibited or directed toward activities that more accurately pertain to the functioning of the overall organization.

SELF- AND PEER APPRAISALS

Most research on judgmental performance appraisal deals with evaluations made by a superior (supervisor, manager). However, there is also information on the value of performance appraisals made by colleagues or peers. Self-evaluations have also been discussed. Our knowledge is somewhat limited, but these methods do offer added understanding of performance.

Self-Assessments

self-assessment
a technique of
performance appraisal
in which individuals
assess their own
behavior

With **self-assessment**, as the term suggests, each employee appraises his or her own performance. The procedure most commonly used is some type of graphic rating scale. Meyer (1980) reported a study in which engineers rated their own performance against their views of the performance of other engineers in the company. On average, each engineer thought he or she was performing better than 75% of the rest of the engineers in the study. Statistically, it is quite a trick to have

100% of the workforce be in the top 25% of job performers. This underscores the biggest problem with self-assessment: positive leniency. Most people have higher opinions of their own performance than others do.

Anderson, Warner, and Spencer (1984) demonstrated in a clever study just how prevalent and pervasive inflation bias is in self-assessments of ability. They asked applicants to rate their own abilities in real clerical tasks as well as in bogus tasks that sounded real but were nonsense. Some of the bogus tasks were "operating a matriculation machine," "typing from audio-fortran reports," and "circumscribing general meeting registers." The clerical applicants rated themselves high on the real tasks (where their ability was not verified) and also on the tasks that did not even exist! Steel and Ovalle (1984) found that there was less positive leniency in self-assessments when there was a high degree of feedback from supervisors. In other words, employees who get little feedback from their supervisors think more highly of their own abilities than employees who receive a lot of feedback. Mount (1984) found that managers evaluate themselves more leniently compared with both how they evaluate their supervisors and how their supervisors evaluate them. Bernardin, Hagan, Kane, and Villanova (1998) suggested that the reason for this pertains to perceptions of factors beyond the control of the individual. When we rate ourselves, we tend not to lower our own evaluations if we perceive that any shortcomings in our performance were beyond our control. However, when other people rate us, they tend to perceive us as being responsible for our performance.

Thornton (1980) reported that despite leniency problems, there are fewer halo errors with self-appraisals. People apparently recognize their own strengths and weaknesses and appraise themselves accordingly. Thornton also reported little agreement in most studies comparing self-assessments and supervisor assessments. Superiors do not evaluate employees in the same way that employees evaluate themselves. This does not mean that one appraisal is "right" and the other "wrong." It just means that the two groups do not agree in evaluating the same performance. Thornton suggested this may be healthy because it provides a basis for discussing differences and may foster an exchange of ideas. Campbell and Lee (1988) concluded that self-assessments were of greater value when used for developmental purposes rather than for administrative purposes. While self-assessments have documented value for developmental purposes, their frequency of use as a component of a performance appraisal process is approximately only 5% among U.S. companies (Atwater, 1998).

Peer Assessments

In **peer assessment**, members of a group appraise the performance of their fellows. According to Kane and Lawler (1978), three techniques are commonly used. One is **peer nomination**, in which each person nominates a specified number of group members as being highest on the particular dimension of performance. The second is **peer rating**, in which each group member rates the others on a set of performance dimensions using one of several kinds of rating scales. The third technique is **peer ranking**, where each member ranks all others from best to worst on one or more performance dimensions.

peer assessment
a technique of performance appraisal in which individuals assess the behavior of their peers or coworkers

peer nomination
a technique of appraising the performance of coworkers by nominating them for membership in a group

peer rating
a technique for appraising the performance of coworkers by rating them on a dimension of their job behavior

peer ranking
a technique of appraising the performance of coworkers by ranking them on a dimension of their job behavior

The method's reliability is determined by assessing the degree of inter-rater agreement. Most studies report high reliabilities (coefficients in the .80s and .90s), indicating that peers agree about the job performance of group members. The validity of peer assessments is determined by correlating the peer assessments with criterion measures usually made later, such as who successfully completed a training program, who got promoted first, the size of raises, and so on. What is uncanny is that group members who have known one another a relatively short time (two to three weeks) can be quite accurate in their long-term predictions about one another. Validity coefficients are impressive, commonly in the .40–.50 range. The peer nomination technique appears best in identifying people with extreme levels of attributes as compared with other members of the group. Peer ratings are the most applicable but have only marginal empirical support. It has been suggested that their use be limited to giving feedback to employees on how others perceive them. Relatively few data are available on the value of peer rankings, though they may be the best method for assessing overall job performance.

There is some evidence that peer assessments are biased by friendship (that is, employees evaluate their friends most favorably), but friendships may be formed on the basis of performance. Also, many work group members do not like to evaluate one another, so part of the method's success hinges on impressing participants with its value. Indeed, Cederblom and Lounsbury (1980) showed that lack of user acceptance may be a serious obstacle to this otherwise promising method. They found that a sample of college professors felt peer assessments were heavily biased by friendship. They thought peers would rate and be rated by their friends more favorably than would be justified. Problems with knowing the people to be rated and fostering a "mutual admiration society" caused the professors to question the value of peer assessment. They also felt that the method should be used for feedback, not for raises and promotions. Despite reluctance to use peer assessments for administrative decisions, research continues to support their predictive accuracy. Shore, Shore, and Thornton (1992) found peer assessments to be superior to self-assessments of job advancement.

Peer assessment, like self-assessment, is part of an overall performance appraisal system. The information generated cannot be isolated from information gained using other methods. Holzbach (1978) showed that superior, peer, and self-assessments all contribute information about performance. But information from each source was subject to halo errors. Borman (1974) showed that peers, superiors, and subordinates (if any) hold unique pieces of the puzzle that portrays a person's job performance. Thus, rather than having raters at just one level of the organization, it is better to have each level contribute the portion it is able to evaluate most effectively. Each performance dimension should be defined precisely enough to obtain the information unique to the relevant source. Overlap with dimensions better assessed by other sources should be avoided. The appraisal system should include compatible and mutually supporting segments. Each segment should be assigned the role to which it is best suited (Kane & Lawler, 1978). Performance appraisal should not be seen as simply selecting the best method. What is "best" varies with the use made of the information, the complexity of the performance appraised, and the people capable of making such judgments.

360-DEGREE FEEDBACK

360-degree feedback
a process of evaluating employees from multiple rating sources usually including supervisor, peer, subordinate, and self ratings

The term **360-degree feedback** refers to the practice of using multiple raters, often including self-ratings, in the assessment of individuals. It is also called multisource feedback. Typically, feedback about a target manager is solicited from significant others, including the individual's coworkers, subordinates, and superiors. The original purpose for 360-degree feedback was to enhance managers' awareness of their strengths and weaknesses to guide developmental planning. However, it is increasingly being used as a method of performance appraisal (Bracken et al., 1997). According to Tornow (1993), 360-degree assessment activities are usually based on two key assumptions: (1) awareness of any discrepancies between how we see ourselves and how others see us enhances self-awareness, and (2) enhanced self-awareness is a key to maximum performance as a manager and thus becomes a foundation for management and leadership development programs.

The term *360-degree feedback* derives from the geometric rationale for the multiple-rater assessment, as shown in Figure 7–6. The target manager is evaluated by other individuals who interact in a social network. The target manager also provides self-assessments. The typical assessment includes evaluations along three dimensions (Van Velsor, Ruderman, & Young, 1991):

1. *People*—dealing effectively with people, building good relationships
2. *Change*—setting, communicating, and implementing a goal or vision
3. *Structure*—structuring and organizing information, time, and work

The multiple raters make their assessments of an individual, and then the assessments are compared. Van Velsor et al. reported the following findings from their study, which are representative of most 360-degree feedback studies:

- Only 10% of the managers saw themselves as others saw them; the rest had substantial discrepancies (i.e., more than half of a standard deviation) on one, two, or three of the scales.
- Overrating oneself was the most common profile across scales. This difference was especially noteworthy in the *People* scale, where overrating was almost twice as common as underrating oneself or showing self–other agreement.
- About 80% of the managers modified their self-assessment in the expected direction on one or more scales after feedback. This change was most pronounced in the area of interpersonal skills.

It is particularly instructive to understand how disagreement among raters in 360-degree feedback is interpreted. The classic measurement perspective treats disagreement among raters as error variance—that is, something undesirable that reduces inter-rater reliability. With 360-degree feedback, differences in rater

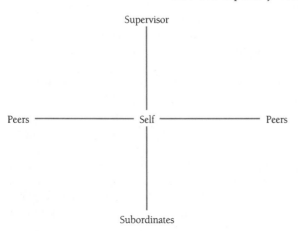

FIGURE 7–6 ■ **360-degree feedback relationships**

perspectives are regarded as potentially valuable and useful and are not treated as variations to be reduced. Such differences provide an opportunity for professional development and personal learning, to understand why individuals are perceived as they are by others.

How important is it that managers see themselves as others see them? Nilsen and Campbell (1993) proposed that job performance is a function of an individual's aptitude, task understanding, decision about how intensely to work, decision about how long to persist in the face of obstacles, and facilitating or inhibiting conditions not under the individual's control. Self-assessments are important because individuals make judgments about themselves that are relevant to these determinants of performance. Individuals have beliefs about their level of aptitude, and whether or not they understand the task they are asked to perform. If individuals overestimate their aptitude, they will devote less effort to the task than is needed to perform it adequately. Additionally, if individuals believe that they fully understand a task, they will probably devote little or no effort to obtaining additional task-relevant information. If, however, individuals do not in fact understand what is expected, they may utilize their aptitude and devote their effort, yet still fail to perform the task correctly. Additionally, London, Smither, and Adsit (1997) believe that 360-degree feedback will have little impact on changing behaviors when (1) the ratees are not accountable for using the feedback, and (2) the raters are not accountable for the accuracy or usefulness of the feedback they provide.

In general, it appears that accurate self-assessors are better able to improve their performance than are inaccurate self-assessors. Self-awareness and self-perception are becoming recognized as critical factors in determining managerial job performance, a job that typically entails working with many other people. However, what exactly people agree or disagree on is not totally clear. Greguras and Robie (1998) found that there is disagreement not only *across* types of raters, but also *within* the same type of rater (e.g., peers). Research has also been conducted on the measurement equivalence of ratings from different sources (Maurer, Raju, & Collins, 1998; Facteau & Craig, 2001). Using sophisticated analytic techniques, the authors concluded that ratings from different sources are comparable, although they may produce differential assessments of the target person.

A disturbing finding regarding the accuracy of multisource feedback was reported by Scullen, Mount, and Goff (2000). Based on a large number of 360-degree assessments, the authors partitioned the total amount of variance in the assessments into three components: the target's actual job performance, the raters' biases in the perception and recall of that performance, and random (uncontrollable) measurement error. The results revealed that only 25% of the variance in multisource feedback is attributable to the target's actual job performance, the intended object of the ratings. More than twice that amount of variance (54%) was due to rater bias in evaluating that performance. Thus, the amount of performance-related variance is only moderate and differs by the perspective of the rater. The authors concluded that what multisource feedback measures is largely the idiosyncratic rating tendencies of the raters. Accordingly, Mount and Scullen (2001) stated that in the context of developmental feedback, rater biases can be interpreted as meaningful information that represents the raters' unique perceptions of the individual.

However, when used to make personnel decisions, multisource feedback ratings should be averaged across types of raters, which will result in a better understanding of the performance level of the individual.

Finally, Brett and Atwater (2001) reported a finding that challenges the very logic of 360-degree feedback. In theory, the presence of negative feedback and discrepant results across raters should motivate positive behavior change in the person being evaluated. In fact, the authors found the opposite effect. Negative and discrepant feedback was perceived as less accurate, less useful, and produced negative reactions among those so rated.

FEEDBACK OF APPRAISAL INFORMATION TO EMPLOYEES

In the final step of appraisal, the employee and his or her superior review and discuss the evaluation, usually referred to by the misnomer "performance appraisal interview." Performance was appraised before the interview; the interview is a means of giving the employee the results. Both superior and subordinate are usually very uneasy about the interview. Employees often get defensive about negative performance aspects. Superiors are often nervous about having to confront employees face to face with negative evaluations. For an appraisal system to be effective, however, interview objectives must be met with the same rigor as the other system objectives.

The interview typically has two main objectives. The first is reviewing major job responsibilities and how well the employee has met them. The second objective is future planning, or identifying goals the employee will try to meet before the next review. Both employee and superior should provide input in setting goals.

There has been much research on factors that contribute to success in meeting the two objectives of the interview. Feedback on job performance has two properties: information and motivation; that is, feedback can tell the employee how to perform better as well as increase his or her desire to perform well. Ilgen, Fisher, and Taylor (1979) showed that how the employee perceives the superior greatly influences his or her response to feedback. They feel that credibility and power are the most important traits here. *Credibility* is the extent to which the superior is seen as someone who can legitimately evaluate performance. It is enhanced when the superior is considered to have expertise about the employee's job and be in a position to evaluate performance. *Power* is the extent to which the superior can control valued rewards. Ilgen and associates believe that credibility and power influence (1) how well the employee understands feedback, (2) the extent to which the feedback is seen as correct, and (3) the willingness of the employee to alter behavior as suggested by the feedback.

Cederblom (1982) found that three factors consistently seem to produce effective performance appraisal interviews: the supervisor's knowledge of the subordinate's job and performance in it, the supervisor's support of the subordinate, and a welcoming of the subordinate's participation. In particular, Cawley, Keeping, and Levy (1998) found that employee participation for the sake of having one's "voice" heard was more important to the employee than participation for the purpose of influencing the end result. However, just conducting a performance appraisal interview will not resolve all problems in evaluating subordinate performance. Ilgen, Peterson, Martin, and Boeschen (1981) found that even after the performance appraisal interview, subordinates and supervisors sometimes disagreed on the level of subordinate performance, with subordinates feeling their performance was at a higher level.

In a review of performance evaluations, Greenberg (1986) identified seven characteristics that contribute to employees' accepting their evaluations and feeling they were fair:

1. Solicitation of employee input prior to the evaluation and using it
2. Two-way communication during the appraisal interview
3. The opportunity to challenge/rebut the evaluation
4. The rater's degree of familiarity with the ratee's work
5. The consistent application of performance standards
6. Basing of ratings on actual performance achieved
7. Basing of recommendations for salary/promotions on the ratings

I fully concur with Greenberg's findings. My experience with effective performance appraisal systems underscores the importance of all of these characteristics and clearly reveals there is much more to performance evaluation than making a check mark on an appraisal instrument. Russell and Goode (1988) concluded that managers' reactions to performance appraisal systems are affected by their overall satisfaction with them (that is, their attitude toward the systems' ability to document the performance of their subordinates) and the appraisal's improvement value. Likewise, Dickinson (1993) found that the most important determinant of employee attitudes about performance appraisal is the supervisor. When the supervisor is perceived as trustworthy and supportive, attitudes about performance appraisal are favorable. Keeping and Levy (2000) concluded that reaction criteria are almost always relevant, and an unfavorable reaction may doom the most carefully constructed appraisal system.

CONCLUDING COMMENTS

The conceptual standards discussed in Chapter 3 on criteria are operationally measured by performance appraisal. The prediction methods discussed in Chapter 4, when united with the topic of standards or criteria, become the basis for making the personnel decisions discussed in Chapter 5. The topic of performance appraisal has attracted strong research interest among I/O psychologists. However, the primary focus of the research has changed over time. Latham, Skarlicki, Irvine, and Siegel (1993) noted that earlier research on performance appraisal tended to address the psychometric properties of the various types of rating instruments. Such studies included the effects of rating scales on reducing rater errors and enhancing accuracy. More recent research has addressed the broader organizational context in which performance appraisals are conducted, including user reactions, perceptions of fairness, and how evaluations can be used to develop employees. Indeed, Mayer and Davis (1999) found that employee trust in the top management of a company increased following the implementation of a more acceptable performance appraisal system. Ilgen, Barnes-Farrell, and McKellin (1993) believe that the major problems facing performance appraisals are not rating scale construction or the cognitive processes raters use to make evaluations; rather, more attention should be given to the values and expectations generated by the social context in which raters find themselves. Factors such as the extent to which raters desire to be liked by ratees and beliefs about freedom to be open and honest in making evaluations are underresearched.

Hauerstein (1998) asserted that many organizations are moving toward performance management rather than performance appraisal. The performance management perspective is that performance appraisal is a formal supervisory activity embedded in the larger context of conducting performance from day to day. For example, athletic coaches do not wait until after the season to evaluate players and give feedback to them. Thus, if managers openly and regularly discuss performance issues, then the yearly evaluation becomes little more than a formality.

CASE STUDY ■ **What Do You Do with Poor Performers?**

Anita Douglass was the regional sales manager for a national chain of fitness centers. Her job was to direct a sales force that sold fitness center franchises to operators. The salesperson's job was to recruit responsible, ambitious people who would invest their own time and money in operating a center. Each operator would pay a franchise fee to the company. The company, in turn, would lease the building, supply all the equipment, and help with the financing, if needed. Sales throughout the nation were very strong, as there was a heavy demand for fitness training. Douglass's sales territory was second best in the nation. All her salespeople were doing very well, except two. Marty Crane and Julie Forester consistently failed to meet their sales goals. Both were running out of excuses and Douglass was running out of patience. Douglass was angry and embarrassed about their poor performance. She figured the only reason her boss hadn't inquired about Crane and Forester was because she could "bury" their performance in the overall performance of her sales territory. If these two salespeople had been at the top of the pile instead of the bottom, her sales territory would be number one in the nation.

Despite their common substandard performance, Douglass viewed the two salespeople somewhat differently. After Crane's first bad performance evaluation, she undertook additional training. Even though the extra training didn't seem to help, at least she tried. Crane seemed to be working hard but getting nowhere—described in her last performance review as "an ineffectual diffusion of energy," otherwise known as "spinning your wheels." Crane had a pleasing demeanor, which may have been part of her problem. Douglass thought that perhaps Crane was more concerned with having people approve of her than making a sale. Maybe Crane would perform better for the company in a job outside of sales, she thought.

Forester, on the other hand, seemed rather indifferent about failing to meet her sales goals and attributed her poor performance to everyone other than herself. If Forester ever worked up a sweat, it went unnoticed by Douglass. Forester conveyed the impression that the company was lucky to have her, although the reasons for this privilege were indiscernible. None of the other salespeople wanted to have anything to do with Forester. They wouldn't trade sales territories with her, and they didn't want Forester covering for them when they went on vacation.

Douglass thumbed through the personnel files of Crane and Forester. It was becoming increasingly difficult to justify not firing them. If only one of them got the axe, Douglass decided it would be Forester. Then Douglass caught herself in midthought. The performance of both these salespeople was equally bad. How could she justify keeping one and firing the other? Douglass surmised that the only difference between Crane and Forester was that she liked one more than the other. Douglass had the reputation of being tough but fair. She couldn't understand why this was becoming a difficult decision for her, and why she was considering being more charitable to Crane than to Forester.

Study Questions

1. What is it about Crane that makes Douglass view her differently from Forester?
2. Are these issues relevant in judging job performance? Should they matter?
3. If you were Douglass, what would you do with Crane and Forester?
4. Do you think Douglass's boss would be critical of Douglass for tolerating poor performance, or admire her for being patient with members of her staff?
5. What other information would you like to have before deciding whether Crane and Forester should be retained or fired?

SUGGESTED INFOTRAC TOPICS

performance evaluation	*rater motivation*
performance appraisal	*self-assessments*
performance feedback	*peer assessments*
halo error	*360-degree feedback*
rater training	*rating scale*

C H A P T E R   8

Organizations and Organizational Change

LEARNING OBJECTIVES

- ■ Explain the three major theories of organization.
- ■ Understand Mintzberg's theory of organizational structure.
- ■ Explain downsizing and its effect on organizations.
- ■ Describe the components of social systems: roles, norms, and culture.
- ■ Discuss the rationale of organizational change.
- ■ Understand the concept of empowerment and why employees resist change.

Many academic disciplines have contributed to the study of organizations, including I/O psychology, sociology, economics, and political science. Their contributions tend to differ in the specific constructs that are investigated. The most common I/O psychological perspective is to examine individual behaviors and attitudes within an organizational context. Before we begin to examine this topic, however, it should be noted that it is not easy to grasp the meaning of an "organization." Organizations are abstract entities, yet they are real and in fact can be considered "alive." When an organization ceases to exist (as a company that declares bankruptcy and goes out of business), it is not unusual to refer to the "death" of this formerly living entity. Authors have tried to use metaphors to understand the meaning of an organization (Morgan, 1997). Metaphors enhance understanding of one concept by invoking reference to a more readily understood second concept. This technique has met with limited success in explaining organizations. One metaphor is to equate an organization with a person. People have a skeletal system and a circulatory system, concepts from physiology that are useful in understanding living organisms. Organizations possess characteristics (such as size and patterns of communication) that are general analogues of these physiological concepts. However, the metaphor is far from totally accurate. What defines the boundary of where a person "ends" and his or her environment begins is our skin. Whatever physiological systems we as humans possess are bounded by the skin covering our bodies. Organizations, in contrast, have no such boundary-defining characteristic as skin. Organizations, unlike humans, have loose or porous boundaries as to where they "end" and their environments (legal, social, political, economic, etc.) begin. If you find that organizations are rather difficult to understand as entities, you are not alone. It is a challenge to those academic disciplines that study organizations to find useful ways to explain what they are.

Davis and Powell (1992) noted that the study of organizations is relatively recent, having begun in the 1950s. During that time period psychologists began to appreciate how much influence organizations exerted on the behavior of employees. It will be recalled from Chapter 1 that it wasn't until 1970 that the profession of "industrial" psychology officially became "industrial/organizational" psychology, thus defining the scope of I/O psychology as we know it today. Formal recognition of the *O* in I/O psychology compelled us to gain a better understanding of the social bases of behavior. This chapter will explain how an organization influences and shapes the behavior of its members. The concepts that we will examine (that is, the unit of analysis) shift from the individual to larger social collectivities. Included are various organizing concepts, ranging from the formal structure of an organization to the dynamics associated with changing the way organizations function.

THREE THEORIES OF ORGANIZATIONS

organization
a coordinated group of people who perform tasks to produce goods or services

It is probably easier to state why organizations exist than to define what they are. In their simplest form, they exist as a vehicle for accomplishing goals and objectives; that is, **organizations** are collectivities of parts that cannot accomplish their goals as effectively if they operate separately. How one chooses to examine the organizing process produces the various schools of thought or theories about organizations. In my opinion, there are three major schools of thought about organizations, with many variations and emphases (Scott, 1992): the classical, neoclassical, and systems theories of organization. These schools of thought take markedly different views of the same phenomenon.

Classical Theory

classical theory
a theory developed in the early 20th century that described the form and structure of organizations

Classical theory, which emerged in the first few decades of the 20th century, focuses mainly on structural relationships in organizations. Classical theory begins with a statement of the basic ingredients of any organization and then addresses how the organization should best be structured to accomplish its objectives. There are four basic components to any organization:

1. *A system of differentiated activities.* All organizations are composed of the activities and functions performed in them and the relationships among these activities and functions. A formal organization emerges when these activities are linked together.
2. *People.* Although organizations are composed of activities and functions, people perform tasks and exercise authority.
3. *Cooperation toward a goal.* Cooperation must exist among the people performing their various activities to achieve a unity of purpose in pursuit of their common goals.
4. *Authority.* Authority is established through superior–subordinate relationships, and such authority is needed to ensure cooperation among people pursuing their goals.

Given that four ingredients are the bases of any organization, classical theory addresses the various structural properties by which the organization should best reach its goals. Four major structural principles are the hallmarks in the history of organizational theory.

functional principle
the concept that organizations should be divided into units that perform similar functions

Functional Principle.   The **functional principle** is the concept behind division of labor; that is, organizations should be divided into units that perform similar functions. Work is broken down to provide clear areas of specialization, which in turn improves the organization's overall performance. Similar work activities are often organized into departments, which enhances coordination of activities and permits more effective supervision and a more rational flow of work. It is the functional principle that accounts for the grouping of work functions into such units as production, sales, engineering, finance, and so on; these labels describe the primary nature of the work performed within each unit. The functional principle relates to the horizontal growth of the organization—that is, the formation of new functional units along the horizontal dimension.

scalar principle
the concept that organizations are structured by a chain of command that grows with increasing levels of authority

Scalar Principle.   The **scalar principle** deals with the organization's vertical growth and refers to the chain of command that grows with levels added to the organization. Each level has its own degree of authority and responsibility for meeting organizational goals, with higher levels having more responsibility. Each

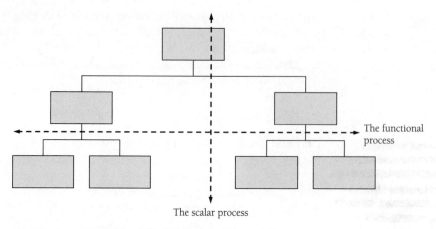

FIGURE 8–1   ■   **Pyramid of organization**

SOURCE: From *Organization Theory: A Structural and Behavioral Analysis* (p. 32) by W. G. Scott, T. R. Mitchell, and P. H. Birnbaum, 1981, Homewood, IL: Richard D. Irwin. Reprinted with permission.

unity of command
the concept that each subordinate should be accountable to only one supervisor

subordinate should be accountable to only one superior, a tenet referred to as the **unity of command**. Classical theorists thought the best way to overcome organizational fragmentation caused by division of labor was through a well-designed chain of command. Coordination among factions is achieved by people occupying positions of command in a hierarchy. Figure 8–1 shows a graphic representation of both the functional and scalar principles.

Line/Staff Principle.

line functions
organizational work that directly meets the major goals of an organization

One way to differentiate organizational work functions is by whether they are line or staff. **Line functions** have the primary responsibility for meeting the major goals of the organization, like the production department in a manufacturing organization. **Staff functions** support the line's activities but are regarded as subsidiary in overall importance to line functions. Typical staff functions are personnel and quality control. That is, while it is important to have good employees and to inspect products for their quality, the organization was not created to provide people with jobs or products to inspect. It was created to manufacture products (a line function), and personnel and quality control are but two staff functions designed to support this larger goal.

staff functions
organizational work that supports line activities

Span-of-Control Principle.

span–of–control principle
the concept that refers to the number of subordinates a manager is responsible for supervising

The **span-of-control principle** refers to the number of subordinates a manager is responsible for supervising. A "small" span of control is 2 subordinates; a "large" span of control might be 15. Large spans of control produce flat organizations (that is, few levels between the top and bottom of the organization); small spans of control produce tall organizations (that is, many levels). Figure 8–2 is a diagram showing how the span of control affects the shape of the organization.

Classical theory is credited with providing the structural anatomy of organizations. It was the first major attempt to articulate the form and substance of organizations in a comprehensive fashion. There is little that is "psychological" about

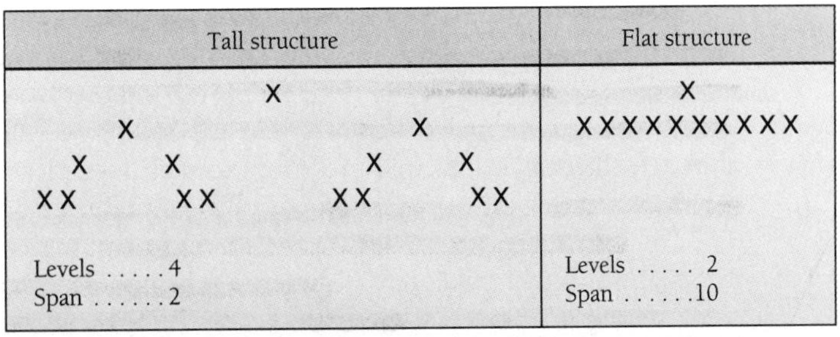

Tall structure				Flat structure
X				X
X			X	X X X X X X X X X X
X	X	X	X	
X X	X X	X X	X X	
Levels 4				Levels 2
Span 2				Span 10

FIGURE 8–2 ■ **Span of control and organizational structure**

SOURCE: From *Organization Theory: A Structural and Behavioral Analysis* (p. 34) by W. G. Scott, T. R. Mitchell, and P. H. Birnbaum, 1981, Homewood, IL: Richard D. Irwin. Reprinted with permission.

this view of organizations; indeed, none of the classical organizational theorists were psychologists. The influence of psychology became apparent in neoclassical theory, the next school of thought. Nevertheless, although current organizational researchers regard classical theory as antiquated, its four principles are deeply ingrained in the real-life structure of organizations. Problems of line/staff relationships, number of organizational levels, division of labor, coordination, and spans of control are still of major concern. Further thinking about organizations occurred because organizations were more complex than the four classical principles suggested. This desire to add richness and realism to organizational theory gave rise to neoclassical theory.

Neoclassical Theory

neoclassical theory
a theory developed in the 1950s that described psychological or behavioral issues associated with organizations

Neoclassical theory was born in the 1950s, but its origins go back to the findings from the Hawthorne studies. It was identified with scholars who recognized the deficiencies in the classical school of thought. In fact, the name *neoclassical* connotes a modernization or updating of the original (classical) theory, while still acknowledging its contributions.

It is a misnomer to call neoclassical theory a "theory" because there really is no formal theory. Rather, it is a recognition of psychological/behavioral issues that question the rigidity with which the classical principles were originally stated. The neoclassicists examined the four major principles of classical theory and found evidence that challenged their apparent unassailability. This evidence was based primarily on either psychological research or an examination of real-life organizational problems.

The neoclassicists noted that while division of labor causes functional interdependence among work activities, it also depersonalizes these activities so that the individual finds little meaning in them. That is, people develop a sense of alienation from highly repetitive work, which ultimately results in dissatisfaction with their work. In turn, this dissatisfaction can result in decreased efficiency caused by lowered productivity and increased absence. In short, the neoclassicists argued for less rigid division of labor and for more "humanistic" work in which people derive a sense of value and meaning from their jobs.

The scalar principle was questioned on the grounds that other systems operate on people in organizations besides those imposed by formal superior–subordinate relationships. Individuals are influenced by interpersonal activities that extend well beyond those prescribed by the formal organizational structure. In short, although the scalar principle prescribes formal lines of authority, in reality many sources operating in an organization influence the individual.

The line/staff principle was perhaps the easiest for neoclassicists to challenge. The black-and-white theoretical distinction between line and staff functions is not always so clear in practice. Take, for example, the sales function. A manufacturing company's purpose is indeed to produce, but if it does not sell what it produces, the company cannot survive. What, then, is the sales function—a major line function or an ancillary staff function? The neoclassicists illustrated that many staff functions are critical to the success of the organization, so the value of the distinction between line and staff is not so great as originally proposed.

Finally, determining a satisfactory span of control is far more complex than picking a number. The neoclassicists noted it depends on such issues as the supervisor's managerial ability (poor managers cannot supervise many subordinates) and the intensity of the needed supervision (one could effectively manage many more subordinates who do not require much direction than those who do require intensive direction). Psychological factors such as leadership style and capacity greatly influence the determination of effective spans of control.

The primary contribution of neoclassical theory was to reveal that the principles proposed by classical theory were not as universally applicable and simple as originally formulated. The neoclassicists drew heavily on behavioral research that revealed the importance of individual differences. They did not overtly reject classical theory. Rather than attempting to change the theory, they tried to make it fit the realities of human behavior in organizations. However, the neoclassicists were limited by basing their conceptualization about organizations on the classical perspective. By the mid-1960s, it became apparent that an entirely new approach to thinking about organizations was necessary. Organizations were more complex than even the neoclassicists portrayed them; this led to the formation of a radically different school of thought called systems theory.

Systems Theory

systems theory
a theory developed in the 1970s that described organizations in terms of interdependent components that form a system

Modern organization theory adopts a complex, dynamic view of organizations called the "systems approach." Systems theory had its origins in the biological sciences and was modified to meet the needs of organizational theory (Kast & Rosenzweig, 1972). Katz and Kahn (1978) were among the early proponents of thinking about organizations as a series of interlocking systems. **Systems theory** views an organization as existing in an interdependent relationship with its environment: "It is impossible to understand individual behavior or the activities of small groups apart from the social system in which they interact. A complex organization is a social system; the various discrete segments and functions in it do not behave as isolated elements. All parts affect all other parts. Every action has repercussions throughout the organization, because all of its elements are linked" (Scott, Mitchell, & Birnbaum, 1981, p. 44). In fact, the idea that all parts of the system are interdependent is the key to understanding the systems approach. All of the parts and their interrelatedness make up the "system," which is how the theory gets its name.

Systems theory asserts that an organizational system is composed of these five parts:

1. *Individuals.* Individuals bring their own personalities, abilities, and attitudes with them to the organization, which influence what they hope to attain by participating in the system.
2. *Formal organization.* The formal organization is the interrelated pattern of jobs that provide the structure of the system.
3. *Small groups.* Individuals do not work in isolation but become members of small groups as a way to facilitate their own adaptability within the system.
4. *Status and role.* Status and role differences exist among jobs within an organization and define the behavior of individuals within the system.
5. *Physical setting.* This is the external physical environment and the degree of technology that characterizes the organization.

Figure 8–3 illustrates the five parts of the system and their interrelatedness. Complex interactions exist among all parts of the system. Individuals interact to form small groups, members of the groups are differentiated by status and roles, the physical environment affects the behavior of individuals and groups, and all exist within the framework provided by the formal organization.

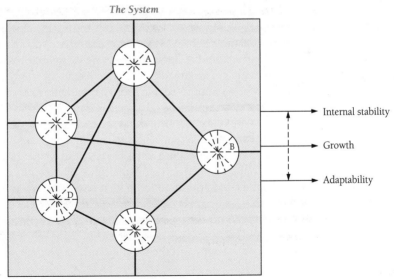

Key:
   1. Circles represent parts of the system.
   2. Broken lines represent intrapart interactions, i.e., individuals with other individuals.
   3. Solid lines represent interpart interaction.
   4. Both the solid and broken lines are the processes that tie the parts of the system together.

FIGURE 8–3 ■ The framework of systems analysis

SOURCE: From *Organization Theory: A Structural and Behavioral Analysis* (p. 48) by W. G. Scott, T. R. Mitchell, and P. H. Birnbaum, 1981, Homewood, IL: Richard D. Irwin. Reprinted with permission.

With all of these parts making up the system, it is necessary to have a means to provide coordination and linkage among them. Such functions are accomplished through communication and decision making; they permit the various parts of the system to "talk" to each other. Organizational communication occurs through a series of networks that often bear little resemblance to formal lines of authority. Similarly, decisions are often made in ways that deviate from formal lines of authority. That is, the reality of how organizations actually conduct themselves is usually quite different from the principles established by classical organizational theory. Also, the Achilles' heel of most large organizations is failure to communicate. This makes considerable sense, given the systems perspective of organizations, because communication is the means by which the system can be responsive to its environment.

Finally, systems theory instructs us that the parts and interactions of a system do not exist for themselves. Rather, they exist to meet the system's larger goals, which are stability, growth, and adaptability. A living organism has to be stable in the sense that its parts are harmoniously integrated. Growth reflects a sense of vitality and vigor. Adaptability is critical if the organism is to respond to environmental changes because adaptability enables the organism to survive in times of rapid change. Thus, a healthy, successful organization is not only "effective" in meeting its business objectives but also stable, growing, and adaptable. These are the characteristics of all living organisms, be they organizations, animals, plants, or societies.

Systems theory offers a radical departure from the classical and neoclassical schools of thought. Systems theory views organizations as any other form of living organism. The purpose of an organization is to reach stability, to grow, and to adapt, as all living organisms must do to survive. Note the abstractness of systems theory. There are no direct references to anything quite as simple as a span of control, for example. This abstractness is deliberate, for only at some degree of generality can one attempt to equate such diverse entities as organizations, plants, and animals. Modern organizational theorists believe that an understanding of something as complex as an organization requires the type of conceptualizations offered by systems theory. A systems perspective of organizations permits us to understand phenomena of organizational life that earlier theories would not permit.

Despite the distinctiveness of the three schools of thought on organizations, each school offered critical concepts that have great relevance today. That is, these schools are more than historical milemarkers in the evolution of organizational theory. In particular, the concept of small groups from systems theory has been greatly amplified to provide a primary focal point of interest, the work team. The concept of work teams and their significance will be discussed in the next chapter.

ORGANIZATIONAL STRUCTURE

Mintzberg (1993) offered a comprehensive and lucid explanation of how organizations evolve to reach a certain form and shape. We refer to these characteristics as the "structure" or formal component of an organization. Various types of structure are possible, and every organization continually seeks to find a structure that is an optimal match to its environment. That is, the structure of an organization is an adaptive mechanism that permits the organization to function in its surroundings. Organizations that have maladaptive structures will ultimately cease to exist. Since individuals assume roles within organizations, individuals (most notably employees) feel the brunt of change caused by the continuing evolution of an organization's structure. It is in this regard that I/O psychology is involved in matters of organizational structure.

Coordinating Mechanisms

structure
the arrangement of work functions within an organization designed to achieve efficiency and control

Mintzberg (1993) defined the **structure** of an organization as "the sum total of the ways in which its labor is divided into distinct tasks and then its coordination is achieved among these tasks" (p. 2). Although many structures are possible for an organization, relatively few are effective structures for a particular organization. Five coordinating mechanisms have been proposed to explain the fundamental ways in which organizations coordinate their work. These are considered the most basic elements of structure, the glue that holds organizations together.

1. *Mutual adjustment.* Mutual adjustment achieves coordination of work by the process of informal communication among employees. As the term implies, it is the process by which employees coordinate their efforts to produce an outcome. Two people paddling a canoe are an example of the mutual adjustment between individuals needed to propel the canoe through water.

2. *Direct supervision.* Direct supervision achieves coordination by having one person take responsibility for the work of others, issuing instructions to them and monitoring their actions. As an organization outgrows its simplest state, it turns to this second mechanism of coordination. In effect one brain coordinates several hands, such as the coxswain (stroke caller) of a six-person rowing crew.

3. *Standardization of work processes.* Work processes are standardized when the contents of the work are specified. The production assembly line of a manufacturing company is an example. A worker inserts a bolt into a holed piece of metal. There is only one action to perform, and there is no room for individual discretion as to how the work is performed. The work is designed in such a way that the same process is followed no matter who is performing the job.

4. *Standardization of work output.* Outputs are standardized when the results of the work—for example, the dimensions of the product or the performance—are specified. The fast-food industry is an example. A hamburger ordered from a particular fast-food vendor should look and taste the same whether it was purchased in the day or at night, in July or December, in Cleveland or San Diego. The work is designed in such a way that the same output is achieved irrespective of differences in time or location.

5. *Standardization of skills and knowledge.* Skills and knowledge are standardized when the kind of training required to perform the work is specified. In this case coordination is achieved before the work is undertaken. Organizations institute training programs for employees to standardize the skills needed to perform work, thereby controlling and coordinating the work. For example, there is rarely communication between an anesthesiologist and a surgeon while removing an appendix in an operating room. They hardly need to communicate because by virtue of their medical training they know what to expect of each other.

According to Mintzberg (1993), these five coordinating mechanisms manifest themselves in a rough order. As organizational work becomes more complicated, the means of coordination shifts from mutual adjustment to direct supervision. This is followed by standardization of work processes, then outputs, and finally skills. A person working alone has no need for any coordinating mechanisms. The addition of a second person requires the two individuals to adjust to each other. As the group gets larger, however, it becomes less able to coordinate informally. A need for leadership arises. Control of the work group passes to a single individual, as direct supervision becomes the favored coordinating mechanism. As the work becomes more involved, a transition occurs toward standardization. When the tasks are simple and routine, the organization relies on the standardization of the work processes themselves. However, increasingly complex work may preclude this, compelling the organization to turn to standardization of the outputs. In very complex work, the outputs often cannot be standardized either. Therefore, the organization must settle for standardizing the skills of the worker.

Organizations cannot rely on a single coordinating mechanism. Most use all five. A certain amount of direct supervision and mutual adjustment is always required. Contemporary organizations simply cannot exist without leadership and informal communication. In the most automated (that is, fully standardized) factory, machines break down, employees fail to show up for work, and schedules must be changed at the last minute. Supervisors must intervene, and workers must be free to deal with unexpected problems.

Classical organization theory emphasized both direct supervision and standardization as coordinating mechanisms. The concepts of span of control, line/staff functions, and unity of command apply to the components of an organization's *formal structure*. Frederick Taylor sought to achieve coordination through standardization, specifying the work operations (such as body movements and when to take work breaks) of pig-iron handlers and coal-shovelers. According to scholars in the beginning of the 20th century, organizational structure defined a set of official, standardized work relationships built around a tight system of formal authority.

However, neoclassical organizational theory revealed the significance of the most primary means of attaining coordination, mutual adjustment. That is, other activities take place among workers that are not in line with the official organizational structure. Thus, the presence of unofficial relationships within work groups (an *informal structure*) established that mutual adjustment serves as an important coordinating mechanism in all organizations. It was not until the creation of systems theory that a balance between the classical and neoclassical perspectives was attained and all five coordinating mechanisms were regarded as viable.

The Five Basic Parts of an Organization[1]

Consistent with systems theory, organizations are structured to define the interrelationships among the parts of the systems. Mintzberg proposed that all organizations consist of five basic parts, as shown in Figure 8–4.

---

[1]Mintzberg (1993) noted that the number five reappears in the study of organizational structure (and is the basis of his book's title, *Structure in Fives*). While the number five is not magical, it is the number of concepts used to explain various aspects of organizational structure. The interested reader is encouraged to read the profound insights Mintzberg offered in his book about organizational structure.

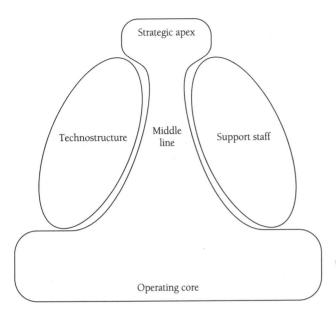

FIGURE 8–4 ■ **The five basic parts of an organization**

SOURCE: From *Structure in Fives: Designing Effective Organizations* (p. 11) by H. Mintzberg, 1993, Englewood Cliffs, NJ: Prentice-Hall.

1. *Operating core.* The operating core of the organization encompasses those members—the operators—who perform the basic work related directly to the production of products and services. The operators secure the inputs needed for production (buy the raw material), turn inputs into outputs (assemble individual parts into complete units), and distribute the outputs (sell the product). The operating core is the heart of every organization, the part that produces the essential outputs that keep it alive.

2. *Strategic apex.* The strategic apex is charged with ensuring that the organization serves its mission in an effective way. Here are found those people charged with *overall* responsibility for the organization: the president and any other top-level managers whose concerns are broad. The strategic apex plays the most important role in providing direction to the organization, serving as the organization's brain.

3. *Middle line.* The strategic apex is joined to the operating core by the chain of middle-line managers who have formal authority. This chain runs from the senior managers to the first-line supervisors, who have direct authority over the operators, and embodies the coordinating mechanism of direct supervision. In theory, one person—at the top of the strategic apex—can supervise all operators. In practice, direct supervision requires close personal contact between manager and operator, with the result that there is some limit to the number of operators any one manager can supervise (the span of control). An organizational *hierarchy* is built, as a first-line supervisor is put in charge of a number of operators to form a basic organizational unit. In turn, another manager is put in charge of a number of these units to form a higher-level unit, and so on. Eventually all the remaining units come under a single person at the strategic apex to form the whole organization.

4. *Technostructure.* In the technostructure are found the analysts who serve the organization by affecting the work of others. These analysts are removed from the operating work flow. They may design the work, plan it, or train the people who do it, but they do not do it themselves. The technostructure is effective only when it can use its analytical techniques to make the work of others more effective. In general, the more standardization the organization uses to facilitate coordination, the more it relies on its technostructure. Standardization of skills plays a major role in coordinating the analysts' own work because analysts are typically highly trained specialists.

5. *Support staff.* The support staff exists to provide services that aid the basic mission of the organization and typically includes the mailroom, switchboard, security, and janitorial services. Many times the support staff is lumped together with the technostructure and labeled the "staff" (vis-à-vis the line/staff distinction).

However, support units are decidedly different from the technostructure. The support staff is not directed toward giving advice; rather, their function is to perform. The support staff does not use a single coordinating mechanism. Each unit relies on whatever mechanism is most appropriate for itself, such as standardization of skills in the legal department and standardization of work processes in the cafeteria.

In many organizations decision-making power is highly centralized; that is, it flows from the strategic apex, down through the middle line of the hierarchy, to the operating core. Centralization is the tightest means of coordinating decision making in the organization. Decisions are made by one person and then implemented through direct supervision. However, there can exist strong pressures to decentralize, to push decision-making power down lower in the organizational hierarchy. Mintzberg (1993) cited three reasons. First is that not all of an organization's decisions can be understood at the strategic apex. Sometimes the necessary information just cannot be brought to the apex. People at the bottom of the hierarchy with the necessary knowledge end up having to defer to managers at the top who are out of touch with the immediate situation. Second is that decentralization allows the organization to respond quickly to local conditions. The transmission of information to the apex and back takes time, which may be critical. Third is that decentralization is a stimulus for motivation. The organization can attract and retain intelligent people only if it gives them considerable power to make decisions. Giving power to middle-line managers trains them in decision making, which is an increasingly important skill as one moves up the organizational hierarchy. However, as Mintzberg cautioned, centralization and decentralization should not be treated as absolutes, but rather as two ends of a continuum. In reality most organizations manifest some of the properties of both, with one being more prominent.

Reorganizing and Downsizing

As noted previously, the structure of an organization is its means of adapting to its environment. Accordingly, when the environment changes (for example, greater competition or regulatory control), it is common for the organization's structure to change in response. Earlier it was stated that the structure of an organization has a great impact on individuals (most notably its employees). Thus, an organization may choose to expand because of greater opportunities to sell its products or services. This necessitates hiring more employees at the operating core and middle-level management and typically more staff employees to serve their needs. It is also possible that as employees move up the organizational hierarchy, reporting relationships may change among the employees. These types of changes in the organizational structure are referred to as **reorganizing,** implying that the organization is reconfiguring itself to better adapt to its environment.

reorganizing
a process of changing the manner in which work is configured in an organization to achieve greater efficiency

There is also another form of reorganization that greatly affects the lives of employees and involves the loss of jobs. The organization may believe it has too many employees to be effectively responsive to its environment. The most common cause for the decision to cut jobs is the conclusion the organization can "do more with less" (i.e., have greater efficiency with fewer employees). For most organizations the single largest expense is the wages and salaries paid to their employees. By eliminating jobs, they reduce costs. Therefore, some organizations have been compelled to reduce jobs just to help assure their economic survival. The work that was done by the departed employees will have to be performed by the remaining employees or through technical changes in work processes (e.g., automation). The terms given to this process of job loss include **downsizing**, *reduction-in-force,* and *right-sizing.* The term *right-sizing* implies that there is a size for the organization that is "right" or correct for its environment. It is not uncommon for large organizations to reduce their size by several thousand employees at one time (see Field Note 1).

Where do the eliminated jobs come from within an organization? All five parts of the organization are targeted, with the greatest losses typically coming from the middle line, technostructure, and support staff. Jobs can also be lost in the operating core, as jobs are automated or reassigned to other countries that pay lower wages. The strategic apex may be reduced, but generally the fewest job losses occur at this level. As noted previously, the support staff consists of such jobs as security personnel and cafeteria workers. Rather than an organization hiring its own employees to work in these jobs, organizations may contract (in effect, "rent") the services of these people through other organizations, such as a company that offers security guards or food preparers to other organizations. Contracting the services of these individuals is less costly to the organization than hiring its own employees to perform these services. Similar reductions occur in the technostructure. With fewer employees to advise (the primary function of the technostructure), there is less need for "advisers." In recent years the number of I/O psychologists working in organizations has decreased, while the number working for consulting firms has increased. In essence, organizations have reduced the number of jobs typically filled by I/O psychologists and in turn contract their services through consulting firms.

downsizing
the process of reducing the size of an organization by the elimination of jobs, and thus employees

---

FIELD NOTE 1   Over-Downsizing

Corporate downsizing has become a conventional response by contemporary organizations that find themselves burdened with economic inefficiencies. For most organizations the single biggest expense is the salaries and benefits paid to their employees. By eliminating jobs, they reduce payroll costs. By eliminating many jobs (4,000–10,000 jobs in some very large companies), organizations can save vast sums of money. But then comes the problem of getting all the work accomplished by the employees who remain. The consequence of restructuring the organization may include greater use of computerization or automation of work, less oversight by supervisory/managerial personnel, greater use of overtime among hourly paid workers, and longer workweeks among salaried employees. These changes are brought about to make the organization operate more efficiently—lower cost per unit of production or service. While downsizing has forced organizations to operate with greater efficiency, some organizations are discovering they cannot reclaim the productive output they had achieved with a larger workforce. In short, the loss of jobs did not strengthen their economic position, rather it weakened it. Organizations that "over-downsized" are sometimes referred to as having "corporate anorexia"—a metaphor based on the medical condition of excessive refusal to eat. Some of these organizations are reestablishing a portion of the jobs they previously eliminated in their original quest to become more successful.

However, it is in the middle line where most of the job loss has occurred. It will be recalled that the middle line serves as a means of direct supervision for lower-level employees. How can an organization survive without the middle line? The answer lies in the coordinating mechanisms. Direct supervision is one of the five coordinating mechanisms. When much of the middle line is eliminated, the coordinating mechanism shifts from direct supervision to standardization. The coordination that was formerly achieved through personal contact with a supervisor is now achieved through greater standardization of the work process, the output, or employee skills.

Another manifestation of reorganization through downsizing is larger spans of control. With larger spans of control, fewer managers are needed, the organizational hierarchy becomes smaller, and the shape of the organization becomes flatter. It is also common for decision making to become more decentralized following a downsizing. Figure 8–5 shows the top part of an organization chart for a manufacturing company before downsizing. The company is structured to be organized by both function (production and sales) and location (California and Texas). There are small spans of control. Each person below the president has two subordinates. A total of 15 people are needed to staff this part of the organization with such a configuration. Figure 8–6 shows the same company following reorganization—in this case, downsizing. A total of eight jobs have been eliminated by this reorganization. The sales function has been consolidated into one job. The plant manager at each of the four locations now reports directly to the vice president. Each plant manager now also provides information directly to the sales manager (as indicated by the broken lines), but administratively the plant managers report to the vice president. The vice president now has a span of control of five.

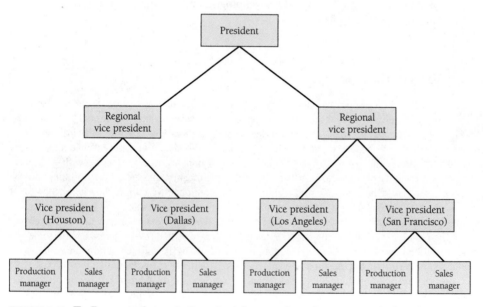

FIGURE 8–5 ■ Top part of organization chart for manufacturing company before downsizing

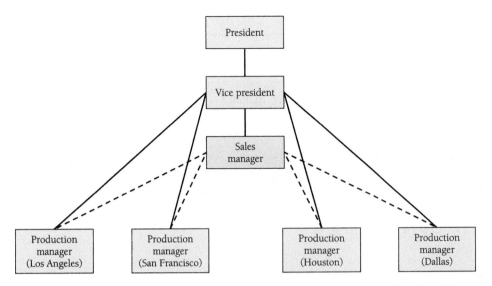

FIGURE 8–6 ■ **Top part of organization chart for manufacturing company after downsizing**

The jobs lost in this reorganization are one vice president, three sales managers, and the entire layer of (middle) managers.

What consequences might we expect from this reorganization? There would be less administrative control from the loss of managerial jobs. There would be greater pressure on the organization's part to coordinate with each other because of the loss of direct supervision. There would probably be more stress placed on the surviving employees to work harder and find new ways to do the work of the employees whose jobs were eliminated. The organization would have fewer salary expenditures associated with the elimination of eight jobs. Eight people would be out of work.

How would you feel if you lost your job because you were fired? Probably not very good, but in all likelihood you received some signals along the way that you were not performing satisfactorily. In turn, you probably had some control over whether you would change your job behavior. How would you feel if you lost your job because it was eliminated? You could have been an exemplary employee, but you lost your job through no fault of your own. *You* were not released, rather the *job* you were filling was eliminated to make the organization more efficient. In Chapter 10 we will examine the psychological reactions to downsizing, from the perspectives of both the survivors and those whose jobs were eliminated.

It was stated previously that organizational structure exerts a great influence on the lives of individuals. When organizations are expanding in size to better adapt to their environments, new jobs are created, leading to the recruitment, selection, training, and appraisal of new employees. When organizations are contracting in size, the overall social order of employment is altered. If, as a rule, organizations reduce the number of middle managers needed to run the business, these displaced middle managers will not simply find new jobs as middle managers in some other companies. Rather the *job* of middle manager is being reduced in frequency, necessitating holders of middle-management jobs to enter new jobs, not new positions in the same job family. This may necessitate professional retraining, learning new skills to fill jobs that continue to exist. Thus, issues of organizational structure affect not only I/O psychology but also the sociology of employment as well as the economics of across-occupational mobility.

Although organizations are defined in large part by their structures, division of labor is not the only concept needed to understand the functioning of organizations. Organizations also have social systems that influence the conduct of their employees. Three components of social systems within organizations will be examined next.

COMPONENTS OF SOCIAL SYSTEMS

social system
the human components of a work organization that influence the behavior of individuals and groups

A **social system** is a structuring of events or happenings; it has no formal structure apart from its functioning. Physical or biological systems (cars or human beings) have structures that can be identified even when they are not functioning (electrical or skeleton structures); that is, they have both an anatomy and a physiology. There is no anatomy to a social system in this sense. When a social system stops functioning, no identifiable structure remains. It is hard for us to think of social systems as having no tangible anatomy because it is easier to understand concepts with concrete and simple components. Social systems do indeed have components, but they are not concrete. They are sometimes referred to as the *informal* component of an organization. We will examine three of them—roles, norms, and culture—while recognizing that they are abstract.

Roles

role
a set of expectations about appropriate behavior in a position

When an employee enters an organization, there is much for that person to learn: expected performance levels, recognition of superiors, dress codes, and time demands. Roles ease the learning process. **Roles** are usually defined as the expectations of others about appropriate behavior in a specific position. Each of us plays several roles simultaneously (parent, employee, club member, and so on), but the focus here will be on job-related roles.

Scott and associates (1981) listed five important aspects of roles. First, they are impersonal; the position itself determines the expectations, not the individual. Second, roles are related to task behavior. An organizational role is the expected behaviors for a particular job. Third, roles can be difficult to pin down. The problem is defining who determines what is expected. Since other people define our roles, opinions differ about what our role should be. How we see our role, how others see our role, and what we actually do may differ. Fourth, roles are learned quickly and can produce major behavior changes. Fifth, roles and jobs are not the same; a person in one job might play several roles.

We learn our role through a role episode, as Figure 8–7 shows. Group members have expectations about job performance, which they communicate either formally or by having the role occupant observe others in similar roles. In stage 3,

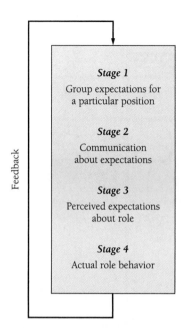

Feedback

Stage 1
Group expectations for
a particular position

Stage 2
Communication
about expectations

Stage 3
Perceived expectations
about role

Stage 4
Actual role behavior

FIGURE 8–7 ■ **The role episode**

SOURCE: From *Organization Theory:
A Structural and Behavioral Analysis* (p. 103)
by W. G. Scott, T. R. Mitchell, and P. H.
Birnbaum, 1981, Homewood, IL: Richard
D. Irwin. Reprinted with permission.

norm
a set of shared group
expectations about
appropriate behavior

the role occupant behaves as he or she believes is appropriate. If the behavior (stage 4) differs widely from the group's expectations (stage 1), the occupant gets feedback from the group regarding the discrepancy. This is intended to alter behavior toward group expectations. The role episode is ongoing. Expectations may change over time, as might the employee's behavior.

Another aspect is role differentiation. This is the extent to which different roles are performed by employees in the same subgroup. One person's job might be to maintain good group relations, such as a work-unit coordinator. His or her role might thus require providing emotional or interpersonal support to others. Another's role might be to set schedules, agendas, and meet deadlines; such a person is usually an administrator. When all the roles in a work group fit together like the pieces of a puzzle, the result is a smoothly running, effective group.

Norms

Norms are shared group expectations about appropriate behavior. While roles define what is appropriate for a particular job, norms define acceptable group behavior. Roles differentiate positions; norms establish the behavior expected of everyone in the group, such as when employees take coffee breaks, how much they produce, when they stop for the day, and what they wear. Norms are unwritten rules that govern behavior. A no-smoking sign is not a norm but a formal written rule of behavior. If employees smoke despite the sign, there is a norm that sanctions such behavior in spite of the formal rule.

Norms have several important properties. First, there is "oughtness" or "shouldness"—that is, prescriptions for behavior. Second, norms are usually more obvious for behavior judged to be important for the group. A norm might exist for the time employees stop work before lunch, but there probably is no norm about what employees eat. Third, norms are enforced by the group. Much expected behavior is monitored and enforced through formal rules and procedures. With norms, group members regulate behavior. Sometimes formal rules and group norms clash. The no-smoking rule and the group norm sanctioning smoking are an example. Unless the organization imposes sanctions on smokers (that is, rule breakers), the group norm probably prevails. Finally, the degree that norms are shared and the degree that deviation is acceptable vary. Not all smokers might smoke in proscribed areas, and those who do not might be as accepted by the group as those who do.

There is a three-step process for developing and communicating norms. The norm must first be defined and communicated. This can be done either explicitly ("Here is the way we do things around here") or implicitly (the desired behavior is observed). Second, the group must be able to monitor behavior and judge whether the norm is being followed. Third, the group must be able to reward conformity and punish nonconformity. Conformity enhances the predictability of behavior within the group, which in turn promotes feelings of group cohesion.

THE FAR SIDE® BY GARY LARSON

"Counterclockwise, Red Eagle! Always counterclockwise!"

Compliance with norms is enforced by positive reinforcement or punishment. Positive reinforcement can be praise or inclusion in group activities. Punishment can be a dirty look, a snide remark, or actual physical abuse. (Workers who exceeded the group norm for productivity in the Hawthorne studies were hit on the arm, which was called "binging.") Another form of punishment is exclusion from group activities. The group often tries to convince the nonconforming employee (referred to as a *deviant*) to change his or her behavior. The group tries to alter the deviant's opinion through increased communication, verbal or nonverbal. The clearer and more important the norm and the more cohesive the group, the greater the pressure. Eventually, the deviant either changes or is rejected. If rejected, the deviant becomes an *isolate,* and the pressure to conform stops. Because the group may need the isolate to perform work tasks, they usually reach a truce; the isolate is tolerated at work but excluded from group activities and relations. Obviously, the isolate can quit the job and try to find a better match between his or her values and a group.

Finally, norms are not always contrary to formal organization rules or independent of them. Sometimes norms greatly promote organization goals. For example, there may be a norm against leaving for home before a certain amount of work has been done. Although quitting time is 5:00 p.m., the group may expect employees to stay until 5:15 or 5:30 to finish a certain task. In this case, the deviant is one who conforms to the formal rule (that is, leaving at 5:00 p.m.) instead of the group norm. When group norms and organization goals are complementary, high degrees of effectiveness can result.

Organizational Culture

culture
the language, values, attitudes, beliefs, and customs of an organization

The concept of culture was originally proposed by anthropologists to describe societies, but we have also found it useful to describe organizations. **Culture** is the languages, values, attitudes, beliefs, and customs of an organization. As can be inferred, it represents a complex pattern of variables that, when taken collectively, gives each organization its unique "flavor." Several definitions of organizational culture have been proposed, but the most straightforward was offered by Deal and Kennedy (1982): "The way we do things around here."

Furnham and Gunter (1993) proposed three features of organizational culture. First, an organization's culture can often be traced to its founders. These people often possess dynamic personalities, strong values, and a clear vision of what the organization should look like. They play a big role in the initial hiring of employees, and their ideas and values are readily transmitted to new employees. Second, culture often develops out of an organization's experience with the external environment. Every organization must establish its own identity in its industry and in the marketplace where it operates. As it struggles to do so, it may find that some values and practices are more effective than others. Third, culture develops from the need to maintain effective working relationships among employees. Depending on the nature of the organization's business and the characteristics of the types of people it must hire, different expectations and values develop.

Deeply ingrained within organizational culture are communication processes, for it is through communication that culture is transmitted. It is through interactions with long-time organizational members that new recruits are enculturated. This is how new members learn the language and appropriate behavior of the group, hear its stories and legends, and observe the organization's rites and rituals. Beyer and Trice (1987) believe the culture of an organization can best be understood by analyzing its tangible and visible rites. They refer to rites of passage (hiring and basic training), degradation (dismissal), renewal (organization development activities), conflict reduction (collective bargaining), and integration (office holiday party). New members must determine what is appropriate dress, how to arrange their office, and how much latitude they have in being on time for appointments and in meeting deadlines (Barnett, 1988). Culture may also be communicated through other channels, such as in-house memos, official policies, statements of corporate philosophy, and any other means of value expression (see Field Note 2).

Schein (1996) asserted that understanding the culture of an organization is critical to making sense of the behavior observed in the organization. A narrow

FIELD NOTE 2   A Clear Message

Organizational culture embraces the values and character of the organization. Sometimes the culture of an organization is communicated in a subtle way, and at other times the communication is loud and unambiguous. I had a client company that was founded about 90 years ago. It started through the efforts of one man who created the company when he was about 30 and served as the company's president until his death at age 80. The company manufactures world-class building supplies. Today its products are sold nationally, and the company employs about 3,000 people. The company was founded on the value of making the finest product in the market, for which it charges a high price. The marketing orientation is strictly top of the line—if you want the best, you think of this company. The culture of the organization today follows the philosophy of the founder. The founder and his philosophy are so revered that the company turned his small office into something of a shrine. Cordoned off with a thick velvet rope, the office is preserved as it was when the founder was leading the company. The office telephone, lamp, desk, chair, briefcase, and fountain pen are all period pieces. The decor of the office is not ostentatious or sumptuous, but rather understated elegance, like the company's products. A 1952 calendar is hanging on the wall. While the office is no longer in active use, it serves an extremely valuable purpose for the company. It is a constant reminder, a physical embodiment, of the person whose values continue to guide the company today, long after his death. The orientation for all new employees includes a visit to this office as a way of communicating the heritage of the company. It doesn't take long for anyone (including an outsider like me) to grasp what this company is all about. Sometimes you have to dig to unearth the culture of an organization. Not this one.

description of behavior, divorced from the cultural context in which it occurs, is of limited value for understanding the organization. For example, Pratt and Rafaeli (1997) examined the types of clothes worn by members of a hospital staff to understand how the hospital views itself. They found that the manner of dress among the staff was symbolic of their sense of organizational identity. Furthermore, differing views among staff members about dress were deeply felt. The authors offered the following two quotations from nurses working in the hospital:

> Head nurse of a rehabilitation unit: "Patients who wear pajamas and see hospital garb around them think of themselves as sick. If *they and their caretakers wear street clothes,* patients will think of themselves as moving out of the sick role and into rehabilitation. They will be ready for life outside the hospital. This is the rehab philosophy, and this is what makes this unit unique." [emphasis added]

> Nurse on the evening shift of the same unit: "We are medical and health professionals. We do professional work. We take care of sick patients, we deal with their bodily fluids and get their slime all over us. So we should all look like medical professionals; *we should be dressed in scrubs.*" [emphasis added] (Pratt & Rafaeli, 1997, p. 862)

Schneider (1996) believes it is the people who populate the organization who most define its culture. That is, people (e.g., employees) are not actors who fill predetermined roles in an established culture, but rather it is the personalities, values, and interests of these people over time that make the organization what it is. Schneider (1987) proposed what he calls the attraction–selection–attrition (ASA) cycle. The ASA cycle proposes that people with similar personalities and values are drawn to (attraction) certain organizations and hired into these organizations (selection), and people who don't fit into the pattern of shared values eventually leave the organization (attrition). However, this process occurs over time, not immediately. There can also be differences among people in the organization in values that are not important. As in the example of the two nurses and their manner of dress, if dress is a deeply held value within the hospital unit, the ASA cycle would predict the attrition of one of the two nurses whose view is not accepted by the rest of the unit. In support of the hypothesis that organizations attract people with relatively homogeneous personalities, Schneider, Smith, Taylor, and Fleenor (1998) found that organizations differ in the modal personality types of their employees. The authors speculate that organizations with different modal personalities may well differ in their organizational cultures and structures. Further evidence of organizations staffing themselves with employees who possess similar personality characteristics was reported by Schaubroeck, Ganster, and Jones (1998), although their findings indicate that various occupations (e.g., sales, clerical, etc.) also influence the ASA process. The tendency for organizations to staff themselves and socialize their members in ways that promote a monolithic culture prompted Morgan (1997) to refer to organizations as "psychic prisons."

Summary of Social System Components

Organizations have physical structures, but these alone do not define organizations. The social fabric—norms, roles, and culture—is a significant influence on the conduct of organization members. These components are not tangible entities, but they are as much attributes of an organization as its size. Organizations differ in norms, roles, and culture. Norms influence behavior, increasing its consistency and predictability. Roles prescribe the boundaries of acceptable behavior and enhance conformity. These constructs help produce uniformity and consistency in individual behavior. This is necessary in part to ensure that all organizational members are pursuing common goals. Individuals give up some freedom when they join an organization, and these constructs represent ways through which freedom is limited. Organizations differ in culture just as individuals differ in personality. Similarly, just as certain personality types are better suited for some jobs, certain cultures foster certain behaviors. Together, these three constructs define an organization's social system; they are intangible but potent determinants of behavior.

ORGANIZATIONAL CHANGE

The first part of this chapter dealt with the concept of an organization and its constituent components. The remainder will deal with an ever-widening area of I/O psychology—the process of effecting change in organizations. It is best to begin this section with a review of why organizations exist in the first place. Organizations are created to fulfill some purpose or objective. They exist in a larger environment that encompasses economic, legal, and social factors. Thus, there must be a fit between the organization and the environment in which it exists. Many business organizations were founded in the first half of the 20th century. They

organization development
a system of planned interventions designed to change an organization's structure and/or processes to achieve a higher level of functioning

enjoyed a period of relative stability in the environments in which they operated. While organizations had to respond to some environmental influences, for the most part the economic and social order was relatively stable until the 1980s. I/O psychology has an area of specialization devoted to the study of facilitating organizations to develop or change themselves in response to environmental influences. It is called **organization development** (OD). From the end of World War II (the mid-1940s) through the 1970s, OD was instrumental in helping those organizations that were, in effect, suffering from some "growing pains" in their own development.

For reasons discussed in Chapter 1, the business world began to change in the 1980s. Among the forces responsible for the change was the adoption and diffusion of computers into worklife, the changing cultural diversity of the workforce, the emergence of advanced communication technologies, the globalization of business, and redistributions of economic power. In Chapter 6 we used the "peg and hole" analogy to describe the need for training. People are pegs who need to be "re-shaped" (i.e., trained) to better fit with changing demands of jobs (the "holes"). We can now extend this analogy. Organizations can also be considered "pegs" that must fit in with ever-changing business environments (the "holes"). While there was always a need for some organizations to change in response to environmental pressures, the past 20 years have witnessed an ever-growing and expanding need for all organizations to respond to the pressures placed on them by changing environmental conditions. Some of the major differences from the past are (1) the greater strength of environmental pressures prompting change, (2) the speed at which change must occur, (3) the acceptance that responsiveness to change is a continuous organizational process, and (4) the pervasiveness of organizations caught up and affected by changing environmental conditions.

In my hometown there is a family-owned ice-cream store that still sells ice cream the way it has for seven decades. On the surface it might appear that this little store has escaped the need to adjust to changes in the last 70 years. To a very large extent this is true, although the store has been compelled to stock low-fat and no-fat dairy products in response to changing customer preferences. For the most part, this store is, in effect, an "organizational dinosaur," one of the last of a rare breed that has not had to change with the times. The broad-scale need for understanding organizational change has produced a shift in how I/O psychology refers to this area of interest. The name "organization development" appears to be giving way to "management of organizational change" (Worren, Ruddle, & Moore, 1999). I will simply refer to it as "organizational change."

Organizations do not change quickly or easily. There is a sense of organizational inertia to maintain the status quo, to keep operating in ways that have served the organization in the past. However, what worked in the past was a product of the conditions in effect in the past, and with changing conditions comes the need to change the organization. In keeping with the ASA model, it is people who give every organization its distinctive culture. Individuals find change to be difficult because it lowers environmental predictability, often produces a sense of anxiety by interrupting the learned "flow" of organizational life. Thus, there is usually resistance, often strong resistance, to change. The area of organizational change is concerned with facilitating the manner in which organizations modify themselves to achieve a better fit with their environments.

Colarelli (1998) stated that organizations that survive are those that fit with their environmental niches. Should their niches change, those organizations will probably perish unless they change. Organizational practices and routines become the organization's tacit knowledge (a concept referenced in Chapter 4 to describe individuals) and thus are difficult to change. These routines are the "genes" of organizational structure. When organizations do change, they do not change on a slow continuous basis, like the growth of a child. Rather organizational change follows a process of *punctuated equilibrium;* that is, change occurs over cycles of stability punctuated by periods of upheaval and transformation. Poor organizational performance or major environmental changes often precipitate discontinuous periods of change. Once a dominant organizational form emerges, its response to the environment becomes more stable, and further change occurs more incrementally.

The magnitude of multinational business is one prime factor in increasing organizational change. Simply put, the challenge is to understand how different national and regional cultures influence the conduct of business and to get the relevant constituents (e.g., employees, managers, customers) to function well together. For example, the manner in which organizations deal with conflict varies in cultures. Tinsley (1998) identified differences in how managers deal with interpersonal conflict in three rather diverse cultures (United States, Germany, and Japan). However, there can also be differences in conflict resolution style among cultures that are close geographically. Cultural differences in the United Kingdom, Denmark, The Netherlands, and Belgium were found regarding the use of power distance (e.g., a manager vs. a secretary) in addressing conflict (van Oudenhoven, Mechelse, & de Dreu, 1998). Even the meanings of the same words, as reflected in employee opinion surveys, differ among people who speak the same language (e.g., Spanish) but are from different (Spain vs. Mexico) cultures (Ryan et al., 1999). Such research findings attest to the sensitivity and care that must be used by organizations as they try to change in response to cross-cultural issues.

There can also be differences of opinion about the effectiveness of organizational change efforts in relation to the criteria used to assess the change. Armenakis and Bedeian (1999) noted that change efforts may produce desired results with regard to such criteria as service quality and productivity in the short run, but employee morale may decline precipitously and limit the likelihood of success of the change in the long run. Researchers have identified mistrust and cynicism among workers about the management of organizations that frequently change. Rousseau and Tijoriwala (1999) found that nurses were skeptical of the formally stated reasons given for change at a hospital (to improve quality) and were more inclined to believe the change was motivated by self-serving reasons on the part of the hospital administrators. Wanous, Reichers, and Austin (2000) reported that employees can develop cynical attitudes about organizational change, learned by experience with previous unsuccessful change efforts and ineffective leadership. In short, while there may be pressing need for organizations to change, the ease, effectiveness, and long-term stability of the change can be problematic for the participants in the change process.

EMPOWERMENT

empowerment

the process of giving employees in an organization more power and decision-making authority within a context of less managerial oversight

As the workforce has become more educated and skilled, organizations need to loosen some of the constraints placed on employees to control and monitor their actions. The need for organizational control systems such as close supervision, strict channels of communication, and chains of command evolved in part because of the perceived differentiation in ability levels between management and workers. The classical perspective (emanating from the era of scientific management) was that management personnel generally had far more ability and insight into organizational issues than workers did. The workers (or, in Mintzberg's terminology, the operating core) were hired to perform the basic work that needed to be done, but they required mechanisms of control, or close supervision. As time passed and the workforce became more educated, it was no longer as necessary to closely control nonmanagerial personnel. It became feasible to push some of the traditional managerial responsibilities (such as decision making) down into the lower levels of the organization. This had the combined effect of giving traditional nonmanagerial personnel managerial-type powers and requiring fewer people in traditional managerial roles. The meaning of **empowerment** comes from "power." When employees are given more power and this power is distributed away from traditional managerial personnel, the downsizing or elimination of mid-level managerial jobs became possible. The power previously vested in these positions has been redistributed in part to the employees, thereby *empowering* them. Liden and Arad (1996) interpret empowerment as the psychological outcome of structural changes in the organization designed to provide power.

Spreitzer (1997) identified four general dimensions of empowerment:

1. *Meaning.* An individual feels a sense of meaning when an activity "counts" in his or her own value system. Empowered individuals derive personal significance from their work. They get "energized" about a given activity and thus become connected through a sense of meaning.

2. *Competence.* Empowered individuals have a sense of self-effectiveness or personal competence. They believe that they have not only the needed skills and abilities but also the confidence that they can perform successfully.

3. *Self-determination.* Self-determination is represented by behaviors that are initiated and regulated through choices as an expression of oneself, rather than behaviors that are forced by the environment. Empowered individuals have a sense of responsibility for and ownership of their activity.

4. *Impact.* Impact is the individual's belief that he or she can effect or influence organizational outcomes. Empowered individuals see themselves as "making a difference"—that is, providing the intended effects of their actions.

Spreitzer asserted that empowered individuals are more likely to be innovative, exert upward influence in the organization, and be effective in their jobs. Empowered individuals are more likely to challenge and question, rather than blindly follow, traditional role expectations. Organizational change interventions are designed to enhance both effectiveness and personal satisfaction. The concept of empowerment provides a potentially useful framework for guiding the intervention. Thus, one outcome of a successful change intervention is to empower the employees. However, this outcome is also dependent on the nature of the work performed by the organization and the ability levels of the employees.

A MODEL OF PLANNED ORGANIZATIONAL CHANGE

As Porras and Robertson (1992) noted, in order to change an organization, one must understand at least two basic sets of variables. The first are those organizational variables that can be manipulated by a change intervention. The second are the outcomes intended by the change effort.

The work setting is made up of four components. The first is the organizing arrangements, the structure, strategies, administrative systems, and reward systems of the organization. The second is the social factors, the organization's culture and management style. Third is the physical setting, the space configuration of the organization, interior design, and physical ambience. Technology is the fourth component and includes equipment, machinery, and work flow design. These four broad categories make up the internal work setting of the organization. The four categories affect one another such that the design of one influences the functioning of the others. Accordingly, a change in one factor usually results in changes in the others. The interaction of the four categories affects the behavior of organizational members. If the different components are congruent, they complement one another. If they are not aligned well, ineffectiveness is the likely result. These four organizational components in turn influence two outcome variables.

1. *Individual development.* The first major outcome of organizational change is enhanced individual development. The nature of the organization in which a person works encourages some types of behavior and inhibits others, which in turn have an important influence on the person's psychological health and personal development. While much of the focus has been on organizations that have a negative impact on their members, organizations can also be designed to provide positive experiences for their members.
2. *Organizational performance.* According to Porras and Robertson, if individual members work hard, take responsibility and initiative, learn their jobs well, and commit themselves to their jobs, it is more likely that the organization as a whole will perform well. A key goal of any change process must be to create work settings that enhance the performance of the organization.

These two outcomes affect each other, and over the long run one cannot improve without the other. The interdependence of the two is reflected in an observation by Mirvis (1988): "In the 1960s, it was assumed that by developing people we could create healthier and more effective organizations. Today many advocate that we must develop organizations to create healthier and more effective people" (pp. 17–18).

The process of intervening in organizational systems, creating changes in organizational components that in turn result in changes in the work behaviors of organizational members, is the primary activity in organizational change (Porras & Robertson, 1992). However, individual behavioral change is not the singular goal of organizational change. Change in individual behavior is necessary to effect change in organizational outcomes. To maintain high levels of one outcome without correspondingly high levels of the other is not possible.

OVERCOMING ORGANIZATIONAL RESISTANCE TO CHANGE

At the core of any change effort is the desire to bring about change. However, change introduces ambiguity into the environment, with the concomitant effects of less predictability and control. Accordingly, organizational members often resist change because of the undesirable effects it has on individuals. Yet, paradoxically, the change is regarded as necessary for the welfare of the organization and thus its members, who are the ones resistant to it. Resistance to change is a major obstacle in any planned change effort.

Dirks, Cummings, and Pierce (1996) proposed a useful framework for understanding the conditions under which individuals promote and resist change. It is based on the concept of psychological ownership, which is the feeling of being psychologically tied to an object and feeling possessive of that object. In this case, the organization is the object in question. The authors proposed three basic human needs that are related to psychological ownership:

1. *Self-enhancement.* Self-enhancement refers to the individual's desire to achieve and maintain high levels of self-esteem. Individuals are likely to avoid those situations that threaten their sense of self-esteem and to seek situations that enhance it.
2. *Self-continuity.* Self-continuity implies that individuals attempt to maintain stability of their self over time and across situations. Individuals actively seek those situations that confirm and preserve their sense of continuity and avoid those that do not.
3. *Control and efficiency.* Individuals have a desire to maintain and demonstrate a sense of control and efficiency. Conditions that allow the individual to have a sense of control and to demonstrate efficiency are psychologically attractive, while those conditions that do not are unattractive.

Furthermore, Dirks et al. delineated three types of organizational change that influence the relationship between psychological ownership and the disposition to either accept or resist change:

1. *Self-initiated versus imposed change.* With self-initiated change the individual undertakes change as a result of his or her own initiative and volition. Imposed change, on the other hand, is change initiated by others to which the individual is forced to react.
2. *Evolutionary versus revolutionary change.* Evolutionary change involves incremental modifications to the organization, and as a consequence, it does not suddenly alter the individual's understanding of, or relationship to, the organization. In contrast, revolutionary change challenges the individual's understanding of the organization because the change alters the organization's existing structure.

3. *Additive versus subtractive change.* Changes may add things to the organization or take them away. Examples of additive change are starting a program and enlarging a job. Conversely, a subtractive change is ending a program or downsizing.

The authors then proposed relationships among the concepts about accepting or rejecting attempts at change. It is proposed that individuals will promote change efforts under conditions that satisfy their needs for self-enhancement, self-continuity, and/or control and efficiency. Conversely, people will resist change efforts when they perceive these needs will be frustrated by the change. Likewise, psychological ownership will be positively related to an individual's disposition toward change under conditions of self-initiated, evolutionary, and additive change. Conversely, psychological ownership will be negatively related to an individual's disposition toward change under conditions of imposed, revolutionary, and subtractive change. The relationships among these concepts are graphically portrayed in Figure 8–8.

Dirks et al. believe these concepts are critical to understanding why organizational change efforts are either accepted or resisted. The theoretical basis is a basic understanding of the self—namely, that people accept conditions that are perceived to enhance them. When employees feel a sense of psychological ownership of their organization, they have a vested interest in conditions that promote the organization and, in turn, themselves. Organizational change that is initiated from

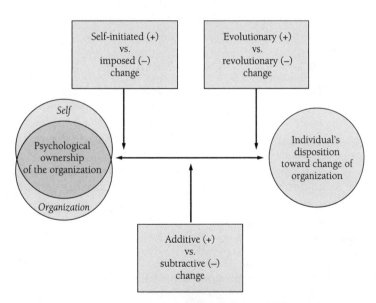

FIGURE 8–8 ■ Effect of psychological ownership or disposition toward change as influenced by type of change

SOURCE: From "Psychological Ownership in Organizations: Conditions Under Which Individuals Promote and Resist Change" by K. T. Dirks, L. L. Cummings, and J. L. Pierce, 1996, in *Research in Organizational Change and Development,* Vol. 9 (pp. 1–24), edited by R. W. Woodman and W. A. Pasmore, Greenwich, CT: JAI Press.

within, does not alter the fundamental relationship to the organization, and is perceived as adding to the reservoir of bonding between the individual and the organization is most likely to be accepted. Change that threatens fundamental psychological needs derived from organizational membership is most strongly resisted. While it is not always possible to orchestrate how change occurs, we have some insights into why and how individuals react to change as they do.

MAJOR ORGANIZATIONAL CHANGE INTERVENTIONS

As noted, there are many intervention strategies for I/O psychologists to draw on. It is beyond the scope of this book to describe all or even most of them. However, the two change interventions described in this section are representative of major types of initiatives in the field. While both of these interventions are large-scale change efforts, all attempts at producing organizational change need not be broad based. Bluedorn, Turban, and Love (1999) examined an issue as elementary as whether meetings among coworkers are conducted with the participants sitting down or standing up. The authors compared five-person groups, half of whom conducted meetings in a standing format while the other half conducted meetings in a seated format. Sit-down meetings were found to be 34% longer than stand-up meetings, but they produced no better discussions than stand-up meetings. While the findings from this study are limited in generalizability to other issues such as larger group size and temporal urgency, change can be brought about in organizations (in this case, regarding time management) in simple and direct ways.

Organizational Culture Change

The culture of an organization embodies its values, beliefs, and attitudes and is the driving force behind its behavior. When the behavior or conduct of the organization no longer serves to attain its larger objectives, it becomes necessary for the organization to behave differently. A change in organizational behavior usually necessitates a change in the organization's culture. It is often difficult to bring about a change in organizational culture because it necessitates altering underlying values and beliefs that have long guided the organization. Although change is difficult to effect, several authors (e.g., Kotter & Heskett, 1992; Appelbaum & Batt, 1993) have identified the following four critical features of the change process:

CNN video

Microsoft reflects a very strong organizational culture.

SOURCE: CNN

1. *A strong leader.* Perhaps the most important feature is a strong leader who can initiate and sustain the cultural change. Leaders must recognize that the environment and organizational members will exert significant energy to maintain the status quo. However, it is critical that leaders do not waver from the plan for change. They must recognize that a vital component of their role is to influ-

ence others to examine prevailing assumptions and values. New approaches or perspectives often threaten or worry organizational members. Nevertheless, the leaders must persevere in their endeavor with missionary zeal. Often the culture change is initiated by one strong leader at the helm, but other influential leaders emerge in the process.

2. *A clear vision of what needs to be done.* It is also critical that there be a sense of vision or direction as to where the organization is headed. It is not enough for a leader to provide intense energy to initiate the culture change. What must also be present is a shared belief in what the new culture will be like. The vision may arise from the values of the leader, or it may emerge out of a crisis that must be handled to save the business. The *process* of cultural change is more important than the *product*. Because change is needed continually by organizations to adapt to their environments, the organization must develop some fluency in learning how to change. While moving from X to Y may be the initial object of attention, eventually the organization will also have to move from Y to Z. The vision process entails not only charting the destination but also generating commitment from all organizational members to be players in the change process. The enrollment of all employees to cultivate change actively is often accelerated by a clear understanding of what will occur if change does not take place. It is not the case that leaders will "punish" employees who fail to participate, but rather the organization as a whole will suffer (most notably through the loss of jobs or the demise of the organization).

3. *Development of new work procedures.* It is necessary for the organization to develop new work procedures that buttress the new cultural values being espoused. If the organization does not "do" anything different besides verbally expressing its desire to do so, it will basically be "business as usual" within the organization. The organization must be prepared to "walk the talk" in the change process. New work procedures help to break the allegiance to the old values from which the organization seeks to depart. These new work procedures may include the extensive use of teams. Moving to team-based operations necessitates major changes in organizational behavior, including communication, cooperation, and decision making, as well as new organizational policies pertaining to selection, training, and compensation. Another possible change in work procedures may be job redesign. In this case the employees will have the structure of their jobs altered, usually giving them greater decision-making authority over their work operations. Such new procedures for performing work provide a venue for organizational members to reframe their values, attitudes, and beliefs about the organization and what it is trying to accomplish. A failure to change how work is performed even though new values and beliefs have been expressed often results in "back-sliding." Back-sliding is the return to the old ways of thinking and feeling, and ultimately behaving, from which the organization needs to evolve.

4. *An organization that is open to learn.* Everyone in the organization, from the leaders on down, must accept the fact that no one has all the answers. The organization must be prepared to go through periods of groping, grasping, and stumbling and to learn from these difficult times. Rather than viewing these occasions as representations of shortcomings in vision, intelligence, or fortitude, the organization must view itself as learning, adaptive, and growing. In so doing mistakes

will be made. However, instead of viewing the mistakes as punishable offenses or signs of weakness, they should be regarded as part of a normal and healthy change process. Senge (1990) spoke to the need for "learning organizations," organizations that not only are comfortable with the growth process but also treat their members in a nurturing, as opposed to a sanctioning, manner. The organization must accept that good ideas and opportunities for growth can and do originate at all levels of the organization, not just from top management.

I heard a presentation by a chief executive officer (CEO) describing what it was like to change a major corporation. The company was a long-time leader in the aerospace industry. It had a long history of profitable years and great organizational prestige. The company then began to lose money because of foreign competition and other external pressures. Two previous CEOs tried and failed to change the culture of the company. Both had been long-time leaders of the company who were successively promoted into the CEO position. Both CEOs failed to change the organizational culture because in part they *were* the culture. Each person had been very influential within the company, and to change the organizational culture entailed "undoing" much of what they had already done.

The company's third attempt at a change in leadership brought in an outsider to the company, someone who was not steeped in its traditions and values. He encountered massive resistance on many fronts and hired two I/O psychologists to facilitate the change process. He successfully persuaded a few top executives to embrace his vision of the company, and the change process began—albeit slowly. The new CEO stated that the company was profitable not because of its actions, but in spite of them. They had relied on their esteemed industry reputation to get away with actions (such as not vigorously developing new products) that hurt them in the long run. When foreign competition increased, the "long run" became the "short run." There was still substantial resistance to the new vision, as some people claimed the company had endured downturns before. On those occasions the company had weathered the storms and eventually returned to economic prosperity. In short, some employees viewed the current crisis as only a temporary problem that would work itself out. It didn't.

Shortly thereafter a major unit of the company was sold off, which affected several hundred employees. Many were laid off by their new employer. This action got the attention of the remaining employees of the company, and the change process began in earnest. The company as a whole came to realize that the need for change wasn't just talk. Many changes began to occur in the way work was performed, particularly with regard to new product development and cost reductions. The company also began to change its self-image, going from self-assured smugness to awareness of its own vulnerability. The new CEO felt other changes would be in the offing but believed the company was more receptive to continued change after having overcome its inertia to change at all.

In an era of multinational organizations, it is often tempting for organizations to try to impose a uniform or standard set of managerial practices in all of the business units in countries where their company is located. The aim is to achieve greater standardization (and thus predictability) of actions. However, research has shown that cultural differences across nations influence attempts to create a singular organizational culture. Robert et al. (2000) examined the degree to which the attempts of a multinational company to bring about an organizational culture change with regard to continuous improvement were effective in four countries (United States, Mexico, Poland, and India). The authors discovered that attempts at organizational change were not uniformly effective across the four countries. They concluded, "The successes of managerial practices and implementation procedures are dependent on an appropriate fit between the assumptions, values, and beliefs inherent in any given managerial practice and the culturally based assumptions, values, and beliefs held by those being managed" (p. 643).

Total Quality Management

Total Quality Management (TQM)
a comprehensive approach to achieving greater organizational efficiency based in part on the use of statistical information to aid in decision making

Total Quality Management (TQM) is a comprehensive approach to organizational change that embraces not only behavioral concepts but also business strategy and the use of statistical information to aid in decision making. The principles of TQM were originally developed for manufacturing organizations but subsequently have been adapted to service organizations (including educational institutions) as well. In service organizations TQM is also referred to as Continuous Process Improvement.

The roots of TQM are varied and from multiple disciplines. From *psychology* is the emphasis on employee involvement in making operating decisions about the organization. That is, as research on participative decision making and leadership reveals, employees have expertise that can be accessed to improve organizational efficiency. Thus, effective decision making is rarely, if ever, a strictly top-down affair. From the field of *statistics* is the concept of statistical quality control. The American physicist W. Edwards Deming is credited with formulating the concept. It uses rudimentary statistical analyses to aid in understanding organizational processes. The most critical statistical index is variation, as discussed in Chapter 2. If an organization wants to provide a high-quality service or product, the quality should not vary across products; that is, consistency is regarded as a precursor of quality. For example, if a fast-food restaurant makes hamburgers that sometimes taste good and sometimes taste bad, there is too much variation in the quality. The hamburgers should taste the same all the time. In addition to reducing variation, the organization should strive to elevate the mean quality of the product. Thus, the goal is to produce hamburgers that always taste the same and always taste good. These two simple statistical concepts of reducing variation and raising the mean are the foundation of using statistical quality control to improve organizational performance. From *marketing* comes the idea that the primary focus of the organization is to satisfy its customers. Satisfied customers are the key to the retention and growth of business. Marketing research reveals that there can be differences between what customers really want from a product (e.g., a tasty hamburger) and what the organization believes its customers want (e.g., a hamburger delivered to the customer in less than 45 seconds). Customer service and satisfaction are the driving forces behind TQM. Finally, from the area of *business* comes the concept that all parts of the organization, including its overall mission, operating technology, support services, organizational culture, and employee training and rewards, must be aligned or work together to produce an effective outcome. For example, it would be dysfunctional for the organization to say it strives to produce a high-quality product yet train and reward employees to produce a large quantity of products irrespective of quality. Thus, TQM is the confluence of concepts and ideas from many disciplines that have been brought together to aid in the development and direction of organizations.

Lawler, Mohrman, and Ledford (1995) concluded that four factors are required in an effective system of employee involvement, upon which TQM is based. The first is the *sharing of information* about business performance, plans, and goals. It is impossible for employees to make good suggestions about how products and services can be improved without access to business information. It is also difficult for employees to alter their behavior in response to changing conditions and get feedback about the effectiveness of their performance. In the absence of business information, individuals are usually limited simply to carrying out prescribed tasks and roles in a relatively automatic way. Thus, it is imperative that relevant business information be shared at all levels of the organization and not be the sole province of upper management.

Second is the need for *developing knowledge*. It is critical that employees at all levels be involved in a continuous process of skill development. Without the proper skills, individuals cannot participate in a business and influence its direction. The skills of group decision making, team building, and leadership are critical because most employee involvement programs make use of meetings, interpersonal interactions, group problem solving, and influencing others.

The third factor needed is *rewarding organizational performance*. Basing rewards on organizational performance is one way to ensure that employees are involved in and care about the performance of their company. Individual incentive plans do not tie the individual into the overall success of the business; moreover, they can interfere with teamwork and problem solving. Team incentives can be supportive of employee involvement activities such as work teams and problem-solving groups. Profit sharing and employee stock ownership are widely used to link employees more closely to the success of the business and reward them for it.

The need for *redistributing power* is the fourth factor. Moving power downward in organizations often requires structural changes. Job enhancement and self-managed work teams involve a substantial change in the basic structure of the organization and are aimed at moving important decisions into the hands of individuals and teams performing the basic manufacturing or service work of the organization. Job enhancement programs are typically targeted at routine assembly and clerical jobs, while self-managed work teams are used in a broader array of jobs.

Lawler et al. (1995) noted that the effective utilization of employee involvement requires the simultaneous use of these four practices, not just the selective use of one or two of them. Interrelated patterns of mutually reinforcing practices are necessary to encourage and sustain employee behavior. Casual or fleeting use of these practices will be ineffectual and will not produce the sustained and systematic efforts needed to produce enduring organizational change.

Lawler et al. conducted a major study of organizations that have adopted TQM. A very high percentage (83%) of those companies report that their experience with TQM programs has been positive or very positive. Responses from their study are summarized in Table 8–1. It seems evident that organizational interest in TQM is not a passing fad or the "flavor of the month" panacea for organizational

TABLE 8–1 ■ Summary of responses to the question "Overall, how positive has your experience been with Total Quality Management?"

	Response Percent
Very negative	0%
Negative	1%
Neither negative nor positive	16%
Positive	66%
Very positive	17%

SOURCE: Adapted from "Creating High Performance" (p.75) by E. E. Lawler, S. A. Mohrman, and G. E. Ledford, 1995, San Francisco: Jossey-Bass. Reprinted by permission.

ills (see Field Note 3). The U.S. government annually grants the Malcolm Baldrige National Quality Award to the company that demonstrates the greatest advances in improving the quality of its products. Competition for the Baldrige Award is intense, and the recipients are highly regarded in the business community.

Reeves and Bednar (1994) noted that there is no universal definition of *quality;* rather, different definitions are appropriate under different circumstances. They believe there are organizational tradeoffs in accepting one definition of quality over another. Despite multiple definitions of *quality,* Vaill (1982) identified eight defining characteristics of high-performing organizations that embody the principles of TQM. Vaill based his findings on a study of diverse organizations, including

FIELD NOTE 3   **Students As Customers?**

ne of the underlying principles of Total Quality Management (TQM) is that the needs and preferences of the customer are of paramount importance. An organization's business strategy is directed toward satisfying the customer, which increases the likelihood of expanding the customer base as well as gaining repeat business among current customers. For example, in the operation of a restaurant, food is prepared to the customers' specific preferences. The goal is to satisfy the customers by increasing their control over the final product. The application of TQM principles in the field of medical practice is not so direct. A medical doctor does not regard patients as "customers," catering to their expressed needs. Rather, the doctor controls the specific form of medical treatment the patient receives—for example, with regard to medi-cation and surgery. In the field of medicine the patients put their faith and trust in the training and experience of the doctors to provide high-quality medical treatment.

Now consider education. Are students more like "customers" (in the restaurant business) or "patients" (in the medical business)? Should educational institutions strive to please their students by giving them more control over the substance and delivery of educational programs? Or should students put their faith and trust in the training of the faculty to know what is in the students' best interests in providing high-quality education? There has been considerable interest in applying TQM principles to educational institutions, but there has also been controversy over how students are to be regarded.

TABLE 8–2 ■ Characteristics of high-performing organizations

1. They are performing excellently against a known external standard.
2. They are performing excellently against what is assumed to be their potential level of performance.
3. They are performing excellently in relation to where they were at some earlier time.
4. They are judged by informed observers to be doing substantially better qualitatively than other comparable systems.
5. They are doing whatever they do with significantly fewer resources than it is assumed are needed.
6. They are perceived as exemplars of the way to do whatever they do, and this becomes a source of ideas and inpiration for others.
7. They are perceived to fulfill at a high level the ideals for the culture within which they exist; that is, they have mobility.
8. They are the only organization that has been able to do what they do at all, even though it might seem that what they do is not that difficult or mysterious a thing.

SOURCE: From "The Purposing of High-Performing Systems" by P. Vaill, 1982, *Organizational Dynamics, 2* (2), pp. 23–39.

universities, a Coast Guard unit, hospitals, marching bands, drug rehabilitation agencies, and stock brokerages. The characteristics are listed in Table 8–2. It is these characteristics that all change programs, directly or indirectly, try to develop in organizations.

EMPIRICAL ORGANIZATIONAL CHANGE RESEARCH

Porras and Robertson (1992) reviewed 63 empirical research studies on organizational change over a 14-year period to assess the impact of interventions. They grouped the interventions into four categories: organizing arrangements, social factors, technology, and physical setting. *Organizing arrangements* included the creation of new committees, task forces, or work teams. *Social factors* most typically included team building and process consultation. *Technology* was most often represented by job redesign. Finally, the *physical setting* involved changes in office layout, such as from a closed-office (e.g., with partitions) to an open-office layout. The dependent variables were individual and organizational outcomes. The results of the study are presented in Figure 8–9. Two findings are evident. First, change interventions resulted in no change more than half the time. Second, the percentage of studies reporting a negative change (i.e., the change intervention produced negative outcomes) was very small. These findings deserve two comments. First, given the problems of accurately measuring change, it is conceivable that at least some of the findings of no change may have been based on measures that were insensitive to the types of change that occurred. Second, it is precisely because specific interventions, such as in technology, produce no change in outcomes that organizations have moved toward large-scale, multifaceted, comprehensive change efforts like TQM. One conclusion that may be drawn from this study is that singular change interventions are not likely to produce large-scale changes in indi-

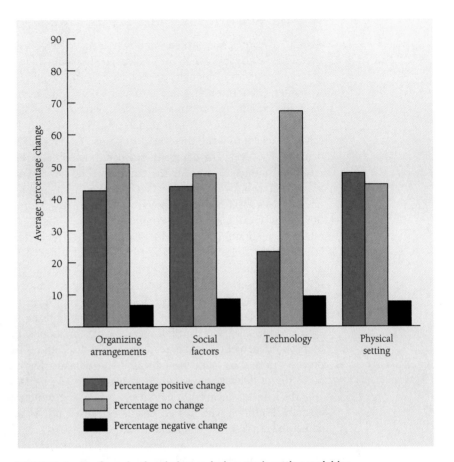

FIGURE 8–9 ■ **Organizational change in key work setting variables**

SOURCE: From "Organizational Development: Theory, Practice, and Research" by J. I. Porras and P. J. Robertson, 1992, in *Handbook of Industrial and Organizational Psychology*, 2nd ed., Vol. 3 (p. 787), edited by M. D. Dunnette and L. M. Hough, Palo Alto, CA: Consulting Psychologists Press.

vidual and organizational outcomes. This is not really surprising given that organizations tend to be resistant to change.

Macy and Izumi (1993) argued that to be successful, organizational change efforts must include systemwide design and transformation strategies. To significantly change and transform organizations, there must be change in the power, control systems, and decision making of the organization. Change efforts that start at the work site (office, plant, production line) are generally not as successful as those that start at the corporate level. TQM and other systemwide initiatives aimed at large-scale organizational change seemingly hold the greatest promise to be successful. There is also evidence (Rodgers & Hunter, 1996) suggesting that different conclusions can be drawn regarding the effectiveness of change interventions depending on the criteria used to render the evaluations.

CASE STUDY ■ The Relative Value of Frogs vs. Grass

About 20 years ago a husband-and-wife team, Helen and Ted McCall, decided to start a new company, which they called The Learning Focus. The business plan was to write books for elementary school teachers that would help them teach children in kindergarten through grade 3. The books would present graphic images and ideas for explaining concepts like colors, letters of the alphabet, and numbers to children in a way they would understand. The McCalls hired former elementary school teachers to write these books because they had experience in teaching students at that level. The company prospered. Eventually the McCalls were ready to retire and found a buyer for the company. The new owner was David Nemeroff, an entrepreneur who recognized a lucrative business opportunity when he saw one. Mr. Nemeroff had never been a teacher; he was a former manufacturing executive with traditional business training. He knew The Learning Focus enjoyed an esteemed reputation in the field as a provider of high-class books for elementary school teachers. He also saw that the potential value of the company was much greater than had been realized under the first owners. The McCalls were former teachers themselves but knew little of the business functions of production, marketing, and sales. It was Nemeroff's intent to transform a "mom and pop" company into a larger scale (and more profitable) business operation. He greatly increased the sales and distribution of the existing books, hired market researchers to propose new books the teachers could use, and upgraded the production process. In a short time he increased the demand for his company's books by 80%. He set delivery dates of new books to his eager customers.

Much to his dismay, Nemeroff discovered the writers repeatedly missed production deadlines. The missed deadlines caused orders not to be filled on time, which in turn led his customers to find other books provided by his competitors. Nemeroff couldn't understand what caused the delays. He would occasionally sit in on design meetings of his writers. What he observed astounded him. At one meeting the writers actively debated for almost three hours on a good way to convey the color "green." Some writers favored the use of frogs to symbolize the color green, while others preferred grass in a lawn. The lawn proponents said some children might never have seen a frog, while the frog proponents said the idea of grass in a lawn was boring and unimaginative. The writers considered this type of debate to be enjoyable and stimulating, and this was regarded as a highlight of their work. However, it was debates about these types of issues that prolonged the production process and caused missed deadlines. Nemeroff couldn't understand how the frogs vs. grass debate, for example, could consume three hours. His opinion was that the book was to convey the concept of the color green; how it did so was of far lesser importance. At least it was not worth a three-hour discussion and inevitable lost revenue.

Nemeroff repeatedly badgered the writers to get their work done on time. The writers said they couldn't rush quality. They believed it was precisely the passion evidenced in the frogs vs. grass debate that led the company to produce such high-quality books when the McCalls ran the business. The McCalls didn't hassle the writers about production deadlines. Nemeroff would reiterate that The Learning Focus was in business to make money, and that prolonged debates that led to production delays hurt the business, not helped it. The writers believed they weren't doing their work just to make money. They felt they had a noble purpose—to help educate children—which was more important than just meeting production deadlines. Nemeroff recognized that The Learning Focus did have a reputation of high-quality products, but he felt that quality would not be greatly sacrificed if the company ran more efficiently. He found himself repeatedly locked in confrontations with his writers, repeatedly facing missed production deadlines, and facing plummeting morale on the part of his writers. Given Nemeroff's apparent values, some writers snidely commented the company should change its name from "The Learning Focus" to "Nemeroff's Money Machine."

Study Questions

1. What are some of the deeply held values by Mr. Nemeroff and the writers that in part define the organizational culture of The Learning Focus?
2. Explain how these differing values produce the conflict among the parties in this case.
3. In an attempt to bring about a change in the organization, what do you think might happen to The Learning Focus if Nemeroff fired all the existing writers and replaced them with new writers?
4. What significance does the legacy of the McCalls have on the way the writers currently view the company?
5. If you were asked to bring about change to benefit The Learning Focus, what change strategies would you follow and why?

SUGGESTED INFOTRAC TOPICS

downsizing

roles

norms

organizational culture

organizational change

empowerment

Total Quality Management

span of control

corporate reorganizing

organizational structure

C H A P T E R   9

eams and Teamwork

LEARNING OBJECTIVES

- ■ Explain why the use of teams is increasing.
- ■ Explain the concept of teamwork.
- ■ Describe the structure and processes of teams.
- ■ Explain how teams make decisions and share mental models.
- ■ Explain how personnel selection, training, and performance appraisal apply to teams.

Historically, I/O psychologists have tended to make individuals the object of their attention. That is, we have been concerned with finding the right person for the job, training the individual, and subsequently monitoring his or her performance on the job. While the existence of informal work groups was acknowledged in the Hawthorne studies, for the most part interest in groups was assigned to the field of social psychology. However, in recent years there has been a tremendous upsurge of interest in using work groups, not just individuals, as the organizing principle through which work is accomplished. Guzzo (1995) noted that there is no real distinction between the words *groups* and *teams.* Psychology has tended to use the term *groups,* as witnessed by the study of group dynamics and group processes. *Teams,* on the other hand, tend to be groups that have a more narrow focus or purpose. I/O psychology is increasingly using the term *teams* or *work teams* in reference to groups. Some authors assert a *team* must have at least three members. The term *dyad* is used to describe a two-person unit.

team
a social aggregation in which a limited number of individuals interact on a regular basis to accomplish a set of shared objectives for which they have mutual responsibility

Teams are bounded social units that work within a larger social system—the organization. A team within an organization has identifiable memberships (that is, members and nonmembers alike clearly know who is a member and who is not) and an identifiable task or set of tasks to perform. Tasks may include monitoring, producing, serving, generating ideas, and doing other activities. The team's work requires that members interact by exchanging information, sharing resources, and coordinating with and reacting to one another in the cause of accomplishing the group task. Furthermore, there is always some degree of interdependence within the members of a team as well as interdependence among different teams in an organization.

ORIGINS OF WORK TEAMS

As we discussed in the previous chapter, organizations are designed for a purpose. Accordingly, the traditional structure of an organization (line/staff relationships, span of control, etc.) was created to conduct and monitor the flow of work. Such traditional organizational structures were in effect and effective for most of the 20th century. In the last two decades of the 20th century, however, several technological, economic, and demographic forces converged, prompting organizations to respond to them. These forces were discussed in Chapter 1 (the discussion continues in Chapter 14) and reflect the changing nature of work. Greater global economic competition and rapid advances in communication technology forced organizations to change the way they performed their work operations. Some automobile companies—Saturn, for example—developed a team approach to the production of cars compared with the traditional assembly line approach. Products had to be developed and brought to market more quickly than in the past. The rapid changes in the business world compelled organizations to be more flexible and responsive to them. To increase their flexibility, companies had to move away from tightly controlled organizational structures, structures that often resulted in a relatively slow work pace. There was increased emphasis on organizations' need to respond quickly in what they did and how they did it. Organizations began to change their structure in response to these environmental forces and use work teams that are held collectively responsible for accomplishing the organization's work (LePine et al., 2000). Concurrently, the decision-making authority concerning the specific means of task accomplishment has been pushed down to these teams. The team members often must decide among themselves who will do the what, where, when, and how of work.

What is it about the contemporary world of work that underlies the creation of teams to accomplish work? Three factors are critical. The first is the burgeoning amount of information and knowledge available. It has been said that society has entered the "information age." Information from multiple sources often has to be absorbed to respond to complex business issues. No one person can have technical expertise in all areas of knowledge; thus, a team approach, representing a pooling of mental resources, becomes more tenable. Second, the working population is becoming increasingly more educated and trained. When the traditional organizational structures of 100 years ago were created (the tenets of classical theory discussed in Chapter 8), the workforce was relatively uneducated. A high school diploma was a level of educational attainment achieved by only a minority of the population. The members of the traditional working class were monitored by members of "management," who often possessed more education or training. One hundred years later our working population is considerably different from their ancestors. The workers of today have achieved a much higher level of education and training. As such, they are more qualified and willing to serve in the types of roles called for in work teams. As an employee who now works in a production team in a manufacturing organization stated, "I'm no longer expected to check my brain at the front gate when I enter the factory." The third factor is the rate of change in work activities. For many years workers had well-defined activities in their jobs that rarely changed. In fact, the static constellation of these work activities served to define the "job." In the current work world there are pressures to make new products, modify services, alter processes to improve quality, and in general be in a continual state of transformation. Rarely today are work activities static, unchanged from years past. Work teams are posited to be responsive and adaptable to these ever-changing conditions of work. As such, the growing conversion from individuals to teams as a means of conducting work is both a product of and a response to the confluence of forces or pressures applied to contemporary organizations.

The evolution of teams and teamwork has compelled I/O psychology to address a host of new issues. Ilgen (1999) identified several critical constructs in understanding teams and why they are effective, including team performance and team composition. Some of what we have learned about individuals in the workplace generalizes to teams, but other issues are more specific to teams. However, teams are *not* universally superior to individuals for conducting work across all relevant performance indices. For example, teams do not necessarily produce better quality decisions than do some individuals. There is nothing magical about transforming individuals into work teams. Teams are merely one means of performing work. In this chapter we will examine teams as a means of accomplishing work, including the factors that lead to successful team performance.

LEVEL OF ANALYSIS

A shift in the focus from individuals to teams as a means of conducting work also requires a shift in the conduct of I/O psychological research. Researchers can and do examine different entities as the object of their investigations. Historically I/O psychology focused on the individual with regard to such factors as desired KSAOs for employment, needed training, and standards of job performance. In such cases the *level of analysis* is the individual; that is, the conclusions drawn by the research are about individuals. However, research questions can also be posed at the team level of analysis and at the organization level of analysis. Consider an organization that has 100 employees. A researcher may be interested in assessing the relationship between the degree to which employees feel a sense of organizational identification with the company and job performance. At the individual level of analysis, the researcher would have a sample size of 100 individuals, obtain measures of organizational identification and job performance, correlate the two variables, and arrive at a conclusion regarding the relationship between them at the *individual* level of analysis. However, the 100 employees could also be organized into 25 four-person work teams. In this case the researcher would have a sample size of 25 (i.e., the 25 teams). Each team would be represented by a score reflecting the sense of organizational identification (as a team) and by their work performance (as a team). The researcher would correlate these two variables and, based upon a sample size of 25, arrive at a conclusion about the relationship between the two variables at the *team* level of analysis. It is also possible to study the relationship between organizational identification and performance at the organizational level of analysis. In this case the 100-employee company would be a sample size of 1. There would be one measure of organizational identification (for the entire company) and one measure of performance (for the entire company). The researcher would then have to collect data from additional organizations. The researcher would correlate these two variables, based upon a sample size of however many organizations were in the study, and arrive at a conclusion about the relationship between the two variables at the *organization* level of analysis. A diagram showing these levels of analysis is presented in Figure 9–1.

The answer to the question, What is the relationship between organizational identification and performance? depends upon the level of analysis under consideration. It is possible to arrive at three different conclusions, depending upon whether the level is the individual, team, or organization. Furthermore, some constructs do not exist at particular levels of analysis. Size is one example. Teams and organizations can differ in their size (i.e., number of members), but individuals cannot. For the most part, I/O psychologists have not focused their research interests on the organization level of analysis. Studying complete organizations and their relationships with other organizations is more traditionally the province of sociology. In fact, there is often a link between a particular scientific discipline and the level of analysis of its research. The field of economics examines variables at the industry (e.g., petroleum, agriculture, manufacturing, etc.) level of analysis, and the field of political science frequently examines variables at the national level of analysis.

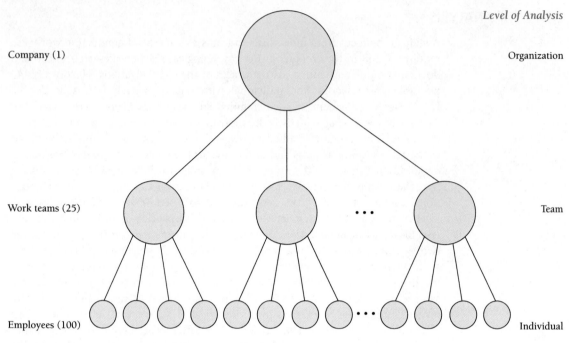

Level of Analysis

Company (1)   Organization

Work teams (25)   • • •   Team

Employees (100)   • • •   Individual

FIGURE 9–1 ■   Three levels of analysis

The term *micro* is often used to describe research at the individual level of analysis, while *macro* is used to describe research at the organizational level of analysis. Research at the team level of analysis is positioned somewhere between the micro and the macro. Rousseau and House (1994) have proposed the term *meso* (meaning "in between," as in the word *mezzanine*) research. Meso research occurs in an organizational context where processes at two levels are examined simultaneously. Thus I/O psychology researchers who study relationships between variables at both the individual and team levels of analysis are engaging in meso research. The entire area of multilevel research and theory is an emerging topic in our profession (e.g., Klein & Kozlowski, 2000). It addresses a fundamental dilemma in understanding human behavior in organizations; namely, we as individuals obtain employment in a larger social collectivity (an organization) and are often members of some smaller level of aggregation (as a team, department, unit, or shift). The dilemma is to disentangle the influences on our behavior from an individual, team, and organizational perspective. It will also be recalled from Chapter 2 that meta-analysis is a frequently used method of research in which investigators combine the results from previously conducted research to distill a conclusion about a topic. Ostroff and Harrison (1999) caution that researchers must be clear about the level of analysis of their investigation because collapsing or combining findings from original studies with differing levels of analysis diminishes the chance of unambiguously interpreting the findings.

TYPES OF TEAMS

problem–solving team
a type of team created for the purpose of focusing on the resolution of a particular problem or issue

creative team
a type of team created for the purpose of developing innovative possibilities or solutions

tactical team
a type of team created for the purpose of executing a well-defined plan or objective

ad hoc team
A type of team created for a limited duration that is designed to address itself to resolving one particular problem

The term *team* has been used in many contexts to describe such types of work operations as project teams, sales teams, new product teams, process improvement teams, cost-reduction teams, and so on. One way to differentiate teams is by their objectives. It is also possible to differentiate teams by other variables, such as the nature of their interactions (e.g., face-to-face vs. virtual). Larson and La Fasto (1989) proposed three basic types of teams.

Problem-solving teams require each member of the team to expect that interactions among members will be truthful and embody a high degree of integrity. Each member must believe that the team will be consistent and mature in its approach to dealing with problems. The members must have a high degree of trust in a process of problem resolution that focuses on issues, rather than on predetermined positions or conclusions. The authors cite diagnostic teams at the Centers for Disease Control as an exemplar of this type.

Creative teams are responsible for exploring possibilities and alternatives, with the broad objective of developing a new product or service. A necessary feature of the team's structure is autonomy. For a creative team to function, it needs to have autonomy from systems and procedures as well as an atmosphere in which ideas are not prematurely quashed. Creative teams need to be insulated within the organizational structure in order to remain focused on the result to be achieved rather than on organizational processes. The IBM PC was developed by a creative team that endured many failures before arriving at a successful product. The design team needed protection from typical organizational pressures that reflect impatience with failure. The "incubation period" for the PC was many years and could not have been shortened by performance expectations imposed by others.

Tactical teams are responsible for executing a well-defined plan. To do so there must be high task clarity and unambiguous role definition. The success of tactical teams depends on a high degree of responsiveness from team members, a clear understanding of who does what, and a clear set of performance standards. An example of a tactical team is a police SWAT team or a cardiac surgical team. Each operational procedure must be well defined, and each task must be highly focused and very specific. Furthermore, the standards of excellence must be clear to everyone, and ways of measuring success or failure must be understood by the entire team. Table 9–1 lists the basic characteristics of the three major types of teams.

We may add a fourth type of team, which is defined primarily by its highly limited life span. It is sometimes called an *ad hoc* (Latin for "to this") team and is basically a hybrid cross between a problem-resolution and a tactical team. An **ad hoc team** is created for a specific purpose, addressing itself to one particular problem. The team members are selected from existing employees in an organization, and after the team has completed its work, the team disbands. Thus, membership in the team (and indeed the life span of the team itself) is finite and then the team no longer exists. Such types of teams are used in organizations that encounter unusual or atypical problems that require an atypical response (the creation of the *ad hoc* team). If the problem tends to repeat itself, there may be pressure to establish the team on a longer-term basis, as a more formalized and permanent unit.

TABLE 9–1 ■ **Characteristics of the three types of teams**

Broad Objective	Dominant Feature	Process Emphasis	Example
Problem resolution	Trust	Focus on issues	Centers for Disease Control
Creative	Autonomy	Explore possibilities and alternatives	IBM PC team
Tactical	Clarity	Directive Highly focused tasks Role clarity Well-defined operational standards Accuracy	Cardiac surgery team

SOURCE: From *Teamwork* (p. 43) by C. E. Larson and F. M. La Fasto, 1989, Newbury Park, CA: Sage. Reprinted by permission of the publisher.

PRINCIPLES OF TEAMWORK

McIntyre and Salas (1995) conducted extensive research on U.S. Navy tactical teams and identified several principles of teamwork that are also relevant for other organizations that use teams. Five of the major principles are listed here.

Principle 1: Teamwork implies that members provide feedback to and accept it from one another. For teamwork to be effective, team members must feel free to provide feedback; that is, the climate within the group must be such that neither status nor power stands as an obstacle to team members' providing feedback to one another. Effective teams engage in tasks with an awareness of their strengths and weaknesses. When team leaders show the ability to accept constructive criticism, they establish a norm that this type of criticism is appropriate.

Principle 2: Teamwork implies the willingness, preparedness, and proclivity to back fellow members up during operations. Better teams are distinguishable from poorer teams in that their members show a willingness to jump in and help when they are needed, and they accept help without fear of being perceived as weak. Team members must show competence not only in their own particular area but also in the areas of other team members with whom they directly interact.

Principle 3: Teamwork involves group members collectively viewing themselves as a group whose success depends on their interaction. Team members must have high awareness of themselves as a team. Each member sees the team's success as taking precedence over individual performance. Members of effective teams view themselves as connected team members, not as isolated individuals working with other isolated individuals. Effective teams consist of individuals who recognize that their effectiveness is the team's effectiveness, which depends on the sum total of all team members' performance.

Principle 4: Teamwork means fostering within-team interdependence. Fostering team interdependence means the team adopts the value that it is not only appropriate but also essential for each team member (regardless of status within the team) to depend on every other team member to carry out the team's mission. Contrary to what may take place in the rest of the organization, interdependence is seen as a virtue—as an essential characteristic of team performance—not as a weakness.

Principle 5: Team leadership makes a difference with respect to the performance of the team. Team leaders serve as models for their fellow team members. If the leaders openly engage in teamwork—that is, provide and accept feedback and supportive behaviors—other team members are likely to do the same. Team leaders are vital and have tremendous influence on teams, and when team leaders are poor, so are the teams.

McIntyre and Salas (1995) believe these principles provide for a theory of teamwork. In their attempts to implement or improve team-based performance, organizations need to think specifically about how organization members can effectively serve in the capacity of team members. A theory of teamwork must be incorporated into the organization's operating philosophy. Teamwork will take place within the organization to the extent that the organization fosters it and builds upon it.

TEAM STRUCTURE

The structure of a team includes variables such as the number of members on the team, demographic composition, and experience of team members. A prominent theme in team structures is the diversity of its members. The term *diversity* is often associated with the gender, race, culture, and age of people. However, such is not strictly the case in describing diversity in a team. Research shows that successful teams manifest diversity in their members, where *diversity* literally means "differentness." In what ways can diversity manifest itself among members on a team? Two manifestations are information diversity and value diversity. Information diversity refers to differences among the members in terms of what they know and what cognitive resources (e.g., factual knowledge, experiences) they can bring to the team. Successful teams often have a pooling of expertise or knowledge among their members. Value diversity reflects more fundamental differences among people with regard to tastes, preferences, goals, and interests. Differences in values among team members can be expressed in a wide range of issues, including the purpose of the team, the willingness to be an active team contributor, and the degree to which membership is valued in the team as a means of accomplishing work. You can think of information diversity and value diversity as the approximate team-level counterparts of the "can do" and "will do" factors described in Chapter 5. Jehn, Northcraft, and Neale (1999) reported that informational diversity positively influenced team performance, but value diversity decreased member satisfaction with the team, intent to remain on the team, and commitment to the team. The authors also found the impact of diversity on team performance was dependent on the type of task. If the task requires great speed and coordination, then information diversity may not positively influence team performance.

Some of the earliest research on team structure was conducted by Belbin (1981). Belbin proposed that diversity within a team was reflected in the members

THE FAR SIDE® By GARY LARSON

**"I've got it, too, Omar ... a strange feeling like
we've just been going in circles."**

filling different roles. Belbin proposed that effective teams were composed of members who served different roles on the team, and their roles were defined by possession of selected mental ability and personality characteristics. Belbin studied eight-person teams and arrived at the following needed roles, as shown in Figure 9–2.

1. *A leader.* The leader of the team has to be responsible for the overall performance of the team, recognizes the team's strengths and weaknesses, and ensures that the best use is made of each team member's potential.
2. *A shaper.* A shaper influences the way team effort is applied, directing attention to the setting of objectives and priorities, and seeks to impose some shape or pattern on the outcome of team activities. Both the leader and shaper roles collectively serve to define the team's direction and output.
3. *A worker.* A worker gets things done by turning concepts and plans into practical working procedures, and carrying out agreed plans systematically and efficiently.

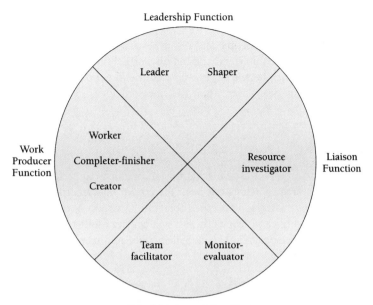

Leadership Function

FIGURE 9–2 ■ Eight team roles distributed over four team functions

4. *A creator.* A creator advances new ideas and strategies with special attention to major issues, and looks for possible new ways to address problems confronting the team.

5. *A resource investigator.* This role reports on ideas, developments, and resources outside of the team and creates external contacts that may be useful to the team in their actions.

6. *A monitor-evaluator.* This role requires analyzing problems and evaluating ideas and suggestions so that the team stays focused on its task. This person often functions as a critic. The more numerous and complex suggestions become, the more important is the role of the monitor-evaluator.

7. *A team facilitator.* A team facilitator supports members in their strengths, helps compensate for their weaknesses, and improves communication between members by fostering team spirit.

8. *A completer-finisher.* This role actively searches for aspects of work that need more than the usual amount of attention, and maintains a sense of urgency within the team.

It is to be remembered, as described in Chapter 8, that these are different roles filled by individuals, and not necessarily different people. That is, while each of these roles may be critical to team success, individuals can serve multiple roles. In teams of fewer than eight people, it is necessary for some team members to play more than one role. Belbin noted there can be more than one worker role on a team, and some roles are more likely pairs than others. That is, one person could well serve in the worker and completer-finisher roles. Some pairs of roles filled by the same individual are less likely, such as facilitator and monitor-evaluator.

Belbin's eight roles can be further reduced to four functions within a team: (1) leadership within a team, (2) work producers, (3) internal team maintenance, and (4) liaison to people and resources outside of the team. Fisher, Hunter, and Macrosson (1998) affirmed the validity of Belbin's team roles in teams with fewer than eight members, and showed that the likelihood of individuals assuming a secondary role was based upon their personalities.

TEAM PROCESSES

As important as the structure of a team is to its functioning, the vast majority of research on teams has been directed to the processes that guide how a team functions. *Processes* are the operations within a team that permit it to function smoothly and efficiently. We will consider four major team processes: socialization, interpersonal, shared mental models, and decision-making.

Socialization

socialization
the process of mutual adjustment between the team and its members, especially new members

Socialization is the process of mutual adjustment that produces changes over time in the relationship between a person and a team. It is the process a person goes through in joining a team, being on a team, and eventually leaving a team. Likewise, the team itself is affected by the arrival, presence, and departure of a team member. The socialization process can range from a formal orientation session to the team to informal one-on-one feedback between a senior team member and the newcomer. The relationship between a senior team member and a newcomer can take on many of the properties of the mentor–protégé relationship discussed in Chapter 6. New team members can be appraised by subtle surveillance of an older team member, or by the newcomer seeking feedback from the team, as "What does it take to be successful on this team?" and "Am I fitting in?"

Moreland and Levine (2001) have proposed an explanatory framework for how the socialization process occurs. It is based on three psychological concepts: evaluation, commitment, and role transition. Evaluation involves attempts by the team and the individual to assess and maximize each other's value. This includes identifying the team goals to which an individual can contribute and evaluating how participation on the team will satisfy the individual's personal needs. Thus the evaluation process is mutual. Commitment is the sense of loyalty, union, and connection between the individual and the team. When the individual is committed to the team, he or she is likely to accept the team's goals, work hard to achieve them, and feel warmly to the team. When a team is strongly committed to an individual, it is likely to accept that person's needs, work hard to satisfy them, and feel warmly toward the person. Changes in commitment transform the relationship between a team and an individual. These transformations are governed by specific levels of commitment that mark the boundaries between different membership roles the person could play in the team. Both the team and the individual will try to initiate a role transition when commitment reaches a certain level. Figure 9–3 shows an individual's commitment to the team over time as he or she

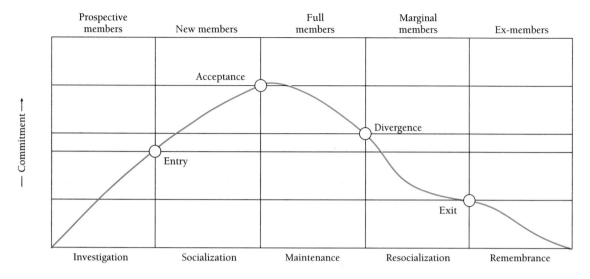

FIGURE 9–3 ■ The socialization process for team members

SOURCE: Adapted from "Socialization in Organizations and Work Groups" by R. L. Moreland and J. M. Levine, 2001, in *Groups at Work* (pp. 69–112), edited by M. E. Turner, Mahwah, NJ: Erlbaum.

passes through five phases of team membership: investigation, socialization, maintenance, resocialization, and remembrance.

During the investigation phase, the team searches for individuals who can contribute to the achievement of team goals. Likewise, the individual, as a prospective member of the team, searches for a team that will be satisfying. If both parties socialization phase begins. In this phase the individual experiences assimilation into the team and the team accommodates itself to the individual. If both parties accept each other, the individual becomes a full member of the team. This acceptance marks the end of the socialization phase and the beginning of maintenance. Now both parties try to maximize their respective needs—the achievement of the team and the satisfaction of the individual. This phase lasts as long as both parties meet their needs. However, as commitment weakens between the team and the individual, another role transition based on the divergence of commitment occurs, resulting in resocialization. During resocialization, the team and the individual try again to influence each other so that the team's needs are more likely to be satisfied. If the resocialization process is not successful, team membership ends with a period of remembrance. The team recalls the individual's contributions to the achievement of its goals, and the individual recalls his or her experiences with the team. Over time, feelings of commitment between the team and the individual often stabilize, usually at a low level.

The socialization process presented by Moreland and Levine reveals the subtleties and phases of group dynamics. Both the individual and the team are mutually trying to influence each other to achieve the same purpose. The socialization process develops over time, although the length of the time period varies across individuals and teams. Teams have "lives" based upon the state of socialization of their members, and this socialization process is constantly evolving.

Interpersonal Processes in Teams

The interpersonal processes in a team have been found to influence the overall performance of teams. Yeatts and Hyten (1998) identified several interpersonal characteristics that are endemic to the high-performing work teams they studied.

Communication.   In successful work teams, interpersonal communication is described as frank, continuous, and regular. Team members often meet briefly and informally to review the day's work. Formal, regularly scheduled weekly meetings are held to discuss team progress. When new information comes to a team member, it is often quickly disseminated among all team members. In high-performing groups, team members communicate problems they are having and freely solicit advice. They rarely "hold back" when it comes to revealing problems. In general, continuous and regular communication within a group results in the team quickly identifying resources that are inappropriate, that are likely to be insufficient to do the work, and that appear to be working best.

Conflict.   Conflict among members is unavoidable in any team. What matters is how the conflict is dealt with in the team, as well as the team's attitude about conflict. Conflict can be viewed either as something the group members actively seek to suppress or as an opportunity to learn from each other. Two types of conflict have been identified: beneficial and competitive. *Beneficial conflict* refers to situations where two or more members have opposing ideas and interests but are motivated to understand the views and interests of the other. The team members try to understand each other's perspectives and seek to fashion a mutually satisfactory decision (see Field Note 1). Such experiences tend to strengthen their relationship, as they become more confident that future conflicts can also be resolved. On the other hand, in *competitive conflict* the disagreeing team members vigorously defend their respective positions and attempt to win over others. They look for weaknesses in each other's arguments as opposed to modifying their own conclusions. They may resort to using superior authority to impose their own solutions. Although not all conflict can be expressed in the beneficial form, Yeatts and Hyten found that high-performing work teams sought to diminish the manifestations of competitive conflict.

Cohesion.   *Cohesion* is the degree to which members of a team feel attracted to their team and are compelled to stay in it. Cohesion is based on two forms of attraction: attraction to the tasks of the team and to the members of the team. With high cohesion of either type, team members are more likely to ask for assistance or defer to others who have more talent with regard to the particular tasks being performed. Team-oriented cohesiveness facilitates decision making because the communication among team members is more open; that is, team members feel "safer" to express differing views and ideas. However, it is possible that once cohesive groups begin to achieve a sense of likemindedness or *groupthink* (to be discussed shortly), additional information important to decision making may be rejected if it is regarded as weakening cohesion. There is also research that suggests greater team cohesion may follow from successful team performance, as opposed to causing the performance to occur. Rewards that focus on team achievements are likely to enhance cohesiveness, whereas individual rewards encourage competition among team members, which weakens cohesiveness. Other teams and individuals within an organization often take notice of cohesive teams and sometimes express the desire to be members of a cohesive unit themselves. Cohesive teams have also been found to exert more influence than less cohesive teams in the running of the organization.

Trust.   Yeatts and Hyten reported that we know less about trust than any of the other interpersonal processes in teams. *Trust* is defined as the belief that even though you have no control over another person's behavior toward you, that person will behave in a way that benefits you. Where trust is reported to be high, team members spend less energy worrying about what others are doing and thinking and more energy directly on doing the work. Furthermore, team members who trust one another are more willing to allow a more talented team member to perform tasks they are less skilled in doing. Team members who have low trust tend to believe that alternatives presented by others in making decisions are designed to benefit only certain members, rather than the team as a whole. In general, trust develops slowly within a team, even among teams with stable memberships. It is also the most fragile of the interpersonal processes. An individual who abuses the norms within a group can quickly destroy any trust with those whose

---

FIELD NOTE 1   Orchestrated Conflict

onflict is often regarded as a negative influence among team members, but this is not always the case. Research reveals the positive value of beneficial conflict. Consider the following case in point. A university had a choice piece of land with an ideal location for many possible uses. An old building that stood on the property was razed, which created an opportunity for new use of the land. Many constituents of the university (students, faculty, alumni, financial supporters, etc.) held differing ideas about what use should be made of the land. The president of the university established an advisory committee to make a formal recommendation to the university on the best use of the land. However, the president did not want the ensuing land use debate to fall strictly along "party lines," such as students versus faculty.

The president did not want to be perceived as favoring one party or subgroup over the rest in making the ultimate decision. The president was to select three faculty members to serve on the advisory committee. The list of possible names was reduced to four finalists, based upon their expressed willingness to serve. Two strong-willed and highly opinionated professors who held similar beliefs about the land use were among the four finalists. The president chose one but not the other. When asked (privately) why both professors were not selected, the president replied, "They think too much alike. At times I believe they have two bodies but share the same brain." Here is one example where a decision was made to increase the likelihood of conflict within the group, in the belief that it would ultimately have a beneficial effect.

trust was violated. Dirks (1999) found that teams with higher levels of trust did not necessarily have better processes and better performance than teams with low levels of trust. Instead, trust appeared to influence how motivation was translated into group process and performance. In high-trust teams motivation was transformed into collaborative or joint efforts and hence better performance, while in low-trust teams motivation was translated into individual efforts.

Yeatts and Hyten noted that these interpersonal processes are often highly interrelated in the workplace. High-performing teams often manifest high levels of communication, constructive means of expressing conflict, cohesiveness, and trust among members of the team. While not all high-performing teams manifest these interpersonal processes to the same degree, the processes are subtle yet enduring mechanisms for facilitating the functioning of the team.

Shared Mental Models

shared mental model
the cognitive processes held in common by members of a team regarding how they acquire information, analyze it, and respond to it

The concept of **shared mental models** refers to team members having some degree of similarity in how they approach problems and evaluate potential solutions. Shared mental models are posited to influence the behavior of the group. How individuals think is reflected in their behavior, and the term given to the thinking process is *cognition*. A team is a social aggregation in which a limited number of individuals interact on a regular basis to accomplish a set of shared objectives for which they have mutual responsibility. The fusion of cognition (as a psychological process) and a team (as an interacting collectivity) produces the concept of shared cognition or shared mental models, which reflects how the team acquires, stores, and uses information (Gibson, 2001).

Cannon-Bowers and Salas (2001) addressed the fundamental question of what is actually shared among team members in establishing mental models. Four broad categories were identified: task-specific knowledge, task-related knowledge, knowledge of teammates, and attitudes/beliefs, as shown in Figure 9–4. Each respective type of knowledge has increasingly broad generalizability across differing tasks. *Task-specific information* is shared information among team members that allows them to act without the need for discussion. Task-specific information involves the particular procedures, sequences, actions, and strategies necessary to perform a task. It can be generalized only to other instances of similar tasks. *Task-related knowledge* refers to common knowledge about task-related processes, but it is not limited to a single task. It is more generalizable, as it applies to knowledge of processes that are used in many specific tasks. *Knowledge of teammates* refers to how well the members understand each other, including their performance, strengths, weaknesses, and tendencies. Thus, team members must learn how the collective expertise of the team is distributed across the members. This type of shared knowledge helps teammates compensate for one another, predict each other's actions, and allocate resources according to member expertise. The final category of *shared attitudes and beliefs* permits team members to arrive at comparable interpretations of the problems they face. It enhances team cohesion, motivation, and consensus. In summary, shared mental models do not refer to a unitary

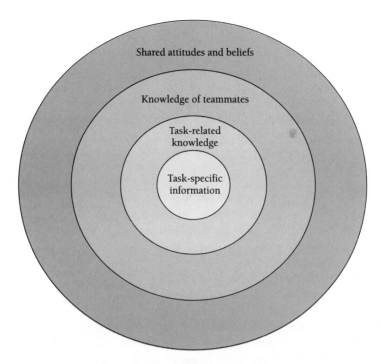

FIGURE 9–4 ■ Generalizability of four types of shared knowledge in mental models

concept. It appears that all of the types of knowledge in these four categories need to be shared in effective teams.

Cannon-Bowers and Salas added there is also not a singular way that knowledge can be "shared" across team members. Some common knowledge must be held by all members of a team, particularly as it relates to task-specific knowledge. Other types of knowledge are shared by being distributed or apportioned across the team members. Certain knowledge is complex or specialized, and it is unrealistic to expect all members of a team to possess this level of knowledge equally. Thus, what is important is that the knowledge resides within the team as a team, not held by each team member. Shared knowledge is common in military combat teams and surgical teams.

As compelling as the evidence is for shared mental models for effective team performance, there is a potential dark side to team members "thinking alike." The phenomenon is called **groupthink**. Noted problems in history that arose from groupthink are the Bay of Pigs invasion of Cuba in the 1960s and the explosion of the Challenger space shuttle in the 1980s. Groupthink refers to a deterioration in cognitive processing caused by team members feeling threatened by external sources. The defects in decision making involve incomplete consideration of options and alternatives, poor information search, and selective information processing. Groupthink is a model of thinking whereby team members consider consensus to be more important than rational, independent thinking. Some symptoms

groupthink
a phenomenon associated with team decision making in which members feel threatened by forces external to the team, resulting in a deterioration in the cognitive processing of information

are the illusion of team vulnerability, the false assumption of the team's morality, stereotyping of opposing groups, the illusion of group unanimity, and the emergence of a process that keeps opposing viewpoints from the team's consideration. The team, under a siege mentality, fails to perceive environments correctly and looks for confirming evidence that it is being threatened. Choi and Kim (1999) noted that the conventional interpretation of groupthink is a negative influence on performance. The term is used in reference to fiascoes like the Bay of Pigs invasion. However, while they found that some dimensions of the groupthink phenomenon (as suppressing dissenting opinions) were related to negative team performance, some other dimensions (as a strong sense of group identity) in fact were related to positive team performance. Turner and Horvitz (2001) concluded that groupthink is more likely found in teams that have a strong sense of social identity. In such cases team members often feel compelled to maintain and enhance their evaluation of the team and its actions. Furthermore, members become motivated to protect the image of the team. When the image is questioned by a collective threat, the response among members is to seek concurrence about the threat and, by virtue of that, attain greater acceptance as bona fide team members. A threat to an individual member of a team is not likely to engender groupthink, as does a threat to the entire team.

In short, effective team performance requires members to operate with similar or complementary knowledge bases, but under conditions of perceived threat to the team, groupthink often produces the opposite effect and can drive the team to undesirable behavior.

While the amount of research on shared mental models is growing, we still have much to learn about the process of forming a "team mentality" and how the performance of a team is affected by it. Marks, Zaccaro, and Mathieu (2000) found that shared mental models provided teams with a common framework from which to perceive, interpret, and respond to novel environments. However, shared mental models were not as critical to team success in routine environments. Research by Mohammed and Dumville (2001) and Rentsch and Klimoski (2001) has expanded our understanding of the conventional statement that "great minds think alike."

Decision Making in Teams

Guzzo (1995) asserted that decision making in teams is distinct from individual decision making. In teams, information is often distributed unequally among members and must be integrated. Choosing among alternatives is made more complicated by having to integrate the often-differing perspectives and opinions of team members. The integration process usually includes dealing with uncertainty, with the effects of status differences among members, and with the failure of one member to appreciate the significance of the information he or she holds. Ambiguity, compressed amounts of time, heavy workloads, and other factors may become sources of stress that affect the group's ability to perform its task.

Hollenbeck, LePine, and Ilgen (1996) described the development of a multilevel theory of team decision making. The theory is called *multilevel* because effective team decision making is related to characteristics of the individuals who make up the team, pairs of people within the team, as well as how the team functions as a team. The theory is based on three concepts. The first is the degree to which team members are adequately informed about the issue they are evaluating. Teams can be well informed on some decisions but poorly informed on others. The general level of how well informed the team is on the issues they must address is called *team informity.* Second, teams are composed of individuals who differ in their ability to make accurate decisions. That is, some individuals can make poor decisions, while others typically make highly accurate decisions. The concept of *staff validity* is the average of the individual team member's abilities to make accurate decisions. The final concept is *dyadic sensitivity.* A team leader must often listen to the differing opinions or recommendations of team members. The relationship between the leader and each team member is a dyad. The leader must be sensitive to weighing each team member's recommendation in reaching an overall decision. Thus, an effective decision-making team leader knows which member's opinion should be given more weight than others. The theory has been tested with computer-simulated military command-and-control scenarios in which the team is asked to decide on the level of threat posed by a series of unidentified aircraft. The results revealed that the three concepts of team informity, staff validity, and dyadic sensitivity explained more variance in team-level decision-making accuracy than other concepts. The authors concluded that getting accurate information, making accurate recommendations, and ensuring that these recommendations are incorporated into the team's overall decision are the core requirements for effective decision making in teams.

VIRTUAL TEAMS

Recent advances in computer technology and electronic communication networks allow for a form of social interaction that was previously unavailable in society. The boundaryless nature of cyberspace has resulted in a new dimension to our lives—the "virtual" environment. The definition of *virtual* is "being in essence or effect, but not in fact." A more concise definition is "almost." One application of the electronic communication technology is evidenced in *"virtual teams."* According to Avolio et al. (2001), virtual teams have several defining characteristics. First, communication among team members primarily takes place electronically. The electronic communication processes use multiple communication channels, which may include text, graphic, audio, and video communication. Second, the team members are usually dispersed geographically. They may be in different cities, nations, or even continents. It is not unusual for the members of a virtual team to never meet face-to-face. Third, virtual team members may interact with each other synchronously or asynchronously. Synchronous interaction occurs when team members communicate at the same time, as in chat sessions or video conferencing (see Field Note 2). Asynchronous interaction occurs when team members communicate at different times, as through e-mail or electronic bulletin boards. Avolio et al. succinctly summarized the major differences between traditional and virtual teams as follows. "If we consider teams along a continuum, at one end of that continuum are teams that came from the same organization, same

One of the consequences of conducting business globally is a greater awareness of the time differences in cities around the world. The world is divided into 24 time zones. In the continental United States there is a 3-hour time difference between the East coast and the West coast. This time difference can be an annoyance for conducting business across time zones during the traditional business hours of 8:00 a.m. to 5:00 p.m. However, the "annoyance" is magnified when conducting business around the world. The use of electronic communication permits asynchronous virtual team meetings. But sometimes virtual team members have to conduct business synchronously; that is, they all have to communicate with each other at the "same time." What time might that be?

I know of a multinational company that has offices in New York, Rio de Janeiro, Rome, and Sydney. Selecting a convenient time when team members could all talk with each other was not easy. They finally agreed upon the following schedule for a weekly conference call: 6:00 a.m. in New York, 8:00 a.m. in Rio de Janeiro, 12:00 p.m. in Rome, and 9:00 p.m. in Sydney. The New York team member didn't like the early hour, and the Sydney team member didn't like the late hour. But any other time only made matters worse for someone. The time issue was compounded by the fact that some cities change time (as from standard time to daylight savings time), while other cities are always on the same time. Also, some cities around the world have times that differ by the half-hour, not the hour. For example, when it's 9:00 a.m. in New York, it's 7:30 p.m. in Calcutta. Most people around the world work during the day and sleep at night. However, "daytime" and "nighttime" lose some of their conventional meaning in global business.

location, and interact face-to-face on a regular basis. At the other extreme end are teams of people who came from different organizations, geographical regions, cultures, and time zones, and are interacting via computer-mediated technology" (p. 340).

Virtual teams face the same challenges as face-to-face teams, including how to develop shared mental models, how to evaluate the team's results, and how to achieve greater team cohesion. The shared mental models are particularly important for providing the virtual team with a sense of coherence regarding its collective expectations and intentions. The team members must learn about each other's backgrounds, aspirations, and goals. They must also reach a mutual understanding of the perceived obstacles that face the team, what norms are acceptable and unacceptable behavior in the team, and what members expect of each other in terms of each other's contribution to the team's work. All of this must be accomplished without the team members ever getting to meet in person.

Weisband and Atwater (1999) reported that because virtual team members cannot benefit from social and nonverbal cues in getting to know each other, the process of developing cohesion is slowed. The interactions among virtual team members often deal less with relationship building and more with logistics and task requirements. There can also be cultural differences among members in the need to establish interpersonal relations as a prerequisite to task performance.

The concept of a virtual work team violates many of the tenets of traditional organizational structure. The most fundamental violation applies to the control and supervision of employees. Cascio (1999) stated that managers of employees in virtual teams are asking, How can I manage them if I can't see them? Wiesenfeld,

Raghuram, and Garud (1999) examined various aspects of virtual teams in conducting work. They described a professional conference attended by individuals whose job responsibilities involved spearheading virtual work programs in their organizations. These virtual work team coordinators reported that the primary obstacle to the expansion of virtual work programs in their own organizations was the resistance of managers—those who must supervise virtual employees. According to the virtual work team coordinators, the resistance of middle managers lowers the rate at which employees participate in, and hinders the success of, virtual work programs. Wiesenfeld et al. also noted that the degree to which employees were satisfied and productive as virtual team members was closely related to whether or not their supervisors were also virtual. Virtual workers who were supervised by virtual managers were more likely to feel trusted, reported being more satisfied and more productive, and were less likely to feel that their virtual status would have a negative impact on their career progress. In contrast, virtual employees whose supervisors were "desked" (i.e., worked from traditional centralized offices) were less satisfied and were more likely to expect that virtual team work would have a negative impact on their careers.

It remains to be seen what role virtual technologies will play in the conduct of work in the future. Current trends indicate they will continue to be implemented, especially in businesses that are global in nature. The costs of international travel alone make virtual work technologies a viable alternative. It seems likely that advances in electronic communication in the future will increase our propensity to use virtual work teams. The growing body of literature on this topic (e.g., Lipnack, 2000; Heneman & Greenberger, 2002) suggests that virtual teams are not a passing fad.

PERSONNEL SELECTION FOR TEAMS

Some of what I/O psychologists have learned about the selection of individuals into organizations is not wholly transferable to the selection of teams. Traditional job analytic methods identify the KSAs needed for individual job performance, yet these methods tend to be insensitive to the social context in which work occurs. Groups or teams, by definition, are social entities that interact in a larger social context. Klimoski and Jones (1995) believe that choosing team members on the basis of individual-task KSAs alone is not enough to ensure optimal team effectiveness. For example, Guzzo and Shea (1992) indicated that considerable interest has been shown in using the Myers-Briggs Type Indicator (which assesses cognitive style) to select team members. Successful teams also depend upon those characteristics of individual members that facilitate team functioning. Consideration should be given to such group process factors as learning ability, tolerance for stress, and risk-taking propensity.

Successful selection of team members requires identifying the best mix of personnel for effective team performance. Thus, the selection requirements for particular individuals may involve complementing the abilities that other individuals will bring to the task. Creating the right mix can also mean considering those factors that account for interpersonal compatibility. Establishing team requirements involves identifying and assessing the congruence among members with regard to personality and values. Prieto (1993) asserted that five social skills are particularly critical for an individual to enhance the performance of the group. Each individual must have these abilities:

1. Gain the group acceptance.
2. Increase group solidarity.
3. Be aware of the group consciousness.
4. Share the group identification.
5. Manage others' impressions of him or her.

We are also learning about the relationship between personality variables and team effectiveness. Barry and Stewart (1997) reported that extraverts were perceived by other team members as having greater effect than introverts on group outcomes. Thus, individuals with more reserved personalities may be less successful in getting the team to accept their ideas and suggestions. A related finding was reported by Janz, Colquitt, and Noe (1997) pertaining to ability. They concluded that especially talented team members are likely to feel frustrated when they must work with lower-ability individuals on interdependent tasks. The introverted team member with high ability may feel particularly vexed in influencing team processes and outcomes. Barrick, Stewart, Neubert, and Mount (1998) reported that extraversion and emotional stability are predictive of team performance and viability (the team's ability to maintain itself over time). Neuman and Wright (1999) extended the validity of the Big 5 personality factors to the prediction of team performance. The authors found the factors of conscientiousness and agreeableness predicted various dimensions of work team performance, while the agreeableness factor predicted ratings of the interpersonal skills of team members. Finally, Stevens and Campion (1999) developed a paper-and-pencil selection test for staffing work teams. The KSAs measured by the test included conflict resolution, collaborative problem solving, communication, and planning. Test scores were found to predict supervisory and peer ratings of teamwork and overall job performance. An unexpected finding was that the teamwork test exhibited a high correlation with traditional aptitude tests, suggesting the new teamwork test had a substantial general mental ability component. Thus, individuals judged to be effective team members also manifested high levels of general mental ability. This finding, established at the team level, corroborates the findings at the individual level, as discussed in Chapter 4.

In general, research results suggest that individuals with outgoing and somewhat dominant personalities strongly influence the functioning of teams, yet a team composed of only such personality types may be thwarted by its own internal dynamics. While this stream of research suggests that the "will do" factors of personality are critical for team success, the "can do" factors of ability cannot be dismissed or minimized. Cognitive and technical skills are also needed. Locke et al. (2001) quoted a leading business executive who said, "A collaboration of incompetents, no matter how diligent or well-meaning, cannot be successful" (p. 503).

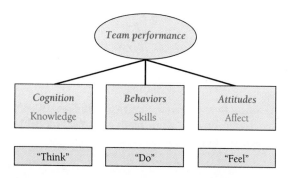

FIGURE 9–5 ■ **The structure of team training**

SOURCE: Adapted from "Methods, Tools, and Strategies for Team Training" by E. Salas and J. A. Cannon-Bowers, 1997, in *Training for a Rapidly Changing Workplace*, edited by M.A. Quinones and A. Ehrenstein, Washington, DC: American Psychological Association.

TRAINING FOR TEAMS

The logic of team training is the same as the logic of individual training, although the mechanisms are somewhat different. The process begins with a job or task analysis, but one aimed at the functioning of teams. Salas and Cannon-Bowers (1997) described a team task analysis as an extension of traditional task analysis to tasks requiring coordination. SMEs are asked to provide information (e.g., ratings of difficulty, importance) on each task in which there is interdependency. The information obtained is then used to specify team training objectives and to develop realistic scenarios for practice.

The results of a team task analysis provide information about the knowledges, skills, and attitudes the team members must possess to be successful. Salas and Cannon-Bowers referred to these three as the *thinking, doing,* and *feeling* needed for the structure of team training, as shown in Figure 9–5. The identification of the criteria for team effectiveness serves to guide instructional activities in team training. The instructional activities focus on providing team members with shared mental models and knowledge structures. These activities are designed to foster common ways for team members to analyze information and make decisions. Cannon-Bowers and Salas (1997) postulated that the next decade will witness rapid growth in computer networking capabilities for team training purposes. Such technologies as video teleconferencing (or distance learning) permit team members who are physically dispersed to receive feedback on their performance.

Much of what we know about team training has come, directly or indirectly, from military applications. The military has been responsible primarily for advanced training technologies (such as intelligent tutoring systems) as well as strategies in team training, such as cross-training. The rationale behind cross-training is that exposure to and practice on other teammates' tasks should result in better team member knowledge about task responsibilities and coordination requirements. I/O psychologists working in military support roles have provided much of our knowledge about team training.

PERFORMANCE APPRAISAL IN TEAMS

Chapter 7 addressed the topic of performance appraisal, primarily as it applies to individual employees. However, the same issues identified at the individual level of analysis have their counterpart at the team level of analysis. Moreover, the team level of analysis includes some additional factors not evidenced at the individual level.

A major issue in team performance appraisal is the extent to which individuals will slacken their performance within the team. A team member may assume

social loafing
a phenomenon
identified in groups
or teams in which
certain individuals
withhold effort or
contributions to the
collective outcome

that individual slacking will not be noticed within the larger social context of a team, or that other members will elevate their performance within the team to achieve a satisfactory team level of performance. The term given to this phenomenon is **social loafing**, and it refers to the demotivating effect on individuals of working in a group or team context. When team outcomes are emphasized, individuals see less connection between their own contributions (time, effort, and skills) and the recognition and rewards they receive (Karau & Williams, 2001). Individual members feel they have less incentive to work hard. Locke et al. (2001) identified three ways in which a lack of individual incentives can contribute to social loafing.

- *Free riding.* In some situations, social loafing derives from a desire to benefit (or free ride) from the efforts of others. When a team task makes individual contributions anonymous and rewards are shared equally, team members can reduce their own individual effort but still enjoy an equal share of the results. Thus, social loafing is more likely to occur when team members believe their own contributions cannot be singled out.
- *The "sucker" effect.* When conditions allow team members to take a free ride, some team members may assume that other group members will do so. Rather than be a "sucker" who contributes more than others, people reduce their effort and match the low level expected from others. Mulvey and Klein (1998) observed the sucker effect in a study of college students working on team-level academic tasks.
- *Felt dispensability.* In some cases, social loafing results from the feeling of being dispensable. Team members may feel dispensable when more able team members are available to accomplish the task, or believe their efforts are redundant because they duplicate the contributions of others. When team members feel dispensable, they often reduce their effort.

Locke et al. observed that these three forms of social loafing share the following characteristics: (1) individual team members are concerned with the impact of their personal contributions on team performance; (2) team members expect some return on their effort; and (3) teamwork can weaken the link between individual effort, contributions to team success, and individual outcomes (see Field Note 3). Therefore, while effective team processes (e.g., interaction, trust, cohesion) are important to achieve team success, it is individuals who make up teams and many organizational rewards (as salary and career progression) are administered at the individual level.

Not all of the research on team performance appraisal is limited to social loafing. Peer appraisals have been found effective at the individual level, and they also appear to have a positive influence at the team level. Druskat and Wolff (1999) found that developmental peer appraisals in work teams had a positive impact on team open communication, task focus, and member relations. As the volume of research on team performance appraisal continues, we will have a firmer basis to examine the generalizability of findings previously established in appraising individuals.

ave you ever been in a class where one of the course requirements was some sort of team project or team presentation? How did you feel about the experience? Did you find it difficult to arrange a time when all the team members could meet? How did you decide who would be responsible for what within the group? Did you feel everyone on the team "pulled their own weight" in the collective effort? Did you detect any social loafing among your team members? Did each member in the team have to evaluate every other team member's contribution to the final product? Did everyone on the team receive the same grade for the product of the team's work? The use of teams in society is escalating [a phenomenon Locke et al. (2001) refer to as "groupism"], and their use in education as a learning mechanism for students is in-creasing as well. If you have ever participated in a team project for a class, your particular team members were probably specific to that class. However, there is a new approach to graduate education in business where students go through the entire degree program (not just in a class) as a team. The name given to this group of students is a "cohort." Each year the admitted students are regarded as a cohort, they all take the same classes in the same sequence and they all graduate at the same time as a group. It is expected the students will stay in touch with each other after they graduate, as they share with each other how they applied their graduate education in their respective careers. The concept of a cohort in education is designed to promote students learning from each other as students and continuing their education of each other after they graduate.

CONCLUDING COMMENTS

The conversion from an individual to a team perspective of work requires that we reexamine our knowledge about many facets of I/O psychology. Furthermore, while some of our concepts might generalize directly from individuals to teams, some procedures might be incompatible (e.g., Campion, Papper, & Medsker, 1996). It will be recalled from Chapter 7 that one purpose of performance appraisal is to identify performance differences across individuals and to reward them differentially. If we strive for teamwork and a sense of unity across team members, we should then *not* differentially reward the "best" individual team members. We will have to develop appraisal and reward processes that treat all members of a group as a single entity, not as individuals. Organizations get what they reward. If they choose to appraise and reward individual job performance, then they should not decry a lack of teamwork and cooperation among their employees (Kerr, 1995). I believe I/O psychology should gird itself for the journey of understanding how work performed by teams requires insight into new psychological concepts, or existing concepts with unknown validity when generalized to teams.

CASE STUDY   ■   **The Grenoble Marketing Company**

It had been a financially tight year for the Grenoble Marketing Company. The company designed printed advertisements and television commercials for its clients. However, with a sagging business economy, increasingly more clients were cutting back on how much they would spend to advertise their products. Grenoble employees were split fairly evenly between the print medium and the electronic (television) medium sides of their business. The print medium team was known as the "Ink Crowd," while the electronic medium team went by the nickname "TV Land." In fact, the employees in the two teams rarely interacted with each other. Each side of the advertising business required very different skills. Each team had separately lobbied the company's vice president, Anthony Prizzio, to hire someone who would solicit new accounts, a generator of new business. Prizzio knew that getting a new position authorized by the president of Grenoble wouldn't be easy given the company's financial situation. However, Prizzio was delighted to hear from his boss that Grenoble would approve adding one new position. Prizzio convened the members of the two teams in a rare joint meeting. He told the respective team members that the president had just authorized adding one new person to the company; that person would be responsible for generating new business. Since the print and electronic media were so different, however, it was extremely unlikely one person could be found who was qualified in both areas. In short, in all likelihood one team would get a new position and the other wouldn't. Prizzio decided to foster what he called "healthy competition" between the two teams. Each team would recruit and recommend for hire its top candidate. Prizzio would then have the ultimate authority and responsibility to select the better of the two candidates. It thus behooved each team to put forth as strong a candidate as it could find.

Each team went about its search for the new person. The position was advertised, leads were followed, and the recruitment process was pursued in earnest. In a brief time TV Land settled on its top candidate. The individual was a proven veteran in the field of television advertising, a person who worked for a competitor of Grenoble and was ready for a career move. Everyone in TV Land was very pleased with their choice and felt reasonably confident Prizzio would likewise be impressed. The Ink Crowd was not so quick to announce its top candidate. In fact, two candidates emerged who split the team with regard to its preference. One was established in the field of print advertising and had the reputation of being a consistent revenue producer. The other was younger and less experienced, but designed extraordinarily creative and powerful advertising copy. A recipient of an industry award for innovation in printing advertising, this was a "can't miss" candidate.

Prizzio asked the Ink Crowd for its decision, but neither half would back down from its enthusiastic preference for its respective choice. The Ink Crowd was deeply divided. Each side accused the other of using pressure tactics, being blind to the obvious talents of the other's choice, and "sabotaging" their chances in the overall competition with TV Land. The members of Ink Crowd realized they were embroiled in *two* competitions—one within their team and one with TV Land. Someone suggested Ink Crowd put forth both candidates for Prizzio's consideration. This idea was rebuked by those who said, "If we can't even make up our own minds about who we like, why wouldn't Prizzio go with TV Land? They know who they like." Another suggestion was to ask Prizzio to hire both candidates from the Ink Crowd, since both were so good in their own way. This idea brought further criticism. One team member said, "Why not propose that Prizzio hire all three candidates since they are all so terrific? I'll tell you why not—it's because we don't have the money to hire more than one of them!" TV Land got word of the conflict going on with the Ink Crowd. TV Land delighted in the news, believing the conflict only increased the chances for their own candidate. A similar sentiment was expressed by a senior member of the Ink Crowd: "TV Land doesn't have to beat us. We are killing ourselves." Meanwhile, Prizzio awaited their response.

Study Questions

1. Do you believe that Prizzio's concept of "healthy competition" can be beneficial for Grenoble, or does deliberately pitting teams against each other inevitably produce a divisive outcome? Why do you feel as you do?
2. Should the Ink Crowd unite behind one of its two candidates "for the good of the team," or is there a way the within-team conflict might benefit Grenoble?
3. Consider the concept of the level of analysis. Can a team "win" and the organization "lose" (or vice versa) in this case? Why?
4. What evidence is there of groupthink operating in this case, and what organizational factors are present that foster its occurrence?
5. If you were an adviser to the president of the Grenoble Marketing Company, what advice would you give to enhance the long-term success of the company?

SUGGESTED INFOTRAC TOPICS

work teams	*conflict*
teamwork	*trust*
socialization	*groupthink*
communication	*virtual teams*
cohesion	*social loafing*

C H A P T E R 10

Organizational Attitudes and Behavior

CHAPTER OUTLINE

LEARNING OBJECTIVES

- Explain the organizational attitudes of job satisfaction, job involvement, and organizational commitment.
- Understand the concept of organizational justice.
- Understand the concept of organizational citizenship behavior and its relationship to other concepts.
- Understand the psychological contract in employment and its changing nature.
- Explain the psychology of mergers and acquisitions.

The preceding chapters have examined several conceptual approaches to organizations and teams, including their structure and configuration and the social mechanisms that enable them to function. This chapter will examine various psychological concepts that have emerged within organizations. In particular, the focus will be on concepts that not only have theoretical value but also have been found to influence a wide array of practical matters relating to work behavior.

The chapter will begin with an examination of three important attitudes employees hold about their work: how satisfied they are with their job, how involved they are with their job, and how committed they are to their organization. Subsequent topics will expand on the psychological constructs that represent the domain of organizational attitudes and behavior.

JOB SATISFACTION

job satisfaction
the degree of pleasure
an employee derives
from his or her job

Job satisfaction refers to the degree of pleasure an employee derives from his or her job. Since work is one of our major life activities, I/O psychologists have had a long-standing interest in job satisfaction. How employees feel about their jobs is highly variable. One hundred years ago employment conditions were, by today's standards, unacceptable. Work was often performed under unsafe conditions, work hours were very long, there were no air-conditioned offices, and benefits we often take for granted today, such as paid vacations, medical insurance, and retirement contributions, did not exist. You might think that the employees of today, who enjoy favorable working conditions, would be highly satisfied with their jobs; however, such is not the case. Some employees derive great pleasure and meaning from their work, while others regard work as drudgery. Why is this so? The answer lies in individual differences in expectations and, in particular, the degree to which a job meets one's expectations. There are broad differences in what people expect from their jobs and thus broad reactions to them. As Hulin (1991) stated, "Jobs with responsibility may be dissatisfying to some because of the stress and problems that covary with responsibility; others may find responsibility a source of positive affect. Challenging jobs may be satisfying to some because of how they feel about themselves after completing difficult job assignments; others may find such self-administered rewards irrelevant" (p. 460). Why people differ in their preferences for job outcomes is posited to be related to their developmental experiences and levels of aspiration.

Research has revealed that people develop overall feelings about their jobs as well as about selected dimensions or facets of their jobs, such as their supervisor, coworkers, promotional opportunities, pay, and so on. I/O psychologists differentiate these two levels of feelings as *global job satisfaction* and *job facet satisfaction*, respectively. Considerable research has been devoted over the years to the measurement of job satisfaction. The two most widely used measures of job satisfaction are the Job Descriptive Index (Balzer, Smith, & Kravitz, 1990) and the Minnesota Satisfaction Questionnaire (Weiss, Dawis, England, & Lofquist, 1967). A version of the Minnesota Satisfaction Questionnaire is shown in Figure 10–1.

Ask yourself: How satisfied am I with this aspect of my job?

Very Sat. means I am very satisfied with this aspect of my job.

Sat. means I am satisfied with this aspect of my job.

N means I can't decide whether I am satisfied or not with this aspect of my job.

Dissat. means I am dissatisfied with this aspect of my job.

Very Dissat. means I am very dissatisfied with this aspect of my job.

On my present job, this is how I feel about . . .	Very Dissat.	Dissat.	N	Sat.	Very Sat.
1. Being able to keep busy all the time	❏	❏	❏	❏	❏
2. The chance to work alone on the job	❏	❏	❏	❏	❏
3. The chance to do different things from time to time	❏	❏	❏	❏	❏
4. The chance to be "somebody" in the community	❏	❏	❏	❏	❏
5. The way my boss handles subordinates	❏	❏	❏	❏	❏
6. The competence of my supervisor in making decisions	❏	❏	❏	❏	❏
7. Being able to do things that don't go against my conscience	❏	❏	❏	❏	❏
8. The way my job provides for steady employment	❏	❏	❏	❏	❏
9. The chance to do things for other people	❏	❏	❏	❏	❏
10. The chance to tell people what to do	❏	❏	❏	❏	❏
11. The chance to do something that makes use of my abilities	❏	❏	❏	❏	❏
12. The way company policies are put into practice	❏	❏	❏	❏	❏
13. My pay and the amount of work I do	❏	❏	❏	❏	❏
14. The chances for advancement on this job	❏	❏	❏	❏	❏
15. The freedom to use my own judgment	❏	❏	❏	❏	❏
16. The chance to try my own methods of doing the job	❏	❏	❏	❏	❏
17. The working conditions	❏	❏	❏	❏	❏
18. The way my coworkers get along with each other	❏	❏	❏	❏	❏
19. The praise I get for doing a good job	❏	❏	❏	❏	❏
20. The feeling of accomplishment I get from the job	❏	❏	❏	❏	❏

FIGURE 10–1 ■ Minnesota Satisfaction Questionnaire (short form)

SOURCE: From *Manual for the Minnesota Satisfaction Questionnaire* by D. J. Weiss, R. V. Dawis, G. W. England, and L. H. Lofquist, 1967, Minneapolis: Industrial Relations Center, University of Minnesota. Used by permission.

Brief (1998) proposed an integrative model of job satisfaction, as depicted in Figure 10–2. It asserts there is a personality dimension of individuals that influences their feelings of job satisfaction. Wright and Staw (1999) refer to this personality dimension as *positive affect*. People who are high in positive affect tend to be active, alert, enthusiastic, inspired, and interested. They are optimistic about life. Such people tend to interpret failure as a temporary setback caused by external circumstances, and are more likely to persevere. People who are low in positive affect are more pessimistic about life and "see the glass as half-empty rather

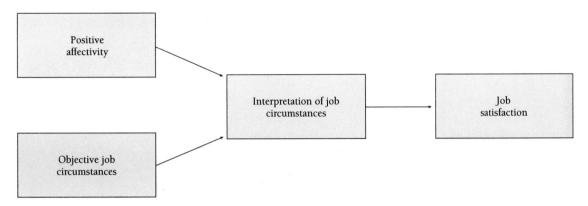

FIGURE 10–2 ■ **Model of job satisfaction**

SOURCE: Adapted from *Attitudes in and Around Organizations* (p. 97) by A. P. Brief, 1998, Thousand Oaks, CA: Sage. Copyright 1998 by Sage Publications. Adapted with permission of Sage Publications, Inc.

than half-full." The second component in Brief's model is objective job circumstances. These are the more factual bases of one's job, including level of pay, hours of work, and physical working conditions. Together these two components (level of positive affect and objective job circumstances) lead to an assessment or interpretation of the job circumstances. The interpretation is based on many considerations, including the perceived adequacy of the pay for the work performed, the level of stress on the job, and the match of the job to the person's skills and abilities. Collectively this interpretation produces a feeling of approval or disapproval, liking or disliking, favor or disfavor, and so on, which constitutes one's attitude (satisfaction) toward the job. A study by Judge, Bono, and Locke (2000) affirmed the validity of job satisfaction being influenced by individual personality characteristics and job characteristics.

Throughout the history of research on job satisfaction, different emphases have been placed on the relative importance of dispositional factors (i.e., positive affect), objective job characteristics, and the interpretive process in forming feelings about one's job. The current state of research acknowledges that all three components are critical to the formation of job attitudes. Recent research has introduced another component to job attitudes: emotions (Fisher & Ashkanasy, 2000). For the most part I/O psychology has not addressed the emotional dimensions of worklife, historically being more interested in cognitive issues (as witnessed by the amount of research on *g*). However, moods and emotions play an undeniable role in how we feel about life, including work. Fisher (2000) proposed that even though moods may not be directly controllable given their somewhat vague and diffuse causes, organizations may be more successful in elevating employees' moods than in raising their overall level of job satisfaction. For example, organizations could concentrate on providing a work environment free of minor irritations and hassles that produce frequent, if mild, feelings of frustration and annoyance. Muchinsky (2000), drawing upon the research of Lazarus and Lazarus (1994), identified five categories of emotions, all of which are (or can be) manifested in the workplace.

TABLE 10–1 ■ **Five categories of human emotions**

Category	Emotion
1. Positive	Happiness
	Love
	Pride
2. Negative	Sadness
	Hopelessness
	Despair
3. Existential	Anxiety
	Guilt
	Shame
4. "Nasty"	Anger
	Envy
	Jealousy
5. Empathetic	Gratitude
	Compassion
	Sympathy

SOURCE: Adapted from *Passion and Reason: Making Sense of Our Emotions* by R. S. Lazarus and B. N. Lazarus, 1994, New York: Oxford.

These five categories of emotions are presented in Table 10–1. In summary, moods and emotions are related but not identical to attitudes. It is possible that intense but short-lived emotional reactions to workplace incidents have an enduring effect on job satisfaction. Fisher and Ashkanasy (2000) concluded that "the study of emotions in the workplace has the potential to add an understanding of behavior in organizations" (p. 123). I/O psychology has much to learn about how emotions influence organizational attitudes and behaviors.

The relationship between job satisfaction and important job-related criteria has been examined extensively. We will discuss three criteria: performance, turnover, and absence. The relationship between job satisfaction and job performance has been researched for over 40 years. The reason is obvious—ideally we would like to be both productive and happy in our work. However, the relationship between satisfaction and performance is not very strong. Iaffaldano and Muchinsky (1985) conducted a meta-analysis of studies that examined this correlation and reported the best estimate of their relationship to be .17. A more recent study by Judge et al. (2001) estimates the satisfaction–performance relationship to be .30. Based on this study the percentage of variance shared between these two concepts (r^2) is 9%, meaning 91% of the variance in one concept is *not* explained by the other. This correlation is not nearly as high as some scholars and practitioners would intuitively believe. Its implication is that organizational attempts to enhance both worker satisfaction and performance *simultaneously* will likely be unsuccessful. The reason is, for the most part, that the two concepts are only mildly related to each other. In fact, some organizational attempts to increase productivity (for example, cracking down on employees through tough supervisory practices) may decrease job satisfaction.

Turnover and absence are often referred to as *withdrawal behavior* because they reflect the employee withdrawing from a noxious employment condition, either temporarily (absence) or permanently (turnover). The relationship between how much you like your job and whether you withdraw from it has attracted considerable interest among I/O psychologists. In general, the research shows that the more people dislike their job, the more likely they are to quit. The magnitude of the satisfaction–turnover correlation, on average, is about $-.40$. However, this relationship is influenced by several factors, including the availability of other work. People would rather endure a dissatisfying job than be unemployed. Conversely, when alternative employment is readily available, workers are more likely to leave unsatisfying jobs (Carsten & Spector, 1987).

The correlation between job satisfaction and absence is considerably lower, approximately $-.25$ (Johns, 1997). Absence from work can be caused by many factors that have nothing to do with how much you like your job, including transportation problems and family responsibilities. However, when researchers control for methodological issues in the design of research addressing this relationship (including whether the absence from work is paid or unpaid, and whether organizational sanctions are imposed on absent workers), a mild but consistent negative relationship emerges between the two. A practical implication of the finding is that if you like your job, you are more likely to make the extra effort needed to get to work (as when you have a cold) than if you are dissatisfied with your job. How people feel about their jobs is also related to how they feel about their life in general. The link between work and family lives will be discussed in Chapter 11.

JOB INVOLVEMENT

job involvement
the degree to which a person identifies psychologically with his or her work and the importance of work to one's self-image

Job involvement refers to the degree to which a person identifies psychologically with his or her work and the importance of work to one's self-image. Brown (1996) asserted that people may be stimulated by and drawn deeply into their work, or they may be alienated from it mentally and emotionally. As others have noted, the quality of one's entire life can be greatly affected by one's degree of involvement in, or alienation from, work. Brown stated: "A state of involvement implies a positive and relatively complete state of engagement of core aspects of the self in the job, whereas a state of alienation implies a loss of individuality and separation of the self from the work environment" (p. 235). Some items from a job involvement questionnaire (Kanungo, 1982) are listed in Figure 10–3.

Research has shown a wide range of correlations between job involvement and other work-related constructs. Brown (1996) conducted a meta-analysis of studies that examined job involvement and reported an average correlation of .45 with overall job satisfaction, .09 with performance, $-.13$ with turnover, and .53 with a personality dimension related to conscientiousness. These results suggest that job involvement is more strongly related to how people view their work and their approach to it and less related to how well they perform their jobs.

> I consider my job to be very critical to my existence.
>
> I am very much involved personally in my job.
>
> Most of my personal life goals are job-oriented.
>
> The most important things that happen in my life involve work.
>
> Work should be considered central to life.
>
> Life is worth living only when people get absorbed in work.

FIGURE 10–3 ■ Sample items from a job involvement questionnaire

SOURCE: From "Measurement of Job and Work Involvement" by R. N. Kanungo, 1982, *Journal of Applied Psychology, 67,* pp. 341–349.

ORGANIZATIONAL COMMITMENT

organizational commitment
the degree to which an employee feels a sense of allegiance to his or her employer

Organizational commitment refers to the extent to which an employee feels a sense of allegiance to his or her employer. Allen and Meyer (1990) proposed three components to this construct. The *affective* component refers to the employee's emotional attachment to, and identification with, the organization. The *continuance* component refers to commitment based on the costs that the employee associates with leaving the organization. The *normative* component refers to the employee's feelings of obligation to remain with the organization. In essence, affective commitment reflects allegiance based on liking the organization, continuance commitment reflects allegiance because it is unlikely the person could get a better job elsewhere, and normative commitment reflects allegiance to the organization out of a sense of loyalty.

Meyer (1997) asserted that in general organizational commitment reflects the employee's relationship with the organization and that it has implications for his or her decision to continue membership in the organization. Committed employees are more likely to remain in the organization than are uncommitted employees. Sample items from a questionnaire (Dunham, Grube, & Castaneda, 1994) measuring organizational commitment are listed in Figure 10–4.

Morrow (1993) proposed that an individual can be committed to different focal points in work—one's job, one's organization, and one's occupation. An occupation represents a constellation of requisite skills, knowledges, and duties that are different from other occupations and are transferable across organizations within an occupation. Occupational commitment is an emotional connection that the person feels with the occupation. Organizational commitment reflects a sense of loyalty to one's particular employer. Finally, job involvement represents the narrowest focal point of commitment, loyalty to one's own job. It would therefore be possible for a person to have high occupational commitment (for example, to nursing), but low organizational commitment. In such a case a person might readily change employers within the larger nursing occupation. Alternatively, a person could have high organizational commitment and low job involvement, indicating the person would be receptive to moving across jobs within the same organization.

I really feel as if this organization's problems are my own.

This organization has a great deal of personal meaning for me.

Too much in my life would be disrupted if I decided I wanted to leave my organization now.

One of the major reasons I continue to work for this company is that leaving would require considerable sacrifice; another organization may not match the overall benefits I have here.

I think that people these days move from company to company too often.

I was taught to believe in the value of remaining loyal to one organization.

Figure 10–4 Sample items from an organizational commitment questionnaire

SOURCE: From "Organizational Commitment: The Utility of an Integrated Definition" by R. B. Dunham, J. A. Grube, and M. B. Castaneda, 1994, *Journal of Applied Psychology, 79,* pp. 370–380.

Morrow developed a model that illustrates the various forms of commitment through a series of concentric circles, as shown in Figure 10–5. At the center of the model is one's work ethic, a personality dimension reflecting how important and central work is to one's life. Working outward from the center of the model is occupational commitment, followed by the continuance dimension of organizational commitment, followed by the affective dimension of organizational commitment, and lastly job involvement. According to Morrow, the innermost forms of commitment are more dispositional in nature, whereas those in the outer circles are determined more by situational factors. While Cohen (1999) did not find strong empirical support for Morrow's conception of work commitment, Lee, Carswell, and Allen (2000) supported the importance of occupational commitment for understanding various aspects of organizational behavior. Meyer and Allen (1997) concluded that employees can feel varying levels of commitment to the different identifications with work (job, organization, occupation), and we must gain a better understanding of what is meant by "work commitment."

Based on a meta-analysis by Brown (1996), the average correlation between organizational commitment and other work-related constructs is similar to the pattern found for job involvement, only stronger. The average correlations were .53 with overall job satisfaction, .11 with performance, −.28 with turnover, and .67 with a personality construct similar to conscientiousness. Brown also estimated a correlation of .50 between job involvement and organizational commitment. The general pattern of results reveals that job satisfaction, job involvement, and organizational commitment are substantially correlated with each other but are only modestly correlated with performance and turnover. Thus, organizational attitudes tend to be substantially intercorrelated. Performance is determined by ability, motivation, and situational constraints, while turnover is determined in part by external economic variables. The linkage between organizational attitudes and behavior is thus moderated by factors beyond the control of the individual.

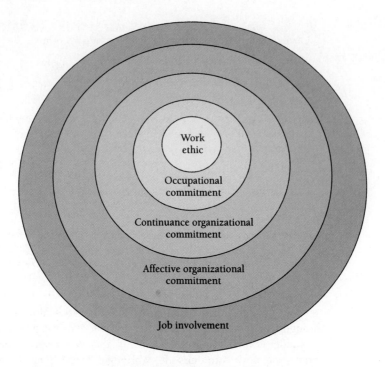

FIGURE 10–5 ■ Concentric circle model of work commitment

SOURCE: Adapted from *The Theory and Measurement of Work Commitment* (p. 163) by P. C. Morrow, 1993, Greenwich, CT: JAI Press. Copyright 1993 by JAI Press. Adapted with permission from Elsevier Science.

Historically, managerial and professional workers have exhibited a high degree of job involvement and organizational commitment. However, as seen in Chapter 8, it is these workers who often lose their jobs during downsizing and reorganization. The loss of work for these people is particularly painful because so much of their personal identity is defined by their work. The reactions of people who lose their jobs due to downsizing will be discussed later in this chapter.

ORGANIZATIONAL JUSTICE

organizational justice
the overarching theoretical concept pertaining to the fair treatment of people in organizations; composed of three types of justice— distributive, procedural, and interactional

Organizational justice is concerned with the fair treatment of people in organizations. It can be thought of as a more limited application of social justice, a concept that has been debated by philosophers for hundreds of years. In an organizational context there are always competing goals and objectives. A case in point is personnel selection. Job applicants are in the role of seeking to obtain employment with an organization. The organization, in turn, is in the role of offering employment to some applicants and denying the opportunity to others. The means by which this decision is made is an assessment of the applicants. Both the outcome of the selection decision (who is offered employment and who isn't) and the process (whether the assessment is rendered via a psychological test, interview, etc.)

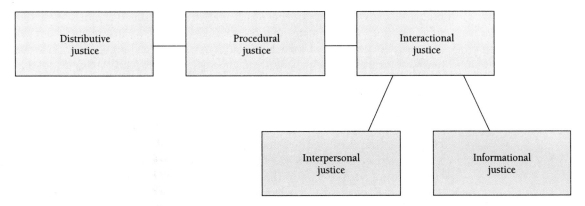

FIGURE 10–6 ■ Categories of organizational justice

can be questioned in terms of fairness. That is, was a just and fair outcome reached through the use of just and fair methods? Organizational justice is a useful concept to examine a wide range of important organizational issues. Justice has been claimed to be "the first virtue of social institutions" (Rawls, 1971, p. 3).

Various configurations or typologies of organizational justice have been proposed over the years (e.g., Greenberg, 1993). However, the most current research and thinking on the topic have yielded the typology shown in Figure 10–6 (Colquitt et al., 2001). Work organizations are highly sensitized to the issue of fairness and have developed mechanisms to increase the likelihood of its occurrence in the workplace (e.g., training employees for dealing with interpersonal conflict, training managers in how to conduct performance appraisals, soliciting employee suggestions and ideas to improve the workplace, and so on). As such, some scholars have proposed that more formal mechanisms are in place to ensure justice at work than might be found in other forms of social collectivity, like families and civic groups. Colquitt et al. believe that organizational justice has been among the most frequently researched topics in I/O psychology in the last decade. This conclusion is most justified since organizational justice has been found to be associated with many of the topics studied in I/O psychology, including performance, turnover, absenteeism, trust, job satisfaction, and organizational commitment.

Distributive Justice

distributive justice
the fairness with which the outcomes or results are distributed among members of an organization

Distributive justice refers to the fairness of the outcomes, results, or ends achieved. Distributive justice, like all forms of justice, is heavily predicated upon values. These values are the rules or standards by which judgments of fairness are rendered. Three such rules have been identified as the basis for distributive justice: equity, equality, and need.

Equity.   The equity distribution rule suggests that people should receive rewards that are consistent with the contributions they make or bring to a situation. Consider a company that is willing to send two of its managers to an expensive and professionally valuable management development program. Using the equity distribution rule, the company decides to send the two managers judged most deserving on the basis of their high job performance. These two individuals are judged to contribute the most to the company in terms of their ability, effort, and judged potential to advance in the company, so they are selected to attend the program. In this case it is "fair" that the two most competent and promising managers are offered the development training.

Equality.   The equality distribution rule suggests that all individuals should have an equal chance of receiving the outcome or reward, regardless of differentiating characteristics such as ability. The truest sense of the equality rule suggests random selection of the developmental training recipients. Since organizations don't make selection decisions randomly, a modified equality rule must be used. In this example there are two openings for participation in the training, so the managers are divided into two categories—for example, by gender. The company then selects the most qualified male manager and the most qualified female manager to attend the program. The "most qualified" consideration is derived from the equity rule, while the one male/one female consideration is derived from the equality rule. In this case it is "fair" that one person from each gender is offered the training program.

Need.   The need distribution rule suggests that rewards should be distributed on the basis of individual need. The special consideration that the needy individual receives is thus perceived as fair. The company therefore selects two managers who are most in need of having their professional skills enhanced by this form of training (irrespective of gender). In this case it is "fair" that the two managers most in need of training are selected to participate.

As you might imagine, there can be legitimate differences of opinion among people regarding which is the "fairest" rule to use in selecting these managers. One possible resolution might be to segment the recipients—that is, to offer one based on merit performance and the other based on need. If the most professionally competent manager is a woman, the other selection could be awarded to the male manager most in need of the training. With such a distribution the training recipients are awarded (in part) on the basis of equity, equality, and need. However, some people might say that it is *unfair* to weight equity and need the same and that both training recipients should be chosen solely on the basis of need (or equity). Arguments could be made that the top performing managers obviously don't need the training—they are already performing very well. Alternatively, the beneficial professional training could be regarded as a reward for being the top two managers in the company, thereby increasing the likelihood that the two best will become even better.

These types of disagreements among people regarding what is fair (and unfair) about distributions are not at all uncommon. Since distribution rules are based on values, no rule is inherently right or wrong. Organizations typically address differences of opinion regarding distribution rules by seeking to gain consensus on which rule is the "fairest" to follow or by distributing different rewards by different rules. Leung (1997) reported a relationship between cultural orientations and reward allocation preferences. Some cultures, as typified by North America, tend to value *individualism* and are concerned more with individual interests, needs, and goals. Other cultures, as typified by Asia, tend to value *collectivism* and are concerned more with the interests, needs, and goals of in-group members. Individualistic cultures prefer the equity rule because of the emphasis on competition and self-gain. Collectivist cultures prefer the equality rule because of the emphasis on solidarity, harmony, and cohesion. Kabanoff (1997) proposed that nations differ in their collective preferences for reward allocation strategies based upon the individualism/collectivism orientation. It is often difficult to reach consensus on fairness, and there can be far-reaching implications for organizations from differing views on what constitutes fairness in their practices (see Field Note 1).

FIELD NOTE 1   What Is "Fair"?

hat does it mean to be "fair"? Most certainly there are many ways to consider fairness, and I was party to one situation that evoked these multiple perspectives. A wealthy individual died and bequeathed $3,000,000 to a university to support students who attended the school. The university invested the $3,000,000 such that it earned 6% interest, or $180,000, per year. Thus, every year the university could grant $180,000 to students to support their education, without having to use the original $3,000,000 gift. The university formed a committee to determine the most fair way of dispersing the $180,000 per year. I was a member of that committee. Three distinct schools of thought emerged as to what constituted the "most fair" disbursement of money.

The first school of thought was to grant a financial award to the most academically talented applicants. As indexed by high school grades and standardized test scores, the "best" applicants were to receive the financial support. This university had highly reputable programs in engineering and agriculture, majors that typically attract more men than women. Because these programs attracted many of the most highly qualified applicants to the university, and because the vast majority of these applicants were men, the financial award recipients would be very heavily represented by men.

Proponents of the second perspective said the university sought to embrace all groups in society—across genders, racial groups, age groups, the physically disabled, and so on. Therefore, the financial support should be intentionally allocated to individual students who

represent the various groups. In this way the university would show its support for recruiting a diverse student body.

The third perspective was to allocate the money based upon financial need. It was proposed that the best use of the money would be to provide a vehicle for students to obtain a college education who could not otherwise afford it. Therefore, the recipients of the financial support would be the financially neediest students.

These were the three basic schools of thought on what was a "fair" strategy to disburse the money. I was struck not only by how different the recipients would be depending upon which strategy was followed, but also by the inherent plausibility of each strategy. That is, I felt each position had some intuitive appeal—each one made some sense to me. The three groups argued over such matters as the difference between a scholarship and financial aid, and what the intentions of the deceased benefactor were in disbursing his money. The final decision by the committee reflected a compromise—a (fair) resolution of conflicting standards of fairness. A portion of the funds were set aside to be allocated on the basis of need. The other funds would be allocated on the basis of academic ability, with members of the various groups being represented in the funding. It was not a decision the committee enthusiastically endorsed, but one it could live with.

If you had been on that committee, what position would you have taken in allocating the funds? Why do you think your position is the "most fair" one?

Procedural Justice

procedural justice
the fairness by which
means are used to
achieve results in
an organization

The second major type of justice is **procedural justice**, which refers to the fairness of the means used to achieve the results. As the name suggests, it deals with the perceived fairness of the policies and procedures used to make decisions. In essence, the distinction between distributive and procedural justice is the difference between content and process that is basic to many of the philosophical approaches to the study of justice.

According to Folger and Greenberg (1985), there are two dimensions to conceptualizing procedural justice. One emphasizes the role of the individual's "voice" in the process. Procedures are perceived to be more fair when affected individuals have an opportunity to either influence the decision process or offer input. Indeed, Schminke, Ambrose, and Cropanzano (2000) found that higher levels of participation in decision making by employees within an organization were associated with higher levels of perceived procedural fairness. The second dimension emphasizes the structural components of the process, whereby procedural justice is a function of the extent to which procedural rules are satisfied or violated. These procedural rules suggest that decisions should be made consistently, without personal biases, with as much accurate information as possible, and with an outcome that could be modified.

In applying the concept of procedural justice to a personnel selection system, for example, one could arrive at several components of what constitutes a "fair" selection process (Gilliland, 1993). Ideally the selection test should be job related (or more precisely from the applicant's view, face valid), should allow the candidate to demonstrate his or her proficiency, and should be scored consistently across applicants. Furthermore, candidates should receive timely feedback on their application for employment, should be told the truth, and should be treated respectfully in the assessment process. Note that these procedural justice issues pertain to the selection process, not the outcome of whether the applicant is accepted or rejected (which is a matter of distributive justice). Leventhal (1980) proposed six criteria by which procedures can be judged as fair. To be considered fair, a procedure should be (1) consistent, (2) bias free, (3) accurate, (4) correctable in case of an error, (5) representative of all concerned, and (6) based on prevailing ethical standards. Folger and Cropanzano (1998) asserted that Leventhal's criteria for procedural justice have been affirmed by subsequent research.

Lind and Tyler (1988) developed a *group-value model* of procedural justice that seeks to explain, in part, why people value membership in social groups. The basic assumption is that group identification is psychologically rewarding. People want to belong to social groups and to establish the social bonds that exist within groups. One reason people seek group membership is that groups provide self-affirmation. Groups provide emotional support and a sense of belonging. Also, groups are important sources of material resources. Lind and Tyler identified three issues that provide a framework for establishing a sense of procedural fairness in group membership.

The first is neutrality. In a long-term relationship, people cannot always have what they want. Instead, they must compromise and sometimes defer to the desires and needs of others. People assume that, over time, all group members will benefit fairly from the application of fair procedures for decision making. The first implication of a group-value perspective is that people will focus on whether the group has created a neutral arena (i.e., a "level playing field") in which to solve their problems or conflicts.

The second issue is trust. The long-term nature of group membership leads people to focus on the intentions of others. Trust involves the belief that the intentions of the group leaders are benevolent, and that they desire to treat people in a fair and reasonable way. Because people are in organizations for the long term, their loyalty depends on their predictions about what will happen to them over time. If they believe that the organization's leaders are trying to be fair and deal equitably with them, they develop a long-term commitment to the group. But when the trust is broken, as when employees lose their jobs through no fault of their own (e.g., downsizing), the sense of procedural fairness is violated.

The third issue is a person's social standing in the group. Interpersonal treatment during social interactions gives people information about their status within the group. Polite and respectful treatment communicates that the leaders of the group regard the members as having high status in the group. If group members are treated rudely, they know the people they are dealing with regard them as having low status in the group. If leaders show respect for individuals' rights as group members, individuals gain knowledge that those rights will be respected, whereas abuse of rights brings their existence into question.

In short, the group-value model assumes that people are concerned about their long-term social relationship with institutions and do not view their relationship as a one-shot deal (Tyler, 1989). Thus, the group-value model posits that continued membership in a group is guided by issues that serve to promote a sense of procedural justice.

Interactional Justice

interactional justice
the fairness with which people are treated within an organization and the timeliness, completeness, and accuracy of the information received in an organization

A third major type of organizational justice has been identified, referred to as **interactional justice.** In turn, interactional justice has two components: interpersonal and informational. *Interpersonal justice* is manifested by showing concern for individuals and respecting them as people who have dignity. Ostensible displays of politeness and respect for citizens' rights enhance their perceptions of fair treatment by authorities, such as the police and the courts. Similarly, apologies enhance interpersonal justice because they involve expressions of remorse and serve to distance individuals from the negative effects of their actions. As Folger and Skarlicki (2001) stated, it rarely costs anything to be polite. The lack of politeness, sensitivity, and caring for the emotional pain inflicted by organizations on employees only adds insult to injury. As we will discuss in the section on workplace violence, employees who seek to physically harm their manager or coworkers often have their vengefulness abetted by a perceived lack of politeness and fairness. Folger and Skarlicki concisely summarized this point: "Politeness costs less than you think, and it stands to reap greater benefits than you might have realized. Paraphrased and shortened, politeness pays" (p. 116).

Informational justice is manifested by providing knowledge about procedures that demonstrate regard for people's concerns. People should be given adequate accounts and explanations of the procedures used to determine desired outcomes. For explanations to be perceived as fair, they must also be recognized as genuine in intent (without any ulterior motives) and based on sound reasoning. Because it is typically the open sharing of information that promotes this form of organizational justice, the term *information* is used to identify it.

A study by Greenberg (1994) illustrates interpersonal and informational justice. Two announcements of a work site smoking ban were made to employees of a large company. The announcements differed in the amount of information given about the need for the ban and the degree of interpersonal sensitivity shown for the personal impact of the ban. Some employees received a great deal of information about the reason for the smoking ban, while others received only the most cursory information. Furthermore, some employees received a personally sensitive message ("We realize that this new policy will be very hard on those of you who smoke. Smoking is an addiction, and it's very tough to stop. We are quite aware of this, and we do not want you to suffer"), while other employees received a message showing less personal concern ("I realize that it's tough to stop smoking, but it's in the best interest of our business to implement the smoking ban. And, of course, business must come first"). Immediately after the announcement, employees completed surveys on their acceptance of the ban. Although heavy smokers were least accepting of the ban, they showed the greatest incremental gain in acceptance after exposure to thorough information presented in a highly sensitive manner. By contrast, nonsmokers' acceptance of the ban was uniformly unaffected by the way it was presented to them. Regardless of how much they smoked, all participants recognized the procedural fairness associated with giving thorough information in a socially sensitive manner.

A major meta-analytic review of 25 years of organizational justice research by Colquitt et al. (2001) concluded that distributive justice, procedural justice, and the two types of interactional justice (interpersonal and informational) each contribute incremental variance to perceptions of fairness in the workplace. Although the different justice dimensions are not totally distinct from each other, each reflects a facet of "what is fair."

ORGANIZATIONAL CITIZENSHIP BEHAVIOR

organizational citizenship behavior
the contributions that employees make to the overall welfare of the organization that go beyond required duties of their job

The classic approach to thinking about a job is in terms of the tasks that make up the job. In fact, one purpose of job analysis (as described in Chapter 3) is to establish or identify these tasks. In turn, performance appraisal (as discussed in Chapter 7) is concerned with assessing how well employees perform the tasks that make up their jobs. However, organizational researchers have discovered that some employees contribute to the welfare or effectiveness of their organization by going beyond the duties prescribed in their jobs. That is, they give extra discretionary contributions that are neither required nor expected. The most frequently used term for this phenomenon is **organizational citizenship behavior.** It is also referred to as **prosocial behavior,** *extra-role behavior,* and *contextual behavior.* We first referenced contextual behavior in Chapter 3 on criteria. Organ (1994) referred to a person who engages in organizational citizenship behavior as a "good soldier."

prosocial behavior
behavior by an individual that goes beyond the formal requirements of the job

There appear to be several dimensions to citizenship behavior (Organ, 1988; Van Dyne, Graham, & Dienesch, 1994). Five dimensions are most frequently proposed by researchers:

1. *Altruism* (also called *helping behavior*) reflects willfully helping specific people with an organizationally relevant task or problem.
2. *Conscientiousness* refers to being punctual, having attendance better than the group norm, and judiciously following company rules, regulations, and procedures.
3. *Courtesy* is being mindful and respectful of other people's rights.
4. *Sportsmanship* refers to avoiding complaints, petty grievances, gossiping, and falsely magnifying problems.
5. *Civic virtue* is responsible participation in the political life of the organization. Civic virtue reflects keeping abreast of not only current organizational issues but also more mundane issues, such as attending meetings, responding to in-house communications, and speaking up on issues. It has been suggested that civic virtue is the most admirable manifestation of organizational citizenship behavior because it often entails some sacrifice of individual productive efficiency.

Employees who exhibit prosocial behavior are highly valued by their managers. Indeed, they should be because they contribute above and beyond the normal requirements and expectations of the job. However, Bolino (1999) raised the possibility that employees who are judged to exhibit prosocial behavior may be "good actors" as well as "good soldiers." Good soldiers act selflessly on behalf of their organizations, while good actors may engage in such prosocial behaviors for the self-serving reason of enhancing their image within the organization. Indeed, Hui, Lam, and Law (2000) demonstrated the strategic value of prosocial behavior for employees. Employees who perceived prosocial behavior as instrumental to getting a promotion and who were promoted were more likely to decline in their prosocial behavior after the promotion. Thus, prosocial behavior has instrumental value for enhancing the likelihood of a promotion, but after the promotion its instrumental value decreases. An empirical study of performance evaluation revealed the degree to which citizenship behavior influences judgments of job performance. MacKenzie, Podsakoff, and Fetter (1991) examined three objective measures of weekly productivity relating to sales volume for a sample of insurance agents. Also obtained for these agents was an evaluation of their dimensions of organizational citizenship behavior as well as a managerial assessment of their overall job performance. The results indicated that the managers' subjective evaluations of the agents' job performance were determined as much by the agents' altruism and civic virtue as by the objective productivity levels. Podsakoff, Ahearne, and MacKenzie (1997) reported that altruism and sportsmanship had substantial effects on the overall quantity of performance of machine crews working in a paper mill, while altruism was related to the quality of performance. Allen and Rush (1998) demonstrated that students gave higher evaluations to teachers who exhibited high organizational citizenship behavior than to teachers who exhibited low organizational citizenship behavior, while controlling for the level of the teachers' task performance.

It is reasonable to question the origins of organizational citizenship behavior; that is, are manifestations of such prosocial behavior a product of our individual dispositions (which are fairly immutable), or can organizations conduct themselves in ways that bring out such behavior in their employees? Research supports both the dispositional and situational antecedents of organizational citizenship behavior.

Support for dispositional antecedents comes from the Big 5 model of personality (as discussed in Chapter 4). Two of the Big 5 dimensions appear relevant to organizational citizenship behavior. One, agreeableness, pertains to the ease or difficulty one has in getting along with people, or how good-natured one is with respect to interpersonal relationships. The second, conscientiousness, pertains to reliability, dependability, punctuality, and discipline. Evidence indicates that some people, given selected aspects of their personality, are more likely to engage in organizational citizenship behaviors than others. As McNeely and Meglino (1994) noted, organizations can promote prosocial behavior by selecting applicants who have high scores on agreeableness and conscientiousness.

The second explanation for organizational citizenship behavior—situational antecedents—has at its basis the concept of organizational justice. It is proposed that if employees believe they are treated fairly, then they are more likely to hold positive attitudes about their work. Organ (1988) hypothesized that fairness perceptions may influence prosocial behavior by prompting employees to define their relationship with the organization as a social exchange. In exchange for being treated fairly, it is proposed that employees would engage in discretionary gestures of organizational citizenship behavior. However, to the extent that unfairness is perceived in the relationship, the tendency would be to recast the relationship as a more rigidly defined exchange. Thus, in a trusting relationship with the organization, the employee contributes more to the exchange than is formally required. However, to the degree the organization is perceived as lacking fairness, the employee retreats to contributing to the exchange only what he or she is obligated.

In a test of this proposition, Moorman (1991) examined the relationship between forms of organizational justice (distributive and procedural) and organizational citizenship behavior. A graphic portrayal of the relationship between organizational justice and prosocial behavior is presented in Figure 10–7. It was proposed that employees engage in citizenship behavior because they perceive the organization to be fair (both distributively and procedurally). Moorman discovered that organizational citizenship behavior was related to perceptions of procedural justice but *not* distributive justice. Furthermore, the courtesy dimension of citizenship behavior was most strongly related to procedural justice. Employees who believed that their supervisors personally treated them fairly appeared to be more likely to exhibit citizenship behaviors.

The major implication of the study is that supervisors can directly influence employees' citizenship behavior. Employees' perception of justice was based on whether supervisors used procedures designed to promote fairness. Moorman concluded that if supervisors want to increase citizenship behavior among their employees, they should work to increase the fairness of their interactions with employees. Subsequent research has strengthened the conclusion of a reciprocal exchange between the employee and the organization. Organizations that are perceived as

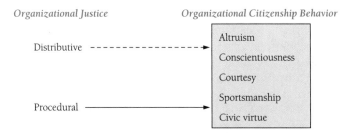

Organizational Justice   *Organizational Citizenship Behavior*

Distributive

Procedural

Altruism

Conscientiousness

Courtesy

Sportsmanship

Civic virtue

FIGURE 10–7 ■ Relationship between organizational justice and organizational citizenship behavior

SOURCE: Adapted from "Relationship Between Organizational Justice and Organizational Citizenship Behaviors: Do Fairness Perceptions Influence Employee Citizenship?" by R. H. Moorman, 1991, *Journal of Applied Psychology, 76*, p. 849.

being equitable and that recognize desirable behavior in their employees reap the benefits of having employees engage in more citizenship behavior.

Research on citizenship behavior reflects the richness of examining workplace behavior from an organizational or social perspective. There are also cross-cultural differences in what constitutes citizenship behavior. Lam, Hui, and Law (1999) found that employees in Hong Kong and Japan were more likely to regard some facets of organizational citizenship behavior as an expected or defined part of the job than were employees from the United States and Australia. Citizenship behavior is related to perceptions of organizational justice and can be viewed as one dimension of the social exchange between the employee and the organization. The next section will examine a related aspect of this social exchange, the psychological contract, and the effects of violating this contract.

THE PSYCHOLOGICAL CONTRACT

psychological contract
the implied exchange relationship that exists between an employee and the organization

Rousseau (1995) described the **psychological contract** as the exchange relationship between the individual employee and the organization. It is not a formal written contract between the two parties but an implied relationship based on mutual contributions. The psychological contract is the employee's perception of the reciprocal obligations that exist within the organization. The employees have beliefs about the organization's obligations to them as well as their obligations to the organization. Thus, employees may believe the organization has agreed to provide job security and promotional opportunities in exchange for hard work and loyalty by the employee. The psychological contract is oriented toward the future. Without the promise of future exchange, neither party has incentive to contribute anything to the other and the relationship may not endure. The contract is composed of a belief that some form of a promise has been made and that the terms and conditions of the contract have been accepted by both parties.

Beliefs or perceptions regarding implied promises and acceptance are the basis of the psychological contract. Each party believes that both parties have made promises and that both parties have accepted the same contract terms (Rousseau, 1989). However, this does not necessarily mean that both parties share a common understanding of all contract terms. Each party believes only that they share the same interpretation of the contract. The psychological contract is made not once but rather is revised throughout the employee's tenure in the organization. The longer the relationship endures and the two parties interact, the broader the array of contributions that might be included in the contract. Rousseau and Parks (1993) found that employment itself is perceived as a promise (the implied contract of continued future employment) and that an employee's performance is perceived as a contribution (a way of paying for the promise). Robinson, Kraatz, and Rousseau (1994) examined how psychological contracts change over time. They found that during the first two years of employment, employees came to perceive that they owed less to their employer, while the employers in turn owed them more.

Rousseau suggested that psychological contracts lie along a continuum ranging from the transactional to the relational. *Transactional contracts* are characterized by short time frames and specific obligations. Financial resources are the primary vehicle of exchange. *Relational contracts* are characterized by long-term relationships with diffuse obligations. Transactional contracts are predicated on total self-interest, whereas relational contracts implicitly acknowledge the value of the relationship itself, in which one party may put the immediate interests of the other party ahead of his or her own. At the relational end of the continuum, obligations are ambiguous and constantly evolving. These contracts are long term and exchange not only financial resources but also socioemotional resources such as loyalty and affiliation. Figure 10–8 shows the continuum of psychological contracts and the range of social behavior within an organization.

There is an element of power in all contracts. Power can be distributed either equally (i.e., symmetrically) between the two parties or unequally (i.e., asymmetrically). Asymmetrical power is most common in employment relationships. Power asymmetries affect the perceived voluntariness of the exchange relationship, dividing the two parties into contract makers (relatively powerful) and contract takers (relatively powerless). As contract takers, employees cannot easily exit the employment relationship. This may result in a perceived loss of control in the relationship, which is likely to intensify feelings of mistreatment and injustice

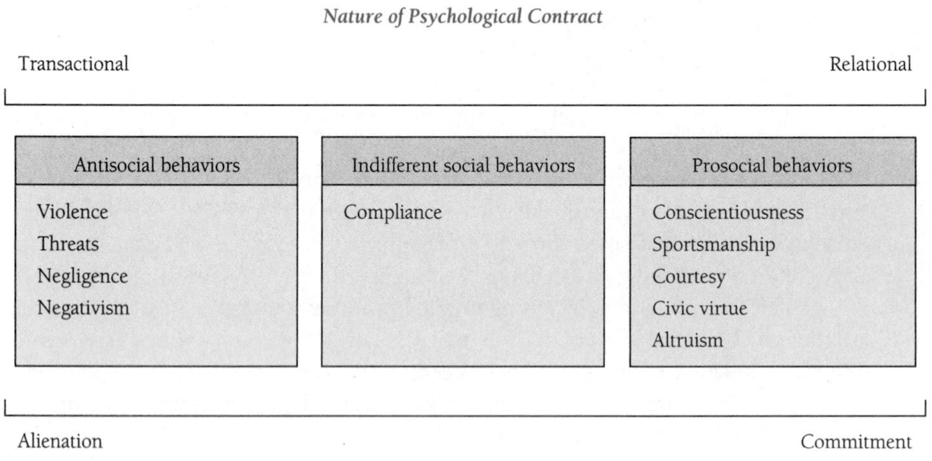

Nature of Psychological Contract

Transactional   Relational

Antisocial behaviors	Indifferent social behaviors	Prosocial behaviors
Violence	Compliance	Conscientiousness
Threats		Sportsmanship
Negligence		Courtesy
Negativism		Civic virtue
		Altruism

Alienation   Commitment

FIGURE 10–8 ■ Relationship between the psychological contract and range of social behaviors

SOURCE: Adapted from "'Till Death Do Us Part . . . ': Changing Work Relationships in the 1990s" by J. M. Parks and D. L. Kidder, 1994, in *Trends in Organizational Behavior,* Vol. 1 (p. 120), edited by C. L. Cooper and D. M. Rousseau, New York: Wiley.

when violations are perceived. Because the employer is the more powerful party, terms of the contract can be dictated to the less powerful employee, who must either accept them or exit the relationship.

Violations of the Psychological Contract

The psychological contract is violated when one party in a relationship perceives another as failing to fulfill promised obligations. Table 10–2 lists typical organizational violations of the psychological contract and related example quotations from employees. The failure of one party to meet its obligations to another can be expected to erode both the relationship and the affected party's belief in the reciprocal obligations of the two parties. Violations by an employer may affect not only what an employee feels he or she is owed by the employer, but also what an employee feels obligated to offer in return. Violation of a psychological contract undermines the very factors (e.g., trust) that led to emergence of a relationship. If the employer reneges on an implied promise, the employer's integrity is questioned. A violation signals that the employer's original motives to build and maintain a mutually beneficial relationship have changed or were false from the beginning. Cavanaugh and Noe (1999) and Turnley and Feldman (2000) found that violations of the psychological contract negatively influenced employees' intent to remain with the employer and job satisfaction. The psychological contract binds the employee and employer—a form of guarantee that if each does his or her part, then the relationship will be mutually beneficial. Thus, violations weaken the bond.

What is the typical employee response to violations of the psychological contract? Robinson et al. (1994) found that psychological contracts become less relational and more transactional following violations. Employees turn away from the socioemotional aspects of work and focus on the monetary benefits of the relationship. This has the effect of increasing the psychological distance between the employee and the employer, making the contract more transactional. A sequential pattern of five employee responses to violations has been identified. The first is *voice:* The employee voices his or her concern over the violation and seeks to reinstate the contract. Dulebohn (1997) found that employees are somewhat reluctant to use formal mechanisms of voice because they fear the mechanisms will expose them to subsequent reprisal by management. People who use formal voice mechanisms (grievance or appeal systems) often are labeled as organizational dissenters and experience retaliation. Instead, employees are more likely to use subtle influence tactics to affect procedural justice. If unsuccessful, voice is followed by *silence.* Silence connotes compliance with the organization, but a loss of commitment. Silence is followed by *retreat,* as indicated by passivity, negligence, and shirking of responsibility. *Destruction* may then occur, whereby the employees retaliate against the employer through theft, threats, sabotage, and in extreme cases, homicidal violence against individuals perceived as contributing to the violation. The topic of workplace violence will be discussed in greater detail later in this chapter. Finally, in the *exit* stage, the employees quit the organization or provoke the organization to dismiss them. Research has shown that justice perceptions exert a role in responses to violations of the psychological contract. In particular, procedural

TABLE 10–2 ■ Types of violations of the psychological contract

Violation Type	Definition	Examples
Training/development	Absence of training or training experience not as promised	"Sales training was promised as an integral part of marketing training. It never materialized."
Compensation	Discrepancies in promised and realized pay, benefits, and bonuses	"Specific compensation benefits were promised. Either they were not given to me, or I had to fight for them."
Promotion	Promotion or advancement schedule not as promised	"I perceived a promise that I had a good chance of promotion to manager in one year. While I received excellent performance ratings, I was not promoted in my first year."
Job security	Promises not met regarding the degree of job security one could expect	"The company promised that no one would be fired out of the training program, that all of us were safe until placement. In return for this security we accepted lower pay. The company subsequently fired four people from the training program."
Feedback	Feedback and reviews inadequate compared with what was promised	"I did not receive performance reviews as promised."
People	Employer perceived as having misrepresented the type of people at the firm, in terms of things such as their expertise, work style, or reputation	"It was promised as dynamic and as having a challenging environment . . . rubbing elbows with some of the brightest people in the business . . . a lie. The true picture started to come out after the initial hype of working at one of the best 100 companies in the country had worn off."

SOURCE: Adapted from "Violating the Psychological Contract: Not the Exception but the Norm" by S. L. Robinson and D. M. Rousseau, 1994, *Journal of Organizational Behavior, 15,* pp. 245–259.

justice is of primary importance to employees whose relational contract was violated. The use of fair and equitable procedures by organizations can lessen the impact of the contract violation on the employee.

Parks and Kidder (1994) noted at least three major underresearched issues regarding the psychological contract. First is the employer side of the contract and employer perceptions of violations by the employees. Most research has examined

FIELD NOTE 2   **Mutual Expectations**

he concept of the psychological contract can be extended from employees in a work organization to students in an educational organization. The psychological contract involves a set of mutual expectations that both parties in a relationship have for each other. What expectations do students have for their professors? Reasonable expectations might include that the professors are qualified to teach the subject matter, they will fairly evaluate the students' performance in class, and they harbor no personal bias against any students. Have you ever been in a class where one or more of these expectations were, in your opinion, unmet? If so, how did it affect your attitude toward the professor, the class, the school? If you felt the basic psychological contract between the students and the professor was violated, it is reasonable that your attitude and perhaps behavior (e.g., attendance, performance in class) were adversely affected. However, the psychological contract consists of *mutual* expectations—in this case, expectations the professors have of students as well. What expectations do professors have for their students? Reasonable expectations might include that the students want to learn, they will complete assignments on time, and they respect the institution of higher learning. Have you ever been in a class where it seemed the professor felt these expectations were violated by the students? If so, how did the professor respond to these perceived violations? The psychological contract applies to both parties in a relationship, but we know less about organizational expectations of their members than vice versa.

the contract from the employee's perspective (see Field Note 2). Second is what happens when the psychological contract is kept. It is unclear whether a contract becomes more relational as goodwill is enhanced by kept promises. Third, we don't know very much about whether, once violated, a psychological contract can be reinstated.

Based on a multinational analysis, Rousseau and Schalk (2000) concluded that the psychological contract as a promise-based exchange is widely generalizable to a variety of societies. Given the rise of global business, it is likely that the nature of cultural differences in the psychological contract will continue to evolve. For example, traditionally Asians prefer to first establish a relationship between parties and then carry out business transactions, while Western cultures prefer to create a relationship through repeated business transactions. In the future it is likely both styles will manifest themselves in new and varied forms.

Next the chapter will examine one of the most fundamental violations of a psychological contract—the organization's decision to reduce employment through layoffs or downsizing. Such decisions demonstrate huge power differentials between employer and employee and involve the complete loss of control by the employee. As noted in Chapter 8, downsizing affects thousands of employees annually and is changing the nature of the psychological contract as we know it.

INDIVIDUAL RESPONSES TO DOWNSIZING

As discussed in Chapter 8, organizational downsizing has targeted middle-level managers and professional staffs as well as blue-collar employees. These developments are harbingers of fundamental change in the evolution and nature of organizational behavior. This section will examine downsizing from the perspective of

DILBERT by Scott Adams

individual employees, both those who have lost their jobs and the survivors (Kozlowski, Chao, Smith, & Hedlund, 1993).

An inherent paradox is associated with downsizing. Downsizing is a deliberate organizational decision to reduce the workforce that is intended to improve organizational performance, yet it has a profound negative impact on the lives of individual employees. At the core of this paradox lies a challenge to a long-standing principle of work and employment—namely, that work can be structured in ways that are beneficial to both the individual and the organization. Downsizing emphasizes the cold and brutal reality that the goals of the individual and the goals of the organization need not necessarily align.

Terminated Personnel

The individuals most directly affected by downsizing are those who lose their jobs. Downsized employees face the immediate prospect of a loss of income. The amount of time employees have between hearing their jobs have been eliminated and the date of their termination is often a matter of weeks and sometimes days. There is often little time to search for a new job. Buss and Redburn (1987) reported that eight years after a plant closing, 27% of the affected workers were still unemployed. Furthermore, those who do find some employment may be able to obtain only less attractive and lower-paying jobs. Individuals with skills that do not readily transfer outside of the organization and those with less education suffer greater financial losses.

Employment has a number of psychological benefits that are lost when an individual becomes unemployed. Individuals who lose their job suffer physical symptoms caused by the strain of unemployment. Some indicators of the stress of unemployment are headaches, stomach problems, and high blood pressure. Unemployed individuals have been found to exhibit patterns of learned helplessness, lower feelings of self-worth, and increased depression. Older, white-collar employees experience particularly acute feelings of betrayal by their organization, demoralization, and cynicism. Issues of stress and well-being will be discussed in greater detail in the next chapter.

Surviving Personnel

Although downsizing has more direct implications for the individuals who lose their jobs, employees who remain with the organization are also affected by downsizing strategies intended to make the organization run more efficiently. Survivors often respond with reduced trust and commitment because the organization broke its psychological contract with them (see Field Note 3). The reactions of these survivors to the downsizing process, as well as their reactions to the organization's treatment of terminated employees, can adversely affect future organizational effectiveness.

Surviving employees are still employed by the organization, but their conditions of employment may be different from before. In order to remain with the organization, some individuals may have to be demoted to lower-level jobs. This may be accompanied by a salary reduction as well. Other downsizing strategies targeted to reduce costs include job sharing, part-time schedules, and reduced hours. Although affected employees may experience a reduction in income, the experience is still less painful than the total loss of employment.

Brockner and Greenberg (1990) developed a conceptual model of survivor reactions to downsizing based upon organizational justice. Survivors may question whether the downsizing was a necessary response to an economic downturn, whether terminated employees were adequately forewarned, whether the rules used to choose those to be laid off were fair, and whether the organization provided "caretaking activities" (e.g., counseling, severance pay) to help individuals adjust to the job loss. Brockner, Davy, and Carter (1985) found that survivors felt

FIELD NOTE 3 **The Loss of Resources**

 o understand the impact of downsizing on the surviving members of an organization, consider an analogy: The employees of an organization are one of its resources (which is why they are often referred to as "human resources"). The organization uses these employees to accomplish its objectives. Individuals have resources as well. One resource that we all have in common is time. Every person has 24 hours in each day to accomplish his or her objectives. Organizational downsizing that results in the loss of 20% of the workforce is not unusual. How would you deal with a 20% loss in your time resources? That is, instead of a 24-hour day, your day has been "downsized" by 20% (or 5 hours) to become a 19-hour day. You still have to do everything you did before, you now just have 5 fewer hours in which to do it. How would you live your life differently? If you normally sleep 8 hours, would you now sleep only 3 hours? If you need 8 hours of sleep and have to continue working an 8-hour day, that leaves only 3 hours for everything else, including eating, transportation time, and recreation. Do you think you would feel stressed under these conditions? Do you think you might not be as fully committed to your activities under these conditions? While we all probably waste some time each day, it is questionable whether we waste 20% of it. Therefore, eliminating 20% of our day would not necessarily make us more efficient. It might compel us to use our time more wisely, but it would also exact a cost on us; that is, we would probably have to "give" on some other aspects of life. Such is the predicament faced by the survivors of organizational downsizing. They face increased pressure to perform the work that was once performed by a larger workforce.

guilt when a fellow worker was laid off, which resulted in increased productivity. However, survivors also feel less commitment to the organization and often seek employment with greater security elsewhere.

In addition to the impact on survivors individually, downsizing affects the functioning of groups. Krantz (1985) described the tendency for groups to engage in defensive behavior to relieve the stress of downsizing. The defensiveness manifests itself in a greater reluctance to be flexible and accommodating in performing group tasks. There is also evidence that work teams become more cohesive and resistant to change in response to environmental threats. Increased resistance to change can greatly impede the functioning of certain types of teams specifically created to be responsive to changing conditions.

Rather than staffing permanent employees, many organizations are making greater use of contingent (temporary) workers (Smither, 1995). Contingent workers perform particular tasks for a specific time period. The need for the services varies as a function of the organization's work flow. Contingent workers may work through temporary employment agencies that allocate their services to organizational clients in need of them. They are the modern-day industrial equivalent of migrant farm workers, people who obtain temporary employment by following the harvesting of crops across the nation. Contingent workers receive lower salaries than if they were permanent employees performing the same work, and they rarely receive fringe benefits such as medical insurance or pensions. Contingent workers are disproportionately young, female, and minority, those who exemplify the transactional psychological contract. They have a short-term outlook on their involvement with an organization because the future holds no promise for them. While contingent workers may increase organizational flexibility and decrease labor costs, there is a price to pay. The price is that workers exhibit fewer prosocial behaviors or, worse, engage in antisocial behaviors.

Another common reaction of surviving employees after downsizing is to feel overworked. Schor (1992) reported that surviving employees often must take up the work slack from the terminated individuals. Additionally, they feel compelled to accept being overworked to ensure their own continued employment. These workers may in turn reassess their *own* psychological contracts and may perceive their own contracts as transactional, whether or not they were intended as such by the employer.

Downsizing has forced both organizations and individuals to reassess the nature of the employment relationship. One consequence has been an apparent increase in transactional psychological contracts, with the accompanying decrease in employees' sense of loyalty and commitment to their employer. It has been argued that downsizing is a necessary response to organizational structures that have become bloated and economically inefficient. Organizations that resist downsizing as a means of addressing their imperiled conditions risk their total demise (and the loss of even more jobs). However, downsizing has become bitter medicine for individuals as a treatment for organizational maladies. Its presence and frequency of use have prompted a major reassessment by I/O psychologists of long-held tenets regarding the nature of the employment relationship.

THE PSYCHOLOGY OF MERGERS AND ACQUISITIONS

organizational merger
the joining or combining of two organizations of approximately equal status and power

acquisition
the process by which one organization acquires or subsumes the resources of a second organization

One strategy organizations can use in response to environmental pressures is to become smaller—that is, to downsize. Another strategy is to become larger. But rather than just becoming a larger version of what the organization already is, organizations can choose to "marry" another organization as a way of increasing their size. The logic behind an organizational marriage is similar to that of the marriage of individuals; that is, the overall quality of life for both parties will be enhanced by the marriage. Organizational marriages encompass both mergers and acquisitions. The technical distinction between mergers and acquisitions is slim. An **organizational merger** is the marriage or joining of two organizations of equal status and power. Their union is mutually decided. Both organizations think they will be more prosperous by their formal association with the other. An **acquisition** is the procurement of property (in this case, an organization) by another organization. The purchasing organization is in the dominant or more powerful role. Unlike a marriage of individuals, an acquisition can be a marriage between two organizations where only one party agrees to the new relationship. The dominant organization thus acquires an unwilling partner to enhance its financial status in what is called a hostile takeover. Other acquisitions are characterized by more friendly relationships between the two organizations, but nevertheless the more powerful organization acquires the less powerful organization. The acquiring organization is referred to as the *parent,* and the organization being acquired is the *target.* For the purpose of this discussion, mergers and acquisitions will be portrayed as the combining of two companies, regardless of the difference in power between the two. There is relatively little research on this topic. What we do know applies mainly to the characteristics of the two organizations as they affect the quality of their marriage and the individual responses of employees to their organization being united with another.

Some characteristics of parent firms have been found to affect the way they implement the integration of the two companies (Hogan & Overmyer-Day, 1994). Two prominent issues are the parent's culture and the parent's arrogance toward the target. Some parent cultures are more likely than others to impose themselves on the target companies. Parent organizations with a strong consensus on beliefs and values, as well as strong socialization of their members into these beliefs and values, are particularly likely to attempt to impose them on targets. The unity of a parent's culture and its tolerance for diversity are related to how the parent treats the target. Some parent companies have been found to exhibit characteristics of arrogance and presumption—they "know what's best" for the target. Jemison and Sitkin (1986) proposed three types of organizational arrogance: interpersonal ("We're better than you"), cultural ("Our values, practices, and beliefs are superior"), and managerial ("Our administrative systems are better"). Arrogance influences parent managers to act condescendingly toward targets, increasing their tendencies to impose solutions and negatively affecting morale, turnover, and performance. Arrogance also increases target resistance to being integrated into the parent company. Buono and Bowditch (1989) suggested that the more important the target to the parent, the more likely the parent is to exert control over the target and thus increase the likelihood of conflict.

The elements of a target's culture pertaining to the identification of its heroes, leadership style, feelings of "family" among workers, and degree of mentoring among managers are likely sources of problems when integration is attempted. It has been suggested that management's attitude toward risk and the degree of responsibility for decision making are areas where cultural clashes are most evident. Each organization's ignorance of the other's culture appears to be responsible for the majority of problems faced when two organizations integrate. During negotiations between the two organizations, issues of *strategic fit* (that is, shared or complementary business strategies, financial goals) typically dominate the discussion. However, issues of *organizational fit* (that is, the compatibility of the cultures and the match between workforces) are often neglected.

Marks and Mirvis (2000) reported that over 80% of corporate mergers fail to achieve projected financial, strategic, and operational goals. The authors recommend the use of some transition structure to help blend the two organizations. A transition structure is a forum in which leaders from combining companies can study and plan for the ways the intended goals can be realized in practice. It is a temporary but formal arrangement in which members represent every area of the two companies and have joint input into the integration of the businesses.

The psychological response of employees to the announcement that their company has been acquired has been compared to the sense of loss experienced by a person following bereavement (Mirvis, 1985). As in models of individual bereavement, it is posited that employees pass through stages of grief beginning with disbelief and denial and followed by anger, emotional bargaining, depression, and finally acceptance. The loss of individuals' identification with their organization may produce stress associated with the loss as well as a nostalgic impulse in employees to hold on to what they have. Collective employee grief is likely to increase cohesiveness and resistance to change and make new cultures even more difficult to introduce.

It has been estimated that during the 1980s at least 25% of the U.S. workforce was affected by merger and acquisition activity (Fulmer, 1986). As with downsizing, I/O psychologists have little experience in dealing with how individuals respond to this type of organizational activity. In the past 20 years, we have had to address new aspects of organizational behavior about which we had little knowledge. The depth and magnitude of these issues on the psychology of work have had a profound impact on the profession of I/O psychology.

ANTISOCIAL BEHAVIOR IN THE WORKPLACE

antisocial behavior
any behavior that brings harm or is intended to bring harm to an organization or its members

Antisocial behavior in the workplace refers to a range of employee behaviors aimed at exacting revenge against the organization or fellow workers for some perceived injustice. Antisocial behavior includes insults, threats, lying, theft, sabotage, physical violence, and occupational homicide. The concept has also been called *organizational deviance* (Bennett & Robinson, 2000) and *workplace incivility* (Pearson,

Andersson, & Porath, 2000). It represents one of the more recent areas of research in I/O psychology.

Andersson and Pearson (1999) proposed a spiraling effect of incivility in the workplace. Workplace incivility is low-intensity deviant behavior with ambiguous intent to harm the target individual, in violation of workplace norms for mutual respect. Uncivil behaviors are characteristically rude and discourteous, displaying a lack of regard for others. The spiraling effect refers to the prospects that incivility can escalate into intense aggressive behavior. Andersson and Pearson state that the spiral of incivility often begins with a thoughtless act or a rude comment. This can be followed by a maligning insult, which prompts a counterinsult. If the spiral of escalation continues, threats of physical attack can follow, ultimately leading to violence. The authors believe there is a "tipping point" in the spiral where the accumulation of minor affronts escalates into coercive action.

Bies, Tripp, and Kramer (1997) described what they call the "thermodynamics of revenge" in organizations. It is predicated on the violation of two underlying concepts previously examined in this chapter: the psychological contract and organizational justice. There is typically a sparking event of one of two types. One is a violation of rules, norms, or promises by the organization. An organizational agent changes the rules or criteria of decision making after the fact to justify a self-serving judgment. The second is status or power derogation, such as destructive criticism or public ridicule intended to embarrass the employee. The employee then "heats up" and experiences anger and bitterness, often feeling a need to satisfy a burning desire for revenge. This is followed by a "cooling down" phase, which can take several forms. One is *venting*, in which the employee talks heatedly and animatedly to friends, "blows off steam," and has little or no intention of acting out his or her feelings. A second is *dissipation*, where the employee gives the harm-doer the benefit of the doubt and searches for plausible explanations for the harm-doer's behavior. A third form is *fatigue*, whereby employees maintain their negative feelings for long periods of time. These people do not forgive, forget, and let go. They often obsessively ruminate and express regret about not getting even with the harm-doer. The final form is *explosion*, which can manifest itself in the employee working harder to prove the critic wrong, mobilizing opposition to the harm-doer, or engaging in physical violence.

Skarlicki and Folger (1997) asserted that organizational agents, particularly managers and supervisors, play prominent roles in reducing employee desires to seek revenge. When managers and supervisors showed adequate sensitivity and concern toward employees, treating them with dignity and respect, the employees were willing to tolerate organizational violations of justice that would otherwise contribute toward retaliatory tendencies (Skarlicki, Folger, & Tesluk, 1999). Such retaliatory behaviors included deliberately damaging equipment or work processes, taking supplies home without permission, and wasting company material. Cropanzano and Greenberg (1997) discovered that workers who were treated in a disrespectful manner by their supervisor stole objects that were of no value to themselves but were of value to their employer. Disrespectful treatment, adding insult to the injury of unfair treatment, encouraged people to retaliate against their employers. The employees sought to harm employers in exchange for being harmed, even if doing so did nothing more than even the score between them symbolically.

Violence in the Workplace

As Bies et al. (1997) noted, one of the responses to perceived violations of organizational justice is physical violence. Physical violence in the workplace is a growing epidemic. Prior to 1980 such terms as "violence in the workplace" and "occupational homicide" did not exist. The U.S. Department of Justice (1998) reported that annually there are over 150,000 violent workplace incidents. From these, more than 1,000 individuals were murdered on the job. The number of employees who killed their managers has doubled in the last decade. Bulatao and VandenBos (1996) reported that homicide is the leading cause of fatal occupational injuries in the retail trade, sales, service, managerial, and clerical occupations. Reporting statistics on crime has the subtle effect of making them appear somewhat dry and impersonal. The following are descriptions of specific acts of violence in the workplace (Mantell, 1994, pp. 2–4):

- A Tampa, Florida, man returned to his former workplace and shot three of his supervisors as they sat eating their lunches. He wounded two others before killing himself.
- A Sunnyvale, California, worker at a defense contractor shot and killed seven people in the office after a female coworker turned down his romantic advances.
- A woman in a Corona, California, hospital opened fire with a .38-calibre handgun, wounding a nurse and spraying the infant nursery with bullets.
- A terminated Woodlawn, Maryland, car mechanic came back to the garage and fired into a crowd of workers, killing two and wounding one.

It may be tempting to dismiss these accounts as somewhat sensationalized reporting of isolated events. However, it appears that the frequency and severity of workplace violence are escalating, both nationally and internationally. Kelleher (1996) described the breadth of the problem as follows: "If you are a gas station attendant, government employee, or retail store clerk, you have a higher probability of being murdered on the job than a police officer in your own community. If you are a secretary or clerk in an office, you are more likely to be murdered at work than a West Virginia miner is likely to be accidentally killed in an industry-related accident" (p. xi). Furthermore, Barling (1996) noted there are both primary and secondary victims of workplace violence—family members of primary victims plus coworkers who themselves were not violated but whose perceptions, fears, and expectations are changed as a result of being vicariously exposed to the violence.

A starting point to understanding the psychology of workplace violence is with the topic of aggression. Cox and Leather (1994) stated, "Human aggression is typically the product of interpersonal interactions wherein two or more persons become involved in a sequence of escalating moves and countermoves, each of which successively modifies the probability of subsequent aggression" (p. 222). Thus, aggressive acts are frequently the retaliatory response to a previous act or acts by the aggressor. A violent act is therefore conceptualized as a step in an integrated series of social acts. The retaliatory response can be understood in part by the concepts of organizational justice and the psychological contract.

Perpetrators of workplace violence often see themselves as victims of some injustice in the workplace. They may be particularly inclined to perceive the organization as having violated the principles of procedural justice. In fact, Johnson and Indvik (1994) posited that violation of the psychological contract is one of the leading causes of workplace violence. A term frequently associated with perpetrators of workplace violence is "disgruntled." Mantell (1994) reported that acts of physical violence are invariably preceded by indications of anger or betrayal, such as verbal threats or sullenness. Actual violence is often preceded by verbal assaults and/or stalking of the victim. However, in most cases of workplace hostility the verbal assaults and stalking do not escalate to homicide. That is, there is a continuum of hostile workplace behaviors, with homicide (or attempted homicide) being the extreme point (Neuman & Baron, 1998). Perpetrators seemingly want more from the organization in terms of personal identity and purpose than the organization can provide, and in turn they personalize a sense of rejection when their needs are unmet. They tend to see themselves as having their relationship (contract) with the organization violated, while accepting little or no responsibility for their own behavior. It also appears that perpetrators of violent workplace crimes often have maladaptive personalities and have experienced interpersonal conflict in other aspects of their lives.

The process of looking for systematic patterns among perpetrators of workplace violence has led to the identification of consistent characteristics among these individuals. A problem with this profile approach is that even though it may indeed describe perpetrators, the identified characteristics may also describe many other individuals. That is, many employees may "fit" the profile but in fact do *not* engage in workplace violence. For example, most employees whose jobs are downsized feel a sense of rejection and injustice, yet they do not commit violent acts. Hindsight or "postdiction" may give the impression that perpetrators were obvious candidates to commit such crimes and therefore should have been identified and deterred from their actions. Folger and Baron (1996) referred to the process of identifying which employees are likely to commit workplace violence as the "popcorn model." They state: "The employee who explodes violently and shoots his or her supervisor is akin to the first kernel of popcorn to explode. Obviously an observer might focus on trying to explain why this particular kernel exploded before all the others. Although all the popped kernels look similar, a microscopic view or chemical assay might help reveal the extent to which each kernel is unique. Similarly, careful study of the individuals in a given workplace may reveal important differences with respect to various personal characteristics previously found to be related to aggression" (p. 62). Despite the prevalence of workplace violence, its occurrence is still relatively rare in the total population of employed individuals. Therefore, the correct prediction of such events is far more problematic than "looking backward" after their occurrence.

Aggression is the product of both individual and situational factors. Among the situational factors identified are population density, noise, heat, and alcohol use. Both laboratory and field research on aggression (e.g., Geen, 1990) indicates that it becomes increasingly likely under conditions of perceived crowding, uncontrollable noise, and high ambient temperatures. However, the research on the relationship between alcohol use and aggression is most declarative (Greenberg &

Barling, 1999). Pernanen (1991) posited that alcohol completely modifies one's ability to understand a social situation. Alcohol leads to both a narrowing of the situation at hand and a dampening of intellectual and verbal ability. Alcohol encourages an overinflated evaluation of one's sense of control, power, and mastery over the world. The inebriated individual may be led into aggression by both a biased interpretation of the situation and increased confidence in being able to cope by largely physical means (Cox & Leather, 1994). Many perpetrators of workplace violence were found to have consumed alcohol prior to their action.

Some researchers believe violence in the workplace is just part of the larger category of psychosocial hazards to which organizations must respond. Cox and Leather (1994) proposed three types of strategies organizations should adopt in dealing with complex hazards such as workplace violence:

- *Preventive strategies* (such as employee training) remove the hazard or reduce its impact on employees or their likelihood of exposure.
- *Reactive strategies* (such as formal organizational emergency plans) improve the organization's ability to recognize and deal with problems as they arise.
- *Rehabilitative strategies* (such as counseling) help employees cope with and recover from problems that exist.

Nicoletti and Spooner (1996) advocate organizational use of threat/violence assessment teams, who train managers to recognize and treat violent behaviors and who implement organized processes for reporting and responding to threats. Root and Ziska (1996) believe the need for such interventions is particularly acute during organizational downsizing.

There is often reluctance on the part of companies to participate in research on workplace violence because it is such a sensitive and volatile subject. Fox and Spector (1999) described a research study addressing workplace violence in which some companies declined to participate. The authors reported: "The primary reason given by companies in declining to participate was that they did not want to 'unsettle' their employees. Employees in precisely such companies might provide the richest information about counterproductive behavioral responses to aversive work environments" (p. 929). Antisocial behavior in the workplace is a complex phenomenon. Baron, Hoffman, and Merrill (2000) assert there are close parallels between violence at work and violence in nonwork areas of life. Like drug use in the workplace, it spills over into other areas traditionally removed from I/O psychology. It remains to be seen how big a role we will play in addressing this topic. If primary emphasis is placed on the act (criminal violence) rather than on its location, then the role of I/O psychology will probably not be large. However, if such violence is examined primarily in terms of its location (the workplace), I anticipate that I/O psychology will be called upon to help understand and control this serious problem.

CASE STUDY ■ Where Should the Ax Fall?

Ted Simmons stared pensively at two personnel files. Simmons was the vice president of finance for Savannah Mills, a long-time business leader in the textile industry. Savannah Mills had endured another difficult year, as sales and profits were again lower than projected. Simmons had just returned from a staff meeting where he was told the company would be downsizing its staff as a way to reduce expenses. Simmons had to eliminate one of his two financial manager positions, and other job losses were to follow down the line in his department. In fact, all the major departments at Savannah Mills would face job losses, some more than others.

Simmons had the pleasure of working with two exemplary managers, and eliminating one of these jobs from the company would be extremely difficult and unpleasant. Warren Davis had been with the company for almost 25 years. He had devoted his entire career to Savannah Mills; he started working there after high school. His dedication and commitment to the company were almost legendary. He had earned a college degree on a part-time basis while holding a job at Savannah Mills, getting a bachelor's degree in general business. Whatever the company asked Davis to do, he did with vigor and good cheer. He willingly accepted assignments where the company needed him and always expressed sincere gratitude for the chance to be with Savannah Mills. His father had been an employee of the company for over 40 years when he retired, and the Davis children grew up playing on company-sponsored recreational teams. Warren Davis was also very active in the community, representing Savannah Mills on various civic projects. Davis was once referred to as a "walking billboard" for the company, so strong was his loyalty to the company that meant so much to him and his family.

The other manager was Barry Steele. Steele had a very different history than Davis. Steele was 29 and had been with Savannah Mills for five years. He had earned an MBA degree from a highly prestigious university in New England. Upon graduation, Steele had had many job offers but chose Savannah Mills because of its expressed intent to more strongly professionalize the financial operations at the company and to give Steele the opportunity to put his talents to work. Steele delivered on all the expectations of him and in fact exceeded these expectations. He revolutionized the company's system of managing financial assets through the use of automated control principles he had learned in graduate school. It was through Steele's shrewd assessments that Savannah Mills avoided even bigger financial losses, and he positioned the company to return to profitability. Steele was known as "the wonder kid" because of his accomplishments, but he never acted arrogant or pompous. He was not active in company or civic affairs, but quietly went about his business. If there was ever a young employee who seemed destined for a highly successful future with Savannah Mills, it was Steele.

Simmons faced a dreadful choice. He didn't have to fire one of his managers because poor job performance was not the issue. Rather, he had to choose to eliminate the job of a person whose contributions to the company were very positive. Simmons argued to the company president on the merits of keeping both managers. His arguments were to no avail because the issue was to reduce expenses, and all departments had to suffer the loss of good employees. Simmons felt this was one of the toughest calls he ever had to make, and no matter which way it went, the decision would speak loudly about what type of employee Savannah Mills valued the most.

Study Questions

1. Recall the concept of the psychological contract. What aspects of the contract are at issue in this case?
2. If Davis's job is eliminated, what message would that send to the other employees at Savannah Mills?
3. If Steele's job is eliminated, what message would that send to the other employees at Savannah Mills?
4. Recall the concept of organizational citizenship behavior. To what degree does this concept influence your thoughts about a just decision in this case?
5. If you were Simmons, whose job would you eliminate, and why?

SUGGESTED INFOTRAC TOPICS

job satisfaction

employee involvement

commitment

distributive justice

procedural justice

psychological contract

corporate mergers

corporate aquisitions

antisocial behavior in the workplace

workplace violence

Occupational Health

LEARNING OBJECTIVES

■ Explain the environmental influences on mental health.
■ Understand the concept of mental health and identify developmental factors in mental health.
■ Discuss the concept of work stress.
■ Discuss how work schedules affect occupational health.
■ Explain the basis of work/family conflict.
■ Explore issues pertaining to dual-career families.
■ Understand the psychological effects of unemployment.

occupational health
a broad-based concept that refers to the mental, emotional, and physical well-being of employees in relation to the conduct of their work

The term **occupational health** refers to the constellation of issues that affect the mental, emotional, and physical well-being of employees as they engage in work. It does not directly include the field of medicine, but medical issues can influence our understanding of this topic. From a psychological standpoint, occupational health often embraces the interplay between the work and nonwork spheres of our lives.

Sigmund Freud was once asked what he thought a "normal" person should be able to do well. He is reported to have said "Lieben und Arbeiten" ("to love and to work"; Erickson, 1963, p. 265). Freud believed that it is through one's family that love-related needs are gratified and that work has a more powerful effect than any other aspect of human life to bind a person to reality. Therefore, Freud's call for a normal person to love and to work can be interpreted as an emphasis on work and family for healthy psychological functioning (Quick, Murphy, Hurrell, & Orman, 1992). The topic of work and the role it plays in our lives has been a subject of interest and controversy down through the ages of recorded history (see Field Note 1). Opinions about various aspects of work are highly varied, as reflected in the following three quotations:

- "Work consists of whatever a body is obligated to do. Play consists of whatever a body is not obligated to do."—Mark Twain
- "The world is full of willing people; some willing to work, the rest willing to let them."—Robert Frost
- "The first sign of a nervous breakdown is when you start thinking your work is terribly important."—Milo Bloom

A person's work and occupational stature play a critical role in an individual's sense of identity, self-esteem, and psychological well-being. Work is the central

---

FIELD NOTE 1   The Meaning of Work

 hy do people work? This seemingly simple question has been debated for centuries from many perspectives, including religion, economics, psychology, and philosophy. Some religious doctrine taught that work was a form of punishment for our original sin. Work was an obligation or duty toward building God's kingdom. Work was thus good, and hard work even better. Work was noble because of its taxing nature and because it is a hardship that strengthens our character. Religious teachings also emphasized work as a means of controlling and restraining our passions. Lack of work, or idleness, fosters unhealthy impulses, which deflect us from more admirable pursuits. Thus, work is thought of as an arduous process, deliberately filled with hardships, a means of facilitating our personal development. The view from an economic perspective is that work provides us with the financial resources to sustain life and the aspiration to improve the quality of our material life. The most commonly accepted definition of work, the exchange of labor services for pay, clearly reflects an economic viewpoint. Work has psychological meaning as well, giving us a source of identity and union with other individuals, in addition to being a source of personal accomplishment. Work also has the effect of providing a temporal rhythm to our lives. Our work gives us our time structure—when we have to leave for work and when we are off work to pursue other activities. Finally, work even provides a philosophical explanation of our mission in life—to derive meaning from creating and giving service to others. As can be inferred, there is no one answer to the question of why we work, but its multiple meanings provide a basis to understand why work is so important.

and defining characteristic of life for most individuals. Work may have intrinsic value, instrumental value, or both. The intrinsic value of work is the value an individual finds in performing the work, in and of itself. The instrumental value of work is in providing the necessities of life and serving as a channel for the individual's talents, abilities, and knowledge.

It has been suggested that the split in a person's work and home identities dates back to the Industrial Revolution era. It was then that it became necessary for a person to leave the home and "go to work." However, work and home commitments need not necessarily be at odds. Kanter (1977) proposed that knowledge of the tension and illness-producing features of one system, either work or family, can be used to understand a person's adjustment to the other system. It seems clear that most workers do not leave the pressures of the job behind when they leave work.

positive psychology
the study of the factors and conditions in life that lead to pleasurable and satisfying outcomes for individuals

Recently there has been a call among psychologists to address what is called **positive psychology.** According to Seligman and Csikszentmihalyi (2000), for the past 60 years psychology has become a science largely about healing. They propose that psychologists should come to understand what makes life worth living, not just how to cope with and heal from negative life events. Diener (2000) believes that society is caught up with materialism, yet the acquisition of material goods is only mildly related to how happy we feel in life. Diener recommends that nations should measure and monitor how frequently and intensely people feel satisfied and happy in various life circumstances and across situations. As long as national indicators focus on the production of goods and services (like the gross national product—GNP), it is those factors that national leaders are likely to consider. If a national indicator of well-being were available, policies could be judged by how they influence happiness. Csikszentmihalyi (1999) posed the question, "If we are so rich, why aren't we happy?" It is because material rewards alone are not sufficient to make us happy. Other conditions, such as having a satisfying family life, intimate friends, and time to reflect and pursue diverse interests, have been shown to be related to happiness. In theory, there is no reason these two sets of rewards—the material and the socioemotional—should be mutually exclusive. In practice, however, it is very difficult to reconcile their conflicting demands. Time is the ultimate scarce resource, and the allocation of time presents difficult choices that eventually determine the content and quality of our lives. Csikszentmihalyi states, "This is why professional and business persons find it so difficult to balance the demands of work and family, and why they so rarely feel that they have not short-changed one of these vital aspects of their lives" (p. 823). As will be seen in this chapter, the fundamental need to balance work and nonwork activities in life often produces stress in people, and the means of striving for balance between the two is often at the core of issues pertaining to occupational health.

ENVIRONMENTAL INFLUENCES ON MENTAL HEALTH

Warr (1987) proposed that a sense of well-being from work must first be understood in terms of the general environmental determinants of mental health. Warr identified nine of these determinants that can be viewed as the bases for psychological well-being.

1. *Opportunity for control.* The first determinant of mental health is assumed to lie in the opportunities an environment provides for a person to control activities and events. Mental health is enhanced by environments that promote personal control. Control has two main elements: the opportunity to decide and act in one's chosen way, and the potential to predict the consequences of action. Absence of the second element produces a specific form of uncontrollability—when a person has freedom to decide and act but cannot predict the outcomes. Not knowing the consequences of behavior, one cannot control what will happen.

2. *Opportunity for skill use.* A second feature is the degree to which the environment inhibits or encourages the utilization and development of skills. Restrictions on skill use may be of two kinds. First are those that prevent people from using skills they already possess, permitting instead only routine behaviors. Second are restrictions on the acquisition of new skills, requiring people to remain at low levels of performance despite their potential for expanding into more complex activity.

3. *Externally generated goals.* The third feature assumed to underlie mental health is the presence of goals or challenges generated by the environment. An environment that makes no demands on a person offers no challenge and encourages no activity or achievement. Conversely, an environment that fosters the establishment and pursuit of goals is assumed to lead to activities that both intrinsically and through their consequences have a positive impact on mental health.

4. *Environmental variety.* Some environments generate goals and associated activities that are repetitive and invariant. Required repetitive activity is unlikely to contribute to mental health to the same degree as more diverse requirements, which introduce novelty and break up routine activity and location.

5. *Environmental clarity.* The fifth feature that underlies mental health is the degree to which a person's environment is clear. Clarity includes two components. First is feedback about the consequences of one's actions. Second is the clarity of role requirements and normative expectations about behavior, and the degree to which standards are explicit and accepted within one's environment.

6. *Availability of money.* Severely restricted access to money can give rise to many processes likely to impair mental health. The presence of money does not ensure mental health, but the absence of money often produces serious psychological problems. Poverty reduces the opportunity for personal control in one's life, which is a previously identified determinant of mental health.

7. *Physical security.* A seventh feature is a physically secure living environment. Environments need to protect a person against physical harm and to provide adequate security with respect to eating, sleeping, and residing. They also need to be reasonably permanent so that occupants can look forward to their continued presence.

8. *Opportunity for interpersonal contact.* Environments differ in the opportunities they provide for contact with other people. Such contact meets needs for friendship and reduces feelings of loneliness. Interpersonal contact also provides social support that is both emotional and instrumental (contributing to the reso-

lution of problems through practical help and advice) in nature. Many goals can be achieved only through the interdependent efforts of several people. Membership in groups makes possible the establishment and attainment of goals that could not be realized by an individual alone.

9. *Valued social position.* The ninth aspect considered to be important is a position within a social structure that receives some esteem from others. Esteem is generated primarily through the value attached to activities inherent in a role and the contribution they make. Role membership also provides public evidence that one has certain abilities and meets certain social obligations. There is often widespread agreement about the level of esteem that derives from a particular position.

Warr (1987) recognized some overlap among these nine dimensions but felt that a recognition of each was necessary to understand how environments affect mental health. If one were interested in changing environments to enhance mental health, these nine features would be productive targets.

THE CONCEPT OF MENTAL HEALTH

Although the nine environmental factors contributing to mental health have been examined, we have not yet defined the concept itself. This is in part because no single definition exists, and it is easier to understand the meaning of mental health by referencing its determinants. Societal standards contribute to the meaning of mental health (with many derived from contemporary Western society), as well as standards proposed by the medical profession regarding mental illness. We will not explore the varied contributions of these sources in conceptualizing mental health. Rather, we will take an overall perspective of mental health as proposed by Warr (1987) and focus on its five major components.

1. *Affective well-being.* Affective well-being has two separate dimensions: pleasure and arousal. A particular level of pleasure may be accompanied by high or low levels of arousal, and a particular level of arousal may be either pleasurable or unpleasurable. Figure 11–1 portrays this two-dimensional model of affective well-being. A feeling of affective well-being derives from both dimensions. For example, "depressed" feelings are characterized by low status on each dimension (located in the bottom left-hand section of Figure 11–1), and "anxious" may be described as low status on pleasure and high status on arousal (in the top left-hand section). The highest levels of affective well-being are associated with the top right-hand section, reflecting high pleasure and high arousal. Terms such as "happy" and "full of energy" (from Figure 11–1) are indicative of high status on these two dimensions. In general, a person's affective well-being can be described in terms of the proportion of time spent in each of the four sections of Figure 11–1.

2. *Competence.* Good mental health is viewed partly in terms of acceptable degrees of success or competence in different spheres of activity, such as interpersonal relationships, problem solving, paid employment, and so on. The competent person has adequate psychological resources to deal with life's pressures. It has been suggested that good mental health becomes apparent only when a person

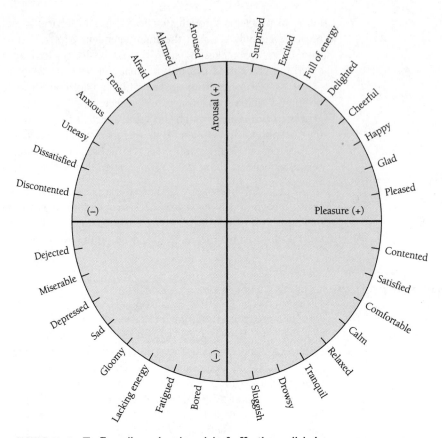

FIGURE 11–1 ■ **Two-dimensional model of affective well-being**

SOURCE: From *Work, Unemployment, and Mental Health* by P. B. Warr, 1987, Oxford: Clarendon. Reprinted by permission.

faces adversity. A successful response to pressures requires having appropriate cognitive and psychomotor skills, as well as beliefs and opinions that are consistent with reality.

3. *Autonomy.* Autonomy refers to a person's ability to resist environmental influences and to determine his or her own opinions and actions. The tendency to strive for independence and self-regulation is a fundamental characteristic of a mentally healthy person. Autonomy is the tendency to feel and act on the assumption that one is influential rather than helpless in the face of life's difficulties. The contribution of autonomy to mental health appears to be given greater importance in Western than in Eastern societies.

4. *Aspiration.* The mentally healthy person is viewed as someone who engages with the environment. He or she establishes goals and makes active efforts to attain them. A raised aspiration level is reflected in high motivation, alertness to new opportunities, and a commitment to meet personal challenges. Conversely, low levels of aspiration are exhibited in reduced activity and an acceptance of the present state no matter how unsatisfactory it appears. In striving to achieve personal goals,

one may face stressful situations, and indeed one may create them by pursuing difficult challenges. The importance of a raised aspiration level to good mental health is particularly clear in circumstances adverse to the individual, where the desire for change is likely to be viewed as central to a healthy response.

5. *Integrated functioning.* The final component of mental health is the most difficult to define and is most unlike the other four. Integrated functioning refers to the person as a whole. People who are psychologically healthy exhibit balance, harmony, and inner relatedness. Consider Freud's statement about love and work: It has been suggested that the healthy person is someone who can balance the importance of the two areas. Integrated functioning may also be considered across time, typically as a balance between accepted strain during difficult phases of goal attainment and relaxation during the intervening periods.

Warr's (1987) portrayal of mental health represents a comprehensive assessment of the major dimensions of psychological well-being. Competence, autonomy, and aspiration reflect aspects of a person's behavior in relation to the environment and often determine a person's affective well-being. For example, an inability to cope with current difficulties (a form of low competence) may give rise to distress (an aspect of low affective well-being). Affective well-being has its roots in medical criteria; the person reports feeling well and also not being impaired psychologically or physically. Integrated functioning, however, deals with the multiple relationships among the four components and covers broader issues. One of the biggest threats to our mental health from an I/O psychology perspective pertains to work stress. The next section of this chapter will address what we have come to learn about work stress and how it affects us.

WORK STRESS

work stress
the response to stimuli that are present on the job that lead to negative consequences, physical or psychological, to the people who are exposed to them

Psychological disorders in the workplace have been identified among the ten leading work-related diseases and injuries in the United States (National Institute for Occupational Safety and Health, 1988). Ilgen (1990) stated, "The health of the work force is one of the most significant issues of our time" (p. 273). Recognition of the psychosocial risk of work has prompted research on medical, psychological, and behavioral stress. Pelletier (1977) reported that stress and psychosocial factors play a far more central role in chronic disorders than they do in acute and infectious diseases. As a consequence, both employees and organizations have become increasingly aware of the negative effects of work-related stress. A nationwide survey by the Northwestern National Life Insurance Company (1991) showed that nearly 46% of American workers felt that their jobs were very or somewhat stressful, whereas nearly 27% reported that their jobs were the single greatest source of stress in their lives. Almost 72% of those surveyed experienced frequent stress-related physical and mental problems.

A large amount of research has been conducted across many disciplines on **work stress.** Research has examined the causes, symptoms, and consequences of work stress, as well as interventions designed to reduce its effect on individuals. Furthermore, there is no agreed-upon definition of stress or how to conceptualize it. For example, not all work demands on individuals are undesirable. If they were, the preferred state of the individual would be inactivity, which we know to be untrue. People seek activity, including the kinds of activities that use abilities they value. However, some activities or situations produce undesirable effects, such as emotional tensions, physical symptoms like sleep disorders, and decrements in job performance. Selye (1982) sought to distinguish "good stress" from "bad stress" by referring to them as "eustress" and "distress," respectively. The focus here will be primarily on distress as we seek to understand its negative effect on individuals.

A Model of Stress

Because of the many issues related to stress, researchers have proposed conceptual models of stress designed to integrate a diverse array of research findings. Many such models have been developed. A most useful model of stress in organizations has been developed by Kahn and Byosiere (1992), which will guide our discussion. The model presented in Figure 11–2 conceptualizes stress in organizations in terms of seven major categories. It should also be noted there are numerous linkages among the categories. This reflects one of the primary research findings about stress: There are complex associations among the antecedents of stress, individual

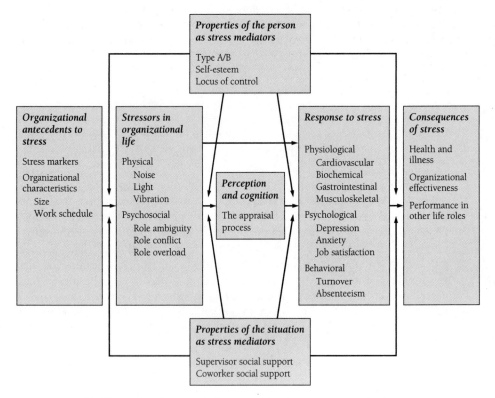

FIGURE 11–2 ■ Theoretical framework for the study of stress in organizations

SOURCE: Adapted from "Stress in Organizations" by R. L. Kahn and P. B. Byosiere, 1992, in *Handbook of Industrial/Organizational Psychology,* 2nd ed., Vol. 2 (p. 592), edited by M. D. Dunnette and L. M. Hough, Palo Alto, CA: Consulting Psychologists Press.

differences in how people respond to stress, and the consequences of stress. A causal sequence is hypothesized to exist among these categories. Each of the seven categories presented in the model will be examined along with findings pertaining to the prevention of stress.

Organizational Antecedents to Stress.   Research on the organizational antecedents to stress is generally directed toward understanding how broad-based and abstract factors induce stress. Brenner and Mooney (1983), for example, examined the relationship between economic conditions (such as economic growth, instability, and unemployment levels) and social indicators of health (such as diseases and death). The variables were examined in what are referred to as "lagged relationships"; that is, changes in economic conditions produce changes in health several years later. The authors examined the relationship between economic change and mortality in nine countries: Australia, Canada, England, Denmark, Finland, France, Germany, Sweden, and the United States. Unemployment and business failures predicted death from heart disease in eight of the nine countries, with a one-year to four-year lag, with controls for such variables as alcohol consumption. Kivimaki et al. (1997) reported on the worklives of employees in Finland when the national unemployment rate reached 18%. The loss of control in their lives (caused by the economy) added to psychosocial illnesses, which resulted in marked increases in absence.

Cobb and Kasl (1977) conducted a longitudinal study on U.S. plant closings for the purpose of understanding the relationship between impending job loss and health. Workers in plants that did not close were compared with workers in plants that were marked for closing. Five waves of data were collected over a two-year period, spanning the sequence of events from rumor to actual job loss and (in most cases) reemployment. Psychological measures of health were collected along with self-reported information. The results showed that the threat of unemployment triggered some physiological changes long before actual job loss occurred and that most physical indicators returned to normal after new job stability was attained. For most people involuntary loss of a job was an event that generated stress, both directly and indirectly.

Stressors in Organizational Life.   The term *stressors* designates stimuli that are generated on the job and have negative consequences, physical or psychological, for significant proportions of people exposed to them. Stress manifests itself

CNN video

Special clothing is needed for working under extremely cold conditions.

SOURCE: CNN

in many forms and is endemic to organizational life. Parker and Sprigg (1999) stated, "The paradox of modern organizations is that people have the opportunity for personal growth, skill development, and connectedness to others, but they also confront a lack of security, ambiguity, competing demands, and unrelenting work pressure" (p. 925). Kahn and Byosiere (1992) reduced the stressors to two major types. The first, *task content,* includes such dimensions as simplicity–complexity and monotony– variety (see Field Note 2). The second, *role properties,* refers

FIELD NOTE 2   Just Waiting Can Be Stressful

 obs that require sustained vigilance have been found to produce marked stress. Research on firefighters indicates that one of their major sources of stress is not responding to fire calls but waiting for a call to come in. The tension and anxiety associated with waiting to use their skills are often far more stress-inducing than responding to hazardous situations. A metropolitan fire department may get several calls per day, usually representing nonthreatening or mildly threatening situations, but occasionally involving large fires or hazardous materials. It is the continuous stream of relatively "minor" incidents that breaks the tedium associated with vigilance and reduces the level of job stress.

Fire departments located at major airports (both commercial and military) face a somewhat different situation than their urban counterparts. Firefighters who work at airports may go several weeks without responding to any incident, but when an incident occurs it is invariably more threatening than rescuing a cat from a tree. Some military planes contain armaments that could explode in the event of a fire or crash landing. The potential loss of life in a commercial airline accident can be very high. When not responding to such potentially perilous situations, airport firefighters endure the stress of waiting for something dramatic to happen. The Greek writer Homer presaged airport firefighters as those who live "between Scylla and Charybdis"—two equally perilous alternatives, neither of which can be avoided without encountering and probably falling victim to the other.

---

to the social aspects of the job and includes supervisory relationships and role conflict.

Research findings have demonstrated relationships between ill health (most notably heart disease) and jobs that are characterized by highly repetitive, monotonous work and sustained vigilance. Shift work also produces stress, which will be discussed later in this chapter. Ill health has been associated with working in air-conditioned offices, a phenomenon referred to as the "sick building syndrome." Hedge, Erickson, and Rubin (1992) reported that sick building syndrome produces the following symptoms: sensory irritation; skin irritation; neurotoxic effects such as headaches, nausea, and drowsiness; and hyperactivity reactions such as runny eyes, runny nose, and asthma-like symptoms. Research has demonstrated that sick building syndrome is not caused solely by indoor pollutants but may be related to the electromagnetic fields from video display terminals, which attract irritating fibers and particles to the screens. The syndrome may be related to respiratory ailments associated with recirculated air. There is a growing body of research (e.g., Soine, 1995; Stenberg & Wall, 1995) that suggests women are more susceptible than men to sick building syndrome. Other research (Hoffman, 1997) has examined the workplace stress associated with HIV disease on infected individuals, coworkers, and members of the caregiving occupations (e.g., medical personnel and counselors).

However, it is with regard to role properties that most organizational stressors have been identified. **Role conflict** refers to perceptual differences regarding the content of a person's role or the relative importance of its elements. Such differences occur between the individual and other people in a work group who do not hold the same role expectations. Role conflict generates negative affect, tension, and

role conflict
the product of perceptual differences regarding the content of a person's role or the relative importance of its elements

often physical symptoms on the part of the focal person. Conflict among the demands of different roles filled by the same individual can also occur. Such conflicts have been reported most often in occupations such as military service, police work, and teaching, where the compartmentalization of time between work and family cannot be easily or dependably arranged. **Role overload** is a variant of role conflict in which conflict is experienced as a necessity to compromise either quantity, time schedule, or quality. For example, consider a supervisor who says to an employee, "I want this report finished by tomorrow and I want it done well." There is conflict between the time deadline and the request for high-quality work. Findings from many studies reveal that overloaded individuals describe their work demands as excessive and their reactions as negative.

role overload
the conflict experienced in a role as a necessity to compromise either the quantity or quality of performance

Schaubroeck, Lam, and Xie (2000) conducted a cross-cultural study of bank tellers who were given more control over how to conduct their jobs. The authors found that increasing job control (i.e., giving the tellers more administrative responsibility) may actually be more disturbing when the worker does not believe that he or she can use the greater control effectively. This finding was observed in both U.S. and Asian cultures.

Perception and Cognition: The Appraisal Process.   The appraisal process seeks to explain that different people react differently to stressors that are objectively the same. Furthermore, the stressors encountered within organizations are often embedded in complex situations. Successful coping requires one to analyze both positive and negative features and to decide upon a course of action. Researchers have examined the stages through which individuals perceive and evaluate situations in assessing stress. Lazarus and Folkman (1984) proposed primary and secondary appraisal processes based on a temporal sequence. *Primary appraisal* consists of the initial determination that a stimulus (person, event, situation) is positive (benign), negative (stressful), or neither (irrelevant) in its implications for well-being. *Secondary appraisal* is a judgment about what can be done to minimize damage or maximize gain. The appraisal process may be cyclical as the individual takes into account a previous coping strategy or some new information.

The importance of the appraisal process as a predictor of stress outcomes is well illustrated by a study of patients who had undergone surgery for breast cancer (Vinokur, Threatt, Vinokur-Caplan, & Satariano, 1990). Neither the objective stage of the disease nor the extent of surgery predicted the person's appraisal of threat, but that appraisal was a major predictor of subsequent anxiety and depression. Other studies as well have indicated that appraisal plays a similar important role in predicting the outcome of job-generated stress.

Response to Stress.   Researchers have identified three major categories of possible responses to stress: physiological, psychological, and behavioral. *Physiological responses* include cardiovascular symptoms such as increased blood pressure and cholesterol level, biochemical measures such as catecholamines and uric acid (both associated with the cause of diseases and disorders), and gastrointestinal symptoms such as peptic ulcers. Faster heart rates have been reported under conditions of role conflict, ambiguity regarding future developments on the job, and overall reported stress at work. Levels of catecholamines change very rapidly and respond to a variety of stimuli. Unpredictability at work, loss of control over pace and method, and distracting noise have all been associated with increased levels of catecholamines. Air traffic controllers, for example, show significant associations between daily levels of cortisol secretion and work variables such as load and pace. Research on gastrointestinal symptoms has shown less consistent results compared with the other two types of physiological response.

Psychological responses to stress at work most typically involve affective variables, with job dissatisfaction being most common. Stress has also been found to influence more intense and aroused affective states such as anger, frustration, hostility, and irritation. More passive, but perhaps no less negative responses include boredom, burnout, fatigue, and depressed mood. The psychological effects of work-related stress have been found to produce lowered self-confidence and self-esteem. Kets de Vries (1999) proposed that work-induced stress can produce a condition in which individuals experience very little (or a total absence of) pleasure. Instead, there is a feeling of emotional numbness. Kets de Vries refers to such individuals as "organizational sleepwalkers."

Behavioral responses to stress at work have not been studied as much as psychological responses. However, five broad categories of behavioral responses have been examined: the work role (job performance, accidents, drug use at work), antisocial behavior at work (theft, purposeful damage), flight from the job (absenteeism, turnover), degradation of other life roles (spouse and child abuse), and self-damaging behaviors (alcohol and drug abuse). Some of the findings have not been studied extensively (such as drug use at work) and may be underreported for reasons of social acceptability or the avoidance of punishment. Dompierre and Lavoie (1994) reflected on the methodological and ethical difficulties of conducting research on work stress and family violence. Nevertheless, the research results indicate that work-generated stressors have behavioral effects that are manifested both on the job and away from it, and they impose substantial costs on organizations.

Consequences of Stress.   The consequences of stress typically affect the performance of the individual on the job and in other life roles. Other ramifications involve the health of the individual, as affected by prolonged exposure to physical stressors and through responses to recurrent psychological stressors. Researchers (Alfredsson & Theorell, 1983) in Sweden, for example, developed standardized measures of job characteristics for 118 occupational groups on a nationwide basis. Men in jobs characterized by high demand and low control (low autonomy) were at twice the risk for heart attacks compared with men in the same age range (40–54) employed in all other occupations. The authors concluded that the next step is to conduct field experiments and interventions to discover ways of reducing such sources of stress.

It is also highly plausible that nonwork stresses can affect attitudes and behavior at work. Research findings suggest such relationships are particularly evident for single-parent families and families in which both parents are employed. Research is also being conducted that shows the combined effects of work and nonwork stressors on health. Frankenhaeuser (1988), for example, showed that the characteristic elevation of catecholamine levels as the stresses of the workday accumulate is sharply reduced at the end of the workday for men, but for married, employed women the elevation persists until the household responsibilities are also fulfilled. Lowman (1996) presented a classification of mental disorders that are specifically work related (i.e., not general mental disorders that carry over to the workplace). The classification includes patterns of undercommitment (underachievement and procrastination), patterns of overcommitment (obsessive-compulsive addiction to the workplace), anxiety in the work role, and work-related depression.

Properties of the Person As Stress Mediators. Individual differences in resistance to stress have long been recognized. Two personality characteristics have been clearly identified as moderating the effects of stress. The first is *personality type.* **Type A** is a personality type that intensifies the effects of job stressors. Type A people walk, eat, and talk rapidly; they are aggressive and competitive and constantly feel under time pressure. **Type B** people are less concerned about time; they play for fun, not to win; and they can relax without guilt. Type A people have a higher standing pulse rate than Type B people and are twice as likely to develop heart disease. Barling and Boswell (1995) identified an irritability dimension to Type A behavior that adversely affects health and concentration. Wright (1988) concluded that Type A people have a high, possibly insatiable need for achievement. They experience early (no later than adolescence) success, which seems to breed a greater than usual sense of hope that striving efforts will eventually pay off. Type A individuals cannot control themselves when exposed to work-related stimuli. In assessing the proclivity of Type A individuals to feel stress from work, Wright said, "What is needed are ways of training ourselves and others to maintain diligence with pacing—that is, to run the race of life like a marathon and not a series of 100-yard dashes" (p. 13).

The second personality characteristic that moderates stress is **locus of control.** Locus of control differentiates people who believe that they themselves are primarily responsible for what happens to them from those who believe that major events in their lives are determined mainly by other people or forces beyond themselves. People whose locus of control is primarily internal respond to stress differently from those whose locus of control is external. Those who are internally oriented are more likely to take action against the source of the stress itself or to mitigate its effects in other ways. Those who are externally oriented are more likely to see effective actions as beyond their powers and thus endure rather than act. Some researchers have also identified a personality construct associated with the capacity to endure negative life events, including job stress. This personality construct has been called ego resilience or hardiness (Kinicki, McKee, & Wade, 1996).

Properties of the Situation As Stress Moderators. In addition to certain characteristics of individuals, certain properties of situations can moderate or buffer the effects of a stressor. The buffering effect reduces the tendency of organizational properties to generate specific stressors, alter the perceptions and cognitions evoked by such stressors, moderate the responses that follow the appraisal process, or reduce the health-damaging consequences of such responses. The primary variable hypothesized to provide this buffering effect is social support. Social

Type A
a personality construct that describes individuals who tend to be aggressive and competitive and feel under chronic time pressures

Type B
a personality construct that describes individuals who tend not to be competitive, intense, or feel under chronic time pressures

locus of control
a personality construct relating to the perceived cause or locus of control for events in one's life, being either internal or external

support reduces the relationship between various job stressors and indicators of mental and physical health (anxiety, depression, and irritation). Social support does not reduce the relationship between job stressors and boredom or job dissatisfaction. Sutton and Kahn (1987) proposed three other situational variables as potential buffers against stress: (1) the extent to which the onset of a stressor is predictable, (2) the extent to which it is understandable, and (3) the extent to which aspects of the stressor are controllable by the person who must experience it. Of these three proposed relationships, the strongest support has emerged for the predictability of a stressor. If the occurrence of a stressful event can be predicted, its absence can also be predicted. Thus, the individual knows when it is safe to relax and need not maintain a constant state of vigilance or anxiety.

Prevention and Intervention

This final category is not part of the model of organizational stress proposed by Kahn and Byosiere (1992), but it does represent a major professional activity in stress management. For the most part stress management has been concerned more with reducing the effects of stress than reducing the presence of stressors at work. As a consequence, the major effort has been directed at increasing individual resistance to stressors generated at work.

Stress management initiatives that are directed at *preventing* stress include onsite physical fitness, exercise, meditation, and time management programs. Ross and Altmaier (1994) reported a growing use of techniques designed to lower arousal to stressors, such as deep breathing, progressive muscle relaxation, biofeedback, and yoga. Stress *intervention* initiatives most typically involve counseling, social support groups, and employee assistance programs.

In general both the quality and quantity of research on the effectiveness of stress management programs fall short of research on other aspects of stress. Nevertheless, there are indications that stress management programs are successful. Those programs that have been rigorously evaluated show significant reductions in subjective work stress and psychophysiological indicators. Their effects on job satisfaction and performance are less clear. Without any question one of the biggest sources of stress in our lives is trying to balance work and family issues. The subject of **work/family conflict** will be discussed next.

work/family conflict
the dilemma of trying to balance the conflicting demands of work and family responsibilities

WORK/FAMILY CONFLICT

As Thomas and Ganster (1995) described, over the past two decades the American family has undergone significant structural and functional changes. These changes have not been accompanied by equally dramatic shifts in organizational policies. Although there are still families in which the father works outside the home while the mother stays home to care for the house and children, many companies continue to be guided by traditional workplace policies that were fashioned when that was the predominant pattern. Today's diverse workplace is increasingly populated with women, single parents, and dual-career couples. The potential for conflict and stress increases as most workers struggle with the demands of balancing paid employment and home responsibilities. A graphic representation of the critical issues associated with changing social conditions and work experiences is presented in Figure 11–3 (Barling & Sorenson, 1997).

Interest in family-related issues by I/O psychologists is relatively new, manifesting itself primarily in the past 15 years. For many years we tended to limit our focus to work-related issues (e.g., tasks, jobs, occupations, organizations) and left the subject of domestic matters (e.g., family) to other areas of professional study. However, I/O psychologists began to see legitimate linkages or connections between the two spheres of work and family and thus have expanded our areas of inquiry. It is also a topic of interest internationally. Watanabe, Takahashi, and Minami (1997) discussed how Japanese families deal with work/family conflict. The following description was offered by a 35-year-old man:

> I am responsible for supporting my family. I leave home early in the morning and usually don't return until my kids are asleep. There is just no time for me to be with my kids. My only free time is on Sundays, but even then I may go play golf with my clients or colleagues. But you know, I don't do this for my own pleasure, but for my family. I think they [my wife and children] are grateful for the kind of life I am providing. Although I spend little time with my kids, I basically trust my wife when it comes to raising and educating them. (pp. 280–281)

The authors reported that the Japanese culture is finding it difficult to depart from the traditional view of men as the primary breadwinners while women stay home

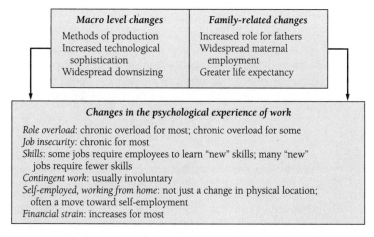

FIGURE 11–3 ■ **Effects of social change on the experience of work**

SOURCE: From "Work and Family: In Search of a Relevant Research Agenda" by J. Barling and D. Sorenson, 1997, in *Creating Tomorrow's Organizations* (pp. 157–170), edited by C. L. Cooper and S. E. Jackson, New York: Wiley.

DILBERT   by Scott Adams

SOURCE: Dilbert® reprinted by permsission of United Feature Syndicate, Inc.

and raise children. However, they believe some Japanese families are moving away from the strict separation of male and female work/family roles.

Zedeck (1992) described the following three topics as targets of research in work/family conflict:

- *The effect of work on family.* This area examines what impact work factors have on family matters. To express this relationship in terms of research design, *work* is regarded as the independent variable and *family* is the dependent variable. This perspective is most typical of I/O psychological research. A common finding is that aspects of work (such as job stress and work schedules) have negative effects on families.

- *The effect of family on work.* This perspective is the opposite of the former and generally focuses on how structural or developmental aspects of the family have an impact on work behavior. For example, some researchers have viewed family life as a "shock absorber" in that, if home life is positive, it blocks disappointment at work. Others view family responsibility as a major determinant of work absenteeism and tardiness.

- *The family–work interaction.* This third perspective views work and family as interacting and concludes that there is no simple or direct causal link between work and family matters. One view of the family–work interaction concerns the compatibility or incompatibility of family–work relationships and their impact on other processes, such as the transition between roles.

Regardless of which of these three perspectives is emphasized, researchers have offered conceptual models to explain the relationship between work and family. Three basic models have been proposed, and they represent different perspectives on how we fill both work and family roles.

- *Spillover model.* The spillover model asserts that there is *similarity* between what occurs in the work environment and what occurs in the family environment. It also proposes that a person's work experiences influence what he or she does away from work. It is assumed that attitudes at work become ingrained and carried over into home life, affecting a basic orientation toward the self and family members. In general, spillover is a notion of positive relationships between work and family variables such that an individual's satisfaction with work enhances family life.

▪ *Compensation model.* The compensation model is most often contrasted with the spillover model. It proposes an *inverse* relationship between work and family. It further assumes that individuals make differential investments of themselves in the two settings so that what is provided by one makes up for what is missing in the other. Thus, deprivations experienced in work are made up or compensated for in nonwork activities.

▪ *Segmentation model.* The segmentation model proposes that the work and nonwork spheres are *distinct* so that an individual can be successful in one without any influence on the other. The two spheres exist side by side and for all practical purposes are separated from each other. This separation, in type, space, or function, allows one to effectively compartmentalize one's life. The dominant view is that the family is the realm of intimacy and empathy, whereas the work world is impersonal and instrumental.

Barling (1990) observed a historical trend in when each of these three models was proposed. Barling concluded: (1) the suggestion that work and family affect each other had emerged by the 1930s; (2) the pervasive assumption during the 1950s was that work and family are independent; (3) by the 1970s the assumption was that work and family roles were intertwined; and (4) today there is considerable empirical evidence attesting to the overlap between work and family for most individuals.

Empirical tests of the three models have generally revealed some support for each. Zedeck (1992) suggested the models need additional refinement and clarity to effectively assess their veracity. Among the unspecified questions underlying the models are these:

▪ Can more than one explanatory model be appropriate for the same individual? That is, can there be spillover for some aspects of the employing organization or family but compensation for others?
▪ If more than one model is applicable to an individual, can the models function simultaneously, or must they be sequential? That is, before there is compensation for some factors, do other factors need to have been spilled over?
▪ Do the models hold at different times or stages for individuals? Both work and family activities develop over time and pass through stages, such as initiation and maturity. What happens to the relationship between work and family if the stages of each are (or are not) synchronized?

Zedeck (1992) believes that reactions to work and nonwork are not totally stable but vary over time and conditions. Furthermore, the relationship is not the same across families. Friedman, Tucker, Neville, and Imperial (1996) offered this description of how the effects of domestic violence do not stay at home: "The battered woman who receives threatening calls or visits by her abuser at work, or who is suffering from the mental and physical bruises of the night before, is likely to have difficulty fulfilling her employer's expectations" (p. 153). There also appear to be meaningful differences between men and women in the effect of work/family conflict on job and life satisfaction. Kossek and Ozeki (1998) reported a stronger correlation between work/family conflict and job satisfaction for women (−.35) than for men (−.29). Likewise, the correlation between work/family conflict and life satisfaction was stronger for women (−.42) than for men (−.32). Thus, women have a greater association than men in resolving issues of work/family conflict and feeling satisfaction. Finally, based on a broad national survey of employees, Frone (2000) reported that employees who experienced work/family conflict were up to 30 times more likely to experience a clinically significant mental health problem than were employees who reported no work/family conflict.

Friedman and Galinsky (1992) noted some of the major changes in the labor force and how organizational efforts have had to change to recruit and retain a productive workforce. By 2000 about two-thirds of the new entrants into the workforce were women, and about three-fourths of them are projected to become pregnant at some time during their working years. More than half of these women return to work before their child's first birthday. An estimated 20% of workers—mostly women—will be responsible for their aging parents. While women still perform most family tasks, 60% of men have wives who work.

The pressures of work and family are accelerating, and families, which already have borne the greater burden of conflicts experienced between home and work, can do little more to sustain the balance. Changes in the social pattern of worker participation have forced companies to make accommodations to their workers. These accommodations are directed toward reducing the conflict between home and family, which if unattended to, ultimately lead to lower efficiency in the work-place. Such inefficiency would be caused by more tardiness, absenteeism, turn-over, and stress-related decrements in job performance.

On-site or near-site child-care centers have been developed to reduce home/family conflict. Companies may develop such centers exclusively for their own employees or in a consortium with other employers for use by several participating companies. There are approximately 1,400 on-site or near-site child-care centers sponsored by employers in the United States. While their number is growing, many companies are too small to have the resources to provide such a center.

Another type of assistance to employees is family leave. In 1993 President Clinton signed into law the Family and Medical Leave Act, whereby employees can withdraw from the workforce to attend to family needs without risking the loss of their jobs. The law gives workers up to 12 weeks of unpaid leave each year for the birth, adoption, or foster care of a child; care for a spouse, parent, or child with a serious health condition; or the employee's own serious health condition. The law is designed to be of particular value to parents of newborn children. Research has shown that the single most important predictor of job retention following child-birth is the availability of job-guaranteed maternity leave. One company with an excellent leave policy found that only 5% of new mothers did not return to their jobs. Grover and Crooker (1995) reported from a national survey of workers that in organizations that offered family-responsive human resource policies such as child-care assistance, employees showed significantly higher organizational commitment and expressed less intention to quit their jobs. The same findings were evidenced for employees *without* children, which the authors interpreted as supporting the theory that offering assistance to employees in need symbolizes concern for employees and positively influences attachment to the organization.

While only a few hundred companies have responded to the elder-care needs of their employees, the number is likely to grow dramatically in the future. Caring for elderly relatives may be more complex than child care because it involves the coordination of a variety of social services, such as transportation, medical, legal, housekeeping, and personal services. Most of the companies that respond to employees' elder-care needs provide information and counseling about the array of available services. Some companies coordinate such services.

DUAL-CAREER FAMILIES

dual-career families families characterized by each adult having his or her own individual career and trying to collectively balance their respective careers

Balancing the demands of work and family can be an arduous task. Issues of adjustment can be further compounded in **dual-career families.** Oakley (1974) estimated that mothers with young children work an average of 77 hours per week in the home. Adding a career to that workload can create extraordinary pressures on both women and men to have fulfilling work and home lives.

Silberstein (1992) concluded that most dual-career couples have a work-oriented lifestyle prior to the birth of children. However, once there are children, the dual-career system undergoes a profound shift. The pragmatic demands of home life increase dramatically and cannot be postponed, rescheduled, or ignored. Both men and women attest that the arrival of children creates the greatest conflict between work and family. For the majority of both men and women, having children translates into fewer hours at work. However, the extent to which this occurs and the meanings of this shift differ for men and women. Karambayya and Reilly (1992), for example, reported that more women than men adjusted their careers to accommodate their families. The felt need to make an accommodation influenced the women's choice of a career (e.g., assuring a flexible schedule) or a work site. However, many women reported that their work environments were not willing or able to bend to the demands of family. Additionally, some women have described hostile reactions from work colleagues to pregnancies.

Men, on the other hand, tend to differentiate their feelings of conflict over family and career from their wives' feelings. This difference between husbands and wives stems from expectations in men that work is primarily for men and family is primarily for women. Silberstein (1992) offered the following statement from a man in his mid-30s:

> I have the suspicion that it's more difficult for a woman. If you're a traditional, career-oriented man, you're supposed to spend a lot of time in the office, and bring work home, and commute long distances. And the man has less time for the family, which is not a good thing, but that's how it is traditionally. Whereas for a woman, there's always the other side of the mirror, which is the woman who is at home, spending hours and hours with her children, and is always there when they need her. And that imposes some degree of guilt on a woman who is successful in her career. (p. 100)

Silberstein (1992) reported that the difference in the degree that wives and husbands accommodate their careers for children has become a central marital tension. Differential investment in career and family is the recurrent issue in arguments, and it demands constant renegotiation. In the dual-career marriage, both spouses arrive at their own definition of what is required for work success and what level of involvement in the family feels right. Each partner, therefore, argues from personal experience about the appropriate balance of work and family, whereas in the one-career marriage, the spheres of wife and husband are less comparable.

Dual-career couples often cite a lack of temporal control over their lives. There appears to be insufficient time to fulfill the obligations of both work and family. The creation of time schedules to coordinate activities can be facilitative, but adherence to the schedules can be a source of tension in itself. Other time-related issues pertain to the lack of personal time for individual activity (such as recreation or leisure) and coordinated social activities. Time constraints are also associated with reformulating role activities in the marriage, such as the division of domestic labor. The lack of time contributes to a couple's decision to seek external support services such as child care and assistance with household chores.

In examining the benefits and costs of dual-career marriages, Silberstein (1992) reported that most marriages are aided by the self-fulfillment each spouse derives from the pursuit of a career. Each spouse experiences an independent source of self-esteem, and the couple benefits from the combined stimulation of each partner's work life. Both partners are also likely to feel that each is contributing in a similar fashion to the welfare of the marriage. However, the costs of dual careers are also considerable, with most sacrifices associated with losses of time and energy. In particular, dual-career couples are likely to save the least amount of time and energy for their own personal relationship, after attending to the demands of work, children, and the managerial aspects of domestic life. This sentiment was expressed by a woman in her early 40s:

> I hesitate to use the analogy, but right now I feel we are more business partners than husband and wife. It's like we operate this small corporation together, but the intimate aspect is somewhat lacking. (Silberstein, 1992, p. 147)

Stress from work can also originate from the schedules we must follow on our jobs. The next section will examine what I/O psychologists have learned about how work schedules influence our attitudes and behaviors.

WORK SCHEDULES

Shift Work

Not all employees work from 8:00 A.M. to 5:00 P.M., Monday through Friday. The nature of the services performed may necessitate other schedules. Police officers, firefighters, and telephone operators provide 24-hour-a-day service. In industrial manufacturing, some technology requires constant monitoring and operation. It isn't practical to shut off furnaces, boilers, and chemical process operations at 5:00 P.M. just because workers go home. In those cases it is advantageous to have

shift work
the period of time a person must perform his or her job; usually an 8-hour period

different shifts work around the clock. About 25% of all working hours in the United States are estimated to be "nontraditional." Psychologists have become interested in how different hours (or **shift work**) affect occupational health.

There are no uniform shift-work hours; companies use different shifts. Usually a 24-hour day is divided into three 8-hour work shifts, like 7:00 A.M.–3:00 P.M.

(day shift), 3:00 P.M.–11:00 P.M. (swing or afternoon shift), and 11:00 P.M.–7:00 A.M. (night shift). Some companies have employees work just one shift, but workers generally don't like the swing and night shifts, so many firms rotate the shifts. Employees may work two weeks on the day shift, two weeks on the swing shift, and then two weeks on the night shift. A shift workweek need not be Monday through Friday. Also, there may be an uneven number of days off between shifts, like two days off after the swing shift and three after the night shift.

Thierry and Meijman (1994) identified the 11 aversive characteristics of shift work that are listed in Table 11–1. The effects are more strongly aversive in some patterns of shift work than in others. Shift workers experience many problems in physiological and social adjustment. Most physiological problems are associated with interruptions of the circadian rhythm; that is, our bodies are "programmed" for a certain time cycle (Aschoff, 1978). Because shift work interrupts the cycle of eating, sleeping, and working, workers often complain of lack of sleep, fatigue, constipation, irritability, and appetite loss. Meers, Maasen, and Verhaagen (1978) reported that the health of a sample of shift workers declined during the first six months of shift work; the decline became more pronounced after four years.

Because most people work during the day and sleep at night, shift workers also have social problems. They often experience difficulties with children, marital relationships, and recreation. Frost and Jamal (1979) reported that shift workers experienced less need fulfillment, were more likely to quit their jobs, and participated in fewer voluntary organizations. Jamal (1981) reported similar findings; workers on fixed work schedules were better off than workers on rotating schedules in terms of mental health, job satisfaction, and social participation.

Shift workers make up a relatively small proportion of the population; they are thus forced to fit their schedules to the rest of society. Dunham (1977) made the interesting point that many social problems would be alleviated by increasing shift work. Society would then make more concessions to the needs of shift workers. Changes might be made in such things as hours of television broadcasting, restaurant service, recreational services, and hours of business operation (banks, supermarkets, gas stations, and the like). In fact, convenience food stores and automated bank machines derive much of their business from employees who work nontraditional hours.

Research indicates that shift work has a strong influence on the lives of people who perform it. As long as certain industries require 24-hour-a-day operations, psychologists will continue searching for ways to improve this particularly difficult person/environment fit. Social problems may be lessened by changing some existing patterns in the community; however, physiological problems will be more difficult to overcome. Monk, Folkard, and Wedderburn (1996) noted that shift workers must face three enduring conditions of *biochronology:* (1) human beings and society are diurnal (awake in the day, asleep in the night), (2) daylight has a cueing effect to initiate wakefulness, and (3) the circadian system is slow to adjust to night work. Any organizational or social policy designed to assist shift workers must address these conditions.

At least one major source of physiological difficulty is the rotation of workers across shifts. If workers were assigned to a fixed shift (day, swing, or night), their behavior would be consistent, which would help them adjust to the circadian

TABLE 11–1   ■   Aversive characteristics of shift work

Characteristic	Definition	Inconveniences
Regularity	Mean number of changes in the starting times of working periods during the week	Unrest, nervous complaints, constipation
Periodicity	Weekly mean of the sum of the accumulated number of successive night shifts plus half of the number of accumulated successive afternoon shifts	Sleeping problems, fatigue, stomach and intestinal complaints
Load per shift	Mean shift length in hours	Fatigue, feelings of overload
Load per week	Mean weekly working time in hours	Fatigue, feelings of overload
Opportunity to rest at night	Mean weekly number of hours off work between 11:00 P.M. and 7:00 A.M.	Sleeping problems, insomnia, fatigue, nervous complaints
Predictability	Cycle time in weeks	Planning/coordination problems
Opportunity for household and family tasks	Weekly mean number of hours off work from Monday through Friday between 7:00 A.M. and 7:00 P.M.	Frustration of partner/ parental role, complaints on limitation of household tasks
Constancy of opportunity for household and family tasks	Variation coefficient of weekly opportunity for household and family tasks	Lack of continuity in partner/parental role and in household tasks
Opportunity for evening recreation	Mean weekly number of hours off work from Monday through Friday between 7:00 P.M. and 11:00 P.M.	Lack of continuity in partner role, limitation of social and recreational activities
Opportunity for weekend recreation	Half of the number of days off work during the weekend per week	Limitation of social and recreational activities
Constancy of opportunity for weekend recreation	Variation coefficient of the number of days off during the weekend per week	Lack of continuity in social and recreational activities

SOURCE: From "Time and Behavior at Work" by H. Thierry and T. Meijman, 1994, in *Handbook of Industrial and Organizational Psychology,* 2nd ed., Vol. 4 (p. 360), edited by H. C. Triandis, M. D. Dunnette, and L. M. Hough, Palo Alto, CA: Consulting Psychologists Press. Reprinted by permission.

rhythm. Some people prefer to work afternoons or nights, so part of the solution may be personnel selection. Workers could choose a shift; if enough workers of the appropriate skill level were placed in the shift of their choice, that would meet both individual and organizational needs. Barton (1994) found that the physical and psychological health of nurses was better when they worked a fixed night shift than when they engaged in night work as part of a rotating-shift schedule. However, fixed shifts are not without their own problems. Bohle and Tulley (1998) found that the night shift was most negatively related to sleep disturbance and work/nonwork conflict. Smith, Reilly, and Midkiff (1989) developed a scale to predict morningness based on circadian rhythms. They concluded that the scale could be used to select workers for the night shift based on their preference for evening activities. Indeed, Jamal and Jamal (1982) found that employees who worked a fixed shift had better mental and physical health than employees on a rotating shift. Using a sample of medical technicians, Blau and Lunz (1999) found that fixed shift day employees experienced a greater variety of work activities and sources of stimulation than did employees on evening, night, or rotating shifts. Rotating shift work seems particularly difficult to adjust to. There is also evidence (Knauth, 1996) that backward rotation (from day to night to afternoon shifts) is more difficult to adjust to than forward rotation (from day to afternoon to night). Totterdell, Spelten, Smith, Barton, and Folkard (1995) reported that nurses felt worse (on such measures as alertness, calmness, and moodiness) on a rest day following a night shift rather than a day shift.

The findings attest to the costs of fatigue and adjustment to and from a nocturnal work routine. In fact, Freese and Okonek (1984) reported that some people who had reached the emotional, mental, and physical breaking point because of rotating shift work were told by their physicians to find jobs with traditional work hours. G. Costa (1996) estimated that 20% of workers have to leave shift work in a short time because of serious disturbances; those remaining show different and varying levels of adaptation and tolerance. Tepas (1993) concluded that organizations should design educational programs for shift workers and their families to better prepare them for the demands imposed by this work schedule. Kogi (1996) proposed that organizations devote substantial resources to occupational health services that support shift workers.

Flexible Working Hours

flextime
a schedule of work hours that permits employees flexibility in when they arrive at and leave work

One variation in work schedules is flexible working hours, popularly known as **flextime**. According to Gottlieb, Kelloway, and Barham (1998), 73% of U.S. employers offer flextime to their workers. The main objective of flextime is to create an alternative to the traditional, fixed working schedule by giving workers some choice in arrival and departure times. The system is usually arranged so that everyone must be present during certain designated hours ("coretime"), but there is latitude in other hours ("flexband"). For example, coretime may be 9:00 A.M. to 3:00 P.M., and flexband may be 6:00 A.M. to 6:00 P.M. Some employees may start working at 9:00 A.M. and work until 6:00 P.M., some may end at 3:00 P.M. by starting at 6:00 A.M.; others work any combination in between. Problems with family commitments, recreation, second jobs, commuting, and stress may be alleviated by flexible working hours. Lateness is virtually eliminated since the workday begins with arrival. Workers can be late only if they arrive after coretime has begun.

In general, the findings on flextime appear quite positive; at least no very adverse effects have yet been reported. The variables examined include satisfaction, productivity, absence, and turnover. Some studies reported more positive results than others. Golembiewski and Proehl (1978) summarized the findings of several studies on flextime; they reported that worker support for adoption or continuation of flextime across nine samples of workers ranged from 80% to 100%. It thus appears that many employees are highly receptive to the idea. Hicks and Klimoski (1981) found that employees did not become more satisfied with their work after flextime was adopted. Nevertheless, they reported other benefits like easier travel and parking, less interrole conflict, more feelings of control in the work setting, and more time for leisure activities.

Narayanan and Nath (1982) examined the impact of flextime at two organizational levels: lower-level and professional employees. They concluded that flextime primarily benefited lower-level employees by giving them more flexibility in their schedules. For professional employees, the flextime system merely formalized the already existing informal system they had with the company. Ralston (1989) found that flextime was especially helpful for working mothers and dual-career couples, two growing segments of the workforce. In a six-year study of flextime, Dalton and Mesch (1990) reported large reductions in employee absenteeism compared with a control group on regular hours. However, the rate of turnover in the two groups was equivalent.

While there is ample evidence that flextime benefits individuals (Gottlieb et al., 1998), it quite possibly could be detrimental to the functioning of teams. If employees must work as a team, the individualized schedules that flextime permits may limit the continuity of the team. However, we need additional research to address this issue. For the present, flextime appears to be highly beneficial in accommodating the scheduling needs of individual employees.

Compressed Workweek

compressed workweek
a schedule of work hours that typically involves more hours per day and fewer days per week

Employees traditionally have worked 8 hours a day, five days a week, for a 40-hour workweek. Some employees work 10 hours a day for four days, however, popularly known as the "4/40." Gottlieb et al. (1998) reported that 21% of U.S. employers have **compressed workweeks**.

There are several obvious advantages to a compressed workweek for both the individual and the organization. Individuals have a three-day weekend, which gives them more recreation time, the chance to work a second job, more time for family life, and so on. Organizations have fewer overhead costs because they are open one day less per week. However, the possible drawbacks include worker fatigue, fewer productive hours, and more accidents.

In a major review of 4/40, Ronen and Primps (1981) reached some conclusions based on many studies. It has a positive effect on home and family life as well as on leisure and recreation. There appears to be no change in employee job performance, however. Finally, there are mixed results with regard to absenteeism, but worker fatigue definitely increases. A few studies have been reported on reactions to a 12-hour shift, typically noon to midnight and then midnight to noon. The results are mixed. Breaugh (1983) reported that nurses on 12-hour shifts experienced substantial fatigue associated with the longer hours. However, the midnight-to-noon shift felt more out of phase with physiological and social rhythms than did the noon-to-midnight shift. Pierce and Dunham (1992) reported significant improvements in work schedule attitudes, general affect, and fatigue in a sample of police officers who switched from a rotating 8-hour shift work schedule to a fixed 12-hour schedule. Duchon, Keran, and Smith (1994) examined underground miners who switched from an 8-hour to a 12-hour schedule. The miners reported improved sleep quality with the new schedule, while fatigue had either no change or slight improvement. The findings from such studies may be influenced by the variety of jobs examined in the research.

Conversion to a compressed workweek is not simply a matter of worker preference. Organizations are limited in altering their work schedules by the services they provide and other factors. For example, a compressed workweek is not viable if customer service must be provided five days a week. The success of organizations that provide services depends partially on accessibility. Dunham, Pierce, and Castaneda (1987) cautioned against blanket support for the 4/40; its success depends on the type of organization and the people in it. Baltes et al. (1999) concluded on the basis of a meta-analysis that there are mixed effects of the compressed workweek related to the specific outcome criterion in question. For example, compressed workweeks seem to increase job satisfaction, but they do not lead to reductions in absences.

ALCOHOLISM AND DRUG ABUSE IN THE WORKPLACE

Alcoholism and drug abuse are global problems that affect all arenas of life. Moore (1994) offered this concise statement: "Alcohol and work. This has always been an uneasy relationship. Genius may be fired by wine. More commonplace talent is often fired because of it" (p. 75). Due to the sensitivity and confidentiality of substance abuse, we do not have a very strong research foundation on which to base our knowledge. That is, it is difficult to collect reliable and valid data on substance abuse, given the delicacy of the issue. What follows is a brief overview of some of the major dimensions of this complex social problem.

substance abuse
the ingestion of a broad array of substances (such as alcohol, tobacco, or drugs) that are deemed to have a harmful effect on the individual

The term **substance abuse** covers a broad array of substances but usually includes alcohol, prescription drugs, and illegal drugs. Some people include tobacco (both smoking and chewing). Most of our knowledge is limited to alcoholism and illegal drugs. It has been estimated that there are over 10 million alcoholic American workers. Tyson and Vaughn (1987) reported that approximately two-thirds of the people entering the workforce have used illegal drugs. Four to 5 million people in the United States use cocaine monthly. The frequency of marijuana use is much higher (Schwenk, 1999). Every year $50 billion is spent on cocaine in the United States—the same amount that companies spend annually on substance abuse programs for their employees. The Americans with Disabilities Act (ADA) regards former drug use as a disability and thus provides legal protection to former drug users. However, current drug users are not covered by the law. By any reasonable standard, substance abuse is a major problem in industry today. Furthermore, substance abuse has long-term negative relationships to work adjustment, both as a cause and as an effect. Galaif, Newcomb, and Carmona (2001) conducted a longitudinal study of polydrug use (alcohol, marijuana, and cocaine). They found that polydrug use predicted lower job satisfaction four years later, and that job instability (i.e., being fired or laid off) predicted subsequent substance abuse.

Although I/O psychologists may approach the topic of substance abuse from several perspectives, a primary area of concern is performance impairment—that is, the extent to which substance abuse contributes to lower job performance. Experts in employee assistance programs estimate that as much as 50% of absenteeism and on-the-job accidents are related to drugs and alcohol use. Drug addiction also contributes to employee theft to support a habit. Thus, we have some knowledge about how substance abuse affects the more global performance criteria of absence, accidents, and theft. Our knowledge of the effects of substance abuse on skill decay is more tentative. Much of what we know is based on industrial accidents in which alcohol or drug use was confirmed. It is also very difficult to make categorical statements about "drugs" in general because of their variety, duration of effects, and interactive properties with other substances. We do know that cognitive skills such as vigilance, monitoring, reaction time, and decision making are adversely affected by many kinds of drugs. We do not know whether these drugs simply lengthen the amount of time needed to perform these cognitive functions, or whether they cause attention to be focused on irrelevant or competing stimuli. Jobs that involve the use of these skills in areas like the transportation industry (for example, pilots and railroad engineers) have regrettably contributed to our knowledge through tragic accidents. Some drugs (such as anabolic steroids) have been found to enhance aspects of physical performance (most notably, strength and speed), but their long-term effects can be very harmful to the individual.

Hollinger (1988) concluded that the employees most likely to work under the influence of alcohol or other drugs are men younger than 30 and that the likelihood of their (or other employees') doing so increases when they feel unhappy about their jobs and socialize frequently with coworkers off the job. Trice and Sonnenstuhl (1988) found not only that employees seek relief from the effects of job stress with alcohol, but also that organizational subcultures establish norms for alcohol use. That is, employees may be expected to consume alcohol after work with their coworkers if there is a norm that encourages such behavior. Harris and Trusty (1997) reported that international cultural norms are less disparaging of alcohol use in work contexts than U.S. norms are, asserting that alcohol use is "part and parcel of business life" (p. 309). Alcohol abuse is an epidemic among workers in the former Soviet Union.

Stein, Newcomb, and Bentler (1988) believe that drug involvement and its adverse consequences are facets of a lifestyle that includes more than drug use only. They think we must appreciate the diverse range of life areas affected by drug use and not treat drug use as an isolated or singular problem in the individual. Bruno (1994) reported that in Italy drug dependence does not limit a person's right to keep a job, even if employees perform tasks dangerous to their own or others' safety. To safeguard others, federal laws require employers to reassign such employees to other tasks. The introduction of drug testing in the workplace in Italy has been delayed because it appears to imply a conflict between the organization's right to safeguard its interest and the individual's right to privacy.

Economic issues are also salient to drug use. Bennett, Blum, and Roman (1994) noted that organizations typically address the problem of drug use at work in two ways. The first is drug testing, designed to exclude drug users from the workplace. The second is employee assistance programs (EAPs). EAPs started after World War II to rehabilitate veterans who came home with alcohol abuse problems. Drug abuse treatment was added to the EAPs mainly after the Vietnam War for veterans returning with drug problems. Currently EAPs address all kinds of adjustment, stress, and family problems faced by workers. Such programs are mandated by the federal government for all employees who receive more than a specified amount of federal funding. Bennett et al. found that organizations in geographic areas with high unemployment rates are more likely to use pre-employment drug testing, while work sites with low turnover more often provide an EAP.

Finally, Normand, Lempert, and O'Brien (1994) offered some staggering estimates of the annual financial costs of alcohol and drug abuse to society. The estimates were based on four factors: the costs of treatment, lowered work productivity, the lost income that would have been earned by individuals who die prematurely from substance abuse, and crime-related costs. The total estimated cost of alcohol abuse is $70 billion; the total estimated cost of drug abuse is $44 billion. These figures have probably increased dramatically in recent years given rising medical costs.

It is very difficult for I/O psychologists to conduct high-quality research on substance abuse. Alcohol or drugs can be administered in an experimental setting only under the most restrictive conditions, given ethical concerns. Reliance on self-report measures are problematic, given the factors of social desirability and accuracy. There are also civil and legal issues associated with drug testing, both in this country and internationally, particularly pertaining to the constitutional rights of individuals to submit to drug testing. As with most complex social problems, researchers and scholars from many professions (such as pharmacology, toxicology, law, and genetics) must take an interdisciplinary approach to addressing these issues. While I/O psychologists will contribute only a small piece of the total picture, I envision our efforts as concentrated in two traditional areas: individual assessment and performance measurement. Perhaps in 20 years an evaluation of working conditions may also include the propensity of certain jobs to induce substance abuse and the likelihood your coworker is under the influence of drugs or alcohol. Whether we are ready for it or not, I believe society will expect I/O psychologists to provide information on problems our predecessors could scarcely have imagined.

THE PSYCHOLOGICAL EFFECTS OF UNEMPLOYMENT

As was discussed in Chapter 8, the possibility of job loss is a major concern for the contemporary worker. Thousands of employees lose their jobs annually through layoffs and organizational downsizing. Perilous economic conditions have resulted in large-scale job loss both domestically and globally. What have we learned about the meaning of work to individuals as a result of involuntary unemployment? We will now present a discussion of the psychological effects of unemployment.

Jahoda (1981) asserted that being employed has both intended and unintended consequences for the individual. Earning a living is the most obvious intended consequence of employment, but the primary psychological meaning of work derives from the unintended or latent consequences. There are five important latent consequences of employment: (1) imposition of a time structure on the waking day, (2) regular shared experiences and contacts with people outside the nuclear family, (3) the linking of individuals to goals and purposes, (4) the definition of aspects of personal status and identity, and (5) the enforcement of activity. Jahoda claimed that these unintended consequences of employment "meet human needs of an enduring kind." Accordingly, when one is unemployed and is deprived of these functions, one's enduring human needs are unsatisfied. It is thus argued that employment is the major institution in society that reliably and effectively provides these supports to psychological well-being.

Fryer and Payne (1986) offered a somewhat different explanation for why unemployment is psychologically devastating based upon a loss of discretionary control. Their explanation is heavily tied to the loss of income associated with unemployment. Financial problems are an outstanding worry for most unemployed people, and lack of money is one of the underlying causes of problems in maintaining relationships. While the loss of adequate income is certain for most unemployed people, there is also uncertainty about how long the low income will persist. The poor resources of the unemployed cause them to have much less discretion or freedom to pursue various decision options, such as food or clothes to purchase. The act of choosing is severely restricted by unemployment. Attempting to solve problems with limited resources frequently means that the quality of the solution is poorer, which can engender a sense of failure and lowered self-esteem. Thus, the loss of financial resources limits choices, thereby enhancing feelings of limited control over one's life. In turn, poorer psychological health follows from this condition.

The explanations offered by both Jahoda (1981) and Fryer and Payne (1986) are represented in Warr's (1987) nine environmental factors needed for mental health (listed at the beginning of this chapter). A loss of employment has been found to trigger changes in eight of the nine environmental determinants of psychological well-being.

Wanberg (1997) reported that the act of job seeking can have a negative effect on mental health. Job search involves putting oneself on the line and dealing with feelings about being judged harshly, evaluated critically, and ultimately rejected. Wanberg believes the best intervention programs for unemployed individuals incorporate exercises that promote feelings of self-esteem, optimism, and control as well as job-seeking skills. Gowan, Riordan, and Gatewood (1999) concluded that individuals who can manage the negative emotions associated with job loss may appear to be stable and confident in interviews, and thus improve their chances of receiving job offers. Finally, Wanberg, Kanfer, and Banas (2000) reported that individual actions directed toward contacting friends, acquaintances, and referrals to get information, leads, or advice on getting a job (i.e., what is popularly referenced as "networking") did not result in more re-employment or faster re-employment speed. While networking is a useful re-employment strategy, it is not a superior method to traditional job-search techniques.

An individual's opportunity for control is clearly lessened by unemployment. Lack of success in job seeking, the inability to influence employers, and increased dependence on social welfare programs all reduce people's ability to control what happens to them. The opportunity to use skills is also likely to be reduced during unemployment. Occupational skills are generally not used during unemployment, although there may be opportunities to use certain skills in domestic activities. People who become unemployed from jobs that demand a high level of skill are likely to suffer a greater reduction in this feature than people whose previous employment required only limited skill. Unemployment reduces externally generated goals because fewer demands are placed on the individual. Since external demands are often linked to particular times (such as family meal times or the start of a workday), a general reduction in demands is often accompanied by a loss of temporal differentiation. Time markers that break up the day or week and indicate one's position in it are no longer as frequent or urgent.

An unemployed person loses variety by having to leave the house less often and also lacks the contrast between job and nonjob activities. Those domestic demands that impinge on the person are likely to be similar and unchanging from day to day, with standard routines and an absence of novelty. Environmental clarity is also likely to be reduced during unemployment. Information relating to the future permits planning within predictable time schedules and reduces the anxiety typically generated by uncertainty. Planning for the future is difficult in view of uncertainty about one's occupational or financial position in the months to come. Payment for work is at the heart of the employment contract, and the standard of living of almost all adults below retirement age is principally determined by income received from a job. Unemployment removes that income and in almost all cases has a serious and wide-ranging impact on the availability of money.

Physical security is usually associated with the availability of money. There appears to be a general need for some personal and private territory that contributes to a stable self-concept and enhanced well-being. Reduced income can give rise to loss of adequate housing or the threat that this will happen. The only determinant of mental health that appears primarily unaffected by unemployment is the opportunity for interpersonal contact. Younger and middle-aged unemployed individuals typically report no change in the amounts of interpersonal contact they have before and after job loss. Some research findings (e.g., Warr & Payne, 1983) indicated that social contacts even *increase* in frequency for these groups during unemployment. They report spending more time with neighbors and family members. However, older individuals (particularly women) report a reduction in social contacts after becoming unemployed, typically spending their days alone at home. On becoming unemployed, a person loses a socially approved role and the positive self-evaluations that go with it. The new position is widely felt to be of lower prestige, deviant, second rate, or not providing full membership in society. Even when social welfare benefits remove the worst financial hardships, there may be shame attached to receiving funds from public sources and a seeming failure to provide for one's family.

Based upon these assessments provided by Warr (1987), there is a strong linkage between unemployment and mental health. Indeed, Murphy and Athanasou (1999) conducted a meta-analysis of longitudinal studies examining how employment affects one's mental health. The results revealed an average correlation of .54 between gaining employment and improved mental well-being, and an average correlation of .36 between losing employment and decreased mental health. Work provides a sense of meaning and purpose to life, and the removal of that purpose lowers the quality of life.

CHILD LABOR AND EXPLOITATION

We conclude this chapter with a facet of occupational health that is rarely addressed by I/O psychology. It pertains to the health of children who are compelled to work. Our awareness of child labor, a disturbing and deplorable aspect of work-life, comes from increased interest in global business practices (Piotrkowski & Carrubha, 1999). While child labor is relatively rare (and illegal in most circumstances) in the United States, it is not rare in many other countries, and some U.S. companies rely on child labor in developing countries to make their products (see Field Note 3).

Child labor refers to economic activities carried out by persons less than 15 years of age. The International Labour Organization (ILO) established in 1996 that

---

FIELD NOTE 3   **Child Labor by U.S. Companies**

▮ n 1909 my maternal grandmother was orphaned as a result of an outbreak of tuberculosis. She was 14 years old at the time. Her mother had taught her how to crochet, a form of knitting. My grandmother found work in a sweatshop in New York City, making doilies, working 14 hours and earning 25¢ *per day.* She also endured abysmal working conditions, but ultimately prevailed through this very difficult period of her life. In 1938 a federal law was passed (the Fair Labor Standards Act—FLSA) that prohibited many of the conditions my grandmother faced in 1909. A standard workweek (40 hours) was established, as was a minimum hourly wage (currently $5.15/hour). The law was passed in part to eliminate the use of child labor in the United States. As a nation we place a very high value on our children, and we have passed other laws over the years to protect their welfare and safety.

It is now almost 100 years since my grandmother toiled in a sweatshop for 25¢ per day. You might think the use of child labor by U.S. companies ended long ago. Not exactly. The FLSA applies to companies operating in the United States. As a means of reducing labor costs (defined in part by the minimum wage), some U.S. companies have sent jobs formerly held by U.S. workers overseas to developing nations with

cheaper labor markets. These nations do not have the same restrictions on employment that are found in the United States. In some countries it is acceptable for children to hold full-time jobs and to be paid a wage that is consistent with the standards of that country. That wage may be, for example, $1.00 per hour. Furthermore, workers in such nations may well be grateful to secure steady employment that pays $1.00 per hour. It might be concluded that the situation appears equitable for all parties concerned. That is, the company lowers its labor costs by not having to pay the U.S. minimum wage, the overseas workers get paid what is to them a fair wage by their standards, and the use of child labor is not illegal.

Some people and advocacy groups have decried this business practice by selected U.S. companies. Even though it is economically feasible, it can be perceived as violating the ethical standards of fair treatment of workers. How do you feel about this issue? Should U.S. companies be prohibited from using child labor overseas to make products for very low wages (by U.S. standards) because it is morally corruptive and defeats the underlying purpose of the FLSA? Or is this an equitable exchange of labor for money, and "everyone wins"?

250 million children worldwide, 5–14 years old, are working, half of them full-time. Child labor is most common is developing countries, particularly those in Asia, Africa, and Latin America. But it occurs in wealthy countries as well. Child workers typically are found in agriculture, working long hours, sometimes under inhumane and hazardous conditions for little or no pay. In Zimbabwe, some children work 60 hours per week picking cotton or coffee. In Nepal, children work on tea estates, some for up to 14 hours per day. In its most extreme form, the exploitation of working children takes the form of slavery or forced labor, still practiced in areas of Asia and Africa. Children's work may be pledged by parents for payment of a debt, the children may be kidnapped and imprisoned in brothels or sweatshops, or they may be given away or sold by families. Child labor is evidenced in the United States by children trafficking in drugs in inner-city neighborhoods.

According to Piotrkowski and Carrubha (1999), child labor is harmful when it interferes with healthy development by imposing inappropriate physical and social demands on children, when it directly exposes children to noxious conditions that harm them physically or psychologically, and when it is detrimental to children's full social and psychological development. Children are especially vulnerable to dangerous or stressful working conditions because they are emotionally, physically, and cognitively immature. Child laborers are too young to understand the physical and psychological hazards they face and are too powerless to escape them. The plight of children around the world confronted with extreme family poverty and crime as precursors to forced labor has been the subject of major initiatives by the United Nations.

Piotrkowski and Carrubha summarized their review of child labor with the following sober conclusion:

> The economic exploitation and maltreatment of defenseless young children are violations of their basic human rights. Even when permitted by law, child labor may be harmful. Insofar as child labor abuses are tied to family poverty, they cannot be tackled alone, without regard for the economic needs of these families. The idea that children are primarily of sentimental value, rather than of economic value, is a fairly recent historical development. Parents may not understand the harms associated with child labor, believing instead that they have a right to make use of all their human resources. Although child labor may help individual families in their day-to-day efforts to survive, ultimately it perpetuates the cycle of poverty. As such, it has enormous social costs. In depriving children of their rights and subjecting them to harm, exploitative child labor has enormous human costs. (p. 151)

I doubt the subject of child labor will become a dominant issue among I/O psychologists, in part because of its inherent social repulsiveness. However, it underscores one of the major reasons we work: Our services have economic and instrumental value. As adults we have the free will to decide how and where we will offer our services to enhance our economic standing in life. Children, on the other hand, do not possess this free will. They are compelled to work to enhance the economic standing of others. Such actions violate the basic tenets of social justice referenced in Chapter 10.

CONCLUDING COMMENTS

Work stress not only is a frequent problem for employees but also appears to be more and more accepted as part of the price individuals pay for employment. The fact that stress management programs are directed not at making work less stressful but at increasing our capacity to deal with stress suggests that few people believe stress can be eliminated or drastically reduced from work. As discussed in Chapter 8, one of the consequences of organizational downsizing is that fewer employees have to do the work that was once performed by a greater number of employees. The prevailing sentiment is that organizations are expected to do more (work) with less (resources). Technological advances (particularly relating to computer-based operations) have also accelerated the speed at which work is performed. These changes have the potential to diminish overall mental health by reducing autonomy or control and thus worker self-esteem (Locke, McClear, & Knight, 1996). In the evolution of work design, employees are becoming increasingly controlled by situational factors, as opposed to exerting control over their own work environments. As research on mental health and stress has revealed, the reduction in self-regulation (i.e., feeling "out of control") impairs psychological well-being (Murphy, Hurrell, & Quick, 1992). Rather than denying the reality of work stress or assuming no responsibility for it, organizations are becoming increasingly committed to addressing it. The annual health care costs in this country alone exceed $500 billion, with business paying about half. The annual cost of stress-related illnesses to the American economy is estimated to be $150 billion (Joure, Leon, Simpson, Holley, & Frye, 1989). It is simply cheaper to promote healthful behavior than to pay the costs associated with not promoting it.

C A S E   S T U D Y   ■   **Two Siblings, Two Lifestyles**

Joe Vesco rarely got to see his older sister, Rita. Although they lived only 70 miles apart, their visits seemed limited to family holidays. Rita was 31, married, and had two boys, ages 6 and 3. She was a supervisor for a telemarketing company, overseeing the work of 15 sales agents. Rita put in long hours, typically 50–60 hours per week. She frequently worked until 8:00 P.M. because many sales calls were made in the early evening. She had a departmental sales quota to reach and also had to monitor the individual sales quotas of each of her agents. Her work was very stressful. She also experienced considerable guilt and anxiety over how her worklife was affecting her family. Her husband picked the children up from day care and fed them dinner. The younger child was often asleep before Rita arrived home. She and her husband had discussed at length whether Rita should look for another job with more conventional hours. It always seemed to come down to money. They needed both incomes to maintain their family, and Rita's job paid particularly well. She was paid partly on commission, and because she frequently exceeded her department's sales quota, Rita received about 20% additional income over her base salary. No other job would pay so well.

Joe had a very different life. He was single, 24, and worked as a surveyor for the county. He had his own apartment, just recently purchased his first new car, and loved his independence. His job didn't pay very well, but the hours were stable. He left work every day at 4:30. Joe didn't worry about being fired or losing his job. The county employed only a few surveyors, and no one could remember anyone in his department ever being fired or laid off. It was a highly secure job, but not very challenging. Joe didn't think he would make a career out of the job, but for the present it suited him very well.

Joe and Rita got together at their parents' anniversary party. Joe hadn't seen Rita for some time and was surprised at how stressed out she looked. He remembered his sister as always being a stabilizing influence on him while they were growing up. She always seemed to be in control of her life. That apparent control, whether real or just imagined by Joe, was no longer evident. Rita complained about not being able to leave her work problems at work; she worried about her children while at work. She acknowledged taking medication to help her get to sleep, which had never been a problem before. Rita also talked about going back to smoking, after having given up cigarettes for almost seven years.

Joe reflected on his own life in comparison to his sister's. He didn't make nearly the money she did, but his biggest concern in life seemed to be which sporting event he would watch on TV when he came home from work. And car payments. Joe remembered his own mother always being home when he got back from school. He wondered how his nephews responded to their mother's absence after school. Joe concluded that Rita was wondering the same thing.

Study Questions

1. What are the primary sources of work/family conflict in Rita's life?
2. To what degree does gender play a role in Rita's work/family conflict? Why?
3. What are the rewards and drawbacks for both Rita and Joe in the jobs they hold?
4. To what do you attribute the difference in lifestyle between Joe and Rita: age, gender, marital status, children, income?
5. Do you think Rita made a conscious choice to pursue her lifestyle, or do you think she was slowly drawn into it over time? What does your answer suggest about the nature of work/family conflict?

SUGGESTED INFOTRAC TOPICS

mental health	*shift work*
work stress	*compressed workweek*
work/family conflict	*alcoholism in the workplace*
dual-career families	*unemployment*
flextime	*child labor*

Work Motivation

LEARNING OBJECTIVES

- ■ Explain five critical concepts central to work motivation.
- ■ Understand the conceptual basis and the degree of empirical support for these work motivation theories: need hierarchy, equity, expectancy, reinforcement, goal setting, self-regulation, and job characteristics.
- ■ Provide an overview and synthesis of the work motivation theories.
- ■ Give practical examples of applying motivational strategies.

Have you ever observed a person who appears "driven" to perform well or succeed? Perhaps you would describe yourself in that way. Such people may or may not have more ability than others, but it appears they are willing to work harder or expend more effort than others. Psychologists refer to this attribute or trait as ambition, or being motivated. Motivation is not directly observable; it must be inferred. Motivational processes can be inferred from an analysis of a continuous stream of behaviors that are determined by both environment and heredity and are observed through their effects on personality, beliefs, knowledge, abilities, and skills.

Work motivation refers to the domain of motivational processes directed to the realm of work. Pinder (1998) offered this definition:

> Work motivation is a set of energetic forces that originate both within as well as beyond an individual's being, to initiate work-related behavior, and to determine its form, direction, intensity, and duration. (p. 11)

There are three noteworthy components to this definition. First, *direction* addresses the choice of activities we make in expending effort. That is, we might choose to work diligently at some tasks and not at others. Second, *intensity* implies we have the potential to exert various levels of effort, depending on how much we need to expend. Third, *duration* reflects persistence of motivation over time, as opposed to a one-time choice between courses of action (direction) or high levels of effort aimed at a single task (intensity). A comprehensive understanding of work motivation requires an integration of these concepts.

Motivation can thus be conceptualized along three dimensions: direction, intensity, and persistence. Each dimension has its associated issues and concerns. In an employment context, each dimension is highly relevant to both the organization and the individual. *Direction* pertains to those activities in life to which you direct your energy. Organizations want employees who will direct themselves to their work responsibilities, and many employees want jobs that will inspire their motivation and commitment. *Intensity* pertains to the amount of motivation that is expended in pursuit of an activity. Organizations want employees who will exhibit high levels of energy. Such people are often referred to as "self-starters" or "self-motivated" individuals, implying they bring a high level of energy to the job and do not require organizational inducements to work hard. Likewise, many employees hope to find jobs that are sufficiently appealing to invite large commitments of energy. The third dimension, *persistence*, pertains to sustained energy over time. It is concerned with how long the energy will be expended. Researchers know the least about this dimension, but it is the focus of more recent motivational theories. You can think of a career as an interrelated series of jobs through which individuals manifest their energies over a working lifetime. Organizations want employees who will persevere through good times and bad. Likewise, employees want jobs that will sustain their interests over the long haul. Each of the three dimensions of motivation has direct implications for both organizations and individuals.

FIVE CRITICAL CONCEPTS IN MOTIVATION

It is relatively easy to misunderstand or confuse several concepts critical to work motivation. The distinctions among these concepts are not always discernible, or at the least they can become blurred. To help you differentiate them throughout the chapter, five critical concepts will be articulated next.

- *Behavior.* Behavior is the action from which we infer motivation. The behavior in question may be typing speed, firing a rifle at a target, or any of a broad constellation of human activities.

- *Performance.* Performance entails some evaluation of behavior. The basic unit of observation is behavior, but coupled with the behavior is an assessment of the behavior as judged against some standard. Thus, if the behavior is typing 60 words per minute, a judgment can be made as to whether this *level of performance* is adequate or inadequate to hold a job. Thus, the behavior is appraised within some organizational context, and 60 words per minute might represent adequate performance in some jobs and inadequate performance in others. Most organizational theories tend to be concerned with performance, not just behavior. Performance, however, is determined by factors that transcend behavior.

- *Ability.* Ability is one of three determinants of behavior. It is generally regarded as fairly stable within an individual and may be represented by a broad construct like intelligence or a more specific construct like physical coordination.

- *Situational constraints.* Situational constraints are the second determinant of behavior. They are environmental factors and opportunities that facilitate or retard behavior (and ultimately performance). Examples include tools, equipment, procedures, and the like, which if present, facilitate behavior, and if absent, diminish it. If no situational constraints are present, it is possible to maximize behavior. Individual behavior manifests itself in some environmental or situational context that influences the conduct of behavior but is beyond the control of the individual.

- *Motivation.* Motivation is the third determinant of behavior. You can think of ability as reflecting what you *can* do, motivation as what you *will* do (given your ability), and the situational constraints as what you are *allowed* to do.

Each of the three components is critical to the manifestation of behavior. Maximum behavior is observed when a person has high ability, exhibits high motivation, and is in an environment that is supportive of such behavior. The judgment of "poor performance" could be attributed to four factors. First, the organization in which the behavior occurs may have high standards, which in another organization may result in a more positive evaluation of the behavior. Second, the individual may lack the needed ability to exhibit the desired behavior. (I was never very good at catching fly balls in baseball.) Third, the individual may lack the motivation to exhibit the desired behavior. (Countless hours of practice didn't seem to enhance my ball-catching behavior.) Fourth, the individual may lack the needed equipment or opportunity to exhibit the behavior. (An expensive new baseball glove didn't help either.)

WORK MOTIVATION THEORIES

Over the past 40 years there has been a profusion of work motivation theories. The theories offer markedly different explanations for the same aspect of human behavior. That is, work motivation theories have been proposed from environmental, social, dispositional, and cognitive perspectives. In the past five to ten years, however, attempts have been made to identify consistency in the psychological constructs that underlie the theories. As you will see, certain psychological constructs coalesce more readily across theories than others.

Seven different theories of work motivation will be presented here. They differ markedly in the psychological constructs that are hypothesized to account for motivation. Each theory will be presented in three sections: a statement of the theory, a presentation of empirical tests, and an evaluation. At the conclusion of the presentation of theories, there will be a discussion of points of convergence among the theories and the fundamental perspectives that have been taken in addressing work motivation.

Need Hierarchy Theory

Statement of the Theory.   One of the major theories of motivation was developed by Abraham Maslow. It is called the **need hierarchy theory**. Most of Maslow's writing was not concerned with work motivation. Only later in his career did he become interested in applications of his theory. Most of its uses were derived from other researchers' examinations of its relevance for organizations.

need hierarchy theory
a theory of motivation based on a sequential ordering of human needs that individuals seek to fulfill in serial progression, starting with psychological needs and culminating in the need for self-actualization

According to Maslow (1987), the source of motivation is certain needs. Needs are biological or instinctive; they characterize humans in general and have a genetic base. They often influence behavior unconsciously. What causes people to behave as they do is the process of satisfying these needs. Once a need is satisfied, it no longer dominates behavior, and another need rises to take its place. Need fulfillment is never ending. Life is thus a quest to satisfy needs.

Much of Maslow's theory identifies needs, but the second component explains how the needs relate to one another. Maslow proposed five types of needs: physiological, safety, social, self-esteem, and self-actualization. *Physiological needs* are the most basic; their fulfillment is necessary for survival. They include the need for air, water, and food. *Safety needs* include freedom from threat, danger, and deprivation. They involve self-preservation. Today most of our safety needs are met, but people experiencing disasters like hurricanes or riots have their safety needs threatened. *Social needs* include the desire for association, belonging, and companionship. These involve an individual's ability to exist in harmony with others. *Self-esteem needs* include self-confidence, recognition, appreciation, and the respect of one's peers. Satisfaction of these needs results in a sense of adequacy; their thwarting produces feelings of inferiority and helplessness. The last type of need is *self-actualization,* the best known and least understood in Maslow's scheme. Self-actualization is realization of one's full potential—in Maslow's words, "to become more and more what one is, to become everything that one is capable of becoming."

FRANK AND ERNEST   by Bob Thaves

SOURCE: Reprinted by permission of Newspaper Enterprise Association, Inc.

As mentioned, the second part of the theory concerns how these needs are related. According to Maslow, they exist in a hierarchy. At the base are the physiological needs, which must be met first and continuously. The remaining needs are placed in order, culminating with the highest need, self-actualization. Physiological and safety needs are referred to as basic needs; social, self-esteem, and self-actualization needs are higher-order needs. The need hierarchy theory is illustrated in Figure 12–1.

Maslow made these propositions about the need hierarchy:

- Behavior is dominated and determined by the needs that are unfulfilled.
- An individual will systematically satisfy his or her needs by starting with the most basic and working up the hierarchy.
- Basic needs take precedence over all those higher in the hierarchy.

The first proposition is fundamental: Once a need is fulfilled, it no longer motivates behavior. A hungry person seeks food, but once the hunger is satisfied, it does not dominate behavior. The second proposition involves fulfillment progression. A person progresses through the needs in order, moving on to the next one only after the preceding one has been fulfilled. We all spend our lives trying to fulfill these needs because, according to Maslow, only a small percentage of people have fulfilled the self-actualization need. Maslow also said this need can never be fully satisfied. The third proposition stresses that the needs basic to survival always have a higher priority.

Maslow's theory has several implications for work behavior. When pay and security are poor, employees will focus on those aspects of work necessary to fulfill their basic needs. As conditions improve, the behavior of supervisors and their relationship with the individual take on increased importance. Finally, in a much improved environment, the supervisor's role diminishes and the nature of the work becomes the focus. Work is now important for self-actualization and not to fulfill basic needs.

The theory also predicts that as people move up in the management hierarchy, they are motivated by increasingly higher-level needs; thus, managers at various levels should be treated differently. Additionally, employees can be expected to always want more. The organization can never give enough in terms of individual growth and development. It is the nature of the self-actualization need that once

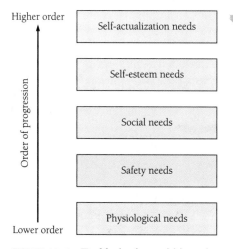

FIGURE 12–1 ■ Maslow's need hierarchy

SOURCE: From *Motivation and Personality*, 3rd ed., by A. H. Maslow, 1987, New York: Harper & Row.

it is activated and satisfied, it stimulates an even greater desire for satisfaction. Thus, it is a continuing source of motivation.

Empirical Tests of the Theory. The ultimate test of any theory is empirical support, but a problem with Maslow's theory involves measuring the variables. Because he did not provide operational definitions of his variables, other researchers must measure them and test the theory.

Betz (1984) found mixed support for the theory. On the negative side, she found that need importance was not related to need deficiency. Yet, as the theory predicts, Betz found a positive correlation between need fulfillment and life satisfaction. Wahba and Bridwell (1976) reviewed all earlier research on Maslow's theory. They concluded that the theory has received little clear or consistent support. Some of Maslow's propositions were totally rejected; others received mixed or questionable support. The most support was for the importance of the basic needs; the least evidence was for the higher-level needs. The number of needs appeared questionable, as did the idea of fulfillment progression.

Evaluation of the Theory. It is tempting to dismiss most of Maslow's theory, given the lack of support, but a few points suggest a more positive verdict. First, it is not a "theory" in the usual sense; Maslow did not propose testable hypotheses. As Wahba and Bridwell (1976) said, "Maslow's need hierarchy theory is almost a nontestable theory" (p. 234). It was based on logical and clinical insights into human nature rather than on research findings. Furthermore, Maslow did not discuss any guidelines for empirical tests of his theory. Many questions remain, and the way the theory is tested is open to interpretation. For example, what is the time span for the unfolding of the hierarchy? Is there a relationship between age and the need we are trying to satisfy? How does the shift from one need to another take place? Do people also seek to fulfill needs by going down the hierarchy? These questions are very important; they affect how we would use the theory in the work environment.

The theory's vagueness also leaves some nagging issues unresolved. According to Maslow, we systematically progress from one need to the next. Yet we all need to eat, drink, and breathe every day. We never really have our physiological needs satisfied. We try to fulfill our self-esteem needs even when our social needs are not fully satisfied. Rather than going through the hierarchy in stages, perhaps we attempt to satisfy all needs concurrently. Maslow did not deal with this speculation.

Pinder (1998) asked whether there is such a thing as a *hierarchy* of needs. There is evidence that different needs exist; however, there is much less empirical support that these needs vary in their relative importance so consistently across individuals that a generalizable hierarchy exists. Such a hierarchy ignores substantial differences among people at various stages in their lives. However, there are some consistencies among people at various life and career stages in the desires they express on the job. It may be that a universal hierarchy of needs is not as valid as a need theory that takes individual and organizational circumstances into account.

Maslow's theory, a highly abstract statement about humankind, is far more philosophical than empirical. But his notion of self-actualization is ingrained in the way we think about our mission in life. His writing has generated a great deal of thought about the nature of humankind in general. While Maslow's theory is deficient in explaining day-to-day behavior at work, his contributions to the field of psychology as a whole should not be ignored.

Equity Theory

Statement of the Theory.
Adams (1965) proposed a theory of work motivation drawn from the principle of social comparison. How hard a person is willing to work is a function of comparisons with the efforts of others. The theory has perceptual and social bases because motivation is a function of how a person sees himself or herself in comparison with others. Adams suggested that motivation has a social rather than a biological origin.

Equity theory has four major parts:

equity theory
a theory of motivation based on the social comparison process of examining the ratio of inputs and outcomes between oneself and a comparison other

1. Because it is a perceptually based theory, the individual perceives himself or herself in comparison with others. The person who does the perceiving is called *Person*.
2. It is postulated that Person compares himself or herself with another individual. This other person is called *Other*.
3. All of the assets Person brings to the job are the third component; collectively, these assets are referred to as *Inputs*. Inputs include Person's education, intelligence, experience, skill, seniority, effort level, health, and so on. They are anything of perceived value or importance that Person brings to the job.
4. All of the benefits Person derives from the job are the fourth component, collectively referred to as *Outcomes*. Outcomes include pay, benefits, working conditions, status symbols, seniority benefits, and so forth. They are those factors Person perceives as being derived from employment.

The theory states that Person forms a ratio of his or her inputs to outcomes and compares it with perceptions of Other's inputs/outcomes ratio. Other can also be conceptualized as Person in a previous job. Thus, the comparison process could involve just Person, comparing what he/she has in a current job with a previous job. Adams assumes that people can quantify both their inputs and outcomes in common scale units. For example, Person will consider all the inputs she brings to the job; let us say they total 50. Person will assess her outcomes in the same manner; again let us assume they total 50 units. Person's ratio is therefore 50:50. Person then compares her ratio with what she perceives Other is putting into his job and deriving in outcomes from it. Let us assume Person assesses Other's inputs and outcomes to be 50 units each. We now have two ratios as assessed by Person:

Person, 50:50   Other, 50:50

The equality of the ratios as perceived by Person represents *equity* (literally, "fair"). If Person perceives Other as deriving 200 units of outcomes from his job (due to more pay and higher status) but also contributing 200 units of inputs (due to more education and more experience), then this also represents equity to her. Other is getting more out of the job than Person but is also putting more into it; that is, 50:50 equals 200:200.

What happens if Person's ratio is different from Other's—that is, 50:50 versus 50:75? Both Person and Other are perceived as contributing the same amount of inputs (50 units), but Other is deriving more outcomes (75 units). According to Adams, this situation represents *inequity,* or "unfairness," in the sense that Person perceives Other to be getting more out of the job, although both are contributing the same inputs.

According to Adams, feelings of inequity cause tension, which Person will be motivated to reduce. The greater the inequity between Person and Other, the greater the tension and the greater the motivation to reduce it. Thus, for Adams, the source of motivation is feelings of tension caused by perceived inequity. Feelings of inequity are necessary for motivation to occur because if Person perceives herself as being in an equitable relationship with Other, she will not be motivated.

underpayment inequity
the sense of unfairness derived from the perception that the ratio of one's own inputs and outcomes is lower than the ratio of a comparison other

overpayment inequity
the sense of unfairness derived from the perception that the ratio of one's own inputs and outcomes is greater than the ratio of a comparison other

Adams proposed two types of inequity. **Underpayment inequity** is when Person perceives herself as deriving fewer outcomes from a job than Other, when both are contributing comparable inputs. An example of underpayment inequity is

Person, 50:50   Other, 50:75

Overpayment inequity is when Person perceives herself as deriving more outcomes from a job than Other, when both are contributing comparable inputs. An example of overpayment inequity is

Person, 50:75   Other, 50:50

Adams felt that people could alter their motivation levels in an attempt to bring feelings of inequity back into line. The drive to reduce the tension caused by inequity manifests itself in more or less effort being put into the job, which is a form of input. Adams said that how inequity is reduced is a function of the method of payment: hourly (wages determined per unit of time, such as $6 per hour) or piece rate (wages determined per unit of production, such as 25¢ per object).

Most research on equity theory was conducted in laboratory or field experiments. To test the theory, researchers induced feelings of overpayment and underpayment in the subjects by using the following manipulations: The experimenter, posing as a manager or supervisor of some fictitious company, placed an ad in a local newspaper announcing part-time job openings. At the employment interview, subjects (who did not know this was a psychology experiment) were told the job paid a certain hourly rate (such as $6 per hour) or piece rate (such as 25¢ per object produced). They then started work at this rate. After a few days the experimenter said, "We just received a large contract from the government, and we can now pay you more money. Starting tomorrow, you will make $8 per hour (or 40¢ per object)." This manipulation was meant to induce feelings of overpayment. Subjects would be paid more for doing the same job. To induce feelings of underpayment, the experimenter said, "We have just experienced a major cutback in financial support due to the loss of a contract. Starting tomorrow, we can pay you only $2 per hour (or 15¢ per object)." These experimental instructions were given to some subjects but not others. Thus, some people would work at the "new" rate, and others would continue to work at the original rate. The first few days of employment were designed to set base rate expectations about the job. After this period, the amount of compensation for the same work went either up (in the overpayment condition) or down (in the underpayment condition). The question to be answered was, What would these people do as a result of feelings of inequity? Given two types of inequity (underpayment and overpayment) and two compensation systems (hourly and piece rate), four sets of hypotheses were proposed for how Person would reduce feelings of inequity:

- *Overpayment—hourly.* Subjects would try to reduce the inequity caused by overpayment by working harder or expending more effort. By increasing their inputs (effort level), they would reduce feelings of inequity. The increased effort was predicted to manifest itself in increased quantity or quality of production.
- *Overpayment—piece rate.* To reduce feelings of inequity, subjects would work harder as a means of increasing their inputs. However, if their increased effort resulted in greater output, the feelings of inequity would be magnified. Thus, subjects in this condition would produce fewer but higher-quality objects than before.
- *Underpayment—hourly.* Subjects would decrease their effort to accommodate the decrease in outcome. Decrements in product quantity and quality would result.
- *Underpayment—piece rate.* To compensate for the loss in pay, subjects would produce more but appreciably lower-quality objects.

Empirical Tests of the Theory.   A fairly large number of studies have tested some or all of the predictions made by equity theory. Researchers used both payment systems in studying the effects of inequity on performance of subjects. Certain groups of subjects were made to feel overpaid or underpaid; others were made to feel they were paid equitably. Most studies found that equity predictions held up best in the underpayment conditions. Also, the results of studies using hourly payment were stronger than those with piece-rate payment. These findings have important implications, which will be discussed shortly.

The original theory proposed that people expend more or less effort to reduce inequity. These are called *behavioral* ways of reducing inequity. As mentioned, one way to reduce inequity is to adjust the level of effort expended—changing one's inputs, as the theory postulates. A second way is to alter one's outcomes, such as asking for a raise if one feels underpaid. A third technique is to get Other to change his or her inputs or outcomes by using peer pressure to get Other to work faster or slower. Finally, if all else fails, Person can always quit a job if it is perceived as too inequitable.

Research has shown, however, that there are also *cognitive* ways to reduce inequity. By cognitive, we mean that a person does not have to "do" anything; rather, he or she reduces inequity through mental processes. One way is for Person to distort views of his or her inputs or outcomes. For example, Person could think, "I'm not really working that hard. After all, I spend a fair part of my day just talking to my friends." Outcomes could be distorted in a similar way. A second technique is for Person to distort Other's inputs or outcomes; for example, "She really has to put up with a lot from her supervisor that I don't have to take." It has also been observed that, given the difficulty of making comparisons across jobs, the distortion of inputs (such as time and effort) is more common than the distortion of outcomes (such as salary increases and promotions). Finally, if a particular Other made Person feel inequitable, Person could always find a new Other for comparison. Equity theory does not state who that Other has to be. Research shows that the selection of Other can be oneself in a previous job, coworkers in the same organization, or people outside of one's own organization. The methods of reducing inequity (both behavioral and cognitive) are listed in Table 12–1.

Most experiments on equity theory have supported the predictions. Problems occur not because the theory is "wrong" but because hypotheses and predictions are not very precise. There are several ways of reducing inequity, and the theory does not specify which way will be chosen. Equity theory states that when people feel a sense of inequity/dissatisfaction, they will do something to alleviate the dissatisfaction. The theory doesn't specify what they will do (i.e., which form of inequity reduction) to relieve the dissatisfaction. A second problem involves time. Many experiments studied behavior for short periods, from 10 minutes to 30 days. As with any motivation theory, we are interested in the long-term effects on behavior. Some of the implications of time will be addressed in the next section.

Evaluation of the Theory.   Numerous authors have expressed concern over the theory's substance and implications. To date, the research on equity theory has addressed financial compensation, yet that is only one of many outcomes derived from a job. We know very little about the effects on motivation of manipulating other outcomes. Most studies have found fairly strong support for the underpayment predictions but less support for the overpayment ones. One consequence of inequity caused by underpayment is an increase in job dissatisfaction. We know that this is associated with increased absenteeism and turnover. We will have accomplished very little in the workforce if, in the name of increased motivation, people feel underpaid and then are absent from work or quit.

TABLE 12–1   ■   Modes of reducing inequity

Behavioral modes of inequity reduction
1. Change inputs.
2. Change outcomes.
3. Get Other to change inputs or outcomes.
4. Quit job for more equitable one.

Cognitive modes of inequity reduction
1. Distort own inputs or outcomes.
2. Distort Other's inputs or outcomes.
3. Change comparison Other.

In theory, feelings of overpayment will cause a person to work harder to produce more or higher-quality products. However, research has shown that such feelings do not last very long. People seem to have a very high threshold for overpayment (that is, it takes a large increment for people to feel overpaid) but a low threshold for underpayment (that is, it takes a small decrement for people to feel underpaid). Given that feelings of overpayment are short-lived, an organization that doubled the wages of its employees every two months to make them feel consistently overpaid would soon be bankrupt. Huseman, Hatfield, and Miles (1987) suggested that individuals differ in their sensitivity to feeling over- or underrewarded. They believe that "benevolents" are employees who more likely feel a sense of being overrewarded than do "entitleds."

Finally, the whole issue of organizations deliberately manipulating their employees to induce feelings of inequity raises serious moral and ethical questions. Few employees would like to work for an organization that willingly made them experience inequity.

Research has shown that the principles of equity theory extend to nonmonetary outcomes. Greenberg (1988) examined employees who were randomly reassigned on a temporary basis to the offices of either higher-, lower-, or equal-status coworkers while their own offices were being remodeled. Relative to those workers reassigned to equal-status offices, those reassigned to higher-status offices raised their performance (a response to overpayment inequity) and those reassigned to lower-status offices lowered their performance (a response to underpayment inequity). Greenberg (1990) measured employee theft rates in manufacturing plants during a period in which pay was temporarily reduced by 15%. Compared with pre- and postreduction pay periods (or with control groups whose pay was unchanged), groups whose pay was reduced had significantly higher theft rates. When the bases for the pay cuts were thoroughly and sensitively explained to employees, feelings of inequity were lessened and the theft rate was reduced as well. In this study, the data supported equity theory's predictions regarding likely responses to underpayment.

The components of equity theory have been substantiated from research. It is evident that people do consider the inputs they bring to the job. "Equity theory assumes that people aggregate their perceived inputs into a sort of psychological total, representing the net value they believe they contribute to the job" (Pinder, 1998, p. 288). It is likewise true that people hold beliefs about the nature and quantity of the consequences or outcomes they receive as a result of doing their work. The process of social comparison is also valid because what we do is in part a product of what others around us do. Consistent with the concept of organizational justice, equity theory postulates that how hard a person is willing to work is in part determined by perceptions of what is fair or just (see Field Note 1). Indeed, the theoretical origins of procedural justice were based on the tenets of equity theory. There should be equity or fairness in the relationship between what you put into a job and what you get out of it, in comparison with other people. Problems with the theory from a motivational perspective pertain to how people deal with feelings of inequity or unfairness. Inequity need not always be resolved by expending greater effort, which cuts to the core of the theory.

FIELD NOTE 1   **Equity Theory Applied to Baseball**

Most formal studies of equity theory have taken place in laboratory experiments. However, some researchers have used the tenets of equity theory to explain naturally occurring phenomena. Lord and Hohenfeld (1979) applied equity theory to explain the on-the-field performance of some major league baseball players.

A major league player signs a contract for a certain duration (say, three years) at a specified salary. At the end of the contract term, both the player and the team must negotiate a new contract. Sometimes the player and the team cannot agree on a new contract because the player feels he is worth more money than the team offers. In short, the player feels underpaid in comparison with what other players are receiving. In that case, the player may engage in a process known as "playing out his option"; that is, he will continue to play for the same team for one more year without a contract. This year is called the "option year." At the end of the option year, the player is free to sign with any other baseball team in the major leagues. However, during the option year, the player receives a lower salary than he did when he was under contract.

Therefore, his feelings of underpayment are intensified for two reasons. First, he feels he is worth more than he was being paid under the old contract. Second, he is paid even less than before during the option year.

According to equity theory, perceptions of underpayment should produce lower performance. Lord and Hohenfeld studied a sample of 23 baseball players who were unable to reach an agreement with their teams for a new contract and thus played out their option year. The authors selected four criteria of job performance: batting average, home runs, runs batted in, and runs scored. They compared the players' performance on these criteria before the option year with their performance during it. Equity theory would postulate that because the players felt underpaid, their performance on these four factors would be lower during the option year. The results supported the hypothesis for the first three performance indices but not for runs scored. The findings were consistent across the players, over time, and over the three performance indices. They indicated that, at least in this sample, feelings of underpayment did produce lower job performance, as equity theory predicted.

Expectancy Theory

expectancy theory
a theory of motivation based on the perceived degree of relationship between how much effort a person expends and the performance resulting from that effort

Statement of the Theory.   **Expectancy theory** originated in the 1930s, but at that time it was not related to work motivation. Vroom (1964) brought expectancy theory into the arena of motivation research. In the past 35 years, expectancy theory has been one of the most popular and prominent motivation theories in I/O psychology. Since Vroom's formulation, several other researchers have proposed modifications. This section will not examine all variations but instead focus on key elements.

This is a cognitive theory. Each person is assumed to be a rational decision maker who will expend effort on activities that lead to desired rewards. Individuals are thought to know what they want from work and understand that their performance will determine whether they get the rewards they desire. A relationship between effort expended and performance on the job is also assumed.

The theory has five major parts: job outcomes, valence, instrumentality, expectancy, and force.

Job outcomes. Job outcomes are things an organization can provide for its employees, such as pay, promotions, and vacation time. Theoretically, there is no limit to the number of outcomes. They are usually thought of as rewards or positive experiences, but they need not be. Getting fired or being transferred to a new location could be an outcome. Outcomes can also be intangibles like feelings of recognition or accomplishment.

Valence. *Valences* are the employee's feelings about the outcomes and are usually defined in terms of attractiveness or anticipated satisfaction. The employee generates valences; that is, he or she rates the anticipated satisfaction from (that is, ascribe a valence to) each outcome considered. Rating is usually done on a +10 to −10 scale. The individual can indicate whether an outcome has positive or negative valence. If the employee anticipates that all outcomes will lead to satisfaction, then varying degrees of positive valence are given. If the employee anticipates that all outcomes will lead to dissatisfaction, then varying degrees of negative valence are assigned. Last, if the employee feels indifferent about the outcomes, a valence of zero is given. The employee generates as many valences as there are outcomes.

Instrumentality. *Instrumentality* is defined as the perceived degree of relationship between performance and outcome attainment. This perception exists in the employee's mind. Instrumentality is like the word *conditional* and means the degree to which the attainment of a certain outcome is conditional on the individual's performance on the job. For example, if a person thinks that pay increases are totally conditional on performance, then the instrumentality associated with that outcome (a pay raise) is very high. If a person thinks that being transferred is totally unrelated to job performance, then the instrumentality associated with that outcome (a transfer) is very low. Like valences, instrumentalities are generated by the individual. He or she evaluates the degree of relationship between performance and outcome attainment on the job. Instrumentalities are usually thought of as probabilities (which therefore range from 0 to 1). An instrumentality of 0 means the attainment of that outcome is totally unrelated to job performance; an instrumentality of 1 means the attainment of that outcome is totally conditional on job performance. An alternative conceptualization of instrumentality is a correlation, which therefore ranges from −1.0 to +1.0. The significance of the correlation conception of instrumentality is that it permits the possibility that increases in performance are, in fact, negatively related to outcome attainment. An example might be when increased job performance *decreases* the likelihood of a promotion: An organization might be reluctant to advance an employee out of a job in which he or she excels. Just as there are as many valences as there are outcomes, there are as many instrumentalities as there are outcomes.

Expectancy. *Expectancy* is the perceived relationship between effort and performance. In some jobs there may seem to be no relationship between how hard you try and how well you do. In others there may be a very clear relationship: The harder you try, the better you do. Expectancy is scaled as a probability. An expectancy of 0 means there is no probability that an increase in effort will result in an increase in performance. An expectancy of 1 means an increase in effort will be followed by a corresponding increase in performance. As with the valence and instrumentality components, the individual generates the expectancy for his or her job. After thinking about the relationship between effort and job performance, the individual makes an assessment (ascribes an expectancy). Unlike the previous components, usually only one expectancy value is generated by the person to reflect the effort–performance relationship.

Force. Force, the last component, is the amount of effort or pressure within the person to be motivated. The larger the force, the greater the hypothesized motivation. Mathematically, force is the product of valence, instrumentality, and expectancy, as expressed by this formula:

$$\text{Force} = E\left(\sum_{i=1}^{n} V_i I_i\right) \qquad \text{[Formula 12–1]}$$

The formula can be explained better with the aid of the information in Figure 12–2. The components that constitute expectancy theory—job outcomes (*O*), rated valences, instrumentalities, and expectancy—are presented for a hypothetical employee. To compute this individual's force, we multiply the valence for an outcome by its corresponding instrumentality and then sum these numbers. Therefore,

$$(7 \times .5) + (6 \times .3) + (2 \times .2) + (9 \times .8) = \sum_{i=1}^{4} V_i I_i = 12.9 \qquad \text{[Formula 12–2]}$$

We then multiply 12.9 by the listed expectancy of .75, which yields a force score of

$$E\left(\sum_{i=1}^{4} V_i I_i\right) = .75(12.9) = 9.7 \qquad \text{[Formula 12–3]}$$

This product—9.7—represents the amount of force within the person to be motivated. It is the end product of the information on valence, instrumentality, and expectancy.

Now that we have this force score, what do we do with it? Think of it as a predictor of how motivated a person is. As with any predictor, the next step is to correlate it with some criterion. Because the force score predicts effort, the criterion must also measure effort. The most common measure of effort is a subjective assessment, usually a rating: The individual renders a self-assessment of his or her

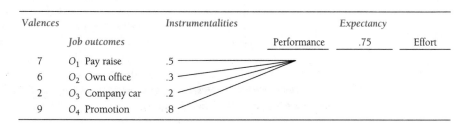

Valences		Instrumentalities		Expectancy	
	Job outcomes		Performance	.75	Effort
7	O_1 Pay raise	.5			
6	O_2 Own office	.3			
2	O_3 Company car	.2			
9	O_4 Promotion	.8			

FIGURE 12–2 ■ **An example of Vroom's expectancy theory**

effort, the individual's supervisor makes the judgment, or peer assessments are used. For example, the number of hours spent studying each week has been used to predict the motivation of students. In one type of validation paradigm of expectancy theory, force scores and criterion measures of effort are calculated for a group of people. If the theory is valid, then the higher the person's force score, the greater the effort should be. The theory's validity is typically assessed by correlating the force scores with the criterion of effort. High correlations between the two variables would substantiate the theory; low correlations would disconfirm it. The validation process will be examined more closely in the next section.

Expectancy theory provides a rich rational basis for understanding motivation in a given job. Each component is a framework for analyzing the motivation process. First, we should consider the outcomes and their rated valences. If a person feels indifferent about the outcomes (a low valence), there is no reason to work hard to attain them. According to expectancy theory, therefore, the first ingredient for motivation is desired outcomes. Second, the person must believe that there is some relationship between job performance and attainment of outcomes (instrumentalities must be high). If a person wants the outcomes but does not see performance as a means of getting them, there is no link between what is done and what is wanted. Reward practices and the supervisor are crucial in establishing high instrumentalities. If a supervisor says, "Your performance has been very good lately; therefore, I will reward you with a raise [or promotion]," the individual will see that the attainment of a pay raise or a promotion is conditional on (instrumental to) good performance. Conversely, if a supervisor says, "We don't give pay raises or promotions on the basis of performance; we grant them only on the basis of seniority," the individual will not be motivated to perform well to attain these outcomes. Perhaps the only motivation will be to work hard enough not to be fired, so these outcomes would eventually be attained through longer service with the organization. When outcomes are made contingent on performance and the individual understands this relationship, expectancy theory predicts that job performance will be enhanced.

Finally, the notion of expectancy is crucial. People must see a relationship (an expectancy) between how hard they try and how well they perform. If expectancy is low, it will make no difference to them whether they work hard because effort and performance seem unrelated. When I first started college, I was a chemistry major. I desired certain outcomes (for example, good grades, a sense of accomplishment). I also realized that attaining these outcomes was conditional on my performance in classes. I had high valences for both the outcomes and the perceived high instrumentalities. However, after three agonizing semesters, my expectancy was near zero. It did not seem to matter how hard I tried; I just could not alter my (low) performance in chemistry classes. My overall motivation fell dramatically along with my performance, and I eventually chose a new major. In retrospect, I realize I lacked the abilities to perform well as a chemist. All the motivation I could muster would not lead to good performance.

The idea of expectancy also explains why some jobs seem to create high or low motivation. On assembly lines, the group performance level is determined by the speed of the line. No matter how hard a person works, he or she cannot produce any more until the next object moves down the line. The employee soon learns that he or she need only keep pace with the line. Thus, there is no relationship between individual effort and performance. In contrast, sales jobs are characterized by high expectancy. Salespeople who are paid on commission realize that the harder they try (the more sales calls they make), the better their performance (sales volume). Expectancy theory predicts that motivation is highest in jobs with high expectancies.

In summary, expectancy theory is very good at explaining the components of motivation. It provides a rational basis on which to assess people's expenditure of effort.

Empirical Tests of the Theory. Research has focused on the specific predictions the theory tries to make. One approach assumes the theory tries to distinguish the "most motivated" from the "least motivated" people in a group. With one force score derived for each person, the person with the highest score should be the most motivated and the person with the lowest score the least motivated. This type of approach is called an *across-subjects design* because predictions are made across people.

The second approach tests the theory differently. Here the theory assumes that each person is confronted with many tasks and then predicts on which tasks the person will work the hardest and on which he or she will expend the least effort. The theory is expanded to derive a force score for each task under consideration, and a criterion of effort is obtained for each. For each person, a correlation is computed between predictions of effort made by the theory and actual amounts of effort expended on the tasks. This type of approach is called a *within-subjects design;* predictions are made for each individual separately.

Validation studies generally find better predictions for the within-subjects design than the across-subjects design. Average validity coefficients for the across-subjects design are usually in the .30s to .40s, while average validity coefficients for within-subjects designs are usually in the .50s to .60s. The theory seems better at predicting the levels of effort an individual will expend on different tasks than at predicting gradations of motivation across different people (Kennedy, Fossum, & White, 1983). These validity coefficients are impressive; they are generally higher than those reported for other motivation theories.

In a major study on incentive motivation techniques, Pritchard, DeLeo, and Von Bergen (1976) reported that a properly designed, successful program for motivating employees will have many of the attributes proposed by expectancy theory. Among the conditions they recommend for a program to be successful are the following:

- Incentives (outcomes) must be carefully sought out and identified as highly attractive.
- The rules (behaviors) for attaining the incentives must be clear to both those administering the system and those actually in it.
- People in the system must perceive that variations in controllable aspects of their behavior will result in variations in their level of performance and, ultimately, their rewards.

In somewhat different words, these three conditions for an effective incentive motivation program reflect the concepts of valence, instrumentality, and expectancy, respectively. The importance of having desired incentives is another way of stating that the outcomes should have high valence. The clarity of the behaviors needed to attain the incentives reflects the strength or magnitude of the instrumentalities. The ability to control performance through different expenditures of effort is indicative of the concept of expectancy. In short, expectancy theory contains the key elements of a successful incentive system as derived through empirical research. Although not all research on expectancy theory is totally supportive, the results have tended to confirm its predictions.

Evaluation of the Theory.   Expectancy theory is a highly rational and conscious explanation of human motivation. The theory has also been used to predict other contexts that involve decisions besides choosing levels of effort. Also included are how people choose an occupation and how they choose to engage in one particular task over others. People are assumed to behave in a way that will maximize expected gains (attainment of outcomes) from exhibiting certain job behaviors and expending certain levels of effort. To the extent that behavior is not directed toward maximizing gains in a rational, systematic way, the theory will not be upheld. Whenever unconscious motives deflect behavior from what a knowledge of conscious processes would predict, expectancy theory will not be predictive. Research suggests that people differ in the extent to which their behavior is motivated by rational processes. This was apparent in one of my own studies (Muchinsky, 1977). I examined the extent to which expectancy theory predicted the amount of effort college students put into each of their courses. In a within-subjects design, the average validity of the theory for all students was .52; however, for individual students it ranged from −.08 to .92. Thus, the theory very accurately predicted the effort expenditure of some students but was unable to predict it for others. This supports the idea that some people have a very rational basis for their behavior, and thus the theory works well for them; others appear to be motivated more by unconscious factors, and for them the theory does not work well (Stahl & Harrell, 1981).

Van Eerde and Thierry (1996) conducted a meta-analysis of the expectancy theory of motivation. They concluded that reduced conceptualization of the theory (not involving the measurement of all the components) resulted in superior predictions of effort compared with the complete VIE model. On a practical level people do not go through life calculating VIE-based force scores, and at a conceptual level it appears equally untenable. However, the underlying concepts of expectancy theory provide one of the dominant explanations of work motivation in I/O psychology. As Pinder (1998) concluded, "At the very least [expectancy theory] is probably an accurate representation of how people form work-related intentions" (p. 359).

reinforcement theory
a theory of motivation based on the schedule of rewards received for behavior that is exhibited

Reinforcement Theory

Statement of the Theory.   **Reinforcement theory** is one of the older approaches to motivation; what is novel is its application to industrial workers. Also referred to as *operant conditioning* and *behaviorism,* reinforcement theory has its origins in B. F. Skinner's work on the conditioning of animals. It was not until the 1970s, however, that I/O psychologists began to see some potential applications of reinforcement theory to the motivational problems of employees.

The theory has three key variables: stimulus, response, and reward. A *stimulus* is any variable or condition that elicits a behavioral response. In an industrial setting, a *response* is some measure of job behavior, like productivity, absenteeism, or accidents. A *reward* is something of value given to the employee on the basis of the elicited behavioral response; it is meant to reinforce the occurrence of the desired response. Most attention has been paid to the response–reward connection. Based on research with animals, four types of response–reward connections or contingencies have been found to influence the frequency of the response:

- *Fixed interval.* The subject is rewarded at a fixed time interval, such as every hour. Those paid on an hourly basis can be thought of as being rewarded on a fixed-interval basis.
- *Fixed ratio.* The subject is rewarded for a fixed number of responses. For example, a real estate salesperson who gets a commission after each sale is rewarded on a fixed-ratio schedule. In this case the reward schedule is said to be continuous.
- *Variable interval.* The subject is rewarded at some time interval that varies. An example is fishing.
- *Variable ratio.* Reward is based on behavior, but the ratio of reward to response is variable. For example, a salesperson might be paid sometimes after each sale and other times after two or three sales. The person is paid on the basis of the response (that is, making a sale), but the schedule of payment is not constant.

Advocates of reinforcement theory believe that the subject's motivation to respond can be shaped by manipulating these reinforcement schedules.

A number of authors have discussed the potential benefits and liabilities of using reinforcement theory as a basis for motivating employees. The theory entails placing the control of employee motivation in the organization's hands, since organizations can "regulate" the energy output of employees by manipulating reinforcement schedules. Most people would like to feel that they are in control of their own lives rather than being manipulated into certain behavior patterns by the organization. The issue of responsibility for controlling behavior is very sensitive because it involves ethical considerations of employee welfare. If employees work to exhaustion by mismanaging their efforts, they are responsible for their actions. However, if they are manipulated into expending excessive effort, they have been victimized by a force beyond their control, and the organization should be held responsible for their condition. Issues of ethical responsibility for behavior are not central to the theory, but they are important when it is applied in daily life. Whenever anything is "done" to someone by an outside agent, the question arises of whose values (the individual's or the agent's) are being optimized.

Empirical Tests of the Theory.   Empirical tests of reinforcement theory have involved determining which schedule of reinforcement has the greatest effect on increasing the occurrence of the desired behavioral response. In a series of studies involving tree planters, Yukl and Latham (1975) and Yukl, Latham, and Pursell (1976) compared the effectiveness of various schedules of reinforcement. Some planters were paid on a fixed-interval schedule (hourly pay); others were paid based on the number of trees they planted. Employees paid on a ratio schedule were significantly more productive (planted more trees). Pritchard, Leonard, Von Bergen, and Kirk (1976) examined the effects of different payment schedules on employees' ability to pass self-paced learning tests of electrical knowledge. Some employees were paid a flat hourly wage, while others were paid according to the number of tests they passed. Two types of ratio payment schedules were used: fixed (the employee was paid after passing every third test) and variable (the employee was paid after passing a variable number). The results of the study are shown in Figure 12–3. Employees who were paid contingently (that is, based on their performance) passed 60% of the tests; those paid by the hour passed about 40%. The results showed no difference in test performance between fixed- and variable-ratio reinforcement schedules. Irrespective of the behavior in question, positive reinforcement, contingently applied, can effectively modify human behavior. Although there are some inconsistencies in results across differing schedules of reinforcement, the success of the theory depends on the appropriate use of positive reinforcement.

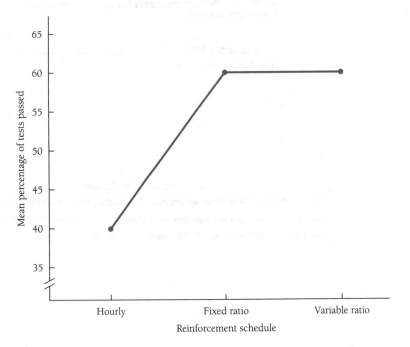

FIGURE 12–3 ■ Percentage of tests passed under different reinforcement schedules

SOURCE: From "The Effect of Varying Schedules of Reinforcement on Human Task Performance" by R. D. Pritchard, D. W. Leonard, C. W. Von Bergen, and R. J. Kirk, 1976, *Organizational Behavior and Human Performance, 16,* p. 218.

Research on reinforcement theory is not limited to measures of productivity. Pedalino and Gamboa (1974) described how the theory could be used to decrease absenteeism. They devised a plan whereby every employee who came to work on time was dealt one card from a poker deck. Each day the attending employees were dealt a new card. At the end of the week, the employee with the best poker hand won $20. In this case the desired response (attendance) was reinforced through monetary reward. Attendance under this plan was higher than it was before the program was introduced.

Evaluation of the Theory. Research clearly indicates that the principles of reinforcement theory do "work"; however, the theory suffers from some limitations in organizational settings. As Mawhinney (1975) noted, current applications of reinforcement theory tend to ignore individual differences in what are valued as rewards. In the Pedalino and Gamboa study, for example, it was assumed that all the employees were interested in playing poker and would respond positively to a gambling or lottery situation. Vast individual differences in preferences would have precluded the success of any such program. In addition, reinforcement has been limited primarily to studies of the quantity of production. We don't know very much about how the quality of performance is affected, the long-term effects of various reinforcement schedules, or people's attitudes toward such incentive methods.

The use of reinforcement theory in industry has both supporters and detractors. Advocates cite its wide applicability for solving problems. Its uses include reducing absence and turnover, increasing productivity, and improving supervisory training. Emery Air Freight is one of the biggest reinforcement theory success stories. Emery reported $3 million in cost savings after adopting a system of positive reinforcement. Other companies have also reported successful applications. In a meta-analysis of reinforcement theory for task performance over a 20-year period, Stajkovic and Luthans (1997) reported an average of 17% improvement in task performance using the theory. Detractors of the theory cite possible ethical questions associated with the reinforcement of behavior. How ethical is it for an organization to use a payment system that increases productivity but may cause adverse side effects? Sweden has condemned piece-rate payment schedules because they cause tension and ultimately damage workers' mental and physical well-being. There is also evidence that workers in short-cycle, monotonous jobs prefer hourly rates to piece rates. They complain that piece-rate systems "control" them (or at least their behavior), which is the precise intent of the system. Despite these legitimate ethical concerns, reinforcement theory has a history of producing desired changes in work behavior. Unlike other motivational theories, its focus is not on the individual but on environmental factors that shape or modify behavior. While implementation problems exist, they address only the theory's applicability rather than its validity (see Field Note 2).

goal-setting theory
a theory of motivation based on directing one's effort toward the attainment of specific goals that have been set or established

Goal-Setting Theory

Statement of the Theory. Goal-setting theory is based on the assumption that people behave rationally. The crux of the theory is the relationship among goals, intentions, and task performance. Its basic premise is that conscious ideas

FIELD NOTE 2   **What Gets Rewarded?**

einforcement theory is premised on rewarding desired behavior. The stronger the link between the behavior and the reward, the greater the probability of the behavior. However, in an organizational context it is sometimes difficult to tie rewards to a particular behavior because many behaviors are typically elicited concurrently. It is thus possible to obscure the connection between the reward and the desired behavior, which decreases the probability of the behavior's occurring. In an extreme case everything gets turned around: The behaviors that organizations have tried to encourage are punished, and those that they have tried to discourage are actually rewarded. Kerr (1995) described how this can happen.

Orphanages are organizations created as residences for children before they are placed in private homes. Orphanages receive state funds to assist them in their operations. Since the primary goal of the orphanage is to place children in good homes, the way the orphanage is run should be directed toward this objective. However, such is not the case—the reward system created by the orphanage's management often drives the process in reverse for these reasons:

- The number of children enrolled in the orphanage often is the most important determinant of the size of its allocated budget.
- The number of children under the director's care affects the size of the support staff, which also is a determinant of the budget.
- The total organizational size largely determines the director's prestige at annual conventions, in the community, and so on.

Therefore, to the extent that staff size, total budget, and personal prestige are valued by the orphanage's executive personnel, it becomes rational for them to make it difficult for children to be adopted. Thus, the reward system reinforces the exact opposite of the behavior for which the orphanage was created—that is, the placement of children.

Vast amounts of research indicate that schedules of reinforcement can indeed motivate behavior to occur in certain patterns. However, the direction of that behavior is not always consistent with organizational goals.

regulate a person's actions. Goals are what the individual is consciously trying to attain, particularly as related to future objectives.

According to Locke and Latham (1990), goals have two major functions: They are a basis for motivation and they direct behavior. A goal provides guidelines for a person deciding how much effort to put into work. Goals are intended behaviors; in turn, they influence task performance. However, two conditions must be met before goals can positively influence performance. First, the individual must be aware of the goal and know what must be accomplished. Second, the individual must accept the goal as something he or she is willing to work for. Goals can be rejected because they are seen as too difficult or too easy or because the person does not know what behaviors are needed to attain them. Acceptance of the goal implies the individual intends to engage in the behavior needed for goal attainment.

Locke and Latham's theory of goal setting states that more difficult goals lead to higher levels of job performance. The authors believe that commitment to a goal is proportional to its difficulty. Thus, more difficult goals engender more commitment to their attainment. Goals can also vary in specificity. Some goals are general (for example, to be a good biology student), and others are more specific (to get an A on the next biology test). The more specific the goal, the more concentrated the individual's effort in its pursuit and the more directed the behavior. It is also important for the person to receive feedback about task performance; this guides whether he or she should work harder or continue at the same pace.

Therefore, according to goal-setting theory, the following factors and conditions induce high motivation and task performance. Goals are behavioral intentions that channel our energies in certain directions. The more difficult and specific the goal, the greater is our motivation to attain it. Feedback on our performance in pursuit of the goal tells us whether our efforts are "on target." The source of motivation, according to goal setting, is the desire and intention to attain the goal; this must be coupled with the individual's acceptance of the goal. Rather than dealing with motivation as a product of innate needs, feelings of inequity, or schedules of reinforcement, goal-setting theory assumes people set acceptable target objectives and then channel their efforts in pursuit of them. In particular, the emphasis in goal-setting theory is on the direction of behavior.

Empirical Tests of the Theory. For the most part, empirical tests of the theory are quite supportive. As an example, Latham and Baldes (1975) studied truck drivers hauling logs to lumber mills. The drivers' performance was studied under two conditions. First, drivers were told only to "do their best" in loading the trucks. After a time, they were told to set a specific, difficult goal of loading their trucks up to 94% of the legal weight limit. (The closer to the legal limit, the fewer trips were needed.) Each truck driver got feedback by means of a loading scale indicating tonnage. Figure 12–4 shows the drivers' performance over a 48-week period. At the onset of goal setting, performance improved greatly; however, the cause is not clear-cut. One explanation may be the effects of goal setting. Another could be a sense of competition among the drivers as to who could load the truck closest to the legal limit. (The decline in performance between the fourth and fifth blocks was due to the truck drivers' "testing" of management to gauge its reaction.) In any case, the study clearly showed that performance under goal setting was superior to the "do your best" condition.

Wright (1990), however, concluded that assigned goals produce greater increases in performance than self-set goals. Also, Hollenbeck, Williams, and Klein (1989) reported that commitment to difficult goals is higher when goals are stated publicly rather than privately. While variation does exist in terms of task behaviors and acceptance of goal setting, research indicates that goal setting produces better performance than the absence of goals or very general goals. As Latham and Marshall (1982) stated, the key issue appears to be not *how* a goal is set but *whether* the goal is set.

Evaluation of the Theory You should be struck by the elegance and simplicity of goal-setting theory. There are no references to innate needs, perceived instrumentalities, or comparison with others. As Latham and Locke (1991) observed, the goal-setting theory lies within the domain of purposefully directed action. The theory focuses on why some people perform better on work tasks than others. If they are equal in ability and environmental conditions, then the cause must be motivational. The theory states that the simplest and most direct motivational explanation of why some people perform better than others is that they have

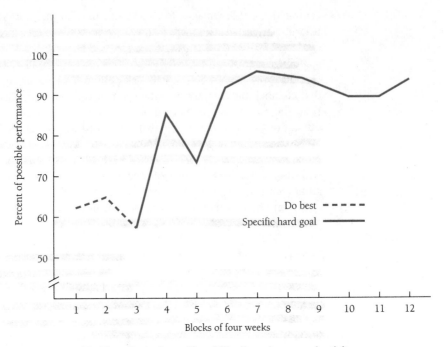

FIGURE 12–4 ■ The effect of specific, difficult goals on productivity

SOURCE: From "The Practical Significance of Locke's Theory of Goal Setting" by G. P. Latham and J. J. Baldes, 1975, *Journal of Applied Psychology, 60,* p. 123.

different performance goals. The difficulty and specificity of the goal influence performance, as do the amount and nature of feedback. There are some differences in performance between goals that are assigned and those that are self-selected. Different types of people also prefer different types of goals, but it is clear that goal setting elicits better performance.

Why is goal setting an effective motivational strategy? Pinder (1998) offered several reasons. Goals direct attention and action. They identify the target of intended behavior, and if they are stated specifically (as is recommended), the focus of the person's effort becomes well defined. Similarly, the condition that goals be made difficult relates directly to the intensity and persistence components of the motivation concept. If a goal is difficult, it normally requires more effort, over a longer period of time, to be attained. One element of persistence is tenacity, which is the refusal to quit trying, despite obstacles, until the goal is achieved. Commitment is one factor that contributes to tenacity, as does the sheer difficulty of the goal itself. Goal setting requires the development of a task-related strategy. When people contemplate a goal, they must also consider the means for its attainment, especially when the goal is seen as difficult. It may be that harder tasks are more likely to stimulate more strategy development than are easy tasks. Pinder believes it makes sense that the more specific the task goal, the more likely it is that people devise specific techniques to achieve it. Rousseau (1997) posited that goal setting is a form of self-management, where people can set their own goals and translate them into action. The acceptance of goals, when they are not self-set, is critical to their attainment. Thus, goal setting places people in control of their own behavior, which can itself serve as an incentive.

Goal setting seems to be generalizable as a theory of motivation. Its application is not limited to highly rational people, although it does assume that people follow through with their intentions. The theory has a cognitive basis: Employees must think about the goals they want to pursue; they must decide whether the goals are acceptable; they must understand what behaviors they have to exhibit to attain the goal; and they must know how to evaluate feedback on their progress. Research on feedback has shown that it is critical for optimal performance but that people differ in their ability to use the information provided. There is also evidence that goal setting is effective for groups. Thus, a work group can set a goal to decrease scrap rate, for example, or to increase productive output. Group goals can be more difficult to attain, however, because in many cases the success of the overall group depends on more than just the success of individual members. A basketball team may set a goal of winning a certain number of games in a season, but its success is determined by more than just the number of points scored by each player. Member coordination and integration must also be considered. One player might help the team by passing, another by rebounding, and the others by shooting.

Locke, Shaw, Saari, and Latham (1981) reviewed 12 years of goal-setting research studies and came to the following conclusion: 90% of the studies show that specific and challenging goals lead to higher performance than easy goals, "do your best" goals, or no goals. Goal setting was found to improve task performance when (1) subjects have sufficient ability, (2) feedback is provided on progress relative to goals, (3) rewards are given for goal attainment, (4) management is supportive, and (5) individuals accept assigned goals. Tubbs (1986) concluded that the concepts of goal difficulty, goal specificity, and participation in the goal-setting process were all supported by empirical research studies. However, the principles of goal setting were empirically supported more often in laboratory than in field studies. Tubbs also discovered that individuals are more willing to accept and work for an extremely difficult goal when they know that they will not have to do so for any extended period. In summary, the overall verdict on the value of goal setting as a theory of motivation is overwhelmingly positive.

Pritchard, Jones, Roth, Stuebing, and Ekeberg (1988) noted that most research on improving productivity through goal setting has studied relatively simple jobs with the individual as the unit of analysis. Because most jobs are more complex and given the interdependencies in work, they feel group-level intervention studies are needed. The authors studied work group productivity for nine months. They introduced a group-level intervention designed to enhance group productivity consisting of three parts: feedback, group goal setting, and incentives (time off from work). Group-level feedback was found to increase productivity by 50% over the baseline, and goal setting plus feedback increased productivity by 75% over the baseline. The combined effect of feedback, goal setting, and incentives increased productivity by 76% over the baseline. The study showed that the principles of goal setting, proven useful with individual performance, also hold for group performance.

Self-Regulation Theory

Statement of the Theory.   There is not a single theory of self-regulation. Rather, it represents a family of theories that share some basic commonalities. A complete description of all the theories and an examination of the specific formulations by which they differ are beyond the scope of this book. Some of the more notable specific theories from this family of theories are self-efficacy theory and control theory. What follows is an explanation of the basic concepts of **self-regulation theory.**

self-regulation theory
a theory of motivation based on the setting of goals and the receipt of accurate feedback that is monitored to enhance the likelihood of goal attainment

At the core of the theory is the idea of goals. It is presumed that people consciously set goals for themselves that guide and direct their behavior toward the attainment of these goals. Furthermore, individuals engage in a process of self-monitoring or self-evaluation; that is, they are aware of their progress in pursuit of the goals they have set. Their awareness of their progress is facilitated by the receipt of feedback. Feedback is information about how successful or "on target" the individual is in progressing toward the goal attainment. The feedback can and often does produce a discrepancy between the individual's current status in pursuing a goal and the desired or needed status to attain the goal. In essence, the feedback can provide an "error message" that the individual is off-track in pursuit of the goal. It is at this point that the individual responds to the information provided by the feedback. The response can be in the form of altering the individual's behavior in anticipation of reducing the magnitude of the discrepancy between the current progress toward attaining the goal and the needed progress toward goal attainment. Alternatively, the feedback received by the individual can yield little or no discrepancy between the actual and desired status in the path toward goal attainment. If the discrepancy is small, the individual has enhanced self-efficacy, a sense of personal control and mastering of the environment, resulting in greater self-confidence that the goal can and will be attained. However, large discrepancies result in a loss of self-efficacy, which decreases the individual's sense of confidence that the goal will be attained. When the discrepancies are large, the individual may engage in goal revision, a process of readjusting or modifying the initial goal to a less difficult or ambitious level. Finally, life is a process of repeatedly pursuing goals in one form or another. With each success we experience in attaining the goals we set, we gain a greater collective sense of self-efficacy. Goal attainment acquires a degree of perceived generalizability, meaning the individual thinks that future goals are more likely to be attained because of his or her success in attaining past goals. The name of this family of theories, *self-regulation theory*, implies that individuals play an active role in monitoring their own behavior, seeking feedback, responding to the feedback, and forming opinions regarding their likelihood of success in future endeavors.

For example, assume an individual sets a goal of losing 30 pounds by dieting and exercising. The 30-pound weight loss is scheduled to occur over a 10-week period, with a loss of 3 pounds per week for 10 weeks. The feedback comes from weighing on a scale. If after 2 weeks, for example, the individual had not lost 6 pounds, a different pattern of eating and exercising may follow. If the individual continued not to meet the weight-loss goal over the ensuing weeks, the individual may revise the stated goal to perhaps 20 pounds over the 10-week period, or extend the 30-pound weight loss over a longer period of time, as perhaps 20 weeks. To the extent the individual is successful in meeting the weight-loss goal, the individual's self-efficacy about personal weight loss is enhanced to seek possible additional weight loss in the future. Furthermore, the sense of self-efficacy regarding the weight loss could generalize to other goals in other aspects of life.

Empirical Tests of the Theory. Self-regulation theory has been tested in a wide variety of contexts as diversified as the various conceptualizations of the theory. Examples include how children learn in school (Zimmerman, 1995), career choice and development (Hackett, 1995), and treatment of addictive behaviors (Marlatt, Baer, & Quigley, 1995). The general pattern of results is very positive. Among the more supportive findings is the perceived importance of personal causation and control over goal pursuit. Self-regulation theory clearly positions the individual as the agent responsible for striving to attain the goal. We are continuing to learn the conditions under which individuals will remain committed to a goal (e.g., Klein, Wesson, Hollenbeck, & Alge, 1999), even when they perceive discrepancies from the feedback regarding their progress in goal attainment. Vande-Walle and Cummings (1997) demonstrated some of the conditions under which individuals seek out feedback. In many cases there are few mechanisms for giving immediate and precise feedback to individuals on the state of their progress, like the scale for providing feedback regarding weight loss.

VandeWalle, Brown, Cron, and Slocum (1999) confirmed a difference between a *learning* goal orientation and a *performance* goal orientation in a study of salespeople. A learning goal orientation is one in which the individual is committed to acquiring new skills and mastering new situations. In a performance goal orientation the individual is committed to demonstrating his or her competence by seeking favorable judgments from others. VandeWalle et al. found that commitment to a learning goal orientation led to increased self-regulation tactics (i.e., seeking feedback, self-monitoring performance, planning future actions) and better on-the-job sales performance than just wanting to appear to others to have high ability. A practical implication of the findings is that organizations should assess the learning goal orientation of job applicants. When the job involves more than the conduct of rote and unchanging job duties, possession of a learning goal orientation will allow employees to learn new duties and responsibilities as the conduct of their work changes. A similar finding related to complex skill-training programs was reported by Brett and VandeWalle (1999). In short, self-regulation theory provides a rich conceptual basis to understand how individuals become motivated to pursue various goals and why they persevere in their pursuit of the goals.

Evaluation of the Theory. While some components of self-regulation theory have not been expressed in earlier theories of motivation, self-regulation theory has several concepts associated with other theories. The importance of setting goals and consciously focusing on their attainment is supported by early research on goal-setting theory. The association between expending effort in pursuit of a goal and ultimately attaining the goal is reflected in the concept of expectancy from expectancy theory. Furthermore, repeated success in goal attainment results in higher self-efficacy, which is the analogue in expectancy theory of perceiving a strong relationship between effort and performance. From reinforcement theory we have learned that rewarded (or reinforced) behavior has a greater probability of occurrence than unrewarded behavior. Repeatedly attaining goals is self-rewarding, which increases the probability that future goals will also be attained. The research on self-regulation theory reveals that we are more likely to be committed to goals that we regard as particularly significant and important to us than to trivial goals.

Finally, Maslow's conception of self-actualization is grounded in the belief that one can master his or her environment to fully realize and achieve one's potential. Likewise, self-efficacy is the belief in one's capabilities and capacity to attain the goals that have been set. In short, much of self-regulation theory is a distillation of previous motivational theories buttressed with new concepts (most notably the feedback/expectation discrepancy; Kluger, 2001) not found in other theories. Furthermore, it emphasizes how cognitive processes become translated or activated in behavior (e.g., Lord & Levy, 1994).

As we stated at the beginning of the description of this theory, there are multiple manifestations of self-regulation theory. Not all of the manifestations make identical predictions of behavior in specific circumstances (e.g., Phillips, Hollenbeck, & Ilgen, 1996). Nevertheless, the basic tenets of the theory, as described, have been shown to explain how people come to learn new tasks in training (e.g., Ford et al., 1998). The concept of self-efficacy does indeed appear to be a very useful and insightful way for us to understand our participation, performance, and persistence in a wide range of human endeavors (see Field Note 3).

FIELD NOTE 3   Conscious or Nonconscious Self-Regulation?

elf-regulation theory asserts that we are constantly engaging in self-monitoring activities. Consistent with other current theories outside the traditional boundaries of I/O psychology, there is an assumption that people are consciously and systematically processing incoming information in order to interpret the world. This information is then used to plan and engage in courses of action. However, some cognitive psychologists are questioning how much of this self-regulation of behavior occurs at the conscious level. Bargh and Chartrand (1999) believe that most moment-to-moment psychological life must occur through nonconscious means if it is to occur at all. They assert that various nonconscious mental systems perform the lion's share of self-regulating behavior. Why? The reasons are varied, but one is that as individuals we are bombarded with vast amounts of information on a continuous basis. It is argued that we would get little accomplished in life if we were so consciously involved in seeking feedback, examining the feedback, and then cognitively processing it. Therefore, the self-regulation process must have a strong nonconscious component to it; namely, we are not aware of our self-regulating behavior even though we are doing it. The research by Bargh and Chartrand introduces a new dimension to our study of motivation: We may not even be actively aware of why we do what we do.

Job Characteristics Theory

Statement of the Theory.   A decidedly different approach to work motivation is represented by **job characteristics theory.** This theory proposes that, for the most part, the locus of control for motivation is not individuals but the environment where work is performed. Thus, this theory proposes that, given the proper design of jobs, work can facilitate motivation in individuals. Therefore, all people can be highly motivated given a work environment that fosters effort expenditure. The theory proposes there are characteristics or attributes of jobs that facilitate motivation. The number of these attributes and their identification have been the subject of extensive research. Early research (i.e., Turner & Lawrence, 1965) identified a set of attributes of job structure that affected motivation. However, the authors also found that not all individuals responded in the same way to the job attributes. That is, there appeared to be individual differences across people that explain why some individuals would respond favorably to a job with a high motivating potential. The process of designing jobs to possess these attributes is called **job enrichment.**

In 1976 Hackman and Oldham proposed the job characteristics model that best exemplifies this approach to motivation. It is among the most heavily researched theories in the history of I/O psychology. The model consists of four major parts. The first part is the specification of the particular job characteristics (also called core job dimensions) that induce motivation:

1. *Skill variety*—the number of different activities, skills, and talents the job requires
2. *Task identity*—the degree to which a job requires completion of a whole, identifiable piece of work—that is, doing a job from beginning to end, with visible results
3. *Task significance*—the job's impact on the lives or work of other people, whether within or outside the organization
4. *Autonomy*—the degree of freedom, independence, and discretion in scheduling work and determining procedures that the job provides
5. *Task feedback*—the degree to which carrying out the activities required results in direct and clear information about the effectiveness of performance

The second part of the model deals with the effect of the core job dimensions on the individual. They are said to influence three critical psychological states. The *experienced meaningfulness of work* is high when the job involves skill variety, task identity, and significance. The *experienced responsibility for work outcomes* is influenced mainly by the amount of autonomy. *Knowledge of results of work activities* is a function of feedback. According to the theory, high levels of the critical psychological states will lead to favorable personal and work outcomes, including high internal work motivation, work performance, and satisfaction, and low absenteeism and turnover.

The third part of the job characteristics model is an individual difference variable called growth need strength (GNS), which reflects a desire to fulfill higher-order needs (in Maslow's sense of needs). Like others before them, Hackman and Oldham felt that people with high needs for personal growth and development

job characteristics theory a theory of motivation based on the presence of dimensions or characteristics of jobs that induce the expenditure of effort

job enrichment the process of designing work so as to enhance individual motivation to perform the work

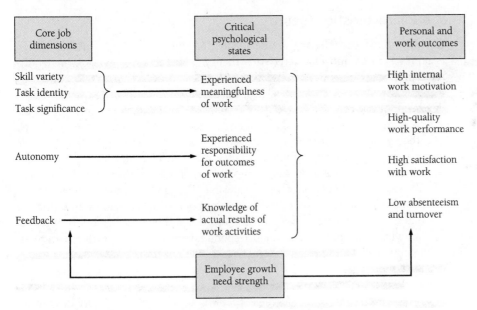

FIGURE 12–5 ■ The job characteristics model

SOURCE: From "Motivation Through the Design of Work: Test of a Theory" by J. R. Hackman and G. R. Oldham, 1976. *Organizational Behavior and Human Performance, 16*, p. 256.

should respond more positively to jobs high on the core dimensions. Only people with high GNS should strongly experience the critical psychological states associated with such jobs. The entire job characteristics model is portrayed in Figure 12–5.

Hackman and Oldham then proposed the fourth part of the model, an equation for indexing the potential of a job to motivate its holder. The equation is based on the five core dimensions. The authors refer to their index as the *motivating potential score* (MPS) and define it as

$$\text{MPS} = \frac{\text{Skill variety} + \text{Task identity} + \text{Task significance}}{3} \times \text{Autonomy} \times \text{Feedback}$$

The first three core dimensions are averaged because they all contribute to the experienced meaningfulness of work, the first critical psychological state. The other two dimensions, autonomy and feedback, reflect the remaining critical states and thus are not averaged.

The job's motivating potential is very high when each component of the formula is high. Because the components are multiplied, low scores on any one yield a low motivating potential score. A score of zero on any of the major components (for example, a job completely lacking in autonomy) reduces the MPS to zero; the job has no potential for motivating incumbents.

Finally, as shown in Figure 12–5, the entire effect of the job characteristics model is moderated by the growth need strength. Only employees who are trying to satisfy higher-order needs will respond favorably to a job high in motivating potential.

In summary, the theory posits that individuals who possess high growth need strength will exhibit high motivation on the job when the job is characterized by a high motivating potential score. It is also proposed that people in such jobs will experience high job satisfaction, another hypothesized outcome of the model.

Empirical Tests of the Theory.   Many studies have tested the relationships and predictions of the model. The empirical support is mixed; certain parts of the model are substantiated more than others.

Hackman and Oldham (1976) provided validation evidence for their own theory. In general, the overall results were moderately supportive:

- The core job dimensions related to the critical psychological states. Skill variety, task identity, and task significance combined to predict the level of perceived meaningfulness. The authors were thus able to identify those factors contributing to "meaningful work," a frequent desire of employees.
- Individual differences in GNS have a moderating effect, as Hackman and Oldham suggested. In particular, high-GNS employees were more likely to have favorable personal and work outcomes after experiencing the critical psychological states.
- The core dimensions of autonomy and feedback were not clearly related to the corresponding critical psychological states of experienced responsibility and knowledge of results. Some of the other dimensions predicted these states as well or better.

In general, the results showed that jobs high on the core job dimensions were associated with high levels of motivation. Individuals with high GNS responded most favorably to these types of jobs. The importance of the intervening critical psychological states was not strongly supported.

Based on a review of over 200 studies that tested the model, Fried and Ferris (1987) arrived at three conclusions. First, research suggests the existence of multiple job characteristics, but it is not clear how many there are. Second, the linkage between the job characteristics and the critical psychological states is not as strong as originally hypothesized. Third, the level of individual motivation specified in the model is indeed related to the job characteristics.

Oldham (1996) proposed some needed research directions with the model. One involves the ongoing effects of job characteristics on individual needs and skills. The characteristics of a job can exert long-term influences on the people performing the job. Furthermore, it is also possible that the design of jobs might affect employees' GNS. For example, employees who work on simple jobs might experience chronic frustration, resulting in lowered GNS.

Loher, Noe, Moeller, and Fitzgerald (1985) reported average correlations between scores on the five core job dimensions of the job characteristics model and reported job satisfaction of around .40. In other words, it seems that the more jobs are enriched (defined as higher scores on the core job characteristics), the more motivated and satisfied the people are who perform them. Campion and Berger (1990) reported that jobs characterized by higher scores on the core job dimensions were associated with higher aptitudes and higher pay. Thus, when organizations want to make jobs more motivating, they should realize that they will need people with more talent and ability to perform them.

Evaluation of the Theory.   As stated previously, the job characteristics model is one of the most heavily researched theories in I/O psychology. The meta-analytic review of the theory by Fried and Ferris (1987) was based on over 200 studies that tested the model. What does the model offer us as a theory of motivation? Its basic approach certainly expands the conception of motivation as proposed by the need hierarchy, equity, and expectancy theories. The job characteristics model asserts that it is properties of the job or the workplace that foster motivation in people. In short, motivation is not a durable personal attribute or a trait that some people possess more of than others, but rather a variable attribute that can be enhanced if properly and intentionally designed within a work environment. However, research reveals that some individual differences across people influence to what degree a potentially stimulating job will motivate them. The GNS component of the model is designed to reflect that individual concept.

Research on the model has been criticized by some because assessments of the job characteristics are subjective, not objective. That is, the level of the job characteristics present in a job is measured by how people perceive and judge the job. They are not objective properties of the work environment, such as the number of hours in a workday or the air temperature at which work is performed. With a crucial reliance on subjective evaluations, the validity of the model is threatened by many of the rating issues discussed in Chapter 7. That is, two people performing the same job may differ (perhaps markedly) in their assessment of how much autonomy (for example) is present in the job. Likewise, it could be possible that over time people with high GNS tend to gravitate toward more complex jobs, while people with low GNS tend to gravitate to more simple jobs. Thus, the "type of job" and "type of person" performing the job in real life are often confounded. Nevertheless, research on the job characteristics model has revealed some important findings about the concept of motivation. Rather than just trying to identify and select highly motivated job applicants, organizations can also design work in a way that fosters or facilitates motivation. The implication is that organizations need not be passive in their desire to identify motivated employees. By the way they design work, organizations can help achieve the very outcomes they strive to attain.

OVERVIEW AND SYNTHESIS OF WORK MOTIVATION THEORIES

After studying the seven theories of work motivation presented, one can reasonably ask whether any unifying themes run through them. Kanfer (1992) proposed that the theories can be examined along a continuum of their conceptual proximity to action. The endpoints of the continuum are distal (i.e., distant) and proximal (i.e., near) constructs. *Distal* constructs such as personality exert indirect effects on behavior. *Proximal* constructs begin with the individual's goals and char-

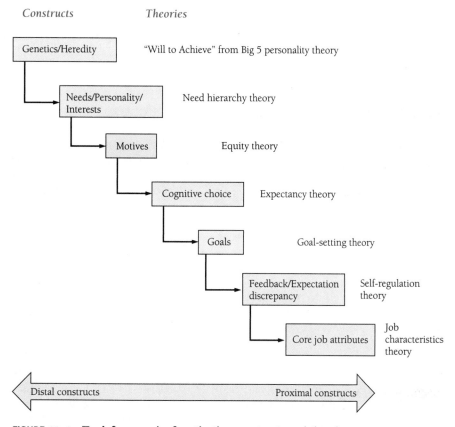

FIGURE 12–6 ■ A framework of motivation constructs and theories

SOURCE: Adapted from "Work Motivation: New Directions in Theory and Research" by R. Kanfer, 1992, in *International Review of Industrial and Organizational Psychology* (p. 4), edited by C. L. Cooper and I. T. Robertson, London: Wiley.

acteristics of the workplace that directly influence behavior. Figure 12–6 portrays the motivation constructs and associated theories arrayed along the distal/proximal continuum proposed by Kanfer.

As illustrated by the arrangement of motivational theories in Kanfer's framework, the array of explanations for motivation is based on consideration of the individual, ranging from genetic predisposition to individual conscious choice. Noticeably absent from Kanfer's framework is where reinforcement theory fits in. Reinforcement theory is predicated upon environmental factors that shape behavior through patterns of reward. The role of the individual, through either genetic makeup or cognitive processes, is not regarded as essential or necessary to understand motivation. Much current thinking in psychology asserts that the cognitive perspective is more insightful for understanding motivation, and believes the operant (reinforcement) perspective is too insensitive to individual differences, particularly with regard to volition. A general summary of the major themes of work motivation discussed in this chapter is presented in Table 12–2.

TABLE 12–2 ■ **Summary and evaluation of work motivation theories**

Theory	Source of Motivation	Empirical Support	Organizational Applicability
Need hierarchy theory	Unconscious, innate needs	Weak: little support for proposed relationships among needs.	Very limited: Theory lacks sufficient specificity to guide behavior.
Equity theory	Drive to reduce feelings of tension caused by perceived inequity	Mixed: Good support for underpayment inequity; weak support for overpayment equity.	Limited: Social comparisons are made, but feelings of inequity can be reduced through means other than increased motivation.
Expectancy theory	Relationship among desired outcomes, performance–reward, and effort–performance variables	Moderate–strong: More strongly supported in within-subjects than across-subjects experiments.	Strong: Theory provides a rational basis for why people expend effort, although not all behavior is consciously determined as postulated.
Reinforcement theory	Schedule of reinforcement used to reward people for their performance	Moderate: Ratio reinforcement schedules evoke superior performance compared with interval schedules, but little difference exists among various ratio schedules.	Moderate: Contingent payment for performance is possible in some jobs, although ethical problems can be present in an attempt to shape employee behavior.
Goal-setting theory	Intention to direct behavior in pursuit of acceptable goals	Moderate–strong: Performance under goal-setting conditions is usually superior to conditions in which no goals are set.	Strong: Ability to set goals is not restricted to certain types of people or jobs.
Self-regulation theory	Self-monitoring of feedback designed to enhance goal attainment	Moderate–strong: Feedback can provide direction for behavior if monitored and acted upon.	Strong: Organizations can provide directive feedback to individuals to facilitate goal attainment.
Job characteristics theory	Attributes of jobs that can facilitate motivation among people with a strong need to achieve	Moderate–strong: Clear support for the validity of the job characteristics but less support for the critical psychological states.	Moderate: It is not clear whether job characteristics are objective properties of jobs that organizations can design or are subjectively perceived by individuals.

At the extreme distal end is the construct of genetics/heredity. This chapter has not formally examined a genetics-based theory of motivation, but we are familiar with it from another area. It will be recalled that a contemporary interpretation of personality is represented in the Big 5 theory. One personality factor of considerable interest to I/O psychologists is conscientiousness. Another name for conscientiousness is "will to achieve" (Digman & Takemoto-Chock, 1981). This name implies that individuals who are attentive to detail, rule abiding, and honest also exhibit high ambition. Accordingly this view of motivation is that the capacity to be motivated is genetically determined, is an enduring component of one's personality, and can be assessed with a paper-and-pencil personality inventory. Indeed, Kanfer and Ackerman (2000) recently developed such a measure, the Motivational Trait Questionnaire. Research continues on the role that personality plays in motivation (e.g., Sackett, Gruys, & Ellingson, 1998).

Maslow's theory is predicated upon a universal set of basic human needs, arranged in a hierarchy, that all individuals have. Inter-individual differences in motivation are attributed to differences in the particular needs that people are trying to satisfy. Equity theory asserts there is a social component to motivation; that is, how hard we are willing to work is in part a function of how we perceive other people in our environment. Based on a social comparison of what other people are giving and getting, we assess how much effort we are willing to exert. Implicit in the equity theory is a sense of fairness (i.e., equity) or justice, which embeds this theoretical perspective of motivation in the same conceptual framework as that offered by the research on organizational justice.

As we continue down the continuum toward proximal constructs, there is increasing reliance on the assumption that people make conscious, deliberate, controllable choices about how much effort they choose to expend. This is the antithesis of a genetic/dispositional orientation toward motivation. Proximal theories are heavily predicated upon a cognitive explanation for motivation. Expectancy theory postulates that individuals are consciously aware of the results or outcomes they wish to attain, perceive relationships between their behavior and attaining those outcomes, and also perceive a relationship between their effort and their behavior. The theory elevates motivation to a conscious choice made by the individual. Goal-setting theory is another example of this orientation and offers motivation as an opportunity to engage in self-control or self-regulation. The capacity to control one's own life was noted in the preceding chapter as one of the determinants of mental health. Goal-setting theory postulates that one way we can take some control over our life is to decide how hard we are willing to work. Locke (1991) offered this description of how important individual choice or volition is in our lives:

> For example, people can choose . . . what their needs are and how to satisfy them; what values they should pursue and the validity of the values other people have told them to pursue; whether and how to apply their values to a specific situation; what goals to set, how to develop plans to reach them, and whether to commit to the goals and plans; what their performance capacity is for a specific task and how to raise it; what their performance means and who is responsible for it; the adequacy of their rewards and the relation of these rewards to their values; the causes of their affective reactions to their performance and rewards; and how to modify these reactions (e.g., by changing their performance or changing their value standards). (pp. 297–298)

The self-regulation theory of motivation is an extension and modification of goal-setting theory. Self-regulation theory also involves consciously setting goals, then obtaining feedback on the degree to which the individual is on target in pursuit of the goal, and then using that feedback to modify or maintain the chosen paths of action to goal attainment. The process of self-monitoring or self-evaluation clearly is predicated upon a conscious, rational, deliberate strategy of using information to guide behavior. Finally, job characteristics theory specifies there are dimensions or components of the job itself that induce motivation. While there are individual differences with regard to how people will respond to these job characteristics, it is the properties of the work environment itself that facilitate energized behavior. Job characteristics theory contains the most proximal constructs, constructs that in fact can be designed or structured by the organization to induce motivation.

A few researchers (e.g., Erez & Earley, 1993) have proposed motivational concepts that originated in non-Western cultures but may be universally applicable. For example, Earley (1997) discussed the concept of *face* (as in "saving face") as a basis of social motivation. Face has been considered a predominantly Asian concept. Earley references face as the evaluation of a person based on self and external social judgments. Face does not lie completely within or outside the individual, as face is both given (by others) and claimed (by the self). Thus, the concept of face is grounded in a social exchange process involving self-presentation. It is proposed that our behavior is guided by efforts to regulate and enhance our self-image. Examples include gaining the sense of prestige derived from a job title, living in an affluent neighborhood, and maintaining a certain physical appearance (e.g., "power dressing"). The loss of face is associated with shame and weakens the network of social relations of which we are all a part. Earley believes the concept of face is a useful framework for understanding our behavior within a social context. We are motivated to enhance face, and our actions can be judged as being instrumental for doing so. This perspective takes a decidedly social view of motivation and has no specific mechanistic tenets such as variable ratio schedules of reinforcement and perceived expectancies. It is most similar to equity theory, which is also based on a social comparison. Although it remains to be seen what role such concepts as face will play in the evolution of motivation theories, Earley's theory presents a cross-culturally based explanation for what is a timeless and boundaryless phenomenon—an understanding of our behavior.

The subject of human motivation is also being addressed from a genetic basis. This view is in marked contrast to considering motivation as a product of job or social influences. Rather, the search is inward to the cellular and genetic levels for the biochemical determinants of human behavior. Ridley (1999) has described the mapping of the human genome, particularly with reference to the gene *D4DR*, which is a component of chromosome 11. This gene determines how receptive neurons are to dopamine, which in turn controls neural electrical discharge and regulates the flow of blood to the brain. Ridley stated, "To simplify grossly, dopamine is perhaps the brain's motivational chemical. Too little and the person lacks initiative and motivation. Too much and the person is easily bored and frequently seeks new adventures. Here perhaps lies the root of a difference in 'personality'" (p. 163). Erez and Eden (2001) succinctly summarized this orientation toward the origins of human behavior. "Although for us as psychologists the jump from chemicals to motivation to personality is a bit abrupt, the trend is clear: We are drawing nearer to the dream—or nightmare—of chemistry-based motivation" (p. 7).

Katzell and Thompson (1990) analyzed the vast body of research and theory on motivation and identified seven practices that can raise the level of motivation of people in work organizations:

1. Ensure that workers' motives and values are appropriate for the jobs on which they are placed.
2. Make jobs attractive and consistent with workers' motives and values.
3. Define work goals that are clear, challenging, attractive, and attainable.
4. Provide workers with the personnel and material resources that facilitate their effectiveness.
5. Create supportive social environments.
6. Reinforce performance.
7. Harmonize all these elements into a consistent sociotechnical system.

As can be inferred from the theories of work motivation presented in this chapter, no one theory strongly addresses all seven of these practices. However, each theory can be adequately directed to some of them, leaving us with the conclusion that each theory of work motivation offers something of value in understanding this most complex construct.

Finally, from the perspective of conducting scientific research, Ambrose and Kulik (1999) noted that many topics in I/O psychology have an *implicit* motivational component even though "motivation" is not explicitly stated. For example, the research on organizational justice reveals that individuals exhibit higher motivation when they feel their employer treats them fairly. It is thus a matter of scientific debate whether our understanding is better enhanced by studying underlying theoretical constructs such as "motivation" or behaviors and contexts in which the constructs are manifested.

THE APPLICATION OF MOTIVATIONAL STRATEGIES

After seven approaches to work motivation have been presented, it is almost inevitable to ask which theory has the greatest practical value or, perhaps more to the point, which theory will "work" for you. While there is no simple answer to this question, some practical guidelines are available to assist in the decision. Mitchell (1997) referred to this process as "matching" motivational strategies with varying organizational contexts.

Mitchell stated we must begin the process with some sort of problem recognition. Behavior has three main causal factors: motivation, ability, and constraints. The preferred point of origin in our analysis is constraints. In many cases, removal of constraints and situational obstacles is the appropriate action and may be far more effective than trying to enhance abilities or increase motivation. The lack of a needed piece of equipment (e.g., a computer) is an example of a situational obstacle.

If problems in behavior persist when situational constraints are removed, the next step is to examine abilities and skills—determine whether ability is an issue (e.g., have you exhibited the desired behavior in the past?). Perhaps you are seeking to behave in ways and in contexts for which you lack the needed abilities, and effort cannot compensate for lack of ability.

If lack of ability does not appear to be a major issue, the problem may have a major motivational component. However, there are several types of motivational problems. Apathy and boredom suggest an arousal problem. If you are working hard but not succeeding, directional processes may be misaligned. If you are not doing enough or following through, intensity and persistence should be the focus of attention.

Ideally there should be room in your environmental context for motivation to manifest itself. There may be organizational constraints that take precedence over inter- or intra-individual differences in motivation. For example, in assembly-line work the speed of the line determines the level of output. You cannot make the assembly line move faster by working harder, nor does the assembly line move faster for harder-working individuals. This type of organizational constraint must be absent for increases in motivation to result in increased performance.

After you have decided you have a motivational problem and have decided which motivational process (e.g., arousal, direction, intensity, persistence) is most involved, you still have a number of issues to consider. At this point Mitchell (1997) refers to the "match" between the motivational strategy you select and the organizational context you face. Organizational contexts differ in many ways—for example, the clarity of the performance criteria by which you will be judged, the frequency and nature of the feedback you receive about your behavior, whether your performance is judged on an individual or group basis, and so on. While goal setting and self-regulation are the most supportable and adaptable motivational strategies, they require accurate and timely feedback. For example, if you set the goal of earning an A in a class but your grade is determined by one comprehensive exam at the end of the course, you will have received no formal feedback on your performance throughout the semester. Instead, you will have to rely on informal feedback for an internal sense of how well you are understanding the course material, which may be inaccurate. In such a case, reinforcement theory may provide you with a motivational incentive, such as rewarding yourself on a biweekly basis for reaching some level of mastery (e.g., doing well on a self-test). Expectancy theory can provide guidance on issues of direction and intensity, such as the perceived degree of association between how hard you try in a class and how well you perform. If the level of association is not high, do you have any insights about factors that determine the low level of association? That is, could you seek the assistance of the professor or a teaching assistant outside of class? Finally, if the class utilizes team projects, can team goals and team rewards be created? Can you use equity theory to judge the contributions (inputs) of other teams and their outcomes compared with your group?

There is probably no single, correct theory of motivation. Rather groups of theories operate in different contexts, differentiated by such factors as simple versus complex tasks and short versus long time frames. Likewise, some motivational theories require fairly extensive self-management, such as having high self-awareness, obtaining feedback, determining strategies, and so on. Self-regulation is one example. Other motivational theories are guided by less obtrusive mechanisms, such as innate needs. There are also individual differences in personality related to motivation. For example, Kanfer and Heggestad (1997) asserted that individuals differ in trait achievement. Persons high in trait achievement are more likely to pursue more challenging situations than persons low in trait achievement. By repeatedly engaging in challenging situations, persons high in trait achievement learn to better regulate their levels of motivation and to generalize this skill to other situations. Conversely, people with low trait achievement tend to avoid challenging situations and thus have fewer opportunities to develop motivational skills.

Finally, Erez (1997) noted the importance of cultural differences in work motivation. Cultures differ in the extent to which they reward individual and collective achievement, and this becomes yet another factor that promotes or inhibits motivation. Scarborough (2001) stated:

> Because values link needs and behavior, motivation is highly culture-specific. The theories of motivation developed and applied in the United States reflect our values. More collectivist cultures prefer evaluation and reward of group performance more than individual performance. Collectivists are less comfortable with great extremes in rewards based on performance or position, and with ostentatious perquisites. . . . Although all this seems very daunting, many managers in the culturally diverse United States are accustomed to coping with different value systems and motivational drives within their own, wholly domestic work forces. The problem in foreign cultures is more in degree than in kinds. (p. 265)

In conclusion, work motivation has a multiplicity of causes and catalysts, and there are no simple solutions or "one correct way" to motivate an individual or group.

CASE STUDY   ■   ## What to Do with Harry?

Joe Collins, Production Manager of York Tool and Die Company, tapped Harry Simpson on the shoulder. "Harry," Collins said, "I'd like to talk to you in my office."

"Right now?" asked Simpson.

"Right now," Collins replied.

Simpson took off his safety goggles and put them on the rack. He was a line foreman, and it was unusual to be called away from his line. He figured it had to be something big; otherwise, Collins would have waited until break.

"Hey, Willie," Simpson yelled at his lead man, "cover for me, will you? I've got to talk to Joe."

Simpson walked into Collins's office and sat down. The look on Collins's face told him it wasn't going to be good news.

"Harry, I've known you for eight years," Collins began. "You've always kept your nose to the grindstone. You've been conscientious and diligent. I've had fewer problems with you than with most of the other foremen. But lately things have been different. You've come to work late five times in the past month. You've been late turning in your weekly production sheets. The scrap rate of your line has been going up, too. I was also told that Willie had to spend a lot of time breaking in the two new guys. That's your job. What's going on, Harry?"

Simpson shuffled his feet and cleared his throat. "I didn't realize these things were happening."

"You didn't know you were late?" Collins was incredulous. "You've been coming to work at seven-thirty for eight years. When you punch in at seven-forty-five, you're late, and you know it."

"I don't know, Joe, I just haven't felt with it lately," Simpson explained. "Doris says I've been moping around the house a lot lately, too."

"I'm not here to chew you out, Harry," Collins replied. "You're a valuable man. I want to find a way to get you back in gear. Anything been bugging you lately?"

"Well, I've finally figured out I'm not going to make it to supervisor. At least not in the near future. That's what I've been working for all along. Maybe I've hit my peak. When Coleman made it to supervisor, I figured I'd be the next one up. But it never happened. I'm not sore—Coleman is a good man and he deserved it. I just feel kind of deflated."

"You're well respected by management, Harry, and your line thinks you're great, too. You've set a tough example to live up to. I want you to keep it up—we need people like you."

"I know I have an important job," said Simpson, "but I figure I can't get ahead anymore, at least not on how well I do my job. I guess it boils down to luck or something."

"What if I give you a new line to run?" Collins asked. "Would that give you a new challenge?"

"No, I wouldn't want that, Joe," replied Simpson. "I like my line, and I don't want to leave them."

"All right, Harry, but here's the deal," Collins stated. "I want you to cut back on the lateness, pronto. Get your production reports in on time, and watch the scrap. With the price of copper going up, we've got to play it tight. Oh, and give Willie a break. He's got enough to do. Does this sound okay to you?"

"Yeah," Simpson said. "You're only telling me to do what I'm supposed to be doing."

"Keep at it, Harry," Collins said with a smile. "In two more years, you'll get a ten-year pin."

Simpson got up to leave. "It won't pay the rent, but I'd like to have it."

Simpson walked back to the line. Willie looked up and saw him coming. "What'd Joe want?" Willie asked.

"Oh, nothing much," Simpson replied.

Willie knew Simpson was hiding something, and Simpson figured Willie knew what it was.

Study Questions

1. Which theory of motivation do you think best explains Simpson's recent behavior?

2. What would equity theory have predicted about Simpson's behavior following Coleman's promotion?

3. In terms of expectancy theory, how would you describe Simpson's valence for a promotion and its instrumentality?

4. What psychological needs did Collins appeal to in talking to Simpson?
5. How might you use reinforcement theory to shape Simpson's behavior in the areas that need attention?

SUGGESTED INFOTRAC TOPICS

motivation	*goals*
incentives	*goal-setting*
needs	*feedback*
ambition	*social comparison*
rewards	*job enrichment*

eadership

CHAPTER OUTLINE

LEARNING OBJECTIVES

- Explain the major topics of interest among leadership researchers.
- Describe the major theoretical approaches to the study of leadership: trait, behavioral, power and influence, situational, transformational and charismatic leadership, implicit leadership, and substitutes for leadership.
- Understand the points of convergence among leadership approaches.
- Discuss cross-cultural leadership issues.
- Discuss diversity issues in leadership.

When you think of leadership, many ideas come to mind. Your thoughts might relate to power, authority, and influence. Maybe you think of actual people—Washington, Lincoln, Kennedy, King—or what effective leaders do. In short, leadership evokes a multitude of thoughts, all of which in some way address the causes, symptoms, or effects of leadership.

This chapter will examine how I/O psychologists have tried to grapple with the multifaceted concept of leadership, particularly as it relates to behavior in the world of work. Research on leadership has been varied because investigators have approached the concept from different perspectives. Some research has examined what strong leaders are like as people by looking at demographic variables, personality traits, skills, and so on. Without followers, there can be no leaders; accordingly, some research has examined leader–follower relationships. Presumably "strong" leaders accomplish things that "weak" leaders do not; thus, other research is on the effects of leadership. An interesting question addresses contextual effects in leadership—for example, is leadership of a prison more demanding than leadership of a business organization? Thus, the situation in which leadership occurs has attracted much attention. Other areas of interest within the domain of leadership research have also been investigated. While such diversity of interest expands our understanding, it also creates ambiguity as to exactly what leadership is all about.

It is a matter of scientific debate whether "leadership" is different from "management" or "administration." Historically and practically, these terms have been used interchangeably. For example, one might readily encounter this sentence: "The leaders of the company manage its resources and are responsible for its administration." A slight variation would be: "The management of the company administers its operations by providing leadership." Other sentences with similar connotative meaning could be written. Are these terms really synonymous? Some researchers think not, believing that management requires administrative oversight, but not necessarily the manifestation of leadership. Leadership implies providing a vision of the future and inspiring others to find ways to make that vision a reality. As such, a large component of leadership is implicitly future-oriented. In contrast, management and administration refer more to present-oriented activities. According to some scholars, leadership has a heroic, larger-than-life quality that differentiates it from related concepts. As such, some people believe that many people can be trained to be managers, but leaders possess unique qualities that may not be created in all individuals. This particular view of leadership will be evidenced in some of the theories presented here.

The scientific study of leadership also embodies two methodological research issues previously discussed in this book. The first pertains to the use of qualitative research methods and the second addresses the issue of differing levels of analysis. Lowe and Gardner (2000) conducted a major review of leadership research done in the past decade. Unlike many areas of research in I/O psychology, the use of qualitative research methods in the study of leadership is fairly common. Lowe and Gardner estimated that about one-third of all leadership research conducted in the past decade utilized qualitative methods. Also, the examination of different levels of analysis is common in leadership research. As will shortly be discussed, the study of leadership can involve the characteristics of leaders, the characteristics of the group that is led, the situation in which leadership occurs, and the interaction of these factors (e.g., certain types of leaders in certain types of situations). Lowe and Gardner assert that all these differing levels of analysis are evident in leadership research.

Interest in leadership concerns the I/O practitioner as well as the scientist. In fact, leadership is one of the richer areas of interplay between the two; it has had a healthy influx of ideas from both camps. Identifying and developing leaders are major concerns of industry today. Companies often train their higher-level personnel in skill areas (interpersonal relationships, decision making, planning) that directly affect their performance as leaders. In Greensboro, North Carolina, there is an organization called the Center for Creative Leadership whose purpose is to enhance, through training, the leadership abilities of key business personnel. Not surprisingly, the military is also greatly concerned with leadership. It sponsors a wide variety of research projects that have the potential for enhancing our understanding of this subject. In summary, the balance between the theory and practice of leadership is fairly even as a result of this dual infusion of interest.

MAJOR TOPICS IN LEADERSHIP RESEARCH

Because of the many facets of leadership, researchers have focused on selected areas. Six major categories of studies will be presented next.

Positional Power

Some investigators view leadership as the exercise of *positional power*: The higher the position in the organizational hierarchy, the more power the position has. In the leadership context, we are most concerned with legitimate power: the formal power given to a position. The positional power of a company president exceeds that of a manager; in turn, the manager has more power than a secretary. Viewing leadership in terms of positional power separates the person from the role. Little attention is given to the individual's attributes; most is focused on the use of positional power. Organizational theorists use such terms as the power of the presidency and administrative clout, issues not really related to the people in such positions. Sometimes history judges leaders on their inability to use all the power their positions give them. Other leaders try to exceed the power granted their positions. In some countries leaders emerge by seizing power through military or political coups. According to this perspective, leadership is inherent in an organizational position based on the concept of power.

In the total spectrum of leadership research, a relatively small number of studies have been done on positional power. Many I/O researchers find it hard to separate leadership itself from the characteristics of people in leadership positions. But research on positional power has shown that some leadership issues transcend individual differences.

The Leader

Characteristics of individual leaders have been one of the most researched areas of leadership. Most leadership theories are based on understanding the differences among personal traits and behaviors. This is almost the opposite of the emphasis on positional power, which minimizes individual differences. Many early studies considered demographic and personality variables. Others studied what behaviors individual leaders exhibit that influence the judgment of whether they are strong or weak leaders. Statements like "Strong leaders radiate confidence" and "Weak leaders are indecisive" reflect the school of thought that stresses the importance of the leader in the leadership process. Research has been done on the selection of people into leadership positions; other research has been devoted to training people to enhance their leadership skills. The significance here is the focus on leader characteristics or behavior and their influence on others. This is a classic I/O psychology perspective, and it is the most popular in leadership research literature.

The Led

Another area of interest is the characteristics of the followers, or the led. This is a shift in emphasis from the preceding area, in that leadership is construed more in terms of who is led than who does the leading. Casual observation suggests that some people are easier for leaders to work with than others. Military leaders have long known that some groups of recruits are more responsive, cohesive, or productive. Teachers have noted variations among student classes. Industrial training directors have found differences among various trainee groups. We thus have evidence that a leader's performance is not the same across different groups of followers. We might label this class of studies "followership" research.

As an example, consider the case of a high school science teacher. The material may remain fairly constant over time, but the teacher's behavior may vary depending on the students. One year the teacher may have a class of bright, motivated students who quickly grasp the material. The teacher may respond by offering the class more advanced topics, laboratory experiments, or field trips. Another year the teacher could have students who have difficulty learning the material. The teacher may have to instruct at a slower pace, use more examples, and hold help sessions. Other variables are class size, disciplinary problems, and student backgrounds. Thus, attributes of the led (the students) as indexed by their intelligence, motivation, number, interpersonal harmony, and background would be examined as factors affecting the behavior of the leader (the teacher).

The Influence Process

Rather than focusing on either the leaders or the led, some researchers have found it instructive to examine the relationship or link between the two parties, particularly as they influence each other. Here researchers give their attention to the dynamics of this relationship, although they may also consider characteristics of both the leaders and the followers. In a general sense, what leaders "do" to a group is influence its members in the pursuit of some goal. Research on the influence process examines how this process is enacted.

The concept of influence entails how one person's actions affect another's. There are several methods of influence, including coercion, manipulation, authority, and persuasion. *Coercion* involves modifying behavior by force. *Manipulation* is a controlled distortion of reality, as seen by those affected. People are allowed to see only those things that will evoke the desired reaction. In the case of *authority,* agents appeal to a mutual decision giving them the right to influence. *Persuasion* means displaying judgment in such a way that those exposed to it accept its value. Researchers study how these methods are used in leader–follower relationships. As an example, Greene and Schriesheim (1980) studied two types of leader behavior: instrumental and supportive. In *instrumental* leadership a leader clarifies the group's goals. A *supportive* leader is friendly and considerate of others' needs. Greene and Schriesheim classified various work groups by size. The results showed that relatively small groups are most influenced by a supportive leader and that instrumental leadership works better in larger groups (perhaps because it brings order and structure to the group).

The Situation

Leadership research has also focused on the situation or context in which leader–group relationships occur. The situation can greatly affect the types of behaviors a leader has to exhibit to be effective. Imagine the leader of a Boy Scout troop, the supervisor of a production crew, and the warden of a prison. Each faces a different situation. Research on situational factors has tried to identify how various contexts differ and what effect they have on leader behavior.

The context in which leadership occurs influences which type of leader behavior is called for. As an example, Green and Nebeker (1977) studied two types of leadership situations: one favorable and one unfavorable. In the favorable situation leaders emphasized interpersonal relationships and were supportive of the group members. However, in the unfavorable situation the leaders became more task oriented and more concerned with goal accomplishment than with interpersonal relationships. Green and Nebeker were able to show that different situations evoke different styles of leadership behavior.

Leader Emergence Versus Leader Effectiveness

The final category considered here is emergence versus effectiveness of leaders. Some leadership researchers are interested in the dynamics of what causes leaders to emerge within a group. This emergence process can be either formal (that is, a person is designated to be the leader) or informal (that is, a person evolves as the leader of a group without having been so designated). Researchers examine such possible characteristics as the leader's age, gender, and physical appearance, or they consider verbal and nonverbal behaviors associated with the subsequent emergence. Also of possible interest might be the characteristics of the group from which the leader emerges. For example, Goktepe and Schneier (1989) reported in a study no difference in the proportion of men and women who emerged as leaders. However, group members with masculine gender-role characteristics emerged as leaders significantly more than those with feminine gender-role characteristics. In short, leader emergence is concerned with the process that results in someone's being regarded as the leader of a group.

Research on leader effectiveness is concerned with the performance of the leader. In this line of research, the characteristics of the leader (or the group) that are associated with evaluations of leader quality and the criteria for effective leaders are of interest. In the former case, effective leaders might be identified as possessing certain characteristics, such as verbal fluency, sensitivity, decisiveness, and so on. In the latter case, effective leadership might be regarded as success in task completion (that is, an effective leader gets the job done) or acceptance by the group (that is, an effective leader has group support). Taggar, Hackett, and Saha (1999) found that individuals who emerged as leaders were characterized as having high general mental ability, followed by the Big 5 personality characteristics of conscientiousness, extraversion, and emotional stability. Issues associated with both leader emergence and leader acceptance have long been of interest to I/O psychologists.

Overview

Leadership researchers do not limit their studies or theories to just one of these six areas. A researcher interested in influence processes might consider in which situations influence attempts will be successful. Interest in leader traits may also include consideration of follower traits. My purpose in describing these areas is to highlight the major categories of leadership research and acknowledge their different units of analysis while realizing that the areas are not mutually exclusive. Table 13–1 summarizes the six major research areas and lists the types of topics and questions each area tends to address.

TABLE 13–1 ■ **Research topics and associated issues in leadership research**

Research Topic	Unit of Analysis	Variables of Interest	Research Questions
Positional power	Organizational roles and positions	Influence tactics; use of power	Under what conditions will organizations resort to strong influence attempts?
The leader	Individual leaders	Personality characteristics; leader behaviors	What traits and behaviors differentiate effective and ineffective leaders?
The led	Work groups and subordinates	Group size; experience of subordinates	What types of subordinates desire close supervision?
Influence process	Superior–subordinate interface	Receptivity to influence; nature of influence attempts	Under what conditions are leaders most susceptible to subordinate influence attempts?
The situation	Environment or context in which leadership occurs	Situational effects on leader behavior; factors defining favorable situations	How do various situations modify behavior?
Leader emergence versus effectiveness	Individual and/or groups	Group dynamics and individual characteristics	How do individuals become recognized as leaders?

THEORETICAL APPROACHES TO LEADERSHIP

Several theoretical approaches have been developed to explain leadership. These orientations will be presented in terms of their dominant focus and contribution to the study of leadership. Yukl and Van Fleet (1992) offered an expanded version of these approaches (and related issues) in their excellent review of leadership research.

The Trait Approach

trait approach
a conception that leadership is best understood in terms of traits held by an individual that account for the observed leadership

The **trait approach** emphasizes the personal attributes of leaders. Early leadership theories attributed success to the possession of abstract abilities such as energy, intuition, and foresight. Some differences were found between leaders and non-leaders on selected traits, but for the most part the relationship between traits and leadership success did not reveal a particular set of universally relevant traits to be successful.

Advances in trait research led to a change of focus from abstract personality traits to specific attributes that can be related directly to behaviors required for effective leadership in a particular situation. This more directed approach revealed that some traits increase the likelihood of success as a leader, even though none of the traits guarantees success (Kirkpatrick & Locke, 1991). The relative importance of different traits for leader effectiveness appears to depend in part on the leadership situation.

Some individual traits that appear to be related to leadership success are high energy level, tolerance for stress, emotional maturity, integrity, and self-confidence. *High energy level* and *stress tolerance* help people cope with the hectic pace and demands of most leadership positions, the frequent role conflicts, and the pressure to make important decisions without adequate information. Leaders with high emotional maturity and integrity are more likely to maintain cooperative relationships with subordinates, peers, and superiors. *Emotional maturity* means that a leader is less self-centered, has more self-control, has more stable emotions, and is less defensive. *Integrity* refers to a person's behavior being consistent with expressed values and the person being honest and trustworthy. *Self-confidence* makes a leader more persistent in the pursuit of difficult objectives, despite initial problems and setbacks. Judge and Bono (2000) reported that the personality factors of extraversion and agreeableness were also associated with success as a leader.

Motivation is another aspect of personality related to leader effectiveness. The classic research of McClelland and his colleagues (e.g., McClelland & Boyatzis, 1982) identified three leader motives: need for power, need for achievement, and need for affiliation. Someone with a high need for *power* enjoys influencing people and events and is more likely to seek positions of authority. Someone with a high need for *achievement* enjoys attaining a challenging goal or accomplishing a difficult task, prefers moderate risks, and is more ambitious in terms of career success. Someone with a high need for *affiliation* enjoys social activities and seeks close, supportive relationships with other people. Similar results were found in another study on managerial motivation conducted by Berman and Miner (1985). Other research reveals that leaders frequently have a high need for power and achievement, but a lower need for affiliation.

A related line of research addresses leader skills, as opposed to the possession of personality traits, in the belief that skill is required to implement the traits in leadership roles. Three basic categories of skills have been proposed: technical, conceptual, and interpersonal. *Technical skills* include knowledge of work operations; procedures and equipment; and markets, clients, and competitors. *Conceptual skills* include the ability to analyze complex events and perceive trends, recognize changes, and identify problems. *Interpersonal skills* include an understanding of interpersonal and group processes, the ability to maintain cooperative relationships with people, and persuasive ability. In general, research supports the conclusion that technical, conceptual, and interpersonal skills are necessary in most leadership positions. However, the relative importance of most specific skills probably varies greatly depending on the situation.

In general, the trait approach was dominant in the early days of leadership research, then fell out of favor for a long time, and only recently has regained some credibility through the recent advances in personality assessment. Traits offer the potential to explain why people seek leadership positions and why they act the way they do when they occupy these positions. It is now evident that some traits and skills increase the likelihood of leadership success, even though they do not ensure success. Despite this progress, the utility of the trait approach for understanding leadership is limited by the elusive nature of traits. Traits interact with situational demands and constraints to influence a leader's behavior, and this behavior interacts with other situational variables to influence group process variables, which in turn affect group performance. It is therefore difficult to understand how leader traits can affect subordinate motivation or group performance unless we examine how traits are expressed in the actual behavior of leaders. Emphasis on leadership behavior ushers in the next era of research on leadership.

The Behavioral Approach

behavioral approach
a conception that leadership is best understood in terms of the actions taken by an individual in the conduct of leading a group

The **behavioral approach** emphasizes what leaders actually do on the job and the relationship of this behavior to leader effectiveness. Two major lines of behavior research are (1) the classification of leadership behaviors into taxonomies and (2) the identification of behaviors related to criteria of leadership effectiveness.

A major question in behavior research is how to classify leadership behavior in a way that facilitates research and theory on leadership effectiveness. Research conducted during the 1950s at Ohio State University sought to identify relevant aspects of leadership behavior and measure these behaviors with a questionnaire completed by subordinates of leaders. The results revealed that the subordinates perceived the behavior of their leader primarily in terms of two independent categories, one dealing with task-oriented behaviors (*initiating structure*) and the other with people-oriented behaviors (*consideration*). The questionnaire that resulted from this research, called the *Leader Behavior Description Questionnaire* (LBDQ), is a hallmark in the history of leadership research. Sample items from the LBDQ are presented in Table 13–2. The two-factor taxonomy of task-oriented and people-oriented behavior provided a good starting point for the conceptualization of leadership behaviors, but the two dimensions eventually proved too abstract for understanding how leaders handle the specific role requirements confronting them.

TABLE 13-2 ■ **Sample items from the Leader Behavior Description Questionnaire**

Structure	*Consideration*
1. He schedules work to be done.	1. He is friendly and approachable.
2. He emphasizes the meeting of deadlines	2. He makes group members feel at ease when talking to them.
3. He lets group members know what is expected of them.	3. He does little things to make it pleasant to be a member of the group.

More recent advances in the assessment of leadership from the behavioral perspective are evidenced in the *Leadership Practices Inventory* developed by Kouzes and Posner (1995). Further progress in behavior research required a shift in focus to more specific aspects of behavior. Yukl, Wall, and Lepsinger (1990) proposed an integrating taxonomy with 11 generic categories of behavior applicable to any leader. They asserted that their relative importance varies across situations, and they can be enacted in different ways in different situations. The taxonomy is presented in Figure 13–1, and the major purposes of the leadership behaviors are listed in Table 13–3.

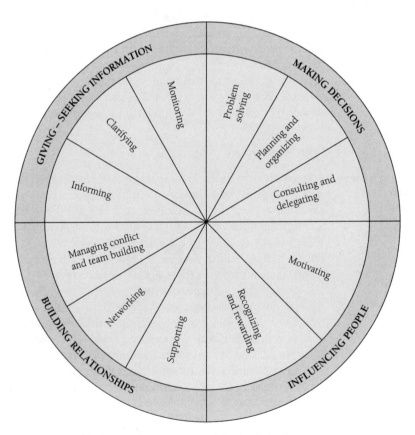

FIGURE 13-1 ■ **Integrating taxonomy of leader behaviors**

SOURCE: From *Leadership in Organizations*. 2nd ed. (p. 129), by G. Yukl, 1989, Englewood Cliffs, NJ: Prentice-Hall. Reprinted by permission.

TABLE 13–3 ■ Major purposes of leadership behaviors in the integrating taxonomy

Managerial Behavior	Internal Context	External Context
Networking	Good relations with subordinates	Good relations with peers, superiors, outsiders
Supporting	Good relations with subordinates, stress tolerance by subordinates	Good relations with peers, superiors, outsiders
Managing conflict and team building	Good relations with subordinates, group cohesiveness, cooperation among subordinates	Good relations with peers, superiors, outsiders
Motivating	Subordinate effort	Cooperation and support from peers, superiors, outsiders
Recognizing and rewarding	Subordinate effort and role clarity, good relations with subordinates	Cooperation and support from peers, superiors, outsiders
Planning and organizing	Unit efficiency and coordination	Adaptation to environment, external coordination
Problem solving	Stability of operations, unit efficiency and coordination	Adaptation to environment, external coordination
Consulting and delegating	Decision quality, subordinate effort	Decision quality and implementation
Monitoring	Detection of problems, evaluation of performance	Detection of problems and opportunities
Informing	Decision quality, unit efficiency and coordination	External coordination, enhance unit reputation
Clarifying	Role clarity, unit efficiency and coordination	External coordination

SOURCE: From *Leadership in Organizations*, 2nd ed., by G. Yukl, 1989. Englewood Cliffs, NJ: Prentice-Hall. Reprinted by permission.

An increasing amount of research has examined how specific types of leadership behavior are related to leader effectiveness. This research suggests that managerial effectiveness is predicted better by specific behaviors (e.g., clarifying, monitoring, and problem solving) relevant to the leadership situation than by broad measures such as initiating structure and consideration. Clarifying is the primary component of initiating structure, and a number of studies have been conducted on the use of clarifying behavior by leaders (e.g., explaining responsibilities, assigning work, giving instructions, and setting priorities, deadlines, and standards). For example, setting specific challenging but realistic goals is an important component of providing clarification, and in the motivation literature there is ample evidence from field experiments that goal setting results in better performance than no goals or "do your best" instructions.

As was found in trait research, behavior research also suffers from a tendency to look for simple answers to complex questions. Most research on leadership effectiveness has focused on behaviors individually rather than on how effective leaders use patterns of specific behaviors. It is likely that specific behaviors interact in complex ways and that leadership effectiveness cannot be understood unless these interactions are studied. For example, monitoring is useful for discovering problems, but unless something is done to solve problems when they are discovered, it will not contribute to the effectiveness of the leader. Delegating is unlikely to be effective unless the leader clarifies the subordinate's new responsibilities, ensures that the subordinate accepts them, monitors progress in an appropriate way, and provides necessary resources.

Because of the growing realization of the importance of influencing others to attain goals, the next major direction in leadership research was to gain a better understanding of leader power and influence.

The Power and Influence Approach

power and influence approach
a conception that leadership is best understood by the use of the power and influence exercised by a person with a group

According to the **power and influence approach,** the power possessed by a leader is important not only for influencing subordinates but also for influencing peers, superiors, and people outside the organization, such as clients and suppliers. Major questions in research on power include an identification of different types of power, an understanding of how different amounts and types of leader power are related to leadership effectiveness, and an understanding of how influence behavior is related to effective leadership.

Power and Leader Effectiveness.   Efforts to understand power usually involve making distinctions among various forms of power. A classic power taxonomy was proposed by French and Raven (1960) that distinguished five types of power: reward, coercive, legitimate, expert, and referent.

1. *Reward power.* This is the capacity of an organization (or a member in a specified role) to offer positive incentives for desirable behavior. Incentives include promotions, raises, vacations, good work assignments, and so on. Power to reward an employee is defined by formal sanctions inherent in a superior's role.

2. *Coercive power.* The organization can punish an employee for undesirable behavior. Dismissal, docking of pay, reprimands, and unpleasant work assignments are examples. This capacity to punish is also defined by formal sanctions inherent in the organization.

3. *Legitimate power.* Sometimes referred to as *authority,* this means that the employee believes the organization's power over him or her is legitimate. Norms and expectations help define the degree of legitimate power. If a boss asks an individual to work overtime, this would likely be seen as legitimate, given the boss's authority. However, if a coworker makes the same request, it might be turned down. The coworker has no legitimate authority to make the request, although the individual might agree out of friendship.

4. *Expert power.* The employee believes that some other individual has expertise in a given area and that he or she should defer to the expert's judgment. Consultants are called on for help in handling problems because they are seen as experts in certain areas. The source of expert power is the perceived experience, knowledge, or ability of a person. It is not formally sanctioned in the organization. There are also differences in the perceived boundaries of expertise. One employee may be seen as the expert on using tools and equipment; others turn to him or her for help with technical problems. However, that expertise may not be seen as extending to other areas, like interpersonal relationships.

DILBERT   by Scott Adams

SOURCE: Dilbert® reprinted by permission of United Feature Syndicate, Inc.

5. *Referent power.* This is the most abstract type of power. One employee might admire another, want to be like that person, and want to be liked by him or her. The other worker is a referent, someone the employee refers to. The source of referent power is the referent's personal qualities. Cultural factors may contribute to these qualities. Younger people will often defer to an older person partly because age, per se, is a personal quality that engenders deference. Norms can also generate referent power. An employee may wish to identify with a particular group and will bow to the group's expectations.

Table 13–4 presents the five sources of power and their likely outcomes in dealing with subordinates. Yukl (1994) noted that the success of an influence attempt is a matter of degree. It produces three qualitatively distinct outcomes. *Commitment* describes an outcome in which an individual (the target) internally agrees with a request from another individual (the agent) and makes a great effort to carry out the request effectively. *Compliance* describes an outcome in which the target is willing to do what the agent asks but is apathetic rather than enthusiastic about it and makes only a minimal effort. *Resistance* describes an outcome in which the target person is opposed to the request, rather than merely indifferent about it, and actively tries to avoid carrying it out.

Research on legitimate power indicates that it is a daily influence on routine matters for managers in formal organizations (Yukl & Falbe, 1991). Research on positive reward behavior, which is based on reward power, finds that it has beneficial effects on subordinate satisfaction. Punishment, which is based on coercive power, can be used to influence the behavior of individuals who jeopardize the mission of the organization or threaten the leader's legitimate authority. Referent and expert power are used to make nonroutine requests and motivate commitment to tasks that require greater effort, initiative, and persistence.

Some researchers have proposed that the manner in which power is exercised largely determines whether it results in enthusiastic commitment, passive compliance, or stubborn resistance. Effective leaders use combinations of power in a subtle fashion that minimizes status differentials and avoids threats to the self-esteem of subordinates. In contrast, leaders who exercise power in an arrogant and manipulative manner are likely to engender resistance.

TABLE 13-4 ■ Sources of leader power over subordinates and likely outcomes

Source of Leader Influence	Type of Outcome		
	Commitment	Compliance	Resistance
Referent power	Likely If request is believed to be important to leader	Possible If request is perceived to be unimportant to leader	Possible If request is for something that will bring harm to leader
Expert power	Likely If request is persuasive and subordinates share leader's task goals	Possible If request is persuasive but subordinates are apathetic about task goals	Possible If leader is arrogant and insulting or subordinates oppose task goals
Legitimate power	Possible If request is polite and very appropriate	Likely If request or order is seen as legitimate	Possible If arrogant demands are made or request does not appear proper
Reward power	Possible If used in a subtle, very personal way	Likely If used in a mechanical, impersonal way	Possible If used in a manipulative, arrogant way
Coercive power	Very unlikely	Possible If used in a helpful, nonpunitive way	Likely If used in a hostile or manipulative way

SOURCE: From *Leadership in Organizations,* 2nd ed., by G. Yukl, 1989, Englewood Cliffs, NJ: Prentice-Hall. Reprinted by permission.

Organizations differ in the extent to which they use the various bases of power. Authoritarian managers rely on reward and coercive power. Managers with a participative style rely on expert and referent power. The military relies heavily on the legitimate power inherent in military rank. Stahelski, Frost, and Patch (1989) reported that university administrators use referent and expert power more than legitimate, reward, or coercive power to influence subordinates.

Ragins and Sundstrom (1989) examined gender differences in the use of power within organizations. They concluded that power seems to grow incrementally through the accumulation of multiple resources over the span of a career. For women, the path to power contains many impediments and barriers that can be characterized as an obstacle course. The path to power for men contains fewer obstacles that derive from their gender and may actually contain sources of support unavailable to their female counterparts.

leader–member exchange (LMX) theory
a theory of leadership based upon the nature of the relationship between a leader and members of the group he or she leads

Leader–Member Exchange Theory.   Graen and his associates (e.g., Dansereau, Graen, & Haga, 1975) proposed a theory of leadership based upon mutual influence, called **leader–member exchange (LMX) theory.** The theory postulates that leaders differentiate their subordinates in terms of (1) their competence and skill, (2) the extent to which they can be trusted (especially when not being watched by the leader), and (3) their motivation to assume greater responsibility within the unit. Subordinates with these attributes become members of what Graen calls the *in-group.* In-group members go beyond their formal job duties and take responsibility for completing tasks that are most critical to the success of the work group. In return, they receive more attention, support, and sensitivity from their leaders. Subordinates who do not have these attributes are called the *out-group;* they do the more routine, mundane tasks and have a more formal relationship with the leader. Leaders influence out-group members by using formal authority, but this is not necessary with in-group members. Thus, leaders and subordinates use different types and degrees of influence depending on whether the subordinate is in the in- or out-group. As expressed by Liden, Sparrowe, and Wayne (1997), "Quite simply, members who receive more information and support from the leader and who engage in tasks that require challenge and responsibility are expected to have more positive job attitudes and engage in more positive behaviors than members whose support is limited to what is required by the employment contract" (p. 60).

In a review of the theory, Dienesch and Liden (1986) concluded there are three psychological bases for the "exchange" between the superior and subordinate. *Personal contribution* refers to the perception of the amount, direction, and quality of work-oriented activity each member puts forth toward the mutual goals of the dyad. *Loyalty* is the expression of public support for the goals and personal character of the other member. *Affect* is the degree of liking members of the dyad have for each other. The authors refer to these three dimensions as the "currencies of exchange" within the dyad. Recently, Liden and Maslyn (1998) identified a fourth dimension of exchange, the level of *professional respect* the parties have for each other.

In a modification of LMX theory, the development of relationships in a leader–subordinate dyad was described in terms of a *life-cycle model* with three possible stages (Graen & Scandura, 1987). The relationship begins with an initial testing phase in which the leader and subordinate evaluate each other's motives, attitudes, and potential resources to be exchanged; changes in the role of the subordinate are negotiated through a series of mutually reinforcing behavior cycles. If the relationship proceeds to the second stage, the exchange arrangement is refined, and mutual trust, loyalty, and respect are developed. Some exchange relationships advance to a third (mature) stage, wherein exchange based on self-interest is transformed into mutual commitment to the mission and objectives of the work unit. Based on a meta-analytic review of LMX theory, Gerstner and Day (1997) concluded that the relationship an employee has with his or her supervisor is "a lens through which the entire work experience is viewed" (p. 840) and is not limited to leader–subordinate relationships. Given the prevalence with which teams are used in the workplace, the theory has recently been expanded to address team–member exchange (TMX), as reported by Liden, Wayne, and Sparrowe (2000).

However, LMX theory has never been clear about the desirability of having sharply differentiated in-groups and out-groups. A sharply differentiated in-group is likely to create feelings of resentment and undermine team identification among subordinates who are excluded from the in-group (Yukl, 1989b). It is likely that effective leaders establish a special exchange relationship with all subordinates, not with just a few favorites. A leader can use some aspects of a special exchange, such as greater delegation of responsibility and sharing of administrative functions with a few subordinates, while also developing a relationship of mutual trust, support, respect, and loyalty with the other subordinates. It is not necessary to treat all subordinates exactly the same, but each should perceive that he or she is an important and respected member of the team rather than a "second-class citizen."

Influence Tactics.   A bridge between the power and behavior approaches is research on influence tactics. The choice of tactics for a particular influence attempt depends somewhat on the status of the target person and the objective of the influence attempt. The most common tactics are listed and defined in Table 13–5.

For example, pressure is used more in downward influence attempts than in lateral or upward influence attempts, consistent with the greater amount of positional power leaders have over subordinates than over peers or superiors. Tactics such as ingratiation, rational persuasion, and personal appeals tend to be used more often in initial influence attempts, whereas tactics such as pressure, exchange, and coalitions tend to be used more often in follow-up influence attempts after the agent has met initial resistance by the target (Yukl & Tracey, 1992).

TABLE 13–5 ■ Definitions of influence tactics

Rational persuasion	The agent uses logical arguments and factual evidence to persuade the target that a proposal or request is viable and likely to result in the attainment of task objectives.
Inspirational appeals	The agent makes a request or proposal that arouses target enthusiasm by appealing to target values, ideals, and aspirations, or by increasing target self-confidence.
Consultation	The agent seeks target participation in planning a strategy, activity, or change for which target support and assistance are desired, or is willing to modify a proposal to deal with target concerns and suggestions.
Ingratiation	The agent uses praise, flattery, friendly behavior, or helpful behavior to get the target in a good mood or to think favorably of him or her before asking for something.
Personal appeals	The agent appeals to target feelings of loyalty and friendship toward him or her when asking for something.
Exchange	The agent offers an exchange of favors, indicates willingness to reciprocate at a later time, or promises a share of the benefits if the target helps accomplish a task.
Coalition tactics	The agent seeks the aid of others to persuade the target to do something, or uses the support of others as a reason for the target to agree also.
Legitimating tactics	The agent seeks to establish the legitimacy of a request by claiming the authority or right to make it, or by verifying that it is consistent with organizational policies, roles, practices, or traditions.
Pressure	The agent uses demands, threats, frequent checking, or persistent reminders to influence the target to do what he or she wants.

SOURCE: From *Leadership in Organizations,* 3rd ed., by G. Yukl, 1994, Englewood Cliffs, NJ: Prentice-Hall. Reprinted by permission.

Some tactics are more effective than others in gaining commitment, although the outcome of any influence attempt will likely depend in part on the specific situation, the relationship between agent and target, the agent's power over the target, and the perceived legitimacy and relevance of the agent's request. Yukl and Tracey reported that the most effective tactics for obtaining target commitment are rational persuasion, consultation, and inspirational appeals; the least effective tactics are pressure, coalition tactics, and legitimating tactics.

In conclusion, influence is a fundamental concept in leadership, and the power and influence approach appears to provide unique insights about the emergence and effectiveness of leadership. The conceptualization of power still remains somewhat unclear, however, because power may be construed as potential influence or enacted influence. That is, power may be viewed either as influence over the attitudes and behaviors of people or as influence over events. We need to learn more about the way power changes over time as a result of the leader's use and misuse of it.

The Situational Approach

situational approach
a conception that leadership is best understood in terms of situational factors that promote the occurrence of leadership

The **situational approach** emphasizes the importance of contextual factors such as the leader's authority and discretion, the nature of the work performed by the leader's unit, the attitudes of subordinates, and the nature of the external environment. Situational research and theory fall into two major subcategories. One line of research treats leader behavior as a dependent variable; researchers seek to discover how the situation influences behavior and how much leader behaviors vary across different positions. The other line of research seeks to discover how situational variables moderate the relationship between leader attitudes (e.g., traits, behaviors) and measures of leader effectiveness. Fiedler (1996) believes it is critical to integrate situational components into an effective program of leadership training and development. Fiedler (1964) was one of the first theorists to propose that the situation or context exerts a strong influence on the type of leader who would succeed in a particular situation.

path–goal theory
a theory of leadership that emphasizes the importance of leaders indicating to followers what behaviors (paths) they need to exhibit to attain the desired objectives (goals)

Path-Goal Theory. According to **path-goal theory** (House, 1971), leaders motivate higher performance in subordinates by acting in ways that influence them to believe valued outcomes can be attained by making a serious effort. Aspects of the situation such as the nature of the task, the work environment, and subordinate attributes determine the optimal amount of each type of leader behavior for improving subordinate satisfaction and performance.

The theory states that a leader must be able to manifest four different styles of behavior, which have been derived from previous research on work behavior.

1. *Directive.* The leader provides specific guidelines to subordinates on how they perform their tasks. The leader should set standards of performance and provide explicit expectations of performance.
2. *Supportive.* The leader must demonstrate concern for subordinates' well-being and must be supportive of them as individuals.

3. *Participative.* The leader must solicit ideas and suggestions from subordinates and invite their participation in decisions that directly affect them (see Field Note 1).

4. *Achievement oriented.* The leader must set challenging goals, emphasize improvements in work performance, and encourage high levels of goal attainment.

Effective leaders need all four of these styles, since each one produces different results. But when should a leader use which style? It depends on two types of situational factors. Some relate to subordinate characteristics, others to environmental factors. Leader behavior is motivating to the extent that it helps subordinates cope with environmental uncertainties or frustrations. What effect do these leader behaviors have? The leader can influence subordinates' perceptions of their jobs by (1) removing obstacles from the paths to the desired goals, (2) rewarding them for attaining their goals, and (3) helping them clarify paths to valued goals. Thus, the leader helps subordinates do the things that must be done to obtain the desired rewards.

However, path-goal theory has a number of conceptual limitations. The theory focuses on subordinate motivation as the explanatory process for the effects of lead-

---

FIELD NOTE 1   Participation As Shared Power

ne leader style proposed by path-goal theory is participative leadership, which refers to allowing subordinates to participate in the decision-making process. I/O psychologists have had considerable difficulty figuring out the conditions under which this style is effective. Many factors seem to contribute to its success. We can start with the leader. Some individuals like to retain the decision-making authority inherent in their leadership roles. One basis for their feelings is that as leaders, they have more expertise than their subordinates, so why dilute the quality of the decision by delegating it to others? Some leaders solve this problem by giving subordinates the authority to make trivial decisions, or what is sometimes called "throwing them a bone."

Another problem is the subordinates. Most of us like to have our feelings solicited in matters that pertain to us, but there are wide individual differences. Some subordinates like to get involved in the fine-grained details of decisions, and others do not. Some subordinates resent having to make all sorts of decisions. If they are going to be burdened with the responsibility for making administrative decisions, then

they want the salary and title that traditionally come with it. When invited by the boss to participate in certain decisions, they are inclined to feel "That's your job, not mine." Willingness to participate is also moderated by the nature of the decision problem. Some problems are fair game for employee involvement, and others are not.

Finally, there are cross-cultural differences in the acceptance of participative leadership. A leading U.S. company once opened a production plant in Latin America. Using the latest leadership ideas from the United States, company officials invited the native employees to participate in a wide range of work-related decisions. Within a short period, turnover became exceedingly high. When the company investigated the cause of the turnover, it was shocked to learn its own management practices were primarily responsible. The employees interpreted management's participative style as evidence of its ignorance about running the plant. The employees were saying, in effect, "We're the workers, not management. If you don't know how to run your own plant, how do you expect us to know?" Effective use of the participative leadership style is more complex than you might think.

ership, and it ignores other explanatory processes, such as a leader's influence on the organization of work, resource levels, and skill levels. It has been suggested that greater empirical support would be found for the theory if some key propositions were stated in more narrowly defined behaviors, such as clarifying work roles, as opposed to the broader concept of initiating structure.

Transformational and Charismatic Leadership

transformational leadership
a conception that leadership is the process of inspiring a group to pursue goals and attain results

charismatic leadership
a conception that leadership is the product of charisma, a trait that inspires confidence in others to support the ideas and beliefs of an individual who possesses this trait

Transformational leadership refers to the process of influencing major changes in the attitudes and assumptions of organization members and building commitment for major changes in the organization's objectives and strategies. Transformational leadership involves influence by a leader over subordinates, but the effect of the influence is to empower subordinates who also become leaders in the process of transforming the organization. Thus, transformational leadership is usually viewed as a shared process, involving the actions of leaders at different levels and in different subunits of an organization.

Charismatic leadership is defined more narrowly and refers to follower perception that a leader possesses a divinely inspired gift and is somehow unique and larger than life. Followers not only trust and respect the leader, but also idolize or worship the leader as a superhuman hero or spiritual figure (Bass, 1985). The indicators of charismatic leadership include a follower's trust in the correctness of the leader's beliefs, unquestioning acceptance of the leader, affection for the leader, and willing obedience. Thus, with charismatic leadership the focus is on an individual leader rather than on a leadership process that may be shared among multiple leaders.

Transformational Leadership. Bass (1998) defined transformational leadership in terms of the leader's effect on followers. Leaders transform followers by making them more aware of the importance and value of task outcomes, by activating their higher-order needs (in Maslow's sense), and by inducing them to transcend self-interest for the sake of the organization. As a result of this influence, followers feel trust and respect toward the leader, and they are motivated to do more than they originally expected to do.

Transformational leaders do more with colleagues and followers than set up simple exchanges or agreements. They behave in ways to achieve superior results by employing one or more of the four components of transformational leadership (Bass, 1998).

- *Idealized influence.* Transformational leaders behave in ways that make them role models for their followers. The leaders are admired, respected, and trusted. Followers identify with the leaders and want to emulate them; leaders are endowed by their followers with extraordinary capabilities, persistence, and determination.
- *Inspirational motivation.* Transformational leaders behave in ways that motivate and inspire those around them by providing meaning and challenge to their followers' work. Leaders get followers involved in envisioning attractive future states; they create clearly communicated expectations that followers want to meet.

- *Intellectual stimulation.* Transformational leaders stimulate their followers' efforts to be innovative and creative by questioning assumptions, reframing problems, and approaching old situations in new ways. New ideas and creative problem solutions are solicited from followers, who are included in the process of addressing problems and finding solutions.
- *Individualized consideration.* Transformational leaders pay special attention to each individual follower's needs for advancement and growth by acting as a coach or mentor. Followers and colleagues are developed to successively higher levels of potential. Individual differences of needs and desires are recognized, and the leader's own behavior demonstrates acceptance of these differences.

A leadership scale has been developed (the *Multifactor Leadership Questionnaire*) that assesses these components of transformational leadership. Research (e.g., Lowe, Kroeck, & Sivasubramaniam, 1996) has supported the construct validity of these components and has revealed that transformational leadership is strongly associated with work unit effectiveness. In particular, the idealized influence component is most strongly related to overall effectiveness. Bass (1997) asserted that these four components of transformational leadership transcend organizational and national boundaries and speak to the "universality of leadership."

Charismatic Leadership.   House (1977) proposed a theory that identifies how charismatic leaders behave, how they differ from other people, and the conditions under which they are most likely to flourish. As noted earlier, the theory specifies indicators of charismatic leadership that involve the attitudes and perceptions of followers about the leader. The theory also specifies leader traits that increase the likelihood of being perceived as charismatic, including a strong need for power, high self-confidence, and strong convictions. Some behaviors typical of charismatic leaders are (1) impression management to maintain follower confidence in the leader, (2) articulation of an appealing vision that defines the task in terms of ideological goals in order to build follower commitment, (3) communication of high expectations for followers to clarify expectations, and (4) expression of confidence in followers' ability to build their self-confidence.

Charismatic leaders are regarded as individuals who give their followers a vision of the future that promises a better and more meaningful life. Conger and Kanungo (1987) believe charismatic leaders are regarded as "heroes" who exhibit unconventional behaviors and transform people to share the radical changes they advocate. Manz and Sims (1991) added that such leaders should also be viewed as hero makers, and the spotlight should be on the achievements of the followers as well as the leaders. House, Spangler, and Woycke (1991) examined the personality and charisma of U.S. presidents and their effectiveness as leaders. The authors concluded that personality and charisma did make a difference in the effectiveness of the presidents. Gardner and Avolio (1998) identified the effective use of "staging" by charismatic leaders. Staging involves attention to the development and manipulation of symbols, including physical appearances, settings, props, and other artifactual displays. For example, a leader may stage a presentation by giving a speech in front of a building that has symbolic significance for the followers (see Field Note 2).

Yorges, Weiss, and Strickland (1999) proposed that leaders who appeared willing to endure hardship for the expression of their beliefs would enhance their influence over followers, while leaders who appeared to achieve personal gain would reduce their influence over others. Research results confirmed their hypothesis. Waldman et al. (2001) found that charismatic leaders were particularly effective under conditions of high situational uncertainty, but not effective under conditions of low uncertainty. The results indicated that the charismatic leaders provide a sense of direction to the organization when it most needs it—that is, when there is no clear path for the organization to follow. However, the effectiveness of a charismatic leader is diminished when the organization is positioned in a system of high situational predictability.

However, Hogan, Raskin, and Fazzini (1990) cautioned there is a "dark side" to charismatic leaders. Because they have excellent social skills, sometimes to the point of being charming, they are readily liked by their followers. But sometimes lurking behind the mask of likability is a person with pronounced adjustment problems. Only after these people fail in their leadership roles do we ever learn of their maladjustment, which was cleverly concealed by their ability to manipulate

---

FIELD NOTE 2   Use of Props by Leaders

 Current research has studied the use of props by leaders and the "staging" of activities designed to enhance communication effectiveness. Several examples of props have been used by U.S. political leaders. When Richard Nixon was Vice President of the United States, he was accused of inappropriately accepting gifts from people who wanted Nixon to use his influence on their behalf. In his defense Nixon appeared on television holding a cocker spaniel puppy named "Checkers." Nixon explained that he returned all the gifts he had received, except the dog, which he noted had become the family pet. The talk by Nixon while holding the dog became long remembered as "Nixon's Checkers speech."

When Dwight Eisenhower was President, he gave a speech on television to outline his philosophy of leadership. A camera was mounted above Eisenhower's head pointing downward at the top of his desk. Eisenhower pulled a piece of string out of his pocket and then demonstrated that if the string were pulled, it would follow his fingers. But if the string were pushed, it would go nowhere. Equating the nation to the string, Eisenhower conveyed that he wanted to lead the nation to prosperity, not push it from behind.

Earl Butz was Secretary of Agriculture under President Nixon. Butz was scheduled to appear before a congressional committee to explain the financial budget of the Department of Agriculture. While seated before the committee, Butz pulled a loaf of sliced bread out from a paper bag. He proceeded to open the bread and stack the slices in various-sized piles, demonstrating symbolically how the agriculture budget was allocated to various directives.

In these examples a dog, a piece of string, and a loaf of bread were used as props by the leaders to explain issues of considerable complexity. The props were remembered long after people had forgotten the content of the speeches. Dunham and Freeman (2000) have suggested that business leaders should learn to utilize some of the techniques of theatre directors in show business to enhance their impact through the use of staging.

people to like them. Musser (1987) described the differences between positive and negative charismatics in terms of whether they seek to instill commitment to ideological goals or to themselves. Conger (1989) described the following problems that can occur with negative charismatics:

- They start grandiose projects to glorify themselves, and the projects are often unrealistic because of the leader's inflated self-assessment and unwillingness to seek and accept advice from others. They tend to ignore or reject evidence that a plan or strategy is encountering serious difficulties, thereby reducing the chance of correcting problems in time to avert a disaster.
- These leaders are willing to spend time in high-visibility activities to promote a vision, but they are unwilling to spend the time necessary to guide and facilitate the implementation of a vision. They tend to vacillate between extremes of loose delegation when things are going well and overcontrolling behavior when trouble occurs with a project.
- They fail to develop competent successors. These leaders try to keep subordinates weak and dependent, and they remove people who have the leadership qualities of a potential successor. Thus, a leadership crisis is likely to occur when the leader dies or departs.

In conclusion, both transformational and charismatic leadership theories identify the importance of leaders having a profound influence over their followers. Charismatic leadership theory tends to emphasize the characteristics of the leader, whereas transformational leadership theory tends to emphasize the processes by which the work group is transformed or developed.

The Implicit Leadership Theory

The previous theories of leadership presume that leadership is something that is really "out there," and the various theories are merely different ways to explain what it is. A radically different view is that leadership exists only in the mind of the beholder, usually the follower. It may be that "leadership" is nothing more than a label we attach to a set of outcomes; that is, we observe a set of conditions and events and make the attribution that leadership has occurred or exists. **Implicit leadership theory** regards leadership as a subjectively perceived construct rather than an objective construct. Implicit leadership theory is also referred to as the *attribution theory of leadership* or *social information processing theory.*

implicit leadership theory
a conception that leadership is a perceived phenomenon as attributed to an individual by others

Lord and his associates have made the greatest contribution to this view of leadership. For example, Lord, Foti, and Phillips (1982) concluded that individuals hold conceptions of prototypic leaders (that is, what they think leaders are like) and then evaluate actual leaders according to their conceptions. People judged as "good" leaders are likely to be those whose actions and demeanors conform to the conception we hold. Thus, "effectiveness" in leadership is determined not objectively but through the confirmation of expectations. Phillips and Lord (1981) discovered that individuals develop global impressions of leader effectiveness and then use those global impressions to describe specific dimensions of leader behavior. Thus, individuals make confident judgments of behavior they have had no opportunity to observe, in much the same way halo error operates in performance appraisal. Meindl and Ehrlich (1987) discussed what they call "the romance of leadership" as it relates to assessments of organizational performance. In their study, subjects gave better evaluations to performance outcomes attributed to leadership factors than they gave to the same outcomes when they were attributed to non-leadership factors. The authors concluded that leadership has assumed a heroic, larger-than-life quality in people's minds. Meindl and Ehrlich believe leadership may serve a symbolic role, causing people to feel assured and confident that the fate and fortune of an organization are in good hands. Thus, the authors contend leadership may not account for as much of an organization's success as we believe, but "leadership" has a symbolic value in producing subordinate support, which may then paradoxically produce organizational effectiveness.

Implicit leadership theory poses a vexing dilemma for the assessment of leaders through questionnaires such as the LBDQ. We don't know if what these questionnaires measure is the actual behavior of the leader or the cognitive set of the rater. While Lord (1985) and Foti and Lord (1987) have proposed strategies to aid in the measurement of leaders, the issues raised by implicit leadership theory challenge the very foundation upon which most of our knowledge of leadership is based.

Substitutes for Leadership

Kerr and Jermier (1978) asked what it is that organization members need to maximize in seeking organizational and personal outcomes. They concluded that employees seek both guidance and good feelings from their work settings. Guidance usually comes from role or task structuring; good feelings may stem from any type of recognition. The authors feel that although these factors must be present, they do not necessarily have to come from a superior. Other sources may provide guidance and recognition as well. In these cases the need for formal leadership is diminished. The authors reference **substitutes for leadership** and highlight the point that a leader is merely a vehicle for providing these services. Indeed, some organizations have been experimenting with abandoning supervisor positions, leaving such traditional leadership roles in the hands of employees organized into special work teams. Podsakoff, MacKenzie, and Bommer (1996) reported that leaders and substitutes for leadership can simultaneously affect work groups. For example, leaders can create less need for formal supervision by carefully selecting employees who can function relatively independently. The authors concluded that such substitutes have very important effects on the work group, but they do not diminish the role of the leader.

There is evidence that the concept of leadership does not have to be vested in a formal position. Howell and Dorfman (1981) tested whether leader substitution can replace or "act in the place of" a specific leader. They examined whether having a closely knit cohesive work group and tasks that provide feedback concerning performance can take the place of a formal leader. The authors found partial support for the substitution of leadership, giving some credence to the idea that leadership need not always reside in a person. Pierce, Dunham, and Cummings

substitutes for leadership
the conception that there are sources of influence in an environment that can serve to act in place of, or be substitutions for, formal leadership

(1984) provided further support for leader substitutes. They examined four environmental sources from which employees get structure and direction in how to perform their work: the job itself, technology, the work unit, and the leader. The authors found that only when the first three sources of structure were weak did the influence of the leader strongly affect employees. It seems that employees can derive typical leader qualities (that is, structure and direction) from inanimate sources in their environments, and that leadership functions need not be associated with someone in authority. It is thus possible to envision a successfully operating leaderless group in which the job itself provides direction in what to do (initiating structure) and the work group members support and tend to one another (consideration).

There is also evidence that some individuals are capable of directing themselves, a concept called *self-leadership*. Manz (1986) found that some employees could lead themselves if their values and beliefs were congruent with those of the organization (see Field Note 3). In summary, the research on substitutes for leadership suggests that leadership can be thought of as a series of processes or functions that facilitate organizational and personal effectiveness. These processes or functions need not necessarily emanate from a person in a formal leadership role but may be derived from characteristics of the work being performed by the group members.

FIELD NOTE 3   Self-Leadership Versus Self-Supervision

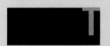he concept of self-leadership is related to many of the issues discussed in Chapter 8 on organizations and Chapter 9 on teams. Among them are the following.

The concept of organizational downsizing has resulted in broader spans of control and flatter organizational structures. As a consequence there is less direct supervision of employees because other control mechanisms must become operative to ensure that organizational goals are met. Small spans of control produce closer supervision but also additional layers in the organization's structure. Reducing the middle-management layer of organizations puts greater pressure on the other parts of the organization to accomplish what middle management once did—providing direction and control.

How might such direction and control be provided? One answer is through different organizing concepts, such as self-managed work teams. The work team provides a sense of direction or structure to the group's efforts and provides feedback and support to the team members. As the literature on substitutes for leadership has revealed, although structure and support are necessary for organizational functioning, they need not emanate from a formal leadership position.

It should also be recognized that today's workforce is more highly educated and trained than ever before. With education and training come the knowledge and skills the employee can bring to the task, thus lessening the need for a supervisor to tell employees what to do and to monitor their performance. Employees who know what needs to be done and have the resources to do it do not need extensive supervision.

Finally, do not equate supervision with leadership. One dimension of leadership is oversight or supervisory responsibilities. However, leadership entails more than just monitoring and directing others. It embraces a sense of vision, an understanding of how the organizational unit can function and even prosper in its environment. Leadership is more inclusive than supervision. Self-directed work teams ameliorate the need for direct supervision, but they do not obviate the need for organizational leadership.

POINTS OF CONVERGENCE AMONG APPROACHES

Despite the profusion of leadership approaches and related empirical findings, Yukl (1994) noted there is some convergence in the findings from different lines of leadership research. Yukl identified three consistent themes in the findings from leadership research.

Importance of Influencing and Motivating.
Influence is the essence of leadership. Much of the activity of leaders involves attempts to influence the attitudes and behaviors of people, including subordinates, peers, and outsiders. Motivating behavior includes a variety of social influence techniques for developing commitment to organizational objectives and compliance with requests. Much of the influence behavior of charismatic leaders falls into the motivating category, including inspiring commitment to new objectives and strategies, modeling exemplary behavior for followers to imitate, and appealing to values and aspirations.

Situational factors determine the importance of leader efforts to motivate subordinates. Leader influence on subordinate motivation is much less important when the task is intrinsically appealing. Motivation is more important for a very difficult task that frustrates and discourages subordinates. For these types of tasks, the subordinate's performance will suffer unless the leader intervenes to arouse enthusiasm and confidence.

Some of the traits and skills that predict leader effectiveness relate to the use of power. Leaders with high need for power and high self-confidence make more influence attempts. Self-confidence, persuasive ability, relevant expertise, and political insight facilitate the effectiveness of influence attempts. Interpersonal skills are necessary to articulate an appealing vision and persuade people of the need for change.

Importance of Maintaining Effective Relationships.
Effective leaders establish cooperative relationships characterized by high levels of mutual trust and loyalty. The power research indicated the importance of referent power as a source of influence over the behavior and commitment of subordinates. Referent power over subordinates is developed gradually over time as a result of dyadic social exchange processes in which the leader demonstrates trust and provides benefits to a subordinate while avoiding forms of influence that cause resentment. The behavior research found that subordinates are usually more satisfied with a leader who is friendly and helpful, shows trust and respect, and demonstrates concern for their needs and feelings. The situational research showed that the effects of leader behavior depend in part on the needs and values of subordinates. Supportive behavior is likely to have a stronger effect on subordinate satisfaction when the subordinate has a stressful, difficult task and lacks self-confidence.

Several of the traits and skills predictive of leadership effectiveness appear important for developing favorable relationships with subordinates, peers, and superiors. Relevant interpersonal skills include tact and diplomacy, listening skills, and social sensitivity. A leader with a positive regard for others is more likely to develop friendly relationships with people. Leaders who are preoccupied with personal ambition tend to do things that jeopardize relationships with people (e.g., betraying a trust or reneging on a promise in order to increase their personal gain).

Importance of Making Decisions.   Much of the activity of leaders involves decision making, but leaders seldom make important decisions at a single point in time, except for problem solving in response to immediate crises. In dealing with day-to-day decisions, effective leaders are guided by their long-term objectives and strategies.

People who effectively solve problems or develop successful strategies gain in status and power as a result. The reputation for expertise gained from successful decisions made in the past gives a person greater influence over subsequent decisions. Situational theories and research on group decision making suggest the conditions under which participation is most likely to improve the quality of a leader's decisions. The potential benefits from group decisions are greater for complex, important decisions than for routine ones. Participation results in better decisions when the participants have relevant information and clear ideas that the leader lacks, when they are willing to cooperate in finding a good solution, and when there is ample time for the participative process to be carried out.

Several of the traits and skills predictive of leadership effectiveness are relevant for decision making. Leaders with extensive technical knowledge and cognitive skills are more likely to make high-quality decisions. These skills are important for analyzing problems, identifying causal patterns and trends, and forecasting likely outcomes of different strategies for attaining objectives. Self-confidence and tolerance for ambiguity and stress help leaders cope with the responsibility for making major decisions on the basis of incomplete information.

CROSS-CULTURAL LEADERSHIP ISSUES

Because of the growing number of organizations that conduct international business, we are learning about cross-cultural issues in leadership. Much of our knowledge comes from situations where international managers are assigned to positions in the United States. Graen and Wakabayashi (1994) studied companies that have manufacturing plants located in both the United States and Japan, such as Toyota. These plants, which use Japanese organization methods and mostly American employees, require cross-cultural leadership to be successful. A *Japanese transplant* is a manufacturing plant owned by a Japanese parent company and located in a foreign country. Leadership presents special problems for Japanese transplants in the United States because of cultural differences between the two countries. Following are some of the problems found in Japanese transplants in the United States as identified by Graen and Wakabayashi:

1. *Language differences complicate communications and cooperation at managerial levels.* Very few domestic managers are able to interpret communications from the Japanese home office, and few Japanese managers can discuss abstract issues in English. Communication is therefore restricted to concrete issues without the ben-

efit of any rationale or subtlety. The array of unresolved language problems keeps managers from confronting underlying cultural issues.

2. *Japanese managers and workers are shocked by what they perceive as American managers' seemingly underdeveloped sense of obligation to their company and coworkers.* Japanese managers often believe that American managers place their personal interests above those of the company and their coworkers. For example, one company launched a new product during deer hunting season and asked its hourly workers to postpone taking days off until the product launch was completed. The Japanese managers were pleased that absenteeism increased by only 5% for production workers, but they were aghast that absenteeism among American managers also increased by 5% during this period. The Japanese managers complained that the American managers should feel a stronger obligation to the company and lead the workers by setting a good example. This perceived underdeveloped sense of obligation makes it difficult for Japanese managers to trust or rely on domestic managers to perform critical tasks.

3. *American managers have difficulty with the absence of punishment for insubordination as an ideal.* According to the Japanese management principles, workers should not necessarily be punished for resisting a legitimate request by their managers. Instead, their philosophy considers the possibility that it is the manager who may be at fault for making a request that is resisted. When insubordination is not a punishable offense, a manager must develop a sense of obligation and ownership in his or her workers through leadership development activities. Such activities build mutual obligations that render insubordination as superfluous.

4. *American managers see a lack of office perks as a loss of status.* The absence of status symbols such as private offices, reserved parking spaces, and management meeting rooms reduces the gulf between hourly workers and management. In addition, some companies require all plant management personnel to work on the shop floor at least one day per month and get their hands dirty. Though domestic managers understand at a conceptual level that such equal treatment helps reduce the social distance between hourly workers and managers, they feel the loss of status associated with a lack of perks at an emotional level. Compared with their cohorts in domestic companies, they feel that their situation is inferior and that they are not treated as well.

5. *American managers do not commit their entire career to a single company.* According to the authors, one of the most serious challenges Japanese transplants face is management mobility in the United States. Japanese transplants very carefully recruit and select domestic managers for home and staff functions. They hope that everyone hired will retire with the company. When domestic managers leave the transplant for another company, Japanese managers feel the loss doubly. First, they must repair their extensive networks by assuming the obligations of their departed peer and prepare for a new person to grow into the numerous company networks. This kind of adjustment is especially difficult for the Japanese leadership system, which is based on stable teams of committed managers. Second, many Japanese managers have difficulty accepting that a domestic manager can proclaim allegiance to a company and then leave within a year or two for another company—especially if it is a direct competitor.

Graen and Wakabayashi believe American and Japanese managers face different fears when confronted with a culture clash. The Americans fear that adopting the Japanese system could subvert traditional American values of individualism. Alternatively, the Japanese fear that adopting the American management system could undermine traditional Japanese values of teamwork. The authors pointed out that functional solutions to this dilemma can be reached when both parties are willing to learn each other's culture and work together to create a hybrid culture. Indeed, House, Wright, and Aditya (1997) and Bond and Smith (1996) contended that cultural differences in societies influence individual expectations and assumptions about their environment, attitudes toward others, and modes of social interaction. They proposed that cultural forces affect the kind of leader behavior that is usually accepted, enacted, and effective within an organization. This view of successful leadership being "culturally dependent" contrasts with the universality of leadership posited by transformational leadership theory.

Lowe and Gardner (2000) stated that leadership research has a technological, modern, and U.S. bias. In fact, the concepts of leader and follower can be traced back to the ancient pharaohs of Egypt. Brodbeck et al. (2000) conducted a study of leaders from 22 European countries. The leaders were asked to indicate the degree to which various traits and behaviors fit into the concept of being an outstanding business leader in their country. The results revealed that preferences for certain leader traits and behaviors were culturally specific. Countries that shared similar cultural values also shared similar leadership concepts. In short, the findings revealed there is not a singular universal conception of leadership.

DIVERSITY ISSUES IN LEADERSHIP

Hogan, Curphy, and Hogan (1994) questioned the role of leadership within organizations in the 21st century. They made the following observations. Historically, the typical American worker has been a white man with a high school education employed in a manufacturing job. Our knowledge of leadership focuses largely on how to lead that kind of person in those kinds of jobs in those kinds of organizations. Demographic trends suggest, however, that the national economy will shift from manufacturing to service jobs and that the workforce will become older, more diverse, and more female (Offerman & Gowing, 1990). The labor market for skilled workers will tighten, and there will be increased competition for talented personnel. As noted in Chapter 8, as organizations shrink, fewer middle managers will be needed and the responsibilities of first-line managers will expand.

Chemers and Murphy (1995) noted that one explanation for gender differences in leadership is cultural. This view holds that because of their roles as family caretakers, women are socialized to be sensitive, nurturing, and caring. When they carry that socialization over into organizational roles, women are likely to be warm, considerate, and democratic leaders. An alternative explanation proposes that observed differences in leadership style between men and women are more a function of biases in the observation process than the result of true differences. If we are more likely to notice and remember behaviors that are consistent with our categorical stereotypes, our observation of male and female leaders may be biased in attention, selection, memory, or recall. While minor differences may exist in leadership styles between men and women, our biases exaggerate the perception of these differences.

We do not have extensive knowledge on the best way to manage female and minority employees in service organizations. Moreover, we will likely have the same percentages of women and minorities in management as are currently in the workforce. Are there significant gender or cultural differences in leadership style, and will these styles be more or less effective for building teams in tomorrow's organizations? Eagly, Makhijani, and Klonsky (1992) provided some answers to these questions. They examined research on the evaluation of men and women who occupy leadership roles. While holding organizational characteristics constant and examining the gender of the leader, the research assessed whether people are biased against female leaders. Although the findings showed only a small overall tendency to evaluate female leaders less favorably than male leaders, this tendency was more pronounced under certain circumstances. Specifically, women in leadership positions were devalued relative to their male counterparts when leadership was carried out in stereotypically masculine styles, especially when this style was autocratic or directive. Also, the devaluation was greater when leaders occupied male-dominated roles and when the evaluators were women. In a meta-analysis of studies examining gender and the effectiveness of leaders, Eagly, Karau, and Makhijani (1995) reported that the congruence of leadership roles with leaders' gender enhanced effectiveness. Men were more effective than women in roles that were defined in more masculine terms, and women were more effective than men in roles that were defined in less masculine terms. Lyness and Thompson (2000) found that women business executives reported more barriers, such as experiencing a lack of organizational fit, being excluded from informal networks, and having greater importance placed on a good track record than did men.

CONCLUDING COMMENTS

As was discussed earlier, sometimes research investigations meld major topics of interest to I/O psychologists. A notable example by Chan and Drasgow (2001) combines motivation and leadership, a study in which the authors addressed the motivation to lead. Chan and Drasgow proposed the existence of an individual difference construct that explains why some people seek leadership positions. Using sophisticated analytic methods, the authors identified three types of people who desire to lead others. The first type sees themselves as having leadership qualities: They are outgoing and sociable (i.e., extraverts), they value competition and achievement, and they are confident in their own leadership abilities. The second type does not expect rewards or privileges to flow from leading but agree to do so because of their agreeable disposition. They value harmony in the group, irrespective of their own leadership experience or self-efficacy. The third type does not necessarily see themselves as having leadership qualities, but they are motivated to lead by a sense of social duty and obligation. The study revealed that the motivation to lead is not a unidimensional construct, but rather people can be drawn to leadership roles for different types of reasons.

Although several approaches have been taken to understand leadership, the approaches agree in the conclusion that leadership is a vital process in directing work within organizations. There appear to be boundary conditions regarding when formal leadership is most effective as well as the processes leaders use to galvanize the members of their organizations. It is also insightful that current thinking about leadership considers leaders as not only heroes but also hero makers. Thus, leadership need not be a phenomenon vested exclusively in upper-level positions; rather, it is a contagious process that can manifest itself throughout all levels of an organization. Bennis (1999) asserts that the turbulent economic and political changes of the 21st century will bring about changes in our conception of leadership. Bennis believes a shift will occur from positioning the leader as responsible for effective organizational change to a position that emphasizes the workforce and its alliance with top leadership. It remains to be seen if these predictions will be borne out. However, they do underscore the importance of the interplay of the major topics that make up the domain of leadership referenced at the start of this chapter.

C A S E   S T U D Y   ■   ## Which Direction Should We Follow?

Wayne LaPoe, President of Americom, studied his notes in preparation for the company's annual business planning and strategy meeting. It was at this meeting that most of the major goals for the next year would be set. As a diversified company in the communications field, Americom could go in several different directions. However, they basically boiled down to two possible avenues. One was to develop a wider range of products in anticipation of changing market needs. The other was to increase the sales and marketing of existing products. Each direction had its own champion within the company, and the decision of which path the company should take would be decided at the meeting where two executive vice presidents would state their cases.

Brandon McQuaid, Vice President of Sales and Marketing, was a dominant force within the company. McQuaid stood 6 feet 4 inches tall, was perfectly trim, always appeared slightly tanned, and had an engaging smile and a resonant voice. He was impeccably dressed in the latest styles. He inspired tremendous loyalty among his staff. Always warm and gregarious, McQuaid was liked by everyone. It would be difficult not to like McQuaid, thought LaPoe. McQuaid had a knack for making everyone feel good about themselves, and he usually got a great deal of support for his ideas.

Ralph Pursell was Vice President of Research and Development. An engineer by training, Pursell was about as different from McQuaid as night from day. Pursell was 5 feet 7 inches tall, at least 30 pounds overweight, and often appeared unkempt. No one ever accused Pursell of making a fashion statement. While his interpersonal skills were minimal, lurking behind his chubby face was the mind of a brilliant product designer. It was under his guidance in product development that Americom captured a huge share of the market in fiber optics. He was the most highly respected employee in the company. While some made snide remarks behind his back about his physical appearance, many employees realized they owed their jobs to Pursell's genius.

LaPoe anticipated how the planning meeting would go. He had seen it unfold the same way in past years. Pursell would make a pitch for developing some new products, using language that only he understood. The other executives in the room would simply take it on faith that Pursell knew what he was talking about. Then McQuaid would have his turn. Radiating confidence and optimism, McQuaid would soon have just about everyone eating out of his hand. He would argue that the company hadn't begun to scratch the surface in marketing Pursell's current trendsetting products. After 15 minutes of this charm, there would be a lot of smiling and head nodding in the room. When all was said and done, it was usually McQuaid's position that the management staff voted to adopt. Pursell would go back to his lab and wonder why the rest of the company didn't see things his way.

LaPoe questioned whether his management staff responded more to McQuaid's form than to Pursell's substance. He didn't want to alienate his staff by overturning their approval of McQuaid's position. Yet LaPoe wondered how much longer Pursell would continue to live with losing battles to McQuaid. LaPoe felt somewhat trapped himself. He needed the loyalty and commitment inspired by McQuaid, yet it was Pursell's ideas that McQuaid sold. LaPoe concluded that if it were possible to combine Pursell's technical ability with McQuaid's interpersonal skills, Americom would probably have a new president.

Study Questions

1. Is the management staff blinded by McQuaid's engaging leadership style, or is charm a legitimate component of leadership?
2. Should all leaders have strong interpersonal skills, or is someone like Pursell entitled to a leadership position on the basis of technical expertise?
3. If you were LaPoe, would you recommend that Pursell get some training in interpersonal skills and communication to enhance his credibility? Why, or why not?
4. Why are so many people at Americom "taken" with McQuaid? What does this suggest about why we accept people as leaders?
5. Is there a difference between having influence and being a leader? In what ways are these concepts related and unrelated?

SUGGESTED INFOTRAC TOPICS

leadership	*decision making*
power	*social participation*
influence	*followers*
traits	*need for achievement*
charisma	*supervision*

The Changing Nature of Work

LEARNING OBJECTIVES

- Understand why emotions in the workplace, adaptability, and genetic influences on work behavior will be potent individual-level factors affecting I/O psychology in the future.
- Understand why technology, the rise of a temporary workforce, and lifelong learning will be potent work-level factors affecting I/O psychology in the future.
- Understand why global economic competition, social values, and time will be influential societal-level factors affecting I/O psychology in the future.

This final chapter is intended to provide a glimpse into the future rather than a capstone summary of the past. It will examine how the nature of work is changing and how these changes are influencing I/O psychology.

Change is inevitable and unavoidable. However, the rate of change can vary from slow to fast, and change can exhibit continuity or discontinuity. It appears that as a society we are in the midst of rapid change of a highly discontinuous nature. As Havel (1994) expressed it, "Many things indicate we are going through a transitional period, when it seems that something is on the way out and something else is painfully being born. It is as if something were crumbling, decaying and exhausting itself, while something else, still indistinct, were arising from the rubble" (p. 27). Discontinuous change implies that the past is no longer a guide to the future. According to Drucker (1993), every few hundred years in Western civilization a sharp transformation creates a very different world. We are in the middle of a transformation that is not yet complete. A primary cause of the discontinuous change is the tremendous growth in knowledge produced by higher levels of education, new technologies, and increased research. This burst of knowledge causes social systems to adapt in fits and starts rather than through a steady stream of continuous change.

Three major dimensions of change affecting I/O psychology will be examined—those pertaining to individuals, work, and society. In turn, each dimension will be represented by three illustrative exemplars. In particular, consideration is given to how these dimensions of change influence the conduct of I/O psychology, as described in the preceding chapters of this book.

INDIVIDUAL DIMENSIONS

If the world of work is going through tumultuous change, it most certainly will influence the type of individuals who will prosper in this new environment. It will also influence the attributes of individuals that organizations find desirable and how job applicants will be assessed.

Emotions in the Workplace

Throughout the history of the scientific study of work, researchers have tended to use a paradigm or approach that is guided by "rationality." Thus, the experience of work is often portrayed through reasoned, analytic concepts, as witnessed by task statements, job specifications, goal objectives, and the like. However, as anyone who has ever worked can attest, "emotions are an integral and inseparable part of everyday organizational life" (Ashforth & Humphrey, 1995, p. 98). Employees are, first and foremost, people, and it is the feeling and expression of emotions that make us human. Elation, gratification, and pride are among the more meaningful positive feelings we derive from our work. However, work can also produce feelings of fear and sadness, as well as the "nasty" emotions of anger, jealousy, and envy. Recently I/O psychologists have come to recognize that emotions influence work-related behaviors, and they accept emotions as a legitimate topic of research.

Kruml and Geddes (2000) offer this statement: "Consider the following scenarios: A service agent displays calm concern and helpfulness to customers who blame her for lost orders; a collections agent exhibits a tough, nonsympathetic and threatening stance toward a delinquent customer. Their jobs require them to manage their personal emotions in order to produce desired customer (or client) responses" (p. 177). This phenomenon is called "emotional labor" and refers to how employees behave when they are required to feel, or at least project the appearance of certain emotions that facilitate their job performance.

Arvey, Renz, and Watson (1998) proposed that (1) emotions are common in the workplace and it is futile to ignore emotions or attempt to eliminate them, (2) emotions produce both positive and negative work outcomes, and (3) people have stable individual differences in their predispositions to experience certain emotions and in the intensity and duration of their expressed and displayed emotions. A person may consistently become angry instead of sad in a variety of situations where either emotion could be elicited. The stable patterns of emotional responses (i.e., individual differences in emotionality) may enable us to predict both the individual's emotional responses to job demands and the resulting behaviors that may affect job performance. The authors also proposed that work performance can be improved by matching people and jobs in terms of emotionality.

George and Brief (1996) asserted that there is an association between emotions and moods in the workplace. Both are based on feelings, but it is the intensity of the feeling that distinguishes moods from emotions. *Emotions* are normally associated with specific events and are relatively intense. Because of their intensity, emotions interrupt cognitive thought processes and behaviors. *Moods,* on the other hand, are typically day-to-day feelings that provide an affective context for thought processes and behaviors without necessarily interrupting them or demanding attention. George and Brief proposed that emotions and moods provide a basis to understand work motivation, just as feelings help determine the causes of actions people take.

In general, recognizing emotions in the workplace reestablishes "workers" as people first, who assume several roles in life, one of which is in an employment context. Given the centrality of work in our lives and the omnipresence of our emotions, this emerging interest is a long-overlooked area of fusion.

Adaptable Employees

Adaptability is a personality construct that relates to a willingness to embrace new situations, one of the Big 5 personality factors. Personality assessment is experiencing renewed popularity in I/O psychology because it can predict the "will do" component of behavior; ability tests assess the "can do" component (Katzell, 1994).

Associated with the ability to adapt to new situations is the ability to adapt to, and relate to, other people. With a growing shift to the use of work teams, it is becoming increasingly important to staff organizations with employees who have effective relational skills. Relational skills include communication, interpersonal relating, conflict resolution, and influencing capabilities. Quite apart from team-based work, organizations want employees who are responsible and conscientious and can get along with their coworkers. Dunn, Mount, Barrick, and Ones (1995) found that managers considered general mental ability and conscientiousness to be the most important attributes related to applicants' hirability. Furthermore, emotional stability, conscientiousness, and agreeableness were the most important attributes that related inversely to insubordination, rule infractions, and theft. It will be recalled that integrity tests measure these attributes. It is therefore reasonable that a selection test battery should include an assessment of both the "can do" (intelligence) and the "will do" (personality) constructs. It is a matter of debate among I/O psychologists whether the selection test battery should assess just these two constructs, or whether additional constructs should be assessed as well. What is agreed upon is that an employee's ability to adapt to change and to relate well to others is becoming as critical to successful job performance as the needed cognitive ability.

Genetic Influences on Work Behavior

Psychology has long been captivated by the nature/nurture debate—the relative degrees to which heredity and the environment influence behavior. For at least the past 40 years, the nurture or environmental perspective has dominated the thinking in psychology. That is, by carefully crafting our environment (such as by providing certain educational experiences for children), we can fashion a society where all people have a high likelihood of attaining selected outcomes, such as good health or satisfying employment. However, recently the pendulum is starting to swing back to the importance of genetic or heredity influences on behavior. That is, because of our individual genetic compositions, we are *not* all equally likely to attain selected outcomes. As Arvey and Bouchard (1994) stated, "biology is back" as an explanation for behavior. Recently researchers have identified genetic structures that account for a wide range of conditions, including obesity and alcoholism.

Arvey and Bouchard described genetic influences on work behavior and the extent to which genetics will play a role in I/O psychology. They presented a descriptive model of how genetic and environmental factors influence concepts important to I/O psychology, as shown in Figure 14–1. As can be seen in the model, genetic differences across individuals are hypothesized to influence such factors as job choice, job performance, how we feel about our work, how we perceive our work environment, our length of service on a job, and our level of income. Research has identified work situations in which individuals with certain genetic makeups are at risk when exposed to radiation and/or certain chemicals. Commercially available tests exist to detect genetic conditions such as sickle-cell anemia, cystic fibrosis, and polycystic kidney disease. Future tests for cancer and hypertension are likely. In addition, methods have been developed to detect a person's susceptibility to environmental work hazards as well as methods to determine whether a worker's chromosomes have been altered by conditions in the workplace.

Genetic studies offer us new insights into serious work problems, such as stress. Research indicates that life stress can be caused by two types of factors: controllable and uncontrollable. Genetic research has shown that the capacity to

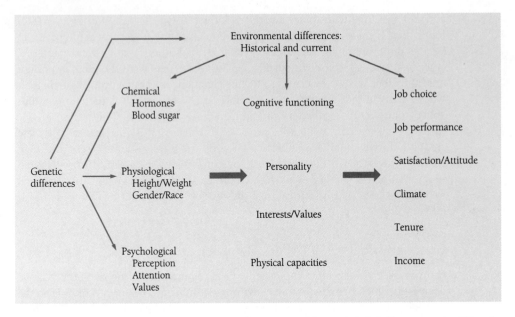

FIGURE 14–1 ■ **Model of genetic and environmental variables and their influence on traditional I/O psychology constructs**

SOURCE: From "Genetics, Twins, and Organizational Behavior" by R. D. Arvey and T. J. Bouchard, Jr., 1994, in *Research in Organizational Behavior,* Vol. 16 (p. 55), edited by B. M. Staw and L. L. Cummings, Greenwich, CT: JAI Press. Used by permission of R. D. Arvey.

control stress has high heritability. However, a critical question is whether organizations should use such information for screening, selection, and placement purposes. Ethical issues abound in this area that have yet to be resolved from a practical standpoint. Among them is the precision of measurement of genetic factors and the likelihood of misclassifying individuals. This is the same issue that applies to the use of psychological tests in making selection decisions. Are the consequences of making true and false positive and negative decisions any different when using genetic tests versus psychological tests? A more extreme ethical concern applies to altering a person's genetic structure through such procedures as gene splicing, gene transfer, and gene replacement. Such interventions are currently being discussed and implemented in medical settings.

It appears we are entering an era where there is growing recognition of the importance of genetic factors in influencing behavior, including in the workplace. It remains to be seen what its degree of impact will be across the full spectrum of concepts studied by I/O psychologists. As was previously discussed in this book, genetics has been proposed as one reason individuals differ in their level of job satisfaction and level of motivation. Future research may identify a gene associated with effective leadership. However, if indeed "biology is back" as an explanation of work behavior, I/O psychologists will have to adjust to the discontinuous change in our own thinking caused by this perspective.

WORK DIMENSIONS

Perhaps more than any other dimension, change is affecting the very nature of how work is performed. These changes in work are profound and reverberate throughout the complete domain of I/O psychology.

Technology

Van der Spiegel (1995) asserted that advances in information technologies (computers and communication systems) are the driving forces behind major changes in how we work. Only a few decades ago computers were accessible to only a privileged few, mainly engineers and scientists. The microprocessor and the personal computer now give a large portion of the population access to new information technologies. As we have moved into the 21st century, portable systems such as cellular phones, faxes, notebook computers, personal digital assistants, and pen-based computers provide multimedia capabilities to the user independent of space or time. Van der Spiegel believes that in the not too distant future we will see the emergence of instruments that can understand natural language instructions and make intelligent decisions. The information technologies will have an impact on office space and facility usage. It may become more efficient to work at home for several days where one can work uninterrupted using a personal desktop computer that provides access to the same resources that are available in the office.

These new technologies are posited to change not only the knowledge, skills, and abilities (KSAs) of individual workers, but also the manner in which we think of KSAs. Davis (1995) suggested that organizations develop differences in their competencies: that is, organizations have their own unique KSAs. Organizational competencies include the sum of knowledge possessed collectively by all employees in the organization. These competencies, particularly core competencies used to coordinate diverse production skills and integrate multiple technologies, have a strategic advantage. Unlike physical assets that deteriorate over time, knowledge grows with use. Hesketh and Bochner (1994) believe that massive technological changes are compelling individuals and organizations to become *multiskilled,* increasing their flexibility to adapt to their dynamic environments. The new information technologies are the driving mechanism behind the changes in the way work is conducted, and the corresponding talents of individuals and organizations needed to adapt to these changes.

The Rise of a Temporary Workforce

According to Cropanzano and Prehar (2001), around 1990 only 100 temporary employment agencies and approximately 470,000 temporary employees existed in the United States. A decade later the number of temporary employment agencies had grown to 1,500, employing more than 1.6 million employees. Employment of a temporary workforce was adopted as a business strategy for many of the same reasons as downsizing was in the past 20 years. In response to ebbing economic cycles and increased labor costs, organizations have turned to temporary workers to meet their staffing needs. Temporary workers typically cost the employer less than regular full-time employees because of reduced expenses for recruitment, selection, training, and compensation. Instead of using temporary employees as replacements for the occasional sick or vacationing employee, many organizations now have jobs that are permanently staffed by temporary workers. The temporary workers work for the employment agency; they are merely assigned to a particular organization to render their services.

As described by Cropanzano and Prehar, the temporary workers of today can come from several sources. One source is a woman with children who is willing to accept lower wages in exchange for a more flexible work schedule and shorter-term commitments. A second source may be a downsized worker looking for permanent employment. Other sources include a retired worker looking for supplemental income and a recent college graduate who is unable to find satisfactory full-time work. When compared with permanent work, temporary work usually pays less, has little or no job security, and offers few opportunities for growth. Approximately 30% of all temporary workers have stable employment, while the remaining 70% hop from assignment to assignment (von Hippel et al., 1997). The organization that employs their services can terminate them at will. Most temporary workers are very dissatisfied with their employment relationship. The job insecurity surrounding temporary work results in a sense of powerlessness. Not knowing when an employment contract will end and not having a regular paycheck to rely on can lead to poorer mental health for the reasons discussed in Chapter 11.

The use of temporary workers to meet the staffing needs of organizations is likely to increase. As economic conditions (industry-based, geographically based, or globally based) become more unpredictable, organizations respond with employment strategies that increase their flexibility. Business conditions that change suddenly demand rapid responses, which can be dampened by the existence of a permanent full-time workforce. However, there are psychological costs for temporary workers engaged in low-pay, unstable employment. The occurrence of workplace violence has been associated with the use of temporary workers. As discussed previously in this book, work can provide an important source of meaning in our lives as well as a sense of remuneration. One can certainly question the long-term gains to be accrued to individuals, organizations, and society by the growing reliance on a temporary workforce as it is currently structured.

Lifelong Learning

The conventional view is that learning is acquired by formal education during the years through college, followed by a relatively brief period of on-the-job learning. Following this phase of knowledge and skill acquisition, you set about "doing" your job, and for the most part your learning days are over. This model of learning (and living) is being replaced by an ethic that emphasizes learning throughout the individual's lifetime. Failure to follow this model will render you more susceptible to job loss and increasingly likely to have difficulty gaining re-employment. Thus, recent college graduates should expect to be involved in various forms of post-college educational experiences, such as programs, short courses, workshops, professional conferences, and the like. One of the fastest-growing areas in educational delivery for universities is the creation of "certificates" (as opposed to degrees). Certificates represent a form of recognition for educational accomplishments beyond the bachelor's degree. They are awarded for periods of study and focus that are more concentrated than a typical postgraduate degree. The changing nature of the psychological contract between employer and employee requires the individual to assume a greater responsibility for career development. Organizations are now far less likely to offer the implicit promise to provide career-advancing opportunities. Organizations are increasingly becoming "vendors of employment" as opposed to incubators of individual professional growth. Consider the following message found posted on the bulletin board of a plant experiencing widespread layoffs (as reported by Hall & Mirvis, 1995):

> We can't promise you how long we'll be in business.
>
> We can't promise you that we won't be bought by another company.
>
> We can't promise that there'll be room for promotion.
>
> We can't promise that your job will exist until you reach retirement age.
>
> We can't promise that the money will be available for your pension.
>
> We can't expect your undying loyalty and we aren't sure we want it. (p. 326)

Hall and Mirvis believe that workers will have to change jobs, companies, and even careers over their lifetimes. Workers who cannot adapt to this kind of change will likely plateau in their worklives or simply be ushered out of the organization. This shift puts a premium on learning how to adapt to new situations. It will become increasingly important for workers to be immersed in a wide variety of professional experiences. The authors assert it is fruitless to try to predict exactly which skills will be required in a given organization in the future. Rather, organizations should encourage employees to learn how to learn so they are capable of gaining job-specific skills as the need becomes apparent. Hall and Mirvis refer to the process of continuous development as "learning a living."

While the general blueprint for such a new system is evident for both individuals and organizations, it is not clear whether both parties have the capability to deliver what is needed. At the individual level we do not know whether people can learn to be adaptable. Is adaptability a characteristic of the individual that is relatively fixed, or can it be developed? Can we measure the ability to be adaptable, and would it predict how people will cope with organizations restructuring and rapid job movement? At the organizational level we need to identify what company practices really help people adapt and learn to learn. In order to become proficient learning centers, companies have to tailor training and work assignments to people's learning styles and set up systems of advanced skill certification, mentoring, and so forth. These are daunting assignments for organizations that are not accustomed to functioning as learning centers. Despite these issues, it is clear that one consequence of continuous change is the need to enhance our capability of responding to it. For that reason lifelong learning is posited as a critical adaptive mechanism for both individuals and organizations.

SOCIETAL DIMENSIONS

Societal dimensions of change are broad-based forces that shape both individuals and organizations. Although they are abstract in nature, their influence can be direct and potent.

Economic Competition

Cascio (1995) stated that wars—World Wars I and II, Korea, Vietnam, and the Persian Gulf—were the driving forces behind geopolitical development in the 20th century. However, in the 21st century economic forces will rule. The competition that is normal and inevitable among nations will be acted out not in war but in commerce. The weapons will be growth rates, investments, trade blocs, and imports and exports.

These changes reflect the impact of globalized product and service markets. In the 1960s only 7% of the U.S. economy was exposed to international competition. By the 1980s that number exceeded 70%. Merchandise exports have risen by 50% since 1986, and every $1 billion in U.S. merchandise that is exported generates approximately 20,000 new jobs. Free-market enterprise in the former Soviet Union will further intensify economic competition. The competition for business has resulted in a worldwide need for a highly skilled workforce. Nations are judged in economic surveys by the quality of their public education, secondary schooling, on-the-job training, and computer literacy. There is thus a global need for a broad, technically literate labor pool.

Changes in the global economy have had profound impacts on jobs in the United States. Over 7 million jobs have been lost permanently since 1987. As a rule companies do not downsize because they are losing money, but rather to strategically improve themselves. Cascio stated that we are moving from an economy where there are many hard-working people to one where there are fewer, smarter-working people. Jobs aren't being lost temporarily because of an economic recession; rather, they are being eliminated permanently as a result of new technology, improved machinery, and new ways of organizing work.

Carnevale (1995) aptly summarized how economic issues have transformed the work world:

> Something happened on the way to the second century of American economic dominance. The globalization of wealth and technology created a whole new economic ball game with new rules and an expanded set of competitive standards. . . . In addition, the globalization of competition assures that if Americans don't deliver on the new competitive standards, someone else will, and that someone else is likely to be a foreign worker in Europe or Asia. The new economy requires profound changes in American institutions. (pp. 238–239)

Although economic issues have always been a driving influence in our society, they have never attained the dominance they now possess. Increased globalization of society has ensured that no country is immune from its effects.

"*The changes are coming much too fast—I never dreamed
I'd see the hully gully in Estonia.*"

Values

The issue of values, particularly values that guide our society, has been hotly debated over the past decade. Values are the basis of legislation and judicial decisions that have profound impacts on our lives. Conflicting values in society regarding such issues as abortion and the separation of church and state generate intense reactions among partisan supporters. Values also pervade employment matters, especially what is meant by "fairness." There are conflicting standards of fairness in employment, standards that seemingly do not lend themselves to a widely endorsed middle ground or compromise position. It has been argued that as a society we do *not* necessarily need a singular concept of fairness and thus a reduction in conflict. That is, open discourse on differing viewpoints that are strongly held is one of the hallmarks of a vibrant and healthy society. However, an alternative view is that if there is not some fusion or coalescence among differing societal values, we will be continually embroiled in the conflict such divergent values produce.

Although there are many ways to conceptualize the conflict about values in employment, a useful framework is the distinction between the standards of equity and equality in social justice. The *equity* standard stems from the position that individuals differ in a wide variety of attributes like intelligence and physical strength. When these attributes are judged critical for performance in societal roles, it is acceptable to base membership in these roles on the attributes. Thus, one role in society is to maintain the security and welfare of its members, as witnessed by police and firefighter jobs. If the attribute of strength is judged critical to performance in this role, it is acceptable to select members of police and fire departments, in part, on the basis of physical strength. Because not all individuals are equally strong, some individuals will be judged more suitable for police and firefighter jobs than others.

The *equality* standard of fairness is predicated upon minimizing differences in individuals and thus ensuring that all individuals in society are treated the same or equally. For example, we all have the same opportunity to vote in an election, and each person's vote counts the same as any other person's vote. Voting is an institution whereby individuals can have a voice in matters that affect their welfare. Another institution affecting individual welfare is employment. It is through employment that we earn a living as well as have the opportunity to better ourselves in life. Accordingly, the opportunity for employment should be extended equally to all members of society.

It is at this point where the two standards of social fairness, equity and equality, frequently clash. The basis for the clash is that the attributes that differentiate individuals (such as strength) are not equally distributed across all the groups in society. That is, there are *group* differences in the attributes that are used to determine individual membership in employment. Members of society can be grouped in several ways, but one major grouping factor is gender. In the case of physical strength, there is a pronounced difference between men and women, with men (as a group) being physically stronger than women (as a group). Thus, it might be reasonable to conclude that if men are physically stronger than women, and if physical strength is an attribute needed to be a firefighter, then men are more suited to be firefighters than women. Thus, because of a difference between the two genders with regard to an attribute, men and women have an *unequal* opportunity to assume membership in the role of firefighter in our society.

Proponents of the equity standard of fairness argue that male-populated fire departments merely reflect the reality that men are stronger than women. Proponents of the equality standard of fairness argue that it is not fair, for a variety of reasons. First, although men are stronger than women, the strongest men are not necessarily the best firefighters. A certain amount of strength may be required, but greater amounts of strength beyond that threshold are unrelated to job performance. Thus, women are not as strong as men, but they may be "strong enough" to perform the job of firefighter. Second, although strength is important to being a firefighter, many other attributes, such as judgment, are also important, which women possess to the same degree as men. Therefore, women shouldn't be disproportionately excluded from the job of firefighter because of one attribute. Third, it can be argued that with the advent of technical advances in firefighting equipment, the equipment exerts the force needed on the job, not the human body.

Thus, the manual aspects of firefighting that require physical strength can be done through technological advances in equipment design, which women can operate as proficiently as men. And fourth, not all jobs in the fire department require the same degree of physical strength. Jobs such as radio dispatcher, fire truck driver, and paramedic within the fire department are less physically demanding than other jobs. Women are as able as men to meet the demands of these types of jobs in the fire department.

While counterarguments can be raised for each of these issues, the clash is evident between the equity and equality standards of fairness with regard to gender and physical strength. The same arguments can be extended to other classifications of societal groups, such as race and age, and the unequal distribution of attributes across these groups. The dilemma is how to be fair to groups that are unequal in selected attributes yet equally deserving of the societal benefits of employment.

Over the past 30 years the pendulum has swung between the equity and equality perspectives. Despite strident claims by proponents of each perspective regarding the "correctness" of their position, the reality is that both perspectives are manifestations of social justice. Whatever the next iteration in societal preference for these two positions will be, the issue will continue to have a major impact on I/O psychology. As a scientific discipline, psychology focuses on how we differ as individuals, which has the effect of gravitating us more toward the equity perspective of justice. However, the philosophic underpinnings of law seem to lean toward the equality perspective of justice. I/O psychology will continue to operate at the cusp of the interplay between these two standards of justice. We will also be compelled to be responsive to the implications of their dictates in the workplace.

Time

A resource possessed by all is time. Each of us has 24 hours in a day, each day, to live our lives. Many resources (both financial and natural) have been the object of inquiry, but we are about to enter an era in which time will be a major focus of our attention. In Chapter 11 we discussed variations in the typical five-day, 40-hour-per-week, 8:00 A.M.–5:00 P.M. work schedule. Variations include flextime, shift work, and the compressed workweek. What all of these variations in scheduling have in common is an attempt to achieve greater efficiency in how organizations and employees use time (Avery & Zabel, 2001). As also discussed in Chapter 11, time pressures are a major source of stress for many workers. We cannot increase the number of hours in a day to accommodate our busy lives; all we can do is find better ways to use the constant 24 hours per day that we all have to live our lives.

There are many manifestations of our interest in time, both scientific and practical. Katzell (1994) asserted that time is one of the major meta-trends in I/O psychology. He pointed to research findings indicating that the accuracy of predictive relationships changes over time. Some aspects of behavior are more predictable in the immediate future than in the distant future. Other aspects of behavior may not be immediately evident but will manifest themselves over time.

One can view these relationships in terms of the specific constructs being measured, or by examining the temporal-based developmental process. Time should also be considered in the issues of career development and motivation. In particular, researchers have examined the stages of a career over time, and they are questioning how the new economic order will affect these stages. While most theories of motivation have typically addressed "how much" motivation a person will exhibit in the pursuit of a goal, more recent research is addressing "how long" a person will persevere in the pursuit of a goal. Also of interest is how time affects group formation. I/O psychologists are becoming more attuned to time as a prominent issue that affects many other constructs. As Katzell (1994) noted, "Paying more attention to consistencies and changes over time contributes to a better understanding of various subjects of interest, and thereby to more effective ways of dealing with them" (p. 8).

There are also cultural differences in how time is valued and treated—either as a precarious resource or as an abundant commodity. Scarborough (2001) observed that "in some places people are driven to make productive use of every available moment and are very punctual, whereas elsewhere it is common to accept with indifference that what does not get done today will get done tomorrow, or someday, and that appointments are more approximations. In the latter case, the passage of time is something to be appreciated, experienced, and even enjoyed rather than lamented" (p. 7). Similarly, Granrose (2000) stated, "Different cultures place different emphasis on the past, the present, or the future. Members of past-oriented cultures focus on tradition, when they interpret events and when they decide what to do in the future. In contrast, ...future-oriented societies such as the United States may require a heavy emphasis on goals, aspirations, and future risks. . . . Those who live in present-oriented societies focus on short-term problem solving and present activities" (pp. 46–47).

Another manifestation of an interest in time is the identification of a personality construct that reflects our preferred use of time. *Serial monochronicity* refers to the pattern of preferring to start and complete one major task before moving on to another. *Polychronicity* is the pattern of preferring to attend to multiple tasks simultaneously. Preferred patterns of time utilization are posited to be predictive of performance in jobs that demand the individual to be responsive to overlaying waves of stimuli from divergent sources.

Time and time management have attracted growing interest as factors that affect the quality of life. Among the memorable statements about the importance of time in our lives are these:

> "How many people on their deathbed wish they'd spent more time at the office?"
> "Time is gone forever, once spent, and is the ultimate equal opportunity employer."

Covey, Merrill, and Merrill (1994) asserted that time-based issues are the leading causes of stress in life. As a way to reduce stress they advocate partitioning issues according to their importance and urgency. They recommend we do not confuse the two: Important but nonurgent issues do not require the same type or speed of response as do important and urgent issues. Covey et al. believe that stress reduction through time management does not involve "working harder" or "working smarter" but being cognizant of the principles that guide our behavior. Although we cannot control events in our lives, we can control how we appraise them and respond to them. Wright (1997) proposed that researchers can gain a better understanding of organizational issues by regarding time as an explanatory concept.

The foregoing discussion is not meant to imply that I/O psychologists have ignored time as an issue in our lives. Rather it reflects expanding one's focus from the particular substantive concepts of interest to include the temporal framework in which they are evidenced. It is also likely that a recognition of time as a precious resource will grow among researchers as we seek ways to cultivate this universal resource. Time is not a *fungible* resource, a resource that can readily be traded or exchanged for another. While we can trade money for goods, we cannot trade money for time. It is anticipated that time will be a critical variable on the research agenda in the 21st century of scientific disciplines that study work (e.g., Cooper & Rousseau, 2000; Mitchell & James, 2001).

CONCLUDING COMMENTS

The axiom that "the best predictor of the future is the past" may have to be modified in the next decades, at least as it applies to I/O psychology. A few caveats or modifiers may be in order, such as "The best predictor of the future is the very recent past." Also, we would be advised to pay close attention to emerging trends. The concept of discontinuous change indicates that the future may look very little like the past. Forces of change are operating with such intensity and velocity that it is indeed very difficult to predict the future, more so now than ever before. This chapter has outlined some of the major dimensions of change in individuals, work, and society. I/O psychology will continue to address human behavior in the work world, and in that sense our mission and purpose as a discipline will not waver. We have much to gain by all that we have learned in the past. However, it seems we will no longer be allowed the luxury of prolonged deliberation over relatively static events and conditions. The pace of change in employment issues will require adaptive responses to mixes of individual, work, and societal factors that are cascading at an accelerated speed.

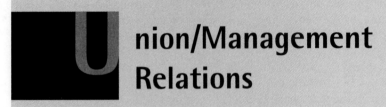

nion/Management Relations

CHAPTER OUTLINE

LEARNING OBJECTIVES

■ Describe the nature and formation of a labor union.
■ Explain the functions of a labor contract.
■ Understand the strategies of impasse resolution in the collective bargaining process.
■ Describe responses to impasse.
■ Describe the nature of grievances and grievance arbitration.
■ Discuss behavioral research on union/management relations.

Over the years, I/O psychologists have studied a broad range of topics relating to work. Strangely enough, one not often addressed is union/management relations. This area cannot be dismissed as "tangential" to work; for many organizations, union-related issues are among the most crucial. Many authors have observed that there is a great imbalance in I/O psychologists' interest between union and management problems. The two are not mutually exclusive, but I/O psychology seems more aligned with management. A listing of some of the professional activities of I/O psychologists testifies to this: managerial consulting, management development, use of assessment centers to identify those with management ability, and cross-cultural managerial issues. However, I/O psychologists have not spurned the advances of unions or been unreceptive to them. Shostak (1964) described the relationship as "mutual indifference." Unions appear reluctant to approach I/O psychologists for help in solving their problems. Rosen and Stagner (1980) think this is caused partly by the belief that I/O psychologists are not truly impartial and partly by reluctance to give outsiders access to union data.

The reasons for the unions' attitudes are numerous. One explanation is that the development of industrial psychology is closely tied to the work of Frederick Taylor. Criticisms of "Taylorism" have been raised by union workers; they see it as exploiting workers to increase company profits. There can be an adversarial relationship between unions and management, a "we/they" perspective. Unions may still see I/O psychologists as a partner of "them." Also, some factors may appear to place I/O psychologists more in the management camp. I/O psychologists are often placed in management-level positions. Management invariably sees the need for, explains the problems to, and pays the consultant. In short, I/O psychology has been more involved with management than with unions (to the point that some authors refer to I/O psychology as a "management tool"). This is most apparent in the conspicuous absence of psychological research on unions. However, another reason has recently been presented by Zickar (2001). One of the major contributions of I/O psychology to employment has been the development and use of psychological assessments of job candidates, the results of which are used to make personnel selection decisions. One notable type of psychological assessment is the personality test. Zickar described an unethical application of

union-busting
a derogatory term used to describe actions taken to prevent a labor union from representing employees

personality testing, that of **"union-busting."** The author noted "that management, in collaboration with some I/O psychologists, initially used personality inventories, not to predict job performance, but to screen potential employees who might be likely to affiliate with unions" (p. 149). Zickar added, "Regardless of the genesis of this practice, it is clear that by the late 1930s psychologists . . . were marketing these [personality] scales for union busting. This alliance with management helped fuel labor's suspicion of social scientists. . . . This partisanship made it difficult for psychologists who wished to implement policies that would ease the tensions between labor and management. Labor unions became suspicious of even the best intentioned psychologists" (p. 161). A list of the major reasons unions distrust I/O psychologists was offered by Huszczo, Wiggins, and Currie (1984) and is presented in Table A–1.

In the past several years interest in unions has increased. Whether the "thaw" will continue and grow remains to be seen. I suspect current interest stems from

TABLE A-1 ■ Reasons unions distrust I/O psychologists

They are associated with management.

They are associated with F. W. Taylor's scientific management (i.e., emphasis on efficiency, time and motion studies).

Unions are ignored in textbooks and journals of I/O psychology.

They are moralistic intellectuals who want social reform.

Methods (e.g., attitude surveys) have been used to avoid or beat union organizing attempts or to lower pay demands.

They are associated with job enrichment techniques that interfere with job classification and standards systems.

Methods of psychological testing emphasize differentiation among workers (hence, antisolidarity and antiseniority systems).

Many psychologists have not had work experience similar to union members', which causes suspicion and communication barriers.

SOURCE: From "The Relationship Between Psychology and Organized Labor: Past, Present, and Future" by G. E. Huszczo, J. G. Wiggins, and J. S. Currie, 1984, *American Psychologist, 39*, pp. 432–440.

the realization that worker/workplace problems need not be dealt with from an either/or perspective. Unions and management can benefit by solving problems that affect them jointly. If our discipline is successful in overcoming its "proman-agement" image, we can and will make greater inroads in understanding unions. Current research suggests that such changes are beginning (see Field Note 1).

This chapter will examine the nature of unions, the factors that influence union/management relations, recent research on unions, and how unionization affects many topics discussed earlier.

WHAT IS A UNION?

Unions are organizations designed to promote and enhance the social and economic welfare of their members. Basically, unions were created to protect workers from exploitation. Unions originally sprang from the abysmal working conditions in this country over 100 years ago. Workers got little pay, had almost no job security, had no benefits, and, perhaps most important, worked under degrading and unsafe conditions. Unions gave unity and power to employees. This power forced employers to deal with workers as a group. Certain federal laws forced employers to stop certain activities (such as employing children) and engage in others (such as making Social Security contributions). Collectively, labor unions and labor laws brought about many changes in the workplace. Although the problems facing the North American worker today are not so severe as they were 75–100 years ago, unions continue to give a sense of security and increased welfare to their members (see Field Note 2).

FIELD NOTE 1   Why Study Unions?

 am of the opinion that unions have been given inadequate attention by educators. When the topic of labor unions comes up, students are more likely to have heard of Jimmy Hoffa (a union leader with reputed criminal connections) than Walter Reuther (a major contributor to organized labor). Why? There are probably many reasons, but one seems fundamental. Schools, colleges, and higher education in general are founded on scholarly intellectual values. They produce learned people, many of whom rise to become business leaders. Unions, on the other hand, got their start representing relatively uneducated workers, rank-and-file employees, rather than business leaders. Rightly or wrongly, unions have had the image of representing the "common man" in labor over the "privileged intellectuals." Some union leaders become suspicious and skeptical of the motives of formally educated people, feeling they are more likely to share values held by management.

Textbooks that offer more than a passing look at organized labor are rarely found in this country. It seems the "we/they" dichotomy between labor and management has also filtered down into textbook writ-

ing; unions simply are infrequently discussed in books. This book, in fact, is one of the few I/O psychology textbooks to discuss union/management issues. On the other hand, the anti-intellectual attitude that some unions hold is costing them in ways beyond exposure in education. Unions rarely hire outside professionals; they generally promote from within their own ranks. If you were an I/O psychologist who wanted to work full time for a union, I doubt you would have many employment possibilities. Furthermore, unions are currently experiencing a decline in membership, an unprecedented number of unions are being decertified, and unions are losing their effectiveness in negotiating for desired employment conditions. In short, I feel unions are in need of some fresh ideas. They could benefit from organizational change interventions. But unless they are willing to look beyond their own ranks for expertise, I doubt that they (like any organization) will have sufficient internal strength to pull themselves up by the bootstraps. The paradoxical split between I/O psychology (the study of people at work) and labor unions (which represent a large portion of workers) has been detrimental to both parties.

Why do workers join unions? What can unions accomplish? According to several authors, unions have consistently contributed to the attainment of certain outcomes. Bok and Dunlop (1970) say unions have made these contributions to worker welfare:

- They have increased wages; in turn, employers have raised the wages of some nonunion workers.
- They have bargained for and gotten benefits such as pensions, insurance, vacations, and rest periods.
- They have provided formal rules and procedures for discipline, promotion, wage differentials, and other important job-related factors. This has led to less arbitrary treatment of employees.

There are other reasons as well: Unions can provide better communication with management, better working conditions, increased employee unity, and higher morale. Other authors cite social reasons, like belonging to a group with whom workers can share common experiences and fellowship. Thus, there are both economic and personal reasons for joining unions.

FIELD NOTE 2   **Is History Repeating Itself?**

n the early years of the 20th century, the use of child labor was prevalent in the United States, particularly in large cities. Children toiled for long hours (10–12 hours per day) in unsafe conditions (unhealthy air to breathe, no heating or cooling) and for minuscule wages (pennies per hour) in what were called "sweat shops." Eventually state and federal labor laws were enacted to prohibit child labor. Then 80–90 years later some U.S. companies moved their production facilities to foreign countries where there are no child labor laws. In some factories children again work long hours in unsafe conditions for minuscule wages (less than $1.00 per hour). How do you feel about this practice? Should U.S. companies follow U.S. labor laws in foreign countries where the laws are much different, particularly with regard to child labor? Should social pressure (e.g., economic boycotts) be exerted against companies that use child labor? Some companies argue that the reduced costs they incur by using child labor are passed on to consumers in the form of lower costs of the products. How should companies in particular and our society as a whole balance economic gain and social conscience? We are finding that history is repeating itself; the conditions that spawned labor laws in this country many years ago are now being exploited by some companies in foreign countries.

UNIONS AS ORGANIZATIONS

Approximately 20 million U.S. citizens belong to labor unions, representing about 25% of the nonagricultural workforce. In Canada membership is over 2 million. The largest labor union is the American Federation of Labor–Congress of Industrial Organizations (AFL-CIO). Other large unions are the United Auto Workers and the United Mine Workers. While historically unions were strongest among blue-collar employees, white-collar workers (particularly government employees and teachers) are now the dominant union base. In recent years there has been a decline in unionization as the number of service jobs has increased and the number of manufacturing jobs (a traditional union stronghold) has decreased.

Each union has a headquarters, but its strength is its many locals. A local may represent members in a geographic area (for example, all tollbooth collectors in Philadelphia) or a particular plant (for example, Amalgamated Beef Packers at Armour's Dubuque, Iowa, slaughterhouse). The local elects officials. If it is large enough, it affords some officials full-time jobs. Other officials are full-time company employees who may get time off for union activities. The shop, or union, steward has a union position equivalent to that of a company supervisor. The steward represents the union on the job site; he or she handles grievances and discipline. Usually the steward is elected by union members for a one-year term.

A union represents an organization (for example, a labor organization) within another organization (the company). The local depends on the company for its existence. Large companies often have a multiunion labor force and thus multiple organizations within themselves. In this case the employer must deal with several collectively organized groups—for example, production workers, clerical workers, and truck drivers. Each union negotiates separately, trying to improve the welfare of its members. A large, multiunion employer is a good example of how organiza-

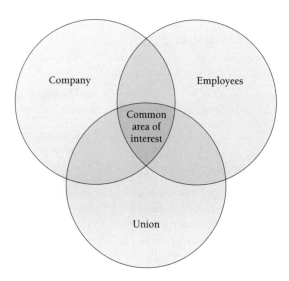

FIGURE A–1 ■ **Management/employee/union relationships**

SOURCE: From *Managing Change in a Unionized Workplace* (p. 65) by K. Blackard, 2000, Westport, CT: Quorum.

tions are composed of interdependent parts. Each union has a certain degree of power, which can influence the behavior of the total organization.

Union members pay membership dues, which are the union's chief resource. The union can also collect money for a strike fund, a pool members can draw from if they are on strike and do not get paid. (Strikes will be discussed in more detail shortly.) Unions use their funds to offer members such things as special group automobile insurance rates or union-owned vacation facilities. Unions are highly dependent on their members. Increased membership gives a union more bargaining clout, generates more revenue, and provides a greater range of services for members. Without members, a union cannot exist; indeed, declining membership can threaten a union's very survival. Blackard (2000) presented a graphic representation of the relationships among the company, the union, and the employees, as shown in Figure A–1.

THE FORMATION OF A UNION

National Labor Relations Board (NLRB)
an agency of the federal government that has responsibility for enforcing laws pertaining to union/management relations

authorization card
a card employees sign authorizing an election to determine whether a union will represent employees in the collective bargaining process

certification election
an election in which employees vote to determine whether a union will represent them in the collective bargaining process

When employees want to consider joining a union, they follow a standard procedure. First, they invite representatives to solicit union membership. Federal law allows organizers to solicit membership as long as this does not endanger employees' safety or performance. Solicitations usually occur over lunch or at break time. It is illegal for employers to threaten physically, interfere with, or harass organizers. It is also illegal to fire employees for prounion sentiments.

Both the union and the company typically mount campaigns on behalf of their positions. The union stresses how it can improve the workers' lot. The company's countercampaign stresses how well off the employees already are, the costs of union membership, and the loss of freedom. Then a federal agency, the **National Labor Relations Board (NLRB)**, becomes involved. The NLRB sends a hearing officer to oversee the union campaign and monitor further developments.

Employees are asked to sign cards authorizing a union election. If fewer than 30% sign the **authorization cards**, the process ends. If 30% or more sign, an election is held to determine whether a union will represent the employees. The NLRB officer must determine which employees are eligible to be in the union and thus eligible to vote. Management personnel (supervisors, superintendents, and managers) are excluded. The hearing officer schedules the election, provides secret ballots and ballot boxes, counts the votes, and certifies the election. As such, this expression of voter preference is termed a **certification election.** If more than 50% of the voters approve, the union is voted in. If the union loses the election, it can repeat the entire process at a later date. A union that loses a close election will probably do so.

Brief and Rude (1981) proposed that the decision to accept or reject a union is not unlike other choices facing an individual. Employees will support a union to the extent that it will provide outcomes important to them without prohibitive costs. Over 50 years ago Bakke (1945) stated this most eloquently:

> The worker reacts favorably to union membership in proportion to the strength of his belief that this step will reduce his frustrations and anxieties and will further his opportunities relevant to the achievement of his standards of successful living. He reacts unfavorably in proportion to the strength of his belief that this step will increase his frustrations and anxieties and will reduce his opportunities relevant to the achievement of such standards. (p. 38)

DeCotiis and LeLouarn (1981) developed the model of the determinants of unionization shown in Figure A–2. The work context includes employee reactions to work, organization climate, perceived organization structure, and supervision. Personal characteristics include age, gender, and race, as well as feelings of job satisfaction. The work context and personal characteristics determine union instrumentality—that is, the extent to which a union is seen as improving the employee's welfare. Instrumentality affects the employee's attitude toward unions; in turn, this affects the employee's intent to vote for a union. The actual vote is determined by the sequence shown in the model. DeCotiis and LeLouarn were able to explain over 54% of the variance in perceptions of union instrumentality with the concepts in their model.

Summers, Betton, and DeCotiis (1986) found that union instrumentality can be lowered when different unions are competing for the right to represent employees. They discovered that employees are likely to take antiunion information more seriously if its source is another union rather than management. Premack and Hunter (1988) carefully studied the unionization decision by means of elaborate statistical methods. They concluded that some employees hold strong attitudes about unions, both pro and con, and their attitudes are usually not altered one

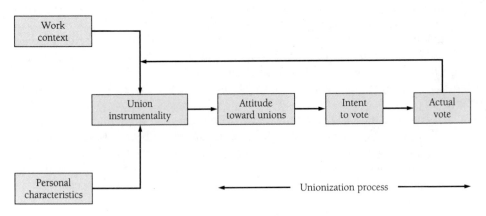

Figure A–2 ■ A model of the determinants of the unionization process

SOURCE: From "A Predictive Study of Voting Behavior in a Representation Election Using Union Instrumentality and Work Perceptions" by T. A. DeCotiis and J. Y. LeLouarn, 1981, *Organizational Behavior and Human Performance, 27,* p. 109.

decertification election

an election in which unionized employees vote to determine whether their union will no longer represent them in the collective bargaining process

way or the other during the course of the organizing campaign. However, other employees are uncertain about their attitudes toward unions, and their attitudes can be altered by the behavior of both parties during the organizing campaign. Premack and Hunter noted that these employees' votes are critical to the outcome of the election because most union representation elections are decided by a small number of votes.

If the employees elect to have a labor union represent them in their negotiations with management, the union must continue to be perceived as instrumental to the employees over time. Some unions have been perceived by employees as having lost their effectiveness in dealing with management. Then employees have the power to remove the union as their representative through a formal vote. Such a vote is called a **decertification election.**

THE LABOR CONTRACT

labor contract

a formal agreement between labor and management that specifies the terms and conditions of employment while the contract is in effect

Once a union is recognized, its officials are authorized to negotiate a **labor contract.** This is a formal agreement between union and management, specifying conditions of employment over a set period.

Both sides prepare a preliminary list of what they want included; the union presents its demands and the employer its offers. The union tends to ask for more than it knows it can get; management tends to offer less. While both sides seek a satisfactory agreement, they often resort to bombast, which is a hallmark of such negotiations. Union officials may allege that management is making huge profits and taking advantage of workers. Management may allege that malicious union leaders have duped the good workers and that their policies may force the company into bankruptcy. Over time, both sides usually come to an agreement; the union often gets less than it wanted and management gives more. When agreement is not reached (an **impasse**), other steps are taken, as will be discussed.

impasse

a point in the collective bargaining process at which both the union and management conclude they are unable to reach an agreement in the formation of a labor contract

Contract negotiations take place between two teams of negotiators. The union side typically consists of local union officials, shop stewards, and perhaps a representative of the national union. Management usually fields a team of a few personnel and production managers, who follow preset guidelines. The contract contains many articles; there are also many issues to bargain over. The issues can generally be classified into five categories: compensation and working conditions, employee security, union security, management rights, and contract duration. Table A–2 lists examples of these issues and the positions typically taken by each side.

In the process each bargaining team checks with its members to see whether they will compromise on the initial positions. Each side may be willing to yield on some points but not others. Eventually the teams reach a tentative agreement. Union members then vote on the contract. If they approve it, the contract is ratified and remains in effect for the agreed-on time (typically two to three years). If members reject the contract, further negotiation is necessary.

Whether a contract will be ratified typically depends on industry practices, community practices, and recent trends. If the union represents truck drivers and a critical issue is wages, the union will collect data needed to judge the proposal: what other companies in the industry pay truck drivers, what other companies in

TABLE A–2 ■ Typical bargaining issues and positions taken by union and management

Issue	Union's Position	Management's Position
Compensation and working conditions	Higher pay, more fringe benefits, cost-of-living adjustments	Lower company expenditures, not yielding to all union demands
Employee security	Seniority is the basis for promotions, layoffs, and recall decisions	Merit or job performance is the basis for these decisions
Union security	A union shop in which employees must join the union when hired	An open shop in which employees can choose to join the union
Management rights	Union wants more voice in setting policies and making decisions that affect employees	Management feels certain decisions are its inherent right and does not want to share them with the union
Contract duration	Shorter contracts	Longer contracts

the community pay them, and whether prices and wages are rising or falling. Stagner and Rosen (1965) classically referred to the area of compromise as the *bargaining zone*; this is illustrated in Figure A–3. Both parties must move toward a compromise without exceeding their tolerance limits; this is the point beyond which the contract will be unacceptable. If both parties reach a compromise within their expectations, there will be agreement. If, however, one side exceeds its tolerance limit, the proposed contract will not be acceptable.

Both sides will use whatever external factors are available to influence the contract in their favor. If there is high unemployment and the company could replace workers who go on strike, management has an advantage. If the company does much of its business at Christmas time, the union may choose that time to negotiate a contract, knowing the company can ill afford a strike then. Each side looks for factors that will bolster its position.

Collective Bargaining and Impasse Resolution

collective bargaining
the process by which labor and management engage in negotiating a labor contract

Whether the **collective bargaining** process runs smoothly often depends on the parties' approaches. Pruitt (1993) distinguished between distributive and integrative bargaining postures. *Distributive bargaining* is predominant in the United States. This assumes a win/lose relationship; whatever the employer gives the union, the employer loses, and vice versa. Because both sides are trying to minimize losses, movement toward a compromise is often painful and slow.

The alternative is *integrative bargaining*. Both sides work to improve the relationship while the present contract is in effect. Contract renewal is not seen as the time and place for confrontation. Instead, both parties seek to identify common

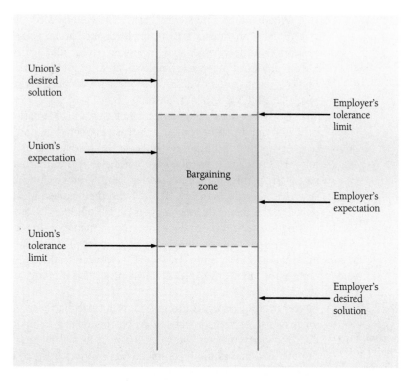

FIGURE A–3 ■ Desires, expectations, and tolerance limits that determine the bargaining zone

SOURCE: From *Psychology of Union–Management Relations* (p. 96) by R. Stagner and H. Rosen, 1965, Belmont, CA: Wadsworth. Reprinted by permission of the publisher. Brooks/Cole Publishing Company, Pacific Grove, California.

problems and propose acceptable solutions that can be adopted when the contract expires.

These bargaining postures are not formally chosen; rather, they are implied by behavior in the workplace. While it is not always a strict either/or decision, distributive bargaining is far more characteristic of union/management relations than is integrative bargaining.

What happens if the two parties cannot reach an agreement? In some cases the labor contract may stipulate what will be done if an impasse is reached. In other cases the union and management must jointly determine how to break the impasse. In either case there are three options, all involving third parties: mediation, fact-finding, and arbitration.

mediation
a method of dispute settlement in which a neutral third party offers advice to the union and management in order to help them agree on a labor contract.

Mediation.   **Mediation** is the most used yet the most informal third-party option. A neutral third party (a mediator) assists the union and management in reaching voluntary agreement. A mediator has no power to impose a settlement; rather, he or she facilitates bringing both parties together.

Where do mediators come from? The Federal Mediation and Conciliation Service (FMCS) provides a staff of qualified mediators. An organization may contact FMCS for the services of such a person. The mediator need not be affiliated with FMCS; any third party acceptable to labor and management may serve. Generally, however, both parties prefer someone with training and experience in labor disputes, so FMCS is often called on.

How a mediator intervenes is not clear-cut. Mediation is voluntary; thus, no mediator can function without the trust, cooperation, and acceptance of both parties. Acceptance is important because the mediator must obtain any confidential information that the parties have withheld. If the information is used indiscriminately, the parties' bargaining strategy and leverage could be weakened. The mediator tries to reduce the number of disputed issues; ideally, he or she reaches a point where there are no disputes at all. The mediator encourages information sharing to break the deadlock. Without a mediator, it is often difficult for parties to "open up" after assuming adversarial roles. The mediator facilitates the flow of information and progression toward compromise. If the mediator is unsuccessful, both parties may engage in the next phase: fact-finding.

fact-finding
a method of dispute settlement in which a neutral third party makes public the respective positions of labor and management with the intention that the public will influence the two sides to resolve their disputes in establishing a labor contract

arbitration
a method of dispute settlement in which a neutral third party resolves the dispute between labor and management by making a decision that is typically final and binding to both parties

interest arbitration
a type of arbitration used in resolving disputes between labor and management in the formation of a labor contract

Fact-Finding.   **Fact-finding** is more formal than mediation. A qualified mediator may also serve as a fact finder, but his or her role is different. In fact-finding the third party reviews the facts, makes a formal recommendation to resolve the dispute, and makes the recommendation public. It is presumed that if the recommendation is public, the parties will be pressured to accept it or use it for a negotiated settlement. However, fact-finding has not produced the desired pressure. Public interest is apparently aroused only when a strike threatens or actually imposes direct hardship on the public.

Fact-finding may be most useful when one party faces internal differences and needs recommendations from an expert to overcome opposition to a settlement. There appears to be a difference in the effectiveness of fact-finding between private- and public-sector employers. In the public sector fact-finding has met with limited success. Parties learn that rejecting a fact-finding recommendation is not politically or economically costly, so they are unlikely to value the opinion of the fact finder. In the private sector fact-finding can be helpful primarily because the final technique of settlement (arbitration) is strongly opposed by unions and management. However, fact-finding is not used very often in the private sector.

Arbitration.   **Arbitration** is the final and most formal settlement technique. Both parties must abide by the decision of the neutral third party. "Final and binding" is usually associated with arbitration. The use of arbitration may be stipulated in the labor contract; it may also be agreed on informally. This is called **interest arbitration** because it involves the interests of both parties in negotiating a new contract.

Arbitrators must have extensive experience in labor relations. The American Arbitration Association (AAA) maintains the standards and keeps a list of qualified arbitrators. Arbitrators listed by AAA often also serve as mediators listed by FMCS. Effective mediators, fact finders, and arbitrators all need the same skills. What distinguishes the services is the clout of the third party.

There are many forms of interest arbitration. With *voluntary arbitration,* the parties agree to the process. It is most common in the private sector in settling disputes that arise while a contract is still in effect. *Compulsory arbitration* is legally required. It is most common in the public sector.

conventional arbitration; final-offer arbitration; total-package arbitration; issue-by-issue arbitration
other forms of arbitration available for dispute settlement between unions and management

There are other types of arbitration. With **conventional arbitration,** the arbitrator creates the settlement he or she deems appropriate. In **final-offer arbitration,** the arbitrator must select the proposal of either union or management; no compromise is possible. For example, suppose the union demands $8 per hour and the company offers $7. In conventional arbitration the arbitrator could decide on any wage but would probably split the difference and decide on $7.50. In final-offer arbitration the arbitrator must choose the $7 or the $8. An additional variation also holds for final-offer arbitration: The arbitrator may make the decision with **total-package arbitration:** He or she chooses the complete proposal of either the employer or the union on all issues. The decision may also be made with **issue-by-issue arbitration.** In this case the arbitrator might choose the employer wage offer but select the union demand on vacation days. Decisions on voluntary versus compulsory arbitration, conventional versus final-offer arbitration, and total-package versus issue-by-issue arbitration are determined by law for public-sector employers and by mutual agreement in the private sector (see Field Note 3).

FIELD NOTE 3   Overuse of Arbitration?

nterest arbitration can be a seductively simple means of resolving impasses—so simple, in fact, that some people fear it is overused. Let us say the union wants a 50-cents-per-hour pay increase and management offers 10 cents per hour. Both sides believe from past experience that an arbitrator would likely split the difference between the two, settling on 30 cents per hour. It has been suggested that the more arbitration is used to resolve impasses and the more splitting that occurs, the more likely it is that parties will not bargain seriously between themselves; that is, they will opt for the effortless remedy, arbitration. Thus, the parties will disregard the mediation and fact-finding stages and go directly to arbitration. Arbitration becomes an addictive response to impasse; this phenomenon has been labeled the "narcotic effect" of arbitration.

How do you weaken the narcotic effect of arbitration? One solution is to have arbitrators not split the difference in making decisions. Arbitrators are free to fashion whatever decisions they think are fair. Splitting the difference is often perceived as the fairest thing to do, and it increases the acceptability of the arbitrator for future cases because neither party will have received preferential treatment. Thus, with each split decision, the narcotic effect becomes stronger. One way to weaken the narcotic effect is to prohibit split decisions, which is what happens in final-offer arbitration. Here, the arbitrator is bound to accept either the 50-cents or 10-cents position and not any figure over, under, or in between. Given this, it has been hypothesized that negotiators will offer more serious, reasonable proposals, knowing the alternative is to have an arbitrator choose one position over the other. An absurd offer would never get chosen. In total-package, final-offer arbitration the arbitrator must choose the entire package of either the union or management, which tends to drive both parties into compromise. The alternative version of issue-by-issue, final-offer arbitration produces its own type of split decisions; that is, since there can be no within-issue splits, the arbitrator splits between issues. Thus, the union position is accepted on one issue and management's position on another. The use of total-package, final-offer arbitration is presumed to have greatly decreased reliance on arbitration for impasse resolution.

Interest arbitration is more common in the public sector. Historically, the private sector has been opposed to outside interference in resolving labor problems that are "private" affairs. Thus, private-sector employers will readily seek the advice of a mediator but shun strategies that require certain courses of action. The public sector, however, is quite different. Strikes in the public sector (for example, police) can have devastating effects on the general public. Since they are often prohibited by law, other means of settlement (fact-finding, arbitration) are used. Some public-sector employees have gone on strike (sometimes legally but usually illegally), but strikes are more often the outcome of impasses in the private sector.

Responses to Impasse

Consider the situation in which union and management cannot resolve their disputes. They may or may not have used a mediator. Assume the private sector is involved because mediation, fact-finding, and arbitration might be required in the public sector. What happens if the two parties cannot agree?

In collective bargaining both sides can take actions if they are not pleased with the outcome. These actions are weapons with which to bring about favorable settlements. The union can call for a **labor strike.** Union members must vote for a strike. If members support a strike and no settlement is reached, they will stop work at a particular time—typically the day after the current contract expires. Taking a strike vote during negotiations brings pressure on management to agree to union demands.

The right to strike is a very powerful tool. The losses from a long strike may be greater than the concessions made in a new contract. Also, unions are skilled in scheduling their strikes (or threatening to do so) when the company is particularly vulnerable (such as at Christmas time in the airline industry). If employees do strike, the company is usually closed down completely. There may be limited production if management performs some jobs. It is also possible to hire workers to replace those on strike. These replacements are called "scabs." Given the time it takes to recruit, hire, and train new workers, replacements will not be hired unless a long strike is predicted.

While a strike hurts management, it is unpleasant for the workers as well. Since they are not working, they do not get paid. The employees may have contributed to a strike fund, but such funds usually pay only a fraction of regular wages. A strike is the price employees pay to get their demands. It sometimes also limits their demands. By the time a union faces a strike, it is usually confronted with two unpalatable options. One is to accept a contract it does not like; the other is to strike. Employees may seek temporary employment while they are on strike, but such jobs are not always available. On the basis of labor economists' studies of the costs of strikes to both employees and employers, it is safe to say that strikes rarely benefit either party. Sometimes the company suffers the most; in other cases the union does. There are rarely any "winners" in a strike. Stagner and Rosen (1965) listed the consequences for both union and management in accepting each other's alternatives, particularly as they relate to a strike (see Table A–3).

One study examined some of the dynamics associated with strikes. Stagner and Effal (1982) looked at the attitudes of unionized automobile workers at sev-

labor strike
a cessation of work activities by unionized employees as a means of influencing management to accept the union position in a dispute over the labor contract

TABLE A–3 ■ Union and company alternatives and related consequences

Company	Union
Alternative 1	
Perceived consequences of giving in to union demands	Perceived consequences of accepting company counteroffer
1. Lessening investor returns	1. Losing membership support
2. Losing competitive standing	2. Losing status within union movement
3. Setting bad precedent	3. Setting bad precedent
4. Avoiding costly strike	4. Avoiding costly strike
5. Avoiding government and public ill will	5. Avoiding government and public ill will
Alternative 2	
Perceived consequences of refusing to accede to union demands	Perceived consequences of sticking to original demands
1. Due to potential strike, lessening investor return	1. Proving strength and determination of union to members
2. Due to potential strike, losing competitive standing	2. Due to potential strike, losing member income
3. Losing government and public goodwill	3. Due to potential strike, losing member support
4. Maintaining company prerogatives	4. Losing government and public goodwill
5. Breaking union power	5. Teaching company a "lesson"

SOURCE: Adapted from *Psychology of Union-Management Relations* (p. 103) by R. Stagner and H. Rosen, 1965, Belmont, CA: Wadsworth. Reprinted by permission of the publishers, Brooks/Cole Publishing Company, Pacific Grove, California.

eral times, including when contracts were being negotiated, during an ensuing strike, and seven months after the strike ended. The authors found that union members on strike (1) had a higher opinion of the union and its leadership than before the strike, (2) evaluated the benefit package more highly after the strike, (3) became more militant toward the employer during the strike, and (4) reported more willingness to engage in union activities. The results of this study support predictions based on theories of conflict and attitude formation.

Management is not totally defenseless in the case of a strike. If it anticipates a strike, it might boost production beforehand to stockpile goods. Most public-sector employees, on the other hand, perform services, and services cannot be stockpiled. This is one reason strikes are illegal in some parts of the public sector. Sometimes a strike uncovers information about the quality of the workforce. When one company replaced strikers with temporary help, new production records were set. In this case the strike revealed a weakness in the employees.

A strike is not the only option available to the union. **Work slowdowns** have also been used. Workers operate at lower levels of efficiency. They may simply put out less effort and thus produce less, or they may be absent to reduce productivity. Since strikes are illegal in the police force, police officers who are dissatisfied

work slowdown
a tactic used by some employees to influence the outcome of union/management negotiations in which the usual pace of work is intentionally reduced

with their contracts may call in sick en masse with what has become known as the "blue flu." Such tactics can exert great pressure on management to yield to union demands.

sabotage
A tactic used by some employees to influence the outcome of union/management negotiations in which company equipment is intentionally damaged to reduce work productivity

Sabotage is another response to impasse in negotiations.[1] Stagner and Rosen (1965) described a situation in which factory production was increased from 2,000 to 3,000 units per day by modifications to a drill press. However, wages were not increased, and workers resented it. They found that bumping the sheet metal against the drill would eventually break the drill. Then the employee handling the drill would have to wait idly for a replacement. By some curious accident, average production continued at around 2,000 units per day. However, management got the "message." While sabotage is not a sanctioned union activity like a strike, it is a way of putting pressure on management to accept demands.

lockout
action taken by management against unionized employees to prevent them from entering their place of work as a means of influencing the union to accept the management position in a dispute over the labor contract

Management also has a major tactic to get the union to acquiesce. It is called a **lockout** and is considered the employer's equivalent of a strike. The company threatens to close if the union does not accept its offer. Employees cannot work and thus they "pay" for rejecting the employer's offer. A threatened lockout may cause a majority of workers to pressure a minority holding out against a contract issue. Like strikes, lockouts are costly to both the company and the union, and they are not undertaken lightly. They are management's ultimate response to an impasse.

Before this section ends, note that labor strikes, work slowdowns, sabotage, and lockouts represent failures in the collective bargaining process. These actions are taken because a settlement was not reached. Like most responses to frustration, they are rarely beneficial in the long run. Some unions may want to "teach the company a lesson"; some companies want to break a union. But both parties have a symbiotic relationship. A company cannot exist without employees; without a company, employees have no jobs. Collective bargaining reflects the continual tussle for power, but neither side can afford to be totally victorious. If a union exacts so many concessions that the company goes bankrupt, it will have accomplished nothing. As Estey (1981) put it, "Labor does not seek to kill the goose that lays the golden eggs; it wants it to lay more golden eggs, and wants more eggs for itself" (p. 83). If management drives employees away by not making enough concessions, it will not have a qualified workforce. Industrial peace is far more desirable for all parties than warfare. Conflict can provide opportunities for change and development; if conflict gets out of hand, however, it can be devastating.

Union/management relations are not all typified by infighting and power plays. Nothing unites opposing factions faster than a common enemy. Because the United States was losing some economic battles to foreign competition, some union/management relations became far more integrative. For example, unions in the auto industry have given up some concessions they gained before the current contract expired. The industry, in turn, used the money saved to become more competitive. By remaining solvent, the industry continued to provide jobs. Both man-

---

[1] The word *sabotage* comes from the French word *sabot,* meaning "shoe." The word derives from an industrial context. Centuries age wooden shoes were worn. A wooden shoe would be intentionally jammed into machinery to prevent its proper operation, thereby *sabotaging* it.

agement and labor could pursue some common goals. Collective bargaining is a delicate process. Neither side should lose sight of the total economic and social environment, even though short-term, narrow issues are often at the heart of disputes.

Grievances

Collective bargaining is mainly directed toward resolving disputes about new labor contracts; however, disputes also occur over contracts that are in effect. No matter how clearly a labor contract is written, disagreements invariably arise over its meaning or extent. Developing a clear and precise contract involves writing skills in their highest form. Despite the best intentions of those involved, events occur that are not covered clearly in a labor contract. For example, companies often include a contract clause stating that sleeping on the job is grounds for dismissal. A supervisor notices that an employee's head is resting on his arms and his eyes are closed. The supervisor infers the employee is asleep and fires him. The employee says he was not sleeping but felt dizzy and chose to rest for a moment rather than risk falling down. Who is right?

grievance
a formal complaint made by an employee against management alleging a violation of the labor contract in effect

If the supervisor dismissed the employee, the employee would probably file a **grievance,** or formal complaint. The firing decision can be appealed through a grievance procedure, which is usually a provision of a labor contract. First, the employee and supervisor try to reach an understanding. If they do not, the shop steward represents the employee in negotiating with the supervisor. This is often done whether or not the steward thinks the employee has a "case"; above all, the steward's job is to represent union members. If the issue is not resolved, the case may then be taken to the company's director of industrial relations, who hears testimony from both sides and issues a verdict. This may be a compromise—such as the employee keeps his or her job but is put on probation. The final step is to call in an arbitrator. He or she examines the labor contract, hears testimony, and renders an opinion. This process is called rights or **grievance arbitration;** it involves the rights of the employee. The labor contract usually specifies that union and management share the cost of arbitration, which may be $3,000 per hearing. This is done to prevent all grievances from being routinely pushed to arbitration. Each side must believe it has a strong case before calling in an arbitrator.

grievance arbitration
a type of arbitration used in resolving disputes between labor and management in interpretation of an existing labor contract

The arbitrator must be acceptable to both sides; this means he or she must be seen as neither prounion nor promanagement. The arbitrator may either decide in favor of one side or issue a compromise decision. The decision is final and binding. If an arbitrator hears many cases in the same company and repeatedly decides in favor of one side, he or she may become unacceptable to the side that always loses. Articles of the labor contract that are repeated subjects of grievance (due mainly to ambiguous language) become prime candidates for revision in the next contract.

Think of grievances as a somewhat contaminated index of the quality of union/management relations. In general, when the working relationship is good, there are fewer grievances. However, as Gordon and Miller (1984) noted, in some organizations work problems are resolved informally between the conflicting parties and never develop into formal grievances. While formal grievances are usually indicative of conflict, their absence does not always reflect a problem-free work environment.

Also, the more ambiguous the labor contract, the more likely conflicts will ensue. A poorly written or inconsistently interpreted contract invites grievances. There can be much grievance activity in a recently unionized organization; employees use grievances to "test" management's knowledge of the labor contract (Muchinsky & Maassarani, 1981). Particularly in the public sector, where collective bargaining is relatively new, government employees are expected to act as "management" even though they have little or no training in dealing with labor. This can contribute to errors in contract administration. Gordon and Bowlby (1989) found employees were more likely to file a grievance when management actions against them were perceived as a threat and when the employee attributed the discipline to a manager's personal disposition (animus toward the worker). Employees were less likely to file a grievance when they perceived managers as simply following rules that required punishment for the specific worker behavior.

Employee concern over capricious management decisions is one of the major reasons employees opt for union representation. Fryxell and Gordon (1989) reported that the amount of procedural justice afforded by a grievance system was the strongest predictor of employee satisfaction with a union. Gordon and Bowlby (1988) also challenged the dictum that grievances are best resolved at the lowest step of the grievance process. Grievants who won their cases at higher levels of the grievance process showed greater faith in the fairness and perceived justice of the dispute resolution process. Klaas (1989) reported that at higher levels in the grievance process managers were influenced by the grievant's work history as documented in their performance appraisals, even when that history was not relevant to evaluating the merits of the grievance. Olson-Buchanan (1996) found that, consistent with procedural justice, employees who had access to a grievance system were more willing to continue working for the organization. Consistent with the equity theory of motivation, employees who had a basis for dispute had lower objective job performance and were less willing to continue working for the organization.

There is also a growing use of arbitration to resolve disputes in nonunion companies. Richey et al. (2001) reported that in the past 20 years there has been a 400% increase in employment litigation and a 2,200% increase in discrimination lawsuits, with a corresponding increase in company costs and negative publicity. With the increased number of lawsuits in the courts, there has been growing support for *alternative dispute resolution* procedures among employees, legislators, and the courts. Arbitration is being proposed as a means of resolving disputes between employees and employers. The arbitration process may be voluntary (i.e., the employee has the option to submit the dispute to an impartial arbitrator) or mandatory (i.e., the employee is required to submit any dispute to an impartial arbitrator as a condition of employment at the company). Likewise, the outcome of the arbitration process can be nonbinding (meaning if the arbitrator's judgment does not satisfy the employee, the employee can choose to pursue the dispute in court) or binding (meaning the outcome of the arbitration process is final and binding and may not be pursued in court). Richey et al. found that job applicants were more inclined to view an employer negatively if they had either mandatory or binding arbitration as a means of resolving disputes. The finding was interpreted as limiting avenues of procedural justice for employees.

In conclusion, while there is much publicity about strike-related issues, union members think the union's highest priority should be better ways of handling grievances. Unions serve many purposes; however, the most pressing need they fill seems to be ensuring fair treatment in employment. Of course, this is a primary reason that unions appeal to workers.

INFLUENCE OF UNIONS ON NONUNIONIZED COMPANIES

Even if they do not have unionized employees, companies are still sensitive to union influence. Companies that are unresponsive to employees' needs invite unionization. A nonunion company that wants to remain so must be receptive to its workers' ideas and complaints. If a company can satisfy its employees' needs, a union is unnecessary; that is, the company does voluntarily what a labor union would force it to do. A given community or industry often has a mix of union and nonunion companies. If unionized employees get concessions from management on wages, benefits, hours, and so on, these become reference points for nonunion-ized employees. Thus, for example, a nonunion company may feel compelled to raise wages to remain competitive. If a labor contract calls for formal grievance procedures, a nonunion company may well follow suit. Workers are aware of employment conditions in other companies, which gives them a frame of reference for judging their own. If a company does not offer comparable conditions, employees may see a union as a means of improving their welfare. This is not to say that nonunion companies must offer identical conditions. There are costs associated with a union (for example, dues); a nonunion company might set wages slightly lower than those paid in a unionized company so the net effect (higher wages minus dues) is comparable. What economists call the **"union/nonunion wage differential"** has been the subject of extensive research. Jarrell and Stanley (1990) reported that the union/nonunion wage differential varied with the national unemployment rate and ranged from 8.9% to 12.4%.

union/nonunion wage differential the average difference in wages paid to union versus nonunion employees across an industry or geographic area for performing the same jobs

Although a prudent nonunion employer keeps abreast of employment conditions in the community and the industry, a company cannot act to keep a union out "at all costs." There is powerful labor relations legislation. Many laws (like the National Labor Relations Act) were enacted to prohibit unfair practices on both sides. For example, an employer cannot fire a worker just because he or she supports a union. The history of labor relations is full of cases of worker harassment by unions or management to influence attitudes toward unionization. But both sides can suffer for breaking the law.

BEHAVIORAL RESEARCH ON UNION/MANAGEMENT RELATIONS

Thus far this appendix has examined the structure of unions, collective bargaining, and various issues in union/management relations. For the most part, psychological issues have not been discussed. With the exception of grievances, there is little behavioral research on union/management relations. However, over the past few years, interest in this area has increased. We are beginning to see an interdisciplinary approach to topics that historically were treated with parochialism (Brett, 1980). This section will examine research on union/management relations with a strong behavioral thrust.

Employee Support for Unions

Numerous studies have examined why employees support a union, particularly with regard to personal needs and job satisfaction. Feuille and Blandin (1974) sampled the attitudes toward unionization of over 400 college professors at a university experiencing many financial and resource cutbacks. The items measured satisfaction with areas like fairness of the university's personnel decisions, adequacy of financial support, representation of faculty interests in the state legislature, and salary. The professors were also asked to rate their inclination to accept a union. Professors who were dissatisfied with employment conditions were much more likely to support a union. Respondents also were consistent in their attitudes toward a union and their perceptions of its impact and effectiveness. Proponents of a union saw it as an effective way of protecting employment interests and as having a positive impact. In general, results indicated that unionization is more attractive as employment conditions deteriorate.

Using a similar research design and sample, Bigoness (1978) correlated measures of job satisfaction, job involvement, and locus of control with disposition to accept unionization. Bigoness also found that feelings of dissatisfaction correlated with acceptance of unionization. In particular, dissatisfaction with work, pay, and promotions each correlated at .35 with attitude toward unionization. Additionally, unionization was more appealing to people who were less involved in their jobs and had an external locus of control. Combining all independent variables in a multiple regression equation, Bigoness accounted for over 27% of the variance in attitudes toward unionization.

Hamner and Smith (1978) examined union activity in 250 units of a large organization. In half the units there had been some union activity; in the other half no activity was reported. Using an immense sample of over 80,000 employees, the authors found that employee attitudes predicted the level of unionization activity. The strongest predictor was dissatisfaction with supervision. Schriesheim (1978) found that prounion voting in a certification election was positively correlated with dissatisfaction; also, dissatisfaction with economic facets was more predictive than dissatisfaction with noneconomic factors. Furthermore, research by Youngblood, DeNisi, Molleston, and Mobley (1984) and Zalesny (1985) showed the importance of two other factors in union support. The first factor is attitude toward collective bargaining in general. The more acceptable unions in general are to a person, the more likely he or she will vote for unionization. The second factor is attitude toward unions as instrumental in enhancing worker welfare. Employees may not be satisfied with their employment conditions, but they may feel that unions can do little to aid them.

These studies all show that dissatisfaction with employment conditions is predictive of support for unionization. The more satisfied workers are, the less likely they are to think a union is necessary or that it can improve their welfare. These results are not surprising. They reveal the types of dissatisfaction associated with a disposition toward unions. Some authors tout the social benefits of unions (for example, association with similar people), but it is mainly the perceived economic advantages that give unions their appeal. Not all support for unions, however, is based on dissatisfaction with economic conditions. Hammer and Berman (1981) found that the faculty at one college wanted a union mainly because they distrusted administrative decision making and were dissatisfied with work content. Prounion voting was motivated by the faculty's desire to have more power in dealing with the administration.

Union Influence

What influence do unions have on enhancing employee welfare? Various studies have produced somewhat different conclusions. Gomez-Mejia and Balkin (1984) found that samples of unionized and nonunionized college teachers were equally satisfied with all job facets except pay; unionized faculty were more satisfied with their wages. Carillon and Sutton (1982) found a strong positive relationship between union effectiveness in representing teachers and their reported quality of worklife. Allegedly, college administrators fear that faculty unionization will affect organization effectiveness. Cameron (1982) dealt with this in 41 colleges; faculty were unionized in 18 colleges and nonunionized in 23. Cameron proposed nine indices of effectiveness for a college, involving student academic development, faculty and administrator satisfaction, and ability to acquire resources. Nonunionized colleges were significantly more effective on three of the nine indices; unionized colleges were not significantly more effective on any. Cameron also collected attitude data from faculty members on four factors relating to their work. These results are presented in Figure A–4. Faculty power and "red tape" were seen as increasing since unionization; collegiality was seen as decreasing. The study revealed some major differences in the effectiveness of union and nonunion colleges;

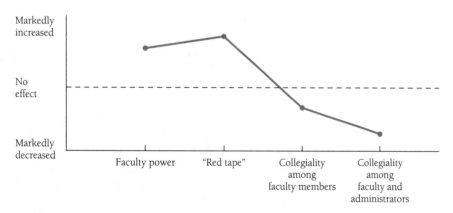

FIGURE A–4 ■ **Perceptions of the effects of faculty unionization**

SOURCE: From "The Relationship Between Faculty Unionism and Organizational Effectiveness" by K. Cameron, 1982, *Academy of Management Journal, 25,* p. 13.

however, the cause was not determined. Unionization may "cause" colleges to be less effective, which would be a strong argument against unions. However, the less effective colleges may turn to unions for improvement, which is obviously an argument supporting unionization. As discussed in Chapter 2, causality is difficult to determine. Raelin (1989) suggested that the literature on this topic indicates that less effective colleges turn to unions in an attempt to restore their professional status, although it is questionable whether a union by itself can return an established profession to its status prior to perceived deprofessionalization.

Fullagar, Gallagher, Gordon, and Clark (1995) tested the proposition that new organizational members are socialized to consider joining a union. There are two types of socialization. The first is *institutional,* which refers to the collective and formal practices organizations use to provide newcomers with a common set of experiences and information to elicit standardized responses. In contrast, *individual* socialization practices are idiosyncratic and informal. Individual socialization is informal in that learning takes place on the job through interactions with other organizational members. Fullagar et al. found that individual socialization practices had a positive impact on both affective and behavioral involvement in the union. However, institutional socialization practices were shown to be either ineffective or counterproductive. The practical implications are that important interactions occur between union officials and new members in developing new members' affective attachment to the union and later participation in union activities. Informal and individual socialization tactics may be undertaken by active or interested rank-and-file members and not necessarily by union stewards. Institutional socialization efforts (e.g., an orientation program to the union) seemingly are more effective in increasing awareness, whereas individual socialization efforts are more effective in producing involvement (Fullagar, Clark, Gallagher, & Gordon, 1994).

Dispute Settlement

As you might imagine, I/O psychologists have examined the process by which disputes are settled in both laboratory and field settings. As in some other areas of I/O research, the generalizability of laboratory findings in this area is somewhat limited. Gordon, Schmitt, and Schneider (1984) think the value of laboratory studies is to prepare people for undertaking actual collective bargaining in the future and to help develop questionnaires for later field use in dispute settlement. They noted that the limitations of laboratory and field research on dispute settlement are the classic ones discussed in Chapter 2. There is questionable generalizability from laboratory studies, and field studies fail to identify causal relationships.

Several studies have looked at mediation and arbitration as means of settling disputes. Bazerman and Neale (1982) asked whether strategies of personnel selection and training can improve negotiating effectiveness. They proposed selecting negotiators on the basis of their ability to take a broad perspective on problems and training them not to be overconfident about effecting a resolution. The authors found that training increased the number of concessions negotiators were willing to make and concluded that it may be a useful tool in dispute settlement. Neale (1984) determined that when the costs of arbitration are high, negotiators are more likely to reach a resolution on their own before they resort to arbitration. However, when cost is not much of an issue, they are more likely to accept arbitration. Researchers have also discovered the behavioral implications of the different types of arbitration. Starke and Notz (1981) reported that subjects who anticipated final-offer arbitration were closer to agreement at the conclusion of their bargaining than subjects who anticipated conventional arbitration. In fact, Grigsby and Bigoness (1982) concluded that final-offer, conventional, total-package, and issue-by-issue arbitration all produced different bargaining outcomes even though they are all variations of the same resolution process (arbitration). These behavioral studies on dispute settlement have enhanced our understanding in ways that traditional labor economic research has been unable to do. In fact, Brett, Goldberg, and Ury (1990) discussed how I/O psychologists can be used to resolve disputes. They proposed that a dispute-system designer organize procedures in a low- to high-cost sequence and work with parties to help them acquire new motivation, negotiation skills, and recourses to new procedures. The individual may even recommend changes in the broader organization that will facilitate the success of a dispute resolution system.

Commitment to the Union

The concept of employee commitment to a union addresses the notion of dual allegiance: Can a person be loyal to both a labor union and the employing company? For several years, researchers have examined the antecedents of both union and company commitment.

union commitment
the sense of identity and support unionized employees feel for their labor union

Our understanding of **union commitment** was enhanced through a major study by Gordon, Philpot, Burt, Thompson, and Spiller (1980). These authors developed a questionnaire for measuring commitment that was completed by more than 1,800 union members. Responses were factor analyzed, and union commitment was found to be composed of four dimensions: loyalty, responsibility to the union, willingness to work for the union, and belief in unionism. The research had at least two major benefits for unions. First, unions could use the questionnaires to assess the effect of their actions and estimate solidarity, especially before negotiations. Second, the research revealed the importance of socialization to new union members. The authors felt that union commitment increases when both formal and informal efforts are made to involve a member in union activities soon after joining. Coworker attitudes and willingness to help are crucial to the socialization process. Improving the socialization of new members improves their commitment, which is one index of union strength. In a follow-up study by Ladd, Gordon, Beauvais, and Morgan (1982), the questionnaire was administered to nonprofessional and professional members of a white-collar union. The results were the same as those from the original study despite the sample differences, although other researchers arrived at somewhat different conclusions (Friedman & Harvey, 1986). Klandermans (1989) found the scale useful for understanding unionism in Holland.

Mellor (1990) studied membership decline in 20 unions. The unions with the greatest decline in membership showed the strongest commitment to the union by the surviving members. Members in locals with more severe losses expressed a greater willingness to participate in future strikes. Fullagar and Barling (1989) reported that union loyalty was best predicted by union instrumentality, extrinsic job dissatisfaction, and early socialization experiences with unions. The authors proposed that greater union loyalty resulted in more formal participation in union activities. In a study of dual allegiance, Margenau, Martin, and Peterson (1988) found that satisfied workers felt allegiance to both the company and the union, whereas dissatisfied workers showed allegiance only to the union.

Tetrick (1995) proposed that union commitment occurs in a context of organizational rights that are provided by the union as well as organizational citizenship behaviors on the part of union members. Tetrick stated that the degree of commitment to the union can be understood in terms of the psychological contract between the employee and the organization, and the role the union plays in maintaining this relationship. Sverke and Kuruvilla (1995) identified two dimensions that explain why employees are committed to a union. The first is *instrumentality*, the perceived value or usefulness associated with union membership. The second is *ideology*, the individual's acceptance and support of the ideals or principles upon which labor unions are based.

Sverke and Sjoberg (1995) developed a typology of union members' commitment to the union based on these two dimensions, as shown in Figure A–5. Each dimension (instrumentality and ideology) is divided into two levels, high and low, resulting in a four-cell classification model. As shown in Figure A–5, the *alienated member* is the noncommitted member who is likely to be nonparticipative and who might intend to withdraw membership. The *instrumental member* can be expected to retain membership and to support union activities directed at improving wages and working conditions. Members committed primarily because of their prounion ideology (*ideological members*) support and take part in union activities, such as attending meetings. The *devoted member* category, representing members with high degrees of commitment on both dimensions, is postulated to contain the most active union members. Other forms of union participation activities include holding office, serving on union committees, and voting in elections (Kelloway, Catano, & Carroll, 1995).

Ideological commitment to the union

	High	Low
High	Devoted member	Instrumental member
Low	Ideological member	Alienated member

Instrumental commitment to the union

FIGURE A–5 ■ **Typology of union commitment**

SOURCE: Adapted from "Union Membership Behavior: The Influence of Instrumental and Value-Based Commitment" by M. Sverke and A. Sjoberg, 1995, in *Changing Employment Relations* (pp. 229–254), edited by L. E. Tetrick and J. Barling, Washington, DC: American Psychological Association.

Finally, Gordon and Ladd (1990) provided a cautionary note about professional ethics to researchers studying dual allegiance. They said researchers should be fully aware of the reasons that either the union or the company would encourage research on allegiance. I/O psychologists should not allow themselves to be "used" by either side to further their own aims by conducting such research. A similar point was raised by Zickar (2001) regarding how I/O psychologists were involved in union-busting by using personality tests to detect "pro-union" job candidates.

I/O PSYCHOLOGY AND INDUSTRIAL RELATIONS

Hartley (1992) proposed that there are many areas in which I/O psychology might contribute to the field of industrial relations. These include many of the issues already examined, including why workers join unions, dispute settlement, and dual commitment. Five traditional I/O topics will be examined from a labor union perspective: personnel selection, training, leadership development, employee involvement, and organizational change.

Personnel Selection.   In both union and nonunion companies, management determines the knowledge, skills, and abilities needed to fill jobs. The personnel office usually determines fitness for employment in lower-level jobs. For higher-level jobs, responsibility is spread throughout various units of the company. However, in a union company the labor contract may stipulate that those hired for jobs represented by the union must join the union after a probationary period. This is a **union shop;** the employee has no choice about joining.[2] In other unionized companies the employee has the choice of joining a union; these are agency or **open shops.** However, considerable pressure can be put on an employee to join. In many cases, it is to the employee's advantage to join the union for the benefits and protection it affords.

Union influence in personnel selection can affect both applicants and companies. Those who do not endorse unions (or who are uncertain about them) may not apply for jobs in unionized companies. Obviously, the applicant pool for unionized companies is smaller if such feelings are widespread. The extent of this problem varies with antiunion sentiment and the availability of other jobs.

Union influence can also work in reverse. One company I know of prides itself on remaining nonunionized. It believes unionization is encouraged by employees who have prior union experience, and therefore it carefully screens job applicants for union membership. Those who have been members are not considered (however, they are not told why). The company wants applicants who have the talent needed, but it places a higher priority on avoiding unions. Whether the company can continue this practice without adversely affecting the quality of its workforce will depend on the job openings and the number of applicants for employment with the company. Thus, from the perspectives of both the applicants and the company, unions can and do ultimately influence who gets hired.

Personnel Training.   One area in which unions have direct and significant influence is personnel training. One of the oldest forms of training is apprenticeship, and unions have a long history of this kind of training, especially in trades and crafts. Apprenticeship is governed by law; at the national level, it is administered by the Department of Labor. The Bureau of Apprenticeship and Training works closely with unions, vocational schools, state agencies, and others. According to the U.S. Department of Labor (1994), there are more than 475 apprenticed

union shop
a provision of employment stipulating that new employees must join the union that represents employees following a probationary period

open shop
a provision of employment stipulating that, although new employees need not join the union that represents employees, in lieu of union dues they must pay a fee for their representation

---

[2] However, currently 21 states have "right to work" laws prohibiting compulsory union membership as a condition of continued employment.

occupations employing over 280,000 apprentices. Apprentices go through a formal program of training and experience. They are supervised on the job and are given the facilities needed for instruction. There is a progressive wage schedule over the course of apprenticeship, and the individual is well versed in all aspects of the trade.

Most apprentice programs are in heavily unionized occupations (construction, manufacturing, transportation); thus, unions work closely with the Bureau of Apprenticeship and Training. For example, Figure A–6 shows the cooperation among various organizations and agencies in the carpentry trade. Although not all unions are involved in apprentice programs, the linkage between unions and apprenticeship is one of the oldest in the history of American labor.

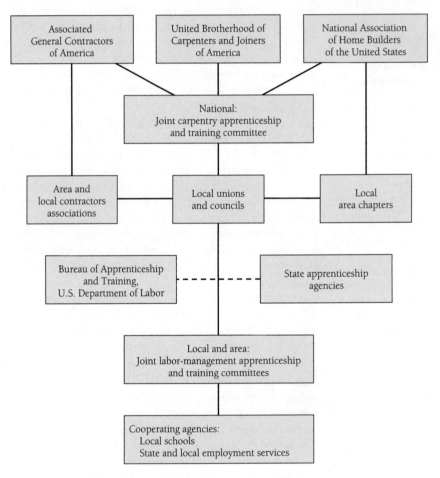

FIGURE A–6 ■ Cooperation among unions, industry, and government in the apprenticeship system of the carpentry trade

SOURCE: From *Apprenticeship: Past and Present* (p. 25) by U.S. Department of Labor, 1994, Washington, DC: U.S. Government Printing Office.

Leadership Development. Often employees elected to leadership roles within their unions (e.g., shop stewards) or within the organization (e.g., supervisors) have had little developmental instruction in how to behave in a position of leadership. Several studies used the tenets of procedural justice as a basis to explain the concept of organizational fairness. Cole and Latham (1997) used a development exercise to teach supervisors to take effective disciplinary action with employees. The supervisors were placed into either a training group or a control group. Following simulated role-playing exercises derived from organizational incidents, both unionized employees and disciplinary subject matter experts (managers, union officials, and attorneys) rated the trained supervisors higher on disciplinary fairness than the supervisors in the control group. Skarlicki and Latham (1996) examined whether training union officers in the skills necessary for implementing principles of organizational justice would increase citizenship behaviors on the part of members of a labor union. The results showed that three months after training, the perceptions of union fairness among members whose leaders were in the training group were higher than those of members whose leaders were in the control group. Skarlicki and Latham (1997) taught shop stewards methods of procedural justice using cases based on organizational incidents. The training improved knowledge of what constitutes fairness and may result in fewer grievances among employees regarding alleged unfairness in work. These examples illustrate how concepts such as procedural justice and organizational citizenship behavior can be used to improve the quality of leadership in organizations with labor unions.

Employee Involvement. Employee involvement embraces some of the newer management concepts such as employee ownership of companies, employee profit-sharing plans, self-managed work teams, and Total Quality Management (TQM). It is reasonable to question whether the increased interest in workers' participation in management has resulted in a reduction of "we/they" attitudes on the part of employees. Kelly and Kelly (1991) concluded that employees express positive attitudes toward particular innovations (self-managed work groups) but that these attitudes are specific to the innovation and do *not* generalize to broader "we/they" attitudes and the industrial relations climate. Kelly and Kelly believe that the proper conditions have not been present for fostering broader cooperative attitudes. They note that attitudes are more likely to change where there is a perception of personal choice and control, but economic conditions and management directives have not provided the conditions to generate employee perceptions of choice and control. That is, there is a perception among workers that management has been compelled because of economic pressures to try new concepts that reduce the power differential between workers and management. Given that, the amount of sincere trust between workers and management is insufficient to increase the cooperation between parties in some companies.

In a related vein, Fields and Thacker (1992) examined changes in union and organizational commitment after the implementation of a joint union–management quality-of-worklife program. The results indicated that company commitment among unionized workers increased only when participants perceived the program as successful, but union commitment increased irrespective of the perception of the program's success. In general, it appears that while unionized employees recognize the benefits of employee involvement programs, participation in them does not mean the boundaries between union and management are less well defined.

Organizational Change.   As was discussed in Chapter 8, it is often difficult to bring about change in any organization. It is even more difficult to bring about change in an organization with employees who are represented by a labor union. Blackard (2000) offered this assessment of the process of managing change in a unionized workplace:

1. Labor/management relations have evolved over time and fall somewhere on a continuum between open warfare and efforts to create labor–management partnerships. Even those relationships near the partnership end of the continuum, however, usually leave much to be desired.
2. Management in a unionized workplace is governed by laws that do not apply in a nonunion environment. These laws, particularly those relating to bargaining and labor contracts, are a major factor in the management of change.
3. Management must face more sources of resistance, more reasons for resistance, and a greater ability to resist in a unionized than a nonunion workplace. (p. 6)

Blackard noted that the need for organizations to change in response to changing environmental conditions (e.g., international competition, increasing costs) is greater today than ever before, a theme identified in Chapter 8. However, in a unionized company change must take place at two levels. First, management must make all the business changes that are necessary to remain competitive in the rapidly changing world. Second, it also needs to change its relationship with its union. A union is in a position to delay, prevent, or make such changes more difficult, and what it elects to do will be determined largely by its relationship with management. According to Blackard, if that relationship is less than positive, management must improve it before the company can effectively make the many business changes that are required. Typically business changes lead to fewer jobs, different roles and responsibilities for existing jobs, new or revised work rules, and changes in pay, benefits, and hours of work. Employees will resist much of the change, both individually and through their elected union representatives. This resistance will confirm their union as a legitimate force in the change process and require management to work not only with employees but also with the union that represents them.

A union may refuse to discuss a company proposal that affects an issue covered by a previously negotiated labor contract, such as wages, hours, or conditions of work. In such a case, the matter is closed to discussion and the union could exercise its right to have a "deal be a deal" until the scheduled termination of the labor contract in effect, which might be several years in the future. When the contract expires, the company may, after appropriate bargaining, implement planned changes at the peril of other union resistance tactics. The psychology of union resistance to change is predicated, in part, upon the union not wanting to appear irrelevant in the relationship between employees and the company (see Figure A–1). Individuals are often reluctant to change because the change represents some loss (or perceived loss) of control over their lives.

The union, therefore, can become an instrument for increasing employee control, even to the possible long-term detriment of the employees. If the union shows little resistance to proposed management changes, the very viability of the union as an agent of the employees can be questioned. Blackard contends that there is a gap in our knowledge about organizational change in unionized companies because such knowledge is based upon understanding both organizational change methods (as discussed in Chapter 8) and labor unions (as presented in this discussion).

CONCLUDING COMMENTS

The role of labor unions in the service and industry sectors of the U.S. economy has changed over the years. The high-water mark of union influence and power was in the 1930s and 1940s. American labor unions have steadily lost membership and influence since the 1970s. Masters (1997) believes unions are at the crossroads in their evolution. Masters notes that three traditional objectives are pursued by unions. The first is to bargain collectively with employers, gaining favorable wages and job conditions for unionized workers. The second is political activity, which is regarded by some scholars as the most prominent objective of European labor unions. Political activity is intended to lead to laws favorable to unions and their members. As such, some labor scholars contend that unions have been more influential in Europe than in the United States because of their greater political and ideological orientation. The third objective is organization activities that generate new members and increased revenues in the form of dues. Each objective adds to the overall strength of the union. Masters asserted that unions must devote more financial and human resources to strengthen their own organizations and reaffirm their value in society. One path of the crossroads faced by unions leads to rejuvenation, while the other path leads to irrelevance.

As a science, I/O psychology can benefit from examining topics from a union perspective in addition to the more traditional management perspective. A case in point is violence in the workplace. The management perspective tends to emphasize detecting workers who are likely candidates to exhibit antisocial behavior. The union perspective, according to King and Alexander (1996), is to place the issue of workplace violence into the total context of workplace safety and health. The workers cite precursors to violence at the work site, such as production pressures, stress, long hours, forced overtime, and fears of plant shutdown or job loss. Furthermore, it is often evidence regarding what needs to be done to alleviate the problems seen on the job that leads to outbreaks of fights and threats on the job site. Unions claim that management is unwilling to respond to the work conditions that are precursors to violence, while the management perspective is to weed out those job candidates who will respond negatively to those conditions. In my opinion, both perspectives have merit, and it is this type of creative interplay between the two views that increases our chances of better understanding the issue of workplace violence.

CASE STUDY ■ **Should We Let in a Labor Union?**

Carl Dwyer and Ann Stovos were faculty members at Springdale College. The college had been in existence for about 30 years, and Dwyer had been on the staff almost since the beginning. Stovos was a relative newcomer, just completing her third year as a faculty member. For the past two years, there had been talk about unionizing the faculty. Much of the interest was sparked by two events. First, the college had experienced financial cutbacks due to low enrollment. Without adequate tuition revenues, it was facing hardships paying the faculty. As a result, six teaching positions had been eliminated. The faculty understood the college's financial problems, but they felt cutbacks should be made in other areas, like some administrative positions. The faculty was also critical of how the college determined which teaching positions were eliminated. The other event was that for the third year in a row, the faculty were given only a 2% raise. Other colleges in the state were giving bigger raises, and some of the Springdale faculty felt they were getting the short end of the stick.

Various union representatives had been on campus; there was enough support for a representation election to be held in about a month. The faculty really seemed divided. Some openly supported a union, some were openly opposed, but the majority did not voice their sentiments. Dwyer was opposed to the idea of collective bargaining; Stovos supported it. Since they were officemates, the topic came up quite often. On this particular day, they were discussing whether the goals of unions were compatible with the goals of higher education.

Dwyer began the conversation: "I just don't think there is any place in a college for burly picketers carrying placards and threatening to beat up anyone who crosses the picket line. A college is a place for quiet, scholarly thought, an opportunity to teach interested students and to contemplate some of the deeper values. I've been here since we had only five buildings and a staff of twenty. I don't want to see this place turned into a playground for skull crushers."

"You've been watching too many movies, Carl," Stovos replied. "No one is going to turn Springdale into a battlefield. I want the same things you do. I didn't come here to be physically intimidated. I wouldn't like that any more than you do. But I also want to be treated fairly by the administration. I'd like some security from arbitrary decisions. There's nothing immoral about that, is there?"

"Do you think a union can prevent layoffs and get us twenty-five percent yearly raises?" Dwyer asked facetiously.

"No, I don't," Stovos countered, "but a union can force the drafting of fair and equitable policies if layoffs have to occur. And if everyone else is getting eight percent raises, maybe they can help us there, too. A union won't work miracles, but it can help prevent injustice."

"You don't understand, Ann. A college is not a factory. Different ideals run a college. It's not profit but scholarship. We have to foster a climate for inquisitive minds, learning, and personal growth. If I were interested only in making a buck, I wouldn't have become a college professor," Dwyer replied.

"Whether you like it or not, Carl, we are employees like all other working people. What's wrong with trying to ensure fair treatment at work? We have bills to pay and families to support just like everyone else. I don't understand why a college is somehow 'different' from all other employers."

"That's the problem in a nutshell," Dwyer rejoined. "A college is not just an employer, and we don't just have jobs. We have careers, and the success of our careers depends on an environment that supports what we are trying to do. Union organizers, picket lines, labor contracts, and mediators have no place in a college."

"I don't see why a college is somehow 'immune' from having to treat its employees fairly like every other employer. What makes a college so special?" Stovos asked.

"Twenty years ago—ten years ago, even—the very thought of a union would have been absurd. The fact that we're now considering one is just proof the quality of education in this country is going downhill. I can just see it now: 'Sorry, class, this is our last meeting. I'm going on strike Monday,'" Dwyer fumed. He got up from his desk, grabbed his coat and hat, and headed off for a meeting.

Stovos shot back, "I suppose you'd feel better if you met your class for the last time because you were one of the ones whose position got eliminated."

Dwyer didn't answer, but he slammed the door on the way out.

Study Questions

1. Do you think Dwyer is correct in believing a union would interfere with the goals of higher education?
2. What benefits does Stovos see from unionization?
3. Do you believe that some organizations, because of their purpose and goals, should not have unionized employees? If so, which ones, and why?
4. Do you think the respective lengths of time that Dwyer and Stovos have spent at the college are related to their attitudes? Why, or why not?
5. When you think of unions, what thoughts come to mind? Why do you feel as you do?

SUGGESTED INFOTRAC TOPICS

labor unions

collective bargaining

labor contract

mediation

fact-finding

arbitration

labor strikes

lockouts

grievances

alternative dispute resolution

GLOSSARY

acquisition the process by which one organization acquires or subsumes (usually through purchase) the resources of a second organization.

actionable knowledge knowledge produced from research that helps formulate policies or action to address a particular issue.

actual criterion the operational or actual standard that researchers measure or assess. Often contrasted with *conceptual criterion*. For example, academic grade point average often serves as the actual criterion for assessing the conceptual criterion of learning.

ad hoc team a type of team created for a limited duration that is designed to address itself to resolving one particular problem.

adverse impact a type of unfair discrimination in which the result of using a particular personnel selection method has an adverse or differential effect on protected group members compared with majority group members. Often contrasted with *disparate treatment*.

affirmative action a social policy that advocates members of protected groups will be actively or affirmatively recruited and considered for selection in employment.

antisocial behavior in organizations any behavior that brings harm or is intended to bring harm to an organization or its members.

apprentice training a method of training in which the trainee (or apprentice) learns to perform a job by serving under the supervision of an experienced worker who provides guidance, direction, and support.

arbitration a method of dispute settlement in which a neutral third party resolves the dispute between labor and management by making a decision that is typi-

cally final and binding to both labor and management.

Armed Services Vocational Aptitude Battery (ASVAB) a test developed in the 1980s by I/O psychologists for the selection and placement of military personnel.

Army Alpha Test an intelligence test developed during World War I by I/O psychologists for the selection and placement of military personnel.

Army Beta Test a nonverbal intelligence test developed during World War I by I/O psychologists to assess illiterate recruits.

Army General Classification Test (AGCT) a test developed during World War II by I/O psychologists for the selection and placement of military personnel.

assessment center a method of assessing job candidates via a series of structured, group-oriented exercises that are evaluated by raters.

authorization card a card employees are asked to sign that authorizes an election to determine whether a union will represent employees in the collective bargaining process.

banding a method of interpreting test scores such that scores of different magnitude in a numeric range or band (e.g., 90–95) are regarded as being equivalent.

BARS acronym for "behaviorally anchored rating scale," a type of performance appraisal rating scale in which the scale points or values are descriptions of behavior.

base rate the percentage of current employees in a job who are judged to be performing their jobs satisfactorily.

behavioral approach to leadership a conception that leadership is best understood in terms of the behaviors or actions taken by an individual in the conduct of leading a group.

behavioral criteria a standard for judging the effectiveness of training that refers to the new behaviors that are exhibited on the job as a result of training.

Big 5 theory of personality a theory that defines personality in terms of five major factors: neuroticism, extraversion, openness to experience, agreeableness, and conscientiousness. Also called the "five factor" theory of personality.

biographical information a method of assessing individuals in which information pertaining to past activities, interests, and behaviors in their lives is recorded.

central-tendency error a type of rating error in which the rater assesses a disproportionately large number of ratees as performing in the middle or central part of a distribution of rated performance in contrast to their true level of performance. Often referenced in the context of performance appraisal.

certification election an election in which employees vote to determine whether a union will represent them in the collective bargaining process.

charismatic leadership a conception that leadership is the product of charisma, a trait that inspires confidence in others to support the ideas and beliefs of an individual who possesses this trait.

classical theory of organizations a theory developed in the early 20th century that described the form and structure of organizations.

classification the process of assigning individuals to jobs based on two or more test scores.

collective bargaining the process by which labor and management engage in negotiating a labor contract.

comparable worth a doctrine or belief that jobs of comparable value to the organization should be compensated equally. Often used in association with the finding of gender differences in levels of compensation.

compensable factor a dimension of work (such as skill or effort) used to assess the relative value of a job for determining compensation rates. Often used in the context of job evaluation.

competency modeling a process for determining the human characteristics (i.e., competencies) needed to successfully perform a job.

compressed workweek a schedule of work hours that typically involves more hours per day and fewer days per week, such as 10 hours per day and four days per week.

computer-based training (CBT) a method of training that utilizes computer technology (such as CD-ROM) to enhance the acquisition of knowledge and skills.

computerized adaptive testing (CAT) a form of assessment using a computer in which the questions have been precalibrated in terms of difficulty, and the examinee's response (i.e., right or wrong) to one question determines the selection of the next question posed to the examinee.

conceptual criterion the theoretical standard that researchers seek to understand through their research. Often contrasted with *actual criterion.*

confidentiality a condition associated with testing pertaining to which parties have access to test results.

construct validity the degree to which a test is an accurate and faithful measure of the construct it purports to measure.

content validity the degree to which subject matter experts agree that the items in a test are a representative sample of the domain of knowledge the test purports to measure.

contextual performance behavior that is exhibited by an employee that contributes to the welfare of the organization but is not a formal component of an employee's job duties. Also called *prosocial behavior* and *extra-role behavior.*

conventional arbitration a form of arbitration in which the arbitrator is free to fashion whatever decision is deemed most fair in resolving a dispute. Often contrasted with *final-offer arbitration.*

correlation coefficient a statistical index that reflects the degree of relationship between two variables.

cost-reduction strategy a business strategy directed at providing customers with low-cost products or services.

creative team a type of team created for the purpose of developing innovative possibilities or solutions.

criteria standards used to help make evaluative judgments about objects, people, or events.

criterion contamination the part of the actual criterion that is unrelated to the conceptual criterion.

criterion deficiency the part of the conceptual criterion that is not measured by the actual criterion.

criterion-related validity the degree to which a test forecasts or is statistically related to a criterion.

criterion relevance the degree of overlap or similarity between the actual criterion and the conceptual criterion.

criterion variable a variable that is a primary object of a research study. It is forecasted by a predictor variable. Usually used in the context of nonexperimental research. Similar to *dependent variable.* Often contrasted with *predictor variable.*

cross-cultural psychology an area of research that examines the degree to which psychological concepts and findings generalize to people in other cultures and societies.

culture the language, values, attitudes, beliefs, and customs of an organization.

decertification election an election in which unionized employees vote to determine whether their union will no longer represent them in the collective bargaining process.

declarative knowledge a body of knowledge about facts and things. Often compared with *procedural knowledge.*

deductive research a research process in which conclusions are drawn about a specific member of a class of objects or people based upon knowledge of the general class under investigation. Often contrasted with *inductive research.*

dependent variable a variable whose values are predicted by the independent variable. Usually used in the context of experimental research. Similar to *criterion variable.* Often contrasted with *independent variable.*

descriptive statistics a class or group of statistical analyses that serve to describe the variables under investigation. Typical descriptive statistics are indices of central tendency and variation.

Dictionary of Occupational Titles (DOT) a classic reference book in I/O psychology that presents information on the content and characteristics of thousands of jobs. The book has been replaced by the O*NET.

disparate treatment a type of unfair discrimination in which protected group members are afforded differential procedures in their consideration for employment compared with majority group members. Often contrasted with *adverse impact.*

distributive justice the fairness with which the outcomes or results are distributed among members of an organization.

downsizing the process of reducing the size of an organization by the elimination of jobs (and thus employees).

drug testing a method of assessment typically based on an analysis of urine that is used to detect illicit drug use by the examinee.

dual-career family a family characterized by each adult having his or her own individual career and trying to collectively balance their respective careers.

dynamic performance criteria aspects of job performance that change (increase or decrease) over time for individuals, as does their predictability.

emic an approach to researching phenomena that emphasizes knowledge derived from the participants' awareness and understanding of their own culture. Often contrasted with *etic.*

emotional intelligence a construct that reflects a person's capacity to manage emotional responses in social situations.

empowerment the process of giving employees in an organization more power and decision-making authority within a context of less managerial oversight.

equity theory a theory of motivation based on the social comparison process of examining the ratio of inputs and outcomes between oneself and a comparison other.

equivalent-form reliability a type of reliability that reveals the equivalence of test scores between two versions or forms of the test.

ethnography a research method that utilizes field observation to study a society's culture.

etic an approach to researching phenomena that emphasizes knowledge derived from the perspective of a detached, objective investigator in understanding a culture. Often contrasted with *emic.*

expectancy theory a theory of motivation based on the perceived degree of relationship between how much effort a person expends and the performance resulting from that effort.

external equity a theoretical concept that is the basis for using wage and salary surveys in establishing compensation rates for jobs. The concept reflects that the compensation rates for jobs in one organization should be fair (equitable) in comparison with the compensation rates paid for jobs by other (external) organizations.

external validity the degree to which the relationships evidenced among variables in a particular research study are generalizable or accurate in other populations or contexts. Often contrasted with *internal validity.*

face validity the appearance that items in a test are appropriate for the intended use of the test by the individuals who take the test.

fact-finding a method of dispute settlement in which a neutral third party makes public the respective positions of labor and management with the intention that the public will influence the two sides to resolve their disputes in establishing a labor contract.

false negative a term to describe individuals who were incorrectly rejected for employment because they would have been successful employees.

false positive a term to describe individuals who were incorrectly accepted for employment because they were unsuccessful employees.

final-offer arbitration a form of arbitration (see *arbitration*) in which the arbitrator is obligated to accept the final offer of either the union or management in their dispute. Often contrasted with *conventional arbitration*, in which the arbitrator has the power to split the difference between the respective labor and management positions in resolving their dispute.

flextime a schedule of work hours that permit employees flexibility in when they arrive at and leave work.

functional job analysis (FJA) a method of job analysis that describes the content of jobs in terms of people, data, and things.

functional principle the concept that organizations should be divided into units that perform similar functions.

g The symbol for "general mental ability," which has been found to be predictive of success in most jobs.

generalizability the extent to which conclusions drawn from one research study spread or apply to a larger population.

goal-setting theory of motivation a theory of motivation based on directing one's effort toward the attainment of specific goals that have been set or established.

graphology a method of assessment in which characteristics of a person's handwriting are evaluated and interpreted.

grievance a formal complaint made by an employee against management alleging a violation of the labor contract in effect.

grievance arbitration a type of arbitration (see *arbitration*) found in resolving disputes between labor and management in interpretation of an existing labor contract. Also called rights arbitration.

group test a type of test that is administered to more than one test taker at a time. Often contrasted with *individual test*.

groupthink a phenomenon associated with team decision making in which members feel threatened by forces external to the team, resulting in a deterioration in the cognitive processing of information.

halo error a type of rating error in which the rater assesses the ratee as performing well on a variety of performance dimensions despite having credible knowledge of only a limited number of performance dimensions. Often referenced in the context of performance appraisal.

Hawthorne effect a positive change in behavior that occurs at the onset of an intervention followed by a gradual decline, often to the original level of the behavior prior to the intervention. First identified in the Hawthorne studies, which is why it is so named.

Hawthorne studies a series of research studies that began in the late 1920s at the Western Electric Company and ultimately refocused the interests of I/O

psychologists to how work behavior manifests itself in an organizational context.

hostile environment sexual harassment a legal classification of sexual harassment in which individuals regard conditions in the workplace (as unwanted touching or off-color jokes) as offensive. Often compared with *quid pro quo sexual harassment*.

I/O psychology an area of scientific study and professional practice that addresses psychological concepts and principles in the work world.

impasse a point in the collective bargaining process at which both the union and management conclude they are unable to reach an agreement in the formation of a labor contract. Impasse (literally meaning "blockage") triggers the use of other means (besides negotiation) to resolve the dispute between the parties.

implicit leadership theory a conception that leadership is a perceived phenomenon as attributed to an individual by others.

independent variable a variable that can be manipulated to predict the values of the dependent variable. Usually used in the context of experimental research. Similar to *predictor variable*. Often contrasted with *dependent variable*.

individual test a type of test that is administered to one individual test taker at a time. Often contrasted with *group test*.

inductive research a research process in which conclusions are drawn about a general class of objects or people based upon knowledge of a specific member of the class under investigation. Often contrasted with *deductive research*.

innovation strategy a business strategy directed at providing customers with innovative or novel products or services.

integrity test a type of paper-and-pencil test that purports to assess a test taker's honesty, character, or integrity.

interactional justice consisting of two components (interpersonal and informational justice), the fairness with which people are treated within an organization and the timeliness, completeness, and accuracy of the information received in an organization.

interest arbitration a type of arbitration (see *arbitration*) used in resolving disputes between labor and management in the formation of a labor contract.

internal-consistency reliability a type of reliability that reveals the homogeneity of the items in a test.

internal equity a theoretical concept that is the basis for using job evaluation in establishing compensation rates for jobs. The concept reflects that compensation rates for jobs should be fair (equitable) based on their relative internal value to the organization.

internal validity the degree to which the relationships evidenced among variables in a particular research study are accurate or true. Often contrasted with *external validity.*

inter-rater reliability a type of reliability that reveals the degree of agreement among the assessments of two or more raters.

invasion of privacy a condition associated with testing pertaining to the asking of questions on a test that are unrelated to the test's intent or are inherently intrusive to the test taker.

inventory a paper-and-pencil method of assessment in which the responses to questions are recorded and interpreted but are not evaluated in terms of their correctness, as a vocational interest inventory. Often contrasted with *paper-and-pencil test.*

issue-by-issue arbitration a form of final-offer arbitration (see *final-offer arbitration*) in which the arbitrator is obligated to accept either the union's position or management's position on an issue-by-issue basis in disputes between the parties. Often contrasted with *total-package arbitration.*

job a set of similar positions in an organization. For example, similar secretarial positions in an organization represent the job of a secretary.

job analysis a formal procedure by which the content of a job is defined in terms of tasks performed and human qualifications needed to perform the job.

job characteristics theory of motivation a theory of motivation based on the presence of dimensions or characteristics of jobs that induce the expenditure of effort.

job enrichment the process of designing work so as to enhance individual motivation to perform the work.

job evaluation a procedure for assessing the relative value of jobs in an organization for the purpose of establishing levels of compensation.

job family a grouping of similar jobs in an organization. For example, the jobs of secretary, bookkeeper, and receptionist represent the clerical job family.

job involvement the degree to which a person identifies psychologically with his or her work and the importance of work to one's self-image.

job rotation a method of learning two or more jobs by performing them in sequence.

job satisfaction the degree of pleasure an employee derives from his or her job.

knowledge compilation the body of knowledge acquired as a result of learning.

KSAOs an abbreviation for "knowledge, skills, abilities, and other" characteristics. Often used in the context of job analysis.

labor contract a formal agreement between labor and management that specifies the terms and conditions of employment while the contract is in effect.

labor strike a cessation of work activities by unionized employees as a means of influencing management to accept the union position in a dispute over the labor contract.

laboratory experiment a type of research method in which the investigator manipulates independent variables and assigns subjects to experimental and control conditions.

leader–member exchange theory a theory of leadership based upon the nature of the relationship (i.e., the exchange) between a leader and members of the group he or she leads.

learning the process by which change in knowledge or skills is acquired through education or experience.

learning criteria a standard for judging the effectiveness of training that refers to the amount of new knowledge, skills, and abilities acquired through training.

leniency error a type of rating error in which the rater assesses a disproportionately large number of ratees as performing well (positive leniency) or poorly (negative leniency) in contrast to their true level of performance. Often referenced in the context of performance appraisal.

level of analysis the unit or level (e.g., individuals, teams, organizations, nations, etc.) that is the object of the researchers' interest and about which conclusions are drawn from the research.

licensure the process by which a professional practice is regulated by law to ensure quality standards are met to protect the public.

line functions organizational work that directly meets the major goals of an organization.

line/staff principle the concept of differentiating organizational work into line (responsible for directly meeting the primary goals of the organization) and staff (responsible for providing support to the line) functions.

linkage analysis a technique in job analysis that establishes the linkage or connection between the tasks performed and the human attributes needed to perform them.

lockout action taken by management against unionized employees to prevent them from entering their place of work (i.e., locking them out) as a means of influencing the union to accept the management position in a dispute over the labor contract.

locus of control a personality construct relating to the perceived cause or locus of control for events in one's life, being either internal (as one's own skill and ambition) or external (as luck and fate).

management development the process by which individuals serving in management or leadership positions are trained (i.e., developed) to better perform the job.

mean the arithmetic average of a distribution of numbers.

median the midpoint of all the numbers in a distribution.

mediation a method of dispute settlement in which a neutral third party offers advice to the union and management for the purpose of helping them agree on a labor contract.

melting pot conception a concept or idea behind facilitating relationships among people of different cultures based upon them relinquishing their individual cultural identities to form a new, unified culture as a means of coexisting. Often contrasted with *multicultural conception*.

Mental Measurements Yearbooks (MMY) a classic set of reference books in psychology that provide reviews and critiques of published tests in the public domain.

mentor typically an older and more experienced person who helps to professionally develop and train a less experienced person (the *protégé*).

meta–analysis a quantitative secondary research method for summarizing and integrating the findings from original empirical research studies.

mode the most frequently occurring number in a distribution.

multicultural conception a concept or idea behind facilitating relationships among people of different cultures based upon them retaining their individual cultural identities as a means of coexisting. Often contrasted with *melting pot conception*.

multiple correlation the degree of predictability (ranging from 0 to 1.0) in forecasting one variable on the basis of two or more other variables. Often expressed in conjunction with multiple regression analysis.

multiple regression analysis a statistical procedure used to predict one variable on the basis of two or more other variables.

National Labor Relations Board (NLRB) an agency of the federal government that has oversight responsibility for enforcing laws pertaining to union/management relations.

need hierarchy theory of motivation a theory of motivation based on a hierarchy or sequential ordering of human needs that individuals seek to fulfill in serial progression starting with psychological needs and culminating in the need for self-actualization.

neoclassical theory of organizations a theory developed in the 1950s that described psychological/behavioral issues associated with organizations.

norm a set of shared group expectations about appropriate behavior.

O*NET abbreviation for the Occupational Information Network, an on-line computer-based source of information about jobs. This network has replaced the *Dictionary of Occupational Titles*.

objective performance criteria a set of factors or standards used to assess job performance that are (relatively) objective or factual in character, such as absences, units of production, and sales volume.

observation a type of research method in which the investigator observes subjects for the purpose of understanding their behavior and culture.

occupational health a broad-based concept that refers to the mental, emotional, and physical well-being of employees in relation to the conduct of their work.

off-site training methods a set of training methods associated with individuals learning how to perform a job at a place removed from the work site. Often contrasted with *on-site training methods*.

on-site training methods a set of training methods associated with individuals learning how to perform a job at the work site. Often contrasted with *off-site training methods*.

on-the-job training a method of learning a job by performing it at the work site.

open shop a provision of employment that stipulates although new employees need not join the union representing employees, in lieu of union dues they must pay a fee for their representation. Often contrasted with *union shop*.

organization a coordinated group of people who perform tasks to produce goods or services.

organization development a system of planned interventions designed to change an organization's structure and/or processes to achieve a higher level of functioning.

organizational analysis a phase of training needs analysis directed at determining whether training is a viable solution to organizational problems, and if so, where in the organization training should be directed.

organizational citizenship behavior the contributions that employees make to the overall welfare of the organization that go beyond the required duties of their job.

organizational commitment the degree to which an employee feels a sense of allegiance to his or her employer.

organizational justice the overarching theoretical concept pertaining to the fair treatment of people in organizations; composed of three types of justice—distributive, procedural, and interactional.

organizational merger the joining or combining of two organizations of approximately equal status and power.

overpayment inequity the sense of unfairness (i.e., inequity) derived from the perception that the ratio of one's own inputs and outcomes is greater than the ratio of a comparison other. Often contrasted with *underpayment inequity*.

paper-and-pencil test a paper-and-pencil method of assessment in which the responses to questions asked are evaluated in terms of their correctness, as a vocabulary test. Often contrasted with *inventory*.

path–goal theory a theory of leadership that emphasizes the importance of leaders indicating to followers what behaviors (paths) they need to exhibit to attain the desired objectives (goals).

peer assessment a technique of performance appraisal in which individuals assess the behavior of their peers or coworkers. Peer assessments include nominations, ratings, and rankings.

peer nomination a technique of appraising the performance of coworkers by nominating them for membership in a group.

peer ranking a technique of appraising the performance of coworkers by ranking them on a dimension of their job behavior.

peer rating a technique for appraising the performance of coworkers by rating them on a dimension of their job behavior.

performance test a type of test that requires the test taker to exhibit physical skill in the manipulation of objects, as a typing test.

person analysis a phase of training needs analysis directed at identifying which individuals within an organization should receive training.

person perception the processes by which individuals form impressions and make inferences about other people.

personnel selection the process of determining those applicants who are selected for hire versus those who are rejected.

physical fidelity a concept from training pertaining to the degree of similarity between the physical characteristics of the training environment and the work environment. Often compared with *psychological fidelity*.

placement the process of assigning individuals to jobs based on one test score.

polygraph an instrument that assesses characteristics of an individual's central nervous system (heart rate, breathing, perspiration, etc.) that are supposedly indicative of giving false responses to questions.

position a set of tasks performed by a single employee. For example, the position of a secretary is often represented by the tasks of typing, filing, and data entry. There are usually as many positions in an organization as there are employees.

Position Analysis Questionnaire (PAQ) a method of job analysis that assesses the content of jobs on the basis of approximately 200 items in the questionnaire.

positive psychology the study of the factors and conditions in life that lead to pleasurable and satisfying outcomes for individuals.

power and influence approach to leadership a conception that leadership is best understood by the use of the power and influence exercised by a person with a group.

power test a type of test that usually does not have a precise time limit. A person's score on the test is the number of items answered correctly. Often contrasted with *speed test*.

predictor cutoff a score on a test that differentiates those who passed the test from those who failed. Often equated with the passing score on a test.

predictor variable a variable used to predict or forecast a criterion variable. Usually used in the context of nonexperimental research. Similar to *independent variable*. Often contrasted with *criterion variable*.

primary research methods a class of research methods that generate new information on a particular research question.

problem-solving team a type of team created for the purpose of focusing on the resolution of a particular problem or issue.

procedural justice the fairness by which means are used to achieve results in an organization.

procedural knowledge a body of knowledge about how to use information to address issues and solve problems. Often compared with *declarative knowledge*.

prosocial behavior behavior exhibited by an individual at work that goes beyond the formal requirements of the job toward increasing the organization's effectiveness. Also referred to as *extra-role behavior* and *organizational citizenship behavior*.

protected group a designation for the members of society who are granted legal recognition by virtue of a demographic characteristic. Protected groups are identified by race, gender, national origin, color, religion, age, and disability.

protégé typically a younger and less experienced person who is helped and developed in job training by a more experienced person (the *mentor*).

psychological contract the implied exchange relationship that exists between an employee and the organization.

psychological fidelity a concept from training pertaining to the degree of similarity between the knowledge, skills, and abilities (KSAs) learned in training and the KSAs needed to perform the job. Often compared with *physical fidelity*.

qualitative research methods a class of research methods in which the investigator takes an active role in interacting with the subjects he or she wishes to study.

qualitative variable an object of study that does not inherently have numerical values associated with them, such as gender. Often contrasted with *quantitative variables*.

quality-enhancement strategy a business strategy directed at providing customers with high-quality products or services.

quantitative variable an object of study that inherently has numerical values associated with them, such as weight. Often contrasted with *qualitative variables*.

quasi-experiment a type of research method for conducting studies in field situations where the researcher may be able to manipulate some independent variables.

questionnaire a type of research method in which subjects respond to written questions posed by the investigator.

quid pro quo sexual harassment a legal classification of harassment in which specified organizational rewards (e.g., a promotion) are offered in exchange for sexual favors. Often compared with *hostile environment sexual harassment*.

range a descriptive statistical index that reflects the dispersion in a set of scores. Arithmetically defined as the difference between the highest score and the lowest score.

rater motivation a concept that refers to organizationally induced pressures that compel raters to evaluate their ratees positively.

rater training the process of training raters to make more accurate ratings of performance, typically achieved by reducing the frequency of halo, leniency, and central-tendency errors.

reaction criteria a standard for judging the effectiveness of training that refers to the reactions or feelings of individuals about the training they received.

recruiting yield pyramid a conceptualization of the recruiting process that reveals the ratio of initial contacts to individuals hired.

recruitment the process by which individuals are solicited to apply for jobs.

regression analysis a statistical procedure used to predict one variable on the basis of another variable.

reinforcement theory of motivation a theory of motivation based on the schedule of rewards received for behavior that is exhibited.

reliability a standard for evaluating tests that refers to the consistency, stability, or equivalence of test scores. Often contrasted with *validity*.

reorganizing a process of changing the manner in which work is configured in an organization to achieve greater efficiency.

research a formal process by which knowledge is produced and understood.

research design a strategy or plan for conducting scientific research for the purpose of learning about a phenomenon of interest.

results criteria a standard for judging the effectiveness of training that refers to the economic value that accrues to the organization as a result of the new behaviors exhibited on the job.

role a set of expectations about appropriate behavior in a position.

role conflict the product of perceptual differences regarding the content of a person's role or the relative importance of its elements.

role overload the conflict experienced in a role as a necessity to compromise either the quantity or quality of performance.

role playing a training method directed primarily at enhancing interpersonal skills in which training - participants adopt various roles in a group exercise.

sabotage a tactic used by some employees to influence the outcome of union/management negotiations in which company equipment is intentionally damaged to reduce work productivity.

scalar principle the concept that organizations are structured by a chain of command that grows with increasing levels of authority.

schema a cognitive approach to processing information that results in making sense of events and actions that in turn influence how decisions are made on the basis of that information.

scientist-practitioner model a model or framework for education in an academic discipline that is predicated upon understanding the scientific principles and findings evidenced in the discipline and how they provide the basis for the professional practice.

secondary research methods a class of research methods that examine existing information from research studies that used primary methods.

selection ratio a numeric index ranging between 0 and 1.00 that reflects the selectivity of the hiring organization in filling jobs. It is the number of people who are selected for a job divided by the number of people who applied for it.

self-assessment a technique of performance appraisal in which individuals assess their own behavior.

self-efficacy a sense of personal control and being able to master one's environment.

self-regulation theory of motivation a theory of motivation based on the setting of goals and the receipt of accurate feedback that is monitored to enhance the likelihood of goal attainment.

sexual harassment unwelcome sexual advances, requests for sexual favors, and other verbal or physical conduct of a sexual nature that creates an intimidating, hostile, or offensive work environment.

shared mental model the cognitive processes held in common by members of a team regarding how they acquire information, analyze it, and respond to it.

shift work the period of time a person must perform his or her job. Usually an 8-hour period of time, typically 7:00 A.M. to 3:00 P.M., 3:00 P.M. to 11:00 P.M., or 11:00 P.M. to 7:00 A.M.

simulation a training method in which selected aspects of the work environment are replicated or modeled in a training environment.

situational approach to leadership a conception that leadership is best understood in terms of situational factors or conditions that promote the occurrence of leadership.

situational exercise a method of assessment in which examinees are presented with a problem situation and asked how they would respond to it.

situational interview a type of job interview in which candidates are presented with a problem situation and asked how they would respond to it.

situational judgment test a type of test that describes a problem situation to the test taker and requires the test taker to rate various possible solutions in terms of their feasibility or applicability.

social loafing a phenomenon identified in groups or teams in which certain individuals withhold effort or contributions to the collective outcome.

social system the human components of a work organization that influence the behavior of individuals and groups.

socialization the process of mutual adjustment between the team and its members, especially new members.

Society for Industrial and Organizational Psychology (SIOP) the professional organization that represents I/O psychologists in the United States.

span-of-control principle the concept that refers to the number of subordinates a manager is responsible for supervising.

speed strategy a business strategy directed at providing customers with rapid delivery of products or services.

speed test a type of test that has a precise time limit (e.g., 10 minutes). A person's score on the test is the number of items attempted in the time period. Often contrasted with *power test.*

staff functions organizational work that supports line activities.

standard deviation a statistic that shows the spread or dispersion of scores around the mean in a distribution of scores.

structure the arrangement of work functions within an organization designed to achieve efficiency and control.

structured interview a format for the job interview in which the questions asked are consistent across all candidates. Often contrasted with *unstructured interview.*

subject matter expert (SME) a person knowledgeable about a topic who can serve as a qualified information source. Often associated with individuals who provide job analysis information.

subjective performance criteria a set of factors or standards used to assess job performance that are the product of someone's (e.g., supervisor, peer) subjective rating of these factors.

substance abuse the ingestion of a broad array of substances (such as alcohol, tobacco, or drugs) that are deemed to have a harmful effect on the individual.

substitutes for leadership the conception that there are factors or sources of influence in an environment that can serve to act in place of, or be substitutions for, formal leadership.

systems theory a theory developed in the 1970s that described organizations in terms of interdependent components that form a system.

tactical team a type of team created for the purpose of executing a well-defined plan or objective.

task typically the lowest level of analysis in the study of work. A task is a basic component of work (such as typing for a secretary).

task analysis a phase of training needs analysis directed at identifying which tasks in a job should be targeted for improved performance.

task-oriented procedure a procedure or set of operations in job analysis designed to identify important or frequently performed tasks as a means of understanding the work performed. Often contrasted with *worker-oriented procedure.*

taxonomy a classification of objects designed to enhance understanding of the objects being classified.

team a social aggregation in which a limited number of individuals interact on a regular basis to accomplish a set of shared objectives for which they have mutual responsibility.

test-retest reliability a type of reliability that reveals the stability of test scores upon repeated applications of the test.

theory a statement that proposes to explain relationships among phenomena of interest.

360-degree feedback a process of evaluating employees from multiple rating sources, usually including supervisor, peer, subordinate, and self ratings. Also called multirater feedback.

total-package arbitration a form of final-offer arbitration (see *final-offer arbitration*) in which the arbitrator is obligated to accept either the union's position or management's position on every issue (i.e., the total package) in a dispute between the parties. Often contrasted with *issue-by-issue arbitration.*

Total Quality Management (TQM) a comprehensive approach to achieving greater organizational efficiency based in part on the use of statistical information to aid in decision making.

training the process through which the knowledge, skills, and abilities of employees are enhanced.

trait approach to leadership a conception that leadership is best understood in terms of traits or dispositions held by an individual that account for the observed leadership.

transfer of training the degree of generalizability of the behaviors learned in training to those behaviors evidenced on the job that enhance performance.

transformational leadership a conception that leadership is the process of transforming or inspiring a group to pursue goals and attain results.

true negative a term to describe individuals who were correctly rejected for employment because they would have been unsuccessful employees.

true positive a term to describe individuals who were correctly selected for hire because they became successful employees.

Type A personality a personality construct that describes individuals who tend to be aggressive and competitive and feel under chronic time pressures. Often contrasted with *type B personality.*

Type B personality a personality construct that describes individuals who tend not to be competitive, intense, or feel under chronic time pressures. Often contrasted with *type A personality.*

underpayment inequity the sense of unfairness (i.e., inequity) derived from the perception that the ratio of one's own inputs and outcomes is lower than the ratio of a comparison other. Often contrasted with *overpayment inequity.*

union-busting a derogatory term used to describe actions taken to prevent a labor union from representing employees.

union commitment the sense of identity and support unionized employees feel for their labor union.

union/nonunion wage differential the average difference in wages paid to union versus nonunion employees across an industry or geographic area for performing the same jobs.

union shop a provision of employment that stipulates new employees must join the union that represents employees following a probationary period. Often contrasted with *open shop.*

unity of command the concept that each subordinate should be accountable to only one supervisor.

unstructured interview a format for the job interview in which the questions asked are different across all candidates. Often contrasted with *structured interview.*

utility a concept reflecting the economic value (expressed in monetary terms) of making personnel decisions.

validity a standard for evaluating tests that refers to the accuracy or appropriateness of drawing inferences from test scores. Often contrasted with *reliability.*

validity coefficient a statistical index (often expressed as a correlation coefficient) that reveals the degree of association between two variables. Often used in the context of prediction.

validity generalization a concept that reflects the degree to which a predictive relationship empirically established in one context spreads or generalizes to other populations or contexts.

variability the dispersion of numerical values evidenced in the measurement of an object or concept.

variable an object of study whose measurement can take on two or more values.

virtual team a type of team in which the members, often geographically dispersed, interact through electronic communication and may never meet face to face.

web-based training (WBT) a method of training that utilizes the World Wide Web as the medium through which individuals acquire knowledge and skills.

work/family conflict the dilemma of trying to balance the conflicting demands of work and family responsibilities.

work samples a type of personnel selection test in which the candidate demonstrates proficiency with a task representative of the work performed in the job.

work slowdown a tactic used by some employees to influence the outcome of union/management negotiations in which the usual pace of work is intentionally reduced.

work stress the response to stimuli that are present on the job that lead to negative consequences, physical or psychological, to the people who are exposed to them.

worker-oriented procedure a procedure or set of operations in job analysis designed to identify important or frequently utilized human attributes as a means of understanding the work performed. Often contrasted with *task-oriented procedure.*

REFERENCES

Ackerman, P. L. (1987). Individual differences in skill learning: An integration of psychometric and information processing perspectives. *Psychological Bulletin, 102*, 3–27.

Ackerman, P. L. (1992). Predicting individual differences in complex skill acquisition: Dynamics of ability determinants. *Journal of Applied Psychology, 77*, 598–614.

Ackerman, P. L., & Heggestad, E. D. (1997). Intelligence, personality, and interests: Evidence of overlapping traits. *Psychological Bulletin, 121*, 219–245.

Ackerman, P. L., & Kanfer, R. (1993). Integrating laboratory and field study for improving selection: Development of a battery for predicting air traffic controller success. *Journal of Applied Psychology, 78*, 413–432.

Adair, J. G. (1984). The Hawthorne effect: A reconsideration of the methodological artifact. *Journal of Applied Psychology, 69*, 334–345.

Adams, J. S. (1965). Inequity in social exchange. In L. Berkowitz (Ed.), *Advances in experimental social psychology* (Vol. 2, pp. 267–299). New York: Academic Press.

Adler, N. J., Doktor, R., & Redding, S. G. (1986). From the Atlantic to the Pacific century: Cross-cultural management reviewed. *Journal of Management, 12*, 295–318.

Alfredsson, L., & Theorell, T. (1983). Job characteristics of occupations and myocardial infarction risk: Effect of possible confounding factors. *Social Science and Medicine, 17*, 1497–1503.

Allen, N. J., & Meyer, J. P. (1990). The measurement and antecedents of affective, continuance, and normative commitment to the organization. *Journal of Occupational Psychology, 63*, 1–18.

Allen, T. D., & Rush, M. C. (1998). The effects of organizational citizenship behavior on performance judgments: A field study and a laboratory experiment. *Journal of Applied Psychology, 83*, 247–260.

Alley, W. E. (1994). Recent advances in classification theory and practice. In M. G. Rumsey, C. B. Walker, & J. H. Harris (Eds.), *Personnel selection and classification* (pp. 431–442). Hillsdale, NJ: Erlbaum.

Alliger, G. M., & Janak, E. A. (1989). Kirkpatrick's levels of training criteria: Thirty years later. *Personnel Psychology, 42*, 331–342.

Alliger, G. M., Lilienfield, S. O., & Mitchell, K. E. (1995). The susceptibility of overt and covert integrity tests to coaching and faking. *Psychological Science, 7*, 32–39.

Alliger, G. M., Tannenbaum, S. I., Bennett, W., Traver, H., & Shotland, A. (1997). A meta-analysis of the relations among training criteria. *Personnel Psychology, 50*, 341–358.

Ambrose, M. L., & Kulik, C. T. (1999). Old friends, new faces: Motivation research in the 1990s. *Journal of Management, 25*, 231–292.

American Educational Research Association, American Psychological Association, & National Council on Measurement in Education. (1999). *Standards for educational and psychological testing*. Washington, DC: American Educational Research Association.

American Psychological Association. (1992). Ethical principles of psychologists and code of conduct. *American Psychologist, 47*, 1597–1611.

Americans with Disabilities Act. (1990). P.L. 101-336, 104 Statute 327, 26 July.

Anderson, C. C., Warner, J. L., & Spencer, C. C. (1984). Inflation bias in self-assessment examinations: Implications for valid employee selection. *Journal of Applied Psychology, 69*, 574–580.

Anderson, J. R. (1985). *Cognitive psychology and its implications* (2nd ed.). New York: Freeman.

Anderson, L., & Wilson, S. (1997). Critical incident technique. In D. L. Whetzel & G. R. Wheaton (Eds.), *Applied measurement methods in industrial psychology* (pp. 89–112). Palo Alto, CA: Consulting Psychologists Press.

Andersson, L. M., & Pearson, C. M. (1999). Tit for tat? The spiraling effect of incivility in the workplace. *Academy of Management Review, 24*, 452–471.

Appelbaum, E., & Batt, R. (1993). *High-performance work systems*. Washington, DC: Economic Policy Institute.

Argyris, C. (1996). Actionable knowledge: Design causality in the service of consequential theory. *Journal of Applied Behavioral Science, 32,* 390–406.

Armenakis, A. A., & Bedeian, A. G. (1999). Organizational change: A review of theory and research in the 1990s. *Journal of Management, 25,* 293–315.

Arthur, W., & Bennett, W. (1995). The international assignee: The relative importance of factors perceived to contribute to success. *Personnel Psychology, 48,* 99–114.

Arvey, R. D. (1986). Sex bias in job evaluation procedures. *Personnel Psychology, 39,* 315–335.

Arvey, R. D., & Bouchard, T. J., Jr. (1994). Genetics, twins, and organizational behavior. In B. M. Staw & L. L. Cummings (Eds.), *Research in organizational behavior* (Vol. 16, pp. 47–82). Greenwich, CT: JAI Press.

Arvey, R. D., & Campion, J. E. (1982). The employment interview: A summary and review of recent research. *Personnel Psychology, 35,* 281–322.

Arvey, R. D., Landon, T. E., Nutting, S. M., & Maxwell, S. E. (1992). Development of physical ability tests for police officers: A construct validation approach. *Journal of Applied Psychology, 77,* 996–1009.

Arvey, R. D., Passino, E. M., & Lounsbury, J. W. (1977). Job analysis results as influenced by sex of incumbent and sex of analyst. *Journal of Applied Psychology, 62,* 411–416.

Arvey, R. D., Renz, G. L., & Watson, T. W. (1998). Emotionality and job performance: Implications for personnel selection. In G. R. Ferris (Ed.), *Research in personnel and human resources management* (Vol. 16, pp. 103–147). Stamford, CT: JAI Press.

Aschoff, J. (1978). Features of circadian rhythms relevant to the design of shift schedules. *Ergonomics, 21,* 739–754.

Ashforth, B. E., & Humphrey, R. H. (1995). Emotions in the workplace: A reappraisal. *Human Relations, 48,* 97–125.

Atwater, L. E. (1998). The advantages and pitfalls of self-assessment in organizations. In J. W. Smither (Ed.), *Performance appraisal* (pp. 331–369). San Francisco: Jossey-Bass.

Austin, J. T., & Villanova, P. (1992). The criterion problem: 1917–1992. *Journal of Applied Psychology, 77,* 836–874.

Author. (1999). Test security: Protecting the integrity of tests. *American Psychologist, 54,* 1078.

Author. (2000). *Deskbook encyclopedia of employment law* (8th ed.). Birmingham, AL: Oakstone.

Avery, C., & Zabel, D. (2001). *The flexible workplace: A sourcebook of information and research.* Westport, CT: Quorum.

Avolio, B. J., Kahai, S., Dumdum, R., & Sivasubramaniam, N. (2001). Virtual teams: Implications for e-leadership and team development. In M. London (Eds.), *How people evaluate others in organizations* (pp. 337–358). Mahwah, NJ: Erlbaum.

Bakke, E. W. (1945). Why workers join unions. *Personnel, 22,* 37–46.

Baldridge, D. C., & Veiga, J. F. (2001). Toward a greater understanding of the willingness to request an accommodation: Can requesters' beliefs disable the Americans with Disabilities Act? *Academy of Management Review, 26,* 85–99.

Baldwin, T. T., & Ford, J. K. (1988). Transfer of training: A review and directions for future research. *Personnel Psychology, 41,* 63–105.

Baldwin, T. T., & Magjuka, R. J. (1991). Organizational training and signals of importance: Effects of pre-training perceptions on intentions to transfer. *Human Resource Development, 2(1),* 25–36.

Baldwin, T. T., Magjuka, R. J., & Loher, B. T. (1991). The perils of participation: Effects of choice of training on trainee motivation and learning. *Personnel Psychology, 44,* 51–66.

Baldwin, T. T., & Padgett, M. Y. (1993). Management development: A review and commentary. In C. L. Cooper & I. T. Robertson (Eds.), *International review of industrial and organizational psychology* (Vol. 8, pp. 35–85). London: Wiley.

Baltes, B. B., Briggs, T. E., Huff, J. W., Wright, J. A., & Neuman, G. A. (1999). Flexible and compressed workweek schedules: A meta-analysis of their effects on work-related criteria. *Journal of Applied Psychology, 84,* 496–513.

Balzer, W. K., Smith, P. C., & Kravitz, D. E. (1990). *User's manual for the JDI and J16 scales.* Bowling Green, OH: Bowling Green State University.

Balzer, W. K., & Sulsky, L. M. (1992). Halo and performance appraisal research. *Journal of Applied Psychology, 77,* 975–985.

Bargh, J. A., & Chartrand, T. L. (1999). The unbearable automaticity of being. *American Psychologist, 54,* 462–477.

Barling, J. (1990). *Employment, stress and family functioning.* Chichester: Wiley.

Barling, J. (1996). The prediction, experience, and consequence of workplace violence. In G. R. VandenBos & E. Q. Bulatao (Eds.), *Violence on the job* (pp. 29–50). Washington, DC: American Psychological Association.

Barling, J., & Boswell, R. (1995). Work performance and the achievement striving and impatience-irritability dimensions of Type A behavior. *Applied Psychology: An International Review, 44,* 143–153.

Barling, J., & Sorenson, D. (1997). Work and family: In search of a relevant research agenda. In C. L. Cooper & S. E. Jackson (Eds.), *Creating tomorrow's organizations* (pp. 157–170). New York: Wiley.

Barnes-Farrell, J. L. (2001). Performance appraisal: Person perception processes and challenges. In M. London (Ed.), *How people evaluate others in organizations* (pp. 135–154). Mahwah, NJ: Erlbaum.

Barnett, G. A. (1988). Communication and organizational culture. In G. M. Goldhaber & G. A. Barnett (Eds.), *Handbook of organizational communication.* Norwood, NJ: Ablex.

Baron, S. A., Hoffman, S. J., & Merrill, J. G. (2000). *When work equals life: The next stage of workplace violence.* Oxnard, CA: Pathfinder.

Barrett, G. V. (2001). *Emotional intelligence: The Madison Avenue approach to professional practice.* Paper presented at the 16th annual conference of the Society for Industrial and Organizational Psychology, San Diego, CA.

Barrett, G. V., Alexander, R. A., & Doverspike, D. (1992). The implications for personnel selection of apparent declines in predictive validities over time: A critique of Hulin, Henry, and Noon. *Personnel Psychology, 45,* 601–617.

Barrett, G. V., Caldwell, M. S., & Alexander, R. A. (1985). The concept of dynamic criteria: A critical reanalysis. *Personnel Psychology, 38,* 41–56.

Barrick, M. R., & Mount, M. K. (1991). The big five personality dimensions and job performance: A meta-analysis. *Personnel Psychology, 44,* 1–26.

Barrick, M. R., Stewart, G. L., Neubert, M. J., & Mount, M. K. (1998). Relating member ability and personality to work-team processes and team effectiveness. *Journal of Applied Psychology, 83,* 377–391.

Barry, B., & Stewart, G. L. (1997). Composition, process, and performance in self-managed groups: The role of personality. *Journal of Applied Psychology, 82,* 62–78.

Bartlett, C. J. (1983). What's the difference between valid and invalid halo? Forced-choice measurement without forcing a choice. *Journal of Applied Psychology, 68,* 218–226.

Barton, J. (1994). Choosing to work at night: A moderating influence on individual tolerance to shiftwork. *Journal of Applied Psychology, 79,* 449–454.

Bashore, T. R., & Rapp, P. E. (1993). Are there alternatives to traditional polygraph procedures? *Psychological Bulletin, 113,* 3–22.

Bass, B. M. (1985). *Leadership and performance beyond expectations.* New York: Free Press.

Bass, B. M. (1997). Does the transactional-transformational leadership paradigm transcend organizational and national boundaries? *American Psychologist, 52,* 130–139.

Bass, B. M. (1998). *Transformational leadership.* Mahwah, NJ: Erlbaum.

Bazerman, M. H., & Neale, M. A. (1982). Improving negotiation effectiveness under final offer arbitration: The role of selection and training. *Journal of Applied Psychology, 67,* 543–548.

Becker, B., & Gerhart, B. (1996). The impact of human resource management on organizational performance: Progress and prospects. *Academy of Management Journal, 39,* 779–801.

Becker, T. E., & Colquitt, A. L. (1992). Potential versus actual faking of a biodata form: An analysis along several dimensions of item type. *Personnel Psychology, 45,* 389–406.

Behling, O. (1998). Employee selection: Will intelligence and conscientiousness do the job? *Academy of Management Executive, 12,* 77–86.

Belbin, R. M. (1981). *Management teams.* New York: Wiley.

Benjamin, L. T. (1997). Organized industrial psychology before Division 14: The ACP and the AAAP (1930–1945). *Journal of Applied Psychology, 82,* 459–466.

Bennett, G. K. (1980). *Test of mechanical comprehension.* New York: Psychological Corporation.

Bennett, N., Blum, T. C., & Roman, P. M. (1994). Pressure of drug screening and employee assistance programs: Exclusive and inclusive human resource management practices. *Journal of Organizational Behavior, 15,* 549–560.

Bennett, R. J., & Robinson, S. L. (2000). Development of a measure of workplace deviance. *Journal of Applied Psychology, 85,* 349–360.

Bennis, W. (1999). The end of leadership: Exemplary leadership is impossible without full inclusion, initiatives, and cooperation of followers. *Organizational Dynamics, 28,* 71–80.

Ben-Shakhar, G., Bar-Hillel, M., Bilu, Y., Ben-Abba, E., & Flug, A. (1986). Can graphology predict occupational success? Two empirical studies and some methodological ruminations. *Journal of Applied Psychology, 71,* 645–653.

Berman, F. E., & Miner, J. B. (1985). Motivation to manage at the top executive level: A test of the hierarchic role-motivation theory. *Personnel Psychology, 38,* 377–391.

Bernardin, H. J., & Cooke, D. K. (1993). Validity of an honesty test in predicting theft among convenience store employees. *Academy of Management Journal, 36,* 1097–1108.

Bernardin, H. J., Cooke, D. K., & Villanova, P. (2000). Conscientiousness and agreeableness as predictors of rating leniency. *Journal of Applied Psychology, 85,* 232–236.

Bernardin, H. J., Hagan, C. M., Kane, J. S., & Villanova, P. (1998). Effective performance management. In J. W. Smither (Ed.), *Performance appraisal* (pp. 3–48). San Francisco: Jossey-Bass.

Bernardin, H. J., & Pence, E. C. (1980). Effects of rater training: Creating new response sets and decreasing accuracy. *Journal of Applied Psychology, 65,* 60–66.

Bersoff, D. N. (1999). *Ethical conflicts in psychology* (2nd ed.). Washington, DC: American Psychological Association.

Betz, E. L. (1984). Two tests of Maslow's theory of need fulfillment. *Journal of Vocational Behavior, 24,* 204–220.

Beyer, J. M., & Trice, H. M. (1987). How an organization's rites reveal its culture. *Organizational Dynamics, 15,* 5–24.

Bhawuk, D. P., & Brislin, R. W. (2000). Cross-cultural training: A review. *Applied Psychology: An International Review, 49,* 162–191.

Bies, R. J., Tripp, T. M., & Kramer, R. M. (1997). At the breaking point. In R. A. Giacalone & J. Greenberg (Eds.), *Antisocial behavior in organizations* (pp. 18–36). Thousand Oaks, CA: Sage.

Bigoness, W. J. (1978). Correlates of faculty attitudes toward collective bargaining. *Journal of Applied Psychology, 63,* 228–233.

Bingham, W. V. (1917). Mentality testing of college students. *Journal of Applied Psychology, 1,* 38–45.

Binning, J. F., & Barrett, G. V. (1989). Validity of personnel decisions: A conceptual analysis of the inferential and evidential bases. *Journal of Applied Psychology, 74,* 478–494.

Black, J. S., & Mendenhall, M. (1990). Cross-cultural training effectiveness: A review and theoretical framework for future research. *Academy of Management Review, 15,* 113–136.

Blackard, K. (2000). *Managing change in a unionized workplace.* Westport, CT: Quorum.

Blau, G., & Lunz, M. (1999). Testing the impact of shift schedules on organizational variables. *Journal of Organizational Behavior, 20,* 933–942.

Bluedorn, A. C., Turban, D. B., & Love, M. S. (1999). The effects of stand-up and sit-down meeting formats on meeting outcomes. *Journal of Applied Psychology, 84,* 277–285.

Blum, M. L., & Naylor, J. C. (1968). *Industrial psychology: Its theoretical and social foundations.* New York: Harper & Row.

Bobko, P. (1994). Issues in operational selection and classification systems: Comments and commonalities. In M. G. Rumsey, C. B. Walker, & J. H. Harris (Eds.), *Personnel selection and classification* (pp. 443–456). Hillsdale, NJ: Erlbaum.

Boehm, V. R. (1980). Research in the "real world"—A conceptual model. *Personnel Psychology, 33,* 495–504.

Bohle, P., & Tulley, A. J. (1998). Early experience of shiftworking: Influences on attitudes. *Journal of Occupational & Organizational Psychology, 71,* 61–79.

Bok, D., & Dunlop, J. (1970). *Labor and the American community.* New York: Simon & Schuster.

Bolino, M. C. (1999). Citizenship and impression management: Good soldiers or good actors? *Academy of Management Review, 24,* 82–98.

Bommer, W. H., Johnson, J., Rich, G. A., Podsakoff, P. M., & MacKenzie, S. B. (1995). On the interchangeability of objective and subjective measures of employee performance: A meta-analysis. *Personnel Psychology, 48,* 587–605.

Bond, M. H., & Smith, P. B. (1996). Cross-cultural social and organizational psychology. *Annual Review of Psychology, 47,* 205–235.

Borman, W. C. (1974). The rating of individuals in organizations: An alternative approach. *Organizational Behavior and Human Performance, 12,* 105–124.

Borman, W. C. (1978). Exploring upper limits of reliability and validity in performance ratings. *Journal of Applied Psychology, 63,* 135–144.

Borman, W. C. (1991). Job behavior, performance, and effectiveness. In M. D. Dunnette & L. M. Hough (Eds.), *Handbook of industrial and organizational psychology* (2nd ed., Vol. 2, pp. 271–326). Palo Alto, CA: Consulting Psychologists Press.

Borman, W. C., & Motowidlo, S. J. (1993). Expanding the criterion domain to include elements of contextual performance. In N. Schmitt & W. C. Borman (Eds.), *Personnel selection in organizations* (pp. 71–98). San Francisco: Jossey-Bass.

Borman, W. C., White, L. A., & Dorsey, D. W. (1995). Effects of ratee task performance and interpersonal factors on supervisor and peer performance in ratings. *Journal of Applied Psychology, 80,* 168–177.

Bracken, D. W., Dalton, M. A., Jako, R. A., McCauley, C. D., & Pollman, V. A. (1997). *Should 360-degree feedback be used only for developmental purposes?* Greensboro, NC: Center for Creative Leadership.

Bramel, D., & Friend, R. (1981). Hawthorne, the myth of the docile worker, and class bias in psychology. *American Psychologist, 36,* 867–878.

Brand, C. (1987). The importance of general intelligence. In S. Modgil & C. Modgil (Eds.), *Arthur Jensen: Consensus and controversy.* New York: Falmer.

Breaugh, J. A. (1983). The 12-hour work day: Differing employee reactions. *Personnel Psychology, 36,* 277–288.

Brenner, M. H., & Mooney, A. (1983). Unemployment and health in the context of economic change. *Social Science and Medicine, 17,* 1125–1138.

Brett, J. F., & Atwater, L. E. (2001). 360° feedback: Accuracy, reactions, and perceptions of usefulness. *Journal of Applied Psychology, 86,* 930–942.

Brett, J. F., & VandeWalle, D. (1999). Goal orientation and goal content as predictors of performance in a training program. *Journal of Applied Psychology, 84,* 863–873.

Brett, J. M. (1980). Behavioral research on unions and union management systems. In B. M. Staw & L. L. Cummings (Eds.), *Research in organizational behavior* (Vol. 2). Greenwich, CT: JAI Press.

Brett, J. M., Goldberg, S. B., & Ury, W. L. (1990). Designing systems for resolving disputes in organizations. *American Psychologist, 45,* 162–170.

Brett, J. M., Tinsley, C. H., Janssens, M., Barsness, Z. I., & Lytle, A. L. (1997). New approaches to the study of culture in industrial/organizational psychology. In P. C. Earley & M. Erez (Eds.), *New perspectives on international industrial/organizational psychology* (pp. 75–129). San Francisco: New Lexington Press.

Brief, A. P. (1998). *Attitudes in and around organizations.* Thousand Oaks, CA: Sage.

Brief, A. P., & Barsky, A. (2000). Establishing a climate for diversity: The inhibition of prejudiced reactions in the workplace. In G. R. Ferris (Ed.), *Research in personnel and human resources management* (Vol. 19, pp. 91–129). New York: Elsevier.

Brief, A. P., & Hayes, E. L. (1997). The continuing "American dilemma": Studying racism in organizations. In C. L. Cooper & D. M. Rousseau (Eds.), *Trends in organizational behavior* (Vol. 4, pp. 89–106). London: Wiley.

Brief, A. P., & Motowidlo, S. J. (1986). Prosocial organizational behavior. *Academy of Management Review, 11,* 710–725.

Brief, A. P., & Rude, D. E. (1981). Voting in a union certification election: A conceptual analysis. *Academy of Management Review, 6,* 261–267.

Brockner, J., Davy, J., & Carter, C. (1985). Layoffs, self-esteem, and survivor guilt: Motivational, affective, and attitudinal consequences. *Organizational Behavior and Human Decision Processes, 36,* 229–244.

Brockner, J., & Greenberg, J. (1990). The impact of layoffs on survivors: An occupational justice perspective. In J. Carroll (Ed.), *Applied social psychology and organizational settings* (pp. 45–75). Hillsdale, NJ: Erlbaum.

Brodbeck, F. C., Frese, M., Akerblom, S., & Audia, G. (2000). Cultural variation of leadership prototypes across 22 European countries. *Journal of Occupational & Organizational Psychology, 73,* 1–29.

Brown, B. K., & Campion, M. A. (1994). Biodata phenomenology: Recruiters' perceptions and use of biographical information in resume screening. *Journal of Applied Psychology, 79,* 897–908.

Brown, S. P. (1996). A meta-analysis and review of organizational research in job involvement. *Psychological Bulletin, 120,* 235–255.

Bruno, F. (1994). Drug and alcohol problems in the workplace in Italy. *Journal of Drug Issues, 24,* 697–713.

Bryan, W. L. (1904). Theory and practice. *Psychological Review, 11,* 71–82.

Bryan, W. L., & Harter, N. (1897). Studies in the physiology and psychology of the telegraphic language. *Psychological Review, 4,* 27–53.

Bryan, W. L., & Harter, N. (1899). Studies of the telegraphic language. *Psychological Review, 6,* 345–375.

Buffardi, L. C., Fleishman, E. A., Morath, R. A., & McCarthy, P. M. (2000). Relationships between ability requirements and human errors in job tasks. *Journal of Applied Psychology, 85,* 551–564.

Bulatao, E. Q., & VandenBos, G. R. (1996). Workplace violence: Its scope and the issues. In G. R. VandenBos & E. Q. Bulatao (Eds.), *Violence on the job* (pp. 1–24). Washington, DC: American Psychological Association.

Buono, A. F., & Bowditch, J. L. (1989). *The human side of mergers and acquisitions: Managing collision between people, cultures, and organizations.* San Francisco: Jossey-Bass.

Burke, M. J., & Day, R. R. (1986). A cumulative study of the effectiveness of managerial training. *Journal of Applied Psychology, 71,* 232–246.

Buss, T. F., & Redburn, F. S. (1987). Plant closings: Impacts and responses. *Economic Development Quarterly, 1,* 170–177.

Callinan, M., & Robertson, I. T. (2000). Work sample testing. *International Journal of Selection and Assessment, 8,* 248–260.

Camara, W. J., & Schneider, D. L. (1994). Integrity tests: Facts and unresolved issues. *American Psychologist, 49,* 112–119.

Cameron, K. (1982). The relationship between faculty unionism and organizational effectiveness. *Academy of Management Journal, 25,* 6–24.

Campbell, D. J., & Lee, C. (1988). Self-appraisal in performance evaluation: Development versus evaluation. *Academy of Management Review, 13,* 302–314.

Campbell, J. P. (1990a). An overview of the Army selection and classification project. *Personnel Psychology, 43,* 231–240.

Campbell, J. P. (1990b). The role of theory in industrial and organizational psychology. In M. D. Dunnette & L. M. Hough (Eds.), *Handbook of industrial and organizational psychology* (2nd ed., Vol. 1, pp. 39–74). Palo Alto, CA: Consulting Psychologists Press.

Campbell, J. P. (1996). Group differences and personnel decisions: Validity, fairness, and affirmative action. *Journal of Vocational Behavior, 49,* 122–158.

Campbell, J. P., Hanson, M. A., & Oppler, S. H. (2001). Modeling performance in a population of jobs. In J. P. Campbell & D. J. Knapp (Eds.), *Exploring the limits in personnel selection and classification* (pp. 307–334). Mahwah, NJ: Erlbaum.

Campbell, J. P., Harris, J. H., & Knapp, D. J. (2001). The Army selection and classification research program: Goals, overall design, and organization. In J. P. Campbell & D. J. Knapp (Eds.), *Exploring the limits in personnel selection and classification* (pp. 31–52). Mahwah, NJ: Erlbaum.

Campbell, J. P., McCloy, R. A., Oppler, S. H., & Sager, C. E. (1993). A theory of performance. In N. Schmitt & W. C. Borman (Eds.), *Personnel selection in organizations* (pp. 35–70). San Francisco: Jossey-Bass.

Campion, J. E. (1972). Work sampling for personnel selection. *Journal of Applied Psychology, 56,* 40–44.

Campion, M. A. (1991). Meaning and measurement of turnover: Comparison of alternative measures and recommendations for research. *Journal of Applied Psychology, 76,* 199–212.

Campion, M. A., & Berger, C. J. (1990). Conceptual integration and empirical test of job design and compensation relationships. *Personnel Psychology, 43,* 525–554.

Campion, M. A., & Campion, J. E. (1987). Evaluation of an interviewee skills training program in a natural field experiment. *Personnel Psychology, 40,* 675–691.

Campion, M. A., Cheraskin, L., & Stevens, M. J. (1994). Career-related antecedents and outcomes of job rotation. *Academy of Management Journal, 37,* 1518–1542.

Campion, M. A., Outtz, J. L., Zedeck, S., Schmidt, F. L., Kehoe, J. F., Murphy, K. R., & Guion, R. M. (2001). The controversy over score banding in personnel selection: Answers to 10 key questions. *Personnel Psychology, 54,* 149–185.

Campion, M. A., Palmer, D. K., & Campion, J. E. (1997). A review of structure in the selection interview. *Personnel Psychology, 50,* 655–702.

Campion, M. A., Papper, E. M., & Medsker, G. J. (1996). Relations between work team characteristics and effectiveness: A replication and extension. *Personnel Psychology, 49,* 429–452.

Cannon-Bowers, J. A., & Salas, E. (1997). A framework for developing team performance measures in training. In M. T. Brannick, E. Salas, & C. Prince (Eds.), *Team performance assessment and measurement: Theory, methods, and applications* (pp. 45–62). Mahwah, NJ: Erlbaum.

Cannon-Bowers, J. A., & Salas, E. (2001). Reflections on shared cognition. *Journal of Organizational Behavior, 22,* 195–202.

Cardy, R. L. (1998). Performance appraisal in a quality context: A new look at an old problem. In J. W. Smither (Ed.), *Performance appraisal* (pp. 132–162). San Francisco: Jossey-Bass.

Carillon, J. W., & Sutton, R. I. (1982). The relationship between union effectiveness and the quality of members' worklife. *Journal of Occupational Behavior, 3,* 171–179.

Carling, P. (1994). Reasonable accommodations in the workplace for persons with psychiatric disabilities. In S. M. Bruyere & J. O'Keeffe (Eds.), *Implications of the Americans with Disabilities Act for psychology* (pp. 103–136). New York: Springer.

Carlson, K. D. Scullen, S. E., Schmidt, F. L., Rothstein, H., & Erwin, F. (1999). Generalizable biographical data can be achieved without multiorganizational development and keying. *Personnel Psychology, 52,* 731–755.

Carnevale, A. P. (1995). Enhancing skills in the new economy. In A. Howard (Ed.), *The changing nature of work* (pp. 238–251). San Francisco: Jossey-Bass.

Carretta, T. R., & Ree, M. J. (2000). General and specific cognitive and psychomotor abilities in personnel selection: The prediction of training and job performance. *International Journal of Selection and Assessment, 8,* 227–236.

Carson, K. P., Becker, J. S., & Henderson, J. A. (1998). Is utility really futile? A failure to replicate and an extension. *Journal of Applied Psychology, 83,* 84–96.

Carsten, J. M., & Spector, P. E. (1987). Unemployment, job satisfaction, and employee turnover: A meta-analytic test of the Muchinsky model. *Journal of Applied Psychology, 72,* 374–381.

Cascio, W. F. (1976). Turnover, biographical data, and fair employment practice. *Journal of Applied Psychology, 61,* 576–580.

Cascio, W. F. (1982). *Applied psychology in personnel management* (2nd ed.). Reston, VA: Reston.

Cascio, W. F. (1989). Using utility analyses to assess training outcomes. In I. L. Goldstein (Ed.), *Training and development in organizations* (pp. 63–88). San Francisco: Jossey-Bass.

Cascio, W. F. (1993). Assessing the utility of selection decisions: Theoretical and practical considerations. In N. Schmitt & W. C. Borman (Eds.), *Personnel selection in organizations* (pp. 310–340). San Francisco: Jossey-Bass.

Cascio, W. F. (1995). Whither industrial and organizational psychology in a changing world of work? *American Psychologist, 50*, 928–939.

Cascio, W. F. (1999). Virtual workplaces: Implications for organizational behavior. In C. L. Cooper & D. M. Rousseau (Eds.), *Trends in organizational behavior: The virtual organization* (Vol. 6, pp. 1–14). New York: Wiley.

Cascio, W. F., Alexander, R. A., & Barrett, G. V. (1988). Setting cutoff scores: Legal, psychometric, and professional issues and guidelines. *Personnel Psychology, 41*, 1–24.

Cascio, W. F., & Phillips, N. F. (1979). Performance testing: A rose among thorns? *Personnel Psychology, 32*, 751–766.

Castellow, W. A., Wuensch, K. L., & Moore, C. H. (1990). Effects of physical attractiveness of the plaintiff and defendant in sexual harassment judgments. *Journal of Social Behavior and Personality, 15*, 547–562.

Cavanaugh, M. A., & Noe, R. A. (1999). Antecedents and consequences of relational components of the new psychological contract. *Journal of Organizational Behavior, 20*, 323–340.

Cawley, B. D., Keeping, L. M., & Levy, P. E. (1998). Participation in the performance appraisal process and employee reactions: A meta-analytic review of field investigations. *Journal of Applied Psychology, 83*, 615–633.

Cederblom, D. (1982). The performance appraisal interview: A review, implications and suggestions. *Academy of Management Review, 7*, 219–227.

Cederblom, D., & Lounsbury, J. W. (1980). An investigation of user acceptance of peer evaluations. *Personnel Psychology, 33*, 567–580.

Chan, K. Y., & Drasgow, F. (2001). Toward a theory of individual differences and leadership: Understanding the motivation to lead. *Journal of Applied Psychology, 86*, 481–498.

Chan, K. Y., Drasgow, F., & Sawin, L. L. (1999). What is the shelf life of a test? The effect of time on the psychometrics of a cognitive ability test battery. *Journal of Applied Psychology, 84*, 610–619.

Chao, G. T., Walz, P. M., & Gardner, P. D. (1992). Formal and informal mentorships: A comparison on mentoring functions and contrast with nonmentored counterparts. *Personnel Psychology, 45*, 619–636.

Chapanis, A., Garner, W. R., & Morgan, C. T. (1949). *Applied experimental psychology*. New York: Wiley.

Chemers, M. M., & Murphy, S. E. (1995). Leadership and diversity in groups and organizations. In M. M. Chemers, S. Oskamp, & M. A. Costanzo (Eds.), *Diversity in organizations: New perspectives for a changing workforce* (pp. 157–188). Thousand Oaks, CA: Sage.

Chen, G., Gully, S. M., Whiteman, J. A., & Kilcullen, R. N. (2000). Examination of relationships among trait-like individual differences, state-like individual differences, and learning performance. *Journal of Applied Psychology, 85*, 835–847.

Childs, A., & Klimoski, R. J. (1986). Successfully predicting career success: An application of the biographical inventory. *Journal of Applied Psychology, 71*, 3–8.

Choi, J. N., & Kim, M. U. (1999). The organizational applications of groupthink and its limitations in organizations. *Journal of Applied Psychology, 84*, 297–306.

Clause, C. S., Mullins, M. E., Nee, M. T., Pulakos, E., & Schmitt, N. (1998). Parallel test form development: A procedure for alternative predictors and an example. *Personnel Psychology, 51*, 193–208.

Cleveland, J. N., & Kerst, M. E. (1993). Sexual harassment and perceptions of power: An under-articulated relationship. *Journal of Vocational Behavior, 42*, 49–67.

Clifford, J. P. (1994). Job analysis: Why do it, and how should it be done? *Public Personnel Management, 23*, 321–338.

Cobb, S., & Kasl, S. V. (1977). *Termination: The consequence of job loss*. U.S. Department of Health, Education and Welfare. Washington, DC: U.S. Government Printing Office.

Cohen, A. (1999). Relationships among five forms of commitment: An empirical assessment. *Journal of Organizational Behavior, 20*, 285–308.

Cohen, D. J. (1990, November). What motivates trainees? *Training and Development Journal*, 91–93.

Colarelli, S. M. (1998). Psychological interventions in organizations: An evolutionary perspective. *American Psychologist, 53*, 1044–1056.

Cole, N. D., & Latham, G. P. (1997). Effects of training in procedural justice on perceptions of disciplinary fairness by unionized employees and disciplinary subject matter experts. *Journal of Applied Psychology, 82*, 699–705.

Colella, A. (2001). Coworker distributive fairness judgments of the workplace accommodation of employees with disabilities. *Academy of Management Review, 26*, 100–116.

Collins, J. M., & Gleaves, D. H. (1998). Race, job applicants, and the five-factor model of personality: Implications for black psychology, industrial/organizational psychology, and the five-factor theory. *Journal of Applied Psychology, 83*, 531–544.

Collins, J. M., & Muchinsky, P. M. (1993). An assessment of the construct validity of three job evaluation methods: A field experiment. *Academy of Management Journal, 36*, 895–904.

Collins, J. M., & Schmidt, F. L. (1993). Personality, integrity, and white collar crime: A construct validity study. *Personnel Psychology, 46*, 295–311.

Collis, J. M., & Messick, S. (Eds.). (2001). *Intelligence and personality: Bridging the gap in theory and measurement*. Mahwah, NJ: Erlbaum.

Colquitt, J. A., Conlon, D. E., Wesson, M. J., Porter, C. O., & Ng, K. Y. (2001). Justice at the millennium: A meta-analytic review of 25 years of organizational justice research. *Journal of Applied Psychology, 86*, 425–445.

Colquitt, J. A., LePine, J. A., & Noe, R. A. (2000). Toward an integrative theory of training motivation: A meta-analytic path analysis of 20 years of research. *Journal of Applied Psychology, 85*, 678–707.

Conger, J. A. (1989). *The charismatic leader: Behind the mystique of exceptional leadership.* San Francisco: Jossey-Bass.

Conger, J. A., & Kanungo, R. N. (1987). Toward a behavioral theory of charismatic leadership in organizational settings. *Academy of Management Review, 12,* 637–647.

Conley, P. R., & Sackett, P. R. (1987). Effects of using high-versus low-performing job incumbents as sources of job analysis information. *Journal of Applied Psychology, 72,* 434–437.

Conway, J. M. (1999). Distinguishing contextual performance from task performance for managerial jobs. *Journal of Applied Psychology, 84,* 3–13.

Cooper, C. L., & Rousseau, D. M. (Eds.). (2000). *Trends in organizational behavior: Time in organizational behavior* (Vol. 7). Chichester: Wiley.

Cooper, W. H. (1981). Ubiquitous halo. *Psychological Bulletin, 90,* 218–244.

Cornelius, E. T., DeNisi, A. S., & Blencoe, A. G. (1984). Expert and naive raters using the PAQ: Does it matter? *Personnel Psychology, 37,* 453–464.

Cortina, J. M., Goldstein, N. B., Payne, S. C., Davison, H. K., & Gilliland, S. W. (2000). The incremental validity of interview scores over and above cognitive ability and conscientiousness scores. *Personnel Psychology, 53,* 325–351.

Costa, G. (1996). The impact of shift and night work on health. *Applied Ergonomics, 27,* 9–16.

Costa, P. T. (1996). Work and personality: Use of the NEO-PI-R in industrial/organizational psychology. *Applied Psychology: An International Review, 45,* 225–241.

Covey, S. R., Merrill, A. R., & Merrill, R. R. (1994). *First things first.* New York: Simon & Schuster.

Cox, T., & Leather, P. (1994). The prevention of violence at work: Application of a cognitive behavioral theory. In C. L. Cooper & I. T. Robertson (Eds.), *International review of industrial and organizational psychology* (Vol. 9, pp. 213–245). London: Wiley.

Craiger, P. (1997). Technology, organizations, and work in the 20th century. *The Industrial-Organizational Psychologist, 34*(3), 89–96.

Cronbach, L. J., Gleser, G. C., Nanda, H., & Rajaratram, N. (1972). *The dependability of behavioral measurements: Theory of generalizability for scores and profiles.* New York: Wiley.

Cronshaw, S. F. (1997). Lo! The stimulus speaks: The insider's view of Whyte and Latham's "The futility of utility analysis." *Personnel Psychology, 50,* 611–616.

Cropanzano, R., & Greenberg, J. (1997). Progress in organizational justice: Tunneling through the maze. In C. L. Cooper & I. T. Robertson (Eds.), *International review of industrial and organizational psychology* (Vol. 12, pp. 317–372). Chichester: Wiley.

Cropanzano, R., & Prehar, C. A. (2001). Emerging justice concerns in an era of changing psychological contracts (pp. 245–269). In R. Cropanzano (Ed.), *Justice in the workplace: From theory to practice* (Vol. 2). Mahwah, NJ: Erlbaum.

Crosby, F. J., & VanDeVeer, C. (Eds.). (2000). *Sex, race, & merit.* Ann Arbor: University of Michigan Press.

Csikszentmihalyi, M. (1999). If we are so rich, why aren't we happy? *American Psychologist, 54,* 821–827.

Cunningham, M. R., Wong, D. T., & Barbee, A. P. (1994). Self-presentation dynamics on overt integrity tests: Experimental studies of the Reid Report. *Journal of Applied Psychology, 79,* 643–658.

D'Adamo, P. J. (1996). *4 blood types, 4 diets: Eat right for your type.* New York: Putnam.

Daft, R. L. (1983). Learning the craft of organizational research. *Academy of Management Review, 8,* 539–546.

Dalton, D. R., & Mesch, D. J. (1990). The impact of flexible scheduling on employee attendance and turnover. *Administrative Science Quarterly, 35,* 370–387.

Daniel, M. H. (1997). Intelligence testing. *American Psychologist, 52,* 1038–1045.

Dansereau, F., Graen, G., & Haga, W. (1975). A vertical dyad linkage approach to leadership in formal organizations. *Organizational Behavior and Human Performance, 13,* 46–78.

Davis, D. D. (1995). Form, function, and strategy in boundary-less organizations. In A. Howard (Ed.), *The changing nature of work* (pp. 112–138). San Francisco: Jossey-Bass.

Davis, G. F., & Powell, W. W. (1992). Organization–environment relations. In M. D. Dunnette & L. M. Hough (Eds.), *Handbook of industrial and organizational psychology* (2nd ed., Vol. 3, pp. 315–375). Palo Alto, CA: Consulting Psychologists Press.

Day, D. V., & Sulsky, L. M. (1995). Effects of frame-of-reference training and information configuration on memory organization and rater accuracy. *Journal of Applied Psychology, 80,* 158–167.

De Corte, W. (1999). Weighing job performance predictors to both maximize the quality of the selected workforce and control the level of adverse impact. *Journal of Applied Psychology, 84,* 695–702.

Deadrick, D. L., & Madigan, R. M. (1990). Dynamic criteria revisited: A longitudinal study of performance stability and predictive validity. *Personnel Psychology, 43,* 717–744.

Deal, T., & Kennedy, A. (1982). *Corporate cultures.* Reading, MA: Addison-Wesley.

DeCotiis, T. A., & LeLouarn, J. Y. (1981). A predictive study of voting behavior in a representation election using union instrumentality and work perceptions. *Organizational Behavior and Human Performance, 27,* 103–118.

DeGroot, T., & Motowidlo, S. J. (1999). Why visual and vocal interview cues can affect interviewers' judgments and predict job performance. *Journal of Applied Psychology, 84,* 986–993.

DeNisi, A. S., & Peters, L. H. (1996). Organization of information in memory and the performance appraisal process: Evidence from the field. *Journal of Applied Psychology, 81,* 717–737.

Dickinson, T. L. (1993). Attitudes about performance appraisal. In H. Schuler, J. L. Farr, & M. Smith (Eds.), *Personnel selection and assessment* (pp. 141–162). Hillsdale, NJ: Erlbaum.

Diener, E. (2000). Subjective well-being: The science of happiness and a proposal for a national index. *American Psychologist, 554,* 34–43.

Dienesch, R. M., & Liden, R. C. (1986). Leader–member exchange model of leadership: A critique and further development. *Academy of Management Review, 11,* 618–634.

Digman, J. M., & Takemoto-Chock, N. K. (1981). Factors in the natural language of personality: Re-analysis and comparison of six major studies. *Multivariate Behavioral Research, 16,* 149–170.

Dipboye, R. L. (1990). Laboratory vs. field research in industrial and organizational psychology. In C. L. Cooper & I. T. Robertson (Eds.), *International review of industrial and organizational psychology* (Vol. 5, pp. 1–34). London: Wiley.

Dipboye, R. L. (1997). Structured selection interviews: Why do they work? Why are they underutilized? In N. Anderson & P. Herriot (Eds.), *International handbook of selection and assessment* (pp. 455–473). Chichester: Wiley.

Dirks, K. T. (1999). The effects of interpersonal trust on work group performance. *Journal of Applied Psychology, 84,* 445–455.

Dirks, K. T., Cummings, L. L., & Pierce, J. L. (1996). Psychological ownership in organizations: Conditions under which individuals promote and resist change. In R. W. Woodman & W. A. Pasmore (Eds.), *Research in organizational change and development* (Vol. 9, pp. 1–24). Greenwich, CT: JAI Press.

Dompierre, J., & Lavoie, F. (1994). Subjective work stress and family violence. In G. P. Keita & J. J. Hurrell (Eds.), *Job stress in a changing workforce* (pp. 213–228). Washington, DC: American Psychological Association.

Dossett, D. L., & Hulvershorn, P. (1983). Increasing technical training efficiency: Peer training via computer-assisted instruction. *Journal of Applied Psychology, 68,* 552–558.

Dotlich, D. L. (1982, October). International and intracultural management development. *Training and Development Journal, 36,* 26–31.

Dovidio, J. F., & Gaertner, S. L. (1996). Affirmative action, unintentional racial biases, and intergroup relations. *Journal of Social Issues, 52,* 51–75.

Dreher, G. F., & Ash, R. A. (1990). A comparative study of mentoring among men and women in managerial, professional, and technical positions. *Journal of Applied Psychology, 75,* 539–546.

Dreher, G. F., Ash, R. A., & Hancock, P. (1988). The role of the traditional research design in underestimating the validity of the employment interview. *Personnel Psychology, 41,* 315–328.

Drucker, P. F. (1993). *Post-capitalist society.* New York: Harper.

Druskat, V. A., & Wolff, S. B. (1999). Effects and timing of developmental peer appraisals in self-managing work groups. *Journal of Applied Psychology, 84,* 58–74.

Duchon, J. C., Keran, C. M., & Smith, T. J. (1994). Extended workdays in an underground mine: A work performance analysis. *Human Factors, 36,* 258–268.

Dulebohn, J. H. (1997). Social influences in justice evaluations of human resources systems. In G. R. Ferris (Ed.), *Research in personnel and human resources management* (Vol. 15, pp. 241–292). Greenwich, CT: JAI Press.

Dunham, L., & Freeman, R. E. (2000). There is business like show business: Leadership lessons from the theatre. *Organizational Dynamics, 29,* 108–122.

Dunham, R. B. (1977). Shift work: A review and theoretical analysis. *Academy of Management Review, 2,* 626–634.

Dunham, R. B., Grube, J. A., & Castaneda, M. B. (1994). Organizational commitment: The utility of an integrated definition. *Journal of Applied Psychology, 79,* 370–380.

Dunham, R. B., Pierce, J. L., & Castaneda, M. B. (1987). Alternative work schedules: Two field quasi-experiments. *Personnel Psychology, 40,* 215–242.

Dunn, W. S., Mount, M. K., Barrick, M. R., & Ones, D. S. (1995). Relative importance of personality and general mental ability in managers' judgments of applicant qualifications. *Journal of Applied Psychology, 80,* 500–509.

Dunnette, M. D. (1998). Emerging trends and vexing issues in industrial and organizational psychology. *Applied Psychology: An International Review, 47,* 129–153.

Dunnette, M. D., & Hough, L. M. (Eds.). (1990). *Handbook of industrial and organizational psychology* (2nd ed., Vol. 1). Palo Alto, CA: Consulting Psychologists Press.

Eagly, A. H., Karau, S. J., & Makhijani, M. G. (1995). Gender and the effectiveness of leaders: A meta-analysis. *Psychological Bulletin, 117,* 125–145.

Eagly, A. H., Makhijani, M. G., & Klonsky, B. G. (1992). Gender and the evaluation of leaders: A meta-analysis. *Psychological Bulletin, 111,* 3–22.

Earley, P. C. (1997). Doing an about-face: Social motivation and cross-cultural currents. In P. C. Earley & M. Erez (Eds.), *New perspectives on international industrial/organizational psychology* (pp. 243–255). San Francisco: New Lexington Press.

Earley, P. C., & Randel, A. E. (1997). Culture without borders: An individual-level approach to cross-cultural research in organizational behavior. In C. L. Cooper & S. E. Jackson (Eds.), *Creating tomorrow's organizations* (pp. 59–74). New York: Wiley.

Ebel, R. L. (1972). *Essentials of educational measurement.* Englewood Cliffs, NJ: Prentice-Hall.

Eby, L. T. (1997). Alternative forms of mentoring in changing organizational environments: A conceptual extension of the mentoring literature. *Journal of Vocational Behavior, 51,* 125–144.

Edwards, J. R., & Bagozzi, R. P. (2000). On the nature and direction of relationships between constructs and measures. *Psychological Methods, 5,* 155–174.

England, P. (1992). *Comparable worth: Theories and evidence.* Hawthorne, NY: Aldine de Gruyter.

Equal Employment Opportunity Commission. (1980). Discrimination because of sex under Title VII of the Civil Rights Act of 1964, as amended; adoption of interim interpretive guidelines. *Federal Register, 45,* 25024–25025.

Erez, M. (1994). Toward a model of cross-cultural industrial and organizational psychology. In H. C. Triandis, M. D. Dunnette, & L. M. Hough (Eds.), *Handbook of industrial and organizational psychology* (2nd ed., Vol. 4, pp. 559–608). Palo Alto, CA: Consulting Psychologists Press.

Erez, M. (1997). A culture-based model of work motivation. In P. C. Earley & M. Erez (Eds.), *New perspectives on international industrial/organizational psychology* (pp. 193–242). San Francisco: New Lexington Press.

Erez, M., & Earley, P. C. (1993). *Culture, self-identity, and work.* New York: Oxford University Press.

Erez, M., & Eden, D. (2001). Introduction: Trends reflected in work motivation. In M. Erez, U. Kleinbeck, & H. Thierry (Eds.), *Work motivation in the context of a globalizing economy* (pp. 1–8). Mahwah, NJ: Erlbaum.

Erickson, E. H. (1963). *Childhood and society* (2nd ed.). New York: Norton.

Estey, M. (1981). *The unions: Structure, development, and management* (3rd ed.). New York: Harcourt Brace Jovanovich.

Facteau, J. D., & Craig, S. B. (2001). Are performance appraisal ratings from different rating sources comparable? *Journal of Applied Psychology, 86,* 215–227.

Fagenson, E. A. (1989). The mentor advantage: Perceived career/job experiences of proteges versus nonproteges. *Journal of Organizational Behavior, 10,* 309–320.

Farr, J. L., & Tesluk, P. E. (1997). Bruce V. Moore: First president of Division 14. *Journal of Applied Psychology, 82,* 478–485.

Farrell, J. N., & McDaniel, M. A. (2001). The stability of validity coefficients over time: Ackerman's (1988) model and the general aptitude test battery. *Journal of Applied Psychology, 86,* 60–79.

Feldman, D. C., Folks, W. R., & Turnley, W. H. (1999). Mentor–protégé diversity and its impact on international internship experiences. *Journal of Organizational Behavior, 20,* 597–611.

Ferdman, B. M. (1992). The dynamics of ethnic diversity in organizations: Toward integrative models. In K. Kelly (Ed.), *Issues, theory, and research in industrial/ organization psychology* (pp. 339–384). Amsterdam: North Holland.

Ferguson, L. W. (1962). *The heritage of industrial psychology.* Hartford, CT: Finlay.

Fetterman, D. M. (1998). Ethnography. In L. Bickman & D. J. Rog (Eds.), *Handbook of applied social research methods* (pp. 473–504). Thousand Oaks, CA: Sage.

Feuille, P., & Blandin, J. (1974). Faculty job satisfaction and bargaining sentiment: A case study. *Academy of Management Journal, 17,* 678–692.

Fiedler, F. E. (1964). A contingency model of leadership effectiveness. In L. Berkowitz (Ed.), *Advances in experimental social psychology* (Vol. 1). New York: Academic Press.

Fiedler, F. E. (1996). Research on leadership selection and training: One view of the future. *Administrative Science Quarterly, 41,* 241–250.

Fields, M. W., & Thacker, J. W. (1992). Influence of quality of work life on company and union commitment. *Academy of Management Journal, 35,* 439–450.

Fine, S. (1989). *Functional job analysis scales: A desk aid* (rev. ed.). Orlando, FL: Dryden.

Fisher, C. D. (2000). Mood and emotions while working: Missing pieces of job satisfaction? *Journal of Organizational Behavior, 21,* 185–202.

Fisher, C. D., & Ashkanasy, N. M. (2000). The emerging role of emotions in work life: An introduction. *Journal of Organizational Behavior, 21,* 123–129.

Fisher, S. G., Hunter, T. A., & Macrosson, W. D. (1998). The structure of Belbin's team roles. *Journal of Occupational & Organizational Psychology, 71,* 283–288.

Fitzgerald, L. F., Drasgow, F., Hulin, C. L., Gelfand, M. J., & Magley, V. J. (1997). Antecedents and consequences of sexual harassment in organizations: A test of an integrated model. *Journal of Applied Psychology, 82,* 578–589.

Flanagan, M. F., & Dipboye, R. L. (1981). Research settings in industrial and organizational psychology: Facts, fallacies, and the future. *Personnel Psychology, 34,* 37–47.

Fleishman, E. A., & Quaintance, M. K. (1984). *Taxonomies of human performance.* Orlando, FL: Academic Press.

Folger, R., & Baron, R. A. (1996). Violence and hostility at work: A model of reactions to perceived injustice. In G. R. VandenBos & E. Q. Bulatao (Eds.), *Violence on the job* (pp. 51–86). Washington, DC: American Psychological Association.

Folger, R., & Cropanzano, R. (1998). *Organizational justice and human resource management.* Thousand Oaks, CA: Sage.

Folger, R., & Greenberg, J. (1985). Procedural justice: An interpretive analysis of personnel systems. In K. Rowland & G. Ferris (Eds.), *Research in personnel and human resources management* (Vol. 3, pp. 141–183). Greenwich, CT: JAI Press.

Folger, R., & Skarlicki, D. P. (2001). Fairness as a dependent variable: Why tough times can lead to bad management. In R. Cropanzano (Ed.), *Justice in the workplace* (Vol. 2, pp. 97–120). Mahwah, NJ: Erlbaum.

Ford, J. K., & Kraiger, K. (1995). The application of cognitive constructs and principles to the instructional systems model of training: Implications for needs assessment, design, and transfer. In C. L. Cooper & I. T. Robertson (Eds.), *International review of industrial and organizational psychology* (Vol. 10, pp. 1–48). New York: Wiley.

Ford, J. K., Quinones, M., Sego, D., & Speer, J. (1991). *Factors affecting the opportunity to use trained skills on the job.* Paper presented at the 6th annual conference of the Society for Industrial and Organizational Psychology, St. Louis.

Ford, J. K., Smith, E. M., Weissbein, D. A., Gully, S. M., & Salas, E. (1998). Relationships of goal orientation, metacognitive activity and practice strategies with learning outcomes and transfer. *Journal of Applied Psychology, 83,* 218–233.

Foti, R. J., & Lord, R. G. (1987). Prototypes and scripts: The effects of alternative methods of processing information on rating accuracy. *Organizational Behavior and Human Decision Processes, 39,* 318–340.

Fox, S., & Spector, P. E. (1999). A model of work frustration—aggression. *Journal of Organizational Behavior, 20,* 915–932.

Fox, S., & Spector, P. E. (2000). Relations of emotional intelligence, practical intelligence, general intelligence, and trait affectivity with interview outcomes: It's not all just "g." *Journal of Organizational Behavior, 21,* 203–220.

Frankenhaeuser, M. (1988). Stress and reactivity patterns at different stages of the life cycle. In P. Pancheri & L. Zichella (Eds.), *Biorhythms and stress in physiopathology of reproduction.* Washington, DC: Hemisphere.

Freeman, R. E. (1990). Ethics in the workplace: Recent scholarships. In C. L. Cooper & I. T. Robertson (Eds.), *International review of industrial and organizational psychology* (Vol. 5, pp. 149–168). London: Wiley.

Freese, M., & Okonek, K. (1984). Reasons to leave shiftwork and psychological and psychosomatic complaints of former shiftworkers. *Journal of Applied Psychology, 69,* 509–514.

French, J. R. P., & Raven, B. (1960). The basis of social power. In D. Cartwright & A. F. Zander (Eds.), *Group dynamics* (2nd ed.). Evanston, IL: Row & Peterson.

Fried, Y., & Ferris, G. R. (1987). The validity of the job characteristics model: A review and meta-analysis. *Personnel Psychology, 40,* 287–322.

Friedman, D. E., & Galinsky, E. (1992). Work and family issues: A legitimate business concern. In S. Zedeck (Ed.), *Work, families, and organizations* (pp. 168–207). San Francisco: Jossey-Bass.

Friedman, L., & Harvey, R. J. (1986). Factors of union commitment: The case for a lower dimensionality. *Journal of Applied Psychology, 71,* 371–376.

Friedman, L. N., Tucker, S. B., Neville, P. R., & Imperial, M. (1996). The impact of domestic violence on the workplace. In G. R. VandenBos and E. Q. Bulatao (Eds.), *Violence on the job* (pp. 153–162). Washington, DC: American Psychological Association.

Frisch, M. H. (1998). Designing the individual assessment process. In R. Jeanneret & R. Silzer (Eds.), *Individual psychological assessment.* San Francisco: Jossey-Bass.

Frone, M. R. (2000). Work-family conflict and employee psychiatric disorders: The national comorbidity survey. *Journal of Applied Psychology, 85,* 888–895.

Frost, P. J., & Jamal, M. (1979). Shift work, attitudes and reported behaviors: Some association between individual characteristics and hours of work and leisure. *Journal of Applied Psychology, 64,* 77–81.

Fryer, D., & Payne, R. (1986). Being unemployed: A review of the literature on the psychological experience of unemployment. In C. L. Cooper & I. Robertson (Eds.), *International review of industrial and organizational psychology* (Vol. 1, pp. 235–278). London: Wiley.

Fryxell, G. E., & Gordon, M. E. (1989). Workplace justice and job satisfaction as predictors of satisfaction with union and management. *Academy of Management Journal, 32,* 851–866.

Fullagar, C., & Barling, J. (1989). A longitudinal test of a model of the antecedents and consequences of union loyalty. *Journal of Applied Psychology, 74,* 213–227.

Fullagar, C., Clark, P. F., Gallagher, D. G., & Gordon, M. E. (1994). A model of the antecedents of early union commitment: The role of socialization experiences and steward characteristics. *Journal of Organizational Behavior, 15,* 517–533.

Fullagar, C., Gallagher, D. G., Gordon, M. E., & Clark, P. F. (1995). Impact of early socialization on union commitment and participation: A longitudinal study. *Journal of Applied Psychology, 80,* 147–157.

Fulmer, R. (1986). Meeting the merger integration challenge with management development. *Journal of Management Development, 5,* 7–16.

Furnham, A., & Gunter, B. (1993). Corporate culture: Definition, diagnosis and change. In C. L. Cooper & I. T. Robertson (Eds.), *International review of industrial and organizational psychology* (Vol. 8, pp. 234–261). London: Wiley.

Galaif, E. R., Newcomb, M. D., & Carmona, J. V. (2001). Prospective relationships between drug problems and work adjustment in a community sample of adults. *Journal of Applied Psychology, 86,* 337–350.

Gardner, W. L., & Avolio, B. J. (1998). The charismatic relationship: A dramaturgical perspective. *Academy of Management Review, 23,* 32–58.

Geen, R. G. (1990). *Human aggression.* London: Open University Press.

George, J. M., & Brief, A. P. (1996). Motivational agendas in the workplace: The effects of feelings on focus of attention and work motivation. In B. M. Staw & L. L. Cummings (Eds.), *Research in organizational behavior* (Vol. 18, pp. 75–109). Greenwich, CT: JAI Press.

Gerhart, B., & Milkovich, G. T. (1992). Employee compensation: Research and practice. In M. D. Dunnette & L. M. Hough (Eds.), *Handbook of industrial and organizational psychology* (2nd ed., Vol. 3, pp. 481–569). Palo Alto, CA: Consulting Psychologists Press.

Gerstner, C. R., & Day, D. V. (1997). Meta-analytic review of leader–member exchange theory: Correlations and construct issues. *Journal of Applied Psychology, 82,* 827–844.

Ghiselli, E. E., & Brown, C. W. (1955). *Personnel and industrial psychology.* New York: McGraw-Hill.

Gibson, C. B. (2001). From knowledge accumulation to accommodation: Cycles of collective cognition in work groups. *Journal of Organizational Behavior, 22,* 121–134.

Gilliland, S. W. (1993). The perceived fairness of selection systems: An organizational justice perspective. *Academy of Management Review, 18,* 694–734.

Goktepe, J. R., & Schneier, C. E. (1989). Role of sex, gender roles, and attraction in predicting emergent leaders. *Journal of Applied Psychology, 74,* 165–167.

Goldberg, S. L., Mastaglio, T. W., & Johnson, W. R. (1995). Training in the close combat tactical trainer. In R. J. Seidel & P. R. Chatelier (Eds.), *Learning without boundaries: Technology to support distance/distributed learning* (pp. 119–133). New York: Plenum.

Goldstein, I. L. (1978). The pursuit of validity in the evaluation of training programs. *Human Factors, 20,* 131–144.

Goldstein, I. L. (1980). Training in work organizations. *Annual Review of Psychology, 31,* 229–272.

Goldstein, I. L. (1991). Training in work organizations. In M. D. Dunnette & L. M. Hough (Eds.), *Handbook of industrial and organizational psychology* (2nd ed., Vol. 2, pp. 507–619). Palo Alto, CA: Consulting Psychologists Press.

Goldstein, I. L., & Ford, J. K. (2002). *Training in organizations* (4th ed.). Belmont, CA: Wadsworth.

Goldstein, I. L., & Gilliam, P. (1990). Training system issues in the year 2000. *American Psychologist, 45,* 134–143.

Goldstein, I. L., Zedeck, S., & Schneider, B. (1993). An exploration of the job analysis–content validity process. In N. Schmitt & W. C. Borman (Eds.), *Personnel selection in organizations* (pp. 3–34). San Francisco: Jossey-Bass.

Goleman, D. (1995). *Emotional intelligence.* New York: Bantam.

Goleman, D. (1998). *Working with emotional intelligence.* New York: Bantam.

Golembiewski, R. T., & Proehl, C. W. (1978). A survey of the empirical literature on flexible workhours: Character and consequences of a major innovation. *Academy of Management Review, 3,* 837–853.

Gomez-Mejia, L. R., & Balkin, D. B. (1984). Faculty satisfaction with pay and other job dimensions under union and nonunion conditions. *Academy of Management Journal, 27,* 591–602.

Gomez-Mejia, L. R., Page, R. C., & Tornow, W. W. (1982). A comparison of the practical utility of traditional, statistical, and hybrid job evaluation approaches. *Academy of Management Journal, 25,* 790–809.

Gordon, M. E., & Bowlby, R. L. (1988). Propositions about grievance settlements: Finally, consultation with grievants. *Personnel Psychology, 41,* 107–124.

Gordon, M. E., & Bowlby, R. L. (1989). Reactance and intentionality attributions as determinants of the intent to file a grievance. *Personnel Psychology, 42,* 309–330.

Gordon, M. E., & Ladd, R. T. (1990). Dual allegiance: Renewal, reconsideration, and recantation. *Personnel Psychology, 43,* 37–69.

Gordon, M. E., & Miller, S. J. (1984). Grievances: A review of research and practice. *Personnel Psychology, 37,* 117–146.

Gordon, M. E., Philpot, J. W., Burt, R. E., Thompson, C. A., & Spiller, W. E. (1980). Commitment to the union: Development of a measure and an examination of its correlates. *Journal of Applied Psychology, 65,* 479–499.

Gordon, M. E., Schmitt, N., & Schneider, W. G. (1984). Laboratory research on bargaining and negotiations: An evaluation. *Industrial Relations, 23,* 218–233.

Gottfredson, L. S. (1994). The science and politics of race norming. *American Psychologist, 49,* 955–963.

Gottlieb, B. H., Kelloway, E. K., & Barham, E. (1998). *Flexible work arrangements.* Chichester: Wiley.

Gowan, M. A., Riordan, C. M., & Gatewood, K. D. (1999). Test of a model of coping with involuntary job loss following a company closing. *Journal of Applied Psychology, 84,* 75–86.

Graen, G. B., & Scandura, T. A. (1987). Toward a psychology of dyadic organizing. In B. M. Staw & L. L. Cummings (Eds.), *Research in organizational behavior* (Vol. 9, pp. 175–208). Greenwich, CT: JAI Press.

Graen, G. B., & Wakabayashi, M. (1994). Cross-cultural leadership making: Bridging American and Japanese diversity for team advantage. In H. C. Triandis, M. D. Dunnette, & L. M. Hough (Eds.), *Handbook of industrial and organizational psychology* (2nd ed., Vol. 4, pp. 415–446). Palo Alto, CA: Consulting Psychologists Press.

Graham, D. (2000). *Online recruiting.* Palo Alto, CA: Davies-Black.

Granrose, C. S. (2000). Alternative ways of describing time in cross-cultural careers research. In C. L. Cooper & D. M. Rousseau (Eds.), *Trends in organizational behavior* (Vol. 7, pp. 45–61). Chichester: Wiley.

Green, S. G., & Nebeker, D. M. (1977). The effects of situational factors and leadership style on leader behavior. *Organizational Behavior and Human Performance, 19,* 368–377.

Greenberg, J. (1986). Determinants of perceived fairness of performance evaluations. *Journal of Applied Psychology, 71,* 340–342.

Greenberg, J. (1988). Equity and workplace status: A field experiment. *Journal of Applied Psychology, 73,* 606–613.

Greenberg, J. (1990). Employee theft as a reaction to underpayment inequity: The hidden costs of pay cuts. *Journal of Applied Psychology, 75,* 561–568.

Greenberg, J. (1993). The social side of fairness: Interpersonal and informational classes of organizational justice. In R. Cropanzano (Ed.), *Justice in the workplace: Approaching fairness in human resource management* (pp. 79–103). Hillsdale, NJ: Erlbaum.

Greenberg, J. (1994). Using socially fair treatment to promote acceptance of a work site smoking ban. *Journal of Applied Psychology, 79,* 288–297.

Greenberg, J., & Scott, K. S. (1996). Why do workers bite the hands that feed them? Employee theft as a social exchange process. In B. M. Staw & L. L. Cummings (Eds.), *Research in organizational behavior* (Vol. 18, pp. 111–156). Greenwich, CT: JAI Press.

Greenberg, L., & Barling, J. (1999). Predicting employee aggression against coworkers, subordinates, and supervisors: The roles of person behaviors and perceived workplace factors. *Journal of Organizational Behavior, 20,* 897–913.

Greene, C. N., & Schriesheim, C. A. (1980). Leader–group interactions: A longitudinal field investigation. *Journal of Applied Psychology, 65,* 50–59.

Greguras, G. J., & Robie, C. (1998). A new look at within-source interrater reliability of 360-degree feedback ratings. *Journal of Applied Psychology, 83,* 960–968.

Grigsby, D. M., & Bigoness, W. J. (1982). Effects of mediation and alternative forms of arbitration on bargaining behavior: A laboratory study. *Journal of Applied Psychology, 67,* 549–554.

Grover, S. L., & Crooker, K. J. (1995). Who appreciates family-responsive human resource policies: The impact of family-friendly policies on the organizational attachment of parents and non-parents. *Personnel Psychology, 48,* 271–288.

Guion, R. M. (1998a). *Assessment, measurement, and prediction for personnel decisions.* Mahwah, NJ: Erlbaum.

Guion, R. M. (1998b). Some virtues of dissatisfaction in the science and practice of personnel selection. *Human Resource Management Review, 8,* 351–366.

Gunter, B., Furnham, A., & Drakeley, R. (1993). *Biodata: Biographical indicators of business performance.* London: Routledge.

Gutek, B. A. (1985). *Sex and the workplace.* San Francisco: Jossey-Bass.

Guzzo, R. A. (1995). Introduction: At the intersection of team effectiveness and decision making. In R. A. Guzzo & E. Salas (Eds.), *Team effectiveness and decision making in organizations* (pp. 1–8). San Francisco: Jossey-Bass.

Guzzo, R. A., Jette, R. D., & Katzell, R. A. (1985). The effects of psychologically based intervention programs on worker productivity: A meta-analysis. *Personnel Psychology, 38,* 275–291.

Guzzo, R. A., & Shea, G. P. (1992). Group performance and intergroup relations in organizations. In M. D. Dunnette & L. M. Hough (Eds.), *Handbook of industrial and organizational psychology* (2nd ed., Vol. 3, pp. 269–313). Palo Alto, CA: Consulting Psychologists Press.

Hackett, G. (1995). Self-efficacy in career choice and development. In A. Bandura (Ed.), *Self-efficacy in changing societies* (pp. 232–258). New York: Cambridge.

Hackman, J. R., & Oldham, G. R. (1976). Motivation through the design of work: Test of a theory. *Organizational Behavior and Human Performance, 16,* 250–279.

Hahn, D. C., & Dipboye, R. L. (1988). Effects of training and information on the accuracy and reliability of job evaluations. *Journal of Applied Psychology, 73,* 146–153.

Haladyna, T. M. (1999). *Developing and validating multiple-choice test items* (2nd ed.). Mahwah, NJ: Erlbaum.

Hall, D. T., & Mirvis, P. H. (1995). Careers as lifelong learning. In A. Howard (Ed.), *The changing nature of work* (pp. 323–381). San Francisco: Jossey-Bass.

Hall, G. S. (1917). Practical relations between psychology and the war. *Journal of Applied Psychology, 1,* 9–16.

Hall, G. S., Baird, J. W., & Geissler, L. R. (1917). Foreword. *Journal of Applied Psychology, 1,* 5–7.

Hammer, T. H., & Berman, M. (1981). The role of noneconomic factors in faculty union voting. *Journal of Applied Psychology, 66,* 415–421.

Hamner, W. C., & Smith, F. J. (1978). Work attitudes as predictors of unionization activity. *Journal of Applied Psychology, 63,* 415–421.

Handbook of human engineering data. (1949). Medford, MA: Tufts College and United States Naval Training Devices Center.

Haney, W. (1981). Validity, vaudeville, and values: A short history of social concerns over standardized testing. *American Psychologist, 36,* 1021–1034.

Harmon, L. W. (1991). Twenty years of the *Journal of Vocational Behavior. Journal of Vocational Behavior, 39,* 297–304.

Harrell, T. W. (1992). Some history of the Army General Classification Test. *Journal of Applied Psychology, 77,* 875–878.

Harris, L. (2000). Procedural justice and perceptions of fairness in selection practice. *International Journal of Selection and Assessment, 8,* 148–157.

Harris, M. M., Smith, D. E., & Champagne, D. (1995). A field study of performance appraisal purpose: Research- versus administrative-based ratings. *Personnel Psychology, 48,* 151–160.

Harris, M. M., & Trusty, M. L. (1997). Drug and alcohol programs in the workplace: A review of recent literature. In C. L. Cooper & I. T. Robertson (Eds.), *International review of industrial and organizational psychology* (Vol. 12, pp. 289–316). New York: Wiley.

Hartley, J. F. (1992). The psychology of industrial relations. In C. L. Cooper & I. T. Robertson (Eds.), *International review of industrial and organizational psychology* (Vol. 7, pp. 201–243). London: Wiley.

Harvey, R. J. (1991). Job analysis. In M. D. Dunnette & L. M. Hough (Eds.), *Handbook of industrial and organizational psychology* (2nd ed., Vol. 2, pp. 71–163). Palo Alto, CA: Consulting Psychologists Press.

Harvey, R. J., & Lozada-Larsen, S. R. (1988). Influence of amount of job descriptive information on job analysis rating accuracy. *Journal of Applied Psychology, 73,* 457–461.

Hattrup, K., Rock, J., & Scalia, C. (1997). The effects of varying conceptualizations of job performance on adverse impact, minority hiring, and predicted performance. *Journal of Applied Psychology, 82,* 656–664.

Hauerstein, N. M. (1998). Training raters to increase the accuracy of appraisals and the usefulness of feedback. In J. W. Smither (Ed.), *Performance appraisal* (pp. 404–444). San Francisco: Jossey-Bass.

Havel, V. (1994, July 8). The new measure of man. *The New York Times,* p. A27.

Hawk, R. H. (1967). *The recruitment function.* New York: AMACOM.

Hazer, J. T., & Highhouse, S. (1997). Factors influencing managers' reactions to utility analysis: Effects of SD_y, method, information frame, and focal intervention. *Journal of Applied Psychology, 82,* 104–112.

Hedge, A., Erickson, W. A., & Rubin, G. (1992). Effects of personal and organizational factors on sick building syndrome in air-conditioned offices. In J. C. Quick, L. R. Murphy, & J. J. Hurrell (Eds.), *Stress and well-being at work* (pp. 286–298). Washington, DC: American Psychological Association.

Hedge, J. W., & Kavanagh, M. J. (1988). Improving the accuracy of performance evaluations: Comparison of three methods of performance appraisal training. *Journal of Applied Psychology, 73,* 68–73.

Hedlund, J., & Sternberg, R. J. (2000). Practical intelligence: Implications for human resources research. In G. R. Ferris (Ed.), *Research in personnel and human resources management* (Vol. 19, pp. 1–52). New York: Elsevier.

Heilman, M. E. (1996). Affirmative actions' contradictory consequences. *Journal of Social Issues, 52*(4), 105–109.

Heilman, M. E., & Alcott, V. B. (2001). What I think you think of me: Women's reactions to being viewed as beneficiaries of preferential selection. *Journal of Applied Psychology, 86,* 574–582.

Heilman, M. E., Block, C. J., & Lucas, J. A. (1992). Presumed incompetent? Stigmatization and affirmative action efforts. *Journal of Applied Psychology, 77,* 536–544.

Heilman, M. E., & Herlihy, J. M. (1984). Affirmative action, negative reaction? Some moderating considerations. *Organizational Behavior and Human Performance, 33,* 204–213.

Heilman, M. E., McCullough, W. F., & Gilbert, D. (1996). The other side of affirmative action: Reactions of nonbeneficiaries to sex-based preferential selection. *Journal of Applied Psychology, 81,* 346–357.

Heilman, M. E., Simon, M. C., & Repper, D. P. (1987). Intentionally favored, unintentionally harmed? Impact of sex-based preferential selection in self-perceptions and self-evaluations. *Journal of Applied Psychology, 72,* 62–68.

Hemphill, H., & Haines, R. (1997). *Discrimination, harassment, and the failure of diversity training.* Westport, CT: Quorum.

Heneman, R. L., & Greenberger, D. B. (Eds.) (2002). *Human resource management in virtual organizations*. Greenwich, CT: Information Age.

Hermans, H. J., & Kempen, H. J. (1998). Moving cultures: The perilous problems of cultural dichotomies in a globalizing society. *American Psychologist, 53*, 1111–1120.

Hesketh, B., & Bochner, S. (1994). Technological change in a multicultural context: Implications for training and career planning. In H. C. Triandis, M. D. Dunnette, & L. M. Hough (Eds.), *Handbook of industrial and organizational psychology* (2nd ed., Vol. 4, pp. 191–240). Palo Alto, CA: Consulting Psychologists Press.

Hicks, W. D., & Klimoski, R. J. (1981). The impact of flexi-time on employee attitudes. *Academy of Management Journal, 24*, 333–341.

Highhouse, S. (1999). The brief history of personnel counseling in industrial-organizational psychology. *Journal of Vocational Behavior, 55*, 318–336.

Highhouse, S., Stierwalt, S., Bachiochi, P., Elder, A. E., & Fisher, G. (1999). Effects of advertised human resource management practices on attraction of African American applicants. *Personnel Psychology, 52*, 425–442.

Hoffman, C. C. (1999). Generalizing physical ability test validity: A case study using test transportability, validity generalization, and construct-related validation evidence. *Personnel Psychology, 52*, 1019–1041.

Hoffman, C. C., Holden, L. M., & Gale, K. (2000). So many jobs, so little "N": Applying expanded validation methods to support generalization of cognitive test validity. *Personnel Psychology, 53*, 955–991.

Hoffman, C. C., & McPhail, S. M. (1998). Exploring options for supporting test use in situations precluding local validation. *Personnel Psychology, 51*, 987–1003.

Hoffman, C. C., & Thornton, G. C. (1997). Examining selection utility where competing predictors differ in adverse impact. *Personnel Psychology, 50*, 455–470.

Hoffman, M. A. (1997). HIV disease and work: Effect on the individual, workplace, and interpersonal contexts. *Journal of Vocational Behavior, 51*, 163–201.

Hoffman, P. J. (1980). On the establishment of an appropriate length for the EPPP. *Professional Psychology, 11*, 784–791.

Hofmann, D. A., Jacobs, R., & Baratta, J. E. (1993). Dynamic criteria and the measurement of change. *Journal of Applied Psychology, 78*, 194–204.

Hofstee, W. K. (2001). Intelligence and personality: Do they mix? In J. M. Collis & S. Messick (Eds.), *Intelligence and personality: Bridging the gap in theory and measurement* (pp. 43–60). Mahwah, NJ: Erlbaum.

Hogan, E. A., & Overmyer-Day, L. (1994). The psychology of mergers and acquisitions. In C. L. Cooper & I. T. Robertson (Eds.), *International review of industrial and organizational psychology* (pp. 247–281). London: Wiley.

Hogan, J. (1991a). Physical abilities. In M. D. Dunnette & L. M. Hough (Eds.), *Handbook of industrial and organizational psychology* (2nd ed., Vol. 2, pp. 753–831). Palo Alto, CA: Consulting Psychologists Press.

Hogan, J. (1991b). Structure of physical performance in organizational tasks. *Journal of Applied Psychology, 76*, 495–507.

Hogan, J., & Brinkmeyer, K. (1997). Bridging the gap between overt and personality-based integrity tests. *Personnel Psychology, 50*, 587–600.

Hogan, J., & Hogan, R. T. (Eds.). (1990). *Business and industry testing: Current practices and reviews*. Austin, TX: Pro-Ed.

Hogan, R. T. (1991). Personality and personality measurement. In M. D. Dunnette & L. M. Hough (Eds.), *Handbook of industrial and organizational psychology* (2nd ed., Vol. 2, pp. 873–919). Palo Alto, CA: Consulting Psychologists Press.

Hogan, R. T., Curphy, G. J., & Hogan, J. (1994). What we know about leadership: Effectiveness and personality. *American Psychologist, 49*, 493–504.

Hogan, R. T., & Hogan, J. (1992). *Hogan Personality Inventory*. Tulsa, OK: Hogan Assessment Systems.

Hogan, R. T., Hogan, J., & Roberts, B. W. (1996). Personality measurement and employment decisions: Questions and answers. *American Psychologist, 51*, 469–477.

Hogan, R. T., Raskin, R., & Fazzini, D. (1990). The dark side of charisma. In K. E. Clark & M. B. Clark (Eds.), *Measures of leadership*. West Orange, NJ: Leadership Library of America.

Hogan, R. T., & Sinclair, R. (1996). Intellectual, ideological, and political obstacles to the advancement of organizational service. *Journal of Applied Behavioral Science, 32*, 378–389.

Hollenbeck, J. R., LePine, J. A., & Ilgen, D. R. (1996). Adapting to roles in decision-making teams. In K. R. Murphy (Ed.), *Individual differences and behaviors in organizations* (pp. 300–333). San Francisco: Jossey-Bass.

Hollenbeck, J. R., Williams, C. R., & Klein, H. J. (1989). An empirical examination of the antecedents of commitment to difficult goals. *Journal of Applied Psychology, 74*, 18–23.

Hollinger, R. C. (1988). Working under the influence (WUI): Correlates of employees' use of alcohol and other drugs. *Journal of Applied Behavioral Science, 24*, 439–454.

Hollinger, R., & Clark, J. (1983). *Theft by employees*. Lexington, MA: Lexington Books.

Holzbach, R. L. (1978). Rater bias in performance ratings: Superior, self-, and peer assessments. *Journal of Applied Psychology, 63*, 579–588.

Hom, P. W., & Griffeth, R. W. (1995). *Employee turnover*. Cincinnati, OH: South-Western.

Honts, C. R. (1991). The emperor's new clothes: Application of polygraph tests in the American workplace. *Forensic Reports, 4*, 91–116.

House, R. J. (1971). A path-goal theory of leader effectiveness. *Administrative Science Quarterly, 16*, 321–338.

House, R. J. (1977). A 1976 theory of charismatic leadership. In J. G. Hunt & L. L. Larson (Eds.), *Leadership: The cutting edge*. Carbondale, IL: Southern Illinois University Press.

House, R. J., Spangler, W. D., & Woycke, J. (1991). Personality and charisma in the U.S. presidency: A psychological theory of leader effectiveness. *Administrative Science Quarterly, 36*, 364–396.

House, R. J., Wright, N. S., & Aditya, R. N. (1997). Cross-cultural research on organizational leadership: A critical analysis and a proposed theory. In P. C. Earley & M. Erez (Eds.), *New perspectives on international industrial/organizational psychology* (pp. 535–625). San Francisco: New Lexington Press.

Howard, A., & Lowman, R. L. (1985). Should industrial/organizational psychologists be licensed? *American Psychologist, 40,* 40–47.

Howell, J. P., & Dorfman, P. W. (1981). Substitutes for leadership: Test of a construct. *Academy of Management Journal, 24,* 714–728.

Howell, W. C., & Cooke, N. J. (1989). Training the human information processor: A review of cognitive models. In I. L. Goldstein (Ed.), *Training and development in organizations* (pp. 121–182). San Francisco: Jossey-Bass.

Huffcutt, A. I., Conway, J. M., Roth, P. L., & Stone, N. J. (2001). Identification and meta-analytic assessment of psychological constructs measured in employment interviews. *Journal of Applied Psychology, 86,* 897–913.

Huffcutt, A. I., & Roth, P. L. (1998). Racial group differences in employment interview evaluations. *Journal of Applied Psychology, 83,* 179–189.

Huffcutt, A. I., & Woehr, D. J. (1999). Further analysis of employment interview validity: A quantitative evaluation of interviewer-related structuring methods. *Journal of Organizational Behavior, 20,* 549–560.

Hui, C., Lam, S. S., & Law, K. S. (2000). Instrumental values of organizational citizenship behavior for promotion: A field quasi-experiment. *Journal of Applied Psychology, 85,* 822–828.

Hulin, C. (1991). Adaptation, persistence, and commitment in organizations. In M. D. Dunnette & L. M. Hough (Eds.), *Handbook of industrial and organizational psychology* (2nd ed., Vol. 2, pp. 445–505). Palo Alto, CA: Consulting Psychologists Press.

Hulin, C. (2001). Applied psychology and science: Differences between research and practice. *Applied Psychology: An International Review, 50,* 225–234.

Hulin, C. L., Henry, R. A., & Noon, S. L. (1990). Adding a dimension: Time as a factor in the generalizability of predictive relationships. *Psychological Bulletin, 107,* 328–340.

Hunt, D. M., & Michael, C. (1983). Mentorship: A career training and development tool. *Academy of Management Review, 8,* 475–485.

Hunter, J. E. (1986). Cognitive ability, cognitive aptitudes, job knowledge, and job performance. *Journal of Vocational Behavior, 29,* 340–362.

Hunter, J. E., & Hunter, R. F. (1984). Validity and utility of alternative predictors of job performance. *Psychological Bulletin, 96,* 72–98.

Hunter, J. E., & Schmidt, F. L. (1990). *Method of meta-analysis: Correcting error and bias in research findings.* Newbury Park, CA: Sage.

Hunter, J. E., & Schmidt, F. L. (1996). Cumulative research knowledge and social policy formation: The critical role of meta-analysis. *Psychology, Public Policy, and Law, 2,* 324–347.

Hurtz, G. M., & Donovan, J. J. (2000). Personality and job performance: The big five revisited. *Journal of Applied Psychology, 85,* 869–879.

Huseman, R. C., Hatfield, J. D., & Miles, E. W. (1987). A new perspective on equity theory: The equity sensitivity construct. *Academy of Management Review, 12,* 222–234.

Huszczo, G. E., Wiggins, J. G., & Currie, J. S. (1984). The relationship between psychology and organized labor: Past, present and future. *American Psychologist, 39,* 432–440.

Iacono, W. G., & Lykken, D. T. (1997). The validity of the lie detector: Two surveys of scientific opinion. *Journal of Applied Psychology, 82,* 426–433.

Iaffaldano, M. T., & Muchinsky, P. M. (1985). Job satisfaction and performance: A meta-analysis. *Psychological Bulletin, 97,* 251–273.

Ilgen, D. R. (1990). Health issues at work: Opportunities for industrial/organizational psychology. *American Psychologist, 45,* 273–283.

Ilgen, D. R. (1999). Teams embedded in organizations: Some implications. *American Psychologist, 54,* 129–139.

Ilgen, D. R., Barnes-Farrell, J. L., & McKellin, D. B. (1993). Performance appraisal process research in the 1980s: What has it contributed to appraisals in use? *Organizational Behavior and Human Decision Processes, 54,* 321–368.

Ilgen, D. R., Fisher, C. D., & Taylor, M. S. (1979). Motivational consequences of individual feedback on behavior in organizations. *Journal of Applied Psychology, 64,* 349–371.

Ilgen, D. R., Peterson, R. B., Martin, B. A., & Boeschen, D. A. (1981). Supervisor and subordinate reactions to performance appraisal sessions. *Organizational Behavior and Human Performance, 28,* 311–330.

Jackson, S. E., & Schuler, R. S. (1990). Human resource planning. *American Psychologist, 45,* 223–239.

Jahoda, M. (1981). Work, employment, and unemployment: Values, theories and approaches in social research. *American Psychologist, 36,* 184–191.

Jamal, M. (1981). Shift work related to job attitudes, social participation, and withdrawal behavior. A study of nurses and industrial workers. *Personnel Psychology, 34,* 535–548.

Jamal, M., & Jamal, S. M. (1982). Work and nonwork experiences of employees on fixed and rotating shifts: An empirical assessment. *Journal of Vocational Behavior, 20,* 282–293.

Jansen, P. G., & Stoop, B. A. (2001). The dynamics of assessment center validity: Results of a 7-year study. *Journal of Applied Psychology, 86,* 741–753.

Janz, B. D., Colquitt, J. A., & Noe, R. A. (1997). Knowledge worker team effectiveness: The role of autonomy, interdependence, team development, and contextual support variables. *Personnel Psychology, 50,* 877–904.

Jarrell, S. B., & Stanley, T. D. (1990). A meta-analysis of the union–nonunion wage gap. *Industrial and Labor Relations Review, 44,* 54–67.

Jawahar, I. M., & Williams, C. R. (1997). Where all the children are above average: The performance appraisal purpose effect. *Personnel Psychology, 50,* 905–925.

Jehn, K. A., Northcraft, G. B., & Neale, M. A. (1999). Why differences make a difference: A field study of diversity, conflict, and performance in workgroups. *Administrative Science Quarterly, 44,* 741–763.

Jelley, R. B., & Goffin, R. D. (2001). Can performance-feedback accuracy be improved? Effects of rater priming and rating-scale format on rating accuracy. *Journal of Applied Psychology, 86,* 134–144.

Jemison, D. B., & Sitkin, S. B. (1986). Corporate acquisitions: A process perspective. *Academy of Management Review, 11,* 145–163.

Jenkins, J. G. (1946). Validity for what? *Journal of Consulting Psychology, 10,* 93–98.

Johns, G. (1994). How often were you absent? A review of the use of self-reported absence data. *Journal of Applied Psychology, 79,* 574–591.

Johns, G. (1997). Contemporary research on absence from work: Correlates, causes, and consequences. In C. L. Cooper & I. T. Robertson (Eds.), *International review of industrial and organizational psychology* (Vol. 12, pp. 115–173). Chichester: Wiley.

Johnson, P. R., & Indvik, J. (1994). Workplace violence: An issue of the nineties. *Public Personnel Management, 23,* 515–523.

Jones, N. (1994). The alcohol and drug provisions of the ADA: Implications for employers and employees. In S. M. Bruyere & J. O'Keeffe (Eds.), *Implications of the Americans with Disabilities Act for psychology* (pp. 151–168). New York: Springer.

Jonson, J. L., & Plake, B. S. (1998). A historical comparison of validity standards and validity practices. *Educational and Psychological Measurement, 58,* 736–753.

Joure, S. A., Leon, J. S., Simpson, D. B., Holley, G. H., & Frye, R. L. (1989, March). Stress: The pressure cooker of work. *The Personnel Administrator, 34,* 92–95.

Judge, T. A., & Bono, J. E. (2000). Five-factor model of personality and transformational leadership. *Journal of Applied Psychology, 85,* 751–765.

Judge, T. A., Bono, J. E., & Locke, E. A. (2000). Personality and job satisfaction: The mediating role of job characteristics. *Journal of Applied Psychology, 85,* 237–249.

Judge, T. A., Higgins, C. A., & Cable, D. M. (2000). The employment interview: A review of recent research and recommendations for future research. *Human Resource Management Review, 10,* 383–406.

Judge, T. A., Higgins, C. A., Thoresen, C. J., & Barrick, M. R. (1999). The big five personality traits, general mental ability, and career success across the life span. *Personnel Psychology, 52,* 621–652.

Judge, T. A., Thoresen, C. J., Bono, J. E., & Patton, G. K. (2001). The job satisfaction–job performance relationship: A qualitative and quantitative review. *Psychological Bulletin, 127,* 376–407.

Kabanoff, B. (1997). Organizational justice across cultures: Integrating organization-level and culture-level perspectives. In P. C. Earley & M. Erez (Eds.), *New perspectives on international industrial/organizational psychology* (pp. 676–712). San Francisco: New Lexington Press.

Kagitcibasi, C., & Berry, J. W. (1989). Cross-cultural psychology: Current research and trends. *Annual Review of Psychology, 40,* 493–531.

Kahn, R. L., & Byosiere, P. B. (1992). Stress in organizations. In M. D. Dunnette & L. M. Hough (Eds.), *Handbook of industrial and organizational psychology* (2nd ed., Vol. 3, pp. 571–650). Palo Alto, CA: Consulting Psychologists Press.

Kane, J. S., Bernardin, H. J., Villanova, P., & Peyrefitte, J. (1995). Stability of rater leniency: Three studies. *Academy of Management Journal, 38,* 1036–1051.

Kane, J. S., & Lawler, E. E. (1978). Methods of peer assessment. *Psychological Bulletin, 85,* 555–586.

Kanfer, R. (1992). Work motivation: New directions in theory and research. In C. L. Cooper & I. T. Robertson (Eds.), *International review of industrial and organizational psychology* (Vol. 7, pp. 1–53). London: Wiley.

Kanfer, R., & Ackerman, P. L. (1989). Motivation and cognitive abilities: An integrative/aptitude–treatment interaction approach to skill acquisition. *Journal of Applied Psychology, 74,* 657–690.

Kanfer, R., & Ackerman, P. L. (2000). Individual differences in work motivation: Further explorations of a trait framework. *Applied Psychology: An International Review, 49,* 470–482.

Kanfer, R., & Heggestad, E. D. (1997). Motivational traits and skills: A person-centered approach to work motivation. In B. M. Staw & L. L. Cummings (Eds.), *Research in organizational behavior* (Vol. 19, pp. 1–56). Greenwich, CT: JAI Press.

Kanter, R. M. (1977). *Work and family in the United States: A critical review and agenda for research and policy.* New York: Russell Sage Foundation.

Kanungo, R. N. (1982). Measurement of job and work involvement. *Journal of Applied Psychology, 67,* 341–349.

Karambayya, R., & Reilly, A. H. (1992). Dual earner couples: Attitudes and actions restructuring work for family. *Journal of Organizational Behavior, 13,* 585–601.

Karau, S. J., & Williams, K. D. (2001). Understanding individual motivation in groups: The collective effort model. In M. E. Turner (Ed.), *Groups at work* (pp. 113–142). Mahwah, NJ: Erlbaum.

Kast, F. E., & Rosenzweig, J. E. (1972). General systems theory: Applications for organization and management. *Academy of Management Journal, 15,* 444–465.

Katz, D., & Kahn, R. L. (1978). *The social psychology of organizations.* New York: Wiley.

Katzell, R. A. (1994). Contemporary meta-trends in industrial and organizational psychology. In H. C. Triandis, M. D. Dunnette, & L. M. Hough (Eds.), *Handbook of industrial and organizational psychology* (2nd ed., Vol. 4, pp. 1–89). Palo Alto, CA: Consulting Psychologists Press.

Katzell, R. A., & Austin, J. T. (1992). From then to now: The development of industrial-organizational psychology in the United States. *Journal of Applied Psychology, 77,* 803–835.

Katzell, R. A., & Guzzo, R. A. (1983). Psychological approaches to productivity improvement. *American Psychologist, 38,* 468–472.

Katzell, R. A., & Thompson, D. E. (1990). Work motivation: Theory and practice. *American Psychologist, 45,* 144–153.

Keeping, L. M., & Levy, P. E. (2000). Performance appraisal reaction: Measurement, modeling, and method bias. *Journal of Applied Psychology, 85,* 708–723.

Keinan, G., & Eilat-Greenberg, S. (1993). Can stress be measured by handwriting analysis? The effectiveness of the analytic method. *Applied Psychology: An International Review, 42*, 153–170.

Kelleher, M. D. (1996). *New arenas for violence: Homicide in the American workplace.* Westport, CT: Praeger.

Kelloway, E. K., Catano, V. M., & Carroll, A. E. (1995). The nature of member participation in local union activities. In L. E. Tetrick & J. Barling (Eds.), *Changing employment relations* (pp. 333–348). Washington, DC: American Psychological Association.

Kelly, J. E., & Kelly, C. (1991). "Them and us": Social psychology and "The new industrial relations." *British Journal of Industrial Relations, 29*, 25–48.

Kennedy, C. W., Fossum, J. A., & White, B. J. (1983). An empirical comparison of within-subjects and between-subjects expectancy theory models. *Organizational Behavior and Human Performance, 32*, 124–143.

Kerr, S. (1995). On the folly of rewarding A, while hoping for B. *Academy of Management Executive, 9*, 7–14.

Kerr, S., & Jermier, J. M. (1978). Substitutes for leadership: Their meaning and measurement. *Organizational Behavior and Human Performance, 22*, 375–403.

Kets de Vries, M. F. (1999). Organizational sleepwalkers: Emotional distress at midlife. *Human Relations, 52*, 1377–1401.

King, J. L., & Alexander, D. G. (1996). Unions respond to violence on the job. In G. R. VandenBos & E. Q. Bulatao (Eds.), *Violence on the job* (pp. 315–326). Washington, DC: American Psychological Association.

Kinicki, A. J., McKee, F. M., & Wade, K. H. (1996). Annual review, 1991–1995: Occupational health. *Journal of Vocational Behavior, 49*, 190–220.

Kirk, R. E. (1996). Practical significance: A concept whose time has come. *Educational and Psychological Measurement, 56*, 746–759.

Kirkpatrick, D. L. (1976). Evaluation of training. In R. L. Craig (Ed.), *Training and development handbook* (2nd ed.). New York: McGraw-Hill.

Kirkpatrick, S. A., & Locke, E. A. (1991). Leadership: Do traits matter? *Academy of Management Executive, 5*(2), 48–60.

Kivimaki, M., Vahtera, J., Thomson, L., Griffiths, A., Cox, T., & Pentti, J. (1997). Psychosocial factors predict employee sickness absence during economic decline. *Journal of Applied Psychology, 82*, 858–872.

Klaas, B. S. (1989). Managerial decision making about employee grievances: The impact of the grievant's work history. *Personnel Psychology, 42*, 53–68.

Klahr, D., & Simon, H. A. (1999). Studies of scientific discovery: Complementary approaches and convergent findings. *Psychological Bulletin, 125*, 524–543.

Klandermans, B. (1989). Union commitment: Replications and tests in the Dutch context. *Journal of Applied Psychology, 74*, 869–875.

Klein, H. J., & Weaver, N. A. (2000). The effectiveness of an organizational-level orientation training program in the socialization of new hires. *Personnel Psychology, 53*, 47–66.

Klein, H. J., Wesson, M. J., Hollenbeck, J. R., & Alge, B. J. (1999). Goal commitment and the goal-setting process: Conceptual clarification and empirical synthesis. *Journal of Applied Psychology, 84*, 885–896.

Klein, K. J., & Kozlowski, S. W. (2000). *Multilevel theory, research, and methods in organizations.* San Francisco: Jossey-Bass.

Kleinmann, M. (1993). Are rating dimensions in assessment centers transparent for participants? Consequences for criterion and construct validity. *Journal of Applied Psychology, 78*, 988–993.

Klimoski, R. J., & Brickner, M. (1987). Why do assessment centers work? The puzzle of assessment center validity. *Personnel Psychology, 40*, 243–260.

Klimoski, R. J., & Donahue, L. M. (2001). Person perception in organizations: An overview of the field. In M. London (Ed.), *How people evaluate others in organizations* (pp. 5–44). Mahwah, NJ: Erlbaum.

Klimoski, R. J., & Inks, L. (1990). Accountability forces in performance appraisal. *Organizational Behavior and Human Decision Processes, 45*, 194–208.

Klimoski, R. J., & Jones, R. G. (1995). Staffing for effective group decision making: Key issues in marketing people and teams. In R. A. Guzzo & E. Salas (Eds.), *Team effectiveness and decision making in organizations* (pp. 291–332). San Francisco: Jossey-Bass.

Klimoski, R. J., & Palmer, S. N. (1994). The ADA and the hiring process in organizations. In S. M. Bruyere & J. O'Keeffe (Eds.), *Implications of the Americans with Disabilities Act for psychology* (pp. 37–84). New York: Springer.

Klimoski, R. J., & Strickland, W. J. (1977). Assessment centers—Valid or merely prescient? *Personnel Psychology, 30*, 353–361.

Kluger, A. N. (2001). Feedback–expectation discrepancy, around and locus of cognition. In M. Erez, U. Kleinbeck, & H. Thierry (Eds.), *Work motivation in the context of a globalizing economy* (pp. 111–120). Mahwah, NJ: Erlbaum.

Kluger, A. N., & DeNisi, A. (1996). The effects of feedback interventions on performance: A historical review, a meta-analysis, and a preliminary feedback intervention theory. *Psychological Bulletin, 119*, 254–284.

Kluger, A. N., Reilly, R. R., & Russell, C. J. (1991). Faking biodata tests: Are option-keyed instruments more resistant? *Journal of Applied Psychology, 76*, 889–896.

Knauth, P. (1996). Designing better shift systems. *Applied Ergonomics, 27*, 39–44.

Kogi, K. (1996). Improving shift workers' health and tolerance to shiftwork: Recent advances. *Applied Ergonomics, 27*, 5–8.

Kohn, L. S., & Dipboye, R. L. (1998). The effects of interview structure on recruiting outcomes. *Journal of Applied Social Psychology, 28*, 821–843.

Komaki, J. L. (1986). Toward effective supervision: An operant analysis and comparison of managers at work. *Journal of Applied Psychology, 71*, 270–279.

Komaki, J. L. (1998). When performance improvement is the goal: A new set of criteria for criteria. *Journal of Applied Behavior Analysis, 31*, 263–280.

Koppes, L. L. (1997). American female pioneers of industrial and organizational psychology during the early years. *Journal of Applied Psychology, 82,* 500–515.

Koppes, L. L. (2002). The rise of industrial-organizational psychology: A confluence of dynamic forces. In D. K. Freedheim (Ed.), *History of psychology.* New York: Wiley.

Kossek, E. E., & Ozeki, C. (1998). Work–family conflict, policies, and the job–life satisfaction relationship: A review and directions for organizational behavior–human resources research. *Journal of Applied Psychology, 83,* 139–149.

Kotter, J. P. (1988). *The leadership factor.* New York: Free Press.

Kotter, J. P., & Heskett, J. L. (1992). *Corporate culture and performance.* New York: Free Press.

Kouzes, J. M., & Posner, B. Z. (1995). *The leadership challenge.* San Francisco: Jossey-Bass.

Kozlowski, S. W., Chao, G. T., & Morrison, R. F. (1998). Games raters play: Politics, strategies, and impression management in performance appraisal. In J. W. Smither (Ed.), *Performance appraisal* (pp. 163–208). San Francisco: Jossey-Bass.

Kozlowski, S. W., Chao, G. T., Smith, E. M., & Hedlund, J. (1993). Organizational downsizing: Strategies, interventions, and research implications. In C. L. Cooper & I. T. Robertson (Eds.), *International review of industrial and organizational psychology* (Vol. 8, pp. 263–331). London: Wiley.

Kraiger, K., & Aguinis, H. (2001). Training effectiveness: Assessing training needs, motivation, and accomplishments. In M. London (Ed.), *How people evaluate others in organizations* (pp. 203–220). Mahwah, NJ: Erlbaum.

Kraiger, K., & Jung, K. M. (1997). Linking training objectives to evaluation criteria. In M. A. Quinones & A. Ehrenstein (Eds.), *Training for a rapidly changing workplace* (pp. 151–176). Washington, DC: American Psychological Association.

Kram, K. E., & Isabella, L. A. (1985). Alternatives to mentoring: The role of peer relationships in career development. *Academy of Management Journal, 28,* 110–132.

Krantz, J. (1985). Group processes under conditions of organizational decline. *Journal of Applied Behavioral Science, 21,* 1–17.

Kravitz, D. A., Harrison, D. A., Turner, M. E., Levine, E. L., Chaves, W., Brannick, M. T., Denning, D. L., Russell, C. J., & Conrad, M. A. (1997). *Affirmative action: A review of psychological and behavioral research.* Bowling Green, OH: Society for Industrial and Organizational Psychology.

Kravitz, D. A., & Klineberg, S. L. (2000). Reactions to two versions of affirmative action among whites, blacks, and Hispanics. *Journal of Applied Psychology, 85,* 597–611.

Kruml, S. M., & Geddes, D. (2000). Catching fire without burning out: Is there an ideal way to perform emotional labor? In N. M. Ashkanasy, C. E. J. Hortel, & W. J. Zerbe (Eds.), *Emotions in the workplace: Research, theory and practice* (pp. 177–188). Westport, CT: Quorum.

Ladd, R. T., Gordon, M. E., Beauvais, L. L., & Morgan, R. L. (1982). Union commitment: Replication and extension. *Journal of Applied Psychology, 67,* 640–644.

Lam, S. S., Hui, C., & Law, K. S. (1999). Organizational citizenship behavior: Comparing perspectives of supervisors and subordinates across four international samples. *Journal of Applied Psychology, 84,* 594–601.

Lance, C. E., LaPointe, J. A., & Fisicaro, S. A. (1994). Tests of three causal models of halo rater error. *Organizational Behavior and Human Decision Processes, 57,* 83–96.

Landy, F. J. (1992). Hugo Münsterberg: Victim or visionary? *Journal of Applied Psychology, 77,* 787–802.

Landy, F. J. (1997). Early influences on the development of industrial and organizational psychology. *Journal of Applied Psychology, 82,* 467–477.

Landy, F. J., & Trumbo, D. A. (1980). *Psychology of work behavior* (rev. ed.). Pacific Grove, CA: Brooks/Cole.

Landy, F. J., & Vasey, J. (1991). Job analysis: The composition of SME samples. *Personnel Psychology, 44,* 27–50.

Larson, C. E., & La Fasto, F. M. (1989). *Teamwork.* Newbury Park, CA: Sage.

Latham, G. P. (1986). Job performance and appraisal. In C. L. Cooper & I. T. Robertson (Eds.), *International review of industrial and organizational psychology* (Vol. 1, pp. 117–155). London: Wiley.

Latham, G. P. (2001). The reciprocal transfer of learning from journals to practice. *Applied Psychology: An International Review, 50,* 201–211.

Latham, G. P., & Baldes, J. J. (1975). The practical significance of Locke's theory of goal setting. *Journal of Applied Psychology, 60,* 122–124.

Latham, G. P., Fay, C. H., & Saari, L. M. (1979). The development of behavioral observation scales for appraising the performance of foremen. *Personnel Psychology, 32,* 299–311.

Latham, G. P., & Finnegan, B. J. (1993). Perceived practicality of instructional, patterned, and situational interviews. In H. Schuler, J. L. Farr, & M. Smith (Eds.), *Personnel selection and assessment* (pp. 41–56). Hillsdale, NJ: Erlbaum.

Latham, G. P., & Kinne, S. B. (1974). Improving job performance through training in goal setting. *Journal of Applied Psychology, 59,* 187–191.

Latham, G. P., & Locke, E. A. (1991). Self-regulation through goal-setting. *Organizational Behavior and Human Decision Processes, 50,* 212–247.

Latham, G. P., & Marshall, H. A. (1982). The effects of self-set, participatively set, and assigned goals on the performance of government employees. *Personnel Psychology, 35,* 399–404.

Latham, G. P., & Saari, L. M. (1979). The application of social learning theory to training supervisors through behavioral modeling. *Journal of Applied Psychology, 64,* 239–246.

Latham, G. P., Skarlicki, D., Irvine, D., & Siegel, J. P. (1993). The increasing importance of performance appraisals to employee effectiveness in organizational settings in North America. In C. L. Cooper & I. T. Robertson (Eds.), *International review of industrial and organizational psychology* (Vol. 8, pp. 87–132). London: Wiley.

Latham, G. P., & Wexley, K. N. (1977). Behavioral observation scales for performance appraisal purposes. *Personnel Psychology, 30,* 255–268.

Latham, G. P., Wexley, K. N., & Pursell, E. D. (1975). Training managers to minimize rating errors in the observation of behavior. *Journal of Applied Psychology, 60,* 550–555.

Lawler, E. E. (1982). Strategies for improving the quality of work life. *American Psychologist, 37,* 486–493.

Lawler, E. E., Mohrman, S. A., & Ledford, G. E. (1995). *Creating high performance organizations.* San Francisco: Jossey-Bass.

Lazarus, R. S., & Folkman, S. (1984). *Stress, appraisal, and coping.* New York: Springer.

Lazarus, R. S., & Lazarus, B. N. (1994). *Passion and reason: Making sense of our emotions.* New York: Oxford.

Lee, K., Carswell, J. J., & Allen, N. J. (2000). A meta-analytic review of organizational commitment: Relations with person- and work-related variables. *Journal of Applied Psychology, 85,* 799–811.

Lee, T. W., Mitchell, T. R., & Sablynski, C. J. (1999). Qualitative research in organizational and vocational psychology, 1979–1999. *Journal of Vocational Behavior, 55,* 161–187.

LePine, J. A., Hansom, M. A., Borman, W. C., & Motowidlo, S. J. (2000). Contextual performance and teamwork: Implications for staffing. In G. R. Ferris (Ed.), *Research in personnel and human resources management* (Vol. 19, pp. 53–90). New York: Elsevier.

Leung, K. (1997). Negotiation and reward allocations across cultures. In P. C. Earley & M. Erez (Eds.), *New perspectives on international industrial/organizational psychology* (pp. 640–675). San Francisco: New Lexington Press.

Leventhal, G. S. (1980). What should be done with equity theory? New approaches to the study of fairness in social relationships. In K. Gergen, M. M. Greenberg, & R. Willis (Eds.), *Social exchange: Advances in theory and research* (pp. 27–55). New York: Plenum.

Levine, E. L., Ash, R. A., Hall, H., & Sistrunk, F. (1983). Evaluation of job analysis methods by experienced job analysts. *Academy of Management Journal, 26,* 339–347.

Levine, E. L., Sistrunk, F., McNutt, K. J., & Gael, S. (1988). Exploring job analysis systems in selected organizations: A description of process and outcomes. *Journal of Business and Psychology, 3,* 3–21.

Liden, R. C., & Arad, S. (1996). A power perspective of empowerment and work groups: Implications for human resources management research. In G. R. Ferris (Ed.), *Research in personnel and human resources management* (Vol. 14, pp. 205–251). Greenwich, CT: JAI Press.

Liden, R. C., & Maslyn, J. M. (1998). Multidimensionality of leader–member exchange: An empirical assessment through scale development. *Journal of Management, 24,* 43–72.

Liden, R. C., Sparrowe, R. T., & Wayne, S. J. (1997). Leader–member exchange theory: The past and potential for the future. In G. R. Ferris (Ed.), *Research in personnel and human resources management* (Vol. 15, pp. 47–120). Greenwich, CT: JAI Press.

Liden, R. C., Wayne, S. J., & Sparrowe, R. T. (2000). An examination of the mediating role of psychological empowerment on the relations between the job, interpersonal relationships, and work outcomes. *Journal of Applied Psychology, 85,* 407–416.

Lind, E. A., & Tyler, T. R. (1988). *The social psychology of procedural justice.* New York: Plenum.

Lipnack, J. (2000). *Virtual teams: People working across boundaries with technology* (2nd ed.). New York: Wiley.

Lobel, S. A. (1993). Sexuality at work: Where do we go from here? *Journal of Vocational Behavior, 42,* 136–152.

Locke, E. A. (Ed.). (1985). *The generalizability of laboratory experiments: An inductive study.* Lexington, MA: D.C. Heath.

Locke, E. A. (1991). The motivation sequence, the motivation hub, and the motivation core. *Organizational Behavior and Human Decision Processes, 50,* 288–299.

Locke, E. A., Jirnauer, D., Roberson, Q., Goldman, B., Latham, M. E., & Weldon, E. (2001). The importance of the individual in an age of groupism. In M. E. Turner (Ed.), *Groups at work* (pp. 501–528). Mahwah, NJ: Erlbaum.

Locke, E. A., & Latham, G. P. (1990). *A theory of goal setting and task performance.* Englewood Cliffs, NJ: Prentice-Hall.

Locke, E. A., McClear, K., & Knight, D. (1996). Self-esteem and work. In C. L. Cooper & I. T. Robertson (Eds.), *International review of industrial and organizational psychology* (Vol. 11, pp. 1–32). Chichester: Wiley.

Locke, E. A., Shaw, K. N., Saari, L. M., & Latham, G. P. (1981). Goal setting and task performance: 1969–1980. *Psychological Bulletin, 90,* 125–152.

Loher, B. T., Noe, R. A., Moeller, N. L., & Fitzgerald, M. P. (1985). A meta-analysis of the relation of job characteristics to job satisfaction. *Journal of Applied Psychology, 70,* 280–289.

Lombardo, M. M., & McCauley, C. D. (1988). *The dynamics of management derailment* (Tech. Report No. 134). Greensboro, NC: Center for Creative Leadership.

London, M. (2001). Social cognition and person perception. In M. London (Ed.), *How people evaluate others in organizations* (pp. 1–3). Mahwah, NJ: Erlbaum.

London, M., & Bray, D. W. (1980). Ethical issues in testing and evaluation for personnel decisions. *American Psychologist, 35,* 890–901.

London, M., Smither, J. W., & Adsit, D. J. (1997). Accountability: The Achilles' heel of multisource feedback. *Group & Organization Management, 22,* 162–184.

Lord, R. G. (1985). An information processing approach to social perceptions, leadership, and behavioral measurement in organizations. In B. M. Staw & L. L. Cummings (Eds.), *Research in organizational behavior* (Vol. 7, pp. 87–128). Greenwich, CT: JAI Press.

Lord, R. G., Foti, R. J., & Phillips, J. S. (1982). A theory of leadership organization. In J. G. Hunt, U. Sekaran, & C. Schriesheim (Eds.), *Leadership: Beyond establishment views.* Carbondale, IL: Southern Illinois University.

Lord, R. G., & Hohenfeld, J. A. (1979). Longitudinal field assessment of equity effects in the performance of major league baseball players. *Journal of Applied Psychology, 64,* 19–26.

Lord, R. G., & Levy, P. E. (1994). Moving from cognition to action: A control theory perspective. *Applied Psychology: An International Review, 43,* 335–367.

Lowe, K. B., & Gardner, W. L. (2000). Ten years of the *Leadership Quarterly:* Contributions and challenges for the future. *Leadership Quarterly, 11,* 459–514.

Lowe, K. B., Kroeck, K. G., & Sivasubramaniam, N. (1996). Effectiveness correlates of transformational and transactional leadership: A meta-analytic review of the MLQ literature. *Leadership Quarterly, 7,* 385–425.

Lowman, R. L. (1996). Work dysfunctions and mental disorders. In K. R. Murphy (Ed.), *Individual differences and behavior in organizations* (pp. 371–415). San Francisco: Jossey-Bass.

Lowman, R. L. (1999). *The ethical practice of psychology in organizations.* Washington, DC: American Psychological Association.

Lubinski, D., & Dawis, R. V. (1992). Aptitudes, skills, and proficiencies. In M. D. Dunnette & L. M. Hough (Eds.), *Handbook of industrial and organizational psychology* (2nd ed., Vol. 3, pp. 1–59). Palo Alto, CA: Consulting Psychologists Press.

Lund, J. (1992). Electronic performance monitoring: A review of research issues. *Applied Ergonomics, 23,* 54–58.

Lyness, K. S., & Thompson, D. E. (1997). Above the glass ceiling: A comparison of matched samples of female and male executives. *Journal of Applied Psychology, 82,* 359–375.

Lyness, K. S., & Thompson, D. E. (2000). Climbing the corporate ladder: Do female and male executives follow the same route? *Journal of Applied Psychology, 85,* 86–101.

Mabe, P. A., & West, S. G. (1982). Validity of self-evaluation of ability: A review and meta-analysis. *Journal of Applied Psychology, 67,* 280–296.

MacKenzie, S. B., Podsakoff, P. M., & Fetter, R. (1991). Organizational citizenship behavior and objective productivity as determinants of managerial evaluations of salespersons' performance. *Organizational Behavior and Human Decision Processes, 50,* 123–150.

Macy, B. A., & Izumi, H. (1993). Organizational change, design and work innovation: A meta-analysis of 131 North American field studies—1961–1991. In W. A. Pasmore & R. W. Woodman (Eds.), *Research in organizational change and development* (Vol. 7, pp. 235–313). Greenwich, CT: JAI Press.

Mael, F. A. (1991). A conceptual rationale for the domain and attributes of biodata items. *Personnel Psychology, 44,* 763–792.

Mael, F. A., Connerly, M., & Morath, R. A. (1996). None of your business: Parameters of biodata invasiveness. *Personnel Psychology, 49,* 613–650.

Mager, R. F. (1984). *Preparing instructional objectives.* Belmont, CA: Pitman Learning.

Mahoney, T. A. (1983). Approaches to the definition of comparable worth. *Academy of Management Review, 8,* 14–22.

Malos, S. B. (1998). Current legal issues in performance appraisal. In J. W. Smither (Ed.), *Performance appraisal* (pp. 49–94). San Francisco: Jossey-Bass.

Mantell, M. (1994). *Ticking bombs: Defusing violence in the workplace.* Burr Ridge, IL: Irwin.

Manz, C. C. (1986). Self-leadership: Toward an expanded theory of self-influence. *Academy of Management Review, 11,* 585–600.

Manz, C. C., & Sims, H. P. (1991). Superleadership: Beyond the myth of heroic leadership. *Organizational Dynamics, 19*(4), 18–35.

Marchant, G., & Robinson, J. (1999). Is knowing the tax code all it takes to be a tax expert? On the development of legal expertise. In R. J. Sternberg & J. A. Howath (Eds.), *Tacit knowledge in professional practice* (pp. 3–20). Mahwah, NJ: Erlbaum.

Margenau, J. M., Martin, J. E., & Peterson, M. M. (1988). Dual and unilateral commitment among stewards and rank-and-file union members. *Academy of Management Journal, 31,* 359–376.

Marks, M. A., Zaccaro, S. J., & Mathieu, J. E. (2000). Performance implications of leader briefings and team-interaction training for team adaptation to novel environments. *Journal of Applied Psychology, 85,* 971–986.

Marks, M. L., & Mirvis, P. H. (2000). Managing mergers, acquisitions, and alliances: Creating an effective transition structure. *Organizational Dynamics, 28,* 35–47.

Marlatt, G. A., Baer, J. S., & Quigley, L. A. (1995). Self-efficacy and addictive behavior. In A. Bandura (Ed.), *Self-efficacy in changing societies* (pp. 289–315). New York: Cambridge.

Martin, S. L., & Terris, W. (1991). Predicting infrequent behavior: Clarifying the impact on false-positive rates. *Journal of Applied Psychology, 76,* 484–487.

Martocchio, J. J. (2001). *Strategic compensation* (2nd ed.). Upper Saddle River, NJ: Prentice-Hall.

Martocchio, J. J., & Baldwin, T. T. (1997). The evolution of strategic organizational training: New objectives and research agenda. In G. R. Ferris (Ed.), *Research in personnel and human resources management* (Vol. 15, pp. 1–46). Greenwich, CT: JAI Press.

Martocchio, J. J., & Harrison, D. A. (1993). To be there or not to be there: Questions, theories, and methods in absenteeism research. In G. R. Ferris (Ed.), *Research in personnel and human resources management* (Vol. 11, pp. 259–329). Greenwich, CT: JAI Press.

Marx, R. D. (1982). Relapse prevention for managerial training: A model for maintenance of behavior change. *Academy of Management Review, 7,* 433–441.

Marx, R. D., & Karren, R. K. (1988). *The effects of relapse prevention training and interactive follow-up on positive transfer of training.* Paper presented at the National Academy of Management Meeting, Anaheim, CA.

Maslow, A. H. (1987). *Motivation and personality* (3rd ed.). New York: Harper & Row.

Masters, M. F. (1997). *Unions at the crossroads: Strategic membership, financial, and political perspectives.* Westport, CT: Quorum.

Matarazzo, J. D. (1987). There is only one psychology, no specialties, but many applications. *American Psychologist, 42,* 893–903.

Mateer, F. (1917). The moron as a war problem. *Journal of Applied Psychology, 1,* 317–320.

Mathieu, J. E., Tannenbaum, S. I., & Salas, E. (1990). *A causal model of individual and situational influences on training effectiveness measures.* Paper presented at the 5th annual conference of the Society for Industrial and Organizational Psychology, Miami.

Maurer, T. J., Raju, N. J., & Collins, W. C. (1998). Peer and subordinate performance appraisal measurement equivalence. *Journal of Applied Psychology, 83,* 693–702.

Mawhinney, T. C. (1975). Operant terms and concepts in the description of individual work behavior: Some problems of interpretation, application, and evaluation. *Journal of Applied Psychology, 60*, 704–712.

Maxwell, J. A. (1998). Designing a qualitative study. In L. Bickman & D. J. Rog (Eds.), *Handbook of applied social research methods* (pp. 69–100). Thousand Oaks, CA: Sage.

Mayer, R. C., & Davis, J. H. (1999). The effect of the performance appraisal system on trust for management: A field quasi-experiment. *Journal of Applied Psychology, 84*, 123–136.

McCall, M. W., & Bobko, P. (1990). Research methods in the service of discovery. In M. D. Dunnette & L. M. Hough (Eds.), *Handbook of industrial and organizational psychology* (2nd ed., Vol. 1, pp. 381–418). Palo Alto, CA: Consulting Psychologists Press.

McClelland, D. C., & Boyatzis, R. E. (1982). Leadership motive pattern and long term success in management. *Journal of Applied Psychology, 67*, 737–743.

McCormick, E. J., & Jeanneret, P. R. (1988). Position analysis questionnaire (PAQ). In S. Gael (Ed.), *The job analysis handbook for business, industry, and government* (Vol. 2, pp. 825–842). New York: Wiley.

McCrae, R. R., & Costa, P. T. (1987). Validation of the five-factor model of personality across instruments and observers. *Journal of Personality & Social Psychology, 56*, 586–595.

McCrae, R. R., & Costa, P. T. (1997). Personality trait structure as a human universal. *American Psychologist, 52*, 509–516.

McDaniel, M. A., Morgeson, F. P., Finnegan, E. B., Campion, M. A., & Brauerman, E. P. (2001). Use of situational judgment tests to predict job performance: A clarification of the literature. *Journal of Applied Psychology, 86*, 730–740.

McIntyre, R. M., & Salas, E. (1995). Measuring and managing for team performance: Lessons from complex environments. In R. A. Guzzo & E. Salas (Eds.), *Team effectiveness and decision making in organizations* (pp. 9–45). San Francisco: Jossey-Bass.

McManus, M. A., & Kelly, M. L. (1999). Personality measures and biodata: Evidence regarding their incremental predictive value in the life insurance industry. *Personnel Psychology, 52*, 137–148.

McNeely, B. L., & Meglino, B. M. (1994). The role of dispositional and situational antecedents in prosocial organizational behavior: An examination of the intended beneficiaries of prosocial behavior. *Journal of Applied Psychology, 79*, 836–844.

Meers, A., Maasen, A., & Verhaagen, P. (1978). Subjective health after six months and after four years of shift work. *Ergonomics, 21*, 857–859.

Meijer, R. R., & Nering, M. L. (1999). Computerized adaptive testing: Overview and introduction. *Applied Psychological Measurement, 23*, 187–194.

Meindl, J. R., & Ehrlich, S. B. (1987). The romance of leadership and the evaluation of organizational performance. *Academy of Management Journal, 30*, 91–109.

Mellor, S. (1990). The relationship between membership decline and union commitment: A field study of local unions in crisis. *Journal of Applied Psychology, 75*, 258–267.

Mero, N. P., & Motowidlo, S. J. (1995). Effects of rater accountability on the accuracy and the favorability of performance ratings. *Journal of Applied Psychology, 80*, 517–524.

Messick, S. (1995). Validity of psychological assessment: Validation of inferences from persons' responses and performances as scientific inquiry into score meaning. *American Psychologist, 50*, 741–749.

Meyer, G. J., Finn, S. E., Eyde, L. D., Kay, G. G., Moreland, K. L., Dies, R. R., Eisman, E. J., Kubiszyn, T. W., & Reed, G. M. (2001). Psychological testing and psychological assessment: A review of evidence and issues. *American Psychologist, 56*, 128–165.

Meyer, H. H. (1980). Self-appraisal of job performance. *Personnel Psychology, 33*, 291–296.

Meyer, H. H., Kay, E., & French, J. R. P., Jr. (1965). Split roles in performance appraisal. *Harvard Business Review, 43*, 123–129.

Meyer, J. P. (1997). Organizational commitment. In C. L. Cooper & I. T. Robertson (Eds.), *International review of industrial and organizational psychology* (Vol. 12, pp. 175–228). Chichester: Wiley.

Meyer, J. P., & Allen, N. J. (1997). *Commitment in the workplace: Theory, research, and application*. Thousand Oaks, CA: Sage.

Michalak, D. F. (1981). The neglected half of training. *Training and Development Journal, 35*, 22–28.

Mintzberg, H. (1993). *Structure in fives: Designing effective organizations*. Englewood Cliffs, NJ: Prentice-Hall.

Mirvis, P. H. (1985). Negotiations after the sale: The roots and ramifications of conflict in an acquisition. *Journal of Organizational Behavior, 6*, 65–84.

Mirvis, P. H. (1988). Organization development: Part I—An evolutionary perspective. In W. A. Pasmore & R. W. Woodman (Eds.), *Research in organizational change and development* (Vol. 2, pp. 1–57). Greenwich, CT: JAI Press.

Mirvis, P. H., & Seashore, S. E. (1979). Being ethical in organizational research. *American Psychologist, 34*, 766–780.

Mitchell, J. L., & McCormick, E. J. (1990). *Professional and managerial position questionnaire*. Logan, UT: PAQ Services.

Mitchell, T. R. (1985). An evaluation of the validity of correlation research conducted in organizations. *Academy of Management Review, 10*, 192–205.

Mitchell, T. R. (1997). Matching motivational strategies with organizational contexts. In B. M. Staw & L. L. Cummings (Eds.), *Research in organizational behavior* (Vol. 19, pp. 57–149). Greenwich, CT: JAI Press.

Mitchell, T. R., & James, L. R. (2001). Building better theory: Time and the specification of when things happen. *Academy of Management Review, 26*, 530–547.

Mohammed, S., & Dumville, B. C. (2001). Team mental models in a team knowledge framework: Expanding theory and measurement across disciplinary boundaries. *Journal of Organizational Behavior, 22*, 89–106.

Monk, T. H., Folkard, S., & Wedderburn, A. I. (1996). Maintaining safety and high performance on shiftwork. *Applied Ergonomics, 27*, 17–23.

Mook, D. G. (1983). In defense of external invalidity. *American Psychologist, 38*, 379–387.

Moore, D. A. (1994). Company alcohol policies: Practicalities and problems. In C. L. Cooper & S. Williams (Eds.), *Creating healthy work organizations* (pp. 75–96). Chichester: Wiley.

Moorman, R. H. (1991). Relationship between organizational justice and organizational citizenship behaviors: Do fairness perceptions influence employee citizenship? *Journal of Applied Psychology, 76,* 845–855.

Moreland, J. L., Eyde, L. D., Robertson, G. J., Primoff, E. S., & Most, R. B. (1995). Assessment of test user qualifications. *American Psychologist, 50,* 14–23.

Moreland, R. L., & Levine, J. M. (2001). Socialization in organizations and work groups. In M. E. Turner (Ed.), *Groups at work* (pp. 69–112). Mahwah, NJ: Erlbaum.

Morgan, G. (1997). *Images of organizations.* Thousand Oaks, CA: Sage.

Morgeson, F. P., & Campion, M. A. (1997). Social and cognitive sources of potential inaccuracy in job analysis. *Journal of Applied Psychology, 82,* 627–655.

Morgeson, F. P., & Campion, M. A. (2000). Accuracy in job analysis: Toward an inference-based model. *Journal of Organizational Behavior, 21,* 819–827.

Morrison, R. F., & Brantner, T. M. (1992). What enhances or inhibits learning a new job? A basic career issue. *Journal of Applied Psychology, 77,* 926–940.

Morrow, C. C., Jarrett, M., & Rupinski, M. T. (1997). An investigation of the effect and economic utility of corporate-wide training. *Personnel Psychology, 50,* 91–119.

Morrow, P. C. (1993). *The theory and measurement of work commitment.* Greenwich, CT: JAI.

Moscoso, S. (2000). Selection interview: A review of validity evidence, adverse impact, and applicant reactions. *International Journal of Selection and Assessment, 8,* 237–247.

Motowidlo, S. J., Hanson, M. A., & Crafts, J. L. (1997). Low-fidelity simulations. In D. L. Whetzel & G. R. Wheaton (Eds.), *Applied measurement methods in industrial psychology* (pp. 241–260). Palo Alto, CA: Consulting Psychologists Press.

Motowidlo, S. J., & Van Scotter, J. R. (1994). Evidence that task performance should be distinguished from contextual performance. *Journal of Applied Psychology, 79,* 475–480.

Mount, M. K. (1984). Psychometric properties of subordinate ratings of managerial performance. *Personnel Psychology, 37,* 687–702.

Mount, M. K., & Scullen, S. E. (2001). Multisource feedback ratings: What do they really measure? In M. London (Ed.), *How people evaluate others in organizations* (pp. 155–180). Mahwah, NJ: Erlbaum.

Mount, M. K., Witt, L. A., & Barrick, M. R. (2000). Incremental validity of empirically keyed biodata scales over GMA and the five factor personality constructs. *Personnel Psychology, 53,* 299–323.

Muchinsky, P. M. (1977). A comparison of within- and across-subjects analyses of the expectancy-valence model for predicting effort. *Academy of Management Journal, 20,* 154–158.

Muchinsky, P. M. (1979). The use of reference reports in personnel selection: A review and evaluation. *Journal of Occupational Psychology, 52,* 287–297.

Muchinsky, P. M. (1993). Validation of intelligence and mechanical aptitude tests in selecting employees for manufacturing jobs. *Journal of Business and Psychology, 7,* 373–382.

Muchinsky, P. M. (2000). Emotions in the workplace: The neglect of organizational behavior. *Journal of Organizational Behavior, 21,* 801–805.

Muchinsky, P. M., & Maassarani, M. A. (1981). Public sector grievances in Iowa. *Journal of Collective Negotiations, 10,* 55–62.

Mulvey, P. W., & Klein, H. J. (1998). The impact of perceived loafing and collective efficacy in group goal processes and group performance. *Organizational Behavior & Human Decision Processes, 74,* 62–87.

Mumford, M. D., & Stokes, G. S. (1992). Developmental determinants of individual action: Theory and practice in applying background measures. In M. D. Dunnette & L. M. Hough (Eds.), *Handbook of industrial and organizational psychology* (2nd ed., Vol. 3, pp. 61–138). Palo Alto, CA: Consulting Psychologists Press.

Münsterberg, H. (1913). *Psychology and industrial efficiency.* Boston: Houghton Mifflin.

Murphy, G. C., & Athanasou, J. A. (1999). The effect of unemployment on mental health. *Journal of Occupational & Organizational Psychology, 72,* 83–99.

Murphy, K. R. (1996). Individual differences and behavior in organizations: Much more than *g.* In K. R. Murphy (Ed.), *Individual differences and behavior in organizations* (pp. 3–30). San Francisco: Jossey-Bass.

Murphy, K. R. (1997). Meta-analysis and validity generalization. In N. Anderson & P. Herriot (Eds.), *International handbook of selection and assessment* (pp. 323–342). Chichester: Wiley.

Murphy, K. R. (2000). Impact of assessments of validity generalization and situational specificity on the science and practice of personnel selection. *International Journal of Selection and Assessment, 8,* 194–206.

Murphy, K. R., & Anhalt, R. L. (1992). Is halo error a property of the rater, ratees, or the specific behaviors observed? *Journal of Applied Psychology, 77,* 494–500.

Murphy, K. R., & Cleveland, J. N. (1995). *Understanding performance appraisal: Social, organizational, and goal-based perspectives.* Thousand Oaks, CA: Sage.

Murphy, K. R., & DeShon, R. (2000). Progress in psychometrics: Can industrial and organizational psychology catch up? *Personnel Psychology, 53,* 913–924.

Murphy, K. R., Osten, K., & Myors, B. (1995). Modeling the effects of banding in personnel selection. *Personnel Psychology, 48,* 61–84.

Murphy, K. R., Thornton, G. C., & Prue, K. (1991). Influence of job characteristics on the acceptability of employee drug testing. *Journal of Applied Psychology, 76,* 447–453.

Murphy, L. L., Impara, J. C., & Plake, B. S. (1999). *Tests in Print V.* Lincoln, NE: Buros Institute of Mental Measurements.

Murphy, L. R., Hurrell, J. J., & Quick, J. C. (1992). Work and well-being: Where do we go from here? In J. C. Quick, L. R. Murphy, & J. J. Hurrell (Eds.), *Stress and well-being at work* (pp. 331–347). Washington, DC: American Psychological Association.

Murray, H. A., & MacKinnon, D. W. (1946). Assessment of OSS personnel. *Journal of Consulting Psychology, 10,* 76–80.

Murrell, A. J., & Jones, R. (1996). Assessing affirmative action: Past, present, and future. *Journal of Social Issues, 52*(4), 77–92.

Musser, S. J. (1987). *The determination of positive and negative charismatic leadership.* Unpublished manuscript, Messiah College, Grantham, PA.

Napoli, D. S. (1981). *The architects of adjustment: The history of the psychological profession in the United States.* Port Washington, NY: Kennikat.

Narayanan, V. K., & Nath, R. (1982). Hierarchical level and the impact of flextime. *Industrial Relations, 21,* 216–230.

National Council on Measurement in Education. (1995). *Code of professional responsibilities in educational measurement.* Washington, DC: National Council on Measurement in Education.

National Institute for Occupational Safety and Health. (1988). *Proposed national strategies for the prevention of leading work-related diseases and injuries—Psychological disorders.* Washington, DC: U.S. Department of Health and Human Services.

Neale, M. A. (1984). The effects of negotiation and arbitration cost salience on bargainer behavior: The role of the arbiter and constituency in negotiator judgment. *Organizational Behavior and Human Performance, 34,* 97–111.

Neuman, G. A., & Wright, J. (1999). Team effectiveness: Beyond skills and cognitive ability. *Journal of Applied Psychology, 84,* 376–389.

Neuman, J. H., & Baron, R. A. (1998). Workplace violence and workplace aggression: Evidence concerning specific forms, potential causes, and preferred targets. *Journal of Management, 24,* 391–419.

Nickels, B. J. (1994). The nature of biodata. In G. S. Stokes, M. D. Mumford, & W. A. Owens (Eds.), *Biodata handbook: Theory, research, and use of biographical information in selection and performance prediction* (pp. 1–16). Palo Alto, CA: Consulting Psychologists Press.

Nicoletti, J., & Spooner, K. (1996). Violence in the workplace: Response and intervention strategies. In G. R. VandenBos & E. Q. Bulatao (Eds.), *Violence on the job* (pp. 267–282). Washington, DC: American Psychological Association.

Nilsen, D., & Campbell, D. P. (1993). Self-observer rating discrepancies: Once an overrater, always an overrater? *Human Resource Management, 32,* 265–282.

Noe, R. A. (1988). An investigation of the determinants of successful assigned mentoring relationships. *Personnel Psychology, 41,* 457–480.

Noe, R., & Ford, J. K. (1992). Emerging issues and new directions for training research. In K. Rowland & G. Ferris (Eds.), *Research in personnel and human resource management* (Vol. 10, pp. 345–384). Greenwich, CT: JAI Press.

Normand, J., Lempert, R. O., & O'Brien, C. P. (Eds.). (1994). *Under the influence? Drugs and the American workforce.* Washington, DC: National Academy Press.

Normand, J., Salyards, S. D., & Mahoney, J. J. (1990). An evaluation of preemployment drug testing. *Journal of Applied Psychology, 75,* 629–639.

Northwestern National Life Insurance Company. (1991). *Employee burnout: America's newest epidemic.* Minneapolis: Author.

Oakley, A. (1974). *The sociology of housework.* New York: Pantheon.

Offerman, L. R., & Gowing, M. K. (1990). Organizations of the future. *American Psychologist, 45,* 95–108.

O'Keeffe, J. (1994). Disability, discrimination, and the Americans with Disabilities Act. In S. M. Bruyere & J. O'Keeffe (Eds.), *Implications of the Americans with Disabilities Act for psychology* (pp. 1–14). New York: Springer.

Oldham, G. R. (1996). Job design. In C. L. Cooper & I. T. Robertson (Eds.), *International review of industrial and organizational psychology* (Vol. 11, pp. 33–60). London: Wiley.

Olson-Buchanan, J. B. (1996). Voicing discontent: What happens to the grievance filer after the grievance? *Journal of Applied Psychology, 81,* 52–63.

Ones, D. S., & Viswesvaran, C. (1998). Gender, age, and race differences on overt integrity tests: Results across four large-scale job applicant data sets. *Journal of Applied Psychology, 83,* 35–42.

Ones, D. S., Viswesvaran, C., & Reiss, A. (1996). Role of social desirability in personality testing for personnel selection: The red herring. *Journal of Applied Psychology, 81,* 660–679.

Ones, D. S., Viswesvaran, C., & Schmidt, F. L. (1993). Comprehensive meta-analysis of integrity test validities: Findings and implications for personnel selection and theories of job performance. *Journal of Applied Psychology, 78,* 679–703.

Organ, D. W. (1988). *Organizational citizenship behavior: The good soldier syndrome.* Lexington, MA: Lexington Books.

Organ, D. W. (1994). Organizational citizenship behavior and the good soldier. In M. G. Rumsey, C. B. Walker, & J. H. Harris (Eds.), *Personnel selection and classification* (pp. 53–68). Hillsdale, NJ: Erlbaum.

Ostroff, C., & Ford, J. K. (1989). Assessing training needs: Critical levels of analysis. In I. L. Goldstein (Ed.), *Training and development in organizations* (pp. 25–62). San Francisco: Jossey-Bass.

Ostroff, C., & Harrison, D. A. (1999). Meta-analysis, level of analysis, and best estimates of population correlations: Cautions for interpreting meta-analytic results in organizational behavior. *Journal of Applied Psychology, 84,* 260–270.

Overton, R. C., Harms, H. J., Taylor, L. R., & Zickar, M. J. (1997). Adapting to adaptive testing. *Personnel Psychology, 50,* 171–185.

Overton, R. C., Taylor, L. R., Zickar, M. J., & Harms, H. J. (1996). The pen-based computer as an alternative platform for test administration. *Personnel Psychology, 49,* 455–464.

Parker, S. K., & Sprigg, C. A. (1999). Minimizing strain and maximizing learning: The role of job demands, job control, and proactive personality. *Journal of Applied Psychology, 84,* 925–939.

Parks, J. M., & Kidder, D. L. (1994). "Till death do us part . . .": Changing work relationships in the 1990s. In C. L. Cooper & D. M. Rousseau (Eds.), *Trends in organizational behavior* (Vol. 1, pp. 111–136). New York: Wiley.

Pearson, C. M., Andersson, L. M., & Porath, C. L. (2000). Assessing and attacking workplace incivility. *Organizational Dynamics, 29,* 123–137.

Pedalino, E., & Gamboa, V. U. (1974). Behavior modification and absenteeism. *Journal of Applied Psychology, 59*, 694–698.

Pelletier, K. (1977). *Mind as healer, mind as slayer: A holistic approach to preventing stress disorders.* New York: Delacorte.

Pernanen, K. (1991). *Alcohol in human violence.* London: Guilford Press.

Peterson, N. G., & Jeanneret, P. R. (1997). Job analysis. In D. L. Whetzel & G. R. Wheaton (Eds.), *Applied measurement methods in industrial psychology* (pp. 13–50). Palo Alto, CA: Consulting Psychologists Press.

Peterson, N. G., Mumford, M. D., Borman, W. C., Jeanneret, P. R., & Fleishman, E. A. (Eds.). (1999). *An occupational information system for the 21st century: The development of the O*NET.* Washington, DC: American Psychological Association.

Peterson, N. G., Mumford, M. D., Borman, W. C., Jeanneret, P. R., Fleishman, E. A., Campion, M. A., Mayfield, M. S., Morgeson, F. P., Pearlman, K., Gowing, M. K., Lancaster, A. R., Silver, M. B., & Dye, D. M. (2001). Understanding work using the Occupational Information Network (O*NET): Implications for research and practice. *Personnel Psychology, 54*, 451–492.

Peterson, N. G., Wise, L. L., Arabian, J., & Hoffman, R. G. (2001). Synthetic validation and validity generalization: When empirical validation is not possible. In J. P. Campbell & D. J. Knapp (Eds.), *Exploring the limits in personnel selection and classification* (pp. 411–452). Mahwah, NJ: Erlbaum.

Phillips, J. M., Hollenbeck, J. R., & Ilgen, D. R. (1996). Prevalence and prediction of positive discrepancy creation: Examining a discrepancy between two self-regulation theories. *Journal of Applied Psychology, 81*, 498–511.

Phillips, J. S., & Lord, R. G. (1981). Causal attribution and prescriptions of leadership. *Organizational Behavior and Human Performance, 28*, 143–163.

Pierce, C. A., Byrne, D., & Aguinis, H. (1996). Attraction in organizations: A model of workplace romance. *Journal of Organizational Behavior, 17*, 5–32.

Pierce, J. L., & Dunham, R. B. (1992). The 12-hour work day: A 48-hour, four-day week. *Academy of Management Journal, 35*, 1086–1098.

Pierce, J. L., Dunham, R. B., & Cummings, L. L. (1984). Sources of environmental structuring and participant responses. *Organizational Behavior and Human Performance, 33*, 214–242.

Pinder, C. C. (1998). *Work motivation in organizational behavior.* Upper Saddle River, NJ: Prentice-Hall.

Piotrkowski, C. S., & Carrubha, J. (1999). Child labor and exploitation. In J. Barling & E. K. Kelloway (Eds.), *Young workers: Varieties of experience* (pp. 129–157). Washington, DC: American Psychological Association.

Plake, B. S., & Impara, J. C. (Eds.) (2001). *The fourteenth mental measurements yearbook.* Lincoln, NE: Buros Institute of Mental Measurements.

Ployhart, R. E., & Ryan, A. M. (1998). Applicants' reactions to the fairness of selection procedures: The effects of positive rule violations and time of measurement. *Journal of Applied Psychology, 83*, 3–16.

Podlesny, J. A., & Truslow, C. M. (1993). Validity of an expanded-issue (Modified General Question) polygraph technique in a simulated distributed-crime-roles context. *Journal of Applied Psychology, 78*, 788–797.

Podsakoff, P. M., Ahearne, M., & MacKenzie, S. B. (1997). Organizational citizenship behavior and the quantity and quality of work group performance. *Journal of Applied Psychology, 82*, 262–270.

Podsakoff, P. M., MacKenzie, S. B., & Bommer, W. H. (1996). Meta-analysis of the relationship between Kerr and Jermier's substitutes for leadership and employee job attitudes, role perceptions, and performance. *Journal of Applied Psychology, 81*, 380–399.

Poortinga, Y. H. (1999). Do differences in behavior imply a need for different psychologies? *Applied Psychology: An International Review, 48*, 419–432.

Porras, J. I., & Robertson, P. J. (1992). Organizational development: Theory, practice, and research. In M. D. Dunnette & L. M. Hough (Eds.), *Handbook of industrial and organizational psychology* (2nd ed., Vol. 3, pp. 719–822). Palo Alto, CA: Consulting Psychologists Press.

Pratt, M. G., & Rafaeli, A. (1997). Organizational dress as a symbol of multilayered social identities. *Academy of Management Journal, 40*, 862–898.

Premack, S. L., & Hunter, J. E. (1988). Individual unionization decisions. *Psychological Bulletin, 103*, 223–234.

Prieto, J. M. (1993). The team perspective in selection and assessment. In H. Schuler, J. L. Farr, & M. Smith (Eds.), *Personnel selection and assessment* (pp. 221–234). Hillsdale, NJ: Erlbaum.

Pritchard, R. D., DeLeo, P. J., & Von Bergen, C. W. (1976). A field experimental test of expectancy-valence incentive motivation techniques. *Organizational Behavior and Human Performance, 15*, 355–406.

Pritchard, R. D., Jones, S. D., Roth, P. L., Stuebing, K. K., & Ekeberg, S. E. (1988). Effects of group feedback, goal setting, and incentives on organizational productivity. *Journal of Applied Psychology, 73*, 337–358.

Pritchard, R. D., Leonard, D. W., Von Bergen, C. W., & Kirk, R. J. (1976). The effect of varying schedules of reinforcement on human task performance. *Organizational Behavior and Human Performance, 16*, 205–230.

Pruitt, D. G. (1993). *Negotiation in social conflict.* Pacific Grove, CA: Brooks/Cole.

Pulakos, E. D. (1997). Ratings of job performance. In D. L. Whetzel & G. R. Wheaton (Eds.), *Applied measurement methods in industrial psychology* (pp. 291–318). Palo Alto, CA: Consulting Psychologists Press.

Pulakos, E. D., Borman, W. C., & Hough, L. M. (1988). Test validation for scientific understanding: Two demonstrations of an approach to studying predictor–criterion linkages. *Personnel Psychology, 41*, 703–716.

Pulakos, E. D., & Schmitt, N. (1995). Experience-based and structured interview questions: Studies of validity. *Personnel Psychology, 48*, 289–308.

Pursell, E. D., Dossett, D. L., & Latham, G. P. (1980). Obtaining valid predictors by minimizing rating errors in the criterion. *Personnel Psychology, 33*, 91–96.

Quick, J. C., Murphy, L. R., Hurrell, J. J., & Orman, D. (1992). The value of work in the risk of distress and the power of prevention. In J. C. Quick, L. R. Murphy, & J. J. Hurrell (Eds.), *Stress and well-being at work* (pp. 3–13). Washington, DC: American Psychological Association.

Quinn, R. E., & Lees, P. L. (1984). Attraction and harassment: Dynamics of sexual politics in the workplace. *Organizational Dynamics, 13*(2), 36–46.

Quinones, M. A. (1995). Pretraining context effects: Training assignment as feedback. *Journal of Applied Psychology, 80,* 226–238.

Quinones, M. A., Ford, J. K., & Teachout, M. S. (1995). The relationship between work experience and job performance: A conceptual and meta-analytic review. *Personnel Psychology, 48,* 485–509.

Raelin, J. A. (1989). Unionization and deprofessionalization: Which comes first? *Journal of Organizational Behavior, 10,* 101–115.

Rafaeli, A., & Klimoski, R. J. (1983). Predicting sales success through handwriting analysis: An evaluation of the effects of training and handwriting sample content. *Journal of Applied Psychology, 68,* 212–217.

Ragins, B. R., & Cotton, J. L. (1991). Easier said than done: Gender differences in perceived barriers to gaining a mentor. *Academy of Management Journal, 34,* 939–951.

Ragins, B. R., & Cotton, J. L. (1999). Mentor functions and outcomes: A comparison of men and women in formal and informal mentoring relationships. *Journal of Applied Psychology, 84,* 529–550.

Ragins, B. R., & McFarlin, D. B. (1990). Perceptions of mentor roles in cross-gender mentoring relationships. *Journal of Vocational Behavior, 37,* 321–339.

Ragins, B. R., & Sundstrom, E. (1989). Gender and power in organizations: A longitudinal perspective. *Psychological Bulletin, 105,* 51–88.

Raju, N. S., Burke, M. J., Normand, J., & Langlois, G. M. (1991). A new meta-analytic approach. *Journal of Applied Psychology, 76,* 432–446.

Ralston, D. A. (1989). The benefits of flextime: Real or imagined? *Journal of Organizational Behavior, 10,* 369–374.

Rawls, J. (1971). *A theory of justice.* Cambridge, MA: Harvard University Press.

Raymark, P. H., Schmit, M. J., & Guion, R. M. (1997). Identifying potentially useful personality constructs for employee selection. *Personnel Psychology, 50,* 723–736.

Ree, M. J., Earles, J. A., & Teachout, M. S. (1994). Predicting job performance: Not much more than g. *Journal of Applied Psychology, 79,* 518–524.

Reeves, C. A., & Bednar, D. A. (1994). Defining quality: Alternatives and implications. *Academy of Management Review, 19,* 419–445.

Rentsch, J. R., & Klimoski, R. J. (2001). Why do "great minds" think alike?: Antecedents of team member schema agreement. *Journal of Organizational Behavior, 22,* 107–120.

Rhodes, S. R., & Steers, R. M. (1990). *Managing employee absenteeism.* Reading, MA: Addison-Wesley.

Richey, B., Bernardin, H. J., Tyler, C. L., & McKinney, N. (2001). The effect of arbitration program characteristics on applicants' intentions toward potential employers. *Journal of Applied Psychology, 86,* 1006–1013.

Ridley, M. (1999). *Genome: The autobiography of a species in 23 chapters.* New York: Harper Collins.

Robert, C., Probst, T. M., Martocchio, J. J., Drasgow, F., & Lawler, J. J. (2000). Empowerment and continuous improvement in the United States, Mexico, Poland, and India: Predicting fit on the basis of the dimensions of power distance and individualism. *Journal of Applied Psychology, 85,* 643–658.

Robertson, I. T., & Kandola, R. S. (1982). Work sample tests: Validity, adverse impact and applicant reaction. *Journal of Occupational Psychology, 55,* 171–183.

Robinson, S. L., Kraatz, M. S., & Rousseau, D. M. (1994). Changing obligations and the psychological contract: A longitudinal study. *Academy of Management Journal, 37,* 137–152.

Robinson, S. L., & Rousseau, D. M. (1994). Violating the psychological contract: Not the exception but the norm. *Journal of Organizational Behavior, 15,* 245–259.

Rodgers, R., & Hunter, J. E. (1996). The methodological war of the "Hardheads" versus the "Softheads." *Journal of Applied Behavioral Science, 32,* 189–208.

Roethlisberger, F. J., & Dickson, W. J. (1939). *Management and the worker.* Cambridge, MA: Harvard University Press.

Rogelberg, S. G., Luong, A., Sederburg, M. E., & Cristol, D. S. (2000). Employee attitude surveys: Examining the attitudes of noncompliant employees. *Journal of Applied Psychology, 85,* 284–293.

Ronen, S. (1997). Personal reflections and projections: International industrial/organizational at a crossroads. In P. C. Earley & M. Erez (Eds.), *New perspectives in industrial/organizational psychology* (pp. 715–731). San Francisco: New Lexington Press.

Ronen, S. (1989). Training the international assignee. In I. L. Goldstein (Ed.), *Training and development in oganizations* (pp. 417–454). San Francisco: Jossey-Bass.

Ronen, S., & Primps, S. B. (1981). The compressed work week as organizational change: Behavioral and attitudinal outcomes. *Academy of Management Review, 6,* 61–74.

Root, D. A., & Ziska, M. D. (1996). Violence prevention during corporate downsizing: The use of a people team as context for the critical incident teams. In G. R. VandenBos & E. Q. Bulatao (Eds.), *Violence on the job* (pp. 353–366). Washington, DC: American Psychological Association.

Rosen, H., & Stagner, R. (1980). Industrial/organizational psychology and unions: A viable relationship? *Professional Psychology, 11,* 477–483.

Rosenthal, R. (1991). *Meta-analytic procedures for social research* (2nd ed.). Newbury Park, CA: Sage.

Rosnow, R. L. (1997). Hedgehogs, foxes, and the evolving social contract in psychological science: Ethical challenges and methodological opportunities. *Psychological Methods, 2,* 345–356.

Ross, R. R., & Altmaier, E. M. (1994). *Intervention in occupational stress.* London: Sage.

Rosse, J. G., Stecher, M. D., Miller, J. L., & Levin, R. A. (1998). The impact of response distortion on preemployment personality testing and hiring decisions. *Journal of Applied Psychology, 83,* 634–644.

Rosse, R. L., Campbell, J. P., & Peterson, N. G. (2001). Personnel classification and differential job assignments: Estimating classification gains. In J. P. Campbell & D. J. Knapp (Eds.), *Exploring the limits in personnel selection and classification* (pp. 453–506). Mahwah, NJ: Erlbaum.

Roth, P. L., & BeVier, C. A. (1998). Response rates in HRM/OB survey research: Norms and correlates, 1990–1994. *Journal of Management, 24,* 97–117.

Rouillier, J. Z., & Goldstein, I. L. (1990). *The determination of positive transfer of training climate through organizational analysis.* Unpublished manuscript.

Rousseau, D. M. (1989). Psychological and implied contracts in organizations. *Employee Responsibilities and Rights Journal, 2,* 121–139.

Rousseau, D. M. (1995). *Psychological contracts in organizations.* Thousand Oaks, CA: Sage.

Rousseau, D. M. (1997). Organizational behavior in the new organizational era. *Annual Review of Psychology, 48,* 515–546.

Rousseau, D. M., & House, R. J. (1994). Meso organizational behavior: Avoiding three fundamental biases. In C. L. Cooper & D. M. Rousseau (Eds.), *Trends in organizational behavior* (Vol. 1, pp. 13–30). New York: Wiley.

Rousseau, D. M., & Parks, J. M. (1993). The contracts of individuals and organizations. In B. M. Staw & L. L. Cummings (Eds.), *Research in organizational behavior* (Vol. 15, pp. 1–43). Greenwich, CT: JAI Press.

Rousseau, D. M., & Schalk, R. (2000). Learning from cross-national perspectives on psychological contracts. In D. M. Rousseau & R. Schalk (Eds.), *Psychological contracts in employment: Cross-national perspectives* (pp. 283–304). Thousand Oaks, CA: Sage.

Rousseau, D. M., & Tijoriwala, S. A. (1999). What's a good reason to change? Motivated reasoning and social accounts in promoting organizational change. *Journal of Applied Psychology, 84,* 514–528.

Roznowski, M., Dickter, D. N., Hong, S., Sawin, L. L., & Shute, V. J. (2000). Validity of measures of cognitive processes and general ability for learning and performance on highly complex computerized tutors: Is the *g* factor of intelligence even more general? *Journal of Applied Psychology, 85,* 940–955.

Ruback, R. B., & Innes, C. A. (1988). The relevance and irrelevance of psychological research. *American Psychologist, 43,* 683–693.

Russell, J. S., & Goode, D. L. (1988). An analysis of managers' reactions to their own performance appraisal feedback. *Journal of Applied Psychology, 73,* 63–67.

Ryan, A. M., Chan, D., Ployhart, R. E., & Slade, L. A. (1999). Employee attitude surveys in a multinational organization: Considering language and culture in assessing measurement equivalence. *Personnel Psychology, 52,* 37–58.

Ryan, A. M., McFarland, L., Baron, H., & Page, R. (1999). An internal look at selection practices: Nation and culture as explanations for variability in practice. *Personnel Psychology, 52,* 359–391.

Ryan, A. M., Ployhart, R. E., & Friedel, L. A. (1998). Using personality testing to reduce adverse impact: A cautionary note. *Journal of Applied Psychology, 83,* 298–307.

Rynes, S. L. (1993). Who's selecting whom? Effects of selection practices on applicant attitudes and behavior. In N. Schmitt & W. C. Borman (Eds.), *Personnel selection in organizations* (pp. 240–274). San Francisco: Jossey-Bass.

Rynes, S. L., & Milkovich, G. T. (1986). Wage surveys: Dispelling some myths about the "market wage." *Personnel Psychology, 39,* 71–90.

Rynes, S. L., McNatt, D. B., & Bretz, R. D. (1999). Academic research inside organizations: Inputs, processes, and outcomes. *Personnel Psychology, 52,* 869–898.

Rynes, S. L., Orlitzky, M. O., & Bretz, R. D. (1997). Experienced hiring versus college recruiting: Practices and emerging trends. *Personnel Psychology, 50,* 309–340.

Rynes, S., & Rosen, B. (1995). A field survey of factors affecting the adoption and perceived success of diversity training. *Personnel Psychology, 48,* 247–270.

Saal, F. E., Downey, R. G., & Lahey, M. A. (1980). Rating the ratings: Assessing the psychometric quality of rating data. *Psychological Bulletin, 88,* 413–428.

Saari, L. M., Johnson, T. R., McLaughlin, S. D., & Zimmerle, D. M. (1988). A survey of management training and education practices in U.S. companies. *Personnel Psychology, 41,* 731–744.

Sackett, P. R., Gruys, M. L., & Ellingson, J. E. (1998). Ability–personality interactions when predicting job performance. *Journal of Applied Psychology, 83,* 545–556.

Sackett, P. R., Schmitt, N., Ellingson, J. E., & Kabin, M. B. (2001). High-stakes testing in employment, credentialing, and higher education: Prospects in a post–affirmative-action world. *American Psychologist, 56,* 302–318.

Sackett, P. R., & Tuzinski, K. A. (2001). The role of dimensions and exercises in assessment center judgments. In M. London (Ed.), *How people evaluate others in organizations* (pp. 111–134). Mahwah, NJ: Erlbaum.

Sackett, P. R., & Wanek, J. E. (1996). New developments in the use of measures of honesty, integrity, conscientiousness, dependability, trustworthiness, and reliability for personnel selection. *Personnel Psychology, 49,* 787–829.

Sackett, P R., & Wilk, S. L. (1994). Within-group norming and other forms of score adjustment in psychological testing. *American Psychologist, 49,* 929–954.

Salas, E., & Cannon-Bowers, J. A. (1997). Methods, tools, and strategies for team training. In M. A. Quinones & A. Ehrenstein (Eds.), *Training for a rapidly changing workplace* (pp. 249–280). Washington, DC: American Psychological Association.

Salgado, J. F. (1997). The five factor model of personality and job performance in the European Community. *Journal of Applied Psychology, 82,* 30–43.

Salgado, J. F. (1998). Sample size in validity studies of personnel selection. *Journal of Occupational & Organizational Psychology, 71,* 161–164.

Salgado, J. F. (2000). Personnel selection at the beginning of the new millennium. *International Journal of Selection and Assessment, 8,* 191–193.

Salovey, P., & Mayer, J. D. (1990). Emotional intelligence. *Imagination, Cognition, and Personality, 9,* 185–211.

Sanchez, J. I. (2000). Adopting work analysis to a fast-paced and electronic business world. *International Journal of Selection and Assessment, 8,* 207–215.

Sanchez, J. I., & Levine, E. L. (2000). Accuracy or consequential validity: Which is the better standard for job analysis data? *Journal of Organizational Behavior, 21,* 809–818.

Sarchione, C. D., Cuttler, M. J., Muchinsky, P. M., & Nelson-Gray, R. O. (1998). Prediction of dysfunctional job behaviors among law enforcement officers. *Journal of Applied Psychology, 83,* 904–912.

Scarborough, J. (2001). *The origins of cultural differences and their impact on management.* Westport, CT: Quorum.

Schaubroeck, J., Ganster, D. C., & Jones, J. R. (1998). Organization and occupation influences in the attraction–selection–attrition process. *Journal of Applied Psychology, 83,* 869–891.

Schaubroeck, J., Lam, S. S., & Xie, J. L. (2000). Collective efficacy versus self-efficacy in coping responses to stressors and control: A cross-cultural study. *Journal of Applied Psychology, 85,* 512–525.

Schein, E. H. (1996). Culture: The missing concept in organizational studies. *Administrative Science Quarterly, 41,* 229–240.

Schippman, J. S., Prien, E. P., & Katz, J. A. (1990). Reliability and validity of in-basket performance measures. *Personnel Psychology, 43,* 837–859.

Schippmann, J. S. (1999). *Strategic job modeling: Working at the core of integrated human resources.* Mahwah, NJ: Erlbaum.

Schippmann, J. S., Ash, R. A., Battista, M., Carr, L., Eyde, L. D., Hesketh, B., Kehoe, J., Pearlman, K., Prien, E. P., & Sanchez, J. I. (2000). The practice of competency modeling. *Personnel Psychology, 53,* 703–740.

Schmidt, F. L. (1991). Why all banding procedures in personnel selection are logically flawed. *Human Performance, 4,* 265–278.

Schmidt, F. L., & Hunter, J. E. (1978). Moderator research and the law of small numbers. *Personnel Psychology, 31,* 215–232.

Schmidt, F. L., & Hunter, J. E. (1980). The future of criterion-related validity. *Personnel Psychology, 33,* 41–60.

Schmidt, F. L., & Hunter, J. E. (1981). Employment testing: Old theories and new research findings. *American Psychologist, 36,* 1128–1137.

Schmidt, F. L., & Hunter, J. E. (1995). The fatal internal contradiction in banding: Its statistical rationale is logically inconsistent with its operational procedures. *Human Performance, 8,* 203–214.

Schmidt, F. L., & Hunter, J. E. (1998). The validity and utility of selection methods in personnel psychology: Practical and theoretical implications of 85 years of research findings. *Psychological Bulletin, 124,* 437–454.

Schmidt, F. L., Hunter, J. E., McKenzie, R. C., & Muldrow, T. W. (1979). Impact of valid selection procedures on work-force productivity. *Journal of Applied Psychology, 64,* 609–626.

Schmidt, F. L., & Rader, M. (1999). Exploring the boundary conditions for interview validity: Meta-analytic findings for a new interview type. *Personnel Psychology, 52,* 445–464.

Schminke, M., Ambrose, M. L., & Cropanzano, R. S. (2000). The effect of organizational structure on perceptions of procedural fairness. *Journal of Applied Psychology, 85,* 294–304.

Schmitt, N., & Chan, D. (1998). *Personnel selection: A theoretical approach.* Thousand Oaks, CA: Sage.

Schmitt, N., Gooding, R. Z., Noe, R. D., & Kirsch, M. (1984). Meta-analyses of validity studies published between 1964 and 1982 and the investigation of study characteristics. *Personnel Psychology, 37,* 407–422.

Schmitt, N., & Landy, F. J. (1993). The concept of validity. In N. Schmitt & W. C. Borman (Eds.), *Personnel selection in organizations* (pp. 275–309). Palo Alto, CA: Consulting Psychologists Press.

Schneider, B. (1987). The people make the place. *Personnel Psychology, 40,* 437–454.

Schneider, B. (1996). When individual differences aren't. In K. R. Murphy (Ed.), *Individual differences and behaviors in organizations* (pp. 548–572). San Francisco: Jossey-Bass.

Schneider, B., Smith, D. B., Taylor, S., & Fleenor, J. (1998). Personality and organizations: A test of the homogeneity of personality hypothesis. *Journal of Applied Psychology, 83,* 462–470.

Schneider, K. T., Hitlan, R. T., & Radhakrishnan, P. (2000). An examination of the nature and correlates of ethnic harassment experiences in multiple contexts. *Journal of Applied Psychology, 85,* 3–12.

Schneider, K. T., Swan, S., & Fitzgerald, L. F. (1997). Job-related and psychological effects of sexual harassment in the workplace: Empirical evidence from two organizations. *Journal of Applied Psychology, 82,* 401–415.

Schoenfeldt, L. F. (1999). From dust bowl empiricism to rational constructs in biographical data. *Human Resource Management Review, 9,* 147–167.

Schor, J. (1992). *The overworked American.* New York: Basic Books.

Schriesheim, C. A. (1978). Job satisfaction, attitudes toward unions, and voting in a union representation election. *Journal of Applied Psychology, 63,* 548–552.

Schuler, H. (1993). Social validity of selection situations: A concept and some empirical results. In H. Schuler, J. L. Farr, & M. Smith (Eds.), *Personnel selection and assessment* (pp. 11–26). Hillsdale, NJ: Erlbaum.

Schwab, D. P., & Wichern, D. W. (1983). Systematic bias in job evaluation and market wages: Implications for the comparable worth debate. *Journal of Applied Psychology, 68,* 60–69.

Schwenk, C. (1999). *Marijuana and the workplace.* Westport: Quorum.

Scott, W. D. (1903). *The theory of advertising.* Boston: Small, Maynard.

Scott, W. D. (1908). *The psychology of advertising.* New York: Arno Press.

Scott, W. D. (1911a). *Increasing human efficiency in business.* New York: Macmillan.

Scott, W. D. (1911b). *Influencing men in business.* New York: Ronald Press.

Scott, W. G., Mitchell, T. R., & Birnbaum, P. H. (1981). *Organization theory: A structural and behavioral analysis.* Homewood, IL: Richard D. Irwin.

Scott, W. R. (1992). *Organizations: Rational, natural, and open systems* (3rd ed.). Englewood Cliffs, NJ: Prentice-Hall.

Scullen, S. W., Mount, M. K., & Goff, M. (2000). Understanding the latent structure of job performance ratings. *Journal of Applied Psychology, 85,* 956–970.

Seashore, S. E., Indik, B. P., & Georgopoulos, B. S. (1960). Relationship among criteria of job performance. *Journal of Applied Psychology, 44,* 195–202.

Secretary's Commission on Achieving Necessary Skills (1991). *What work requires of schools: SCANS report for America 2000.* U.S. Department of Labor. Washington, DC: U.S. Government Printing Office.

Seligman, M. E., & Csikszentmihalyi, M. (2000). Positive psychology: An introduction. *American Psychologist, 55,* 5–14.

Selye, H. (1982). History and present status of the stress concept. In L. Goldberger & S. Breznitz (Eds.), *Handbook of stress* (pp. 7–17). New York: Free Press.

Senders, J. W., & Moray, N. P. (1991). *Human error: Cause, prediction, and reduction.* Hillsdale, NJ: Erlbaum.

Senge, P. (1990). *The fifth discipline: The art and practice of the learning organization.* New York: Doubleday/Currency.

Shadish, W. R. (1996). Meta-analyses and the explanation of causal mediating processes: A primer of examples, methods, and issues. *Psychological Methods, 1,* 47–65.

Shaffer, M. A., & Harrison, D. A. (2001). Forgotten partners of international assignments: Development and test of a model of spouse adjustment. *Journal of Applied Psychology, 86,* 238–254.

Shore, T. H., Shore, L. M., & Thornton, G. C. (1992). Construct validity of self- and peer evaluations of performance dimensions in an assessment center. *Journal of Applied Psychology, 77,* 42–54.

Shostak, A. B. (1964). Industrial psychology and the trade unions: A matter of mutual indifference. In G. Fisk (Ed.), *The frontiers of management psychology.* New York: Harper & Row.

Silberstein, L. R. (1992). *Dual-career marriage: A system in transition.* Hillsdale, NJ: Erlbaum.

Silvester, J., & Chapman, A. J. (1997). Asking "why" in the workplace. In C. L. Cooper & D. M. Rousseau (Eds.), *Trends in organizational behavior* (Vol. 4, pp. 1–14). London: Wiley.

Siskin, B. R. (1995). Relation between performance and banding. *Human Performance, 8,* 215–226.

Skarlicki, D. P., & Folger, A. (1997). Retaliation in the workplace: The roles of distributive, procedural, and interactional justice. *Journal of Applied Psychology, 82,* 434–443.

Skarlicki, D. P., Folger, R., & Tesluk, P. (1999). Personality as a moderator in the relationship between fairness and retaliation. *Academy of Management Journal, 42,* 100–108.

Skarlicki, D. P., & Latham, G. P. (1996). Increasing citizenship behavior within a labor union: A test of organizational justice theory. *Journal of Applied Psychology, 81,* 161–169.

Skarlicki, D. P., & Latham, G. P. (1997). Leadership training in organizational justice to increase citizenship behavior within a labor union: A replication. *Personnel Psychology, 50,* 617–654.

Smith, C. S., Reilly, C., & Midkiff, K. (1989). Evaluation of three circadian rhythm questionnaires with suggestions for an improved measure of morningness. *Journal of Applied Psychology, 74,* 728–738.

Smith, E. M., Ford, J. K., & Kozlowski, S. W. (1997). Building adaptive expertise: Implications for training design strategies. In M. A. Quinones & A. Ehrenstein (Eds.), *Training for a rapidly changing workplace* (pp. 89–118). Washington, DC: American Psychological Association.

Smith, M., Farr, J. L., & Schuler, H. (1993). Individual and organizational perspectives on personnel procedures: Conclusions and horizons for future research. In H. Schuler, J. L. Farr, & M. Smith (Eds.), *Personnel selection and assessment* (pp. 333–351). Hillsdale, NJ: Erlbaum.

Smither, J. W. (1995). Creating an internal contingent workforce: Managing the resource link. In M. London (Ed.), *Employees, careers, and job creation.* San Francisco: Jossey-Bass.

Smither, J. W., Reilly, R. R., Millsap, R. E., & Pearlman, K. (1993). Applicant reactions to selection procedures. *Personnel Psychology, 46,* 49–76.

Soine, L. (1995). Sick building syndrome and gender bias: Imperiling women's health. *Social Work in Health Care, 20,* 51–65.

Solomonson, A. L., & Lance, C. E. (1997). Examination of the relationship between true halo and halo error in performance ratings. *Journal of Applied Psychology, 82,* 665–674.

Spector, P. E., Brannick, M. T., & Coovert, M. D. (1989). Job analysis. In C. L. Cooper & I. T. Robertson (Eds.), *International review of industrial and organizational psychology* (Vol. 4, pp. 281–328). London: Wiley.

Spool, M. D. (1978). Training programs for observers of behavior: A review. *Personnel Psychology, 31,* 853–888.

Spreitzer, G. M. (1997). Toward a common ground in defining empowerment. In W. A. Pasmore & R. W. Woodman (Eds.), *Research in organizational change and development* (Vol. 10, pp. 31–62). Greenwich, CT: JAI Press.

Spreitzer, G. M., McCall, M. M., & Mahoney, J. D. (1997). Early identification of international executive potential. *Journal of Applied Psychology, 82,* 6–29.

Sredl, H. J., & Rothwell, W. J. (1987). *Professional training roles and competencies* (Vol. II). Amherst, MA: HRD Press.

Stagner, R., & Effal, B. (1982). Internal union dynamics during a strike: A quasi-experimental study. *Journal of Applied Psychology, 67,* 37–44.

Stagner, R., & Rosen, H. (1965). *Psychology of union–management relations.* Belmont, CA: Wadsworth.

Stahelski, A. J., Frost, D. E., & Patch, M. E. (1989). Use of socially dependent bases of power: French and Raven's theory applied to workgroup leadership. *Journal of Applied Psychology, 19,* 283–297.

Stahl, M. J., & Harrell, A. M. (1981). Modeling effort decisions with behavioral decision theory: Toward an individual differences model of expectancy theory. *Organizational Behavior and Human Performance, 27,* 303–325.

Stajkovic, A. D., & Luthans, F. (1997). A meta-analysis of the effects of organizational behavior modification on task performance, 1975–1995. *Academy of Management Journal, 40,* 1122–1149.

Standards for educational and psychological testing. (1985). Washington, DC: American Psychological Association.

Stanton, J. M. (1998). An empirical assessment of data collection using the Internet. *Personnel Psychology, 51,* 709–725.

Starke, F. A., & Notz, W. W. (1981). Pre- and post-intervention effects of conventional versus final offer arbitration. *Academy of Management Journal, 24,* 832–850.

Steel, R. P., & Ovalle, N. K. (1984). Self-appraisal based upon supervisory feedback. *Personnel Psychology, 37,* 667–686.

Steele-Johnson, D., Osburn, H. G., & Pieper, K. F. (2000). A review and extension of current models of dynamic criteria. *International Journal of Selection and Assessment, 8,* 110–136.

Stein, J. A., Newcomb, M. D., & Bentler, P. M. (1988). Structure of drug use behaviors and consequences among young adults: Multitrait-multimethod assessment of frequency, quantity, work site, and problem substance abuse. *Journal of Applied Psychology, 73,* 595–605.

Steiner, D. D., & Gilliland, S. W. (1996). Fairness reactions to personnel selection techniques in France and the United States. *Journal of Applied Psychology, 81,* 134–141.

Stenberg, B., & Wall, S. (1995). Why do women report "sick building symptoms" more often than men? *Social Science and Medicine, 40,* 491–502.

Sternberg, R. J. (1997). The concept of intelligence and its role in lifelong learning and success. *American Psychologist, 52,* 1030–1057.

Sternberg, R. J., & Horvath, J. A. (Eds.). (1999). *Tacit knowledge in professional practice.* Mahwah, NJ: Erlbaum.

Stevens, M. J., & Campion, M. A. (1999). Staffing work teams: Development and validation of a selection test for teamwork settings. *Journal of Management, 25,* 207–228.

Stokes, G. S., Mumford, M. D., & Owens, W. A. (Eds.). (1994). *Biodata handbook: Theory, research, and use of biographical information in selection and performance prediction.* Palo Alto, CA: Consulting Psychologists Press.

Stone, D. L., & Kotch, D. A. (1989). Individuals' attitudes toward organizational drug testing policies and practices. *Journal of Applied Psychology, 74,* 518–521.

Strasser, S., & Bateman, T. S. (1984). What we should study, problems we should solve: Perspectives of two constituencies. *Personnel Psychology, 37,* 77–92.

Streufert, S., Pogash, R. M., Roache, J., Gingrich, D., Landis, R., Severs, W., Lonardi, L., & Kantner, A. (1992). Effects of alcohol intoxication on risk taking, strategy, and error rate in visuomotor performance. *Journal of Applied Psychology, 77,* 515–524.

Stricker, L. J. (2000). Using just noticeable differences to interpret test scores. *Psychological Methods, 5,* 415–424.

Sulsky, L. M., & Balzer, W. K. (1988). Meaning and measurement of performance rating accuracy: Some methodological and theoretical concerns. *Journal of Applied Psychology, 73,* 497–506.

Sulsky, L. M., & Day, D. V. (1992). Frame-of-reference training and cognitive categorization: An empirical investigation of rater memory issues. *Journal of Applied Psychology, 77,* 501–510.

Summers, T. P., Betton, J. H., & DeCotiis, T. A. (1986). Voting for and against unions: A decision model. *Academy of Management Review, 11,* 643–655.

Sutton, R. I., & Kahn, R. L. (1987). Prediction, understanding, and control as antidotes to organizational stress. In J. W. Lorsch (Ed.), *Handbook of organizational behavior.* Englewood Cliffs, NJ: Prentice-Hall.

Sverke, M., & Kuruvilla, S. (1995). A new conceptualization of union commitment: Development and test of an integrated theory. *Journal of Organizational Behavior, 16,* 505–532.

Sverke, M., & Sjoberg, A. (1995). Union membership behavior: The influence of instrumental and value-based commitment. In L. E. Tetrick & J. Barling (Eds.), *Changing employment relations* (pp. 229–254). Washington, DC: American Psychological Association.

Sweetland, R. C., & Keyser, D. J. (Eds.). (1991). *Tests: A comprehensive reference for assessments in psychology, education, and business* (3rd ed.). Kansas City, MO: Test Corporation of America.

Taggar, S., Hackett, R., & Saha, S. (1999). Leadership emergence in autonomous work teams: Antecedents and outcomes. *Personnel Psychology, 52,* 899–926.

Tangri, S. S., Burt, M. R., & Johnson, L. B. (1982). Sexual harassment at work: Three explanatory models. *Journal of Social Issues, 38*(4), 33–54.

Tannenbaum, S. I., & Yukl, G. (1992). Training and development in work organizations. *Annual Review of Psychology, 43,* 399–441.

Taylor, F. W. (1911). *The principles of scientific management.* New York: Harper.

Tenopyr, M. L. (1996). The complex interactions between measurement and national employment policy. *Psychology, Public Policy, and Law, 2,* 348–362.

Tenopyr, M. L. (1998). Measure me not: The test taker's new bill of rights. In M. D. Hakel (Ed.), *Beyond multiple choice: Evaluating alternatives to traditional testing for selection* (pp. 17–22). Mahwah, NJ: Erlbaum.

Tepas, D. I. (1993). Educational programmes for shiftworkers, their families, and prospective shiftworkers. *Ergonomics, 36,* 199–209.

Tesluk, P. E., & Jacobs, R. R. (1998). Toward an integrated model of work experience. *Personnel Psychology, 51,* 321–355.

Tetrick, L. E. (1995). Developing and maintaining union commitment: A theoretical framework. *Journal of Organizational Behavior, 16,* 583–595.

Tharenou, P. (1997). Managerial career advancement. In C. L. Cooper & I. T. Robertson (Eds.), *International review of industrial and organizational psychology* (Vol. 12, pp. 39–94). New York: Wiley.

Tharenou, P., Latimer, S., & Conroy, D. (1994). How do you make it to the top? An examination of influences on women's and men's managerial advancement. *Academy of Management Journal, 37,* 899–931.

Thierry, H., & Meijman, T. (1994). Time and behavior at work. In H. C. Triandis, M. D. Dunnette, & L. M. Hough (Eds.), *Handbook of industrial and organizational psychology* (2nd ed., Vol. 4, pp. 341–413). Palo Alto, CA: Consulting Psychologists Press.

Thomas, D. A. (1990). The impact of race on managers' experiences of developmental relationships (mentorship and sponsorship): An intra-organizational study. *Journal of Organizational Behavior, 11,* 479–492.

Thomas, D. A. (1993). Racial dynamics in cross-race developmental relationships. *Administrative Science Quarterly, 38,* 169–194.

Thomas, K. W., & Tymon, W. G., Jr. (1982). Necessary properties of relevant research: Lessons from recent criticisms of the organizational sciences. *Academy of Management Review, 7,* 345–352.

Thomas, L. T., & Ganster, D. C. (1995). Impact of family-supportive work variables on work–family conflict and strain: A control perspective. *Journal of Applied Psychology, 80,* 6–15.

Thompson, D. E., & Thompson, T. A. (1982). Court standards for job analysis in test validation. *Personnel Psychology, 35,* 865–874.

Thornton, G. C., III. (1980). Psychometric properties of self-appraisals of job performance. *Personnel Psychology, 33,* 263–272.

Tinsley, C. (1998). Models of conflict resolution in Japanese, German, and American cultures. *Journal of Applied Psychology, 83,* 316–323.

Tokar, D. M., Fisher, A. R., & Subich, L. M. (1998). Personality and vocational behavior: A selective review of the literature, 1993–1997. *Journal of Vocational Behavior, 53,* 115–153.

Tornow, W. W. (1993). Perceptions or reality: Is multi-perspective measurement a means or an end? *Human Resource Management, 32,* 221–230.

Totterdell, P., Spelten, E., Smith, L., Barton, J., & Folkard, S. (1995). Recovering from work shifts: How long does it take? *Journal of Applied Psychology, 80,* 43–57.

Tracey, J. B., Tannenbaum, S. I., & Kavanagh, M. J. (1995). Applying trained skills on the job: The importance of the work environment. *Journal of Applied Psychology, 80,* 239–252.

Triandis, H. C. (1975). Culture training, cognitive complexity, and interpersonal attitudes. In R. Brislin, S. Bochner, & W. Lonner (Eds.), *Cross-cultural perspectives on learning* (pp. 39–77). Beverly Hills, CA: Sage.

Triandis, H. C. (1994). Cross-cultural industrial and organizational psychology. In H. C. Triandis, M. D. Dunnette, & L. M. Hough (Eds.), *Handbook of industrial and organizational psychology* (2nd ed., Vol. 4, pp. 103–172). Palo Alto, CA: Consulting Psychologists Press.

Triandis, H. C. (1995). A theoretical framework for the study of diversity. In M. M. Chemers, S. Oskamp, & M. A. Costanzo (Eds.), *Diversity in organizations* (pp. 1–36). Thousand Oaks, CA: Sage.

Triandis, H. C., Kurowski, L. L., & Gelfand, M. J. (1994). Workplace diversity. In H. C. Triandis, M. D. Dunnette, & L. M. Hough (Eds.), *Handbook of industrial and organizational psychology* (2nd ed., Vol. 4, pp. 769–827). Palo Alto, CA: Consulting Psychologists Press.

Trice, H. M., & Sonnenstuhl, W. J. (1988). Drinking behavior and risk factors related to the work place: Implications for research and practice. *Journal of Applied Behavioral Science, 24,* 327–346.

Tubbs, M. E. (1986). Goal setting: A meta-analytic examination of the empirical evidence. *Journal of Applied Psychology, 71,* 474–483.

Turner, A. N., & Lawrence, P. R. (1965). *Industrial jobs and the worker: An investigation of response to task attributes.* Cambridge, MA: Harvard University Press.

Turner, M. E., & Horvitz, T. (2001). The dilemma of threat: Group effectiveness and ineffectiveness under adversity. In M. E. Turner (Ed.), *Groups at work* (pp. 445–470). Mahwah, NJ: Erlbaum.

Turnley, W. H., & Feldman, D. C. (2000). Re-examining the effects of psychological contract violations: Unmet expectations and job dissatisfaction as mediators. *Journal of Applied Psychology, 84,* 594–601.

Tyler, T. R. (1989). The psychology of procedural justice: A test of the group-value model. *Journal of Personality and Social Psychology, 57,* 830–838.

Tyson, P. R., & Vaughn, R. A. (1987, April). Drug testing in the work place: Legal responsibilities. *Occupational Health and Safety,* 24–36.

U.S. Civil Service Commission. (1977). *Instructions for the Factor Evaluation System.* Washington, DC: U.S. Government Printing Office.

U.S. Department of Justice. (1998). *Bureau of Justice Statistics special report on workplace violence 1992–1996.* Washington, DC: The Bureau.

U.S. Department of Labor. (1994). *Apprenticeship: Past and present.* Washington, DC: U.S. Government Printing Office.

U.S. Department of Labor, Employment, and Training Administration. (1991). *Dictionary of occupational titles* (4th ed.). Washington, DC: U.S. Government Printing Office.

Vaill, P. (1982). The purposing of high-performing systems. *Organizational Dynamics, 2*(2), 23–39.

Van De Water, T. J. (1997). Psychology's entrepreneurs and the marketing of industrial psychology. *Journal of Applied Psychology, 82,* 486–499.

Van der Spiegel, J. (1995). New information technologies and changes in work. In A. Howard (Ed.), *The changing nature of work* (pp. 97–111). San Francisco: Jossey-Bass.

Van Dyne, L., Graham, J. W., & Dienesch, R. M. (1994). Organizational citizenship behavior: Construct redefinition, measurement, and validation. *Academy of Management Journal, 37,* 765–802.

Van Eerde, W., & Thierry, H. (1996). Vroom's expectancy models and work-related criteria: A meta-analysis. *Journal of Applied Psychology, 81,* 575–586.

van Oudenhoven, J. P., Mechelse, L., & de Dreu, C. K. (1998). Managerial conflict management in five European countries: The importance of power distance, uncertainty avoidance, and masculinity. *Applied Psychology: An International Review, 47*, 439–455.

Van Velsor, E., Ruderman, M. N., & Young, D. P. (1991). *Enhancing self objectivity and performance on the job: The role of upward feedback.* Paper presented at the 6th annual conference of the Society of Industrial and Organizational Psychology, St. Louis.

VandeWalle, D., Brown, S. P., Cron, W. L., & Slocum, J. W. (1999). The influence of goal orientation and self-regulation tactics on sales performance: A longitudinal field test. *Journal of Applied Psychology, 84*, 249–259.

VandeWalle, D., & Cummings, L. L. (1997). A test of the influence of goal orientation on the feedback-seeking process. *Journal of Applied Psychology, 82*, 390–400.

Varca, P. E., & Pattison, P. (1993). Evidentiary standards in employment discrimination: A view toward the future. *Personnel Psychology, 46*, 239–258.

Vinokur, A. D., Threatt, B. A., Vinokur-Caplan, D., & Satariano, W. A. (1990). The process of recovering from breast cancer in younger and older patients. *Cancer, 65*, 1242–1254.

Visweswaran, C., & Schmidt, F. L. (1992). A meta-analytic comparison of the effectiveness of smoking cessation methods. *Journal of Applied Psychology, 77*, 554–566.

Von Hippel, C., Magnum, S. L., Greenberger, D. B., Heneman, R. L., & Skoglind, J. D. (1997). Temporary employment: Can organizations and employees both win? *Academy of Management Executive, 11*(1), 93–104.

Vroom, V. H. (1964). *Work and motivation.* New York: Wiley.

Wagner, R. K. (1997). Intelligence, training, and employment. *American Psychologist, 52*, 1059–1069.

Wagner, S. H., & Goffin, R. D. (1997). Differences in accuracy of absolute and comparative performance appraisal methods. *Organizational Behavior and Human Decision Processes, 70*, 95–103.

Wahba, M. A., & Bridwell, L. T. (1976). Maslow reconsidered. A review of research on the need hierarchy theory. *Organizational Behavior and Human Performance, 15*, 212–240.

Wainer, H. (2000). *Computerized adaptive testing* (2nd ed.). Mahwah, NJ: Erlbaum.

Waldman, D. A., Ramirez, G. G., House, R. J., & Puranam, P. (2001). Does leadership matter? CEO leadership attributes and profitability under conditions of perceived environmental uncertainty. *Academy of Management Journal, 44*, 134–143.

Walker, C. B., & Rumsey, M. G. (2001). Application of findings: ASVAB, new aptitude tests, and personnel classification. In J. P. Campbell & D. J. Knapp (Eds.), *Exploring the limits in personnel selection and classification* (pp. 559–576). Mahwah, NJ: Erlbaum.

Wallace, S. R. (1965). Criteria for what? *American Psychologist, 20*, 411–417.

Wanberg, C. R. (1997). Antecedents and outcomes of coping behaviors among unemployed and reemployed individuals. *Journal of Applied Psychology, 82*, 731–744.

Wanberg, C. R., Kanfer, R., & Banas, J. T. (2000). Predictors and outcomes of networking intensity among unemployed job seekers. *Journal of Applied Psychology, 85*, 491–503.

Wanek, J. E. (1999). Integrity and honesty testing: What do we know? How do we use it? *International Review of Selection and Assessment, 1*, 183–195.

Wanous, J. P., Reichers, A. E., & Austin, J. T. (2000). Cynicism about organizational change: Measurement, antecedents, and correlates. *Group & Organization Management, 25*, 132–153.

Wanous, J. P., Sullivan, S. E., & Malinak, J. (1989). The role of judgment calls in meta-analysis. *Journal of Applied Psychology, 74*, 259–264.

Warr, P., Allan, C., & Birdi, K. (1999). Predicting three levels of training outcome. *Journal of Occupational and Organizational Psychology, 72*, 351–375.

Warr, P. B. (1987). *Work, unemployment, and mental health.* Oxford: Clarendon.

Warr, P. B., & Payne, R. L. (1983). Social class and reported changes in behavior after job loss. *Journal of Applied Social Psychology, 13*, 206–222.

Wasti, S. A., Bergman, M. E., Glomb, T. M., & Draggon, F. (2000). Test of the cross-cultural generalizability of a model of sexual harassment. *Journal of Applied Psychology, 85*, 766–778.

Watanabe, S., Takahashi, K., & Minami, T. (1997). The emerging role of diversity and work–family values in a global context. In P. C. Earley & M. Erez (Eds.), *New perspectives on international industrial/organizational psychology* (pp. 276–318). San Francisco: New Lexington Press.

Weekley, J. A., & Gier, J. A. (1989). Ceilings in the reliability and validity of performance ratings: The case of expert raters. *Academy of Management Journal, 32*, 213–222.

Weekley, J. A., & Jones, C. (1997). Video-based situational testing. *Personnel Psychology, 50*, 25–49.

Weisband, S., & Atwater, L. (1999). Evaluating self and others in electronic and face-to-face groups. *Journal of Applied Psychology, 84*, 632–639.

Weisinger, H. (1998). *Emotional intelligence at work.* San Francisco: Jossey-Bass.

Weiss, D. J., Dawis, R. V., England, G. W., & Lofquist, L. H. (1967). *Manual for the Minnesota Satisfaction Questionnaire.* Minneapolis: Industrial Relations Center, University of Minnesota.

Weiss, H. M. (1990). Learning theory and industrial and organizational psychology. In M. D. Dunnette & L. M. Hough (Eds.), *Handbook of industrial and organizational psychology* (2nd ed., Vol. 1, pp. 171–221). Palo Alto, CA: Consulting Psychologists Press.

Werner, J. M., & Bolino, M. C. (1997). Explaining U.S. court of appeals decisions involving performance appraisal: Accuracy, fairness, and validation. *Personnel Psychology, 50*, 1–24.

Westin, A. F. (1992). Two key factors that belong in a macroergonomic analysis of electronic monitoring: Employee perceptions of fairness and the climate of organizational trust or distrust. *Applied Ergonomics, 23*, 35–42.

Wherry, R. J. (1957). The past and future of criterion evaluation. *Personnel Psychology, 10,* 1–5.

Whetten, D. A., & Cameron, K. S. (1991). *Developing management skills* (2nd ed.). New York: HarperCollins.

Whetzel, D. L., & McDaniel, M. A. (1997). Employment interviews. In D. L. Whetzel & G. R. Wheaton (Eds.), *Applied measurement methods in industrial psychology* (pp. 185–206). Palo Alto, CA: Consulting Psychologists Press.

Whittington, D. (1998). How well do researchers report their measures? An evaluation of measurement in published educational research. *Educational and Psychological Measurement, 58,* 21–37.

Whyte, G., & Latham, G. (1997). The futility of utility analysis revisited: When even an expert fails. *Personnel Psychology, 50,* 601–610.

Wiener, R. L., & Hurt, L. E. (2000). How do people evaluate social sexual conduct at work? A psychological model. *Journal of Applied Psychology, 85,* 75–85.

Wiesenfeld, B. M., Raghuram, S., & Garud, R. (1999). Managers in a virtual context: The experience of self-threat and its effects on virtual work organizations. In C. L. Cooper & D. M. Rousseau (Eds.), *Trends in organizational behavior: The virtual organization* (Vol. 6, pp. 31–44). New York: Wiley.

Wigdor, A. K., & Sackett, P. R. (1993). Employment testing and public policy: The case of the General Aptitude Test Battery. In H. Schuler, J. L. Farr, & M. Smith (Eds.), *Personnel selection and assessment* (pp. 183–204). Hillsdale, NJ: Erlbaum.

Williams, C. R., & Livingstone, L. P. (1994). Another look at the relationship between performance and voluntary turnover. *Academy of Management Journal, 37,* 269–298.

Williams, K. M., & Crafts, J. L. (1997). Inductive job analysis. In D. L. Whetzel & G. R. Wheaton (Eds.), *Applied measurement methods in industrial psychology* (pp. 51–88). Palo Alto, CA: Consulting Psychologists Press.

Williamson, L. G., Campion, J. E., Malos, S. B., Roehling, M. V., & Campion, M. A. (1997). Employment interview on trial: Linking interview structure with litigation outcomes. *Journal of Applied Psychology, 82,* 900–912.

Woehr, D. J. (1994). Understanding frame-of-reference training: The impact of training on the recall of performance information. *Journal of Applied Psychology, 79,* 524–534.

Woehr, D. J., & Huffcutt, A. I. (1994). Rater training for performance appraisal: A quantitative review. *Journal of Occupational and Organizational Psychology, 67,* 189–205.

Worren, N. A., Ruddle, K., & Moore, K. (1999). From organizational development to change management: The emergence of a new profession. *Journal of Applied Behavioral Science, 35,* 273–286.

Wright, L. (1988). The Type A behavior pattern and coronary artery disease: Quest for the active ingredients and the elusive mechanism. *American Psychologist, 43,* 2–14.

Wright, P. M. (1990). Operationalization of goal difficulty as a moderator of the goal difficulty–performance relationship. *Journal of Applied Psychology, 75,* 227–234.

Wright, T. A. (1997). Time revisited in organizational behavior. *Journal of Organizational Behavior, 18,* 201–204.

Wright, T. A., & Staw, B. M. (1999). Affect and favorable work outcomes: Two longitudinal tests of the happy-productive worker thesis. *Journal of Organizational Behavior, 20,* 1–24.

Wright, T. A., & Wright, V. P. (1999). Ethical responsibility and the organizational researcher: A committed-to-participant research perspective. *Journal of Organizational Behavior, 20,* 1107–1112.

Yeatts, D. E., & Hyten, C. (1998). *High-performing self-managed work teams.* Thousand Oaks, CA: Sage.

Yorges, S. L., Weiss, H. M., & Strickland, O. J. (1999). The effect of leader outcomes on influence, attributions, and perceptions of charisma. *Journal of Applied Psychology, 84,* 428–436.

Yost, E. (1943). *American women of science.* New York: Stokes.

Youngblood, S. A., DeNisi, A. S., Molleston, J. L., & Mobley, W. H. (1984). The impact of work environment, instrumentality beliefs, perceived labor union image, and subjective norms on union voting intentions. *Academy of Management Journal, 17,* 576–590.

Yukl, G. A. (1989a). *Leadership in organizations* (2nd ed.). Englewood Cliffs, NJ: Prentice-Hall.

Yukl, G. A. (1989b). Managerial leadership: A review of theory and research. *Journal of Management, 15,* 251–289.

Yukl, G. A. (1994). *Leadership in organizations* (3rd ed.). Englewood Cliffs, NJ: Prentice-Hall.

Yukl, G. A., & Falbe, C. M. (1991). The importance of different power sources in downward and lateral relations. *Journal of Applied Psychology, 76,* 416–423.

Yukl, G. A., & Latham, G. P. (1975). Consequences of reinforcement schedules and incentive magnitudes for employee performance: Problems encountered in an industrial setting. *Journal of Applied Psychology, 60,* 294–298.

Yukl, G. A., Latham, G. P., & Pursell, E. D. (1976). The effectiveness of performance incentives under continuous and variable ratio schedules of reinforcement. *Personnel Psychology, 29,* 221–232.

Yukl, G. A., & Tracey, J. B. (1992). Consequences of influence tactics used with subordinates, peers, and bosses. *Journal of Applied Psychology, 77,* 525–535.

Yukl, G. A., & Van Fleet, D. D. (1992). Theory and research on leadership in organizations. In M. D. Dunnette & L. M. Hough (Eds.), *Handbook of industrial and organizational psychology* (2nd ed., Vol. 3, pp. 147–197). Palo Alto, CA: Consulting Psychologists Press.

Yukl, G. A., Wall, S., & Lepsinger, R. (1990). Preliminary report on validation of the management practices survey. In K. E. Clark & M. B. Clark (Eds.), *Measures of leadership* (pp. 223–238). West Orange, NJ: Leadership Library of America.

Zalesny, M. D. (1985). Comparison of economic and noneconomic factors in predicting faculty vote preference in a union representation election. *Journal of Applied Psychology, 70,* 243–256.

Zedeck, S. (1992). Introduction: Exploring the domain of work and family careers. In S. Zedeck (Ed.), *Work, families, and organizations* (pp. 1–32). San Francisco: Jossey-Bass.

Zedeck, S., & Cascio, W. F. (1982). Performance appraisal decisions as a function of rater training and purpose of the appraisal. *Journal of Applied Psychology, 67,* 752–758.

Zedeck, S., Outtz, J., Cascio, W. F., & Goldstein, I. L. (1995). Why do "testing experts" have such limited vision? *Human Performance, 8,* 179–190.

Zeidner, J., & Johnson, C. D. (1994). Is personnel classification a concept whose time has passed? In M. G. Rumsey, C. B. Walker, & J. H. Harris (Eds.), *Personnel selection and classification* (pp. 377–410). Hillsdale, NJ: Erlbaum.

Zickar, M. J. (2001). Using personality inventories to identify thugs and agitators: Applied psychology's contribution to the war against labor. *Journal of Vocational Behavior, 59,* 149–164.

Zimmerman, B. J. (1995). Self-efficacy and educational development. In A. Bandura (Ed.), *Self-efficacy in changing societies* (pp. 202–231). New York: Cambridge.

NAME INDEX

SUBJECT INDEX

Page references in **boldface** indicate
where the entry is defined in the margin.

TO THE OWNER OF THIS BOOK:

We hope that you have found *Psychology Applied to Work, Seventh Edition,* useful. So that this book can be improved in a future edition, would you take the time to complete this sheet and return it? Thank you.

School and address: _____

Department: _____

Instructor's name: _____

1. What I like most about this book is: _____

_____

_____

2. What I like least about this book is: _____

_____

_____

3. My general reaction to this book is: _____

_____

4. The name of the course in which I used this book is: _____

_____

5. Were all of the chapters of the book assigned for you to read? _____

    If not, which ones weren't? _____

6. In the space below, or on a separate sheet of paper, please write specific suggestions for improving this book and anything else you'd care to share about your experience in using the book.

_____

_____

_____

_____

_____

Optional:

Your name: _____ Date: _____

May Wadsworth quote you, either in promotion for *Psychology Applied to Work* or in future publishing ventures?

Yes: _____ No: _____

Sincerely,

Paul Muchinsky